MARKEDNESS

'Markedness' refers to the tendency of languages to show a preference for particular structures or sounds. This bias towards 'unmarked' elements is consistent within and across languages, and tells us a great deal about what languages can and cannot do. This pioneering study presents a groundbreaking theory of markedness in phonology. De Lacy argues that markedness is part of our linguistic Competence, and is determined by three conflicting mechanisms in the brain: (a) pressure to preserve marked sounds ('preservation'), (b) pressure to turn marked sounds into unmarked sounds ('reduction'), and (c) a mechanism allowing the distinction between marked and unmarked sounds to be collapsed ('conflation'). He shows that, due to these mechanisms, markedness occurs only when preservation is irrelevant. Drawing on examples of phenomena such as epenthesis, neutralization, assimilation, vowel reduction, and sonority-driven stress, *Markedness* offers an important new insight into this essential concept in the understanding of human language.

PAUL DE LACY is Assistant Professor in the Department of Linguistics, Rutgers University. He has contributed to a wide range of books and journals, and is editor of the forthcoming *Cambridge Handbook of Phonology* (to be published by Cambridge University Press, 2006).

In this series

73 JOHN A. HAWKINS: *A performance theory of order and constituency*
74 ALICE C. HARRIS and LYLE CAMPBELL: *Historical syntax in cross-linguistic perspective*
75 LILIANE HAEGEMAN: *The syntax of negation*
76 PAUL GORREL: *Syntax and parsing*
77 GUGLIELMO CINQUE: *Italian syntax and universal grammar*
78 HENRY SMITH: *Restrictiveness in case theory*
79 D. ROBERT LADD: *Intonational morphology*
80 ANDREA MORO: *The raising of predicates: predicative noun phrases and the theory of clause structure*
81 ROGER LASS: *Historical linguistics and language change*
82 JOHN M. ANDERSON: *A notional theory of syntactic categories*
83 BERND HEINE: *Possession: cognitive sources, forces and grammaticalization*
84 NOMI ERTESCHIK-SHIR: *The dynamics of focus structure*
85 JOHN COLEMAN: *Phonological representations: their names, forms and powers*
86 CHRISTINA Y. BETHIN: *Slavic prosody: language change and phonological theory*
87 BARBARA DANCYGIER: *Conditionals and prediction*
88 CLAIRE LEFEBVRE: *Creole genesis and the acquisition of grammar: the case of Haitian creole*
89 HEINZ GIEGERICH: *Lexical strata in English*
90 KEREN RICE: *Morpheme order and semantic scope*
91 APRIL MCMAHON: *Lexical phonology and the history of English*
92 MATTHEW Y. CHEN: *Tone Sandhi: patterns across Chinese dialects*
93 GREGORY T. STUMP: *Inflectional morphology: a theory of paradigm structure*
94 JOAN BYBEE: *Phonology and language use*
95 LAURIE BAUER: *Morphological productivity*
96 THOMAS ERNST: *The syntax of adjuncts*
97 ELIZABETH CLOSS TRAUGOTT and RICHARD B. DASHER: *Regularity in semantic change*
98 MAYA HICKMANN: *Children's discourse: person, space and time across languages*
99 DIANE BLAKEMORE: *Relevance and linguistic meaning: the semantics and pragmatics of discourse markers*
100 IAN ROBERTS and ANNA ROUSSOU: *Syntactic change: a minimalist approach to grammaticalization*
101 DONKA MINKOVA: *Alliteration and sound change in early English*
102 MARK C. BAKER: *Lexical categories: verbs, nouns and adjectives*
103 CARLOTA S. SMITH: *Modes of discourse: the local structure of texts*
104 ROCHELLE LIEBER: *Morphology and lexical semantics*
105 HOLGER DIESSEL: *The acquisition of complex sentences*
106 SHARON INKELAS and CHERYL ZOLL: *Reduplication: doubling in morphology*
107 SUSAN EDWARDS: *Fluent aphasia*
108 BARBARA DANCYGIER and EVE SWEETSER: *Mental spaces in grammar: conditional constructions*
109 MATTHEW BAERMAN, DUNSTAN BROWN and GREVILLE G. CORBETT: *The syntax-morphology interface: a study of syncretism*
110 MARCUS TOMALIN: *Linguistics and the formal sciences: the origins of generative grammar*
111 SAMUEL D. EPSTEIN and T. DANIEL SEELY: *Derivations in minimalism*
112 PAUL DE LACY: *Markedness: reduction and preservation in phonology*

Earlier issues not listed are also available

CAMBRIDGE STUDIES IN LINGUISTICS

General editors: P. AUSTIN, J. BRESNAN, B. COMRIE,
S. CRAIN, W. DRESSLER, C. J. EWEN, R. LASS,
D. LIGHTFOOT, K. RICE, I. ROBERTS, S. ROMAINE,
N. V. SMITH

Markedness
Reduction and Preservation in Phonology

MARKEDNESS

REDUCTION AND PRESERVATION IN PHONOLOGY

PAUL DE LACY
Rutgers University

CAMBRIDGE UNIVERSITY PRESS
Cambridge, New York, Melbourne, Madrid, Cape Town, Singapore, São Paulo

Cambridge University Press
The Edinburgh Building, Cambridge CB2 2RU, UK

Published in the United States of America by Cambridge University Press, New York

www.cambridge.org
Information on this title: www.cambridge.org/9780521839624

© Paul de Lacy 2006

This publication is in copyright. Subject to statutory exception
and to the provisions of relevant collective licensing agreements,
no reproduction of any part may take place without
the written permission of Cambridge University Press.

First published 2006

Printed in the United Kingdom at the University Press, Cambridge

A catalogue record for this publication is available from the British Library

ISBN-13 978-0-521-83962-4 hardback
ISBN-10 0-521-83962-9 hardback

Cambridge University Press has no responsibility for the persistence or accuracy of URLs for external or third-party internet websites referred to in this publication, and does not guarantee that any content on such websites is, or will remain, accurate or appropriate.

**In memory of my father, Reg
(1928–2004)**

and

**my brother, Grant
(1973–1993)**

Contents

	Preface	*page* xi
	Acknowledgments	xv
	Symbols and abbreviations	xvii
1	**What is markedness?**	**1**
1.1	Aims	1
1.2	Challenges for markedness	4
1.3	Solutions	10
1.4	Implications and diagnostics	27
1.5	Markedness: an outline	31
2	**Theory**	**33**
2.1	Aims	33
2.2	Markedness hierarchies	34
2.3	Theory and formalism	46
2.4	Discovering hierarchies	72
2.5	Summary	75
3	**Markedness reduction**	**78**
3.1	The visibility of markedness reduction	78
3.2	Consonant epenthesis	79
3.3	The output of neutralization	110
3.4	Methodology and exceptions	133
3.5	Conclusions	144
4	**Preservation of the Marked**	**146**
4.1	Introduction	146
4.2	Neutralization and inventories	148
4.3	Undergoers of assimilation	173
4.4	The form of faithfulness constraints	202
4.5	Summary: overt and covert markedness	206

5	**Conflation in reduction**	**208**
5.1	Introduction	208
5.2	PoA conflation	210
5.3	Conflation prevention and vowel sonority	224
5.4	Alternatives	244
5.5	Summary	249
6	**Markedness conflation in preservation**	**252**
6.1	Introduction	252
6.2	Preservation conflation in Swedish voicing	254
6.3	Preservation conflation in Pali coalescence	262
6.4	Domain faithfulness and the majority rules problem	279
6.5	Summary	284
7	**Markedness conflict: vowels**	**286**
7.1	Introduction	286
7.2	Vowel epenthesis	287
7.3	Vowel inventories and neutralization	306
7.4	Prosodification	328
7.5	Summary	331
8	**Predictions and alternatives**	**333**
8.1	Introduction	333
8.2	Predictions	335
8.3	Markedness exists	348
8.4	Representational complexity is not markedness	355
8.5	Non-contrastive markedness	380
8.6	Markedness is absolute	387
8.7	Markedness is expressed in both output and preservation constraints	395
8.8	Conclusions	402
9	**Conclusions**	**404**
9.1	Markedness	404
9.2	Markedness in the future	407
	References	409
	Subject index	440
	Language index	444

Preface

This book presents a new theory of markedness, a concept that is central to understanding human language. The domain of discussion is phonology (the mental representation and computation of speech sounds), but the theory applies to syntax and morphology as well.

Many linguistic phenomena show a bias towards certain segments or structures. For example, consonants are often inserted to meet prosodic requirements. Such epenthetic consonants always have coronal or glottal place of articulation (e.g. [t ʔ h] and so on); they are never dorsal (e.g. [k g x ŋ]) or labial (e.g. [p b m]). Other phenomena like neutralization also produce glottals and coronals, but never labials and dorsals. To explain this consistent bias there is often an appeal to a concept of 'markedness': dorsals and labials are designated as 'marked', glottals and coronals are 'unmarked', and phonological processes can only ever turn marked segments and structures into unmarked ones.

Three leading ideas about markedness are presented in this book. One is that the term 'markedness' has often been used to refer to very different phenomena. This book is about the human Language Faculty, so a major aim is to distinguish markedness as it relates to grammatical Competence from other uses of the term.

Another central proposal is that there is pressure to preserve marked elements. This principle of 'Preservation of the Marked' (PoM) can prevent highly marked elements from being eliminated in phonological phenomena like neutralization and assimilation. PoM has a significant effect: it allows markedness to only be apparent when preservation is irrelevant. For example, epenthetic consonants have no corresponding input form so preservation is irrelevant; markedness will therefore be evident in consonant epenthesis. The practical effect of PoM is that many phenomena thought to show markedness effects actually do not, including segmental inventories and undergoers of processes like neutralization and assimilation.

The third central proposal is 'conflation': that is, distinctions between markedness categories can be collapsed. For example, dorsals are more marked than coronals, so some languages may favour coronals over dorsals, while others may treat them as equally marked. However, hierarchical markedness relations can never be reversed, so no language will favour dorsals over coronals. Conflation is crucial to understanding markedness. It explains why markedness is apparently ignored in a variety of situations.

One final point that recurs throughout the book is that there is no such thing as the 'least-marked segment'. Neither [t], [ʔ], or [b] is the least marked consonant, and neither [a] nor [ə] is the least-marked vowel. Markedness does not impose relations at the segmental level, but rather among feature values. In addition, there is no meta-restriction that all markedness hierarchies be consistent at the segmental level. So, while glottal is the least-marked place of articulation, other markedness hierarchies favour non-glottals over glottals. Whether glottals or coronals are treated as least marked in a language depends on which markedness hierarchy dominates. In addition, some markedness hierarchies vary with prosodic context. The result is that there is variation in terms of what may be the least-marked segment in a particular language, even though that variation is limited.

The leading ideas in this book are implemented within Optimality Theory (Prince & Smolensky 1993; McCarthy & Prince 1995). The theory of markedness presented here consists of proposals about the form of feature values and restrictions on the constraint component CON. In essence, a markedness hierarchy is realized as two different sets of constraints. One set places restrictions on output structures: for every element in the hierarchy, there is an output constraint that bans that element and every more marked element. The other set restricts the input → output mapping: specific constraints preserve marked elements, and there is no constraint that preserves a relatively unmarked element without also preserving all more marked elements. All the constraints can be ranked freely.

The empirical phenomena discussed and analysed in this book include epenthesis, neutralization, assimilation, vowel reduction, and sonority-driven stress. Diachronic processes, loanword adaptation, language acquisition, and disordered phonology are not discussed as they fall outside the bounds of a Competence theory of markedness, as explained in chapter 1.

Audience

Even a cursory examination of linguistic phenomena reveals numerous asymmetries; the theory presented in this book provides a way to explain them. This book will therefore be relevant to any scholar interested in human language, from the perspective of theoretical or descriptive linguistics, or in allied fields such as anthropology, computer science, neurology, psychology, and philosophy.

While this book is accessible to anyone with a general background in linguistics and for adherents of any phonological theory, a full understanding of the approach requires knowledge of current linguistic theory, especially Optimality Theory (for introductions, see Kager 1999 and McCarthy 2001b). Those who are interested in syntax will also find this book useful; the proposals in their most general form apply to syntactic mechanisms as well as phonological ones. It is important to point out that this book is not a history of markedness (cf. Battistella 1990, Rice in prep.); the aim here is to present a theory.

Use

As it discusses a central idea in phonological theory, this book can be used in advanced courses in phonology and Optimality Theory. Parts of it can also be used in courses on general linguistics.

History of this book

This book comes at a particularly contentious time for markedness theory. There are several competing theories of markedness set in Optimality Theory (e.g. Prince & Smolensky 1993; Rice 1999a,b, 2004a,b, 2006) and many set in other frameworks (e.g. underspecification theory). In addition, recent work has also questioned whether markedness even exists, or at least whether it is relevant for a theory of linguistic Competence (Hume 2003, 2004; Blevins 2004).

A good deal of my work over the past five years has focused on markedness. For my previous work on markedness hierarchies, see de Lacy 2000a, 2000b. For conflation and stringent constraint form, see de Lacy 2000a, 2002a, 2004. Some of the central theoretical proposals in this book were developed at the University of Massachusetts, Amherst, and formed part of my doctoral dissertation (de Lacy 2002a). However, a great deal of this book reports new research I undertook at the University of Cambridge and Rutgers University. Unlike my previous work, this book focuses on the Competence-Performance distinction, determining markedness diagnostics, vowel markedness in neutralization and epenthesis, conflation in place of articulation, and comparison with other theories of markedness. For the phenomena discussed in previous work (e.g. consonant epenthesis), much of the empirical base has been extended. A great deal of new and important work for markedness has emerged very recently, and I have attempted to discuss and refer to as much of it as possible, including Blevins 2004, Howe & Pulleyblank 2004, Hume 2003, 2004, Kiparsky 2004, and Rice 1999a,b, 2004a,b, 2006, in prep.

Acknowledgments

This book represents the culmination of work over the last eight years in three different places: the University of Massachusetts, Amherst, the University of Cambridge, and Rutgers University. Consequently, there are many people I need to thank.

First and foremost I thank my family. My wife Catherine is top of the list. She listened patiently to my rants about markedness, proof-read the book three times, carefully checked all the references, and made many suggestions for its improvement.

My mother, Mary, continues to inspire me; she is incredibly hard-working and intelligent, the most capable person I know, and always encouraged me wherever my interests turned. My father, Reg, was one of the most brilliant people I have ever known. I regret that he died before I could thank him in print for being such an inspiration. I also must thank my brother, Grant. From him I learnt how to persevere.

I also thank many colleagues.

John McCarthy has commented extensively on everything I have ever written about markedness leading up to this book. John taught me to think critically and concisely. His influence can be seen in the good parts of this book; the rough parts can be ascribed to my baser nature.

Alan Prince's theoretical proposals inform many aspects of the theory presented here. He also commented on a great deal of the work that led up to this book. I am also deeply grateful for the kindness he and Jane Grimshaw have shown to Catherine and myself.

I also owe Lisa Selkirk and John Kingston thanks for detailed comments on previous related work and providing the inspiration for many of the proposals found here.

For this book, I am especially grateful to Kate Ketner, Michael O'Keefe, and Sarah Murray for all the time they spent carefully critiquing and correcting the manuscript. Their comments made this book significantly better in both theory and presentation.

A number of people have commented on various aspects of this theory, either in this book or in my previous work. I therefore thank Ricardo Bermúdez-Otero, Lee Bickmore, Mark Feinstein, Michael Kenstowicz, Paul Kiparsky, Linda Lombardi, Sarah Murray, Steve Parker, Joe Pater, Keren Rice, Ellen Woolford, and Moira Yip.

I consulted with native speakers or experts for a great deal of the data presented in this book. My deepest thanks go to: Shimauli Dave (Gujarati), José Elías-Ulloa (Panoan languages), Eugene Helimski (Nganasan), Roger Higgins (English dialects), Arthur Holmer (Seediq), Eva Juarros (Catalan), Makoto Kadowaki (Japanese), Shigeto Kawahara (Japanese), Minjoo Kim (Korean), Steve Parker (South American languages), Varun Patel (Gujarati), Jack Reuter (Moksha Mordvin), Keren Rice (Chipewyan), Mariko Sugahara (Japanese), Olga Vaysman (Nganasan) and Gene Buckley (Kashaya).

I also thank Kathy Adamczyk, Lynn Ballard, Ariel Knapman, Joanna Stoehr, and George Puttner for moral and practical support at the various stages of this project. My thanks also to Ian Roberts for encouraging me to write this book in the first place.

I am also grateful to my colleagues and graduate students in the Rutgers linguistics department for making it such an intellectually inspiring environment.

Finally, I wish to thank my editor at Cambridge University Press – Helen Barton. Her kindness and understanding helped make writing this book a tolerable burden.

Symbols and abbreviations

/ /	= underlying form
[ ]	= surface form
| |	= encloses a markedness hierarchy
|| ||	= encloses a constraint ranking
〉	= 'is more marked than'
»	= 'outranks'
»»	= 'universally outranks' (i.e. outranks in every grammar)
DTE	= Designated Terminal Element
MoA	= manner of articulation
OT	= Optimality Theory
PoM	= Preservation of the Marked
PoA	= place of articulation
CoMP	= an abbreviation for the theory proposed in this book (i.e. <u>C</u>ompetence, <u>C</u>onflation, Hierarchy <u>C</u>onflict, <u>M</u>arkedness, and <u>P</u>reservation of the Marked)
☞	= the winner in a tableau
💣	= a winner that is not the attested form in a particular language
☠	= a winner that is never the attested form in any language

Chart of the International Phonetic Alphabet (revised 1993, updated 1996)

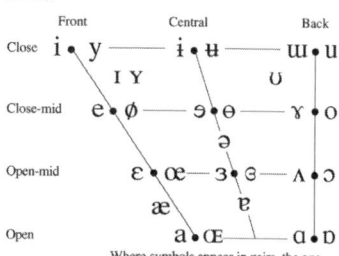

1 *What is markedness?*

1.1   Aims

This book is about the concept of 'markedness' in human language. Certain structures are often avoided while others are generated; the avoided structures are called 'marked' while the generated ones are 'unmarked'. As an example, many languages have processes which turn the phonological segment /k/ into [?]. In a sense, this process avoids [k] and favours [?], so [k] (or some component of [k]) can be said to be more marked than (some component of) [?].

The focus here is on phonology, but the general conclusions and theoretical devices extend to other linguistic domains as well. While the leading ideas proposed here are applicable to a wide range of theories of linguistic Competence, they are particularly suited to formal expression within Optimality Theory (Prince & Smolensky 1993).

Markedness has a very long history in phonological theory (Trubetzkoy 1931, 1939; Jakobson 1941; Chomsky & Halle 1968:ch. 9; Stampe 1972; Prince & Smolensky 1993; see Battistella 1990, 1996 for an overview). Even so, an important question remains: Which processes are sensitive to markedness and which ones are not? While many phenomena have been proposed as being markedness diagnostics, there has as yet been no explanation of which particular phenomena should show markedness effects. This book presents a theory of markedness that answers this question. Behind the theory are four leading ideas, summarized in (1).

(1)   (a) *Competence markedness*
        Markedness is part of grammatical Competence (i-language).
        Markedness in Competence is distinct from sometimes apparently similar Performance-related phenomena.

      (b) *Preservation of the Marked*
        There is grammatical pressure to preserve marked elements. If x is more marked than y, x can be unaffected by a process while y is forced to undergo it.

(c) *Markedness conflation*
Markedness distinctions can be conflated (i.e. ignored), but never reversed. If a language treats *x* as more marked than *y*, another language can treat *x* and *y* as being equally marked; however, no language will treat *y* as less marked than *x* (caveat: subject to (d) below).
(d) *Hierarchy conflict*
Markedness hierarchies can conflict: one hierarchy may favour *x* over *y* while another favours *y* over *x*.

The following chapters will argue that there are formal objects called 'markedness hierarchies', following much previous work (markedness hierarchies are enclosed by | |, and the symbol ⟩ means 'is more marked than'). For example, the hierarchy for major place of articulation (PoA) is given in (2), building on work by Lombardi (1995, 1998) and others.

(2)   Major place of articulation markedness hierarchy
       | dorsal ⟩ labial ⟩ coronal ⟩ glottal |

The PoA hierarchy is related to a set of output constraints in (3) (building on work by Prince 1997a,b,c,d, 1998, 1999; de Lacy 2000a, 2002a, 2004) and a set of faithfulness constraints in (4). The PoAs 'dors', 'lab', 'cor', and 'gl' are abbreviations of dorsal, labial, coronal, and glottal respectively.

(3)   Output constraints for major place of articulation
       (a) *{dors}   'Assign a violation for each [dorsal] feature.'
       (b) *{dors,lab}   'Assign a violation for each [dorsal] and each [labial] feature.'
       (c) *{dors,lab,cor}   'Assign a violation for each [dorsal], each [labial], and each [coronal] feature.'
       (d) *{dors,lab,cor,gl} 'Assign a violation for each [dorsal], each [labial], each [coronal], and each [glottal] feature.'

Together, the output constraints in (3) express the PoA hierarchy. For example, dorsals are more marked than other PoAs, and *{dorsal} is violated by dorsals like [k] but not by other segments like [p], [t], and [ʔ]. Labials are never less marked than coronals, so every constraint that coronals violate is also violated by labials (i.e. *{dor,lab,cor}, *{dors,lab,cor,gl}). In this way relative markedness relations are translated into violations of the PoA output constraints.

The constraints in (3) differ from Prince & Smolensky's (1993) theory of markedness in not imposing any universally fixed rankings – the constraints can be ranked in any way. Fixed ranking is shown to have undesirable empirical consequences in §1.3.3 and §5.2.2.

(4)   Faithfulness constraints for major place of articulation
        IDENT {dors}   'If x is dorsal, then x' has the same PoA as x.'
        IDENT {dors,lab}   'If x is dorsal or labial, then x' has the same PoA as x.'
        IDENT {dors,lab,cor}   'If x is dorsal, labial or coronal, then x' has the same PoA as x.'
        IDENT {dors,lab,cor,gl} 'If x is dorsal, labial, coronal, or glottal, then x' has the same PoA as x.'
        • Segment x' corresponds to segment x

Because the feature dorsal is the most marked PoA, there are specific constraints that preserve it and no other. The effect is that dorsals can be exempted from undergoing a PoA-altering process like neutralization or assimilation while other PoAs undergo it. Labial is the next most marked PoA, so there is a constraint IDENT {dors,lab} that preserves it and the more marked PoA dorsal, and so on down through the PoA hierarchy.

To make one thing clear, the theory presented here is not a necessary consequence of Optimality Theory's formalism. The OT framework is not committed to any particular theory of markedness, or even to expressing markedness at all. For example, OT could in principle allow freely rankable *{dors}, *{lab}, *{cor}, and *{gl}, so disregarding PoA markedness. OT's relationship to the theory presented here is analogous to Chomsky & Halle's (1968) formalism and the theory of markedness in their chapter 9: the theory presented here does not derive from fundamental properties of the OT framework, but rather imposes restrictions on its constraint component and feature representation.

As a terminological note, confusion could arise because 'markedness constraint' is used in OT to mean a constraint that is violated if a particular structure is present in an output candidate (Prince & Smolensky 1993; McCarthy 2001b:14). Because such constraints do not necessarily express markedness relations, I hereby rename them 'output constraints' for the rest of this book.

To be clear from the outset, this book is not a history of markedness (cf. Battistella 1990, 1996; Rice to appear); its aim is to present a markedness theory. Of course, a great deal of work on markedness has preceded this book, including the Prague School's work (e.g. Trubetzkoy 1939; Jakobson 1941, 1949a,b, 1978), Greenberg (1966, 1975, 1978), Natural Phonology (Stampe 1972), Kean (1975), Cairns & Feinstein (1982), and work in Underspecification Theory (e.g. Kiparsky 1982; Archangeli 1984, 1988). The formalism owes much to work in OT: the proposals take from Prince & Smolensky (1993) the insight that markedness relations can be formally expressed by constraints, they adopt Smolensky's (1994) proposal that markedness asymmetries can be explained through constraint interaction, and they build on Prince's (1997a,b,c,d, 1998, 1999) and my previous work (de Lacy 2002a, 2004) in using constraint forms to express markedness hierarchies (cf. Prince & Smolensky 1993). All of these theories will be discussed when they shed light on the theory; explicit comparison is provided in chapter 8.

It is also not the aim of this book to identify all the markedness hierarchies that exist; instead, a methodology for discovering them is provided. In a related vein, it is not the aim to determine whether markedness hierarchies are entirely innate or derive from functional factors (Chomsky & Lasnik 1977:435ff.; Lasnik 1990; Bermúdez-Otero & Börjars 2005 cf. articles in Hayes, Kirchner & Steriade 2004; Bybee 2001:194ff.). Instead, the purpose of this book is to present a theory that explains why the Competence mechanisms specific to phonology exhibit markedness effects.

So, what is markedness? Before giving an answer it is necessary to identify the phenomena that a theory of markedness must explain, then the mechanisms that provide the explanation must be identified. To do this, §1.2 identifies three major challenges for a theory of markedness. The solutions are given in §1.3; in effect they identify the empirical scope of the theory. The theoretical proposals are also given in brief; they are used to identify valid and invalid diagnostics for markedness in §1.4. With the necessary background in place, §1.5 provides a definition of markedness and outlines how the theory is developed in the rest of the book.

Markedness hierarchies only refer to features and their values, not to segments as a whole. However, for convenience I will occasionally refer to 'unmarked segments' instead of saying 'segments that have some particular unmarked feature value', and make statements such as '[k] is very marked' instead of 'some feature value in [k] is very marked'.

1.2   Challenges for markedness

The term 'markedness' has been used to refer to many different linguistic concepts. One of the most common uses relates to observations about asymmetries in the output, triggers, and undergoers of certain processes.[1] 'Unmarked' elements can be the sole output of processes, fail to trigger alternations, and undergo processes alone. In contrast, 'marked' elements are rarely the output, are often the only triggering elements, and are often exempt from undergoing processes.

---

1 In OT, the term 'process' refers to a situation involving an unfaithful input→output mapping.

For example, (2) expressed the claim that glottals and coronals are commonly accepted as having a relatively unmarked Major place of articulation while labials and dorsals are relatively more marked. The output of consonant epenthesis is always a coronal (e.g. [t n ɹ]) or glottal ([ʔ h]), and never a labial or dorsal (e.g. [p f m], [k x ŋ]) (§3.2; Lombardi 2002). Similarly, if coronal consonants force a preceding segment to assimilate, then so do labials and dorsals (i.e. if /mt/→[nt] then /mk/ must become [ŋk]). However, the reverse is not true: if dorsals trigger assimilation, then coronals do not have to do so: /mk/→[ŋk] does not imply that /mt/→[nt] (Mohanan 1993; Jun 1995; de Lacy 2002a:ch. 7). So, coronals and glottals behave differently from labials and dorsals in many different situations and languages. Therefore it seems reasonable to appeal to an overarching principle that treats glottals and coronals differently from labials and dorsals — i.e. markedness. Glottals and coronals can be said to be 'unmarked' relative to labials and dorsals.

As in a great deal of previous work, markedness relations can be expressed as a hierarchy like the one in (2). 'Dorsal' is the most marked element and 'glottal' is least marked; evidence for the hierarchy's details will be provided in the following chapters (esp. §2.2.1). Elements are marked or unmarked relative to some other element on the same hierarchy. So, dorsals are relatively marked in comparison to coronals. The terms 'marked' or 'unmarked' have often been used as if referring to an absolute state; however, no segment or prosodic structure is ever 'not marked' — it is only comparatively less marked than some other segment or structure. There are many markedness hierarchies, including ones for voice, sonority, and tone; markedness relations between prosodic structures have also been identified, but are not the focus of this book. Of course, a pressing question is 'How do we discover markedness hierarchies?' This question can only be answered after a theory of markedness effects is introduced and used to identify valid diagnostics for markedness. The theory will be discussed below and valid diagnostics identified in §1.4.

A central issue for markedness is whether it is a formal concept or merely an informal descriptive term. In other words, is it necessary to employ special Competence mechanisms to account for the phonological asymmetries observed in natural language? The proposals in this book take the view that there are i-language devices that produce markedness effects: there are formal objects that are the equivalent of markedness hierarchies and formal mechanisms that relate constraints to those hierarchies.

However, there is a great deal of disagreement and even scepticism about markedness. An alternative to having a Competence account is to allow the phonological and syntactic components to produce virtually any output. External pressures like restrictions on language learning are then used to explain why some outputs are infrequent or non-existent (e.g. Hale & Reiss 2000; Blevins 2004). §8.3.2 argues that this approach is not adequate in accounting for all markedness phenomena.

Those who agree that markedness asymmetries require a Competence-based explanation often disagree on the details. For example, Rice (1996) proposes that velars can be less marked than coronals, while they are seen as more marked here and in Paradis & Prunet 1990, Lombardi 2002, and here. Views also differ as to which phenomena give insight into markedness (e.g. §1.4; Greenberg 1966; Rice 1999a,b, 2006).

A great deal of the scepticism about markedness and the variation in what is considered unmarked seems to be due to three apparent problems: (a) some markedness diagnostics do not work all the time, (b) *marked* elements are favoured for some phenomena, and (c) markedness distinctions can be ignored. The following three subsections expand on each of these. §1.3 provides solutions and shows how they give insight into a formal theory of markedness.

1.2.1   Some markedness diagnostics do not work all the time

A significant difficulty in providing a comprehensive account of markedness is that many processes do not treat categories in an asymmetrical way; they seem to ignore markedness hierarchies.

For example, there are no height asymmetries in vowel epenthesis. Epenthetic vowels may be high [i ɨ], mid [e ɛ ə], or low [a] (§7.2; Lombardi 2003). The only asymmetry relates to roundness: [round] vowels cannot be epenthetic (factoring out interfering processes like round harmony – §7.2.5).

There are almost no implicational universals for segmental inventories; almost every possible set of segments is attested (§3.3). The term 'inventory' is used here to refer to the output segments found in a language. For example, Hawaiian and Yellowknife Chipewyan have the voiceless stops [k p], which are highly marked in PoA, and the relatively unmarked [ʔ], but have no intermediately marked coronal [t] (Elbert & Pukui 1979; Haas 1968 respectively). In contrast, Tahitian has [p t ʔ] and no [k] (Coppenrath & Prévost 1974), Ayutla Mixtec has only [k t ʔ] in native words and no [p] (Pankratz & Pike 1967), and Māori has [k p t] but no [ʔ] (Bauer 1993).

Similarly, there are no implicational universals relating to the undergoers of assimilation; both marked and unmarked segments can assimilate while other segments do not (§4.3). For example, only coronals undergo assimilation in

Catalan; labials and dorsals do not (§4.3.1; Mascaró 1976; Wheeler 2005a). In contrast, only labials and dorsals undergo assimilation in Sri Lankan Portuguese creole while coronals do not (§4.3.2; Smith 1978; Hume & Tserdanelis 2002).

There are also no asymmetries relating to the output of segment coalescence: if two segments are fused into one the resulting segment may retain either the marked or the unmarked value of the input segments (§6.3). For example, coalescence of /bʰ/ and /t/ in Pāli yields [dːʰ] – an output that preserves the unmarked coronal PoA of the /t/ (e.g. /labʰ-ta/ → [ladːʰa] 'take' {passive perfect participle}). In contrast, Pāli's coalescence of /k/, /ʃ/, and [t] results in preservation of the more marked PoA: [kːʰ] (e.g. /a-sakː-ʃ-ti/ → [asakːʰi] {aorist-'be able'-aorist-3sg}).

The proposal that vowel epenthesis, inventories, undergoers of assimilation, and coalescence do not show markedness effects disagrees with a number of previous claims (e.g. de Haas 1988; Paradis & Prunet 1991a; Mohanan 1993; Jun 1995; Lombardi 2003). Evidence to support the view here is provided in the following chapters (see the sections cited above for specific discussion).

So, does the lack of markedness sensitivity in the phenomena just mentioned mean that there is no such thing as markedness? This question broaches a much broader issue: which phenomena give insight into markedness and which do not? Only once this latter question is answered is it possible to address the former. Consequently, this book aims to identify the phenomena that can be expected to show markedness effects, and – more importantly – to provide principles that can be used to determine whether a particular phenomenon will exhibit markedness asymmetries. To put it slightly differently, this book will provide a theory in which the phenomena listed above are insensitive to markedness distinctions. Before discussing the solution, though, there are two more challenges to markedness to consider.

1.2.2 Marked elements are favoured

Another apparent difficulty for markedness is that occasionally *less* marked elements can be eliminated while *more* marked elements remain. This situation is apparently contrary to expectations: the traditional notion behind markedness is that grammars seek to eliminate highly marked structures – i.e. markedness reduction.

The Nepalese language Yamphu provides a relevant example of preservation of marked place of articulation (see §4.2 for details). The coronal stop /t/ debuccalizes to [ʔ] in codas while the more marked /k/ and /p/ remain unchanged. The first three forms in (5a) have an underlying /t/, the second two have an underlying geminate /tː/. The data are from Rutgers 1998. In an unrelated process, voiceless stops become voiced inter-vocalically (e.g. /hæːt-u-ŋ/ → [hæːduŋ]).

(5)   Yamphu /t(ː)/-debuccalization (Rutgers 1998)
    (i) /t/ → [ʔ], /tː/ → [ʔ]
       (a) [namːiʔ]   'daughter-in-law'
          cf. [namːid-æʔ] {instrumental/ergative}
       (b) [tʰeʔ-nani] 'I don't lift you(sg.)'
          cf. [tʰed-a] 'I lifted him'
       (c) [triʔ-ma] 'contrary+{infin.}'
          cf. [kap-trid-u] 'he has (unexpectedly)'
       (d) [imːeʔ-na] 'I had caused to buy you(sg.)'
          cf. [imːet:-uŋ] 'I caused to buy him'
       (e) [siʔ-ma]   'hit+{infin.}'
          cf. [sitː-a] 'hit+past', [sitː-iŋ] 'hit+exp.'
    (ii) /p/→[p]
       (a) [kʰap]   'language'
       (b) [kep-ma] 'stick+{infin.}'
    (iii) /k/→[k]
       (a) [æʔlik]   'bendy'
       (b) [kʰaːk-pa] 'scrape one's throat+perform act'
       (c) [hæk-ma]   'cut with a knife or sickle+{infin.}'
       (d) [aktok]   'like that'
    (iv) /ʔ/ →[ʔ]
       (a) [asiʔ]   'previously'   cf. [asi.ʔ-em-ba] 'before'
       (b) [jiːw-æʔ-mu] 'river-poss.-down' cf. [kaniŋ-æʔ-æ] 'we-poss.'

The challenge raised by Yamphu is why the more marked dorsals and labials are exempt from debuccalization while the less marked coronals are not.

Similar situations are found in assimilation and coalescence. Chapter 4 describes cases where coronals undergo assimilation but dorsals and labials do not. A famous case is Catalan, in which the coronal /n/ assimilates while the labial /m/ and dorsal /ŋ/ do not (§4.3). There are also many cases of segment coalescence where the most marked feature value is retained. For example, when Attic Greek vowels coalesce the resulting output vowel keeps the marked [+round] feature: /mistʰo+εːte/ → [mistʰɔːte] 'you may hire out', *[mistʰεːte] (de Haas 1988; de Lacy 2002a:ch. 8).

On the other hand, all of the processes just cited also allow the most marked element to be eliminated while the least marked element is retained. For example, the highly marked dorsal /k/ is eliminated in Standard Malay codas while the less marked labial /p/ and coronal /t/ are faithfully preserved §3.2. Sri Lankan

Portuguese creole is the exact opposite to Catalan: labials [m] and dorsals [ŋ] assimilate while coronals [n] do not (§4.3.2; Smith 1978; Hume & Tserdanelis 2002). Finally, the unmarked value can emerge in coalescence, as noted for Pāli in §1.2.1 (also §6.3).

The challenge that these phenomena raise for markedness is that marked and unmarked elements seem to be treated in the same way. Both marked and unmarked features can be eliminated (through neutralization, assimilation, and so on), and both marked and unmarked features can survive in coalescence. Lack of sensitivity to markedness makes it seem that there is no use for a marked–unmarked distinction. However, the proposals in this book will argue that markedness is at the heart of phenomena like those above. Marked elements can be selectively retained because there is a principle of Preservation of the Marked: highly marked elements can be preserved while less marked ones are not. However, such preservation only applies in phenomena for which preservation of the input is possible. It is noteworthy that there is no phenomenon which only ever produces marked elements (cf. de Haas 1988); this fact follows from the theory presented here. Before discussing the proposal in more detail, one other challenge to markedness needs to be mentioned.

1.2.3 Markedness distinctions are conflated

The idea that markedness relations are universally invariant faces a challenge in apparent markedness reversals: for example, some languages treat coronals as more marked than glottals, while others treat them in the opposite way. Another challenge relates to markedness distinctions in particular hierarchies: while some languages treat labials as more marked than coronals, others seem to conflate or ignore this markedness distinction. Markedness reversal and conflation can also occur in different phenomena within the same language.

A markedness reversal can be seen in neutralization. While input glottals become coronal in Korean codas, coronals become glottal in Yamphu (§3.3). The following chapters will argue that markedness reversal is due to conflicting markedness hierarchies. There is no meta-restriction that all markedness hierarchies have to be consistent as to which segment or feature value is the least marked. So while glottals are less marked than coronals on the PoA hierarchy, coronals are less marked than glottals in other hierarchies. Languages, and even different processes in the same language, may differ as to which hierarchy they favour; the result is that there is some variation as to which segment is the 'least marked'. It is important to point out that markedness hierarchies do not conflict over everything — there are some feature values and segments that are not least marked on *any* hierarchy; for this reason markedness effects are visible in natural language.

Markedness conflation is an entirely different issue. To give an example, the PoA markedness hierarchy has dorsals as more marked than coronals, and coronals more marked than glottals. Markedness can therefore make sense out of a situation in which dorsals and coronals become glottals, as in Kashaya codas: e.g. /mihjoq/ → [mihjo?] 'woodrat', /sulemat/ → [sulema?] 'rope' (§5.2). However, glottals are blocked from appearing before other glottals. If the coda neutralization process is indeed one of simply reducing markedness, it is reasonable to expect two things in pre-glottal environments: (a) coronals should remain coronals, as there is nothing less marked for them to become, but (b) dorsals should become coronals, as this would achieve at least partial markedness reduction. However, in Kashaya dorsals remain dorsals in this situation: /mihjoq+?/ → [mihjoq?], *[mihjot?] 'it's a woodrat'. The reason for dorsal survival is that Kashaya coda neutralization treats dorsals and coronals as being equally marked, so there is no motivation for either to change in situations where they cannot become glottals.

There are many other situations where markedness distinctions on a particular hierarchy are ignored or conflated. Examples can be found in languages where stress is sensitive to sonority, discussed in §5.3.2.

Markedness conflation seems to pose a problem because it suggests that there is no such thing as universality in markedness hierarchies. Nevertheless, this book will argue that markedness hierarchies are universal, as are the theoretical devices that refer to them. Markedness distinctions may be conflated in a principled way within the same hierarchy. Such collapse follows from the form of the theoretical devices that refer to markedness hierarchies. Crucially, it is not possible for a hierarchy to be reversed, showing that it is not possible to get rid of the concept of markedness altogether.

1.3 Solutions

Part of the solution to the apparent problems identified in §1.2 is that 'markedness' has been used to refer to several distinct concepts. One use refers to linguistic Competence, or 'i-language' mechanisms (Chomsky 1986). The other relates to Performance. This book aims to provide an account of markedness in a theory of linguistic Competence, so all asymmetrical effects that are not due to Competence mechanisms must be eliminated from the discussion. This point is developed in §1.3.1.

For phenomena that are governed by Competence mechanisms, the main proposal is that there is 'Preservation of the Marked' (PoM): marked elements can be the specific targets of preservation so that they can avoid undergoing otherwise general processes. The desire to preserve marked elements can conflict with the pressure to eliminate marked elements ('markedness reduction'). When PoM dominates in a grammar marked elements appear in the output intact while relatively unmarked ones are eliminated. When PoM is subordinate to markedness reduction, unmarked elements remain while relatively more marked ones are eliminated. The result is that certain phenomena show no overt sensitivity to markedness. The only situation in which markedness reduction is seen clearly is when preservation is irrelevant.

The issue of markedness conflation can be recast as the question 'Are markedness distinctions always the same for individual languages, and even for individual processes?' This book adopts the long-standing proposal that markedness hierarchies are universal. However, it differs in its conception of the relation of markedness. Informally, a markedness relation like | α 〉 β | should not be read as 'α is more marked than β', but rather as 'β is never more marked than α'. In visual terms the symbol ≥ would be more appropriate than 〉. So, distinctions between contiguous categories in a markedness hierarchy can be collapsed. Such 'conflation' is shown to follow from the form of feature values and the constraints that refer to them.

The following subsections expand on the solutions outlined above. They also introduce the basic formalism of the theory.

1.3.1 Competence

Following Chomsky (1965, 1968, 1986), work in the generative framework has established the importance of the Competence-Performance distinction (see Newmeyer 1998, 2003 for overviews). 'Competence' refers to a speaker's internal knowledge of language, called 'i-language' (Chomsky 1986). Given the phonological focus of this book, 'Competence' and 'i-language' can in practice be read here as 'the phonological component of the Language Faculty'; but of course the theoretical proposals here relate equally to the syntactic and other i-language components. 'Performance' refers to how language is used (Chomsky 1965:§2) – i.e. to everything outside the i-language components of the Language Faculty; the term covers mechanisms of perception (i.e. the means by which external stimuli are converted into phonological structures), limits on phonetic implementation (i.e. articulation), memory limitations, shifts of attention, errors, and so on. The Competence–Performance distinction will be assumed to be valid here without discussion; it will turn out to be crucial in making sense of markedness.

A central problem with markedness is that it has not only been used to refer to asymmetries in Competence-related phenomena, but also for phenomena that reflect language use. So, there is a formalist sense of 'markedness' which is relevant to a theory of grammatical Competence, and a use of 'markedness' which refers to certain asymmetries that result from influences outside i-language. When it is necessary to be clear about the two uses of 'markedness', the Competence concept will be called 'c-markedness', and markedness as used otherwise will be called 'p-markedness'.[2]

1.3.1.1   P-markedness

Generalizations about markedness are often about p-markedness, not c-markedness. For example, the frequency of a particular segment is often used to argue for its markedness (Greenberg 1966, 1975; Kean 1975; Paradis & Prunet 1991a:1, cf. Trubetzkoy 1975:162). There are several different senses of frequency (Paradis & Prunet 1991a:§2.4.4); one of the most commonly cited is typological inventory frequency: the more languages a particular segment or segment type appears in, the less marked it is assumed to be. Others include 'text frequency' – the more a segment occurs within a corpus of natural speech, the less marked it is assumed to be. However, factors external to i-language can profoundly affect all of these notions of frequency. Consequently, they give insight into Performance, and not necessarily into Competence. The same can be said for diachronic change, loanword adaptation, order of language acquisition, and phonological disorders. All these phenomena are discussed below.

1.3.1.1.1   Typological frequency

It is not necessarily the case that Competence mechanisms have any impact on the typological frequency of occurrence of particular linguistic phenomena (also see Rice 1999b:§5.3, 2006). In contrast, Performance factors have a direct influence.

---

2 Hale & Reiss (2000) express related concerns about evidence for Competence mechanisms. Their conclusion is that 'many of the so-called *phonological universals* (often discussed under the rubric of markedness) are in fact epiphenomena deriving from the interaction of extragrammatical factors like acoustic salience and the nature of language change'. The following discussion also emphasizes the importance of determining which empirical phenomena are relevant to Competence mechanisms, but is less extreme than Hale & Reiss' proposal in accepting that synchronic alternations provide evidence. For further discussion see §8.3.

To illustrate, almost every language in the world has a [t]. The exceptions are few: Hawaiian (Elbert & Pukui 1979), colloquial Samoan (Mosel & Hovdhaugen 1992), Luangiua (Salmond 1974), Kiowa Apache (Bittle 1963:77), Yellowknife Chipewyan (Haas 1968; Rice 1978), Chama (Key 1969), Orokolo (Brown 1986), and several Austronesian languages discussed by Blust (1990) and Lynch et al. (2002:54ff.). For this reason [t] is often assumed to be less marked than other stops (e.g. [p k ʔ]), and perhaps all other consonants. In a similar vein, for plain fricatives there are 196 languages with [s], 180 with [f], and 94 with [x] according to Maddieson's (1992) UPSID database of 451 languages. If typological frequency relates to markedness, coronal fricatives are therefore less marked than labials, which are less marked than dorsals. For vowels, the system [i a u] is often considered to be less marked than the inventory [i a] because the former appears much more frequently than the latter (Schwartz et al. 1997).

However, inventory frequency does not give insight into c-markedness, as Competence alone does not determine frequency; there are many influencing factors that have nothing to do with i-language. At the most removed, migration patterns, disease, war, and a variety of other factors influence the frequency of individual sounds. If all the speakers of a dialect that lacks [t] are wiped out, the relative frequency of inventories with [t] increases. As an example, the speakers of proto-Eastern Polynesian were particularly adventurous in settling many different islands over the last thousand years or so. The consequence is that few of its daughter languages have [s] while almost all have [f] (Clark 1976). The high frequency of [f] relative to [s] in this language group therefore does not give insight into i-language mechanisms.

More internally, but still not i-language, is the effect of the learning process. Learning is influenced by errors in perception and articulation; if a sound is misperceived, its language-internal frequency may decrease, and perhaps lead to its elimination (Blevins 2004). Similarly, if a sound requires significant articulatory effort to produce it, there is good reason from the child's point of view to learn it 'imperfectly', again lowering its lexical frequency and eventually eliminating its existence in the inventory. With all these e(xternal)-language factors influencing frequency, it is at least unclear what frequency implies for i-language.

Certainly, the infrequency of a phonological structure is irrelevant in determining the form of i-language. Very few languages lack a [t], but nevertheless the phonological component must be able to generate grammars with [t]-less inventories.

1 What is markedness?

So do i-language mechanisms have any influence on typological frequency? One (often implied) hope is that external influences can be factored out of human languages so that the influence of Competence will show through. However, there is little reason to be hopeful. According to SIL's Ethnologue, 38.5% of the world's languages are either Austronesian or in the Niger-Congo family. In terms of numbers of speakers, just a few languages – e.g. English, Spanish, French, Mandarin, and Cantonese – are spoken by a large portion of the world's current population. These language families have areal characteristics that almost certainly skew any expected 'normal distribution' of diversity. It is not clear that careful typological sampling will help as it is not clear at which level the skewing occurs (i.e. at the level of the language family, phylum, or some other stage). There is no guarantee that the current set of languages is a representative sample of what i-language is capable of generating.

While it might not be possible to factor external influences out of inventory frequency, it is legitimate to ask whether Competence markedness would be relevant to inventory frequency even if such factors were eliminated. For example, if [s] is less c-marked than [f] and all external factors were in some way eliminated, would [s] then appear in more inventories than [f]?

To give this idea of a Competence-frequency relation some content, suppose typological frequency followed from the number of distinct outputs based on all possible permutations of a ranking (Coetzee 2002). Idealizing, suppose further that there are just two [s]-related constraints: one that bans [s] (*[s]) and one that prevents /s/ from deleting (MAX). With just these two constraints and two possible rankings, 50% of the world's languages should have [s] while the other 50% should not. Unfortunately, external factors influence the final frequencies. Performance factors, such as ease of articulation, may mean that some rankings are incredibly rare, such as the ranking that permits every possible segment to appear in the output of some language; other factors, such as the need to transmit information, will prevent rankings that neutralize all consonants to [s]. Consequently, it would be surprising if 50% of languages had [s].

As a more concrete example, there are very few or even no languages that demand onsets for all syllables (usually the word- or prosodic word-initial syllable is allowed to be onsetless) (Blevins 1995, 2004). However, there are many rankings which would produce such a situation (i.e. all rankings in which ONSET outranks some appropriate faithfulness constraint). Of course, there is a vast amount of evidence to show that syllables with onsets are less marked than onsetless syllables (from allophony, epenthesis, deletion, reduplication, allomorphy, and so on). Again, this is a frequency issue: although the constraint ONSET *can* produce languages where all syllables have onsets, there is no Competence imperative that there *must* be many (or even one) language that has this property.

In addition, rankings differ in that some require positive evidence to acquire while others do not. If the learner's Initial State has all output constraints outranking all faithfulness constraints (Tesar & Smolensky 1998), there should be a bias towards maintaining this ranking, as positive evidence can clearly be ignored in language transmission (as evinced by the fact that languages change). The result would be that languages in which preservation is more common than alteration of underlying forms will be less frequent than the alternative.

In short, it is undeniable that inventory frequency gives insight into factors outside i-language – most probably into perception, production, and the learning process. However, there is no easy way to remove these effects so that the influence of Competence mechanisms can be seen clearly. In fact, Competence markedness may have no effect at all on inventory frequency. De Boer's (2001) work on vowel inventories shows that their typological frequency follows from mechanisms that have nothing to do with i-language restrictions.

1.3.1.1.2 Other frequencies

'Text frequency' refers to how often a particular segment or structure occurs in the speech (or lexicon) of a language (called 'Occurrence Frequency' in Paradis & Prunet 1991a:11). Again, nothing necessitates a relation between c-markedness and text frequency (Trubetzkoy 1975:319; Schwartz 1979:319; Andrews 1990:ch. 4; Newmeyer 1998:§4.6, cf. Greenberg 1966:60ff., 1975:81). For example, [t] and [k] have the same frequency in a set of spontaneous Māori speech I recorded in 2001. However, [t] is epenthetic, not [k] (de Lacy 2003). Moreover, there is no language in which [k] is epenthetic, nor is there any language in which /t/ neutralizes to [k], although there are languages in which /k/→[t] (§3.3.2).

A final frequency-related issue is 'inventory frequency'. For Greenberg (1966:59), 'the number of phonemes with the marked feature is always less than or equal to the number with the unmarked feature'. To give an example, voicing is clearly more marked than voicelessness in obstruents: voiced obstruents neutralize to voiceless ones, but the opposite is never true; epenthetic obstruents can be voiceless, but are never voiced, and so on. However, languages can have more voiced stops than voiceless ones. Table (6) goes further in showing that there is no relation between the two in terms of the number of segments.

(6) Voicing oppositions in stops
    (a) More voiced than voiceless
        Buriat native words in onsets: [tʰ] vs. [b d g] (Poppe 1960:9–10)[3]
    (b) More voiceless than voiced
        Taiof: [p t c k] vs. [b d g] (Ross 2002)
    (c) Equal numbers of voiced and voiceless
        Gujarati: [p t ṭ c k] vs. [b d ḍ ɟ g] (Mistry 1997)
    (d) The same number, but disjoint sets in terms of PoA
        Berber: [t tˤ k kʷ q qʷ] vs. [b d dˤ g gʷ] (Kossman & Stroomer 1997:467).

The generalization is also not valid even if markedness is allowed to vary from language to language. Buriat has fewer voiceless consonants than voiced ones in onsets, so voiced consonants could be considered unmarked using the phoneme inventory frequency diagnostic. However, voiced consonants devoice in codas, indicating that voiceless consonants are less marked than voiced ones (e.g. /bulag/→[bulak] 'well', cf. [bulag-ai] 'of the well' – Poppe 1960:10–11, 38).

There is good reason why the inventory frequency diagnostic is not valid: many different phenomena can affect different manners of articulation in different ways. For example, voiceless stops can undergo PoA neutralization alone, and voiced stops can undergo lenition alone. The outcome is fewer segments of one manner of articulation or the other, but by means of incidental phonological phenomena, not of a general markedness principle.

1.3.1.1.3 Diachronic change and loan phonology

Like frequency, diachronic change has been cited as showing markedness effects (Greenberg 1966:69ff., 1975:82ff.; Jakobson 1941). There is no doubt that Competence restrictions have an effect on the result of diachronic change: no set of diachronic changes could result in a grammar that violates Competence restrictions (for detailed discussion, see Kiparsky 2004). Therefore, an adequate theory of Competence must be able to generate all states of languages at each point of change. However, the result of change is different from the nature of the changes. Performance factors certainly can influence the changes that segments and structures undergo. Consequently, a historical change of a parent language [t] to daughter language [k] is not evidence that [t] is more c-marked than [k].

The idea that all diachronic changes are possible synchronic processes seems to stem from the idea that diachronic change can only result from a grammar-internal unfaithful mapping. For example, Proto-Eastern Polynesian *t is realized as [k] in its daughter language Hawaiian (Clark 1976:20; Elbert & Pukui

---

3 Buriat has [pʰ] in some interjections, but mostly in loans; [kʰ] is found only in loanwords.

1979) (e.g. Hawaiian [kanaka] 'person', cf. Māori [taŋata]). In this case, the assumption would be that there was some Hawaiian learner who learnt and stored the proto-[t] correctly as /t/, then applied a phonological process to make it [k] on the surface. This view relies on the idea that learners never make perceptual errors.

The idea that diachronic change always gives insight into Competence mechanisms is similar to ideas about loanword adaptation (cf. Paradis & LaCharité 2001 and many others). Again, the idea is that foreign words are correctly perceived (i.e. correctly mapped to the native language's phonetic categories), correctly mapped to phonological primes, and serve as an input to the grammar, which then modifies it. In other words, Competence mechanisms are seen as the only relevant factor in loanword adaptation. For example, Māori [kɪˈɾihiˌmete] is borrowed from English [ˈkɹɪsməs]. In the Māori borrower's grammar, was there ever a mapping in which /kɹɪsməs/ → [kɪˈɾihiˌmete]? Work by Silverman (1992), Dupoux et al. (1999), Peperkamp & Dupoux (2003), and Peperkamp (in press) suggests otherwise: foreign words can be misperceived, and this misperception may be a source of adaptation (also see Yip 2002; Kang 2003). Since errors can be made 'pre-phonology', phonological processes need not be responsible for every change in linguistic transmission. If this latter view is correct, loanword adaptations cannot be trusted to give evidence for c-markedness. The same is true for diachronic change. Change may be due to misperception (e.g. Guion 1996) or misanalysis, whereby the speech signal could be analysed in different phonological ways (famously, as in *an ewt* being analysed as *a newt*). So, the change of *t to [k] in Hawaiian does not imply that the phonological component must generate a grammar in which /t/→[k].

It is therefore unsurprising that there are differences between diachronic changes and synchronic processes. For example, it is not uncommon for [t] to become [k] in a daughter language. Apart from Hawaiian, this change occurred independently in other Polynesian languages (Luangiua – Salmond 1974; colloquial Samoan – Clark 1976:21; Mosel & Hovdhaugen 1992). It also took place in several other Austronesian languages (Blust 1990), and outside Austronesia in Chipewyan (Li 1946; Haas 1968; Rice 1978), Chama (Key 1969), and Orokolo (Brown 1986). In Classical Fuzhou, the change only occurred in codas (Chen 1973; Chan 1985). However, there are no synchronic non-assimilative alternations in which underlying /t/ surfaces as [k] (§3.3). In all relevant cases, /k/ becomes [t] or [ʔ] in neutralization. Consequently, it is likely that some Performance effect (e.g. a perception or articulatory factor) is responsible for the *t→k diachronic change, and not a Competence mechanism. C-markedness always treats [k] as more marked than [t].

To make one thing clear, I do not mean to imply that loanword adaptation and diachronic change provide no insight into Competence mechanisms. As noted above, Competence mechanisms must be able to generate the *result* of diachronic change, so restrictions on the result of diachronic change in terms of the grammar as a whole can provide useful insights (see, e.g., Kiparsky 1988, 1995, 2004). As Greenberg (1978:65) observes, 'if there are limitations on synchronic linguistic types, then change must proceed from lawful type to lawful type'. However, the outcome of change is different from the process: change of *α to β does not imply that there is a synchronic grammar in which /α/→[β]. Diachronic processes are influenced by factors outside Competence, and it is difficult to tease i-language and external influences apart. The same can be said of loanword adaptation: while some elements of borrowed words may be due to misperception, others may well be due to active phonological constraints. At the present state of understanding, it is difficult to be sure which explanation applies to which particular loanword adaptations and diachronic changes.

1.3.1.1.4 Language acquisition and disorder

It has been claimed that language learners acquire unmarked sounds before marked ones (Jakobson 1941; Greenberg 1975, and many others; for second language acquisition, see Battistella 1996:117ff.).[4] This evidence is in the same vein as diachronic change. While there is no doubt that competence mechanisms influence the acquisition of language, it is difficult to see how performance mechanisms can have no influence. For example, it is common for labials to be learned early on in the acquisition process. Miyakoda (2005) reports that in Japanese 'the general tendency seems to be that vowels and bilabial consonants are acquired at an early stage'. However, there is no evidence that labials are the least c-marked element on the PoA hierarchy (ch. 3; §8.2.3; Paradis & Prunet 1991a; cf. Hume & Tserdanelis 2002); there are no synchronic neutralization processes in which PoA neutralizes to labial, for example. It is possible that early acquisition of labials is due to Performance factors, such as the ability to control lip articulations more effectively than tongue articulations, or — from a visual perception point of view — that lip movement is more clearly visible than tongue movement. In another markedness inversion, Beckman, Yoneyama, and Edwards (2003) report a case of Japanese acquisition in which [k] is acquired

---

4 A more complex idea is that contrastiveness is a crucial part of the order of acquisition (Jakobson & Halle 1956; Fikkert 1994; Dresher 2003c). In this approach there is a restriction on the order of acquisition of contrasts, which is analogous to requiring that unmarked contrasts develop earlier than marked ones.

earlier than [t]. As discussed with regard to loanword adaptation and diachronic change above, there is no evidence from synchronic processes that [k] is less c-marked than [t]. Nicolaidis et al. (2004) suggest that this acquisition may be due to Performance factors, namely the child's sensitivity to lexical frequency as there are a large number of [k]-initial words available to the child.

For further discussion of the role of Performance factors influencing order of acquisition, including discussion of production abilities and familiarity with lexical items, see Strange & Broen 1980. For work that directly compares Competence and Performance factors in language acquisition (i.e. markedness vs. frequency), see Stites, Demuth, & Kirk 2004.

Language disorders are claimed to be typified by late development of marked structures (see Bernhardt & Stemberger 2006 for an overview). Therefore, unmarked structures should develop first. However, while there is evidence to suggest that disorders involve Competence mechanisms, it is likely that the mechanisms that convert the speech signal into abstract representation are also relevant. So, it is not surprising that 'some children with atypical phonological systems have been reported to show better development of the apparently marked value of a feature than of the unmarked value' (Bernhardt & Stemberger 2006: §2.2).

Again, I do not mean to imply that Competence mechanisms have no effect on language acquisition and phonological disorders (far from it: see, e.g., Demuth 1995; Pater 1997; Stemberger & Stoel-Gammon 1991; Bernhardt & Stemberger 2006). However, it would be remarkable if Performance factors played no role in these phenomena. Consequently, they show a mix of Performance and Competence influences that prove difficult to tease apart. At the very least, the effects of Competence are non-obvious, and not everything that happens in language acquisition and disorders is due to c-markedness.

1.3.1.1.5 Summary

It is crucial to distinguish i-language mechanisms from those that are external to the Language Faculty (cf. Bybee 2001:194). The proposals in this book are about Competence mechanisms, specifically those mechanisms that are responsible for output asymmetries. Consequently, speech-related asymmetries that are caused by factors external to i-language are not relevant to the theoretical proposals made here. While there is need for a Performance theory which can account for all the observed asymmetries and to help tease apart the effects of Performance and Competence, such a theory is outside of the scope of this book. For present purposes, it is enough to identify the phenomena that are relevant to c-markedness.

1.3.1.2 C-markedness and synchronic alternations

The best evidence for markedness asymmetries caused by i-language mechanisms comes from synchronic alternations. An 'alternation' describes a situation with an observable unfaithful mapping, typically from input to output but also from paradigmatic base to derived form, base to reduplicant, and so on. Alternations contrast with static phonotactic generalizations in which the outcome of the unfaithful mapping is not observable (e.g. New Zealand English does not have surface [mk] within words and there are no alternations to show what happens to underlying /mk/).

Synchronic alternations exhibit asymmetries that must be explained by a formal theory of markedness. For example, neutralization of PoA in codas is highly restricted: dorsals can become coronals, but coronals never become dorsals (§3.3). This asymmetry can be captured if the phonological mechanisms that force neutralization and determine its output are constrained so that dorsals are more marked than coronals.

One could object that synchronic alternations are influenced by diachronic change, and so are just as likely to be influenced by p-markedness as c-markedness. However, if it can be demonstrated that an input→output mapping /α/→[β] exists, it must be the case that there are i-language phonological mechanisms that motivate this change. Even if Performance factors did influence the diachronic development of the /α/→[β] synchronic mapping, the fact is that it exists and so an adequate phonological theory must allow it to happen.[5]

A more serious objection relates to non-occurring phenomena. Is /t/→[k] never observed because there is no state of the phonological component that allows it, or because no series of diachronic changes could ever motivate the change? If the diachronic angle is taken, lack of /t/ → [k] is therefore accidental from a Competence point of view. The problem with this particular case is that there are diachronic changes of *t to [k]. This issue is discussed further in §8.3.2. Suffice to say that it is possible to separate at least some diachronic and synchronic effects.

It is important to emphasize the significance of alternations as opposed to static phonological generalizations. For example, Hawaiian only has [k p ʔ] as stops, and lacks a [t]. This fact alone tells us nothing about the relative markedness of [t] vs. [k], [p], and [ʔ]. If there was a synchronic alternation where /t/ surfaces as [k], then that *would* give insight into markedness: for /t/ to surface as [k] there must be some markedness reduction process that treats

---

5 McMahon (2000) has suggested that diachronic change can create synchronic phenomena that cannot be modelled within a theory of markedness. See §8.3 for discussion.

[t] as more marked than [k]. However, without alternations there is no way to know what sort of markedness relation Hawaiian [t] bears to [k].[6] After all, /t/ may delete, become [l], or any of a myriad of other options.

Some static phonotactic generalizations can have bearing on markedness; an example is discussed in §4.2.2, where it is demonstrated that glottals and coronals of the same manner of articulation cannot both be eliminated by PoA neutralization. Nevertheless, the best way to establish a markedness relation is through synchronic alternations. To be clear, as mentioned above, loanword adaptations are not necessarily alternations in this sense because an adaptation of a segment 'α' of L2 into a different segment 'β' of L1 does not necessarily imply that there is a grammar in which /α/→[β].

The one misgiving in putting aside factors other than synchronic alternations is that they occasionally agree with c-markedness. For example, synchronic coda neutralizations show that [k] is more c-marked than [t] (§3.3.2). Similarly, typological frequency suggests that [k] is more p-marked than [t]. However, correlation is not causation: just because c-markedness and Performance factors happen to converge on similar results there is no reason to attribute the form of c-markedness to Performance, or Performance to c-markedness. It is unsurprising that p- and c-markedness often agree: similarities should abound if Performance factors have ever influenced the evolutionary development of the language faculty, and thereby Competence mechanisms (Newmeyer 2003).

However, there are many mismatches as well. For example, Maddieson's (1992) UPSID database of 451 languages has 450 with a voiceless coronal stop while only 216 have [ʔ]. Nevertheless, there is strong evidence that the PoA markedness hierarchy favours glottals over coronals: /t/ often neutralizes to [ʔ] in synchronic alternations (§3.3). As the output of neutralization is a diagnostic for c-markedness, [t] is therefore more c-marked than [ʔ]. Rice (1999b:§5.3) makes the same point for central vowels: they can be the output of neutralization but are often not present in vowel inventories; so while typological frequency treats central vowels as marked, they are unmarked relative to other vowels for c-markedness (§7.3).

To conclude, the Competence–Performance distinction for markedness is crucial to understanding the nature of the phenomenon and what sort of evidence is relevant for establishing c-markedness relations.

---

6 For some phonological theories the lack of a surface [t] implies that there is never any input /t/. In OT, however, Richness of the Base requires that every possible input have an output mapping in every language (Prince & Smolensky 1993:chs.4,9; McCarthy 2001b:70–1, 2003a).

1.3.2 Preservation of the marked

A number of apparent problems for the concept of markedness fall by the wayside when the Competence–Performance distinction is taken into account. However, there still remain challenges for a theory of c-markedness (hereafter just 'markedness'). The standard conception is that there is just one markedness-related influence on linguistic phenomena: the pressure to become unmarked, called 'markedness reduction' here. Markedness reduction accounts for a wide range of disparities between inputs and outputs: inputs are forced to surface unfaithfully if there is pressure on them to become less marked. It also accounts for the 'direction' of change: /k/ can become [t] because coronals are less marked than dorsals, but /t/ never becomes [k] in a non-assimilative environment because such a change would be an increase in markedness.

In Optimality Theory markedness reduction can be modelled by restricting constraint form. For dorsals to become coronals in non-assimilative neutralization there must be some output constraint that penalizes dorsals but not coronals: e.g. *{dorsal}. As coronals never become dorsals, there can be no constraint that penalizes coronals without also penalizing dorsals: i.e. there is no *{coronal}, but *{dorsal, labial, coronal} is acceptable because it treats dorsal and coronal equally. Consequently, the PoA hierarchy in (2) can be expressed as the set of freely rankable constraints in (3). The form of the constraints will be discussed in §1.3.3.

The constraints in (3) can be used to produce markedness reduction. For example, if *{dorsal} outranks all constraints that preserve dorsals, dorsals will be eliminated. The insight that markedness hierarchies can be formally expressed in terms of constraints and their ranking is due to Prince & Smolensky (1993). However, the means of expression here is different: while Prince and Smolensky use universally fixed rankings to express markedness relations, the theory here uses constraint form instead, along with Prince (1997 a,b,c,d, 1998, 1999), and de Lacy (2000a, 2002a, 2004) (see §2.3.1.3).

In short, 'markedness' is two innate formal devices: (a) markedness hierarchies and (b) a constraint-generation schema that relates markedness hierarchies to constraints.

The challenge for markedness reduction is that some synchronic phenomena do not show any markedness asymmetries. For example, any PoA can undergo neutralization in coda position, and there are no implicational relations between PoAs: /t/ neutralizes in Yamphu but /k/ and /p/ do not, while /k/ neutralizes in Malay and /t/ and /p/ do not, and so on (see §4.2.2 for a fuller typology).

The solution to this apparent problem is to recognize a further pressure imposed by markedness: the pressure to preserve marked elements. Such

'Preservation of the Marked' (PoM) accounts for situations in which highly marked elements are left unchanged by an otherwise general process. For example, the relatively highly marked dorsals and labials are untouched by an otherwise general debuccalization process in Yamphu codas – this exemption can be attributed to an overriding pressure in the language to retain marked PoAs. In contrast, coronals undergo the process because as low-marked elements they are afforded no special protection.

To summarize in (7), there are two major influences in markedness:

(7)   Markedness pressures
       (a) Markedness reduction
           There is pressure for output segments to have unmarked features.
       (b) Preservation of the Marked (PoM)
           There is pressure for marked inputs to be preserved faithfully.

The combined effect of (7a) and (7b) is to reduce the number of phenomena that are traditionally thought to show markedness effects.

(7a) is formally expressed through the constraints banning marked segments, as in (3). (7b) is expressed through constraints enforcing faithfulness to marked features. To complement the set of output constraints in (3), there is a set of faithfulness constraints that implement PoM, called 'marked-faithfulness' constraints. For example, the constraints in (4) implement PoM for major place of articulation. The constraints are schematic because they do not mention the dimension of correspondence: there are separate sets of constraints for each of the pairs input-output, base-reduplicant (McCarthy & Prince 1995), output-output (Benua 1997), sympathy-output (McCarthy 1999), and so on.

A constraint such as IDENT{dors,lab} prevents both dorsals and labials from changing. For example, for voiceless stops IDENT{dors,lab} is violated by mappings from /k/ to anything but [k], and from /p/ to anything but [p]; /k/→[p], /p/→[k], /k/→[t], /p/→[t], /k/→[?], and /p/→[?] all incur violations of the constraint. The formalism is discussed in detail in chapter 2 (see esp. §2.3.1.2).

PoM reduces the opportunities for markedness effects to show through clearly. Nevertheless, the need for markedness is still clear in two situations. One is when preservation is irrelevant, as markedness reduction will be the only influence. For example, epenthetic segments cannot be influenced by preservation demands because they are not present in the input. Putting aside assimilation and dissimilation, the sole influence on them will therefore be the pressure to keep marked features at a minimum – i.e. markedness reduction. Epenthesis is predicted to produce only unmarked elements (see §3.2).

24   *1 What is markedness?*

The other clear influence of markedness is seen in the 'direction' of change. While marked inputs can become unmarked, unmarked inputs cannot become more marked under the influence of output constraints once incidental processes like assimilation and dissimilation are factored out. For example, /t/ never neutralizes in codas to become [k] or [p].

1.3.3   *Markedness conflation and stringent form*

Hierarchical markedness relations are invariant across languages, but individual languages – and even individual processes – can collapse markedness distinctions. For example, a markedness relation like | dorsal) coronal | does not mean that coronals will be treated as less marked in every environment for every process; the distinction can be collapsed. However, the relation can never be reversed.

In formal terms, conflation is effected by the stringent form of constraints, building on Prince (1997a,b,c,d, 1998, 1999) and de Lacy (2000a, 2002a, 2004). Essentially, two constraints are stringently related if one assigns a subset of the other's violations. Of present concern is how stringency can produce markedness effects.

For example, the constraints in (3) are stringently related, as is evident in quasi-tableau (8). A 'quasi-tableau' shows relative violation marks, whereas standard tableaux illustrate constraint conflict.

(8)   Stringent markedness

	*{dors}	*{dors,lab}	*{dors,lab,cor}	*{dors,lab,cor,glottal}
ʔ				*
t			*	*
p		*	*	*
k	*	*	*	*

No matter how the PoA output constraints are ranked they will always have the same effect: dorsals will incur a proper superset of violations of all other PoAs, while glottals will incur a proper subset. As explained above, the violations mean that markedness relations will never be reversed: for example, there is no way to rank the constraints so that labials win over coronals. However, the constraints do allow markedness distinctions to be conflated. If only the constraint *{dorsal,labial,coronal} is active in a language for a particular competition, no markedness distinction will be made between these three categories as they all violate this constraint equally. For examples, see chapter 5.

1.3 Solutions 25

The same point can be made for the faithfulness constraints in (4). The constraint IDENT{dorsal,labial} treats preservation of labials and dorsals as equally important. If only this constraint is active, some other constraint must be called upon to make the crucial decision between preserving dorsals or labials in cases where both cannot be realized. The case studies involving coalescence make use of faithfulness conflation in chapter 6.

Generalizing, markedness conflation will be shown to occur when two markedness categories incur the same violations of active constraints. For example, if *{dorsal,labial} is the only active constraint, the distinction between dorsals and labials is eliminated as they both incur the same violations of this constraint. This approach to formally expressing markedness relations contrasts with OT approaches that employ universally fixed constraint ranking. Chapters 5 and 6 show that fixed ranking cannot produce all attested conflations (also see de Lacy 2004).

1.3.4   Markedness reversals
Markedness hierarchies may conflict. This is to be expected: markedness hierarchies refer to features, not segments, and there is no principle that requires markedness hierarchies to be consistent at the segmental level.

Hierarchy conflict accounts for the variation seen in phenomena that are sensitive to markedness, a point made previously by Waugh (1979:157), Dressler (1989:118), and Battistella (1990:54ff.), among others. Exactly which segment is favoured in which environment in a particular language depends on which markedness hierarchy dominates in that language. For example, in German the obstruent voicing hierarchy has sway over the sonority hierarchy, so /g/→[k] in codas (i.e. /taːg/→[taːk] 'day', cf. [taːg-ə]). However, in Dakota the sonority hierarchy takes precedence, so that /k/ becomes the more sonorous [g] in codas: e.g. /ʃok/→[ʃog] 'thick, solid', cf. [ʃok-a] (§4.2.2.3; Shaw 1980:367,374).

Hierarchy conflict means that statements like 'segment x is marked' are not valid. Strictly speaking, markedness relations should be qualified as 'y is never more marked than x with respect to feature F in the F-hierarchy in environment E'. For example, the question 'is [v] more marked than [t]?' is unanswerable. In contrast, the question 'is [t] never more marked than [v] with respect to the PoA hierarchy in onsets?' is answerable: coronals are less marked than labials on the PoA hierarchy, so [t] will never be treated as more marked than [v] in terms of this hierarchy. Similarly, voiced obstruents are more marked than voiceless ones, so [v] is more marked than [t] on the obstruent voicing hierarchy. Again, [v] proves to be more marked than [t] on the sonority hierarchy, but only in onset position: onsets prefer segments with lower sonority over those with higher sonority (Prince & Smolensky 1993; de Lacy 2000b; Smith 2002). However, codas prefer higher sonority elements over lower sonority ones; so [v] is *less* marked than [t] with respect to the sonority hierarchy in codas. In short, there is no way to answer whether [v] is more marked than [t]; [v] happens to be more marked than [t] for many hierarchies, but [v] is less marked than [t] for at least one hierarchy in one environment.

Hierarchy conflict does *not* mean that *every* segment can be the 'default' in a particular language – i.e. the output of epenthesis, neutralization, and so on. A segment x can only be the default if for every other segment y there is a hierarchy in which y is more marked than x. For example, [ʔ] can have least marked status in a language because coronals, labials, and dorsals are more marked on the PoA hierarchy, and other glottals (like [h]) are more marked in sonority. Some segments simply never fulfil the two criteria. For this reason, [ɣ] will never be epenthetic in a language (unless assimilation or dissimilation intervenes – see §3.2.1 re Brahui). The coronal [t] beats the dorsal [ɣ] on the PoA hierarchy, and [t] is less marked in terms of sonority, and there is no hierarchy in which [ɣ] is less marked than [t].

As a more complex example, while the voiced approximant [ɦ] has the least-marked PoA, so does the voiceless [h], and there is no other feature value for which [ɦ] is less marked than [h]. In contrast, [h] is less marked than [ɦ] in terms of the voicing hierarchy. Consequently, [ɦ] will never be epenthetic or the result of neutralization through markedness reduction (although it may inadvertently appear through voicing assimilation to a vowel).

So, because markedness hierarchies refer to features, there is apparent conflict over which segment is least marked. [k] is less marked than [g] on the voice hierarchy, but in terms of sonority [g] is less marked than [k] (§3.2.3). If the voice hierarchy takes precedence over the sonority hierarchy, /g/ will become [k]. In OT, if the voice hierarchy 'takes precedence' over the sonority hierarchy, the output constraints that relate to the voice hierarchy outrank those that relate to the sonority hierarchy. If sonority takes precedence, /k/ will become [g].

A final source of apparent markedness reversals is that phenomena like assimilation and dissimilation can interfere with markedness reduction. For example, [t] is less marked than [k], but /t/ can become [k] before another dorsal through assimilation. In practice, these influences on markedness reduction are often easy to detect (see §4.2.2.3); they do not obscure evidence for markedness.

To summarize, markedness hierarchies are universally consistent. There are no language-specific hierarchies; apparent markedness disagreements arise through different choices about which hierarchies take precedence in a particular language.

1.4 Implications and diagnostics

The proposals about constraint form outlined above are a formal implementation of c-markedness. Markedness is two innate formal devices: (a) markedness hierarchies and (b) a schema that relates markedness hierarchies to constraints. Markedness reduction occurs when an output constraint that is related to a markedness hierarchy outranks all antagonistic faithfulness constraints. For example, the ranking of *{dorsal} over all dorsal-preserving faithfulness constraints produces 'markedness reduction' of dorsals. The theory is restrictive because it prohibits certain types of constraints. For example, there is no way to generate a constraint *{coronal} from the PoA (or any other) hierarchy, so there can be no system in which markedness reduction forces coronals to become more marked, factoring out assimilation and dissimilation. As a descriptive term, 'markedness' refers to the effects on outputs due to the constraints derived from markedness hierarchies. When taken together, the output and faithfulness constraints allow certain phenomena and prevent others from occurring.

1.4.1 Valid diagnostics

Now that the theory has been introduced, it is possible to return to the question 'Which processes are sensitive to markedness, and which are not?' The answer is that a synchronic phenomenon will exhibit effects of a markedness hierarchy if (a) it is not subject to constraints on preservation (i.e. faithfulness constraints) of that hierarchy and (b) the phenomenon is not influenced by a directly conflicting markedness hierarchy. The phenomena in table (9) fit these requirements, so they are valid markedness diagnostics. Of course, table (9) is not exhaustive – it only includes phenomena that are discussed in this book or in closely related work.

There is a significant abbreviation in (9), relating to segments and features. The phrase 'there is some markedness hierarchy in which segment [β] is more marked than segment [α]' is more correctly 'there is some hierarchy in which some feature of [β] is more marked than the corresponding feature of [α]'. Markedness hierarchies do not refer to segments but to features and their values. Consequently, if /α/ and /β/ neutralize to [α], then [α] and [β] have different values for some feature F and there is some markedness hierarchy in which [β]'s F value is more marked than [α]'s F value. For example, /k/ neutralizes to [t] in a Taiwanese reduplication, [k] and [t]'s value for PoA is different and they do not differ in any other feature, so dorsals must be more marked than coronals on some hierarchy.

28 1 What is markedness?

(9) Valid markedness diagnostics
  (a) Neutralization: outputs
  If /α/ and /β/ undergo structurally conditioned neutralization to output [α], then there is some markedness hierarchy in which [β] is more marked than [α].[7]
  (§3.3; Trubetzkoy 1939, 1968:27–8; Jakobson 1941; Greenberg 1966:60ff.; Cairns 1969; Paradis & Prunet 1991a:§2.4.2; cf. Rice 2006)
  (b) Deletion
  If /β/ undergoes structurally conditioned deletion and /α/ does not, then there is some markedness hierarchy in which [β] is more marked than [α].
  (§8.7.2; Rice 1999a,b; de Lacy 2002a:§6.4.2)
  (c) Consonant Epenthesis
  If consonant [α] is epenthesized and [β] is not, then there is some markedness hierarchy in which [β] is more marked than [α].
  (§3.2; Archangeli 1984, 1988; McCarthy & Prince 1994; Lombardi 2003; cf. Rice 2006)
  (d) Assimilation: triggers
  If /γ/ assimilates to /β/ in terms of some feature F, but /γ/ does not assimilate to /α/'s F-value, then there is some markedness hierarchy in which [β] is more marked than [α].
  (Mohanan 1993:75,76; Jun 1995:78; de Lacy 2002a:§7.5)
  (e) Prosodification: mutual influence
  If some prosodic constituent P is attracted to or attracts [α] and ignores [β], there is some markedness hierarchy in which [β] in constituent P is more marked than [α] in constituent P.
  (§5.3.2, §7.4; for tone and stress: Goldsmith 1987; de Lacy 1999, 2002b; sonority and stress: Kenstowicz 1996; de Lacy 2002a, 2006; sonority and syllable structure: Prince & Smolensky 1993 and references cited therein)
  (f) Inventory structure
  If the presence of [α] in a segmental surface inventory always implies the presence of [β] but not vice versa, then there is some markedness hierarchy in which [β] is more marked than [α].
  (§4.2.2; Jakobson 1941; Trubetzkoy 1939; Greenberg 1966)

Table (9) summarizes a great deal of information that is discussed at length in the following chapters. It identifies positive evidence that can be used to establish markedness hierarchies.

---

[7] The term 'structurally conditioned' is adapted from Trubetzkoy (1939:235ff.). A process is structurally conditioned if (i) it takes place in some prosodic position (e.g. coda, onset, stressed syllable) and (ii) no surrounding elements are involved in triggering the process. For example, if [k] deletes in codas regardless of the surrounding environment, it undergoes structurally conditioned deletion. If [k] only deletes before other dorsals, it is not structurally conditioned since a non-prosodic element – i.e. the other dorsal – is crucial in triggering the unfaithful mapping.

1.4 Implications and diagnostics

Negative evidence can also provide evidence for markedness relations. If /α/ never neutralizes to [β], then it may be the case that there is no markedness hierarchy in which [β] is more marked than [α]. For example, /k/ never neutralizes to [p], so it could be that no markedness hierarchy ever favours a distinct property of [p] (e.g. its [labial] PoA) over the corresponding property of [k]. However, there is another reason why /k/ may never neutralize to [p]: there could always be a more harmonic alternative. For example, the PoA hierarchy will never force /k/ to neutralize to [p] because [t] and [ʔ] are even less marked than [p], and there is no feature that [p] and [k] share that [t] or [ʔ] do not also share with [k]. Consequently, even though /k/ never neutralizes to [p], this does not prevent a markedness hierarchy in which some property of [k] is more marked than the corresponding property of [p].

In short, phonological phenomena that show markedness asymmetries are just those for which marked preservation is irrelevant. There are no doubt many other phenomena that exhibit markedness asymmetries apart from those in (9). Vowel and consonant harmony, dissimilation, tone sandhi, and various prosodic processes are not mentioned above, yet they too should show markedness asymmetries when preservation is irrelevant. Similarly, Walker's (1998, 2000) work on nasal harmony suggests that transparency and blocking are sensitive to the sonority hierarchy; the relation of transparency to markedness is discussed more generally by Steriade (1987b) and Paradis & Prunet (1994).

Of course, markedness is not the only factor that influences output form. Others include the pressure for certain features in adjacent elements to agree (i.e. assimilation) or disagree (i.e. dissimilation). Markedness reduction is not an absolutely overwhelming force, so the pressure to agree may take precedence. For example, the PoA assimilation in /anpa/→[ampa] results in an increase in /n/'s PoA markedness in order to satisfy the demand that coda consonants have the same PoA as the onset's. In other words, processes may mask the effect of markedness; fortunately, these processes are usually easily detectable by their context (§4.2.2.3).

1.4.2 Invalid diagnostics

The phenomena listed in table (10) are not valid markedness diagnostics. The source of their insensitivity is Preservation of the Marked. If PoM outranks markedness reduction it can prevent marked features from being eliminated. However, if markedness reduction dominates, only unmarked features will survive. The result is that the output of the phenomena listed below can be either a set of marked or unmarked segments.

(10) Invalid markedness diagnostics due to marked faithfulness
    (a) Inventory structure
        If there is some segmental inventory that has [α] but not [β], then it is not necessarily the case that there is a markedness hierarchy in which [β] is more marked than [α].
        (§4.2; cf. Trubetzkoy 1939; Jakobson 1941; Greenberg 1966)
    (b) Neutralization: undergoers
        If /β/ undergoes neutralization but /α/ does not, then it is not necessarily the case that there is a markedness hierarchy in which [β] is more marked than [α].
        (§4.2; cf. Jakobson 1941; Trubetzkoy 1939; Cairns 1969)
    (c) Assimilation: undergoers
        If in some language α undergoes assimilation and β does not, then it is not necessarily the case that β is more marked than α.
        (§4.3; cf. Kiparsky 1985:97–8; Avery & Rice 1988, 1989b; Mohanan 1993:63,76; Cho 1991, 1999; Jun 1995:33,70ff.)
    (d) Coalescence
        If α and β coalesce to form β, it is not necessarily the case that β is more marked than α.
        (§6.3; cf. de Haas 1988; Causley 1999:ch. 5)

Another set of phenomena which do not exhibit markedness asymmetries are those which are influenced by conflicting markedness hierarchies. If one markedness hierarchy favours [α] over [β] and another favours [β] over [α], then either [α] or [β] could appear depending on which hierarchy is dominant in the particular language. This is the case for vowel epenthesis, discussed in §7.2: there are several conflicting vowel markedness hierarchies with the result that many different vowels can be epenthesized. Consequently, vowel epenthesis provides only partial evidence for markedness (cf. Archangeli 1984, 1988; McCarthy & Prince 1994; Lombardi 2003).

Finally, there is another class of invalid diagnostics — those that are heavily influenced by Performance. As discussed in §1.3.1, the influence of factors external to i-language means that they do not offer unambiguous evidence for c-markedness.

(11) Invalid markedness diagnostics due to Performance influences
    (a) Diachronic change
        If proto-language *β becomes [α] in a daughter language, then it is not necessarily the case that there is some hierarchy in which [β] is more marked than [α].
        (cf. Greenberg 1966:69ff., 1975:82ff.; Jakobson 1941)

(b) Pidgins/creoles
If a pidgin or creole's segmental inventory contains [α] but not [β], it is not necessarily the case that there is some markedness hierarchy in which [β] is more marked than [α].
(Lefebvre 2000:128; cf. Bickerton 1984)

(c) Order of language acquisition
If segment [α] is acquired before segment [β], it is not necessarily the case that there is some markedness hierarchy in which [β] is more marked than [α].
(cf. Jakobson 1941; Greenberg 1975)

(d) Loanword adaptation/L2 acquisition
If a source language's [β] is converted into a target language's [α], it is not necessarily the case that there is some markedness hierarchy in which [β] is more marked than [α].
(see Battistella 1996:117ff.)

(e) Typological frequency
If [α] appears in more languages than [β], then [α] is not necessarily less marked than [β].
(Trubetzkoy 1975:319; Newmeyer 1998:§4.6; cf. Greenberg 1966:60ff., 1975:81)

(f) Text frequency
If [α] appears more frequently in a corpus/the lexicon of a particular language than [β], then [α] is not necessarily less marked than [β].
(Trubetzkoy 1975:319; Schwartz 1979:319; Newmeyer 1998:§4.6; cf. Greenberg 1966:60ff., 1975:81; Paradis & Prunet 1991a:11)

The claims about which diagnostics are valid and invalid above do disagree with a great deal of previous work (as indicated). For some, though, there is general agreement. Ever since the Prague School's work, the output targets of neutralization have been thought to be unmarked (though cf. Rice 2004a, 2006). Overall, the claim here is that there are far fewer phenomena that exhibit markedness asymmetries than is traditionally thought. Some phenomena do not exhibit such asymmetries because they are influenced by PoM, and others do not provide clear insight into Competence mechanisms.

The remainder of this book is devoted to showing how the implications identified in this section follow from the proposals made above.

1.5 Markedness: an outline

So what is markedness? In its relation to i-language, 'markedness' refers to the empirical effects of the restrictions on constraint form outlined above. The restrictions express the leading ideas of markedness reduction and Preservation of the Marked: both output and faithfulness constraints must refer to a contiguous range of a hierarchy starting with its most marked member; no constraints can refer to the hierarchy in any other way.

Chapter 2 presents the details of the formal theory of markedness reduction, Preservation of the Marked, and markedness conflation. It also identifies the markedness hierarchies used in this book.

Chapters 3 to 7 explore the leading ideas behind the theory. Chapter 3 shows how the theory deals with markedness reduction. It discusses phenomena that are valid markedness diagnostics, and shows why they exhibit markedness asymmetries.

Chapter 4 deals with Preservation of the Marked. It focuses on cases where marked elements survive while unmarked ones do not. Combined with markedness reduction, marked preservation results in phenomena that do not exhibit markedness asymmetries at all.

Conflation is discussed in chapters 5 and 6. Chapter 5 focuses on the collapse of markedness distinctions in markedness reduction. It discusses cases where two or more markedness categories are treated as equally marked when undergoing a general markedness-reducing process. In contrast, chapter 6 discusses conflation in preservation. The cases discussed here are those where there is a conflict over which of two elements to preserve: in such cases the two categories can be treated as equally marked for purposes of preservation, so allowing other influences to determine the surface form.

Chapter 7 discusses markedness reversals in vowel-related phenomena. Unlike consonant markedness, vowel markedness is influenced by several directly conflicting hierarchies. The conflict is shown to obscure markedness effects in phenomena that are not subject to PoM: i.e. epenthesis and direction of neutralization. Even so, markedness can still be seen in phenomena related to prosodic structure.

Chapter 8 discusses predictions of the present theory and compares them to other theories of markedness. It argues that markedness is relevant to i-language, and that it is not related to representational complexity or contrastiveness.

Chapter 9 summarizes the book's findings and identifies areas for further research.

2 *Theory*

2.1   Aims

This chapter contains the theoretical core of this book. It shows how the leading ideas of markedness reduction, Preservation of the Marked, and markedness conflation are formalized in Optimality Theory.

Section 2.2 identifies some of the markedness hierarchies that will be discussed in this book. In particular, the form of the hierarchy for major place of articulation (PoA) | dorsal ⟩ labial ⟩ coronal ⟩ glottal | is examined, building on Lombardi (1998) and many others.

Section 2.3 presents the three distinct aspects of the theory. One is that every markedness hierarchy is formally expressed as a feature; each element on a hierarchy corresponds to a feature value. The second proposal relates to how the constraints refer to those feature values. Due to the form of the schema that produces such constraints, the result is a set of freely rankable output constraints in stringency relations and a corresponding set of freely rankable faithfulness constraints. The proposal is briefly schematized in (1).

(1)   For a markedness hierarchy $|\alpha \rangle \beta \rangle \gamma |$, there are two sets of constraints:
 (a) Output constraints: $*\{\alpha\}$, $*\{\alpha,\beta\}$, $*\{\alpha,\beta,\gamma\}$
 (b) Faithfulness constraints: IDENT$\{\alpha\}$, IDENT$\{\alpha,\beta\}$, IDENT$\{\alpha,\beta,\gamma\}$

The set members should be read disjunctively: $*\{\alpha,\beta\}$ is violated for every segment that is either α *or* β in a candidate. For example, $*\{\alpha,\beta\}$ is violated twice by each of the candidates [$\alpha\beta$], [$\beta\alpha$], [$\alpha\alpha$], and [$\beta\beta$].

The remaining proposal is about how hierarchies are related to different phonological environments: only prosodic markedness hierarchies like sonority and tone can combine with prosodic elements to form constraints; hierarchies involving subsegmental features like PoA cannot.

Finally, §2.4 presents a guide to discovering markedness hierarchies.

The theory is presented in this chapter in its entirety so lengthy formal excurses can be avoided in the case studies. For those readers who would prefer to move quickly on to the case studies, I recommend reading the description of the PoA hierarchy in §2.2.1 and the overview of the formalism in the introduction to §2.3 before reading chapter 3.

2.2 Markedness hierarchies

There is a broad consensus in the phonological literature that there are markedness hierarchies, and even a good deal of agreement as to many of the details of those hierarchies. For example, there is almost universal agreement that the obstruent voicing hierarchy has voiced obstruents as more marked than voiceless ones (recent work includes Lombardi 1991, 1995, 1996, 1999; Gnanadesikan 1997; Wetzels & Mascaró 2001). There is also widespread agreement that there is a hierarchy for segmental sonority, though there are many disagreements over the details (see Parker 2002 and the extensive discussion therein). Of course, while widespread consensus is suggestive and a helpful guide, it is far more helpful to determine how markedness hierarchies can be discovered and evaluated. This is the aim of the following discussion, with focus on the PoA hierarchy.

The ease of discovering markedness hierarchies is related to the pervasiveness of markedness reduction. Under the most extreme view, markedness reduction is responsible for all divergences from underlying forms. In formal terms, this means that every output constraint is directly related to a markedness hierarchy. It is therefore easy to discover markedness hierarchies under this approach: if there is a synchronic alternation such that segment /α/ surfaces unfaithfully as [β], there must be a markedness hierarchy in which some property of [α] is more marked than some related property of [β].

A more moderate view is to recognize several different forces acting on the output of the phonological component. Markedness reduction is one of the forces responsible for 'horizontally' context-free alternations. An alternation is horizontally context free if the output constraint that is responsible for causing it does not mention surrounding segments, only prosodic constituents. For example, *ONSET/glottal is horizontally context free, while Pater's (1996) constraint *NÇ, in which the voicing of the onset consonant contextually depends on the preceding nasal, is not.

Other forces include those that require agreement and disagreement in nearby segments' feature values. There is a fair amount of (often implicit) disagreement over whether assimilation and dissimilation can be considered a type of markedness reduction. For example, some work in autosegmental theory sees markedness reduction as elimination of structural complexity (an idea rejected in §8.4). As assimilation comes about through feature deletion and subsequent spreading and deletion is reduction of structural complexity, assimilation is therefore a type of markedness reduction in this theory (see Cho 1999 and references cited therein). Recent approaches in OT by Lombardi (1999) and Baković (1999a) argue that assimilation is caused by a set of constraints that require feature identity between adjacent segments (called AGREE[F]); this view essentially regards assimilation as unrelated to the sort of markedness reduction produced by constraints like *{dorsal}. In contrast, the theory presented in this book argues that assimilation is a form of markedness reduction (see §4.3). Therefore, it takes the extreme view – markedness reduction is responsible for almost all unfaithfulness, and consequently almost all output constraints are related to a markedness hierarchy.

However, not all phonological alternations are caused by markedness reduction. Restrictions on prosodic structure are fundamentally different from those on segmental form. In general terms, prosodic heads demand more structure and non-heads demand less. In contrast, there is no subsegmental neutralization process that forces a segment to become more featurally elaborate, such as taking on a secondary articulation. In short, I consider processes involving the form of prosodic constituents to derive from entirely different principles than subsegmental ones. Constraints like ONSET, NOCODA, FTBIN (Prince & Smolensky 1993:§6) therefore do not relate to markedness hierarchies, and so the following theory will make no attempt to derive them from hierarchies. Given the scope of this book, I will reserve further discussion of prosody for future work.

2.2.1 The PoA hierarchy

The PoA hierarchy in (2), repeated from chapter 1, closely follows Lombardi (1995, 1998, 2002), with one change discussed below. The hierarchy has its foundations in a great deal of previous work starting with the Prague School (Jakobson 1941) and has figured prominently in phonology since then (Battistella 1990:121; Paradis & Prunet 1991b and references cited therein; Prince & Smolensky 1994:ch.9§1.2,§2; Smolensky 1993; Gnanadesikan 1995; Prince 1997c, 1999; and Pater & Werle 2003, to name but a few).

(2)   The major place of articulation (PoA) hierarchy
        | dorsal 〉 labial 〉 coronal 〉 glottal |

'Dorsal' refers to velars and uvulars (e.g. [k q ŋ N]). 'Labial' refers to both bilabials and labio-dentals (e.g. [m ɱ β v]). 'Coronal' covers interdental, dental, alveolar, and palato-alveolar places of articulation. 'Glottal' refers to the glottals [ʔ h ɦ] and to the *anusvara* [N], discussed in §2.2.1.1.

The hierarchy does not mention secondary articulations such as labialization, palatalization, and velarization; these will be discussed where appropriate. It does not distinguish minor PoA distinctions such as bilabial vs. labio-dental; similarly, dentals, alveolars, and palato-alveolars are all treated as 'coronal', and so on. There was no need to make distinctions among these minor PoAs in the case studies. Of course, it is highly probable that there are other hierarchies that mention minor PoAs (e.g. see §3.2.4.3).

McCarthy (1994) argues that there is a class of consonants which all share the feature [pharyngeal]: uvulars [q ɢ ɴ ʀ χ ʁ], glottals [ʔ h ɦ], pharyngeals [ħ ʕ], and epiglottals [ʕ ʔ ʜ]. In the present work, glottals are least marked in the PoA hierarchy, but the exact place of uvulars, pharyngeals, and epiglottals is left unaddressed here. Pharyngeals and epiglottals are rare, so it is difficult to find clear evidence as to their relative markedness. As for uvulars, there is some evidence that they are more highly marked than velars (§5.2.4). In contrast, there is ample evidence that glottals are least marked: many languages have PoA neutralization to glottal (§3.3.3). The lack of resolution does not affect any of the major points in this book. I note that Lombardi (2002) proposes that all [pharyngeal] sounds are least marked in terms of PoA, but apart from glottals the evidence for this claim is unclear.

There is controversy over whether palatals are coronal, corono-dorsals, dorsal, or a class unto themselves, and there is great variability in the descriptive use of the term (Hall 1997). The issue is not absolutely crucial to the theory, so the position of palatals on the PoA hierarchy will be discussed in the case studies when necessary.

The PoA hierarchy in (2) is not the only one that has been proposed. Paradis & Prunet (1991b) and many others consider coronal to be the least marked PoA; chapter 3 presents evidence from neutralization and epenthesis that glottals are less marked than coronals. A less popular view is that velars can be less marked than coronals (Williamson 1977:698; Kaye, Lowenstamm, & Vergnaud 1985, 1989:74; Trigo 1988; Harris 1990:264; Rice 1996, 1999a,b; Oostendorp 1999); evidence against this idea is discussed in §8.4.2. Finally, Hume & Tserdanelis (2002) and Hume (2003) argue that labial can be least marked; this proposal is rejected in §8.2.1.1.

PoA markedness does not depend on prosodic context: dorsal segments are highly marked for PoA regardless of whether they are in an onset, coda, stressed syllable, or any other prosodic constituent (see §2.3.1.1 and §8.4.2, cf. Trigo 1988).

2.2.1.1 Glottals

The PoA hierarchy in (2) distinguishes four main classes of PoA. As the coronal, labial, and dorsal classes are generally accepted in a great deal of previous work, the 'glottal' class is the focus of this section. Glottals are special in several ways, and so they require extra discussion.

It is uncontroversial that the class of glottals includes the glottal stop [ʔ] and the fricatives/approximants [h ɦ]. I will argue that there are two glottal nasal segments as well. One is the equivalent of the 'placeless nasal glide' or *anusvara*, discussed in detail by Trigo (1988). I identify the *anusvara* as the nasalized glottal continuant [ɦ̃]. The other is a glottal nasal stop, which will be represented as [N] here. This stop is phonetically realized with an oral constriction in the velar~uvular region, similar to a velar [ŋ] or uvular [ɴ].

The voiced glottal approximant [ɦ̃] — or the 'nasal glide' — is reported in a number of languages, including word-final codas in many Japanese dialects (McCawley 1968; Trigo 1988). Trigo describes it as a 'glide-like transitional element'. In Gujarati it is said without occlusion in the oral cavity, just like a nasalized [ɦ] (Cardona 1965). [ɦ̃] is also reported to occur in a number of Peruvian languages. In Arabela it is clearly nasal because it motivates progressive nasal harmony, just like [m] and [n]: e.g. [ɦ̃ãnũʔ] 'to fly', cf. [nũw̃ãʔ] 'partridge', [mõnũʔ] 'kill' (Rich 1963). Finally, just like [h], [ɦ̃] continues the articulations of preceding vowels. For example, McCawley (1968:84) describes the Japanese [ɦ̃] as 'a nasalized prolongation of the preceding vowel'.

I propose that there is also a stop version of [ɦ̃] — the glottal nasal stop, represented as [N]. [N] contrasts with [ɦ̃] solely in terms of the feature [continuant]. The term 'glottal nasal stop' may seem like an oxymoron: after all, an oral glottal is produced with occlusion in the glottis and nasal sounds are said with airflow through the nasal cavity, so a glottal nasal stop would seem to require an articulatory impossibility. However, I argue that a revised understanding of the phonetic interpretation of [glottal] allows glottal nasal stops to be produced. In any case, there is compelling phonological evidence that there is a glottal nasal stop [N] and that it is distinct from the velar [ŋ] and uvular [ɴ].

2.2.1.1.1 Interpretation of [glottal][1]

Ohala & Lorentz (1977:585) argue that the main feature that distinguishes PoA in nasals is the difference in the size of the oral cavity. A bilabial [m] has the largest oral cavity, then [n]; [ŋ] has the smallest, as illustrated in (3). The '•'

---

[1] My thanks to John Kingston for his comments on the proposals in this section.

indicates primary airflow, while 'o' indicates airflow deviation into the oral cavity.

(3)   Vocal tract shape for [m], [n], [ŋ], from Ohala & Lorentz (1977:586)

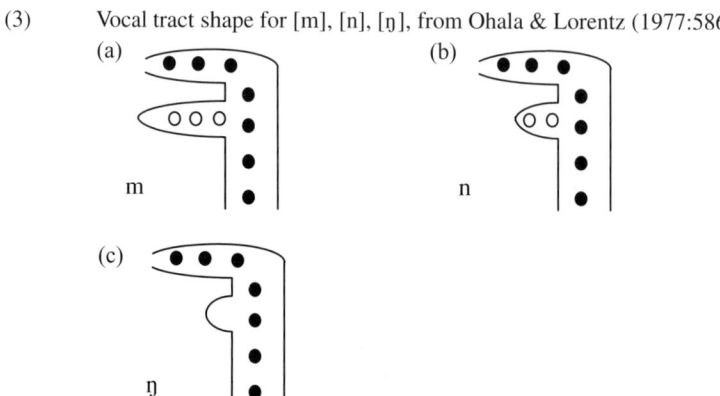

Following a suggestion by John Kingston, the [glottal] feature can be interpreted as requiring an absence of consonantal constriction downstream from the sound source.[2] For oral consonants, there must be no consonantal constriction in the oral cavity. In contrast, for nasal consonants the velum must be lowered (i.e. there must be access to the nasal cavity). A further requirement is that there must be no deviation from the primary resonating chamber. For oral glottals, the nasal passages must be blocked off, but for nasal glottals the *oral* cavity must be blocked. In short, the implementation of [glottal] for nasals effectively calls for the most direct route from the glottis to the nostrils via the pharyngeal and nasal airways. Therefore, the size of oral cavity must be restricted. As shown in the diagrams above, a constriction in the velar or post-velar region is the best that can be done in this regard – i.e. (3c). Coincidentally, this happens to be the same as [ŋ]'s phonetic realization.

The implementation of [N] can be compared with [h]: like the proposal for [N], [h] is produced by creating the most direct route from the glottis to the sound radiation point and the nasal cavity is closed off.

In short, a nasal stop phonologically specified as [glottal] is not articulatorily impossible given the revised interpretation of [glottal]. In practical terms, this proposal means that the two phonologically distinct segments [ŋ] and [N] have a similar phonetic realization, but for quite different reasons. The phonological

---

2 The ban on a *consonantal* constriction – a constriction related to the production of a consonant – allows for coarticulation of glottals with vowels (as typically happens). My thanks to John Kingston for discussion of this point.

2.2 *Markedness hierarchies*   39

specifications of [ŋ] issue a directive for velar constriction; in contrast, the phonological specifications of [N] merely require a direct route from source to radiation point, and velar constriction happens to be necessary to achieve this goal. Because no exact target for [N]'s occlusion is specified, it is possible that it may vary between velar and uvular. As the focus here is on phonology, identifying the degree of variation in the phonetic realization of [N] will be left to future work.

2.2.1.1.2 Phonological evidence for [N]

The phonetic similarity of [N] and [ŋ] has resulted in a great deal of descriptive confusion: many languages are reported to have [ŋ], but really have [N].

For example, many languages neutralize nasal PoA contrasts to [N] in coda position, but are reported as neutralizing to 'ŋ': e.g. Huallaga Quechua (Weber 1989), Genovese (Ghini 2001:173), Kagoshima Japanese (Haraguchi 1984; Trigo 1988), Seri (Marlett 1981:20), Yamphu (Rutgers 1998), Makassarese (Aronoff et al. 1987), and the San Marcos dialect of Misantla Totonac (MacKay 1994:380). Since [N] is realized with velar constriction, the apparent result is often a coda nasal inventory described as [ŋ] (but is really [N]), or [m ŋ] if only coronals neutralize (i.e. [m N]) as in Yamphu (§4.2.1). That the nasals are [N] rather than [ŋ] is evident from their phonological behaviour.

For example, many of the languages just cited also have neutralization of oral stops to the glottal [ʔ] and/or fricatives to [h]. Kagoshima Japanese coda nasals neutralize to [N] while all other segments become [ʔ] (Shigeto Kawahara p.c.; Trigo 1988:34–5; Haraguchi 1984; Fallon 2002:182ff.).

(4)   Kagoshima Japanese coda neutralization
     (a) /kuʦu/   → [kuʔ] 'shoe'
                           cf. [kuʦu-ʃita] 'socks (shoe-under)'
     (b) /miʣu/   → [miʔ] 'water'
                           cf. [miʣu-tamaɾi] 'puddle (water-group)'
     (c) /hiɾu/   → [hiʔ] 'noon'
                           cf. [hiɾu-gohaN] 'lunch (noon-food)'
     (d) cf. /kami/ → [kaN] 'hair'
                           cf. [kami-sori] 'razor (hair-shaver)'

If the neutralized nasal in (d) was really velar [ŋ], one could expect stops to neutralize to [k], not [ʔ] (i.e. /kuʦu/ → *[kuk]). Even if Kagoshima Japanese was an exception, at least *one* language should exist in which stops and/or fricatives neutralize to [k] and [x] while nasals neutralize to 'ŋ'. However, there is no such language (see §3.3, §8.4.2). Whenever nasals are reported to neutralize to 'ŋ', stops and/or fricatives neutralize to [ʔ] and [h] respectively. If the 'ŋ' is really glottal [N], it is clear why oral stops become [ʔ] and fricatives become [h]. If the 'ŋ' is really velar [ŋ], the lack of parallelism for oral stops and fricatives is inexplicable.

Epenthesis also provides evidence for [N]. The oral stops [ʔ] and [t] are commonly produced by epenthesis, as is the glottal [h]; in contrast, [k] and [x] are never epenthetic. As discussed in §3.2, Uradhi provides an example of epenthesis that produces 'ŋ', supporting the proposal that this is phonologically [N].

Assimilation also shows that there are glottal nasal stops. In Yamphu, oral stops become [ʔ] before another glottal: e.g. /mo-dok-ha/ → [modoʔha] 'like those', *[modokha]; /læ:t-he-ma/ → [læ:ʔhema] 'to be able to do' (Rutgers 1998:48). Nasal stops also assimilate to glottals, and the result is analysed here as a glottal [N]: /pen-ʔi/ → [peNʔi] 'he's sitting'; /hen-he:-nd-u-æn-de/ → [heNhe:ndwende] 'can you open it?' (Rutgers 1998:44). If Yamphu [N] is really velar [ŋ], this assimilation is inexplicable – again one would expect stop assimilation to result in [k] before [ʔ]: i.e. /læ:t-he-ma/ → *[læ:k.he.ma]. From a broader perspective, assimilation of PoA always results in agreement of PoA features. Therefore, the nasal that appears before [h] in Yamphu must be phonologically [glottal].

[N] behaves like other glottals in triggering processes. Gutturals – glottals, pharyngeals, and uvulars – can force an adjacent vowel to have a retracted tongue root ([RTR]). For example, Arabic verb stems must have a low vowel next to a guttural in the imperfect: e.g. [faʕal]/[ja-fʕal] 'do', *[faʕil] (McCarthy 1994). The generalization holds for uvulars [ʁ χ], pharyngeals [ʕ ħ], and glottals [ʔ h], but not for velars. Similarly, Miogliola's vowels must be RTR when followed by a tautosyllabic moraic glottal nasal [N] (Ghini 2001:ch.4). Coda [N] is usually non-moraic (e.g. [feᵘN] 'fine'), but becomes moraic when a consonant follows (e.g. [fɛᵘNᵗd͡z]) or after a stressed vowel. The only vowels allowed before moraic [N] are the RTR vowels [ɛ œ a ɔ]; ATR [i y e æ ɑ o u] are not allowed. As velars never cause vowels to lower, it must be the case that Miogliola [N] is post-velar – i.e. glottal.[3]

[N] has the same distribution as other glottals. It is common for glottals to be banned from onset position. For example, Chamicuro and Macushi Carib do not allow [h] in onsets (Parker 1994b). Similarly, Buriat's [N] is allowed only in codas while [n] and [m] appear in onsets (Poppe 1960). If Buriat [N] is

---

3 An alternative analysis is that [N] nasalizes the preceding vowel, and nasal vowels must be [−high]. However, Ghini does not report any such nasalization, and vowels do not lower before other nasals (e.g. [ɪɲ.d͡ʒénw] 'naïve', *[ɪɲ.d͡ʒɛ́nw]).

actually a velar [ŋ], it is difficult to explain why [k], [g], and [x] can all appear in onset position. In fact, there is no language that bans velars like [k g x ɣ] in onsets but allows them in codas; glottals excepted, every PoA that is allowed in codas is also allowed in onsets (§3.2.3; Goldsmith 1990; Beckman 1998). So, the fact that Buriat's 'ŋ' is only allowed in codas indicates that it is really glottal [N]. Miogliola [N] has the same distribution, consistent with its vowel-lowering behaviour mentioned above (Ghini 2001:§5.1).

[N] also alternates with other glottals. For example, [h̃] appears in Aguaruna onsets, but is realized as [N] in codas: [suŋkuN] 'influenza', cf. [suŋ.ku.h̃-ãn] 'influenza+accusative' (D. L. Payne 1990:162). If this [N] is really velar [ŋ], the motivation for the alternation is unclear; alternations involving [h] in other languages produce coronals (e.g. Korean – §3.3.2).

In summary, there is a great deal of evidence that there is a phonologically glottal nasal [N]. However, because its phonetic realization is somewhat similar to [ŋ], it has often been misdescribed as velar.

2.2.1.1.3 Comparison with Trigo (1988)

The proposal here that there are glottals [h̃] and [N] owes a great deal to Trigo's (1988:45ff.) work. However, there are important differences. For Trigo, there is no glottal nasal stop; there is only a nasal glide, equivalent to [h̃] here. To account for the fact that this sound is realized with velar constriction in some languages, Trigo proposes that 'the dorsal articulation of place-less consonants is acquired to implement the [+consonantal] feature' (p.49). In other words, glottal nasals always start off as /h̃/ and are converted to velar nasal stops [ŋ] at some point in the derivation (p.55).

Trigo's view is not adopted here for three reasons. One is that there is no evidence that a glottal [N] is ever velar [ŋ] at any point in the derivation. Trigo's proposal means that an underlying glottal /h̃/ could act like a glottal (i.e. trigger and undergo glottal-related processes), but after it is converted to velar [ŋ] it could act like a velar. In contrast, Yamphu [N] behaves as if it were glottal at all points in the derivation.

Another reason relates to the markedness of velars. Trigo (1988:ch.2) argues that the phonological rule that inserts dorsals applies to placeless consonants generally, not just /N/. With an opaque derivation, this implies that placeless oral stops and oral fricatives could also be given a [dorsal] feature. As Trigo shows, the result of this prediction is that [k] can be epenthetic and a target of neutralization: for epenthesis, a placeless consonant is inserted, then assigned a [dorsal] feature to produce [k]. For neutralization, stop consonants first debuccalize then the output is assigned a dorsal feature, predicting that [k] and [x] can be the output of place neutralization. Although Trigo argues that cases supporting these predictions exist, none withstand scrutiny – there is never epenthesis of [k] or [x], and these segments are never the output of neutralization (§3.2.5, §8.4.2; Paradis & Prunet 1990, 1994).

A final issue is the representation of glottals. I follow McCarthy (1994) in assuming that glottals have a [glottal] feature – they do not lack Place features or a Place node. For further discussion of representation and markedness, see §8.4.

2.2.2 Evidence for hierarchies

The PoA hierarchy is particularly interesting because it has more than two members. Such multi-valued hierarchies raise two issues: (1) how can the dominance relations among the hierarchy members be verified? and (2) is it a single hierarchy or the result of several smaller (perhaps binary) hierarchies?

2.2.2.1 Evidence for dominance

As discussed in §1.3.1.2, evidence for the dominance relations in the PoA hierarchy – and in any markedness hierarchy – come from synchronic alternations. For example, Malay /k/ becomes [?] in codas, as in /baik/ → [bai?], cf. [bai.k-an] (§3.3.1). The maximum that can be reasonably deduced from such an alternation is that there is some property of [k] which is more marked than the equivalent property of [?] on some markedness hierarchy. The PoA hierarchy provides a potential source: with dorsal as more marked than glottal, /k/→[?] can be seen as a reduction of markedness on the PoA hierarchy.

There are several assumptions behind this view of markedness relations. One is that markedness relates to features rather than segments. [k] is not more marked than [?] in Malay; rather it is [k]'s PoA value that is more marked than [?]'s. Here, this idea is encoded directly by relating markedness hierarchies to features. Of course, it may happen that a particular segment never fares better than another segment on any markedness hierarchy; for example, every feature value of [p] is either equally or more marked than every feature value of [t] on every hierarchy. Therefore, it is in a sense legitimate to say that the segment [p] is more marked than the segment [t], as long as it is understood that there is no direct formal markedness relation between the two segments as a whole.

Another assumption is that markedness is not transitive across hierarchies: it is only possible to talk of relative markedness with respect to a single hierarchy. For example, [k] is more marked than [?] in terms of the PoA hierarchy. However, [?] may well be more marked than [k] for some other hierarchy (and it is, for sonority – §3.2.3). This lack of transitivity is expressed by placing no limit on constraint formation for a particular hierarchy. Consequently, markedness relations in one hierarchy have no bearing on the relations in another hierarchy.

Suppose that /α/→[β] in some language or process but /β/→[α] in another. Do these alternations mean that [α] and [β] are equally marked, or do they indicate that there are two markedness hierarchies, one in which [α] is more marked than [β] and another in which the opposite holds? The theory requires that the latter be true. For /α/ to surface as [β] there must be some constraint that penalizes [α] and not [β], while for /β/ to surface as [α] there must be a constraint that favours [α] over [β]. Therefore, there is some hierarchy in which | α 〉 β | and at least one in which | β 〉 α |. In short, such alternations show that there are conflicting markedness hierarchies. It is not possible to say that [α] and [β] are 'equally marked' – this would require that none of the features of [α] and [β] are ever mentioned on any markedness hierarchy. If this is the case, then the theory predicts that there is no output constraint that distinguishes [α] from [β], so there will never be any motivation for [α] to become [β] or vice versa.

A final point is that for a markedness relation to be direct the elements must be phonologically related. For example, 'labial' can be legitimately seen as more marked than 'coronal' because they are both values of PoA. However, there can be no direct markedness relation between labials and liquids, for example. The theory of constraint formation proposed here derives this limitation by formally encoding markedness hierarchies as features (§2.3.2.1): markedness is a relation that can only hold directly between two values of the same feature; no markedness hierarchy can mention different features.

The PoA hierarchy presented above follows all of the limits just given. There are alternations that justify the dominance relations in the PoA hierarchy. For example, Kelantan Malay /k/, /p/, and /t/ all become [ʔ] in codas (Teoh 1988; Trigo 1988), thus establishing the ranking of non-glottals over glottals. In a Taiwanese secret language, /k p/ appear as [t], so showing the relation of dorsals and labials to coronals (§3.2). Evidence for the relation between dorsals and labials is harder to come by, but is suggested by triggering effects in assimilation (de Lacy 2002a: §7.5).

2.2.2.2 Binary vs. multi-valued hierarchies

One other important concern for hierarchies is whether a set of markedness relations is derived from a single hierarchy or is a composite of several hierarchies.

44   2 Theory

This question has not arisen many times for PoA, but is a recurring concern for the sonority hierarchy (e.g. de Lacy 2004:§3.6.2). Even so, it is a logical possibility that instead of a four-member PoA hierarchy, | dorsal ⟩ labial ⟩ coronal ⟩ glottal |, there are three binary subhierarchies: | dorsal ⟩ {labial, coronal, glottal} |, | {dorsal, labial} ⟩ {coronal, glottal} |, and | {dorsal, labial, coronal} ⟩ glottal |.[4] In concert, the sub-hierarchies would penalize dorsals more than any other feature, labials next, then coronals, then glottals.

There is way to distinguish between the two approaches if it assumed that each member on a hierarchy is a natural class; this assumption follows from the theory proposed here (§2.3.2). The single hierarchy | dorsal ⟩ labial ⟩ coronal ⟩ glottal | implies that there are four classes of PoA. In contrast, a subhierarchy like | dorsal, labial ⟩ coronal, glottal | implies that dorsal and labial form a natural class, and coronal and glottal form a natural class.

Natural classes should be able to assimilate, dissimilate, and otherwise participate in phonological processes. However, if dorsal and labial forms a natural class, many unattested predictions result. Suppose there was assimilation to the {dorsal,labial} class: coronals would become either labial or dorsal before a dorsal: e.g. /anka/ → [amka] or [aŋka]. If the language banned [ŋ], the result would be that a coronal becomes a labial when it precedes a dorsal (i.e. /anka/ → [amka]); this sort of assimilation is unattested: in all cases of PoA assimilation, adjacent segments *agree* in major PoA.

In short, if hierarchies relate to natural classes, proliferation of hierarchies means proliferation of natural classes, and every natural class should be able to participate in assimilation, dissimilation, and other such processes. Therefore, the way to determine whether a hierarchy is unified or really several smaller hierarchies is to see whether the natural classes defined by those hierarchies participate in attested subsegmental processes.

2.2.3   Markedness and environment

The dominance relations for some markedness hierarchies vary depending on their environment. Sonority is probably the most well-known example: high-sonority elements are less marked than low-sonority ones in syllable nuclei, while the opposite is true in syllable onsets (§7.4; Prince & Smolensky 1993). In contrast, PoA markedness relations remain the same regardless of

---

4   It is not possible to claim that all hierarchies refer only to two types of PoA. The subhierarchies | dorsal ⟩ labial |, | dorsal ⟩ coronal |, and | dorsal ⟩ glottal | do not have the same effects as the hierarchy | dorsal ⟩ labial, coronal, glottal |. | dorsal ⟩ coronal | results in the constraints *{dors} and *{dors,cor}; *{dors,cor} favours labials over coronals, so subverting the relationship between coronals and labials.

2.2 Markedness hierarchies

the environment. The issues to be addressed are therefore: (a) which markedness hierarchies differ depending on environment and why?, (b) what are the environments? and (c) how do hierarchies differ in different environments?

This book is primarily focused on establishing the fundamental mechanisms behind markedness reduction, preservation, and conflation. Consequently, presenting a detailed theory of markedness hierarchies and their relation to environment is beyond the scope of this work (cf. de Lacy 2002a:chs.2–4; Zec 2000). Nevertheless, the issue of hierarchies and environment arise in chapters 5 and 7 for vowel markedness. So, some observations will be made here, starting with the ones in (5).

(5) Markedness and environment: observations
   (a) Prosody-feature split
       Subsegmental feature hierarchies (e.g. PoA, voicing) never combine with prosodic constituents to form constraints. Suprasegmental feature hierarchies (e.g. tone, sonority) always combine with prosodic constituents to form constraints.
   (b) Heads vs. non-heads
       Suprasegmental hierarchies combine with prosodic heads and non-heads in constraints (more specifically, Designated Terminal Elements – Liberman 1975; Liberman & Prince 1977; de Lacy 2002a).
   (c) Hierarchy reversal
       Markedness relations in heads are the opposite of those in non-heads.

With respect to (5a), I propose that markedness relations for subsegmental relations like PoA, voicing, nasality, and so on remain constant in every environment. For example, the PoA hierarchy is the same in both onsets and codas: glottals are always least marked, then coronals, and so on. In contrast, suprasegmental features like sonority and tone are sensitive to their prosodic environment.

Observations (5b) and (5c) have been proposed or implied in a great deal of previous work (e.g. Prince & Smolensky 1993; Kenstowicz 1996; de Lacy 2002a, 2004, 2006). Prince & Smolensky (1993) have two sets of constraints that relate sonority to environment: one combines sonority with syllable nuclei (i.e. the head mora of syllables) and the other combines sonority with onsets (i.e. not the heads of syllables). More directly, Kenstowicz (1996) combines sonority with foot heads and foot non-head syllables (also see Zec 2000; de Lacy 2004). In all of these combinations, the markedness relations for sonority in head position are the exact opposite of the relations in non-head position. This is not just the case for sonority: I argued the same for tone and its relation to heads in de Lacy 2002b.

Of course, such claims require a good deal of evidence. Some will be provided in chapters 5 and 7. More detail on this issue can be found in Zec 2000 and de Lacy 2002a,b, 2004, 2006.

As a final note, the following proposals provide no account of why subsegmental features fail to combine with prosodic constituents in forming output constraints; the generalization is simply stipulated in the theory here with the hope that it may be reduced to other factors in the future.

2.3 Theory and formalism

This section presents a theory that formally expresses markedness hierarchies and allows for markedness reduction, marked preservation, and markedness conflation. The theory is set in the framework of Optimality Theory (Prince & Smolensky 1993) and also relies on Correspondence Theory (McCarthy & Prince 1995). The following discussion assumes a basic knowledge of OT; for an introduction to the framework, see Kager 1999 and McCarthy 2001b.

Essentially, this section shows how to get from a markedness hierarchy (as in (6a)) to output constraints (as in (6b)) and faithfulness constraints ((6c)), repeated from §1.1.

(6)   (a) Hierarchy: | dorsal 〉 labial 〉 coronal 〉 glottal |
      (b) Output constraints:
          *{dors}, *{dors,lab}, *{dors,lab,cor}, *{dors,lab,cor,gl}
      (c) Faithfulness constraints:
          IDENT{dors}, IDENT{dors,lab}, IDENT{dors,lab,cor},
          IDENT{dors,lab,cor,gl}

A central part of the theoretical proposal is that each markedness hierarchy is related to a feature, such as PoA or [±voice]. Each element on the hierarchy is a feature value. Constraints refer to these feature values in such a way as to produce markedness effects, to be detailed below.

For ease of exposition, the theoretical proposals have been split into three parts. The first two deal with related but separable aspects of the markedness-referring constraints: violation profiles (i.e. how they can be violated) and structural descriptions. To illustrate the difference, there is general agreement regarding the violation profile of the well-known constraint ONSET (Prince & Smolensky 1993): ONSET assigns a violation for each vowel-initial syllable. However, there is controversy regarding the structural description of ONSET: it has been formulated negatively (*$_\sigma$[V – McCarthy & Prince 1993b) and positively within the ALIGN schema (i.e. ALIGN-L(σ,C) – McCarthy & Prince 1993a). Even so, the controversy over the structural description does not in any way affect the need for a constraint that assigns a violation to vowel-initial syllables. In other words, the violation profile of a constraint and its structural description can be examined separately. The proposals about the violation profiles of constraints that refer to hierarchies are presented in §2.3.1, and their structural descriptions are discussed in §2.3.2. The validity of the proposals in this section do not depend on the validity of the proposals about violation profiles in the preceding section, and vice versa.

Finally, §2.3.3 discusses elaborations of the constraints, showing how different types of constraints can combine with prosodic constituents and other features to form constraints.

2.3.1 Constraint violations

The formal equivalent of the informal notion 'hierarchy' will be argued to be a feature in §2.3.2, with markedness relations expressed through feature values. For the purposes of this section a 'hierarchy' is an ordering of phonological feature values.

For every markedness hierarchy H, there is a set of output and a set of faithfulness constraints that refer to H.[5] The aim of this section is to provide a precise characterization of such hierarchy-referring constraints.

The theory has two goals. One is to correctly translate the dominance relations expressed by hierarchy into constraint-violation terms. As discussed in chapter 1, this 'correct translation' must allow for markedness conflation as well. So, for the markedness relation between dorsals and coronals, the theory seeks to explain why (a) dorsals can be treated as more marked than coronals, (b) dorsals can be treated as equally marked as coronals (i.e. dorsals and coronals can be conflated), and (c) dorsals are never treated as less marked than coronals.

The other goal is to have a theory with faithfulness and output constraints that can be ranked freely; no constraints are in a universally fixed ranking. Prince (1997a,b,c, 1998, 1999), de Lacy (2002a, 2006), and chapter 5 argue that free ranking of output constraints is essential in producing certain types of conflation. Chapter 6 shows that free ranking of faithfulness constraints is essential for certain types of assimilation and coalescence.

The following two subsections present a theory that both expresses the dominance relations in markedness hierarchies and has fully permutable constraint

---

5 While it is imaginable that there may be some hierarchy or hierarchy levels for which there are no corresponding constraints, this possibility is untestable, so it is put aside here. I have found no markedness hierarchy for which it could be proven that there is only a set of output constraints and no faithfulness constraints, or vice versa.

ranking. Section 2.3.1.1 is devoted to output constraints and §2.3.1.2 to faithfulness constraints.

A generalization to emerge is that both output and faithfulness constraints refer to the same sets of hierarchy elements, as expressed in (7).

(7)   The Marked Reference Hypothesis (MRH)
      If a constraint C refers to markedness hierarchy H,
      C refers to a contiguous range of H
      and that range always includes the most marked member.

The meaning of the term 'refer' differs depending on the type of constraint. The MRH requires output constraints to assign a violation to the most marked hierarchy element. For faithfulness constraints, the MRH requires preservation of the most marked member of the hierarchy in every constraint.

2.3.1.1   Hierarchies and output constraints

The relation of markedness hierarchies to output constraints can be informally expressed by the schema in (8). The proposals build on work by Prince (1997 a,b,c,d, 1998, 1999) and de Lacy (2000a, 2002a, 2006), and less directly on Green (1993).

Schema (8) applies to subsegmental hierarchies – hierarchies that refer to subsegmental features such as place of articulation and [voice]. Features that apply to segments as a whole (e.g. sonority) and are independent of segments (e.g. tone) are discussed in §2.3.3.

(8)   Subsegmental hierarchy-referring output constraints
      (a) For every markedness hierarchy H, and every member p of H, there is an output constraint o.
      (b) o assigns a violation for each segment in a candidate that either
          (i) contains p
          or (ii) contains any member more marked than p in hierarchy H.
      (c) Every output constraint that refers to H respects (b).

(8a) requires that (i) there is a set of output constraints for every markedness hierarchy and (ii) there are as many output constraints for a hierarchy H as there are elements in H. For the PoA hierarchy | dorsal ⟩ labial ⟩ coronal ⟩ glottal | there are therefore four output constraints.

By (8b), if an output constraint o refers to the element p in hierarchy H, it will assign a violation to p and all elements that are more marked than p in H (8bi). So for PoA, if an output constraint refers to labials it also has to refer to dorsals. In the by now familiar notation, this particular output constraint can be written as *{dors,lab}. The constraint *{dors,lab} will assign a violation for every segment that contains a dorsal or labial feature. In the output forms [paka], [kaka], and [papa] it will therefore assign two violations to each form, while for [pata], [kata], and [ka] it will assign just one violation. Of course, *{dors,lab} does not assign violations to any element lower on the hierarchy – i.e. coronals and glottals. The result for PoA is the set of output constraints *{dors}, *{dors,lab}, *{dors,lab,cor}, and *{dors,lab,cor,gl}.[6]

The constraints assume that segments are fully specified for PoA – no segment is 'placeless'. Arguments against placeless segments are given in §8.4.

The result is more straightforward for binary hierarchies. The obstruent voicing hierarchy | voiced obstruent 〉 voiceless obstruent | has the output constraints *{+voiced obstruent} and *{+voiced obstruent,*−voiced obstruent}; crucially, there is no constraint *{−voiced obstruent}.

Clause (c) is crucial. There are no other hierarchy-referring constraints apart from those that follow (8). So, there is no *{coronal}, no *{−voice}, and so on.

2.3.1.1.1 Formal schema

Schema (8) is expressed in more precise terms in (9). The definition assumes that a constraint is a function from a candidate to a set of violation marks (after Prince & Smolensky 1993).ABut, 'o (CAND)→V' is the constraint function o from a candidate CAND to a set of violation marks V. The number of violation marks in the set V is the same as the number of distinct x's in the candidate where x is any element that is equally or more marked than the hierarchy element in question. Conditions (c) and (d) restrict the definition.

(9) Subsegmental hierarchy-referring output constraints (formal)
    (a) For every hierarchy H, there is a set of output constraints O.
    (b) For every member p of H, there is some $o \in O$ such that for all q in H such that q is equally or more marked than p in H, o(CAND) → V
       • CAND is a candidate
       • V is a set of violation marks
       • the cardinality of V is the same as the number of distinct q's in CAND.
    (c) There are no other members of O.
    (d) There is no output constraint that refers to H and does not obey (a) and (b).

Condition (d) prevents another set of output constraints apart from O from referring to H in a way that is inconsistent with (9a–c). Importantly, (d) does not prevent H from being mentioned in combination with some other hierarchy.

---

[6] This theory disagrees with Gouskova's (2003) proposal that markedness-referring constraints never ban the least marked element in a hierarchy. For discussion, see §8.7.3.

For example, §4.3.2.1 presents a set of constraints that combine the place of articulation hierarchy with itself; these constraints are distinct from the set that refers only to the PoA elements and to nothing else. Similarly, §2.3.3 discusses prosodic hierarchies, where a single hierarchy combines with many different structural elements.

2.3.1.1.2 Stringency and conflation

The schemas in (8) and (9) incorporate the proposals of Prince (1997a,b,c,d, 1998, 1999) about maintaining hierarchy dominance relations while allowing free ranking – i.e. the constraints are 'stringently related'. This point can be illustrated using the place of articulation hierarchy's constraints, given above. Quasi-tableau (10) shows the constraints in action. A quasi-tableau compares harmonic bounding relations between forms rather than demonstrating winners under a particular ranking.

(10)   Quasi-tableau showing stringency

	*{dors}	*{dors, lab}	*{dors, lab, cor}	*{dors, lab, cor, gl}
k	*	*	*	*
p		*	*	*
t			*	*
ʔ				*

Quasi-tableau (10) shows how the output constraints impose a harmonic order on segments that differ in PoA without recourse to universally fixed constraint ranking. No matter which of the constraints is active in a given situation, dorsals always incur the same or a more significant violation than all other PoAs. Thus dorsals are the least favoured by these constraints. Similarly, regardless of the ranking, labials are never favoured above coronals – every constraint that coronals violate is also violated by labials, and there is one constraint that labials violate and coronals do not.

The reason that constraint ranking is irrelevant relates to the relationship between constraint violations: in terms of the PoA-referring output constraints, glottals incur a proper subset of the violations of every other PoA. So, after the mark-cancellation procedure (whereby violation marks common to both candidates in a pairwise competition are eliminated) glottals will not have any violations of the output constraints above, unlike the other PoAs.

In OT terms, the situation presented above is a type of harmonic bounding. A candidate α is a harmonic bound for β if α incurs a proper subset of β's violations (Samek-Lodovici 1992; Prince & Smolensky 1993:ch.9; McCarthy 2001b:§1.3.1).[7] In such a situation, no grammar will ever output β since α will always be more harmonic than β. Prince & Smolensky (1993:ch.9) show that harmonic bounding reduces to properties of the mark-cancellation procedure. If α has a subset of β's marks, then after mark cancellation β will still have violations while α does not, therefore dooming β to 'loser' status. Adopting terminology from Samek-Lodovici & Prince (1999), α is a harmonic bound for β if no constraint favours β over α and some constraint favours α over β. A constraint C favours α over β if α incurs fewer violations of C than β does.

The constraints presented above impose a type of harmonic bounding, but localized to just the output constraints for the PoA hierarchy. Thus, [p] may win in some grammar, but only through the action of some non-'PoA markedness' constraint (e.g. a faithfulness constraint like IDENT{dorsal,labial}). In terms of the PoA-output constraints alone, [t] is a harmonic bound for [p]. Such a relation between a set of constraints is called 'local harmonic bounding' here.

The local harmonic bounding relation is essential in allowing the constraints' ranking to be permutable. If the PoA output constraints were not in such a relation, their ranking could not be fully permutable and maintain the hierarchy's hierarchical relations. For example, suppose CON contained a constraint *CORONAL; this favours dorsals and labials over coronals. No longer is [t] a local harmonic bound for [p] and [k]: with *CORONAL ranked above the other constraints, the harmonic relations are reversed so that [t] can be less harmonic than [p] and [k]. A similar story holds for *LABIAL – again, this constraint favours dorsals over labials, potentially reversing the ranking between the two.

In short, local harmonic bounding is essential for having freely ranked hierarchy-referring output constraints that maintain the relationships encoded in markedness hierarchies.

It is important to point out that this proposal differs from the approach to hierarchies proposed by Prince & Smolensky (1993) and adopted in much subsequent work. Prince & Smolensky's theory imposes a universally fixed ranking between constraints that referred to individual elements of a hierarchy. For PoA, the result is the constraints and universal rankings ||*dorsal»»*labial»»*coronal»»*glottal|| (the symbol '»»' marks a universally fixed ranking). For discussion of the problems with the 'Fixed Ranking' theory, see §5.2.2 and §6.2.3.

---

7 Samek-Lodovici & Prince (1999) identify another type of harmonic bounding – 'collective' harmonic bounding – in which a candidate always incurs a subset of the combined violations of two or more other candidates. This type of harmonic bounding is not relevant here.

2.3.1.2 Hierarchies and faithfulness constraints

For every hierarchy there is also a set of faithfulness constraints. Faithfulness constraints require identity between segments in related forms, such as input and output, base and reduplicant, paradigmatic bases and derived forms, and so on. Faithfulness constraints refer to ranges of a markedness hierarchy in the same way that output constraints do. Consequently, they all preserve the most marked members of hierarchies.

The informal schema in (11) shows how markedness hierarchies are related to faithfulness constraints (cf. §8.7.2).

(11) Subsegmental hierarchy-referring faithfulness constraints (informal)
    (a) For each hierarchy H, for every element p in H, there is a faithfulness constraint f.
    (b) f preserves p and all elements in H that are more marked than p, i.e. f assigns a violation for every element q that
        (i) is equally or more marked than p in H
        and (ii) has a correspondent that is not identical to q.
    (c) Every faithfulness constraint that refers to H respects (b).

As with the output constraints, the schema in (11) requires as many faithfulness constraints as there are hierarchy members. If a faithfulness constraint preserves an element p in the hierarchy, it also preserves every more marked element. So for PoA there is some faithfulness constraint that preserves the mapping from a labial to its correspondent: it assigns violations to mappings from a labial to a non-labial. However, it also preserves all more marked elements – i.e. dorsals – in the same way. The notion 'mapping' is expressed in terms of Correspondence Theory (McCarthy & Prince 1995).

The schema in (11) does not place any restrictions on the dimension of faithfulness: there are separate sets of hierarchy-referring faithfulness constraints for all dimensions (Input→Output, Base→Reduplicant, Output→Output, and so on).

The result for PoA is a set of faithfulness constraints that refer to the same sets of elements as the output constraint counterparts. One constraint per dimension preserves dorsals alone; it will be called IDENT{dors} here. Another preserves both dorsals and labials – IDENT{dors,lab}; this constraint is violated for every input dorsal or labial that does not retain its feature specifications in the output. For example, /kapa/ → [tata] incurs two violations of IDENT{dors, lab}. It is important to point out that the constraint requires *identity* between correspondents: the mappings /k/→[p] and /p/→[k] also incur a violation of IDENT{dors,lab}, so /kapa/ → [paka] violates IDENT{dors,lab} twice as well. The other two PoA faithfulness constraints are IDENT{dors,lab,cor} and IDENT{dors,lab,cor,gl}.

The effect of the form of these constraints can be seen in quasi-tableau (12). The 'candidates' are input→output mappings from different underlying PoAs. Each mapping is unfaithful; exactly how it is unfaithful is irrelevant, so the outputs are designated [¬x], where [¬x] is some segment that differs from /x/ in PoA.

(12)

	IO-IDENT {dors}	IO-IDENT {dors,lab}	IO-IDENT {dors,lab,cor}	IO-IDENT {dors,lab,cor,gl}
/k/ → [¬k]	*	*	*	*
/p/ → [¬p]		*	*	*
/t/ → [¬t]			*	*
/ʔ/ → [¬ʔ]				*

Quasi-tableau (12) shows the mappings to be in a local harmonic bounding relation, as described in §2.3.1.1. So, the constraints ensure that unfaithfulness to dorsals incurs more serious violations than unfaithfulness to every other PoA. Consequently, unfaithfulness to the least marked elements – glottals – is least significant. The empirical relevance of local harmonic bounding for faithfulness is discussed in chapter 6, which discusses conflation in preservation.

There is a clear symmetry between the form of markedness and faithfulness constraints: for each output constraint there is a faithfulness constraint that refers to the same set of hierarchy elements. The result is that the elements that violate the most output constraints are also those that are most preserved. The effects of this implication are discussed in chapter 4's discussion of Preservation of the Marked.

As with the output constraints, in order for faithfulness constraints to be in a local harmonic bounding relation there can be no faithfulness constraint that preserves a hierarchy element without also preserving all more marked ones. A constraint such as IDENT {coronal}, for example, will preserve mappings from /t/ but not from /k/ or /p/. This predicts that there could be a system in which /t/'s excite greater faithfulness than /p/ and /k/, potentially preventing them from undergoing processes that other PoAs undergo. Chapter 4 presents evidence that such a constraint has undesirable empirical consequences.

Again, (11) describes the only way that faithfulness constraints can refer to hierarchies. There can be no constraint IDENT{coronal}, for example, or IDENT{−voice}, and so on.

2.3.1.2.1 Formal schema

A more precise version of (11) is provided in (13). The 'dimension' variable D refers to Input→Output, Base→Reduplicant, Output→Output, and so on. The aim of (a) is to require a separate set of constraints for every different dimension, but restrict constraints to only one set per dimension.

(13) Subsegmental hierarchy-referring output constraints
    (a) For every hierarchy H, for every dimension D there is a set of faithfulness constraints F.
    (b) For every element p in H, there is some f∈F such that for all elements q in H such that q is equally or more marked than p, D-f(CAND) → V
- CAND is a candidate
- V is a set of violation marks
- the cardinality of V is the number of distinct /q/→[r] mappings along dimension D such that $q \neq r$
- D is a dimension: e.g. input-output, base-reduplicant, etc.

    (c) There are no other members of F.
    (d) There is no faithfulness constraint that refers to H on dimension D and disobeys (b) of this schema.

2.3.1.3 Previous theories

A leading idea in the present theory is that the ranking of hierarchy-referring constraints is unrestricted. As shown above, this requirement necessitates sets of constraints that impose local harmonic bounding relations between candidates. There are a number of precursors to this idea in pre-OT work. For example, Clements (1990) argues that the sonority of a segment is calculated by reference to the features [sonorant], [approximant], [vocalic], and [syllabic]. The features are in subset–superset relation with each other: if a segment is [+vocoid], it is also [+approximant] and [+sonorant], and so on for each feature value. To clarify, Clements' (1990:292) table is reproduced here (O=obstruent, N=nasal, L=liquid, G=glide).

(14) Clements (1990): sonority calculation

O	< N	< L	< G	
−	−	−	−	'syllabic'
−	−	−	+	vocoid
−	−	+	+	approximant
−	+	+	+	sonorants
0	1	2	3	rank (relative sonority)

In Clements' theory there is no need to refer to a hierarchy of features to determine a segment's sonority – no particular feature has primacy over the others precisely because the features' values are related to each other in a subset–superset manner. The present approach is loosely related to this idea – there is no fixed ranking because constraints are in a local harmonic bounding relation.

The local harmonic bounding idea can also be found in early OT work in specific analyses. For example, Kiparsky (1994) uses faithfulness constraints similar to the ones above to deal with PoA assimilation in Catalan (an approach discussed in detail in §4.3.1), while Green (1993) uses sonority constraints analogous to the ones discussed above to deal with syllabification. Finally, Beckman's (1998) theory of positional faithfulness employs faithfulness constraints that refer to morpheme classes in a special–general relation, rather than in a fixed ranking.[8]

As mentioned above, the most extensive discussion of stringent constraints in previous OT work is in a series of lectures by Alan Prince (Prince 1997a,b,c, 1998, 1999). Prince shows that stringent constraints can express hierarchical relationships, just like constraints in a fixed ranking. I have also argued the same point for hierarchies, primarily in the context of prominence-driven stress (de Lacy 1997, 2000a, 2002a, 2004). Prince also identifies the crucial empirical difference between the stringent constraints and Fixed Ranking theories – they differ in their ability to produce conflation (also de Lacy 1997, 2000a, 2004). This point is discussed in more detail in chapter 6 (also see de Lacy 2002a:ch.3, 2006).

To summarize, the requirements that hierarchy-referring constraints be freely permutable and effect hierarchical relations can be achieved by invoking harmonic bounding. Harmonic bounding in turn necessitates that hierarchy-referring constraints have particular properties: they must assign violations to a contiguous part of the hierarchy, and always to the same endpoint. In short, the violation profile of hierarchy-based constraints must be such that they produce local harmonic bounding in the way described above. The requirements provide a guide to determining the structural description of constraints, a matter to which we can now turn.

2.3.2 Structural descriptions

The previous section presented proposals about the way in which hierarchy-referring constraints assign violation marks. This section focuses on the constraints' structural description. Informally speaking, it is concerned with how

---

[8] Beckman (1998) proposes that there are faithfulness constraints to roots and non-specific faithfulness constraints (e.g. Root-IDENT[F] vs. IDENT[F]). Beckman's stringently related constraints achieve the same result as McCarthy & Prince's (1995) fixed ranking ||FAITH-root » FAITH-affix||.

constraints refer to elements in markedness hierarchies, rather than how the constraints assign violations to candidates.

Section 2.3.2.1 proposes that the structural description of hierarchy-referring constraints is most easily stated using a multi-valued feature, generalizing proposals by Selkirk (1984), Green (1993), Gnanadesikan (1997), and others. Section 2.3.2.2 discusses the form of the hierarchy-referring constraints using multi-valued features.

2.3.2.1 Multi-valued features

An approach to feature values is adopted here that is related to Prince's (1983) grid theory: a feature value is a string of x's and o's (also see Green 1993). This approach allows for a formally definable notion of relative similarity; this point will prove to be important in providing a formal definition of the structural description of hierarchy-referring constraints (§2.3.2.2).

I propose that a feature's value is a string that has the form $x_0 o_0$, where $_0$ stands for '0 to any number'. For example, valid feature values are x, o, xo, $xxooo$, but not xox or ox. This approach will be called the 'xo theory'.

Every value shows the extent of a hierarchy – a hierarchy of n distinctions has xo-values of length $n - 1$. For example, the feature [nasal] has two values, traditionally [+nasal] and [−nasal], so the present approach represents the distinction as [x nasal] and [o nasal]. For ternary features, such as Gnanadesikan's (1997) consonantal stricture, a string of length 2 is used to distinguish xx, xo, and oo values.

The xo theory offers a straightforward way to express hierarchies formally. A hierarchy is simply a multi-valued feature. For example, the PoA hierarchy | dorsal ⟩ labial ⟩ coronal ⟩ glottal | is expressed by the feature [Place]. There are four distinctions, so [Place] has a feature value string of length 3. The feature values in (15) match the points on the hierarchy.

(15)   Multi-valued place of articulation features
      [*xxx*Place]   dorsal
      [*xxo*Place]   labial
      [*xoo*Place]   coronal
      [*ooo*Place]   glottal

In short, hierarchies are expressed as features. The most marked value of the hierarchy is assigned a string value consisting entirely of x's. Every less marked value differs from the most marked value in terms of its proportional x content, as seen in the PoA features in (15).

To recap, a grid theory for feature values is employed here, with some slight changes: (a) a feature string has the form $x_0 o_0$, not just x_0, and (b) all features employ this formalism, not just stress or multi-valued features. Hierarchies are therefore expressed as multi-valued features.

The *xo* representation of features is only part of a theory of hierarchies. The other part is the form of the constraints that refer to them; these are discussed in §2.3.2.2. The following section discusses the desirability of having multi-valued features.

2.3.2.1.1 Multi-valued and binary features

The most popular views of feature values are that they are binary or privative (Jakobson, Fant, & Halle 1952; Jakobson & Halle 1956; Chomsky & Halle 1968; Creider 1986; Steriade 1995b:147–57). However, the proposal that there are multi-valued features has a long history. Its origins can be traced back to some of the earliest proposals in markedness theory which allowed for 'gradual oppositions', characterized by varying degrees of a property like vowel height and backness (Trubetzkoy 1939:75ff.). Chomsky & Halle (1968) employ a multi-valued feature for stress, and a number of researchers have in effect argued for a multi-valued [Sonority] feature (Steriade 1982; Selkirk 1984; van der Hulst 1984; Durand 1990; Green 1993). Ladefoged (1975) and Williamson (1977) propose multi-valued laryngeal features, and Stahlke (1975) and many others have multi-valued features for tone (cf. Odden 1995). Recently, Gnanadesikan (1997) has argued that several features are ternary-valued, and Clements' (1991) [open] feature can be 'stacked', effectively producing multiple distinctions in vowel height (also see Lindau 1978; Clements & Hume 1995). In short, these theories have expanded the set of feature values to include many more distinct elements (usually represented by the natural numbers $\{0,1,2,\ldots\}$, for convenience).

The 'natural number' approach is only one way to allow multi-valued features. Prince's (1983) grid theory provides another method (with precursors in Kiparsky 1979 and Selkirk 1984). Instead of an n-valued [stress] feature, a string of x's specifies relative stress among syllables or moras. The grid-theory approach to multi-valued features has frequently been extended to other features: for example, it has been used for sonority, with gridmarks standing for different sonority levels (van der Hulst 1984; Milliken 1988; Zec 1988; Parker 1989; Clements 1990, 1992; Green 1993).[9] In the present work, the grid-theory approach to features is adopted, and extended as detailed in the previous section.

---

9 Grid theory is unlike multi-valued features in that gridmarks (and even some multi-valued features) are construed as representing *relative* values for the feature (stress, sonority) (see esp. Selkirk 1984:112, 121). This conception sets it apart from Gnanadesikan's feature value theory, in which features can be ternary-valued with each value expressing an absolute, not relative, value (although Gnanadesikan's *constraints* have the effect of relative values).

58   2 Theory

The few explicit comparisons of the virtues of binary and multi-valued features are Sommerstein (1977), Creider (1986), and McCarthy (1988). In the most recent and detailed account, McCarthy (1988:94) states the following, comparing binary- with multi-valued features:

(16)   'Are there any differences, then, between these two very different theories of
         essentially the same problem? Explicit discussion of this question is rare,
         and the arguments raised are unpersuasive, tending to emphasize
         methodological rather than empirical differences.' (McCarthy 1988:94)

McCarthy (1988) observes that arguments presented for one or the other approach are not based on empirically testable issues, but instead rely on appeals to theory-internal simplicity or ease of implementation (e.g. Chomsky & Halle's 1968 evaluation metric). Objections to multi-valued features often rest on the assumption that multi-valued features automatically introduce the full power of arithmetic to the grammar, allowing features to be incremented or decremented by any number. McCarthy points out that this assumption is not warranted: the algorithms that manipulate feature values are not determined by the form of feature values. The same goes for the objection that there is no obvious limit to the number of distinctions allowed per feature; again the issue of the maximum number of distinctions per feature is entirely separate from the form of the features themselves. Certainly, the *xo* proposal does not introduce the full power of arithmetic operations commonly associated with integers, as shown below.

More concretely, McCarthy compares a theory with a single multi-valued [Place] feature and one that has a non-terminal Place node which dominates several independent features ([coronal], [labial], [dorsal], etc.). He concludes that 'all arguments in favour of the class node Place apply with equal force to the *n*-ary feature [Place]' (McCarthy 1988:94); the reader is referred to this work for further discussion.

However, McCarthy does raise one argument in favour of the privative Place feature approach. Labial cooccurrence restrictions in Arabic apply across intervening segments; thus a stem /btf/ is blocked from appearing faithfully. He argues that this follows straightforwardly if [labial] and [coronal] are on different tiers, illustrated in (17) from McCarthy (1988).

(17)   Tiers and multi-valued features (McCarthy 1988: Fig. 2.2)

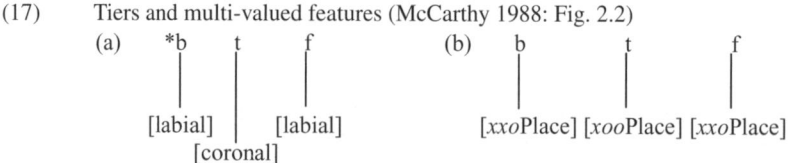

2.3 Theory and formalism 59

If [labial] and [coronal] are on different autosegmental tiers, it is a straightforward matter to explain why labials cannot appear in the output even when non-adjacent: their [labial] features are adjacent on a tier, and thus are subject to the Obligatory Contour Principle (OCP – Goldsmith 1976); the OCP bans adjacent identical elements. In contrast, a theory with a single [Place] feature (17b) clearly cannot appeal to tier-adjacency.

This is clearly a strong argument within autosegmental theory. However, recent approaches to similar problems have been resolved in non-representational ways (e.g. Alderete's 1997 local self-conjunction, Suzuki's 1998 generalized OCP constraint, Fukazawa 1999). These constraints do not appeal to tier-adjacency, so they can employ either multi-valued or privative Place features.

In short, there is no compelling phonological reason to reject multi-valued features in favour of binary/privative ones. There also seems to be no strong reason to reject binary/privative features in favour of multi-valued ones, although chain shifts have been argued to provide evidence for multi-valued features (e.g. Gnanadesikan 1997 and works cited therein; cf. Creider 1986; Kirchner 1996).

As a concluding observation, the proposal that there are multi-valued features by no means precludes the existence of binary or privative ones. However, §2.2.2 argued that it is not possible to decompose all multi-valued features into several independent binary features (also see de Lacy 2004:§2.4).

2.3.2.2 Constraint form

One part of the theory of markedness proposed here is the form of feature values, and the other is restrictions on the form of constraints. The schema in (18) gives the form of hierarchy-related output constraints. F is a feature, and v is its value (i.e. a string of x's and o's).

(18)   Subsegmental hierarchy-related output constraint definition
        *[vF] $=_{def}$ Incur a violation for every segment that is [wF]
        (i) v is a substring of w
        (ii) v does not contain o elements

In a constraint like *[xPlace], x is the value of [Place]. Therefore, *[xPlace] is violated by every segment whose [Place] value contains x: i.e. [xooPlace], [xxoPlace], and [xxxPlace], but not [oooPlace].

As noted, v may only contain x's. Context-free output constraints do not refer to o values, though other constraints may (§2.3.3.1). Following Green (1993), schema instantiation is assumed to be 'complete'; there is a constraint *[vF] for every possible length of v, implying that there are also *[Place], *[xPlace], *[xxPlace], and *[xxxPlace] constraints. Completeness is incorporated into the schemas (9b) and (13b). Together, the *[vPlace] constraints – with the restrictions stated above – have the desired harmonic bounding effect. Quasi-tableau (19) illustrates this result.

(19)   Harmonic bounding for PoA constraints

	*[Place]	*[xPlace]	*[xxPlace]	*[xxxPlace]
?[oooPlace]	*			
t [xooPlace]	*	*		
p [xxoPlace]	*	*	*	
k [xxxPlace]	*	*	*	*

As (19) shows, the constraints are in a local harmonic bounding relation with each other. *[xPlace] is violated by all segments except glottals, while *[xxPlace] is violated by only the relatively marked labials and dorsals. Every constraint assigns violations to a contiguous part of the hierarchy, and every element is a harmonic bound for elements higher on the hierarchy in terms of the PoA constraints.

The *xo* theory of feature values plays an important role in the hierarchy-referring constraints' formulation. To produce harmonic bounding, the structural description of the hierarchy-referring constraints needs to refer to a relation of inclusion between the members of the hierarchy. So, any structural description that includes [p] must also include [k], and so on. The *xo* theory allows reference to inclusion in a straightforward way via the substring relation.

2.3.2.2.1 Disjunction

Theories without the *xo* representation offer no easy formal way to refer to sets of features. For example, a theory with a set of privative PoA features – [glottal], [coronal], [labial], and [dorsal] – offers no straightforward method of referring to the set {[dorsal], [labial]}. A constraint such as *{[dorsal], [labial]} 'Assign a violation to a segment that is either [dorsal] or [labial]' introduces a significant new formal apparatus to the theory of constraint form – i.e. a disjunction operator.

Such an operator may not be seen as far removed from Smolensky's (1993) 'local conjunction': a locally conjoined constraint such as *[labial]&*[dorsal] is violated only if both *[labial] and *[dorsal] are each violated within the same domain. In contrast, the constraint *{[labial],[dorsal]} is a single constraint with disjoined elements. However, it could be recast as a disjoined pair of constraints, so that *[labial]∨[dorsal] would be violated if either *[labial] or *[dorsal] is violated within the domain of a single segment (cf. Crowhurst & Hewitt 1997). The problem with such a 'local disjunction operator' is that it greatly expands the possible space of constraints and goes no way toward explaining why it is that *[labial] and *[dorsal] form a disjunctive constraint while, for example, *[coronal] and *[dorsal] do not.

The proposal presented above does not covertly implement a disjunction operator in constraint form. Certainly, the interpretation of the constraints does allow for a disjunctive evaluation: *[*xx*Place] effectively assigns violations to segments that are [*xxo*Place] *or* [*xxx*Place]. However, this formalism has nothing of the power of a disjunction operator. For example, there is no way to disjoin different features — constraints can only refer to different values of the same feature. Moreover, the present approach does not allow just any pair of feature values to be disjoined: only a range of values starting with the most marked one are effectively disjoined. For example, there is no constraint that assigns a violation to a segment only if it is [*xoo*Place] or [*xxx*Place], since [*xoo*] and [*xxx*] are not contiguous feature values. In short, while the effect of the present approach has the flavour of disjunction, it has very little of the power of a disjunctive operator.

As one final comment, the output constraints here are expressed negatively – i.e. they incur a violation for the presence of a certain structure. Yip (2001) argues that at least some markedness-related constraints should be positively formulated. A positive PoA constraint would have the form *Place→[xxxPlace]*, which is violated for all PoA features that are not [*xxx*Place]. The reason that the constraints are expressed negatively here is due to an empirical problem with positive constraints, called the 'pile-up problem'. Positive constraints demand the presence of structure, so they predict that more structure is less marked. For example, one way to satisfy separate demands for PoA to be dorsal and labial is for a segment to have both, like the complex segment [k͡p]. So, the best way to satisfy positive PoA constraints would be to 'pile up' whatever PoA each required. The empirical effect is to predict neutralization of simplex to complex segments, which never occurs. In contrast, negative constraints force reduction of structure. For related discussion, see de Lacy 2002a: §3.5.1.3.

2.3.2.2.2 Faithfulness
Schema (20) is for hierarchy-referring faithfulness constraints; again F is a feature and *v* is its value.

(20) Subsegmental hierarchy-related faithfulness constraint definition
IDENT[vF] = $_{def}$ Incur a violation for every segment S that is [wF] while its correspondent S′ is [zF], where $z \neq w$
(i) w is a substring of v
(ii) w does not contain o elements

For example, IDENT[xPlace] requires every input segment with a Place value that includes x to retain its input specification in the output. So, IDENT[xPlace] requires coronals ([xooPlace]) to surface as coronals, labials ([xxoPlace]) as labials, and dorsals ([xxxPlace]) as dorsals, but is not violated if glottals ([oooPlace]) fail to surface faithfully. Similarly, IDENT[xxPlace] is violated only if input labial and dorsal segments do not have output correspondents with the same PoA; it is not violated if glottal or coronal PoA is not preserved. The empirical effects of this schema are discussed in detail in chapters 4 and 6.

To summarize, constraints that refer to hierarchies are standard output and faithfulness constraints with the structural description given in (18) and (20). The proposal that hierarchies are expressed as multi-valued features almost reduces the theory of hierarchy-referring constraints to a simple generalization: there is a separate markedness and faithfulness constraint for every value of every feature. For example, the place of articulation hierarchy is expressed by a set of constraints that refers to all four values of the [Place] feature. The restriction is that constraints may only refer to x values (except for special circumstances discussed in §2.3.3), and do so in the substring manner encoded in the constraint schemas. Thus, the majority of the theory of markedness presented here reduces to the theory of multi-valued features and how they relate to hierarchies.

2.3.3 Environment and subcategories

Certain hierarchy-referring constraints can mention a prosodic environment. For example, Prince & Smolensky (1993) propose that the positions 'syllable peak' and 'syllable margin' are combined with the sonority hierarchy to produce sets of constraints. Similarly, Kenstowicz (1996) argues that the sonority hierarchy can combine with the structural position 'foot head' (i.e. the stressed syllable of a foot) and 'foot margin', and I have done the same for tone and feet (de Lacy 2002b).

Section 2.3.3.1 presents a proposal that the structural elements found in hierarchy-referring constraints are always one of two elements: the Designated Terminal Element (DTE) and non-DTE, adapted from Liberman & Prince (1977).

Section 2.3.3.2 proposes that there are general restrictions on which constraints may combine with structural positions in constraints: prosodic hierarchies must combine with structural elements while subsegmental hierarchies must not.

In a similar vein, hierarchy constraints may limit themselves to particular classes. For example, there could be a set of constraints that relate PoA to a particular manner of articulation: i.e. *{dorsal}/continuant, *{dors,lab}/continuant, and so on. This issue is discussed in §2.3.3.3.

2.3.3.1 DTEs and non-DTEs

I propose that markedness-related constraints can mention only two structural elements: the Designated Terminal Element (DTE) and non-DTE (Liberman 1975; Liberman & Prince 1977). A 'DTE' is similar to the notion 'prosodic head': the DTE of a prosodic category Π can be found by following the path of prosodic heads down to its terminal node. For example, the DTE of a syllable is the head root node that is dominated by the head mora of a syllable. The DTE of a foot is the head root node that is dominated by the head mora of a foot's head syllable, and is circled in (21). The + marks heads and − marks non-heads.

(21)

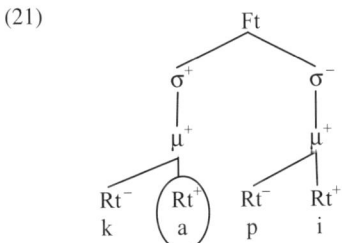

Every node on the prosodic plane is marked as a head or non-head; moras, syllables, and feet are marked for headedness, as are root nodes. As the definition of the DTE crucially relies on the notion 'prosodic head' it inherits the 'uniqueness' property of heads: for every prosodic node Π there is only one DTE of Π (Selkirk 1984, 1995; Ito & Mester 1992; cf. Crowhurst 1996).

The 'DTE' here is based on Liberman's (1975) and Liberman & Prince's (1977) proposal, but differs in two important ways. One is that DTEs can refer to two elements: p-DTE$_\Pi$ refers to the node that is of type p and dominated by an unbroken chain of prosodic heads to Π. For example, $_\mu$DTE$_{Ft}$ (read as 'the mora-DTE of a foot') refers to all those head moras that are dominated by head syllables that are dominated by feet. The other difference is that there are 'non-DTEs'.

The DTEs mentioned above are root node DTEs; other elements on the prosodic plane can also be DTEs. For example, the leftmost mora in (21) is the mora-DTE of the foot, and the leftmost syllable is the syllable-DTE of the foot. Reference to mora-DTEs is essential for elements that associate directly to moras, like tones. In contrast, reference to Root node DTEs is essential for properties that are part of the root node, like sonority. Since sonority is the focus of the hierarchies in this book, DTEs will be assumed to be root node DTEs unless stated otherwise; for further discussion, see chapter 7. A definition of DTEs is given in (22).

(22)   Definition of DTE
       $_p\text{DTE}_\Pi =_{def}$ A node n of prosodic type p is the DTE of prosodic category Π iff the path from n to Π consists entirely of prosodic heads.

A 'path' from n to Π consists of node n and all nodes that (a) dominate n and (b) are dominated by Π. The arguments p and Π can be any member of the prosodic hierarchy, from the root node to the Utterance Phrase node (and possibly also 'Focus' – see Truckenbrodt 2006). There are constraints that relate tone and DTEs of every prosodic category (de Lacy 1999); Zec (2000) has explored a similar idea for sonority.

Non-DTEs are the complement of DTEs. A root node non-DTE of prosodic category Π is every root node inside Π that is not Π's DTE. [k], [p], and [i] are root node non-DTEs of the foot in (21). Non-DTEs are defined in (23).

(23)   Definition of non-DTE
       $_p\text{non-DTE}_\Pi =_{def}$ A node n of prosodic category p is a non-DTE of Π iff
       (i) n is (transitively) associated to Π
       and (ii) n is not a $_p\text{DTE}_\Pi$.

The non-DTE definition in (23) can also be expressed in terms of paths: n is a non-DTE of Π if the path from n to Π (including n but not Π) contains one or more non-heads.

To clarify, DTEs are not a new element on the prosodic hierarchy. Instead, they are a way to refer to prosodic structure. So, the DTE proposal has no bearing on whether elements may be extra-prosodic, or whether feet may be ternary, and the like. It also makes no commitment to particular models of the syllable; a moraic one is used here for convenience. Compatible theories of representation are those that distinguish heads from non-heads.

Part of the usefulness of DTEs is that a node may be a DTE of one category but a non-DTE of another category. This dual nature proves to have significant empirical consequences, as discussed in chapter 7. In fact, the majority of elements are both DTEs and non-DTEs of some category. The DTE of the Utterance Phrase (the highest prosodic category) is the only element that is not a non-DTE of any category. Some elements are perpetual non-DTEs, though. For example, the onset [k] in (21) is not a DTE of any category since it is a non-head of the lowest prosodic level (i.e. μ).

The dual DTE-nature of terminal elements is evident in large structures, as in the prosodic word (ω) in (24). The figure below identifies the root-node DTEs and non-DTEs.

(24)   Root-DTEs and root-non-DTEs in the prosodic word (ω)

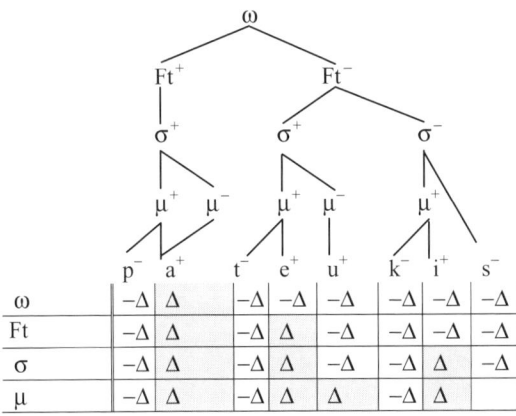

[a] is the root node DTE of the prosodic word in (24), while every other element is a $-\Delta_\omega$. Similarly, [a] and [e] are DTEs of a foot, while all other root nodes are foot non-DTEs. This table makes it clear that an element may be a DTE for one constituent but not for another.

Another point that emerges in (24) is that it is possible for a root node to have no DTE status with respect to some constituent. The word-final [s] in (24) is neither a Δ_μ nor a $-\Delta_\mu$ since it is not dominated by a mora. So, no constraint of the form $*\Delta_\mu \leq x$ or $*-\Delta_\mu \geq x$ will apply to it. This situation is only possible when strict layering is violated. The empirical effects of this fact are discussed in chapter 7.

Traditional notions such as 'syllable peak' and 'margin' can be expressed as DTEs and non-DTEs. For example, the peak (i.e. nucleus) of a syllable is Δ_σ, while the margin (onset and coda) is $-\Delta_\sigma$. Further constituents such as onset, rime, and coda can also be expressed in this system (as $-\Delta_\mu$, Δ_μ/Δ_σ, and $-\Delta_\sigma$ respectively).

A final question is why DTEs are used here and not 'heads'. The problem with the term 'head' is that it has been used in a variety of different ways, and some uses are mutually inconsistent. By using 'DTE' and 'non-DTE', any confusion that the different meanings of 'head' may cause can be avoided.

2.3.3.1.1 Constraint form

DTEs and non-DTEs form the structural prominence hierarchy $|\ _\beta\Delta_\alpha \rangle\ _\beta{-}\Delta_\alpha\ |$, generalizing Prince & Smolensky's (1993) peak-margin structural hierarchy. There are many (non-)DTE hierarchies, one for each possible specification of α and β: i.e. $|\ _\mu\Delta_\sigma \rangle\ _\mu{-}\Delta_\sigma\ |$, $|\ _\mu\Delta_{Ft} \rangle\ _\mu{-}\Delta_{Ft}\ |$, and so on for each pair of prosodic categories. Every DTE structural hierarchy combines with every prosodic hierarchy to form sets of constraints.

The tone hierarchy will be used to illustrate the constraints here (Ping 1996, 1999; de Lacy 1999, 2002b). The tone hierarchy has three distinctions: | Low ⟩ Mid ⟩ High |. The feature [Tone] represents this hierarchy, with the values: [ooTone] = High, [xoTone] = Mid, and [xxTone] = Low.

Because tone is suprasegmental, constraints that refer to the tone hierarchy must mention DTEs. Schematically, the DTE-tone constraints are as in (25). Recall that the hierarchy reverses in combination with non-DTEs.

(25)   DTE-Tone constraints
       (a) DTE constraints: $*_\mu\Delta_\Pi/xx$Tone, $*_\mu\Delta_\Pi/x$Tone, $*_\mu\Delta_\Pi/$Tone,
       (b) Non-DTE constraints: $*_\mu{-}\Delta_\Pi/$Tone, $*_\mu{-}\Delta_\Pi/o$Tone, $*_\mu{-}\Delta_\Pi/oo$Tone

The constraints in (25) follow the general schema for prosodic output constraints, given in (26).

(26)   Prosodic output constraints with DTEs
       $*_p\Delta_\Pi/[vF]$ =$_{def}$ Incur a violation for every segment that
            (a) is a p-DTE of Π
       and (b) is [wF]
       (i) v is a substring of w
       (ii) v does not contain o elements

For example, the constraint $*_\omega\Delta_\mu/[x$Tone$]$ is violated by every mora-DTE of the prosodic word that has a [Tone] specification that contains an x: i.e. [xxTone], [xTone]. In other words, the constraint is violated by mid- and low-toned primary stressed syllables.

As Prince & Smolensky (1993) observe, the relation of hierarchies to structural combinations is reversed in non-DTE constraints. In their example, voiceless stops are the most marked syllable peaks, but least marked margins (Dell & Elmedlaoui 1988). In the case above, low tone is the most marked element for DTEs, while it is the least marked for non-DTEs. The hierarchy reversal is formally expressed by a difference in the feature value used: for DTEs it is x while for non-DTEs it is o.

(27) Prosodic output constraints with non-DTEs
$*_p - \Delta_\Pi/[vF] =_{def}$ Incur a violation for every segment that
 (a) is a p-non-DTE of Π
and (b) is [wF]
 (i) v is a substring of w
 (ii) v does not contain x elements

It could be that $-\Delta$ constraints have the form 'Incur a violation if v is *not* a substring of w' where v refers only to x's; this would eliminate the need to refer to o values. However, this formulation introduces negation – a potentially undesirable operation in constraint form.

As an example, the tone non-DTE constraints for ω non-DTEs are $*-\Delta_\omega/$[ooTone] (a ban on high-toned non-DTEs), $*-\Delta_\omega/$[oTone] (banning high- and mid-toned ω non-DTEs), and $*-\Delta_\omega/$[Tone] (which bans all tones on ω non-DTEs). The difference between DTE and non-DTE constraints does not follow from any part of the theory – it must be stipulated that hierarchies reverse.

In principle every value of α,β for DTEs can be combined with hierarchies to form constraints. However, most of these constraints will be vacuously satisfied depending on the nature of the hierarchy. For example, on the assumption that tone associates to moras, only mora-DTEs and non-DTEs (i.e. $_\mu\Lambda_\alpha$ and $_\mu-\Lambda_\alpha$) will be relevant for the tone hierarchy. In contrast, sonority is a property of Root nodes, so the only relevant DTEs and non-DTE combinations are $_{Rt}\Delta_\alpha$ and $_{Rt}-\Delta_\alpha$.[10] Since it will be evident which type of DTE is relevant depending on the hierarchy discussed below, the β part of the DTE definition will not be supplied from now on unless it is directly relevant.

A more extended example uses the sonority hierarchy; this hierarchy is the focus of chapter 7 and used in chapter 5. Twelve distinctions are recognized here, after Kenstowicz (1996) (especially for the vocalic part), Walker (1998)

---

10 This fact limits the number of constraints that can be active in a grammar in a practical sense. However, this in no way inhibits generation of the constraints. Given a prosodic hierarchy with nine levels and two structural levels (Δ, $-\Delta$), there are $162n$ output constraints for each prosodic hierarchy with n elements. As pointed out above, effectively only $18n$ constraints are useful for each hierarchy. Of course, this means that CON contains a large number of hierarchy-referring constraints. The sheer number of constraints is of no concern though: what is important is that (a) the constraints make restrictive predictions and (b) the constraints have a common well-defined source – i.e. the schemas identified in this chapter (cf. McCarthy & Prince's 1993a ALIGN and McCarthy & Prince's 1995 IDENT, which also describe large numbers of constraints).

(especially for the consonantal part), and de Lacy (2004, 2006). The sonority hierarchy is broken in two in (28) for convenience only; it is a single hierarchy.

(28)   The sonority hierarchy
        (a) Consonant sonority
        voiceless   voiced   voiceless   voiced
            ⟩   ⟩   ⟩   ⟩   nasals ⟩ liquids ⟩ glides ⟩ glottals
          stops   stops   fricatives fricatives
        (b) Vowel sonority
          high   mid   high   mid-high   mid-low   low
         central ⟩ central ⟩ peripheral ⟩ peripheral ⟩ peripheral ⟩ peripheral
         vowels   vowels   vowels   vowels   vowels   vowels

The hierarchy has fourteen distinctions, so there is a feature [Sonority] with a feature value string of length 13. Voiceless stops are [*xxxxxxxxxxxxx*Sonority], while [a] is [*ooooooooooooo*Sonority]. As this notation is difficult to read, the symbol ≥ will be used to mean 'equally or more marked than' and ≤ to mean 'equally or less marked than'. The DTE equivalent of Prince & Smolensky's (1993) peak and margin constraints are given below. A syllable peak is equivalent to the DTE of a syllable (Δ_σ), while syllable margins are equivalent to the non-DTE of a syllable ($-\Delta_\sigma$). A capitalized coronal member stands for the entire manner of articulation for consonants (e.g. T stands for voiceless stops, from [t]); representative members of vowel sonority classes are used to represent the whole class. The sonority hierarchy is reversed in combination with non-DTEs: the best peak is the worst margin, and vice-versa.

(29)   DTE-sonority constraints
        (a) *$\Delta_\sigma \leq$T, *$\Delta_\sigma \leq$D, *$\Delta_\sigma \leq$S, *$\Delta_\sigma \leq$Z, *$\Delta_\sigma \leq$N, *$\Delta_\sigma \leq$L, *$\Delta_\sigma \leq$?,
             *$\Delta_\sigma \leq$ɨ, *$\Delta_\sigma \leq$ə, *$\Delta_\sigma \leq$\{i,u\}, *$\Delta_\sigma \leq$\{e,o\}, *$\Delta_\sigma \leq$\{ɛ,ɔ\}, *$\Delta_\sigma \leq$a
        (b) *$-\Delta_\sigma \geq$a, *$-\Delta_\sigma \geq$\{ɛ,ɔ\}, *$-\Delta_\sigma \geq$\{e,o\}, *$-\Delta_\sigma \geq$\{i,u\}, *$-\Delta_\sigma \geq$ə,
             *$-\Delta_\sigma \geq$ɨ, *$-\Delta_\sigma \geq$?, *$-\Delta_\sigma \geq$L, *$-\Delta_\sigma \geq$N, *$-\Delta_\sigma \geq$Z, *$-\Delta_\sigma \geq$S,
             *$-\Delta_\sigma \geq$D, *$-\Delta_\sigma \geq$T

As an example, *$\Delta_\sigma \leq$\{ə\} assigns violations to root-DTEs of σ nodes (i.e. syllable nuclei) with sonority of less than or equal to mid central vowels.

Of course, the sonority hierarchy does not only combine with syllable DTEs, but with DTEs of every other level. These constraints will be discussed in chapters 5 and 7.

All DTE-referring constraints are freely permutable. There is no fixed ranking between constraints based on the type of DTE element; constraints that refer to *$_\beta \Delta_\alpha$ do not universally outrank *$_\beta - \Delta_\alpha$ constraints or vice versa. Similarly, there is no need to impose a fixed ranking between constraints that differ in their value for α or β: $*_\beta \Delta_\alpha$ constraints do not universally outrank constraints that refer to $*_\beta \Delta_{\alpha+1}$, or vice versa.

To re-emphasize a point made in chapter 1, the proposal that hierarchies combine with DTEs and non-DTEs in different ways means that the traditional notion of 'markedness' does not apply directly to certain hierarchies. For example, it is not valid to say that the sonority category 'low vowel' is unmarked. Markedness of prosodic hierarchies depends on the structural element with which they combine, so 'low vowel' is the least marked category in terms of DTEs, but the most marked for non-DTEs.

In contrast, markedness is easily applied to subsegmental hierarchies: since subsegmental hierarchies do not combine with DTEs, the least marked element remains consistent across contexts. So, 'glottal' is always the least marked PoA element. This point is discussed next.

2.3.3.2 Subsegmental and prosodic hierarchies

Some markedness hierarchies never combine with DTEs to form constraints. For example, the PoA and voicing hierarchies do not vary with environment: neutralization of voicing always results in voiceless obstruents regardless of whether it occurs in the coda or onset, or in a stressed syllable and so on. The same is true of PoA (§8.4.2).

In contrast, some hierarchies must be combined with DTEs in constraints. For example, there is no evidence that the sonority hierarchy forms a set of context-free constraints of the form *[vSonority], where v is some value. So, a theory of hierarchies must identify the hierarchies that must appear with DTEs and the hierarchies that must not. I propose the restriction in (30).

(30)   The Hierarchy-Structure Combination Restriction
      (a) Hierarchies that refer to prosodic properties (e.g. tone, sonority) always combine with prosodic elements in constraints.
      (b) Hierarchies that refer to subsegmental properties (e.g. voice, place of articulation) never combine with prosodic elements in constraints.

Prosodic hierarchies refer to features that are not dependents of the Root node (e.g. tone, sonority) and prosodic structure. Subsegmental hierarchies include those features commonly regarded as dependents of the root node (e.g. [voice], Place, [nasal], and so on). So, there are no constraints of the form $*\Delta \leq [v\text{Place}]$, or $*-\Delta \geq [v\text{Nasal}]$, and so on. Similarly, all constraints on sonority or tone must mention a (non-)DTE.

As stated above, the prosodic hierarchies include the Tone hierarchy and Sonority hierarchy. Tone has not been considered a subsegmental feature since Leben (1973) and Goldsmith (1976). Sonority is commonly considered a property of entire segments (or root nodes), unlike subsegmental features like place of articulation. This idea follows the spirit of McCarthy's (1988) proposals that major class features reside in the root node, and that major class features are essential in defining sonority (Clements 1990; Rice 1992). Thus, sonority is a property of the root node rather than being a dependent feature, unlike [voice] or [nasal]. These hierarchies are dubbed 'prosodic' here, with the further claim that only these sorts of hierarchies can combine with structural hierarchies while subsegmental hierarchies cannot.

The generalization made above has broad consequences. It prevents positional output constraints on subsegmental features: there are no constraints like $*\Delta_\omega \leq $[labial], or $*\Delta_\mu/$[−voice].

Inside the syllable, a number of researchers have argued that output constraints that refer to the relation between constituents and subsegmental features are necessary (e.g. Ito 1986; Zoll 1998). The Hierarchy-Structure Combination Restriction rules out such approaches, instead necessitating an analysis using positional faithfulness constraints (Beckman 1998) coupled with context-free output constraints (see §4.3.1 for an example). As a note on positional faithfulness theory, it may seem that (30a) precludes positional faithfulness constraints such as onset-IDENT[voice] since this faithfulness constraint refers to a prosodic position and a subsegmental feature. However, this is outside the scope of (30). (30) prevents the general algorithm that relates constraints to hierarchies from producing full sets of (non-)DTE-referring hierarchy constraints. However, the proposal does not prevent an entirely different procedure from producing DTE-referring constraints. Beckman's positional faithfulness theory is just such another algorithm – it combines a small set of prosodic positions with hierarchies in a totally independent way from the hierarchy-combination processes proposed here. Note that the set of prosodic elements that positional faithfulness allows to combine with hierarchies is a small subset of those of the DTE theory (i.e. onsets, stressed syllables), and even elements that are not definable using DTEs and non-DTEs (e.g. root-initial syllables). In short, the Hierarchy-Structure Combination Restriction and positional faithfulness can coexist.

For the purposes of this book (30) is taken to be axiomatic; its reduction to other principles is left for future work.

2.3.3.3 Manner of articulation: subcategories of constraints

The PoA constraints presented in §2.3.1 are the basis for all PoA-referring output constraints. It is possible that there are elaborations on the PoA constraints as long as markedness relationships are not reversed. One such elaboration is given in §4.3.2 for assimilation. Another relates to manner of articulation (MoA), which is the focus of discussion here.

There is no relation between different MoAs for PoA. For example, Māori has the voiceless stops [p t k] and the voiceless fricatives [f h] (Bauer 1993); there clearly is no implicational relationship between the existence of dorsal and coronal voiceless stops and the existence of those same PoAs for voiceless fricatives. Colloquial Samoan shows that the opposite also does not hold: this language has [f s] and [k p ʔ], showing that the existence of a coronal voiceless fricative does not imply the presence of a coronal voiceless stop (Clark 1976; Mosel & Hovdhaugen 1992). Similarly, Hawaiian has the voiceless stops [k p ʔ], nasals [m n], and fricative [h] – the existence of a coronal nasal does not imply the presence of a coronal voiceless stop or voiceless fricative in any of the other manners of articulation (Elbert & Pukui 1979). Conversely, colloquial Samoan has the voiceless fricatives [f s] and nasals [m ŋ] – here the presence of a coronal voiceless fricative does not imply the presence of a coronal nasal. To expand on this point, table (31) lists languages in which the PoA contrasts for a particular MoA are a proper subset of those found in another MoA. For example, PoA contrasts in Murut voiceless fricatives are a proper subset of the voiced stop contrasts: the former has just the coronal [s], while the latter has [b d g]. Conversely, voiced stop contrasts are a proper subset of voiceless fricative contrasts in Wintu. The gaps for voiced fricatives are probably accidental – due to the relative rarity of voiced fricatives cross-linguistically. As table (31) shows, there are no implicational relations between different MoAs for PoA contrasts.

(31)   PoA proper subset relations among different MoAs

⊂	−vd stops	+vd stops	−vd fricatives	+vd fricatives	nasals
−vd stops		Nganasan [tk(ʔ)]~[bdg]	Ormuri [ptk]~[fsxχh]	–	Vanimo [pt]~[mnŋ]
+vd stops	Djapu [d]~[ptṯʲtk]		Wintu [bd]~[fsxχh]	Anejom̃ *none* ~[vɣ]	Central-Eastern Tundra Nenets [bd]~[mnŋ]
−vd fricatives	Tongan [fsh]~[ptkʔ]	Murut [s]~[bdg]		Sudest [s]~[vʷvðɣʷ]	Kewa [s]~[mnɲ]
+vd fricatives	E. Mari [zʒ]~[ptk]	Boazi [vz]~[bdg]	W. Mari [zʒ]~[fsʃx]		Harar Oromo [z]~[mnɲ]
nasals	Mordvin [mnɲ]~[ptck]	Komi [mnɲ]~[bdɟg]	Hungarian [mnɲ]~[fsʃxh]	Mountain Slave [mn]~[vzʒɣ]	

72 2 Theory

References: Anejom̃ (Lynch 2000), Boazi (Foley 1986:61), Central-Eastern Tundra Nenets (Salminen 1998), Djapu Yolngu (Morphy 1983), Harar Oromo (Owens 1985:10), Hungarian (Abondolo 1998a:433), Kewa (Foley 1986:60–1), Komi (Hausenberg 1998:309), Mari (Kangasmaa-Minn 1998:221), Mordva (Zaicz 1998:185–6), Mountain Slave (Rice 1989:30), Murut (Prentice 1971:16), Nenets (Salminen 1998:522–3), Nganasan (Helimski 1998:483–4), Ormuri (Efimov 1986), Sudest (Anderson & Ross 2002), Tongan (Churchward 1953), Vanimo (Ross 1980), Wintu (Broadbent & Pitkin 1964).

The theoretical implication of the observation is that it is likely that there are manner-specific PoA constraints. Output constraints of this type may have the form *{dors,lab,cor}/nasal (i.e. *{ŋ,m,n}), *{dors,lab,cor}/[−vd stop] (i.e. *{k,p,t}), and so on. For example, to account for the fact that there is a velar [k] in Mordva but no velar nasal [ŋ], *{dors}/nasal would outrank all velar-preserving faithfulness constraints while *{dors}/{−vd stop} would not.

A separate issue is whether there are manner-specific faithfulness constraints to complement the output constraints (e.g. IDENT{dors,lab,cor}/nasal vs. IDENT{dors,lab,cor}/stop). The cases discussed in the following chapters do not provide much insight into this issue. In any case, if the constraints did exist, they would not affect the results of the following chapters, which focus on more fundamental properties of the constraints such as conflation, Preservation of the Marked, and so on. It is difficult to separate the effects of manner-specific markedness and faithfulness constraints. If there were manner-specific faithfulness constraints, one could expect them to block a process for a particular manner of articulation while allowing others to undergo it. For example, nasals assimilate in PoA in English while fricatives and stops do not. This fact may indicate that IDENT{dors,lab,cor}/{stop,fricative} outranks all assimilation-triggering constraints while IDENT{dors,lab,cor}/nasal is ranked lower. On the other hand, it may indicate that there are nasal-specific assimilation-triggering constraints. Since this issue is tangential to the main point of this book, it is left for future research.

For the sake of brevity, the PoA output constraints used in later chapters will not have any manner specifications; the MoA will be mentioned only when it is directly relevant.

2.4 Discovering hierarchies

Now that the theory of markedness has been presented, it is possible to turn to a methodological issue: how to discover markedness hierarchies.

2.4.1 Neutralization

The theory predicts that if there is a synchronic non-assimilative, non-dissimilative neutralization /β/→[α] in some prosodic environment, there is a markedness hierarchy in which a feature value of β is more marked than a related feature value of α. The easiest way to determine the particular feature is to examine minimally different segments. For example, /m/→[n] must involve PoA because this is the only feature by which [m] and [n] differ. Consequently, there must be a hierarchy in which | labial ⟩ coronal |.

The theory places even stronger restrictions about what can be in a hierarchy. A hierarchy is a single feature and its elements are feature values; so unrelated features cannot be in a markedness hierarchy. For example, the Misantla Totonac neutralization /ł/→[h] cannot imply that there is a hierarchy | +lateral ⟩ glottal |. Instead, the change must involve the neutralization of other hierarchies (i.e. the PoA hierarchy).

2.4.2 Multi-valued hierarchies

The relation to a feature also helps determine how many elements a hierarchy has. For example, if /β/→[α] and /γ/→[α], there is a single hierarchy that contains α, β, and γ if and only if α, β, and γ are all different values of a single feature.

The theory also predicts that hierarchies completely order all elements of a hierarchy. If α, β, and γ are part of a single hierarchy, the hierarchy cannot have the form | α, β ⟩ γ |, where there is no relation between α and β.

Neutralization is a useful markedness diagnostic because the theory predicts that every hierarchy can undergo neutralization. However, the theory also predicts that the output of neutralization will always be the least marked member available. So, a hierarchy | γ ⟩ β ⟩ α | will result in the neutralizations /γ/→[α] and /β/→[α], but never /γ/→[β] unless [α] is eliminated by some other hierarchy. For example, /k/ never neutralizes to [p], so neutralization gives no evidence for the PoA relation | dorsal ⟩ labial |. We only know of the relation | dorsal, labial ⟩ coronal | because glottals (the least marked PoA element) can be eliminated by the sonority hierarchy.

At this point, some other diagnostic is needed. For PoA, the triggers of assimilation follow a hierarchy: dorsals always trigger assimilation, while if labials trigger assimilation, so do dorsals. This provides evidence that | dorsal ⟩ labial |.

2.4.3 Supra- and subsegmental hierarchies

The theory claims that prosodic features are always related to DTEs and non-DTEs in constraints, while constraints on subsegmental features never mention prosodic structure.

Due to the nature of the DTE and non-DTE constraints, the theory predicts that if a neutralization of a prosodic feature /β/→[α] is seen in a DTE, the neutralization /α/→[β] should also appear in a non-DTE. For example, if low tones become high tones in foot DTEs in some language, then there must be a language in which high tones become low tones in foot non-DTEs (de Lacy 2002a).

2.4.4 Hierarchy conflict

There are few restrictions on inter-hierarchy conflict. If | α ⟩ β | in one hierarchy, it may be the case that | β ⟩ α | in another.

However, for subsegmental features there is an important restriction that effectively ensures that hierarchy conflict is always partial. It is not possible for there to be two completely contradictory hierarchies like | α ⟩ β | and | β ⟩ α |. As hierarchies are encoded as features, two contradictory hierarchies require that there are two different features that encode the same contrasts. For example, there cannot be two hierarchies | +voice ⟩ −voice | and | −voice ⟩ +voice | because these would have to be realized as two features [±voiced] and [±voiceless], which are identical except that their feature values are reversed. Consequently, hierarchy conflict is always partial and inadvertent. For example, the sonority hierarchy partially conflicts with the voicing hierarchy – the former favours voiced stops in DTEs over voiceless stops, while the latter favours voiceless stops. However, they both favour voiceless fricatives over voiced stops. In addition, the voicing hierarchy refers to a subsegmental feature, while the sonority hierarchy refers to a prosodic feature; the features just happen to overlap at the segmental level.

For prosodic features, the theory predicts that conflict will occur, but only in environments that are both DTEs and non-DTEs.

2.4.5 Non-existing hierarchies

The theory makes it somewhat difficult to directly prove the lack of existence of a hierarchy. If there is never a neutralization in which /α/→[β], then there are two options. One is that there is no hierarchy in which | α ⟩ β |. The other is that there is a hierarchy in which | α ⟩ β |, but β is not the least marked element: i.e. | α ⟩ β ⟩ γ |. As mentioned above, such a hierarchy only allows neutralization of /α/→[γ] and /β/→[γ], unless [γ] is eliminated by some other hierarchy.

However, relating hierarchies to features has the implication that features participate in processes such as assimilation/harmony, dissimilation, and so on. This idea automatically restricts phenomena that are relevant for possible hierarchies. For example, is it possible to interpret the Misantla Totonac neutralization /ɬ/→[h] as being due to a feature [φ] in which [+φ] is interpreted as [lateral] and [−φ] is interpreted as [glottal], so allowing a hierarchy | +φ ⟩ −φ |? In this case, /ɬ/→[h] could be seen as neutralization of [φ].

The problem with this idea is that as a feature [φ] must participate in assimilation/harmony, dissimilation, and so on. A feature [φ] predicts that there could be dissimilation of [φ] so that /h . . . h/ (i.e. [−φ . . . −φ]) sequences would become [h . . . ɬ] (i.e. [−φ . . . +φ]). There is no evidence that such a dissimilation, and therefore such a feature, exists.

2.4.6 Prosodic markedness

As mentioned in §2.2, the proposals say nothing about markedness relations between prosodic structures. They mention prosodic feature such as tone and sonority, but say nothing about syllable structure, foot structure, and so on.

The reason is that hierarchies are equated with feature values here, and prosodic structures are not features. Consequently, asymmetries in prosody should not derive from the same factors as featural markedness. In fact, there is little reason to think that prosodic and featural markedness relate to the same principles: the unmarked state of prosodic heads is to branch, and there is no clear analogue for subsegmental features. Determining the form and cause of prosodic markedness will be left to later work.

2.5 Summary

To summarize, for every markedness hierarchy involving subsegmental features there is both a set of output constraints and a set of faithfulness constraints. The two sets refer to contiguous parts of the hierarchy starting with the most marked element. For the PoA hierarchy in (32a), the result is the output constraints in (32b) and the faithfulness constraints in (32c).

(32) PoA hierarchy and constraints
    (a) | dorsal ⟩ labial ⟩ coronal ⟩ glottal |
    (b) *{dors}, *{dors,lab}, *{dors,lab,cor}, *{dors,lab,cor,gl}
    (c) IDENT{dors}, IDENT{dors,lab}, IDENT{dors,lab,cor},
        IDENT{dors,lab,cor,gl}

The informal notion 'hierarchy', as in (32a), was argued to be formally expressed as a feature. Order between elements in the hierarchy was argued to relate to the form of feature values and how constraints refer to them.

Output constraints like those in (32b) formally express markedness reduction: the constraints favour less marked elements over more marked ones. For PoA, the output constraints collectively favour glottals over all other elements. Coronals incur a subset of the constraints violations that the more marked labials and dorsals do, and labials incur a subset of dorsal violations. So, the more marked the PoA, the more seriously it will violate the PoA output constraints. Markedness reduction is therefore the result of the dominance of one or more of these constraints over the pressure to preserve inputs, formally implemented as faithfulness constraints.

Faithfulness constraints like those in (32c) formally express marked preservation: collectively, unfaithfulness to marked elements will incur a superset of violations compared with unfaithfulness to unmarked elements. For PoA, all the constraints militate against the most marked dorsal PoA becoming non-dorsal. Every constraint that demands that coronals be preserved also requires the more marked labials and dorsals to be preserved, and so on. Marked preservation is therefore the situation where a faithfulness constraint that preserves only marked elements blocks those elements from undergoing an otherwise general process.

Both sets of constraints can formally express markedness conflation. For example, a constraint like *{dorsal,labial} makes no distinction between dorsals and labials – both violate this constraint equally. Consequently, if only this constraint is active in a grammar and no constraint that distinguishes dorsals from labials (e.g. *{dorsal}) is active, then the two categories will be treated identically. The same point holds for IDENT{dorsal,labial}. The empirical consequences of this conflation can be seen in chapters 3 and 4 for markedness reduction and preservation respectively.

Restrictions on the combination of hierarchies were identified. Hierarchies that refer to subsegmental features cannot combine with prosodic constituents in constraints, while prosodic hierarchies (e.g. sonority, tone) must.

A final point is that the theory places strong restrictions on possible hierarchy-referring constraints in OT. Every constraint that refers to a markedness hierarchy H must conform to the restrictions specified in §2.3.1. So, there is no constraint *{coronal}, no *{−voice}, and no *Δ_{Ft} /mid vowels because all of these constraints fail to mention all more marked members on the PoA, voicing, and sonority hierarchies respectively. The theory's restrictions on constraints are crucial because occasionally there arises a misunderstanding that OT allows any imaginable output, and so is inherently unsuited to expressing markedness asymmetries (e.g. Hume 2003:§4). This is not so (see, e.g., McCarthy 2001b:§1.3.1). For example, dorsals could only ever be 'less marked' than coronals if a constraint like *{coronal} exists: this constraint favours dorsals over coronals, so the ranking ||*{coronal} » *{dorsal}|| would produce a language in which /t/ neutralized to [k], and so on. However, if no constraint that favours coronals over dorsals exists in CON, there is no way for /t/ to ever neutralize to [k]. In the theory presented here, there is no way to generate an output constraint like *{coronal} because there is no markedness hierarchy in which coronals are more marked than dorsals. Consequently, there is no ranking of *any* constraints in CON that will allow /t/→[k]. In more technical terms, the mapping /t/→[t] is a harmonic bound for /t/→[k] in all possible rankings (Samek-Lodovici & Prince 1999).

Chapters 3 to 7 provide empirical evidence for the theory presented in this chapter. Chapter 8 compares the theory with alternative theories of markedness. Chapter 9 provides a summary.

3 *Markedness reduction*

3.1 The visibility of markedness reduction

Marked elements can be singled out for preservation, so obscuring the effects of markedness reduction. Consequently, markedness effects are only clearly visible when preservation is irrelevant. The aim of this chapter is to identify such situations. In addition, it shows that there are many interacting markedness hierarchies, some of which conflict. Consequently, a variety of segments can have 'least marked' status.

Section 3.2 identifies the most obvious situation in which preservation is irrelevant: when there is nothing to preserve. The empirical focus is consonant epenthesis (e.g. McCarthy & Prince 1994; Lombardi 2002). Epenthesis describes a situation where there is a segment in the output form that does not correspond to any input element. Rice (1989:133) identifies a case in Hare Slave: underlying /icẽ/ 'we sing' surfaces as [hicẽ] in order to avoid a ban on onsetless syllables (cf. /t-icẽ/ → [ticẽ] 'we start to sing', *[thicẽ], *[tʰicẽ]). Once influences like assimilation and dissimilation are put aside, the form of epenthetic consonants clearly shows the influence of markedness hierarchies such as place of articulation, voice, and sonority. Because markedness hierarchies can conflict, there is a range of possible epenthetic consonants. However, all hierarchies agree to the extent that many consonants can never be epenthetic.

Section 3.3 shows that preservation is also irrelevant in determining the output of neutralization. Consequently, neutralization only ever produces unmarked outputs (Trubetzkoy 1939; Greenberg 1966, 1975, 1978). As an example, Lapoliwa (1981:88–9) shows that Standard Malay /k/ surfaces as [ʔ] when it appears in syllable codas: e.g. /baik/ → [baiʔ] 'good' (cf. /kə-baik-an/ → [kə.bai.kan]). PoA preservation is irrelevant in choosing whether /k/ will turn into [p], [t], or [ʔ], because none of these options preserves the input segment better than any other. Consequently, markedness reduction has full control over the PoA of the segment that /k/ becomes. Examination of a range of cases of neutralization shows that PoA neutralization can only produce glottals or coronals;

this generalization is shown to follow from the form of the PoA hierarchy constraints. The outputs of consonant epenthesis and consonant neutralization are the same, as expected if there is a single set of markedness hierarchies.

Section 3.4 discusses a methodology for identifying solid cases of epenthesis and neutralization from other phonological and morphological processes. This methodology eliminates a number of apparent problems for the empirical generalizations and theoretical predictions (cf. Rice 1996; Vaux 2003). Section 3.5 provides a summary and conclusions.

3.2 Consonant epenthesis

Consonant epenthesis presents a situation where preservation is irrelevant: as no input elements correspond to the epenthetic element, constraints on input–output identity have no effect. So, markedness reduction is often the driving force in determining the feature content of epenthetic consonants. Consequently, consonant epenthesis provides valuable insight into markedness relations and the constraints that express them.

Section 3.2.1 presents a typology of epenthetic consonants. When processes like place assimilation and dissimilation are factored out, there are few possibilities: i.e. [ʔ t n N h ɹ r w j]. There are clear restrictions in PoA: non-approximant epenthetic consonants can only be glottal or coronal.

Sections 3.2.2 and 3.2.3 argue that variation is due to partially conflicting hierarchies. For example, the PoA hierarchy | dorsal ⟩ labial ⟩ coronal ⟩ glottal | favours glottals over all other PoAs, so accounting for why epenthetic consonants can be glottal. However, glottals are highly sonorous, so when constraints against high sonority segments dominate, glottals are eliminated as possible epenthetic elements. Following Lombardi's (2002) proposals, this elimination allows coronals to be 'promoted' to least marked status.

The manner of articulation of epenthetic consonants is discussed in §3.2.4. Epenthetic [h], [n N], rhotics, and [j], [w] are argued to get their manner of articulation through assimilation to an adjacent vowel, while markedness reduction produces stops.

The predictions of the present approach are discussed in §3.2.5 with a focus on why certain consonants — like [p] and [x] — are never epenthetic.

3.2.1 An epenthetic typology

Processes like assimilation and dissimilation can interfere with markedness reduction's influence on epenthesis. For example, epenthetic elements can assimilate in PoA and manner to adjacent segments (see Rosenthall 1995: §4.2

for a general discussion). An example of both manner and PoA assimilation is found in Dakota: epenthetic consonants are [j] before the front (i.e. coronal) vowels [i e] and [w] before back (i.e. dorsal) vowels [a o u] (Shaw 1980:90). Similarly, the epenthetic consonant in Brahui assimilates to low back vowels in dorsality, voice, and continuancy, resulting in [ɣ] (e.g. [lumːa-ɣ-aːk] 'mother {masc.pl}') (Elfenbein 1997); epenthesis is blocked in other environments.

However, once assimilation and dissimilation are factored out, cases of 'default' epenthesis remain (Greenberg 1966:59). For example, as mentioned in §3.1, the epenthetic consonant in Hare and Bearlake Slave is always [h], no matter what the surrounding vowels are (Rice 1989:133). Of course, a language can have both 'default' and assimilative/dissimilative consonant epenthesis in different environments. For example, a number of languages have epenthetic homorganic glides next to non-low vowels, but have default epenthesis of [ʔ] elsewhere (Dutch – Booij 1995:191; Tamil – Wiltshire 1998; Kaliniga – Rosenthall 1995:180; Malay – Cohn 1989; Cohn & McCarthy 1994).

'Default' consonant epenthesis shows markedness asymmetries. As argued in a great deal of previous work, default epenthetic consonants are drawn from a very small set (Lombardi 1995, 1998, 2003). The list in (1) identifies the possible epenthetic consonants as glottals [ʔ h N], coronals [t n ɹ r], the palatal [j], and the labio-dorsal [w], building on work by Kitto & de Lacy (1999) and Lombardi (1998, 2002).

(1) Default Consonant Epenthesis Typology

	Language	Reference
ʔ	Chadic	Frajzyngier & Koops 1989
	Cupeño	Crowhurst 1994
	Larike	Laidig 1992
	Misantla Totonac	MacKay 1994: §2.7.1
	Mohawk	Hale & White Eagle 1980
	Tsishaath Nootka	Stonham 1999
t	Axininca Campa	Payne 1981
	French	Tranel 1981; Pagliano 2004
	Māori	de Lacy 2004 & references cited therein
	Odawa Ojibwa	Piggott 1993; Lombardi 1998
h	Ayutla Mixtec	Pankratz & Pike 1967
	Chipewyan	Li 1946
	Huariapano	Parker 1994a:100–1, 1998
	Slave (Bear Lake, Hare)	Rice 1989:133
	Tigré	Rose 1996
	Tucanoan (utterance-final)	Welch & Welch 1967:18
	Yagua	Payne & Payne 1986:438

3.2 *Consonant epenthesis* 81

N	Uradhi	Hale 1973; Crowley 1983; Trigo 1988:57ff.; cf. Paradis & Prunet 1994
	Kaingáng	Yip 1992 (cit. Lombardi 1998:14)
n	Murut	Prentice 1971:113[1]
	Tunica	Haas 1946; Lombardi 1998
ɹ	Anejom̃	Lynch 2000:29
	Boston English	McCarthy 1993
	Japanese	Mester & Ito 1989; Lombardi 1998
r	Southern Tati	Yar-Shater 1969
j	Uyghur	Vaux 2003
w	Chamicuro	Parker 1989, 1994b

Table (2) shows attested default epenthetic consonants. Consonants with a double-lined circle only ever appear in syllable codas.

(2)   Possible 'default' epenthetic consonants

	labial	coronal		retroflex	palatal	velar	uvular	pharyngeal	glottal
oral stops	p	(t)		ʈ	c	k	q		(ʔ)
	b	d		ɖ	ɟ	g	G		
affricates	p͡f	t͡s	t͡ʃ			k͡x			
	b͡v	d͡z	d͡ʒ			g͡ɣ			
nasals	m ɱ	((n))		ɳ	ɲ	ŋ	N		((N))
fricatives	ɸ f	θ s	ʃ	ʂ	ç	x	χ	ħ	(h)
	β v	ð z	ʒ	ʐ	j	ɣ	ʁ	ʕ	ɦ
lateral fricatives		ɬ							
		ɮ							
l. approximants		l		ɭ	ʎ	ʟ			
rhotics		(ɹ r ɾ)		ɽ					
glides	(w) ʋ				j	ɰ			

[1] Murut epenthetic [n] appears mainly in the environment /aː+V/, but also at some other V+V junctures.

Epenthesis is always forced by some general prosodic requirement in the languages listed above. The most common motivation for epenthesis is the demand for syllables to have onsets. Epenthetic consonants can also appear in codas. For example, Ayutla Mixtec requires the initial syllable of the prosodic word to be bimoraic (i.e. CVC) (Pankratz & Pike 1967). This requirement is usually satisfied by geminating the following consonant: [tos.so] 'a floral arch', [tim.ma?] 'candle', [cel.le] 'scissors', [naj.ja?] 'a dog'. However, stops are not permitted in codas, so when a stop follows an [h] is inserted: [tuh̲.tʲa] 'atole (a type of porridge)', *[tut.tʲa], [ʃah.ku?] 'a few', [kah.t͡ʃi] 'cotton'. Similarly, Huariapano provides an example of [h] epenthesis in codas to make foot heads bimoraic (Parker 1994a, 1998).

Uradhi dialects have an epenthetic glottal nasal stop [N] in codas (Trigo 1988:57ff.; Hale 1973; Crowley 1983). All Uradhi utterances end in a consonant; in OT terms, this condition can be implemented by a version of FINAL-C (McCarthy & Prince 1994: §5). This condition is met by insertion of [N] after vowel-final words: e.g. [iwi-N] 'morning bird', [juku-N] 'tree'. Words can also end in a coronal nasal; in such a case, the coronal remains unchanged: [nanimun] 'ground-ablative' (Crowley 1983:325). For further discussion, see Trigo (1988).[2]

Coda epenthesis is rarer than onset epenthesis, so it is difficult to make solidly supported generalizations. However, all attested cases of epenthetic codas involve high sonority elements [? h N]. See §3.2.4.1 for discussion.

3.2.2 Glottal epenthesis: PoA beats sonority

Many languages have [?] as a default epenthetic element. An example is Mabalay Atayal; the data and the formal motivation for epenthesis are taken from Lambert 1999. Mabalay Atayal has the consonants in table (3), adapted from Lambert 1999:6.

---

2 Paradis & Prunet (1991a:12) propose that the epenthetic segment is simply a floating [+nasal] feature that acquires dorsality from the preceding vowel. More recent views of vowel features do not consider all vowels to be [dorsal], so this approach is put aside here (Clements & Hume 1995). Having said this, Uradhi offers some interesting further complexities. Final nasals – both underlying and epenthetic – can be optionally denasalized if the preceding consonant is oral. The result is [?] or [k], depending on the dialect. This complication is left for future research.

(3)   Mabalay Atayal segments

	labial	laminal-alveolar	palatal	velar	pharyngeal	glottal
stops	p	t t͡s		k		ʔ
fricatives	β	s	ʒ	x ɣ	ħ	
nasals	m	n		ŋ		
liquids		ɬ ɾ				
glides	w		j			

Mabalay Atayal syllables have the shape CV, CVC, or CVVC. Codas can contain any consonant except the voiced fricatives [β ʒ ɣ] and flap [ɾ]. Of crucial importance is the fact that all lexical words end in a consonant. When a word is underlyingly vowel-final, a [ʔ] is inserted. Stress marks in the forms below are not transcribed by Lambert – they are inserted following her stress description.

(4)   Mabalay Atayal final [ʔ] epenthesis (Lambert 1999:86)
    (a) /an-βakħa/ → [βa.nak.'ħɐʔ]   cf. [βak.ħɐ-.'un], *[βak.ħɐ.'ʔun]
    'break+{perfective}'   'break+{trans.loc.}'
    (b) /am-satu/ → [sa.ma.'tuʔ]   cf. [sa.tu-.'an]
    'send+{intrans.}'   'send+{trans.loc.}'
    (c) /sinħi/ → [sin.'ħəiʔ]   cf. [sin.ħə-.'un]
    'believe+{intrans.}'   'believe+{trans.pat.}'
    (d) /m-paŋa/ → [ma.pa.'ŋaʔ]   cf. [pa.ŋa-.'an]
    'carry on back+{intrans.}'   'carry on back+{trans.loc.}'
    (e) /am-sβu/ → [sa.ma.'βuʔ]   cf. [βu-.'an]
    'shoot+{intrans.}'   'shoot+{trans.loc.}'

The underlined glottal stops in (4) cannot be present underlyingly. If, for example, 'shoot' (4e) had an underlying /ʔ/, there would have to be a process of intervocalic ʔ-deletion to account for [βu-an], *[βuʔan]. The problem is that [ʔ] *is* allowed intervocalically, as shown in the second column in (5).

(5)   Mabalay Atayal underlying /ʔ/s
    (a) /p-kaniʔ/ → [pa.ka.'niʔ]   cf. /p-kaniʔ-i/ → [pak.ni.'ʔi]
    '{cause}+eat'   '{cause}+eat+{jussive}' (Lambert 1999:83)
    (b) /maʃʲaʔ/ → [ma.'ʃʲaʔ]   cf. /p-maʃʲaʔ-an/ → [p-a.ʃʲa.'ʔ-an]
    'laugh'   '{cause}+laugh+{trans.loc}'

Lambert (1999:183ff.) observes that the final syllable of a word is always stressed, and so proposes that [ʔ] epenthesis is motivated by the need for a

84   3 *Markedness reduction*

stressed syllable to be heavy, or in foot terms for there to be a perfect iamb – i.e. a light and heavy syllable. Epenthesis in Mabalay Atayal is therefore motivated by a prosodic requirement.

Three constraints are at the core of the motivation for epenthesis:

(6)   ALIGN-σ́-R   'The main stressed syllable must be rightmost'
                              (after McCarthy & Prince 1993a)
       STRESS-TO-WEIGHT   'Stressed syllables must be heavy'
                              (Fitzgerald 1997)
       DEP-IO   'Every segment in the output must have an input
                              correspondent' (McCarthy & Prince 1995)

Tableau (7) shows how the constraints force epenthesis. Candidate (a) loses because it does not have rightmost stress, while (b) loses because it does not have a bimoraic stressed syllable. As DEP-IO is ranked below these constraints, candidate (c) with rightmost stress and a heavy syllable wins.

(7)   Mabalay Atayal I

/sinɦi/	ALIGN-σ́-R	STRESS-TO-WEIGHT	DEP-IO
(a) 'sin.ɦi	*!		
(b) sin.'ɦi		*!	
☞ (c) sin.'ɦiʔ			*!

Other options for producing a heavy word-final syllable are blocked. It is not possible to lengthen the vowel as long vowels are not permitted in Mabalay Atayal (i.e. *Vː is ranked above appropriate faithfulness constraints). MAX-IO outranks DEP-IO because final heavy syllables are not achieved through deletion: e.g. /sinɦi/ does not surface as *['sin].

Now that the motivation for epenthesis has been presented, it is possible to turn to the constraints that determine the feature content of the epenthetic consonant. Mabalay Atayal allows many consonants in coda position [p t k ʔ s x ɦ m n ŋ ħ ʐ j w], but only [ʔ] is epenthesized.

Importantly, faithfulness constraints have no influence on the form of the epenthetic consonant. For example, a constraint like IDENT[dorsal] demands that every dorsal input segment have an output correspondent that is also dorsal. Since epenthetic elements do not correspond to any input segment, IDENT[dorsal] will always be vacuously satisfied by epenthetic segments. In fact, a mapping like /pao/ → [paʔo] or [pako] or [pato] or [papo] violates no feature-faithfulness constraints at all. So, the determination of featural content of epenthetic segments is the sole responsibility of output constraints.

The one situation where faithfulness might matter in epenthesis is when an epenthetic element copies the features of another segment (see Kitto & de Lacy 1999). Another type of faithfulness constraint that could influence epenthetic form are those that refer to correspondence relations between features (Howe & Pulleyblank 2004). Such constraints are not employed here for reasons discussed in §8.7.

In its essentials the analysis below follows Lombardi 2002. As shown in chapter 2, the PoA markedness hierarchy has the form | dorsal ⟩ labial ⟩ coronal ⟩ glottal |, and is expressed by the output-oriented constraints *{dors}, *{dors,lab}, *{dors,lab,cor}, and *{dors,lab,cor,gl}. In terms of the PoA markedness hierarchy, [ʔ], [h], and [N] are therefore the least marked of all consonants, as shown in tableau (8). (I assume that the pharyngeal [ħ] classes with glottals – nothing at all hinges on this assumption.)

(8)   Mabalay Atayal II: Epenthetic [ʔ]

/sinħi/	*{dors}	*{dors,lab}	*{dors,lab,cor}	*{dors,lab,cor,gl}
(a) sin.'ħik	*!	*	* * *	* * * *
(b) sin.'ħip		*!	* * *	* * * *
(c) sin.'ħit			* * *!	* * * *
☞ (d) sin.'ħiʔ			* *	* * * *

Every ranking of the PoA constraints will favour [ʔ] over [p t k] because there is no PoA constraint which favours [k], [p], or [t] over [ʔ], and there is at least one constraint which favours [ʔ] over [k p t]. In comparison with non-PoA constraints, a language with an epenthetic glottal consonant is one in which the glottal-favouring PoA output constraint *{dors,lab,cor} is the most highly ranked influence on PoA markedness. This PoA constraint outranks all other output-oriented constraints that contradict it, including constraints that demand assimilation and require low sonority.

In the current ranking, ALIGN-ó-R and STRESS-TO-WEIGHT must outrank *{dors,lab,cor,gl}, otherwise epenthesis would be blocked (see §8.7.3 for discussion of constraints that ban all members of a hierarchy). Apart from this, ranking the PoA output constraints may be ranked in any position with respect to DEP and ONSET. All violations are shown for *{dors,lab,cor,gl} below for clarity.

86 3 Markedness reduction

(9)   Mabalay Atayal III

/sinhi/	ALIGN-ó-R	WEIGHT-TO-STRESS	*{dors,lab,cor,gl}
(a) 'sin.hi	*!		* * *
(b) sin.'hi		*!	* * *
☞ (c) sin.'hi?			* * * *

The anti-deletion constraint MAX-IO must outrank all the PoA constraints in order to prevent deletion of [t], [p], and [k]. The ranking so far is given in (10).

(10)   Mabalay Atayal [?] epenthesis: Interim ranking

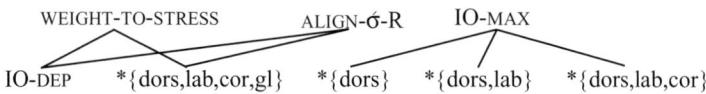

3.2.2.1 Manner of articulation

PoA markedness is only one of many hierarchies in the grammar. Another hierarchy that will figure prominently in later sections is sonority. As a prosodic feature, sonority combines with prosodic constituents to form constraints (§2.3.3.2). Prince & Smolensky (1993) propose that sonority combines with the position 'syllable margin', which is equivalent to the non-DTE of a syllable $(-\Delta_\sigma)$ here. Glottals are highly sonorous consonants, so there is a constraint $*-\Delta_\sigma/\{\text{glottal}\}$ which bans them in syllable margins.

The constraint $*-\Delta_\sigma/\{\text{glottal}\}$ conflicts with the PoA hierarchy because it favours voiceless stops [k p t] over glottals [?] while *{dors,lab,cor} does the exact opposite. So, *{dors,lab,cor} must outrank $*-\Delta_\sigma/\{\text{glottal}\}$, as illustrated in tableau (11).

(11)   Mabalay Atayal IV

/sinhi/	*{dors,lab,cor}	$*-\Delta_\sigma/\{\text{glottal}\}$
(a) sin'hit	* * *!	
☞ (b) sin'hi?	* *	*

The ranking so far favours glottals over all other PoAs. The next step is to identify the ranking responsible for favouring an epenthetic oral stop [?] over a nasal stop [N] or a fricative [h]. The choice between [?] and [h] is due to the emergent effect of assimilation constraints. [?] is less marked than [h] in terms of continuancy, while [h] – unlike [ʔ] – agrees with the following vowel in continuancy. The choice between [h] and [ʔ], then, comes down to the relative ranking of *{+continuant} and AGREE[continuant]. For Mabalay Atayal, the former outranks the latter, so [ʔ] wins. In contrast, for Ayutla Mixtec, AGREE[continuant] outranks *{+continuant}, so [h] wins. [N] is more marked than [ʔ] in terms of margin sonority, and it is less similar to vowels than [h]. Consequently, [N] offers no markedness gain compared to [h] and [ʔ] in Mabalay Atayal (except in codas – §3.2.4.1).

3.2.2.2 The subordination of assimilation and dissimilation
Finally, it is important to account for the fact that assimilation and dissimilation do not affect the quality of Mabalay Atayal's epenthetic element. All constraints that promote assimilation (e.g. AGREE[PoA]) must be outranked by the PoA output constraints that favour glottals. The opposite ranking would force the epenthetic consonant to take on the PoA of the preceding vowel. In tableau (12) both the labial [p] and the dorsal [k] are superior to [ʔ] in terms of assimilation to [u], assuming that [u] is both labial (i.e. [+round]) and dorsal (i.e. [+back]).

(12)   Mabalay Atayal v

/am-sβu/	*{dors,lab,cor}	AGREE[PoA]
(a) samaβup	* * * *!	
(b) samaβuk	* * * *!	
☞ (c) samaβuʔ	* * *	*

To conclude the ranking, both AGREE[PoA] and *−Δ_σ/{glottal} must be outranked by WEIGHT-TO-STRESS and ALIGN-σ́-R; the opposite ranking would prevent epenthesis. The final ranking diagram is given in (13); the part of the ranking that ensures that the epenthetic consonant is [ʔ] is underlined.

(13)   Mabalay Atayal epenthesis: Final ranking

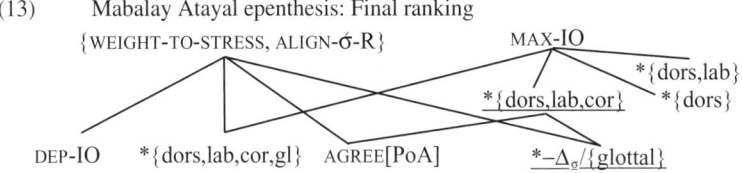

In short, glottal epenthesis takes place when the PoA constraint *{dors,lab,cor} outranks conflicting sonority and feature-agreement constraints.

3.2.3 Coronal epenthesis: sonority beats PoA

The only other voiceless stop that can be epenthetic is [t]. A well-known case is in Axininca Campa, where [t] is inserted to ensure that every output syllable has an onset. [t] is inserted between vowels at root-suffix and suffix-suffix junctures, as shown in (14a,b). Epenthesis also occurs when a syllable is added to a mono-vocalic root in order to satisfy the minimal word restriction (14c). Epenthesis does not take place between prefix and stem boundaries; deletion occurs instead (14d). The data below is taken from Payne 1981 and Spring 1990; for a detailed analysis of Axininca Campa phonology, see Payne 1981 and McCarthy & Prince 1993b. Roots are preceded by the '√' symbol in the data below. Epenthetic segments are underlined, and reduplicants are double-underlined.

(14)   Axininca Campa [t] epenthesis
(a) Root+suffix juncture

/i-N-√koma-i/ →	[iŋkomati]	'he will paddle'
/i-N-√koma-aː-i/ →	[iŋkomataːti]	'he will paddle again'
/i-N-√koma-ako-i/ →	[iŋkomatakoti]	'he will paddle for'
/i-N-√koma-ako-aː-i-ro/→	[iŋkomatakotaːtiro]	'he will paddle for it again'
/iN-√kim-√piro-i/ →	[iŋkimpiroti]	'he will really hear'
/√piro-aːntʃʰi/ →	[pirotaːntʃʰi]	'verity+infinitive'
/√na-aːntʃʰi/ →	[nataːntʃʰi]	'carry+infinitive'
cf. /i-N-√tʃʰik-i/ →	[intʃʰiki]	'he will cut'
/i-N-√tʃʰik-aː-i/ →	[intʃʰikaːti]	'he will cut again'

(b) Suffix+suffix juncture

/i-N-√tʃʰik-aː-i/ →	[intʃʰikaːti]	'he will cut again'
/i-N-√tʃʰik-ako-i/ →	[intʃʰikakoti]	'he will cut for'
/i-N-√tʃʰik-ako-aː-i-ro/ →	[intʃʰikakotaːtiro]	'he will cut for it again'
/no-N-√tʃʰik-wai-i/ →	[nontʃʰikawaiti]	'I will continue to cut'
/√na-√RED-wai-ak-i/ →	[nata-nata-waitaki]	'I will continue to carry it'
/no-√tʃʰik-√RED-akiri/ →	[notʃʰikatʃʰikatakiri]	'I cut it and cut it'
/no-N-√kow-√RED-iro/ →	[noŋkowakowatiro]	'I will search for it'

(c) Minimal word augmentation

/√na/ →	[nata]	'carry'
	(cf. /no-na+RED/ →	[nonanona])
/√tʰo/ →	[tʰota]	'kiss, suck'
	(cf. /non-tʰo+RED/ →	[nontʰonontʰo])

(d) Prefix+Root boundary: deletion

/no-√ana-ni/ → [nanani] 'my black dye'

(e) Root+Root boundary: no change

/√asi-√RED/ → [asi-asi] 'cover'
/√oːk-√RED/ → [oːka-oːka] 'abandon'

Payne (1981) explains why a deletion analysis is not possible. Vowel epenthesis breaks up underlying heterorganic consonant clusters: e.g. / . . . tʃʰik-wai . . . /→[tʃʰikawai]. So, if the future morpheme is underlying /ti/ rather than /i/, vowel epenthesis should occur between a consonant-final root and the future: i.e. /tʃʰik/ + putative /ti/ should become *[tʃʰikati]; however, it surfaces as [tʃʰiki]. If there is instead [t]-epenthesis, the form of [tʃʰiki] follows straightforwardly: i.e. /tʃʰik+i/→[tʃʰiki].

The other deletion option is that the underlined [t]'s in (14) belong to the roots or preceding suffixes: i.e. 'paddle' is underlyingly /komat/. The problem with this idea is that vowel epenthesis should again occur when a consonant-initial suffix is added: i.e. /komat/ + /wai/ should surface as *[komatawai] 'continue to paddle' but the attested form is [komawai]. Consequently, an epenthesis analysis is the only viable option.

It is important to show that there is a phonologically adequate analysis of Axininca Campa epenthesis. As Lombardi (2002) and §3.4 emphasize, apparently epenthetic segments may in fact be morphemes or due to other phonological processes. Consequently, the first step is to identify the prosodic motivations and restrictions on epenthesis.

The following analysis owes a great deal to Payne (1981), McCarthy & Prince (1993b), and Lombardi (2002). McCarthy & Prince propose that the constraint that motivates hiatus-avoidance by both deletion at prefix+root boundaries and epenthesis elsewhere is ONSET 'Incur a violation for every syllable without an onset'. Deletion at prefix+root boundaries can be caused by having ONSET and DEP-IO outrank MAX-IO, as shown in tableau (15).

(15) Axininca Campa I

/no-√ana-ni/	ONSET	DEP-IO	MAX-IO
(a) no.a.na.ni	*!		
(b) no.ta.na.ni		*!	
☞ (c) na.na.ni			*

Another revealing competitor is *[nonani], where the root's initial /a/ deletes. This candidate is eliminated by MAX-Stem, a constraint that bans deletion inside the morphological constituent that contains the root and suffixes. MAX-Stem has another use: it explains why ONSET causes epenthesis at other boundaries, not deletion. Tableau (16) illustrates with the form /i-N-koma-i/ → [iŋkoma<u>t</u>i].

(16)   Axininca Campa II

/i-N-koma-i/	ONSET	MAX-STEM	DEP-IO	MAX-IO
(a) iŋ.ko.ma.i	* *!			
(b) iŋ.ko.ma	*	*!		*
☞ (c) iŋ.ko.ma.<u>t</u>i	*		*	

The initial vowel in all the candidates causes ONSET to be violated at least once. However, candidate (a) fatally violates it twice with the final onsetless [i]. Candidate (b) is ruled out by MAX-Stem because it resolves ONSET by deleting part of the stem; the candidate *[iŋkoma] is ruled out for the same reason. Candidate (c) is the only one remaining, with epenthesis.

The fact that the winner has an initial onsetless syllable brings up the issue of candidates like *[koma<u>t</u>i] and *[ti<u>ŋ</u>koma<u>t</u>i]. *[koma<u>t</u>i] violates MAX-Stem, so is ruled out. *[ti<u>ŋ</u>koma<u>t</u>i] can be eliminated by DEP-σ₁ – a positional faithfulness constraint which bans epenthesis in prosodic word-initial syllables, as shown in tableau (17)'s candidate (a). Candidate (b) attempts to avoid both DEP-σ₁ and ONSET violations by deleting the root-initial vowel, but fatally violates MAX-STEM. The only way left to avoid initial epenthesis and root-deletion is to have an onsetless syllable, as in (c).

(17)   Axininca Campa III

/i-N-koma-i/	DEP-σ₁	MAX-STEM	ONSET	DEP-IO
(a) <u>ti</u>ŋkoma<u>t</u>i	*!			* *
(b) ko.ma.<u>t</u>i		* *!		*
☞ (c) iŋkoma<u>t</u>i			*	*

The same approach can be used to explain why ONSET fails to force epenthesis at root-root boundaries: /√asi-√RED/→ [asi-asi] 'cover' cannot become *[{<u>t</u>asi}{<u>t</u>asi}] as DEP-σ₁ would be violated on the assumption that the roots are in two separate prosodic words.

3.2 Consonant epenthesis

A final significant competitor is *[iŋ.ko.mai], where the suffix is incorporated into a syllable with the root-final [a], so avoiding an ONSET violation; this form beats the winner [iŋ.ko.ma.ti] in faithfulness. An explanation is that diphthongs are emergently avoided in Axininca: *DIPTH favours [iŋ.ko.ma.ti] over *[iŋ.ko.mai].

(18)   Axininca Campa IV

/i-N-koma-i/	*DIPTH	DEP-IO
(a) iŋ.ko.mai	*!	
☞ (b) iŋ.ko.ma.ti		*

However, *DIPTH is blocked morpheme-internally by a constraint that requires morpheme-internal input adjacency relations to be preserved: IO-CONTIG-M (Kenstowicz 1994; McCarthy & Prince 1995). Tableau (19) illustrates with the word for 'bee' [airi]. Morpheme-internal deletion (e.g. *[ari], *[iri]) is blocked by MAX-STEM.

(19)   Axininca Campa V

/airi/	IO-CONTIG-M	*DIPTH	DEP-IO
(a) atiri	*!		*
☞ (b) airi		*	

A similar ranking involving *V: can account for /i-N-√koma-ako-i/ → [iŋkomatakoti] and not *[iŋkomaːkoti].

The other constraint that indirectly motivates consonant epenthesis is FTBIN 'Feet must be binary at the syllabic or moraic level' (Prince & Smolensky 1993; McCarthy & Prince 1993b:46). This constraint forces monosyllabic inputs like /na/ to have two syllables in the output, and ONSET requires that the inserted syllable start with a consonant, thus /na/→[na.ta] (for analysis of epenthetic vowel qualities see §7.2).

(20)   Axininca Campa VI

/tʰo/	FTBIN	ONSET	DEP-IO
(a) (tʰo)	*!		
(b) (tʰo.a)		*!	
☞ (c) tʰo.ta			**

92   3 *Markedness reduction*

The ranking so far is summarized in (21).

(21)   Motivating Axininca epenthesis

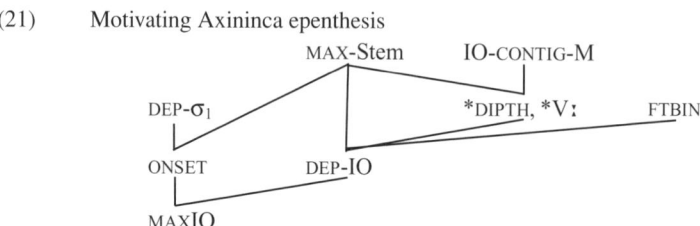

The ranking shows that Axininca Campa's epenthesis is motivated by general prosodic concerns: i.e. ONSET and, less directly, FTBIN. The fact that it fails to apply in some environments is due to environment-specific faithfulness constraints like MAX-Stem and DEP-σ_1. This point is important, as Lombardi proposes that coronal epenthesis is fundamentally different from glottal epenthesis: '[coronals] are never the general, purely syllabification-driven epenthetic consonant of a language' (2002:1). Lombardi claims that coronal epenthesis only occurs in 'particular morphological situations'.

This claim has significant bearing on the proposal that coronal epenthesis is due to output constraints. If an apparently epenthetic coronal consonant only ever appears in a specific morphologically restricted environment, it may not be epenthetic. Instead, it is more likely to be a morpheme that has specific morphological subcategorization requirements, so accounting for its limited distribution (see §3.4.1). Lombardi discusses Gokana [r]/[n] epenthesis in this regard (Hyman 1982, 1985): [n] appears when nasals are adjacent, and [r] otherwise. She observes that [n]/[r] appear only with two suffixes: the second person plural subject and the logophoric. It is therefore quite possible that the [r]/[n] is part of the underlying form of these suffixes, so accounting for their restricted morphological distribution. In addition, Lombardi notes that Gokana also has an epenthetic [ʔ].

Nevertheless, the Axininca Campa case cannot be given a 'morphological' solution. While [t]-epenthesis does not happen in every environment, the restrictions are due to phonological requirements. For example, [t] is not epenthesized before root-initial vowels, but this is due to an environment-specific ban on epenthesis. Epenthesis does not happen at prefix+root boundaries, but this is arguably not due to some special restriction on epenthesis, but on a general faithfulness requirement that targets specific morphological or phonological constituents. In short, Axininca Campa does have an epenthetic [t]. While there is no doubt that coronal epenthesis is much rarer than glottal epenthesis,

3.2 Consonant epenthesis

frequency is irrelevant – the constraints merely tell us which consonants *may* be epenthesized, not how often they will appear.

3.2.3.1 Why [t]?

Of concern is why Axininca Campa does not epenthesize a glottal – either [ʔ] or [h]. [ʔ] does not occur at all on the surface, so a ranking needs to be identified to account for this fact. In contrast, [h] is allowed (e.g. [haka] 'here', [apaːha] 'wait'), but is not epenthesized; the preference of [t] over [h] also needs an explanation.

As discussed briefly in §3.2.2 above, a solution can be found in hierarchy conflict. Specifically, the sonority hierarchy favours coronals over glottals. The relevant part of the hierarchy for consonants is given in (22) (§2.3.3.1).

(22)   *Consonant sonority*
        voiceless stops ⟩ voiced stops ⟩ voiceless fricatives ⟩ voiced fricatives ⟩ nasals ⟩ liquids ⟩ glides ⟩ glottals

In onsets, less sonorous elements are less marked (Prince & Smolensky 1993; de Lacy 2000b; Smith 2002; Parker 2002). Consequently, voiceless stops are the least marked consonant type. This is therefore a point of conflict between the PoA and sonority hierarchies – while [ʔ] is the least marked of all the stops for PoA, it is highly sonorous and therefore highly marked in onsets. Therefore, if margin-sonority constraints dominate, [ʔ] will be eliminated as a possible epenthetic element. In this case, a voiceless stop will be chosen; of the remaining [p t k], the least marked in terms of PoA is [t], so [t] will be epenthesized, following the spirit of Lombardi's (1998, 2002) proposals.

The ranking for Axininca Campa is therefore very similar to the one used for Mabalay Atayal. The crucial difference is that the ranking of the sonority and PoA output constraints are reversed, so [t] instead of [ʔ] is epenthesized. In tableau (23), the demand for low sonority onsets outranks the PoA constraints. So, the other voiceless stops are favoured over glottals, as shown in tableau (23).

(23)   Axininca Campa VII

/√na/	ONSET	*–Δ_σ/glottal	*{dors,lab,cor}	DEP-IO
(a) na.a	*!		*	*
(b) naʔa		*!	*	**
(c) naha		*!	*	**
☞ (d) nata			**	**

94   3 Markedness reduction

Sonority makes no distinction among non-glottal PoAs: *−Δ$_\sigma$/glottal equally favours [p], [k], and [t] over [ʔ] and [h]. So, the PoA constraints must determine which of [k], [p], or [t] is epenthesized. As [t] is the next least marked in terms of PoA, it wins:

(24)   Axininca Campa VIII

/na/	*{dors,lab}	*−Δ$_\sigma$/glottal	*{dors,lab,cor}
(a) naʔa		*!	*
(b) naka	*!		**
(c) napa	*!		**
☞ (d) nata			**

The final issue is why [t] is epenthesized rather than any of the other coronals. The PoA constraints have nothing to say about this issue: [t d s z n r ɾ l ɹ] all incur the same violations of the PoA constraints. In contrast, the sonority constraints all favour the least sonorous segment − i.e. [t] − over all the others. For example, *−Δ$_\sigma$/{liquids,glides,glottals} rules out [l ɹ], and so on; this issue is discussed further in §3.2.4.

The remaining issue of interest is underlying /ʔ/. /ʔ/ does not surface faithfully and there are no alternations that show what happens to it, so a number of outcomes are possible. However, /h/ surfaces faithfully as [h], so MAX outranks *−Δ$_\sigma$/glottal. It is possible that a [ʔ]-specific constraint forces neutralization of /ʔ/ to [h]. Whatever /ʔ/'s fate, the point of this section holds: [ʔ] is less marked than [t] in terms of PoA, but [t] is less marked than [ʔ] in onset position in terms of sonority. If *−Δ$_\sigma$/glottal outranks the PoA constraint *{dors,lab,cor}, an epenthetic coronal will result.

3.2.3.2   Glottal sonority

The analysis of epenthetic coronals rests on the claim that there is a markedness hierarchy that favours non-glottals over glottals, identified as the sonority hierarchy above. A great deal of previous work has argued that high sonority elements are avoided in onsets (see references cited in de Lacy 2000b, 2002a: §6.5.2.2; Smith 2002), so it will be assumed to be correct here. It therefore remains to provide evidence for why glottals are highly sonorous, specifically that [ʔ] is more sonorous than [p t k] and [h] is more sonorous than [f s x]. One option that can be put aside at this point is that glottals are placeless, and that there are constraints that require segments to have PoA features − arguments against this proposal are given in §8.4.

The sonority status of glottals is disputed. Previous work that supports the proposal that glottals are highly sonorous includes Pike 1954, Chomsky & Halle 1968:301, Pinker & Birdsong 1979, Levin 1985, Trigo 1988:46, Parker 1989, 2002, Inkelas & Cho 1993:552, Churma & Shi 1995, and Gnanadesikan 1995, 1997. However, Clements (1990:322) claims that glottals 'behave arbitrarily in terms of the way they class with other sounds', effectively having no sonority value (also van der Hulst 1984; Boersma 1998). A number of authors have argued that glottals have low sonority – effectively the same sonority as obstruents (Heffner 1950; Lass 1976; Dogil & Luschützky 1990; Dogil 1992; Zec 1988; Lombardi 2002: §3.2). To help resolve the issue, the following paragraphs identify phonological evidence that glottals class with highly sonorous elements like glides and liquids.

In transparency effects, glottals consistently class with high sonority segments like glides and liquids. For example, Walker (1998, 2000) shows that the ability of segments to undergo nasal harmony follows the sonority hierarchy, with more sonorous elements more susceptible to nasalization. Notably, the glottals are at the top of this list, classed with glides (Walker 1998: §2.2.3, p.56). For example, nasality can only spread through glides, laryngeals, and nasals in a Malay dialect: [mẽw̃ãh] 'prosperous', [mãj̃ãt] 'corpse', [mãh̃ãl] 'expensive', [mã̃ʔãp] 'forgive' (Teoh 1988:60). Given Walker's proposal, this implies that these segments are higher sonority than those which block nasal spreading: i.e. fricatives and stops.

Similarly, Gafos & Lombardi (1999) show that vowel feature spreading follows the sonority hierarchy, with glides more willing to allow features to spread through them than liquids, liquids more susceptible than nasals, and so on. Notably, glottals stand at the top of this hierarchy. For example, height and roundness features can spread leftward in Harar Oromo (Owens 1985), but only through glides, [h], and [ʔ], as shown in (25).

(25)   Harar Oromo Height Harmony (Owens 1985:21)
    /tah-e/   → [tehe]   'he became'
    /tah-u/   → [tohu]   'he becomes (dependent form)'
    /dʒaʔ-e/ → [dʒeʔe]   'he said'
    /dʒaʔ-u/ → [dʒoʔu]   'let him say {jussive}'
    /d'agaj-e/ → [d'ageje] 'he heard'
    cf. [barar-ne] 'we flew' *[barerne]; [dameː] 'branch', *[demeː]

An objection may be that glottals are good transparent elements because they are representationally minimal, not because of their sonority. For arguments against this proposal, see §8.4.

In sonority-distance restrictions, glottals usually act like highly sonorous elements. For example, Gujarati allows only glides, liquids, and [h] as the second member of onset clusters: [kjal] 'opinion', [krupa] 'kindness', [kleʃ] 'fatigue', [khərəc] 'cost' (Cardona 1965:31ff.). In contrast, it is rare that [h] has the same distribution as other fricatives: compare English [slɪt] 'slit', [flɪt] 'flit', *[hlɪt]. For further discussion of glottals and syllabification, see Churma & Shi 1995.

Zec (1988, 1995) and Churma & Shi (1995:30) also observe that codas tend to house high sonority segments. They list several cases where only high sonority elements (glides, liquids, nasals) and glottals are permitted in coda position. For example, Cayapa only allows nasals, continuants, and [ʔ] to appear in codas (Lindkoog & Brend 1962).

To conclusively show that glottals are highly sonorous all glottal behaviour would have to be examined, especially where glottals apparently do not act like highly sonorous elements. I will touch on one relevant situation. Section 4.3 shows that less marked elements can undergo assimilation while more marked ones do not. Since glottals are the least marked in terms of PoA, this predicts that they should be very prone to assimilation. More generally, because glottals are the least marked elements in terms of PoA, they excite least faithfulness. So, the fact that glottals make such chequered appearances in inventories therefore could derive from the fact that they undergo so many processes because of their unmarked status.

3.2.3.3 Glottal Elimination is not related to PoA

Further support for the idea that Glottal Elimination is sonority-related is the fact that it behaves differently from processes that eliminate other PoAs. A striking difference relates to the 'subset' relation between onsets and codas. A number of authors have argued that there is a relation between PoA contrasts in onsets and codas: the PoA contrasts found in codas are always a subset of those found in onsets (Trubetzkoy 1939; Goldsmith 1990; Beckman 1998, and references cited therein).

The PoA-subset generalization is valid if attention is restricted to non-glottal PoAs: if a language has a dorsal in the coda there is also one in the onset; the same is true for labials and coronals. For example, there is no language with [p t] in its onset but [k p t] in the coda. This generalization is based on a survey of the languages cited in the language index to this book.

In contrast, Parker (2001b) shows that the subset generalization is not true for glottals: if a language allows glottals in its coda, this does not necessarily mean that it also permits them in onsets. For example, the Peruvian language

Chamicuro allows the voiceless fricatives [s h] in codas but only [s] in onsets (also Parker 1994b, 2001b). A more extreme case is Macushi Carib, which allows [s] but not [h] in onsets and [h] but not [s] in codas (Abbott 1991). For stops, Standard Malay allows [ʔ] in codas but not in onsets (§3.3.1). In contrast, some languages have glottals in onset position but not in codas. For example, Yuma has [k p t ʔ] in onsets but only [k p t] in codas (Halpern 1946). Similarly, Lamani allows [s h] in onsets, but only [s] in codas. In short, non-glottal PoAs obey the subset generalization, but glottals do not. This difference is summarized in (26). The table shows that any configuration of glottals is permitted. There are languages that allow glottals in (a) both onsets and codas (Apalai Carib), (b) onsets only (Yuma for [ʔ]), (c) codas only (Chamicuro for [h]), and (d) neither in onsets nor codas (Māori for [ʔ]).

(26) Glottals and the subset generalization

(a) Glottal Distribution			(b) Non-Glottal Distribution		
onsets	*codas*	*language*	*onsets*	*codas*	*language*
✓	✓	Apalai Carib	✓	✓	English [k p t]
✓	✗	Yuma [ʔ]	✓	✗	Toba Batak [k p t]
✗	✓	Chamicuro [h]	✗	✓	–
✗	✗	Māori [ʔ]	✗	✗	Djapu (fricatives)

Apalai Carib (Koehn & Koehn 1986), Yuma (Halpern 1946), Chamicuro (Parker 1994b), Māori (Bauer 1993), Toba Batak (Hayes 1986), Djapu (Morphy 1983)

In contrast, for non-glottal PoA there are languages that allow non-glottals in both onsets and codas (e.g. English), and there are languages that allow non-glottals in onsets but not codas (e.g. Kelantan Malay has [k p t] in onsets but just [ʔ] in codas). However, there is no language that allows a particular non-glottal PoA in codas but bans it in onsets: for example, no language allows [k] in codas but not in onsets.

There are also languages that ban all non-glottal fricatives in both codas and onsets (e.g. Djapu). There is no analogous case for stops, but this is probably due to functional reasons. Of course, there are languages that ban a *subset* of non-glottal stops in both onsets and codas (e.g. Ayutla Mixtec bans [p] in both positions (Pankratz & Pike 1967)).

The theoretical implication is that the constraints that ban glottals are different from those that militate against other PoAs. Beckman's (1998) approach to the subset generalization for non-glottals employs context-free output constraints coupled with onset-specific faithfulness constraints. With such constraints, there is no way to eliminate dorsals in onsets alone, for example.

3 Markedness reduction

However, since glottals can be eliminated in onsets alone, there must at least be onset-specific constraints against glottals (see, e.g., Parker 2001b; Broselow 2001). Here, the constraint is $*-\Delta_\mu$/glottal 'Incur a violation for glottals in the non-DTE of moras (i.e. an onset)'. There is also a constraint against glottals in margins ($*-\Delta_\sigma$/glottal), as used above. The rankings that produce the possible systems are given in (27).

(27) Crucial rankings for glottal distribution
 (a) No glottals in onsets or codas
  ‖ $*-\Delta_\sigma$/glottal » IDENT{dors,lab,cor,gl}, onset-IDENT{dors,lab,cor,gl} ‖

 (b) Glottals in onsets but not in codas

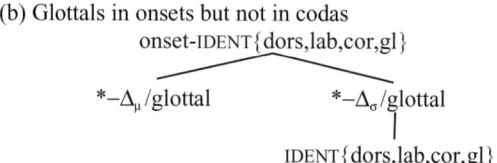

 (c) Glottals in codas but not in onsets

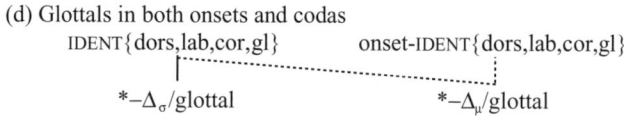

 (d) Glottals in both onsets and codas
  IDENT{dors,lab,cor,gl}   onset-IDENT{dors,lab,cor,gl}
   | ⋮
  $*-\Delta_\sigma$/glottal $*-\Delta_\mu$/glottal

Dotted line indicates that one of the rankings must exist.

Finally, §2.3.3.2 proposed that output constraints can only combine prosodic positions with sonority values, not subsegmental features. So, in a constraint $*-\Delta_\mu$/glottal the 'glottal' must be a sonority value, not a feature.

3.2.3.4 Summary

In summary, coronals are epenthetic when glottals are prevented from appearing. In ranking terms, a constraint that favours non-glottals over coronals ($*-\Delta_\sigma$/glottal, $*-\Delta_\mu$/glottal) outranks all constraints that favour coronals over glottals (e.g. *{dors,lab,cor}). The variability in glottal and coronal epenthesis illustrates a fact about markedness: markedness hierarchies can conflict.

3.2.4 Other epenthetic segments

The previous sections have shown why [ʔ] and [t] can be epenthetic: [ʔ] is the least-marked segment in terms of PoA and beats [h] in continuancy markedness, while [t] is less marked than [ʔ] in terms of sonority and beats [p k] in terms of PoA. However, several other default epenthetic segments are attested: [n N h ɹ w j]. There are three reasons why not all epenthetic elements are [ʔ] or [t]. One is that sonority requirements in codas are different from sonority requirements in onsets. The other is that assimilation to vowels can override sonority and PoA markedness. The remaining reason is that for approximants, coronals have an Achilles' heel for markedness – they are liquids. Each point is discussed in turn.

3.2.4.1 Coda Sonority

Coda consonant epenthesis is rarer than onset epenthesis. All coda epenthesis cases may be motivated by metrical restrictions. For example, coda [h] epenthesis in Ayutla Mixtec, discussed in §3.2.1, makes a stem-initial syllable bi-moraic. In Tunica, [n] is epenthesized phrase-finally, and this may be due to it having phrase-level stress (Haas 1946; Lombardi 2002: §3.2.2).

Coda consonants have a dual nature in terms of DTEs. Consonants that are dominated by a mora are the DTE of a mora but a non-DTE of the syllable (§2.3.3.1). As a syllable non-DTE, there are constraints that seek to minimize its sonority (i.e. the margin-sonority constraints of Prince & Smolensky 1993). As a mora DTE, there are constraints that demand that they have high sonority (also see Morén 1999:§2.2.1). In some languages, the mora-DTE demand wins out and codas are forced to have high sonority elements. The most striking evidence of this high-sonority preference is found in languages where segments are forced to become more sonorous in codas. For example, in Squliq Atayal codas /z/ becomes [j] (28a) and /g/ becomes [w] (28b) (Huang 2004).

(28) Increase of coda sonority in Squliq Atayal (Huang 2004)

Input	Active	Passive	Gloss
(a) /z/ → [j]			
/ʔubuz/	[ʔu.buj]	[bu.z-an]	'continue, connect'
/hapuz/	[p-ha.puj]	[pu.z-an]	'cook'
cf. /takuj/	[ta.kuj]	[tku.j-an]	'fall'
(b) /g/ → [w]			
/htug/	[htuw]	[htg-an]	'come out'
/luhug/	[lu.huw]	[lu.hu.g-an]	'thread a needle'

A similar process where stops are turned into the more sonorous nasals in codas is found in Dakota (§4.2.2.3; Shaw 1980:367,374): e.g. /xap/ → [xam] 'be stripped', cf. [xap-a]; /ja-zit͡ʃ/→[jazin] 'elastic, flimsy', cf. [ja-zi.t͡ʃ-a].

The epenthetic counterparts of Squliq Atayal and Dakota are those languages with epenthesis of high-sonority coda elements (e.g. Ayutla Mixtec, Tunica). The constraints that promote high sonority mora-DTEs are high ranked. Tunica is a particularly interesting case because [n] is epenthesized phrase-finally: e.g. /hatika/ → [hatikan] 'again' (Haas 1946; Lombardi 2003:§3.2.2). Lombardi proposes that the motivation is a phrasal version of McCarthy's (2000) FINAL-C, which requires prosodic words to end in a consonant. An alternative is that the language is like Mabalay Atayal: phrase-final syllables are stressed and stressed syllables must be heavy; further investigation is warranted.

The epenthesis of nasals shows the conflict between the mora-DTE and syllable-non-DTE constraints. Constraints that ban non-DTEs with more sonority than nasals prevent anything more sonorous than a nasal from being epenthesized: $*-\Delta_\sigma \geq \{\text{liquid}\}$. At the same time, constraints that ban DTEs with less sonority than nasals prevent anything less sonorous from nasals from being epenthetic: $*\Delta_\mu \leq \{\text{fricative}\}$. These two constraints outrank all other sonority constraints that ban nasals from coda position (e.g. $*-\Delta_\sigma \geq \{\text{nasal}\}$, etc.). This type of sonority conflict is discussed in detail in chapter 7.

(29)   Tunica I

/hatika/	$*-\Delta_\sigma \geq \{\text{liquid}\}$	$*\Delta_\mu \leq \{\text{fricative}\}$
(a) hatika<u>t</u>		*!
(b) hatika<u>r</u>	*!	
(c) hatika<u>h</u>	*!	
☞ (d) hatika<u>n</u>		

MAX outranks the constraints in tableau (29), preventing them from causing deletion.

The result is that, because some constraints demand high sonority and others low sonority, epenthetic coda consonants are predicted to have almost any sonority level. At the moment, the known cases have high sonority glottals (e.g. Ayutla Mixtec) and mid sonority nasals (e.g. Tunica [n], Uradhi [N]). No cases have been reported with epenthetic coda consonants of other sonority (e.g. glides, liquids, fricatives, stops); but this lack may be due to the rarity of coda epenthesis cases.

3.2.4.2 Manner assimilation

Coda sonority constraints account for some variation in the manner of articulation of some epenthetic consonants, but not all. Epenthetic onset consonants can also have high sonority: i.e. rhotics, [w], [j], and [h]. These epenthetic consonants owe their feature values to assimilation: unlike [ʔ] and [t], they are partially assimilated in manner of articulation to adjacent vowels. Specifically, they agree with adjacent vowels in terms of the feature [+sonorant], and may also agree in [+approximant]. Such manner assimilation comes about when manner-assimilation constraints outrank antagonistic sonority constraints.

Southern Tati provides an example of manner of articulation assimilation (Yar-Shater 1969). All dialects have the same epenthesis facts (p.53ff.). The rhotic trill [r] is epenthesized in hiatus after [a] and [aː], as shown in (30). The data are from Yar-Shater (1969:54). Rhotic epenthesis is also found in many dialects of English (e.g. McCarthy 1991, 1993; Baković 1999c) and Anejoñ (Lynch 2000:29). In some of the examples cited, [r] is epenthesized *before* [a] as well (e.g. [u-r-aːʃin] 'throw up'); it is not clear whether this varies according to dialect.

(30)   Southern Tati [r] epenthesis
      (a) [ruazaː-r-ijoːm]   'my grandson, too'
      (b) [dʒuaː-r-a de-r-e] 'it is in that one'
      (c) [dʒuaː-r-eːn]   'from those'

A fact about Southern Tati that lends credence to the idea that epenthetic consonants assimilate to vowel features is that the epenthetic consonants before non-low vowels clearly copy the PoA and assimilation features of the following vowel. After non-round vowels, [j] is epenthesized: e.g. /bi-æ/ → [bijæ] 'she made', [mirine-j-ø miaː] 'he is scattering (seed) and coming'. [w] is epenthesized after round vowels: e.g. [sywar] 'horseman', [ruwæn] 'ghee'.[3]

In short, Southern Tati epenthetic consonants clearly attempt to copy the PoA and manner of articulation of the following vowel. So, [j] appears after [i] because [j] and [i] have the same value for [sonorant] and [approximant], and both are palatal; [w] copies the [u]'s labial and manner features.

After [a] the epenthetic consonant is an approximant [r] because it copies the vowel's manner of articulation. For discussion of the feature composition of trills and other rhotics and their identification as sonorants or approximants, see Walsh Dickey 1997 and Wiese 2001. However, it cannot copy the vowel's PoA

---

3 Some cases of a 'connective [h]' are also cited (Yar-Shater 1969:54), but its appearance does not seem to be systematic, so it is therefore not epenthetic.

because [a] has no PoA features (Clements & Hume 1995).[4] In this situation, the epenthetic vowel has no choice but to take on a default PoA feature – coronal.

Epenthesis in Southern Tati is clearly motivated by ONSET; as in Axininca Campa, ONSET and MAX-IO must outrank DEP-IO.

To get the right epenthetic consonants, AGREE[approx(imant)] must outrank all constraints that seek to keep onset sonority low, including all the margin-sonority constraints like $*\Delta_\sigma/\{\text{glottal,glide,liquid}\}$. In addition, AGREE[PoA]$_{VC}$ must outranks all PoA output constraints, ensuring that [j] and [w] are epenthesized after [i] and [u] respectively. AGREE[PoA]$_{VC}$ applies to vowel+consonant clusters. These rankings are illustrated in tableau (31). As both AGREE constraints dominate both PoA and sonority output constraints, the winner has an epenthetic segment that agrees entirely in PoA.

(31)   Southern Tati I

/ru-æn/	AGREE[PoA]$_{VC}$	AGREE [approx]	*{dors,lab}	$*-\Delta_\sigma/\{\text{glottal, glide,liquid}\}$
(a) ru.hæn	*!			*
(b) ru.ræn	*!			*
(c) ru.pæn		*!	*	
☞ (d) ru.wæn			*	*

Before [a], the epenthetic consonant again becomes an approximant due to AGREE[approx]. However, [a] has no PoA features, so AGREE[PoA] is irrelevant, and output constraints must determine the form of the epenthetic consonant. If the PoA constraints were dominant, a glottal [ʔ] or [h] would be epenthesized. In fact, this is exactly what happens in Tamil, where the epenthetic consonant is [j] adjacent to front vowels, [w] before back vowels, and [ʔ] before the central vowel [a] (Wiltshire 1998); the same happens in Kalinga (Rosenthall 1995:180). However, with the constraint $*-\Delta_\sigma/\text{glottal}$ outranking *{dors,lab,cor}, the best option is to epenthesize a coronal approximant – i.e. [r].

(32)   Southern Tati II

/dʒuaː-eːn/	$*-\Delta_\sigma/\text{glottal}$	*{dors,lab}	*{dors,lab,cor}
(a) dʒuaː-ɦ-eːn	*!		**
(b) dʒuaː-w-eːn		*!	***
☞ (c) dʒuaː-r-eːn			***

---

[4] At least, [a] is neither palatal, labial, nor dorsal. It may have some other PoA feature (e.g. pharyngeal).

In other words, [r] — and the other high sonority segments — are epenthetic because the demand for adjacent segments to agree in manner of articulation outranks the sonority requirements. Rhotics can be epenthetic when glottals are eliminated and the requirement that epenthetic consonants agree in PoA is irrelevant.

The epenthetic [ɹ] found in many dialects of English is similar to Southern Tati's in that it only appears after non-high vowels. Many view epenthetic rhotics with scepticism (e.g. Hale & Reiss 2000:§2.2; Vaux 2003). For example, McCarthy (1993:189) states that 'r is demonstrably not the default consonant in English'. I suspect that the source of the scepticism is the notion of 'default consonant'. The problem with this concept is that there is no such thing as an 'unmarked/default consonant', and pure markedness is rarely ever on display. Any epenthetic consonant is subject to many different influences: markedness reduction, assimilation, dissimilation, and so on. Epenthetic rhotics are the perfect example: the majority of features in an epenthetic rhotic are influenced by assimilation; markedness reduction only shows in their PoA. In this way, they are simply a compromise between being entirely influenced by their environment (like glides) and having entirely unmarked features (like [t ʔ]).

Apart from rhotics, the other default epenthetic approximants are [h], [j], and [w]. [h]/[ɦ] is epenthesized because it has the least marked PoA, and it agrees in continuancy with a following vowel. Default epenthesis of [j] and [w] pose a more interesting issue as they have highly marked PoAs — palatal and labio-dorsal. This issue is addressed in the next section.

It is now possible to ask what the theory predicts for manner of articulation of epenthetic consonants. For codas, this question has already been answered: since there are conflicting sonority demands on codas, epenthetic coda consonants are predicted to have any sonority level — stops, fricatives, nasals, liquids, and glides.

For onsets, the prediction is quite different. The only pressure in the grammar is for onsets to have low sonority (de Lacy 2000b; Smith 2002 and references cited therein). The least sonorous manner of articulation is 'voiceless stops', so they can be epenthesized: i.e. effectively just [t]. Epenthetic consonants can be forced to be more sonorous by the PoA constraints: i.e. [ʔ]. All other manners of articulation must come from assimilation. Vowels are approximants, so it is unsurprising that the other epenthetic onset segments are also approximants: [ɹ j w h].

Many manners of articulation are not possible in epenthetic consonants, though. For example, the theory cannot produce a language with an epenthetic nasal in onsets (unless an adjacent segment is also nasal) as an epenthetic onset consonant cannot get a [+nasal] feature through assimilation to oral vowels, and nasals are not the least sonorous segment type. Without knowing exactly which manner features consonants and vowels can share, it is difficult to be more precise about the impossibility of other epenthetic manners of articulation. Assuming that consonants cannot share the feature [voice] with a following vowel, it is therefore impossible for there to be an epenthetic voiced stop — voiceless stops will be more harmonic in terms of sonority. Similarly, if consonants cannot share the feature [continuant], there should be no epenthetic fricatives. In other words, with the most conservative assumptions about feature agreement, the theory predicts that epenthetic onset consonants can only be glottals, voiceless stops, and approximants.

3.2.4.3 Epenthetic labials and palatals

The preceding sections have argued that coronal can be 'promoted' to least-marked status when glottal is eliminated by sonority constraints. The remaining issue is whether other PoAs like labial and dorsal can ever be promoted in a similar way. For most manners of articulation, epenthetic consonants can never be anything but coronal or glottal — they cannot be labial, retroflex, palatal, dorsal, or pharyngeal. This is due to the nature of the proposed constraints: there is no constraint that favours a labial or dorsal over a coronal. All the PoA constraints favour coronals over every PoA apart from glottal, and the sonority constraints do not distinguish PoAs. However, there is one situation where non-coronals can be promoted to least-marked status: when coronals necessarily have some independently marked value.

This situation arises for approximants. The glottal approximant [h] can be ruled out by $*-\Delta_\sigma$/glottal. This leaves the laterals and rhotics, but they have an incidentally marked property — they are also liquids. If liquids are banned and glottals are avoided, then an epenthetic approximant must have either labial or dorsal PoA. Such a situation happens in Uyghur (Hahn 1991; Vaux 2003).[5] The palatal [j] is inserted to satisfy ONSET, as shown in (33). Note that [j] is inserted regardless of the rounding of the following or preceding consonant, so its PoA is not the result of assimilation. There is free variation between inserting [j] and [r] in some environments; this may be morphologically conditioned.

(33) Uyghur [j] epenthesis (Vaux 2003)
 (a) /oqu+al/ → [oqujal] 'to be able to read'
 (b) /iʃlæ+al/ → [iʃlæjæl] 'to be able to work'
 (c) /juːb/ → [jujup] 'wash and ...'

---

5 My thanks to Bert Vaux for bringing this case to my attention.

(d) /suːm/ → [syjym] 'my liquid'
(e) /sijaː-m/ → [sijajim]/[sija̠rim] 'ink+1ˢᵗ person',
    cf. [sija-si] {3rd pers.}
(f) /toxuː-ŋ/ → [toxujuŋ]/toxu̠ruŋ] 'chicken+2nd pers.',
    cf. [toxusi]
cf. /bahaːɹ/ → [bahaːrim] 'spring+1st pers.',
    cf. [bahari] {3rd pers.}

The epenthetic consonant's manner of articulation agrees with the following vowel – it is an approximant, indicating that AGREE[approx] outranks all sonority constraints that promote low sonority segments.

The palatal [j] is epenthesized because both glottals and liquids can be banned for independent markedness reasons. The only remaining option is for another approximant to be epenthetic, such as a palatal [j], or labial [w ʋ], or dorsal [ɰ]. Assuming [j]'s major PoA to be coronal (see Hall 1997 for discussion), it is the next best choice even though its minor PoA (i.e. [–anterior]) is marked compared with [+anterior] alveolar coronals.

In constraint terms, glottals are ruled out by *–Δ_σ/glottal, and liquids by a ban on liquids, called *liquid for convenience. There is no question that palatals are more marked than alveolars as palatals neutralize to alveolars in some languages (e.g. Korean /nac/→[nat] 'daytime' – Kim-Renaud 1974); the opposite neutralization never takes place. So, the constraint against palatals – *[–anterior] – must be outranked by the ban on liquids. The following tableau summarizes these rankings.

(34)   Uyghur palatal epenthesis

/oqu+al/	AGREE [approx]	*–Δ_σ/glottal	*{dors,lab}	*liquid	*[–anterior]
(a) oquta̠l	*!		*	*	
(b) oquha̠l		*!	*	*	
(c) oquwal			**!	*	
(d) oquɹal			*	**!	
☞ (e) oqujal			*	*	*

In other words, palatal approximants can be promoted to least-marked status because both glottals and alveolars can be ruled out by other constraints. The ranking does not mean that liquids are banned in the language. If IDENT[liquid] outranks *liquid, the avoidance will be emergent.

The one problem with palatals is that they can be ruled out emergently by *[−anterior]. If this is the case, then there is no choice but to resort to the next available segment in terms of PoA markedness — a labial approximant. This situation occurs in Chamicuro (Parker 1987, 1989, p.c.).⁶ In this language, onsetless syllables are avoided. If there is hiatus between a high vowel and a following vowel, the high vowel becomes a glide. Otherwise, an epenthetic [w] is inserted.

(35)   Chamicuro [w] epenthesis (Parker 1987, 1989)
         (i) High vowels become glides before vowels
            (a) /u-atʃiki/   → [watʃíki] 'I grab'   cf. [u-kamáni] 'I wash'
            (b) /u-iːla/   → [wíːla] 'my blood'   cf. [u-tódlo] 'my forehead'
            (c) /i-atʃiki/   → [jatʃíki] 's/he grabs'   cf. [i-kamáni] 's/he washes'
            (d) /i-iːla/   → [jíːla] 'his/her blood'   cf. [i-tódlo] 'his/her forehead'

         (ii) Otherwise [w] is inserted
            (a) /a-atʃiki/   → [awatʃíki] 'we grab'   cf. [a-kamáni] 'we wash'
            (b) /a-eʃtihki/ → [aweʃtíhki] 'we tie up'
            (c) /a-usmuski/ → [awusmúski] 'we run'
            (d) /a-oʔti/   → [awóʔti] 'we give'
            (e) /a-iːla/   → [awíːla] 'our blood'
            (f) /a-enopine/ → [awenopíne] 'lemon'

Parker (p.c.) argues against a deletion analysis whereby the underlined [w] belongs to the morphemes for 'we' and 'our' – i.e. /aw/. The problem with this analysis is that underlying /w/'s demonstrably do not delete in codas – they devoice: e.g. [káw̥.sa] 'smoke', [s̩aw̥kolo] 'thick'.

The Chamicuro epenthetic consonant is [w] regardless of the context: any of [a e o i u] can follow it. It would be ideal to show that any vowel can also precede it, but the only affixes that end in a non-high vowel have /a/. It could therefore be the case that the epenthetic consonant is [w] because it assimilates to the preceding /a/'s [+back] or [dorsal] feature. However, Ohala & Lorentz (1977) argue that [w] is always specified as [labial], and never [dorsal]. If they are correct, Chamicuro [w] cannot be [w] through assimilation to [a].

In ranking terms, Chamicuro [w] emerges as the winner if the ranking in (34) is changed so that *[−anterior] outranks *{dors,lab}.

---

6 I am indebted to Steve Parker for providing additional examples and an extensive discussion about Chamicuro epenthesis. The analysis builds on Parker's comments.

(36)   Chamicuro I

/a+iːla/	AGREE [approx]	*−Δ_σ/glottal	*[−anterior]	*liquid	*{dors,lab}
(a) aʔiːla	*!			*	
(b) ahiːla		*!		*	
(c) ajiːla			*!	*	
(d) aliːla				* *!	
☞ (e) awiːla				*	*

To summarize, epenthetic approximants provide interesting insight into the form of PoA markedness because they show how various PoA values can be promoted to relatively least-marked status. If PoA markedness dominates, glottals will be epenthesized. If glottals are eliminated, then coronals will be epenthetic. If alveolars are eliminated for an incidental reason (only relevant for approximants), palatals or labials can be promoted to least-marked status. The end result is an array of epenthetic onset segments [ʔ h t r ɹ j w].

3.2.5 Impossible epenthetic segments

The preceding sections have focused on accounting for attested epenthetic segments, claiming that the interaction of markedness hierarchies and constraints on assimilation determines the feature content of epenthetic segments. This section focuses on providing an account of unattested epenthetic consonants.

As an example, [p] is never epenthetic. In constraint terms, the only way it could be epenthetic is if [t] and [ʔ] could be eliminated by a careful arrangement of conflicting markedness hierarchies. However, with the markedness hierarchies discussed above such a conflict can never occur – there is always some other consonant that performs better than [p] in terms of markedness. Specifically, there is no property of [p] that is less marked on any hierarchy than any of [t]'s corresponding properties: [p] is equally as marked as [t] in sonority, and more marked in terms of PoA. The result is that no matter how markedness-related constraints are ranked, [p] will never be favoured over [t] for markedness, and therefore never be epenthetic. Of course, assimilation and dissimilation are factored out of the preceding discussion. A labial like [p] may be epenthesized in order to agree with an adjacent segment's PoA.

Conversely, as [p] is never epenthetic, there must therefore be no markedness hierarchy that favours [p] over [t] or [ʔ]. So, there can be no freely rankable constraint *{coronal}. If there were, it would be straightforward to get [p] epenthesis, as shown in tableau (37).

(37) Why there is no *{coronal}

/a/	*{coronal}	*{dors}	*{dors,lab}
(a) ta	*!		
(b) ka		*!	*
☠ (c) pa			*

In constraint terms, [t] is a harmonic bound for [p] (Samek-Lodovici & Prince 1999). There is no ranking of output-oriented constraints which favours [p] over [t]: no PoA constraint assigns [t] a violation without also assigning [p] one (e.g. *{dors,lab,cor}, *{dors,lab,cor,gl}). Of the sonority constraints, there is no constraint that favours [p] over [t]. Consequently, if no output-oriented output constraint ever favours [p] over [t], [p] can never be the result of a process driven by markedness reduction.

It is useful to compare this situation with those for epenthetic approximants. Alveolar approximants just happen to have a property that is highly marked on another markedness hierarchy: | +liquid ⟩ −liquid |. Consequently, the coronal approximants [ɹ ɻ l] can be eliminated, allowing [w] or [j] to be epenthesized. The situation contrasts with stops because [t] has no special marked feature that distinguishes it from [p] apart from PoA.

The points made above still hold when there is no coronal in a language's inventory. For example, even in a Hawaiian-like language where there is no [t], labials and dorsals can never be epenthetic. The reason is that no language can eliminate both coronals and glottals for every manner of articulation. As both coronal and glottal are less marked PoAs than labial and dorsal, there will always be an alternative with a less marked PoA. As further discussion of this point necessarily refers to neutralization and PoM, it will be taken up again in §4.2.2.2.

3.2.5.1 Epenthetic [d s z l]
A remaining question is why coronals like [d], [s], [z], and [l] are not attested as epenthetic. Cases of [l]-epenthesis have been proposed for Bristol English

(Wells 1982) and certain dialects in the north-eastern USA (Gick 1999). However, Bermúdez-Otero & Börjars (2005:§6.5) argue that the quality of the [l] is due to assimilation – therefore it is not a case of default epenthesis. The problem that these consonants face is that they are neither least sonorous nor most similar to vowels. While epenthetic consonants can be coronal, their manner of articulation is determined by sonority constraints and assimilation. In onsets, low sonority is preferred, so [t] will win. In codas, higher sonority is favoured, so either glides, nasals, or rhotics will win. For assimilation, the most assimilated consonants are approximants.

The fricative [s], on the other hand, is neither least sonorous nor most like a vowel. Even so, it could be possible for [s] to be epenthetic under certain conditions because it is the least sonorous segment that agrees with vowels in terms of continuancy, assuming that vowels are specified as [+continuant]. Similarly, [z] is the least sonorous consonant that agrees with vowels in both continuancy and voice, and [d] is the least sonorous consonant that agrees with vowels in [+voice]. Also, [l] is the most sonorous coronal segment apart from rhotics. In short, the theory predicts that all of these consonants could be epenthetic, as long as vowels are [+continuant] and their voicing feature is the same one that is found in obstruents. The lack of epenthetic [d s z l] may be due to the complex ranking that needs to be present to bring them about – i.e. a mixture of emergent assimilation and onset-sonority constraints and the related learnability issues. Alternatively, vowels may not have a [+continuant] feature and their voicing may be fundamentally different from the [voice] feature of obstruents (see, e.g., Gnanadesikan 1997). Whatever the reason, the focus here is on PoA, and it is clear that both coronals and glottals can be epenthetic.

3.2.6 Summary

To summarize, default consonant epenthesis presents a situation in which the effects of markedness reduction are clearly visible. The discussion has underscored the point that there is no 'least marked segment' – there are a number of interacting markedness hierarchies which partially disagree about which segment is least marked. The conflict, along with manner assimilation, produces the range of attested epenthetic consonants. However, while markedness hierarchies conflict to a small extent, they often agree. Consequently, no ranking will ever produce epenthetic consonants like [k] and [p].

The preceding sections have also shown that processes like assimilation and dissimilation can interfere with epenthesis. Assimilation can cause epenthetic

110   3 *Markedness reduction*

elements to take on almost all features of the following vowel, as in glide epenthesis. There are less pervasive assimilations, too. For example, assimilation of PoA alone causes the epenthetic consonant to have the same PoA as a following consonant, but the least marked manner. Assimilation of manner alone causes epenthetic consonants to have the same manner as a vowel, but unmarked PoA, as for [h].

In short, this chapter has shown that consonant epenthesis exhibits asymmetries. All of the attested epenthetic consonants can be ascribed to the action of markedness hierarchies and assimilation/dissimilation processes. The reason that markedness hierarchies are so influential in consonant epenthesis is that preservation is irrelevant: no constraint on input preservation can influence epenthetic segments, so epenthesis shows the effects of markedness reduction; this point is developed in chapter 4.

3.3   The output of neutralization

The term 'neutralization' is used here to refer to a change in a feature value that is not influenced by adjacent segments. Neutralization is often conditioned by prosodic context; for example, PoA often neutralizes in syllable codas. However, neutralization can also occur in every environment, in which case it defines the inventory of a particular language. In Trubetzkoy 1939, neutralization is synonymous with 'loss of contrast'. Here, the phrase '*x* neutralizes to *y*' means that /x/ becomes [y] even when a loss in contrast is not involved. For example, Malay /k/→[ʔ] in codas does not lose contrast because [ʔ] does not contrast with [k] elsewhere (i.e. in onsets). For further discussion of the present theory's rejection of the role of contrast in markedness, see §8.5.

Trubetzkoy (1939) argued that neutralization provides insight into markedness relations (also see Greenberg 1966:14ff.). The output target of neutralization is always the least-marked available element on some markedness hierarchy. So, /t/ can neutralize to [ʔ] because [ʔ] is less marked than [t] in terms of PoA, but /t/ can never neutralize to [k] as [k] is not less marked than [t] on any markedness hierarchy. This section builds on Trubetzkoy's proposal; it argues that the neutralization generalization follows from the markedness theory proposed here because faithfulness constraints cannot distinguish between unfaithful competitors. Consequently, markedness reduction is decisive in selecting the output form.

Only the PoA neutralizations in (38) are possible once Glottal Elimination is taken into account (§3.2.3).

(38) Possible outputs of PoA neutralization

Input	Output	Example	Language
dorsal	glottal	/baik/ → [bai?] cf. [kə-baik-an]	Malay codas (Lapoliwa 1981)
	coronal	/l-k'ak-RED/ → [lak-k'it] /ogi-ʔapur/ → [ot.ʔapur]	Taiwanese secret language codas (Li 1985) Basque codas (Hualde 1991)
labial	glottal	[m-rataʔ-ratap]	Ulu Muar Malay reduplicant codas (Hendon 1966)
	coronal	/l-ɕap-RED/ → [lap-ɕit]	Cantonese secret language codas (Yip 1982)
coronal	glottal	/namːit/ → [namːiʔ] cf. [namːid-æʔ]	Yamphu codas (Rutgers 1998)
glottal	coronal	/tʃoːh-kʰo/ → [tʃoːt-kʰo] cf. [tʃoːh-uni]	Korean codas (Kim-Renaud 1986)

As an example, /k/ can neutralize to the least marked PoA [ʔ]. /k/ can also neutralize to [t] when [ʔ] is ruled out by margin sonority constraints. However, /k/ can never neutralize to [p] because there is always a less-marked element available – either [t] or [ʔ].

Section 3.3.1 identifies the two major factors responsible for the neutralizations listed above. One relates to the form of the output constraints: as glottal is less marked than (i.e. a local harmonic bound for) all other PoAs, glottals will always be favoured as outputs over other segments. The other reason relates to the form of the PoA faithfulness constraints: the constraints assign the same violations to all unfaithful elements. Together, these two factors result in the least-marked PoA emerging as the target of neutralization: the form of the faithfulness constraints ensures that output constraints will determine the output's form, and glottals harmonically bound all other PoAs, so the output of neutralization will typically be glottals.

Section 3.3.2 discusses the effect of glottal elimination on the output of neutralization. This section shows that glottal elimination can force neutralization to a coronal, even when a glottal is present in the language.

Section 3.3.3 discusses cases where glottals are neutralized through Glottal Elimination. The outcome is the next least-marked PoA – coronal. The only time that labials are ever the output of neutralization is when they are approximants: i.e. [w], as discussed in §3.3.4.

112   3 *Markedness reduction*

Section 3.3.5 discusses predictions of the theory for language-internal consistency of neutralization and promotion of labials and dorsals to least-marked status. This section shows that even if coronals are eliminated by some incidental process, labials and dorsals can never be the least-marked PoA, and therefore never the target of neutralization. It also shows that if dorsals neutralize to glottals in a language, the proposals presented here require labials to become glottals in the same environment, if labials neutralize at all. So, a language in which /k/→[ʔ] in codas and /p/→[t] in the same environment is predicted to be impossible.

The table also emphasizes that the principles of markedness reduction operate on dimensions other than input→output. The Ulu Muar Malay, Taiwanese, and Cantonese cases all involve neutralization of base segments in the reduplicant.

3.3.1   *The irrelevance of faithfulness for neutralization outputs*

Neutralization of PoA to glottal (also called 'debuccalization' – McCarthy 1994) is possible for two reasons: (1) the PoA-output constraints favour glottal over all other types, and (2) the PoA faithfulness constraints do not distinguish between different types of PoA-unfaithfulness. These points will be illustrated through an analysis of Standard Malay /k/-neutralization, described by Lapoliwa (1981), Onn (1980), Teoh (1988), and Trigo (1988:§1.3).

Standard Malay onsets allow the voiceless stops [k p t], but codas permit only [p t ʔ]. Alternations show that input /k/ neutralizes to [ʔ] in codas. The data in (39) are from Lapoliwa (1981:88–9) (also see Onn 1980:9; Teoh 1988:98ff.). The suffix -*an* expresses a result: e.g. [didik-an] is 'the result of educating', [-i] is a transitivizer.

(39)   Malay codas [p t ʔ] (Lapoliwa 1981:88–9)[7]
        (a) /k/→[ʔ] in codas

Root	Final codas	Medial codas	Onsets
/baik/	baiʔ 'good'	baiʔ.-lah 'all right'	kə-bai.k-an
/didik/	di.diʔ 'educate'		di.di.k-an
/duduk/	du.dʊʔ 'sit'	du.dʊʔ.-kan 'to seat'	du.du.k-i
/gərak/	gə.raʔ 'move'	gə.raʔ.-lah 'move it'	gə.ra.k-an
/pendek/	pen.dɛʔ 'short'	pə.ndeʔ.-ɲa 'in short'	kə.-pən.de.k-an
/sorak/	so.raʔ 'shout'	so.raʔ.-ɲa 'way he shouted'	so.ra.k-i

---

7 Lapoliwa also cites the free variants [gərak-lah], [sorak-ŋa], [baik-lah] (but never *[pəndek-ɲa]). The variable appearance of [k] rather than [ʔ] in these forms may be due to the development of onset clusters, so that /baik-lah/ can be syllabified as [bai.klah] or [baiʔ.lah] (but not *[pənde.k-ɲa] for sonority-distance reasons). Such clusters are found only in loans and as the result of certain syncope processes (cf. Hendon 1966:32–3). In all unambiguous coda positions – i.e. word-finally – /k/ becomes [ʔ].

(b) /p t/ surface faithfully
[i.kat]   'to tie'   [a.tap]   'roof'
[sa.kat]   'parasitic plant'   [lə.tup] 'to explode'
[su.ŋut]   'grumble'

Teoh (1988) differs from Lapoliwa in reporting that underlying /k+V/ sequences surface as [ʔkV]: e.g. /masak-an/ → [ma.saʔ.kan] 'dish' (p.103), cf. /ikat+an/→[i.ka.tan] 'ties', *[i.kaʔ.tan]. However, all underlying stem-final stops geminate before V-initial suffixes in slow speech: /lətup+an/→[lə.top.pan] 'explosion', /ikat+i/→[i.kat.ti] 'to tie' (pp.106–7). Teoh argues that gemination of input /k/ produces a coda [k] which is forced to neutralize, yielding /k+V/→[k.kV]→[ʔ.kV]. In parallelist terms, the underlying /k/ breaks into two segments: the one in the coda neutralizes to [ʔ] as expected, and the one in the onset is realized faithfully as [k]. In short, in both Teoh and Lapoliwa's dialects, all /k/s debuccalize in codas. The issue of present importance is why Malay codas neutralize to [ʔ] rather than [t] or [p].

To neutralize /k/ to [ʔ], an output constraint that favours [ʔ] over [k] must outrank all faithfulness constraints that preserve /k/ (at the very least – see §4.2.1.3). Almost all PoA-output constraints favour [ʔ] over [k], so any would do at this point. *{dors} will be used here – the reason for this choice will become apparent below. All faithfulness constraints preserve /k/'s PoA, so *{dors} must outrank them all.

(40)   Malay I: Neutralization of coda /k/

/baik/	*{dors}	IDENT {dors}	IDENT {dors,lab}	IDENT {dors,lab,cor}	IDENT {dors,lab,cor,gl}
(a) baik	*!				
☞ (b) baiʔ		*	*	*	*

As tableau (40) shows, candidate (a) is eliminated because it contains a dorsal, so fatally violating *{dors}. All the dorsal-preserving faithfulness constraints are ranked lower, so the input dorsal cannot survive. To force neutralization and not deletion, MAX must outrank all of the IDENT constraints.

The fact that /p/ and /t/ do not neutralize in codas shows that some labial- and coronal-preserving constraints (i.e. IDENT{dors,lab,cor}, IDENT{dors,lab,cor,gl}) outrank all output constraints that would favour [ʔ] over [p] and [t] (i.e. *{dors,lab}, *{dors,lab,cor}). This ranking is illustrated in tableau (41).

114   3 *Markedness reduction*

(41)   Malay II: No neutralization of /p/ and /t/

/atap/	*{dors}	IDENT{dors,lab,cor}	*{dors,lab}	*{dors,lab,cor}
☞ (a) atap			*	**
(b) ata?		*!		*

Neutralization of /k/ in onsets is blocked by an onset-specific faithfulness constraint, as proposed by Lombardi (1995, 1999), and Beckman (1998). A /k/-preserving onset-IDENT constraint outranks *{dors}, so preventing /kepeh/ from neutralizing to *[?epeh] or *[tepeh].[8] The opposite ranking would produce a language that bans [k] in onsets as well as codas. In tableau (42), the onset-faithfulness constraint onset-IDENT{dors} is used, but it could well be any of the other PoA-preserving onset-IDENT constraints.

(42)   Malay III: Preserving the onset

/ikat/	onset-IDENT{dors}	*{dors}	IDENT{dors}
(a) itat	*!		*
☞ (b) ikat		*	

With the basic neutralization ranking established, it remains to show why Standard Malay /k/ turns into [?] rather than [t] or [p]. On the markedness side, [?] is a local harmonic bound for all other segment types in terms of the PoA-output constraints, so it will emerge triumphant regardless of ranking. This result is illustrated in the 'broken' tableau (43). Broken tableaux show two different ranking arguments using one set of candidates; they can be read as two different tableaux, one with the constraints in the left half and one with the constraints on the right half.

(43)   Malay IV

/baik/	*{dors}	IDENT {dors}	*{dors,lab}	*{dors, lab, cor}	*{dors, lab, cor,gl}
(a) baik	*!		**	**	**
(b) baip		*	**!	**	**
(c) bait		*	*	**!	**
☞ (d) bai?		*	*	*	**

[8] The primary ranking arguments in this section stand regardless of whether positional markedness or positional faithfulness motivates coda place neutralization (Beckman 1998; cf. Zoll 1996). If a set of coda-specific PoA constraints (e.g. *coda/{dorsal}, etc.) were used to motivate neutralization, the ranking needed would be the same.

So, the output of neutralization partly depends on the form of output constraints. Since /k/ neutralizes to [ʔ] and not [t] or [p] in Malay, there must be some constraint or constraints that favours [ʔ] over both [t] and [p] (*{dors,lab,cor} here). Similarly, since /k/ never neutralizes to [p] in any language, there cannot be any constraint that favours [p] over both [t] and [ʔ]. In more concrete terms, there can be no freely rankable constraints like *{coronal,glottal} or *{coronal}. The same is true for neutralization to [k]: since [k] is never the target of neutralization, freely rankable constraints that favour [k] over both [t] and [ʔ] cannot exist in CON. For discussion of a theory that avoids this problem through universally fixed ranking, but encounters other problems, see §5.2.2 and §6.2.3.

3.3.1.1 Faithfulness

The form of faithfulness constraints also plays an important role in determining the target of neutralization. A crucial aspect of tableau (43) is that the faithfulness constraint IDENT{dors} assigns the same violation marks to all unfaithful forms, so allowing the PoA output constraints to be solely responsible for the outcome of neutralization. This equal treatment of unfaithful forms is why the output of neutralization provides insight into markedness − faithfulness constraints are of no use in helping choose between the possible outputs of PoA neutralization, so markedness reduction (in the form of the PoA output constraints) is entirely responsible for the decision.

To develop this point further, suppose that faithfulness constraints assigned different violations based on the degree of difference along the hierarchy; such 'gradient' faithfulness constraints will be called ✻IDENT, to distinguish them from the standard IDENT constraints. For example, [k] and [p] are only one step away on the PoA hierarchy, so ✻IDENT{dorsal} would assign one violation to the mapping /k/→[p]. Since [t] is two steps away from [k], /k/→[t] would incur two violations of ✻IDENT{dorsal}, and /k/→[ʔ] would incur three violations. With this type of 'gradient' faithfulness constraint, neutralization could produce the next least-marked element on a hierarchy, as shown by Gnanadesikan (1997). Tableau (44) illustrates this situation.

(44)   Malay v

/baik/	*{dors}	✻IDENT {dors}	*{dors,lab}	*{dors, lab, cor}	*{dors, lab, cor,gl}
(a) baik	*!		**	**	**
☞ (b) baip		*	**	**	**
(c) bait		**!	*	**	**
(d) baiʔ		***!	*	*	**

The tableau shows that gradient faithfulness constraints, ranked above all output constraints, can prevent markedness from having any say in the output of neutralization. Since /k/→[p] neutralization is not attested, gradient faithfulness constraints cannot exist.[9]

Not only does the lack of /k/→[p] neutralization doom the type of gradient faithfulness just mentioned, it means that CON cannot contain any faithfulness constraint that favours /k/→[p] over /k/→[t] and /k/→[ʔ]. For example, suppose there were a faithfulness constraint IDENT[–coronal]. This constraint would not assign a violation to /k/→[p], but would assign one to /k/→[t]. In a language with Glottal Elimination, /k/ could therefore neutralize to [p]. Therefore, there can be no constraint IDENT[–coronal].

Generalizing, CON cannot contain faithfulness constraints that favour $/m_1f/\rightarrow[m_2f]$ over $/m_1f/\rightarrow[uf]$, where $[m_1f]$ and $[m_2f]$ are different marked elements on the same hierarchy and $[uf]$ is the unmarked hierarchy element. The problem with IDENT[–coronal] is that it favours /k/→[p] (i.e. the neutralization of a marked feature to another marked feature) over /k/→[t] (i.e. the neutralization of a marked feature to an unmarked feature).

In the theory here, the PoA-faithfulness constraints conflate unfaithful categories. From input /k/, the outputs [p], [t], and [ʔ] are all equally unfaithful – they all incur exactly the same violations of IDENT{dors}, IDENT{dors,lab}, IDENT{dors,lab,cor}, and IDENT{dors,lab,cor,gl}. This property is illustrated in the violations of IDENT{dors} in tableau (44). Because all unfaithful candidates are equally unfaithful, they allow the lower-ranked output constraints to make the crucial decision.

Of course, I do not mean to imply that faithfulness constraints can never be relevant in deciding between possible winners. Faithfulness constraints can play a role in preserving manner of articulation and voicing in neutralization, and so on. However, in terms of a single hierarchy – e.g. PoA – preservation constraints are irrelevant in winnowing down the set of unfaithful forms.

3.3.1.2 Ranking summary

The final ranking for Malay codas is summarized in (45). The dotted lines indicate that at least one of the dotted rankings must hold: so either IDENT{dors,lab,cor} or IDENT{dors,lab,cor,gl} (or both) must outrank *{dors, lab,cor}; either IDENT{dors,lab}, IDENT{dors,lab,cor}, or IDENT{dors,lab,cor, gl} must outrank *{dors,lab,}

---

9 Gnanadesikan (1995:ch.3) argues that faithfulness constraints with a similar effect account for chain shifts: where /x/→[y] but /y/→[z]. For an alternative approach to chain shifts, see Kirchner 1996.

3.3 The output of neutralization 117

(45) Malay coda neutralization ranking

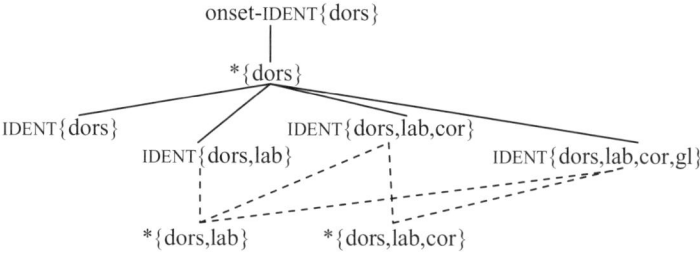

The ranking of the output constraint *{dors,lab,cor,gl} is irrelevant because it does not favour any segment over any other type. The topmost faithfulness constraint could be any onset-IDENT constraint, as all preserve /k/.

The diagram gives a sense of the ranking needed to neutralize and preserve. To neutralize /k/ to [?], some constraint that favours [?] over [k] must outrank over all /k/-preserving faithfulness constraints: this is shown in the diagram, where *{dors} outranks all the faithfulness constraints above. The diagram shows that the other PoAs survive because some relevant faithfulness constraint outranks all relevant output constraints.

In terms of neutralization outputs, the crucial point is that faithfulness constraints for a particular hierarchy are only able to distinguish between faithful and unfaithful candidates; they cannot make further distinctions between unfaithful forms. Consequently, output constraints – i.e. the formal embodiment of markedness reduction – are solely responsible for choosing among the unfaithful winners.

Of course, Malay is not unique – neutralization of PoA to glottal is probably the most common neutralization pattern. Other examples are found in Cockney English (Sivertsen 1960), Kagoshima Japanese (Trigo 1988:34–5; Haraguchi 1984; Fallon 2002:182ff.), Selayarese (Mithun & Basri 1986), West Tarangan (Nivens 1992), and Yamphu (Rutgers 1998). Neutralization to [h] is found in Caribbean Spanish (Trigo 1988) and Navaho (Kari 1976). Examples of neutralization to the glottal [N] are given in §2.2.1.1 and §8.4.2.

3.3.2 Coronal promotion

Coronals can also be the output of PoA neutralization. Neutralization to coronal occurs when glottals are eliminated from contention for reasons detailed in §3.2.3. Glottal Elimination can be either overt or emergent. In overt cases, glottals are banned from the inventory. For example, /m/ neutralizes to the coronal [n] in Misantla Totonac (Yecuatla dialect) and this language has no glottal [N]

(§8.4.3; MacKay 1994:33). In emergent cases, glottals are permissible surface segments, but dorsals and/or labials still neutralize to coronal. This situation is found in a Taiwanese secret language: dorsal and labial stops in reduplicants neutralize to [t] in codas despite the fact that [ʔ] is available (Li 1985). This case also shows that neutralization can happen on the base-reduplicant dimension just as it happens on the input-output dimension.

Li (1985) describes a Taiwanese secret language which involves reduplication with neutralization and melodic overwriting. There are three major changes: (a) the reduplicant's vowel is neutralized to [i], (b) if the base's coda consonant is dorsal or labial, the reduplicant has a coronal, and (c) the base's initial consonant is replaced with [l] before oral vowels and [n] before nasal vowels. To clarify the changes, (46) informally describes them as a series of steps.

(46)　　Taiwanese secret language[10]
　　　　Input /pak/:

Reduplication	[pak pak]
Replace base's initial consonant with [l]	[lak pak]
Neutralize reduplicant vowel to [i]	[lak pik]
Neutralize labial and dorsal reduplicant coda	[lak pit]

Relevant data is provided in (47); the reduplicant is underlined. For the forms with glottal codas it is important to note that glottals are optionally eliminated before other consonants, but always appear in word/phrase-final codas. For discussion about the status of coda glottals in Taiwanese, see Roberts & Li 1963 and Yip 1995:19.

(47)　　Taiwanese secret language (Li 1985)
　　　　(a) Vowel-final roots

/be t͡s'ai/	→ [le bi lai t͡s'i]	'buy food, go to the market'
/e hiau/	→ [le i liau hi]	'able'
/pẽ ĩ/	→ [nẽ pĩ nĩ ĩ]	'hospital'

　　　　(b) Coronals, labials, and dorsals become coronals

/t'at/	→ [lat t'it]	'to kick'
/t͡sap ap/	→ [lap t͡sit lap it]	'ten boxes'
/kam tsia/	→ [lam kin lia tsi]	'sugarcane'
/t͡sin t'iam/	→ [lin t͡sin liam t'in]	'very tired'
/pak k'ak/	→ [lak pit lak k'it]	'to peel, to crack open'
/p'ɔŋ hɔŋ/	→ [lɔŋ p'in lɔŋ hin]	'flatus ventritus'

　　　　(c) Glottals remain glottal

/piaʔ/	→ [lia(ʔ) piʔ]	'wall'
/ho k'eʔ/	→ [lo hi le(ʔ) kiʔ]	'good guest'

---

10 This language game is similar in form to the well known Pig Latin. For example, Pig Latin [pæk] 'pack' is reduplicated, the base's onset is overwritten with [ʔ], and the reduplicant's rime is overwritten with [ej]: [pækpæk] → [ʔækpak] → [ʔækpej].

3.3 *The output of neutralization*   119

The alternative to the proposal that reduplicant codas neutralize to coronals is melodic overwriting – where a coronal ghost consonant morpheme coalesces with the reduplicant-final consonant (see Alderete et al. 1999 for examples). However, the melodic overwriting analysis fails to explain why there is no coronal in vowel-final words: e.g. [e] becomes [le i], not *[le it]. Note that the [l] – which *is* melodic overwriting – appears regardless of whether the base has an onset consonant. In addition, if the final coda of reduplicants was overwritten with a coronal, the reduplication of /pia?/ should be *[lia(?) pit], not [lia(?) pi?].

The issue raised by this case is why labials and dorsals neutralize to coronal and not to [?] since it is available. For example, /pak/ could be realized as *[lak pi?], yet the result is [lak pit]. In other words, although [?] is allowed in Taiwanese it is clearly not less marked than [t] for neutralization purposes.

The following analysis focuses on the aspects of the secret language that are of interest here; a more detailed analysis would be an unnecessary tangent. The approaches to reduplication developed by McCarthy & Prince (1995) and to fixed segmentism in Alderete et al. 1999 are adopted. The Taiwanese secret language consists of a morpheme /l/ which prefixes to the base, and the reduplicant undergoes neutralization through ranking output constraints above base-reduplicant faithfulness constraints.

Tableau (48) summarizes the reduplication. The input consists of a prefix /l/, the root, and a reduplicant. The main competitors to the winner [lin t͡sin] are forms in which both base and reduplicant are identical: a form without realizing the prefix /l/ (a), and one that both realizes the prefix and copies it (b). Candidate (a) is ruled out by MORPHREAL (Samek-Lodovici 1993): this constraint requires every underlying morpheme to be realized distinctively, and /l/ is not so realized. Candidate (b) violates IR-MAX, a constraint that requires every input segment to have a correspondent in the reduplicant – fatally, the input's /t͡s/ has no correspondent in the reduplicant. In contrast, the winner [lin t͡sin] both realizes /l/ and every segment in the input has a reduplicant correspondent.

(48)   Taiwanese I

/l-tsin-RED/	MORPHREAL	IR-MAX	BR-MAX
(a) t͡sin t͡sin	*!		
(b) lin lin		*!	
☞ (c) lin t͡sin			*

To produce coda neutralization, PoA output constraints must outrank the constraints that demand identity between the base and reduplicant. However, to prevent neutralization in the base's coda those same PoA output constraints must be outranked by input-output faithfulness constraints, as illustrated in tableau (49).

Candidate (a) neutralizes all dorsals, and so fatally violates IO-IDENT{dors,lab}. In contrast, candidate (b) does not neutralize enough, and incurs more violations of *{dors,lab} than candidate (c). Candidate (c) wins because it compromises – it preserves the base's dorsal but eliminates the reduplicant's.

(49)   Taiwanese II

/l+hɔŋ+RED/	IO-IDENT{dors,lab}	*{dors,lab}	BR-IDENT{dors,lab}
(a) lɔn-hin	*!		
(b) lɔŋ-hiŋ		* *!	
☞ (c) lɔŋ-hin		*	*

Analogous to Malay neutralization, an onset-specific faithfulness constraint prevents neutralization of onset non-coronals: i.e. /k'ak/ → [lak k'it], *[lak t'it]. This constraint refers to the input-reduplicant relation: IR-onset-IDENT{dors,lab}.

A similar ranking can be used to neutralize the reduplicant's vowel to [i]. IO-IDENT[high,back] can outrank constraints against back and non-high vowels (e.g. *[+round] and *[−high] – see chapter 7 for details). The output constraints can in turn outrank their equivalent BR-faithfulness constraints, so reduplicant vowels will neutralize to [i].

The next step is to explain why dorsals and labials become coronals, not glottals, and why glottals remain glottal. Neutralization to coronal is the result of Glottal Elimination. With glottals emergently banned by $*-\Delta_\sigma$/glottal, coronals will be 'promoted' to least-marked PoA status. $*-\Delta_\sigma$/glottal must outrank all constraints that favour glottals over coronals – i.e. *{dors,lab,cor}, as shown in tableau (50).

(50)   Taiwanese III

/t͡sap-RED/	$*-\Delta_\sigma$/glottal	*{dors,lab,cor}
(a) lap- t͡siʔ	*!	* * *
☞ (b) lap- t͡sit		* * * *

Both (a) and (b)'s reduplicant codas are equally unfaithful to the base's coda [p], so the lower-ranked output constraints must make the crucial decision. As

*−Δ_σ/glottal favours non-glottals over glottals, candidate (a) is eliminated, leaving the candidate with coronal PoA (b) as the winner.

The ranking does not ban glottals generally, either in bases or in reduplicants. With both IO-IDENT{dors,lab,cor,gl} and BR-IDENT{dors,lab,cor,gl} outranking *−Δ_σ/glottal, [?] is preserved in base and reduplicant codas:

(51)   Taiwanese IV

/l-pia?-RED/	IO-IDENT {dors,lab,cor,gl}	BR-IDENT {dors,lab,cor,gl}	*−Δ_σ/glottal
(a) liat-pit	*!		
(b) lia?-pit		*!	*
☞ (c) lia?-pi?			**

Of course, *{dors,lab} must outrank BR-IDENT{dors,lab,cor,gl} in order to get dorsals and labials to neutralize to coronals. All the rankings are amalgamated in (52). The dotted lines mean that at least one of the IO-IDENT constraints must outrank *{dors,lab}.

(52)   Taiwanese Secret Language coda neutralization ranking

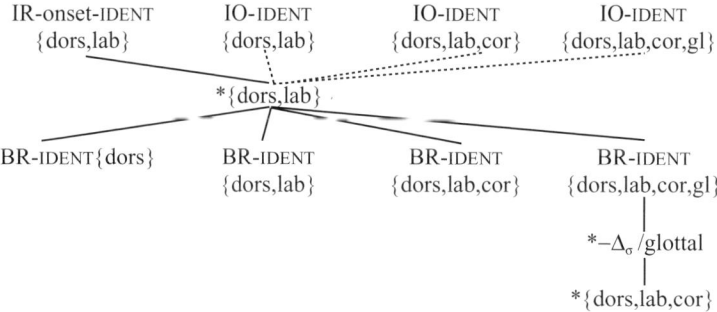

There are several other PoA rankings that prevent other neutralizations. For example, at least one of IO-IDENT{dors,lab,cor} and IO-IDENT{dors,lab,cor,gl} outranks *{dors,lab,cor} so as to prevent coronals from being debuccalized in all positions.

In short, Glottal Elimination can have an emergent effect in a language, forcing neutralization to coronals even though glottals are available. This ranking results from a ban on glottals outranking *{dors,lab,cor} − the PoA constraint that favours glottals over coronals.

A number of other languages also neutralize PoA to coronal. For example, Basque codas can contain only coronals (Hualde 1991:13). So when a consonant appears in coda position due to stem-final vowel deletion in derivational contexts, it becomes [t]: [ogi] 'bread', cf. [ot.-apur] 'bread crumb', [sagu] 'mouse' vs. [sat.-or] 'mole', [idi] 'ox' vs. [it-zain] 'ox-driver' (Hualde 1991:81). Similarly, Castilian Spanish nasals neutralize to [n] in codas: e.g. /desdeɲ/ → [desden] 'disdain' (cf. [des.de.ɲ-ar] 'disdain+verbalizer'), /adam/ → [adan] 'Adam' (cf. [a.da.m-is.mo]) (Trigo 1988:77). The same sort of neutralization is also found in Somali (Saeed 1999:10) (e.g. /ním/ → [nín] 'man', cf. [ním-an] 'men'; vs. /sán/ → [sán] 'nose', cf. [sanán] 'noses').

3.3.2.1 More on conflict: voicing and sonority

The analyses of coronal epenthesis and neutralization to coronal presented here and in §3.2.3 relies on the idea that the sonority and PoA hierarchies partially conflict. While PoA has been the focus here, many similar partial conflicts exist. For example, the sonority hierarchy also partially conflicts with the voicing hierarchy. The voicing hierarchy favours voiceless obstruents over voiced ones; however, codas favour high sonority segments (§3.2.4.1) and voiced stops are more sonorous than voiceless ones.

When the voicing hierarchy dominates the coda sonority hierarchy, voiced stops and fricatives become voiceless, as in Standard German:

(53) *German devoicing: Voicing hierarchy beats sonority hierarchy*
    (a) /liːb/ → [liːp] 'fond'   cf. [liːb-ən] 'love+{infinitive}'
    (b) /fɛld/ → [fɛlt] 'field'   cf. [fɛld-əs] 'field+{genitive}'
    (c) /taːg/ → [taːk] 'day'   cf. [taːg-ə] 'day+{plural}'
    (d) /motiːv/ → [motiːf] 'motive'   cf. [motiːv-iːʀən] 'motivation'
    (e) /bəwaiz/ → [bəwais] 'proof'   cf. [bəwaiz-ən] 'proof+{infinitive}'
    cf. /ʃtʏk/ → [ʃtʏk] 'piece'   cf. [ʃtʏk-ə] 'piece+{plural}'

The neutralizing part of German's ranking is given in tableau (54). The constraint *{+voice} is derived from the obstruent voicing hierarchy | +voice 〉 −voice | in the usual way. The faithful candidate (a) fatally violates *{+voice}. Candidate (b)'s violations show that it is crucial for *{+voice} to outrank both faithfulness to voicing *and* the sonority constraint *$\Delta_\mu \leq$ {−vd stop}; this constraint bans everything with equal or less sonority than a voiceless stop in the DTEs of moras; the analysis assumes that German codas are moraic. Devoicing can be blocked in onsets by ONSET-IDENT[voice], after Beckman (1998).

(54) German devoicing: voicing beats coda sonority

/taːg/	*{+voice}	*$\Delta_\mu \leq$ {−vd stop}	IDENT[+voice]
(a) taːg	*!		
☞ (b) taːk		*	*

3.3 *The output of neutralization* 123

The opposite ranking applies in Somali (Saeed 1999). The consequence is that underlying voiceless stops become voiced in codas, as shown in (55). Note that there is a vowel deletion process whereby /CVCVCV/ words become [CVC.CV] (e.g. /hilib-o/ → [hil.bo], *[hilibo] 'meats').

(55) Somali stop voicing
    (a) voiceless stops voice in codas
        /gunut̪/ → [gú.nud̪] 'knot (it)!' cf. [gun.t̪-aj] '(I) knotted it'
        /ilik/ → [i.lig] 'tooth' cf. [il.k-ó] 'teeth'
        /arak/ → [a.rag] 'see!' cf. [ar.k-aj] '(I) saw'
    (b) voiced stops remain voiced
        /hílib/ → [hí.lib] 'meat' cf. [hil.b-ó] 'meats'
        /t͡ʃiríd̪/ → [t͡ʃi.ríd̪] 'trunk' cf. [t͡ʃir.d̪-ó] 'trunks'
    (c) Voiceless fricatives remain voiceless
        [ʕá.kis] 'hinder' cf. [ʕa.ki.s-aj] '(I) hindered'
        [fe.teʃ] 'search' cf. [fe.te.ʃ-aj] '(I) searched'
        [ʃiiχ] 'sheikh' [χál] 'vinegar'
        [sáħ] 'correctness' [ħabːad] 'bullet'
        [sáʕ] 'cow' [ʕèel] 'well'
        [léh] 'having, owning' [húb] 'weapon'

The Somali voicing process is an increase in coda sonority: $*\Delta_\mu \leq \{-\text{vd stop}\}$ forces voiceless stops to become the more sonorous voiced stops. In this way, Somali is similar to Squliq Atayal (§3.2.4.1); the difference is that Somali's voiceless stops only need to become voiced stops to become adequately sonorous, while Squliq Atayal's must become glides.

(56) Somali: sonority beats voicing

/arak/	$*\Delta_\mu \leq \{-\text{vd stop}\}$	$*\{+\text{voice}\}$	IDENT[+VOICE]
(a) a.rak	*!		
☞ (b) a.rag		*	*

At this point one may wonder whether there are any voicing markedness relations. What is the difference between the hierarchy partial-conflict approach and simply saying that there is no voicing hierarchy, so that any type of voice neutralization can occur?

The crucial difference is that the sonority and voicing hierarchies only *partially* conflict; in some aspects they agree. Specifically, the voicing hierarchy favours both voiceless stops and fricatives over voiced stops and fricatives; consequently, voiceless stops and fricatives in German become voiceless. In contrast, the sonority hierarchy in codas favours voiced stops over voiceless fricatives, but it favours voiceless fricatives over voiced stops. In other words, there is no sonority constraint that can cause both voiceless stops and fricatives to become voiced. To illustrate, tableau (57) shows that the Somali ranking does not force voiceless fricatives to become voiced.

(57)   Somali voicing: sonority beats voicing

/ʕákis/	*Δ$_μ$≤{−vd stop}	*{+voice}	IDENT[+voice]
(a) ʕá.kiz		*!	*
☞ (b) ʕá.kis			

The only way to force voiceless fricatives to become voiced is to use the sonority constraint *−Δ$_μ$≤{−vd fricatives}. However, this constraint will force voiceless stops to become voiced fricatives, not voiced stops. In short, there is no sonority constraint that will cause voiceless stops to become voiced stops and voiceless fricatives to become voiced fricatives.

This same pattern is argued to be found in Lezgian: voiceless stops voice in codas, but fricatives do not (Haspelmath 1993; Yu 2004). However, Kiparsky (2004: §4.2) argues that the data is misanalysed.

The Somali situation is analogous to the fact that the PoA and sonority hierarchies only partially conflict: PoA favours glottals over coronals, while sonority favours coronals over glottals, but the hierarchies do not disagree about the relations between coronals, labials, and dorsals.

For further evidence that coda stop voicing processes are caused by sonorization, see the discussion of Dakota in §4.2.2.3.

3.3.3   Glottal neutralization

Glottals can also neutralize. For example, Korean /h/ surfaces as the coronal [t] in codas. The theory predicts that this neutralization cannot be forced by the PoA output constraints. As glottals are less marked than coronals on the PoA hierarchy, it is impossible for the hierarchy to motivate a change from glottal to coronal. Consequently, all cases where glottals become coronals must be due to some non-PoA restriction. This is certainly the case for Korean − not only [h] but all fricatives are banned in codas. As shown in (58), both /s/ and /h/ are neutralized to the stop [t] (Kim-Renaud 1986:10,16 (KR); Iverson 1989:287 (I); Lee 1998:146 (L)).

(58)   Korean coda continuant neutralization
     (a) /s/ → [t]
        /os/ 'clothes'   [osɨn] 'as for the clothes'   (KR10,L146)
                           [os-e] 'clothes+locative'
                           [otˀ-k'wa] 'clothes and'
        /pus/ 'swell up'   [pus-ə]   (L161)
                           [putˀ-k'o] 'swell up and'

3.3 *The output of neutralization*   125

/is'/ 'exist, have'	[is'-ə] 'I have it'	(KR10)
	[it̚-k'o] 'exist and'	
/nas/ 'sickle'	[nat̚] 'sickle'	(L151)
	[nat̚-kwa] 'sickle and'	
cf. /soki/ 'inside'	[soki] {nominative}	(L146)
	[sok̚-t'o] 'inside also'	
	[sok̚] {phrase-final form}	

(b) /h/ → [t]

/tʃoːh/ 'good'	[tʃoːh-ɯni] 'as (it's) good'	(I287)
	[tʃoːt̚-kʰo] 'good and'	
	[tʃoːt̚-tʰa] 'good (decl.)'	
/suh/ 'male'	[sut̚-pʰəm] 'male tiger'	(KR16)
/nəh/ 'insert'	[nət̚-tʰ a] 'to insert'	(KR16)
/nah/ 'bear'	[nat̚-kʰo] 'bear and'	(KR16)

Kim-Renaud (1986:16) reports that neutralization in some registers is restricted to word-final codas: [h] appears pre-consonantally in 'slow, bookish, emphatic pronunciation'; it is deleted in faster and colloquial speech. Word-final /h/ always surfaces as unreleased [t̚] (Ahn 1998:93).

The PoA output constraints cannot motivate neutralization of glottals. However they are instrumental in determining the output of glottal neutralization: i.e. why the glottal /h/ neutralizes to the coronal [t]. The first step is to explain why fricatives are eliminated in Korean codas. The ranking || onset-IDENT[±continuant] » *+continuant » IDENT[±continuant] || will achieve this result, as shown in tableau (59).

(59)   Korean I

	/suh/	onset-IDENT[±cont]	*+continuant	IDENT[±cont]
	(a) tut	*!		* *
	(b) suh		* *!	
☞	(c) sut		*	*

The next issue is why /h/'s PoA becomes coronal. This is due to the PoA hierarchy — 'coronal' is the next least-marked available PoA. /h/ cannot neutralize to [ʔ] because glottal stops are banned in Korean (Ahn 1998:55). The ban can be formally implemented by a stop-specific version of *−Δ_σ/glottal: i.e. *−Δ_σ/ʔ. /h/ is then left with the choice of [k p t]. Other alternatives — like aspirated consonants, tense consonants, and palato-alveolars — are independently banned in codas. So, /h/ neutralizes to [t] rather than [p] or [k] because [t] has the next least marked PoA, as shown in tableau (60). After Clements (1999), [t͡ʃ] is taken to be [−continuant].

126   3 *Markedness reduction*

(60)   Korean II

/tʃoːh/	*[+continuant]	*−Δ_σ/?	*{dors, lab,cor}	*{dors}	*{dors,lab}
(a) t͡ʃoːh	*!				
(b) t͡ʃoː?		*!			
(c) t͡ʃoːk			*	*!	*
(d) t͡ʃoːp			*		*!
☞ (e) t͡ʃoːt			*		

In short, neutralization of glottals to coronals is not caused by PoA neutralization, but an incidental process (like continuancy neutralization in Korean). However, if the target manner of articulation of such a neutralization does not have a glottal, glottals can be forced to become coronals − just as in epenthesis, coronals can be promoted to least marked status.

3.3.3.1   Miogliola /N/ → [n]

Another relevant case is neutralization of glottal [N] to coronal [n] in Miogliola onsets (Ghini 2001:80ff.). There are two reasons to think that Miogliola [N] is glottal and not velar [ŋ]. One is its distribution: as is common for glottals, /N/ can only appear in codas (e.g. [fɛNdz] 'to pretend', [rœNp] 'to break' − *[Náp] (Ghini 2001:155)). The other reason is that /N/ causes a preceding vowel to become RTR when it is forced to be moraic (Ghini 2001:ch.4). For example, /feN-dz/ surfaces as [fɛNdz], with the ATR vowel /e/ becoming RTR [ɛ] (cf. [feN]). Consequently, moraic [N] only ever appears after the RTR vowels [ɛœ a ɔ], never after the ATR vowels [i y e o u æ ɑ]. This sort of lowering is a well-known effect of glottals, pharyngeals, and uvulars (e.g. McCarthy 1994; Bessell 1998), but not velars (§2.2.1.1).

The data in (61) is from Ghini 2001:81, except that [N] replaces Ghini's transcription as 'ŋ'. The forms in (a) show neutralization of /N/ to [n]. The forms in (b) show that underlying /n/, /m/, and /ŋ/ surface faithfully.

(61)   Miogliola /N/ → [n] neutralization
    (a)   UR   *masc.sg.* *fem.sg.* *fem.pl.* *gloss*
       (i)   /feN/   feN   fɛ́ː.na   fɛ́ː.nɛ   'fine'
      (ii) /øN/   øN   œː.na   œː.nɛ   'one'
     (iii) /saN/   saN   sáː.na   sáː.nɛ   'healthy'
     (iv) /boN/   boN   bɔ́ː.na   bɔ́ː.nɛ   'good'
    (b)   UR   *masc.sg.* *fem.sg.* *fem.pl.*
       (i)   /tun/   tún   tú.na   tú.nɛ   'dumb'
      (ii) /boːrɲ/ bóːrɲ boːr.ɲa boːr.ɲɛ 'stupid'
     (iii) /grɑːm/ grɑ́ːm grɑː.ma grɑː.mɛ 'nasty'

3.3 The output of neutralization

When /N/ would appear in an onset – i.e. when a suffix vowel follows – it becomes a coronal [n]. Ghini shows that the [N] in (a) cannot be an underlying coronal, palatal, or labial. If 'fine' was really /fen/ underlyingly, then it should be *[fen] in the masculine singular, just like [tun]. The same argument goes for palatals (bii) and labials (biii). In other words, onsets allow only alveolars, palatals, and labials, while codas permit glottals, alveolars, palatals, and labials. So, Miogliola is a case where glottals neutralize to coronals.

Miogliola can be analysed in the same way as Korean. Elimination of glottal [N] in onset position is caused by $*-\Delta_\mu$/glottal – this constraint assumes that onset consonants are associated to a mora while coda consonants do not. By outranking both IDENT{dors,lab,cor,gl} and onset-IDENT{dors, lab,cor,gl}, this constraint eliminates /N/ in onsets, as shown in tableau (62). *{dors,lab} favours coronals over all other PoAs.

(62)   Miogliola I : /N/→[n] in codas

/saN-a/	$*-\Delta_\mu$/glottal	IDENT{dors,lab,cor,gl}	*{dors,lab}
(a) 'saː.Na	*!		
(b) 'saː.ma		*	*!
☞ (c) 'saː.na		*	

Glottals appear in codas, so IDENT{dors,lab,cor,gl} outranks $*-\Delta_\sigma$/glottal.

So, Miogliola presents another example of coronal promotion. When glottals are eliminated in some environment, the next least marked PoA – i.e. coronal – is promoted to 'least marked' status.

As a final comment, according to McCarthy (1994), uvulars, pharyngeals, and glottals share the feature [pharyngeal]. Consequently, if glottals are banned but faithfulness to [pharyngeal] is high ranked, glottals could neutralize to uvulars or pharyngeals. Evidence that faithfulness to [pharyngeal] is possible is provided in §5.2.4.

3.3.4 Neutralization to [w]

To complete the typology, there is one situation in which PoA can be neutralized to labial. As discussed in §3.2.4, the labial approximant [w] can be promoted to least-marked status if both the glottals [h ɦ] and coronals [ɹ l] are eliminated.

Polish nasal neutralization provides an example. In a variety of situations nasals and liquids optionally become glides (Czaykowska-Higgins 1988, 1992; Trigo 1988:§2.1.4). For example, /n/ optionally becomes [w̃] before continuant obstruents: e.g. ko[n]flik~tko[w̃]flikt 'conflict', ša[n]sa~ša[w̃]sa 'chance',

128   3 *Markedness reduction*

o[n]*vidiźi*-o[w̃]*vidźi* 'he sees'. This change is clearly not just PoA neutralization – it is primarily assimilation of continuancy. The issue is why [w̃] is chosen rather than a liquid or some other segment. As in §3.2.4, [l] is ruled out by its liquid status: /n/→[l] is unfaithful to /n/'s lack of a lateral feature; consequently coronal approximants are ruled out. The next least-marked approximant in terms of PoA is [w̃].

(63)   /n/→[w̃] in Polish

/ton xa/	AGREE[cont]	IDENT[lateral]	IDENT{dors,lab,cor}
(a) ton xa	*!		
(b) tol̃ xa		*!	
☞ (c) tow̃ xa			*

In short, neutralization of PoA to labial can only happen with approximants; this is due to the coronal approximants (i.e. the liquids) inadvertently having a marked property that can cause them to be eliminated from competition.

There are other cases that potentially involve neutralization of approximants to [w]. For example, Brazilian Portuguese /l/ becomes a labial approximant in syllable codas (Harris 1997:316). The same thing happens in New Zealand English codas and nuclei ([kəw] 'kill', cf. [kə.l-ə] 'killer', [bærw] 'battle', cf. [bæt⁷lən] 'battling').[11] It may be that these cases show avoidance of laterals resulting in neutralization to the approximant with the 'next least-marked' PoA – i.e. [w]. On the other hand, it may indicate that [l] and [w] have some special affinity. In either case, [w] can be promoted to 'least-marked approximant' status, just as in epenthesis.

3.3.5   Can labials and dorsals be promoted?

The preceding sections have shown how both coronals and glottals can be the output of neutralization and epenthesis. Essentially, coronals are favoured when glottals are blocked by the sonority constraints, and glottals are favoured when the PoA constraints dominate the sonority hierarchy. The remaining question is whether labials and dorsals can be promoted to least-marked status. This section shows that they cannot: there is no way for both coronals and glottals to be avoided in neutralization, so allowing labials or dorsals to be the least-marked option available.

11 My thanks to Catherine Kitto for providing data for New Zealand English.

3.3 The output of neutralization   129

Labials and dorsals cannot be promoted because there is no constraint or set of constraints that favours them over both coronals and glottals. As an example, consider what it would take to get neutralization of nasals to [m]. On the PoA hierarchy, both the coronal [n] and glottal [N] are less marked. It is possible to get rid of [N] as a contender by invoking the sonority hierarchy – i.e. *–Δ_σ/glottal, so Glottal Elimination leaves just [p] and [t]. Is it now possible to eliminate [t] from the running, and have neutralization of /k/ to [p]? There is no markedness hierarchy which favours labials over coronals, so there is no constraint *{coronal}. The only option is to rely on an incidental process, like vowel-nasal coalescence. In a number of languages, /Vn/ becomes [Ṽ]. So if /n/ is eliminated by vowel-nasal coalescence, could /ŋ/ neutralize to [m]? The answer is no – there is no possible grammar in which both /Vn/→[Ṽ] and coda /ŋ/ becomes [m]. The reason is that the ranking needed to produce /Vn/→[Ṽ] establishes that the optimal response to coda consonants is to coalesce. It is therefore impossible to force /ŋ/ to neutralize rather than coalesce. To expand on this point, vowel-nasal coalescence comes about when NOCODA outranks UNIFORMITY, a constraint that bans coalescence, as in tableau (64). For details on how coalescence works, see §6.3. Coalescence in onsets is blocked by ONSET.

(64)

/a₁n₂/	NOCODA	UNIFORMITY	IDENT{dors,lab,cor}
(a) an	*!		
☞ (b) ã₁,₂		*	*

One crucial assumption is that the nasal's PoA – or at least C-Place – features are lost in vowel coalescence. So, IDENT{dors,lab} prevents /m/ from coalescing, as in tableau (65).

(65)

/a₁m₂/	IDENT{dors,lab}	NOCODA	UNIFORMITY	IDENT{dors,lab,cor}
(a) ã₁,₂	*!		*	*
☞ (b) am		*		

The ranking establishes that coda nasals face two choices: faithfulness or coalescence. To get neutralization of /ŋ/, *{dors} must outrank all dorsal-preserving constraints, including IDENT{dors,lab}. However, nothing can prevent /ŋ/ from coalescing instead of neutralizing, as shown in tableau (66).

(66)

/a₁ŋ₂/	*{dors}	IDENT {dors,lab}	NOCODA	IDENT {dors,lab,cor}	UNIFORMITY
(a) aŋ	*!		*		
(b) am		*	*!	*	
☞ (c) ã₁,₂		*		*	*

The problem /ŋ/ faces is that it is not possible to force it to neutralize rather than coalesce given the constraints above. Both coalescence and neutralization violate faithfulness (i.e. IDENT{dors, lab}), and the mapping /Vn/→[Ṽ] already establishes that coalescence is more optimal than neutralization. The only way to force /ŋ/ to become [m] in this situation is if /ŋ/ would preserve some feature F by becoming [m] that it would lose if it became [n] or coalesced. However, there is no such feature value.

There is only one other possible approach. If there is a specific ban on coalescing dorsals – i.e. UNIFORMITY{dorsal} – could /ŋ/ be forced to become [m]? Interestingly, it cannot – it must become [n]. If /aŋ/ → [ã] is blocked by uniformity{dorsal}, it can either become [am] or [an]. No IDENT constraint will decide between the two as they are equally unfaithful; the deciding constraint will therefore be an output one. All output constraints favour coronals over labials, so it is inevitable that /ŋ/ will become [n], as shown in tableau (67).

(67)

/a₁ŋ₂/	*{dors}	UNIFORMITY{dors}	*{dors,lab}
(a) aŋ	*!		*
(b) ã₁,₂		*!	
(c) am			*!
☞ (d) an			

In summary, there is no way to produce neutralization to labials using the stringent output constraints, even if both glottals and coronals are eliminated by other phenomena. The same goes for neutralization to dorsal PoA. This result does not depend on the inventory, either. In the hypothetical language just discussed, the coda inventory desired consists of just [m], yet it is impossible to force /ŋ/ to neutralize to [m].

The same point holds for epenthesis. Suppose there is a language in which [ʔ] is banned by the sonority constraints, and /t/ lenites to [ɾ] post-vocalically. It is still not possible for [p] to be epenthesized. To demonstrate schematically, lenition is caused by a general constraint LENITE which targets all PoAs equally

3.3 The output of neutralization 131

(also see Kirchner 1998). To block lenition of /k/ and /p/ both IDENT{dors,lab} and *{β,ɣ} must outrank LENITE, as shown in tableau (68).

(68)

/abada/	IDENT{dors,lab}	*{β,ɣ}	LENITE	*{β,ɣ,ɾ}
(a) aɾaɾa	*!			* *
(b) aβaɾa		*!		* *
(c) abada			* *!	
☞ (d) abaɾa			*	*

If ONSET forces epenthesis, the constraints identified so far will favour epenthetic [ɾ] over [p] or [k]. In tableau (69) candidate (b) has an epenthetic labial consonant that satisfies the lenition requirement, but fatally violates the lenition-blocking constraint *{β,ɣ}. In contrast, candidate (c) has an unlenited epenthetic [p], but loses for that reason – for violating LENITE. Candidate (d)'s epenthetic [t] is ruled out for the same reason. The 'least-marked' epenthetic segment is therefore [ɾ] – this segment is least marked because it satisfies the output requirements best – it not only beats labials in terms of PoA, it also satisfies the other requirements – i.e. LENITE – better.

(69)

/ta-i/	ONSET	*{β,ɣ}	LENITE	*{β,ɣ,ɾ}
(a) ta.i	*!			
(b) taβi		*!		*
(c) tapi			*!	
(d) tati			*!	
☞ (e) taɾi				*

To summarize, the form of epenthetic consonants and neutralization outputs is determined by output requirements. There is no markedness-related constraint that favours labials over coronals, and all other processes (like assimilation, coalescence, and lenition) that force coronals to change also apply to labials. The result is that epenthetic consonants and the output of neutralization will always undergo the same processes that coronals otherwise undergo. It will therefore never be more harmonic for an epenthetic consonant to avoid what is otherwise a general process in the language.

3.3.5.1 Language-internal consistency

A related point is that languages must be internally consistent in their neutralization and epenthesis. For example, if dorsals neutralize to glottals, so will labials and coronals (if they undergo neutralization at all – see §4.2); there is no language in which dorsals neutralize to glottals in codas while labials neutralize to coronals. The neutralization target within an individual language is consistent.

The within-language consistency of neutralization target follows from basic principles of markedness and certain properties of faithfulness constraints. Schematically, if /α/ neutralizes to [δ] and not [γ], then some output constraint O that favours [δ] over [γ] must outrank all output constraints that do the opposite. If that is so, then neutralization of /β/ in the same environment must also be to [δ] and not [γ] – [γ] cannot win as O favours [δ] over [γ]. More concretely, if /k/ neutralizes to [ʔ], then *{dors,lab,cor} must outrank *−Δ_σ/glottal. So, /p/ can only neutralize to [ʔ] – [t] is eliminated by *{dors,lab,cor}.

The markedness side is only part of the story, though; this result depends heavily on the form of faithfulness constraints. Schematically, if some faithfulness constraint is not violated by /β/→[γ] but is violated by /β/→[δ], then /β/ could neutralize to [γ] while /α/ neutralizes to [δ]. For example, if there is a faithfulness constraint F that penalizes /k/→[ʔ] but is not violated by either /k/→[t] or /p/→[ʔ], the ranking || F » *{dors,lab,cor} » *−Δ_σ/glottal || will produce a language where /k/ neutralizes to [t] but /p/ neutralizes to [ʔ]. As this does not take place, there are no such faithfulness constraints.

3.3.6 Summary

This section showed that the form of the markedness and marked-faithfulness constraints permit only a restricted set of values to be the output of neutralization. PoA neutralization can produce glottals because glottal is a harmonic bound for all other PoAs in terms of the PoA hierarchy. Neutralization can also produce coronals because they can be promoted to least-marked status by Glottal Elimination. In contrast, no process eliminates both coronals and glottals, so dorsals and labials can never be the outcome of neutralization.

The form of faithfulness constraints is crucial to this result. Faithfulness constraints cannot favour mappings to a more-marked element over a less-marked one. For example, there can be no faithfulness constraint that penalizes the mapping /k/→[t] but not /k/→[p]. The marked-faithfulness constraints have this character. For example, IDENT{dorsal} is violated equally by /k/→[p] and /k/→[t]. Accordingly, the PoM-faithfulness constraints cannot determine the target of neutralization – this is left entirely to output constraints.

The results of this section also apply to hierarchies other than for PoA. Neutralization should always produce the least-marked element available. So, for any hierarchy H = | γ 〉 β 〉 α |, [α] will always be the output of neutralization of H elements. Similarly, for binary hierarchies the least-marked element should always be the target of neutralization. If [β] or [γ] are ever outputs of a neutralization process, it will not be due to neutralization of H but some other hierarchy. For example, the obstruent voicing hierarchy | +voice 〉 −voice | only ever neutralizes to [−voice] (e.g. German coda devoicing); when voiceless stops become voiced, it is demonstrably due to the sonority hierarchy.

3.4 Methodology and exceptions

The claim that only glottals and coronals can be epenthetic and the output of neutralization (except for approximants − §3.2.4.3) has been disputed in a variety of recent work (Rice 1999a,b, 2004a,b, 2006; Vaux 2003; Hume 2003; Blevins 2004). This section shows that the counter-examples can be ascribed to either (a) misapplication of the terms 'epenthesis' and 'neutralization' (§3.4.1), (b) misanalysis of morphological phenomena (§3.4.2), or (c) misidentification of the glottal nasal [N] as a velar (§3.4.3).

3.4.1 Synchronic alternations

The only clear evidence for markedness effects is from synchronic alternations. Static phonotactics – or non-alternating inventories – provide little or no evidence about neutralization targets. Take a language that only has [b] in coda position and no other voiced stops. Optimality Theory's principle of Richness of the Base forces consideration of input /d/; as [d] does not appear on the surface, some output constraint must force unfaithfulness to /d/. However, there is no way to know that /d/ neutralizes to [b], or any other segment, without alternations. There are a multiplicity of other options, such as devoicing (/d/→[t]), lenition (/d/→[l] or [ð]), or deletion or coalescence of [d].

As another example, the coronal nasal [n] never occurs in Chaoyang codas, resulting in a nasal coda inventory of [ŋ m] (Yip 1994). However, this does not mean that /n/ becomes [m] or [ŋ]. Instead, it is possible that it coalesces with the preceding vowel, as nasal vowels are in complementary distribution with [Vm]$_\sigma$ and [Vŋ]$_\sigma$ sequences: e.g. [pʰaŋ] 'fragrant', [ŋiam] 'surname', [mẽ:] 'fast', *[pʰan], *[ŋiãm], *[pʰãŋ] (Yip 1994:§3.1). Synchronic alternations in other languages show this same effect. For example, in Chickasaw underlying /Vn/ surfaces as a nasalized vowel: /cholhkan-a-n/ → [cholhkanã] 'spider-object', cf. [apa-ta-m] 'eat-question-past'. The result is that only [m] and [ŋ] appear in codas (Munro & Ulrich 1985; Trigo 1988:111; for analysis see de Lacy 2002a:§6.5.1.3). However, even though Chickasaw /n/ demonstrably coalesces in codas, this does not mean that Chaoyang /n/ does the same. There is simply no direct way of knowing without synchronic alternations.

Diachronic changes are not helpful in this regard. For example, Pre-Hawaiian *t has become Hawaiian [k] (e.g. Proto-Eastern Polynesian *taŋata → [kanaka] 'man' — Clark 1976 and references cited therein). The same is true for loanword adaptation: Hawaiian adopts English [t] in loanwords as [k] (Adler 2004). However, neither the diachronic nor loanword changes imply that there was any synchronic grammar in which /t/ neutralized to [k]. As discussed in §1.3.1, these alterations can come about through misperception. It is notable that all cases of /t/-elimination that have synchronic alternations result in [ʔ], and never [k] (e.g. Cockney English, Yamphu, Refugee Tibetan – see §4.2.3.1).

In a related vein, Vaux (2003) claims that epenthetic [b ʃ ʒ] occur in various dialects of Basque, citing Hualde & Gaminde 1998. The data derive from a comparison of how different dialects respond to a vowel hiatus involving a stem + the singular determiner [a]. However, Hualde & Gaminde (1998:42) state that their data lists 'the output for each of the historical (or, if one wishes, "underlying") sequences'. They make no claim that the consonants are produced by synchronic epenthetic processes. In all cases, it is clear that the 'epenthesis' is not 'default': [b] appears between only /u+a/ sequences in four of the dialects while [ʒ] appears between /i+a/, and there is no epenthetic consonant for the other hiatus situations (/a+a/, /e+a/, /o+a/). At the very least the restrictions suggest some effect of assimilation.

The closest case of synchronic coronal to dorsal neutralization is reported by Trigo (1988) for the Maracaibo dialect of Venezuelan Spanish. Guitart (1981) reports that coda stops neutralize to [k] and fricatives to [x]: *obsekio* [oksekio], *este* [exte]. However, these forms are in free variation with neutralizations to [ʔ] and [h]: i.e. [oʔsekio], [ehte]. It is therefore unclear whether this constitutes evidence for neutralization of glottals to dorsals or of dorsals to glottals.

I have found no cases where fricatives neutralize to the velar [x]. Neutralization to a uvular has been reported for Surinam Carib (Hoff 1968; Gildea 1995:65). Due to a process of apocope, consonants may end up in coda position. In this environment, they neutralize to [χ] before obstruents and to [ʔ] before sonorants: [enaːpɨ] 'eat', cf. [enaːχ-potɨ] 'eat repeatedly', [enaʔ-neŋ] 'he ate' (Hoff 1968:58; Gildea 1995). It seems that the uvular [χ] is at least treated like a glottal in this situation since it parallels [ʔ] in the neutralization pattern above. In fact, [χ] is in complementary distribution with [h] – the latter appears in onsets while the former appears in codas. It is thus inviting to consider [χ] not a true uvular, but perhaps a glottal [h] with a strident secondary articulation. Alternatively, Lombardi's (2003) proposal that [pharyngeal] sounds are the least marked PoA could be adopted, as uvulars have a [pharyngeal] PoA. It may be significant that Gildea's (1995) survey of debuccalization in other Carib languages shows that the target of neutralization in all other cases is a glottal. Without close phonetic analysis, further speculation about Surinam Carib is unwarranted.

In short, synchronic alternations are crucial in establishing markedness relations.

3.4.2 Morphemes and epenthesis

Some cases of apparently epenthetic labials and dorsals are better analysed as involving morphemes. Lombardi (2002) makes this same point for several cases of coronal epenthesis. Broadly speaking, there are two situations in which morphological phenomena can seem 'epenthetic'. One involves mono-segmental morphemes (§3.4.1.1), and the other involves phonologically conditioned suppletion (§3.4.1.2).

3.4.2.1 Mono-segmental morphemes in Koḍava and elsewhere

Blevins (2003) proposes that Southern Oromo has an epenthetic [m]. It is found in reduplication of frequentative verbs: e.g. [eːm-eːge] 'he waited long', [tam-tataːniː] 'they stayed and stayed', [fuːm-fuːgite] 'she raised some children' (Stroomer 1987). There are several problems with calling this [m] 'epenthetic'. One is its restricted morphological distribution: it is only found with frequentative reduplication. The other is the phonological unnaturalness of the motivation for epenthesis – [m] is 'epenthesized' to fill a coda, acting against NOCODA. There are other reasons why coda epenthesis can happen (e.g. to make a stressed syllable bimoraic), but [m] appears even when a consonant from the base could have been copied: e.g. [ham-harkifte] 'he pulled frequently', *[har-harkifte]. The [m] in Southern Oromo has all the hallmarks of a morpheme – it is morphologically restricted and appears in phonologically unmotivated environments. Following Alderete et al.'s (1999) analysis of similar cases of reduplicant pre-specification, it is clear that the Southern Oromo [m] can be analysed as a morpheme: i.e. /RED-m-tataːni/ → [ta-m-tataːni].

The Dravidian language Koḍava provides a more complex example: a putative epenthetic [k] is better treated as a mono-segmental morpheme. Koḍava has the voiceless stops [p t̪ t ʈ tʃ k]. Syllable structure is CVX, where X is either a consonant or vowel; onsets are optional word-initially. Ebert (1996:9) reports that 'euphonic [k] is inserted between roots ending in a vowel or [n] and a

136   3 *Markedness reduction*

following [a]', with the additional proviso that [k] voices after nasals. Of course, if [k] is truly epenthetic, the typology in §3.2.1 is incorrect, as is the theory behind it. Examples are given in (70); [ɯ] is epenthesized after root-final consonants. Voiceless stops are banned after nasals, so accounting for the 'euphonic' [g] in (d) and (e).

(70)   Koḍava euphonic [k] (Ebert 1996)

    (a) /kuḍi-a/ → [kuḍika]   'let's drink' (cf. [kuḍi] 'drink')
    (b) /aḷa-ate/ → [aḷakate]   'without sitting down' (cf. [aḷa] 'sit')
    cf. /ʌḷɯd-ate/ → [ʌḷɯdate]   'don't write', *[ʌḷɯdkate] (cf. [ʌɯdɯ] 'write')
    (c) [koḍɯkate] 'do not give!'
    (d) [tingadɯ] 'let him eat'
    (e) [kanga] 'see you!'

The reasoning for treating [k] as epenthetic in [aḷakate] is that: (a) the bare root is realized as [aḷa], not *[aḷak], and (b) the suffix is [ate], as can be seen in [ʌḷɯd-ate].

However, the major problem with treating [k] as epenthetic relates to the environment that triggers its insertion. If [k] were truly epenthetic, it should be inserted for phonotactic reasons, such as a requirement that syllables have onsets. However, epenthesis after /n/-final roots is prosodically unnecessary: /kan-a/ could surface as *[ka.na], since this form satisfies ONSET; yet [g] is epenthesized: [kan-g-a]. Not only is there no prosodic motivation for dorsal epenthesis here, but the epenthesis creates a prosodically undesirable syllable – i.e. one with a coda.

Moreover, euphonic [k] is severely restricted in its distribution. It can only appear between a verb root and suffix. For example, /√kondɯn-avÃ/→[kondɯnavÃ], *[kondɯnkavÃ] 'one who killed'; /√ʌḷɯd-ɯn-ʌ/→[ʌḷɯdɯnʌ], *[ʌḷɯdɯnkʌ] 'I wrote'. In short, [k] does not behave like epenthetic consonants in other languages.

If [k] is a morpheme, a good deal of sense can be made of its distribution. Like other morphemes, /k/'s distribution can be morpho-syntactically restricted so keeping its appearance to the verb root + suffix juncture. With [k] as a (perhaps semantically empty) morpheme, the only challenge is to explain why it does *not* appear after every verb stem. The answer to this is straightforward: [k] is deleted when it would create a phonotactic problem. If there is a conflict between realizing a verb root segment or [k], the verb root wins. For example, /ʌḷɯd-k-ate/ does not surface as [ʌḷɯdkate] because the cluster [dk] is banned in Koḍava (as is [dg]). In contrast, /k/ does surface in /tin-k-ad/ → [tingadɯ] because NC clusters are permitted on the surface.

3.4 Methodology and exceptions   137

Finally, treating /k/ like a morpheme has ample precedent: many languages have semantically contentless 'thematic' morphemes (e.g. Attic Greek – Lupas 1972).

The final reason for treating [k] as epenthetic in this language is that glides are epenthesized in other hiatus situations (e.g. [elːi-j-uː] 'wherever', [boṇḍu-w-aː] 'is it necessary?' – Ebert 1996:9).

I have discussed Koḍava [k] in detail because several other languages have been claimed to have epenthetic velars, but on closer inspection the velars are morpheme-like rather than phonological. Trigo (1988) argues that two languages show epenthesis of velars: [k] and [ŋ] in Uradhi (Hale 1976; Crowley 1983), and [g] in Murut (Prentice 1971). One other relevant case is in Seri (Marlett 1981).

In Seri, Marlett (1981:56) reports that [k] is epenthesized in a very specific morphological and phonological environment: $\emptyset \rightarrow$ [k] / $C^{coronal}\_C^{nasal}$ +. In other words, [k] is epenthesized after [t] and before a nasal that is part of a prefix: e.g. /ʔa-tm-aɬχ/ → [ʔatkmaɬχ] '1pS-ABIL-go/pl', /ʔp-tm-kap/ → [ʔptkomkap] '1sS-ABIL-fly' (p.56); /m-t-m-aa/ → [imtkmaa] 'don't you know it', /i-t-m-piː/ → [itkompiː] 'didn't he taste it' (p.72). As in Koḍava, it is unclear what prosodic restriction motivates the 'epenthesis'. [k] is not epenthesized to avoid an ONSET or NOCODA violation. Moreover, it may be accompanied by [o]-epenthesis: [itkompiː] (see §7.2 for discussion). It is unclear in this case why the output is not simply [itompiː] – this solves the problem of [tm] adjacency and avoids creating marked syllables.

As in Koḍava, Seri [k]-'epenthesis' is limited to a very specific morphological environment – between prefixal elements (e.g. /i-t-√/mis/ → [itmis], *[itkmis] 'OM-RL-resemble' (Marlett 1981:56)). In fact, it effectively only appears in two cases: after the morpheme /tm/ and between the morphemes /t/ and /m/. In short, Seri [k] does not act like an epenthetic element; its distribution may reasonably be called idiosyncratic, much like a morpheme's.

Paradis & Prunet (1994) have provided a detailed reanalysis of Uradhi; the reader is referred to their work for further details.

As for Murut, Trigo (1988:59ff.) argues that a [ɣ] that appears with certain reduplicants is epenthetic. Data from Prentice 1971:121 includes /RED+aŋ kup/ → [gaɣ aŋ kup] {no gloss}, /RED+insilot/ → [giɣ insilot] 'toothpick' (cf. [bu-βulud] 'ridges in which tuberous crops are planted'). Note that [ɣ] reduplicates as [g] – this is due to the fact that voiced stops and voiced fricatives are in complementary distribution – voiced stops are forced to spirantize intervocalically.

The appearance of Murut [ɣ] poses a number of puzzles if it is epenthetic. One is why a segment that is less marked in manner is not epenthesized; the voiceless stop [k] is an excellent candidate: it is acceptable in stem-initial position and intervocalically (e.g. [kabul] 'fan', [kutupus] 'bangs, explodes' (Prentice 1971: 99); [naka-β̱ala?] 'has informed' (Prentice 1971:17)). The other issue is that [ɣ]'s appearance is unpredictable. It only occurs with some vowel-initial reduplicants. Others employ infixation: e.g. /RED +ulampoj/ → [ulalampoj] {*no gloss*}, /RED+indimo/ → [ind̲idimo] 'about five times'. If [ɣ] appears to satisfy a general prosodic requirement, it is difficult to see why it should only appear for some roots and not others. Like the other cases cited above, [ɣ]'s distribution is idiosyncratic and unpredictable. It is therefore much more reasonable to propose that it is a morpheme that selects for particular morphosyntactic environments, rather than being an epenthetic segment.

To conclude, a number of apparent cases of epenthesis are better analysed as morphemes. Unlike usual epenthetic segments, 'epenthetic' morphemes can only appear in extremely limited morphosyntactic environments and do not appear for phonological reasons. There are therefore no convincing cases of epenthesis of dorsals, and therefore no reason to posit an output constraint that favours dorsals over coronals. The lack of such a constraint ensures that neutralization can never produce dorsals, only glottals and coronals.

No doubt other cases of putative epenthetic dorsals and labials will come to light in the future. However, if the 'epenthesis' is limited to a particular morpheme or class of closely related morphemes, the 'epenthetic segment' is likely to be a morpheme. If the environment in which apparent epenthesis occurs is not phonologically well defined, then the 'epenthetic' segment again is likely to be a morpheme. A convincing case of an epenthetic labial or dorsal would be one in which the epenthetic segment is inserted solely for prosodic reasons (e.g. to fill an onset, to make a stressed syllable heavy) *and* it is not morphosyntactically restricted (i.e. it must be able to appear anywhere in some phonologically definable domain). No case of epenthetic labials or dorsals that I have seen so far fits these criteria.

The final point is language-internal consistency. As observed in §3.3.5, if consonant *x* is default-epenthetic, then *x* will be the only epenthetic segment in the language. So, if a language has two or more 'epenthetic' consonants, one must be a morpheme.

3.4.2.2 Suppletion

Suppletion can account for some cases that are apparently epenthesis. Suppletive morphemes have more than one underlying form. For example, the Italian masculine definite article is variously [il], [lo], and [l] (Mascaró 1996).

There is no single underlying form for the masculine definite article. If the sole underlying form was /il/, for example, the ouput [lo] would have to be derived by otherwise unmotivated processes of initial [i]-deletion and [o] epenthesis. Alternatively, if the sole underlying form was /lo/, the output [il] would have to be produced through inter-consonantal [o] deletion and pre-lateral [i] epenthesis. None of these processes have any support in the phonology of Italian or cross-linguistically. Even so, the allomorphs' appearance is conditioned by phonology: [lo] appears before sibiliant-initial stems (e.g. *lo stato* 'the state', *lo zingaro* 'the gypsy'), [il] appears before other consonants (e.g. *il ragazzo* 'the boy'), and [l] appears before vowels (e.g. *l'amico* 'the friend'). The realization is tied to syllabification: the allomorph that allows the most desirable output syllable appears (e.g. [la.mi.ko] avoids an onsetless syllable, cf. *[i.la.mi.ko], *[lo.a.mi.ko]; [los.ta.to] allows avoidance of a complex onset *[il.sta.to], and *il* otherwise appears).

In some cases phonologically conditioned suppletion offers a viable – and even desirable – alternative to an apparent case of epenthesis. An example is found in Buriat (Poppe 1960), which is cited as having an epenthetic dorsal (Rice 2004b). The exact featural content of the 'epenthetic' consonant varies depending on the environment: it is velar [g] before front vowels, uvular [ʁ] between back vowels, and uvular [ɢ] after front and before back vowels. Buriat's other stops in native words include [tʰ b d] ([pʰ] and [kʰ] are only found in loanwords). Poppe (1960:20) states that a [g]/[ʁ]/[ɢ] is epenthesized at stem-suffix junctures in certain situations of vowel hiatus. However, there are several problems with this proposal: (a) the 'inserted' consonant varies – it is sometimes dorsal and sometimes [j], (b) the phonological environment for the consonant is not consistent among different suffixes, and (c) deletion is the default strategy for hiatus-resolution, not epenthesis. The alternative account presented here is that the allomorphs with [g] are suppletive.

The allomorphs of the reflexive possessive (RP) in (71) illustrate the issues (Poppe 1960:46). Note that vowel harmony accounts for the vowel changes, and stem-final /n/ deletes before this morpheme (though not before other morphemes). The bare root is given in the left column, and its RP form in the right.

(71)   Buriat Reflexive Possessive (RP) allomorphy
      (a) After consonants other than [n] = /aː/
         [ger] 'house'   [ger-eː]
         [ɢar] 'hand'   [ɢar-aː]
         [nom] 'book'   [nom-oː]
         [aŋ g] 'wild animal' [aŋ g-aː]

(b) After long vowels and diphthongs = /ɢaː/
   [taχaː] 'hen'   [taχaː-ʁaː]
   [dyː] 'younger brother'   [dyː-ɢeː]
   [ɢaχai] 'pig'   [ɢaχai-ɢaː]
   [ɢaluːN] 'goose'   [ɢaluː-ɢaː]
(c) After suffixes ending in [n] = /ɢaː/
   [noχoi-N] 'of the dog'   [noχoi-N-ɢoː]
   [aχ-iːN] 'of the elder brother'   [aχ-iːN-ɢaː]
(d) After a short vowel = /jaː/
   [aχa] 'elder brother'   [aχa-jaː]
   [modoN] 'tree'   [modo-joː]
   [moriN] 'horse'   [mori-joː]

Comparing the examples in (71a) and (71b), there are three possible analyses. One is that the RP is like Italian *il-lo* – it is suppletive, with several different underlying forms, including /ɢaː/, /jaː/, and /aː/; as in Italian, the RP's allomorphs appear in complementary phonological environments.

Another option is that there is one underlying form /aː/ and a dorsal is epenthesized after long vowels and diphthongs. The third alternative is that the underlying form is /ɢaː/ and the /ɢ/ deletes after a consonant. However, the forms in (71c) present a significant problem for both the deletion and epenthesis analyses. The epenthesis approach faces the problem of why [ʁ] is inserted in [taχaː-ʁaː] 'own hen' but [j] appears in [aχa-j-aː]. The deletion approach faces the problem of determining whether the underlying form of the RP is /ɢaː/ or /jaː/: [taχaːʁaː] suggests the former, and [aχajaː] suggests the latter. The final problem faced by both approaches relates to the environment. The environment for epenthesis in (71b) and (71d) is inter-vocalic, and for deletion it is post-consonantal. However, the environment in (71c) is 'after suffix-final n', which is not a natural prosodic environment to expect epenthesis; it is a quirk that does not easily fit either analysis.

There are some other surprising quirks, too. One is that the suffix forces deletion of root-final /n/, as in [moriN] 'horse' and [mori-joː], *[morin-oː]. Root-final /n/ does not delete before many other suffixes: e.g. [morin-oi] 'of a horse', [morin-hoːn] 'from one's own horse', [morin-to-joː] 'together with one's own horse'.

For present purposes, the important point is that the [g]/[ɢ]/[ʁ] in (71b) and in (71c) is not clearly an epenthetic consonant; [j] has an equal claim to epenthetic status from (71d).

The problems disappear when a suppletive analysis is considered. In such an analysis, the reflexive possessive has three distinct underlying forms: /aː/, /ɢaː/, and /jaː/. The choice of allomorph depends on phonological conditions. The

/aː/ allomorph is preferred after stem-final consonants because the alternatives would produce a consonant cluster. Why [gaː] is chosen over [jaː] and vice versa is less clear, but supports the approach: suppletive allomorphy often exhibits idiosyncrasies.

There is a variety of evidence to support the idea that the apparently epenthetic dorsal is actually part of the underlying form of a suppletive allomorph in Buriat. There are only three morphemes that exhibit an 'epenthetic' dorsal. One is the RP, another is the instrumental /(g)aːr/, and the other is the possessive /(g)ai/. Of these three, the possessive has clearly suppletive allomorphs /(g)aːi/ and /iːn/: /iːn/ is used with stems ending in /iː/ and diphthongs, while /ai/ is used after consonants, and /gai/ appears after long vowels (Poppe 1960:36). The instrumental is less overtly suppletive: /gaːr/ is used with stems ending in all long vowels and diphthongs, while /aːr/ is used elsewhere. Suppletion for these morphemes is unsurprising as it is rife among many other Buriat morphemes; for example, the causative is realized as [uːl] after stems with short vowels, [ga] after stem-final liquids, [χa] after stem-final [d], and [lga] after long vowels and diphthongs (Poppe 1960:99).

A further problem for the epenthesis analysis is that the 'epenthetic' dorsal appears in different environments for different morphemes. For example, it appears with the instrumental /aːr/ after all long vowels and diphthongs, whereas it only appears with the possessive after long vowels, excluding /iː/ and diphthongs.

A final problem is that deletion, not epenthesis, is clearly the preferred response to vowel hiatus in Buriat. In the majority of situations with a short stem vowel followed by a long suffix vowel, the short stem vowel deletes: e.g. /aχa-iːn/ → [aχiːN] 'of the elder brother', /jaba-uːl/ → [jabuːl] 'go+causative' (Poppe 1960:100). The reflexive possessive is exceptional in this regard (i.e. [aχa-jaː], cf. [aχiːN], *[aχajiːN]), supplying more evidence that its allomorph [jaː] is suppletive. Finally, the default strategy even for long vowels is deletion. For example, a stem-final short vowel deletes before the 'pure relational noun' /iːji/, as expected: e.g. /xana-iːji/ → [xaniːji] 'the wall', /dere-iːji/ → [deriːji] 'the pillow'. In contrast, the suffix's long vowel deletes after a stem-final long vowel or diphthong: e.g. /ʃereː-iːji/ → [ʃereːji] 'the table', /dalai-iːji/ → [dalaiji] 'the sea' (Poppe 1960:37). The same happens with the suppletive allomorph /iːn/ of the possessive: /dalai-iːn/ → [dalain] 'of the elder brother' (Poppe 1960:36). If deletion is the usual response to hiatus, then the dorsal in [taχaː-ʁaː] cannot be epenthetic.

In short, an analysis of Buriat dorsals as epenthetic faces a number of significant problems. One is that there is no consistent environment for dorsal epenthesis. Another is that there is abundant evidence that deletion is the preferred hiatus-resolution strategy, both for short and long vowels. The other is that [j] would also have to be analysed as epenthetic in the reflexive possessive. The alternative is to regard all dorsal-containing allomorphs as suppletive. In this case, deletion can be seen as the hiatus-resolution strategy, and appearance of [g/ʁ/ɢ] and [j] in various environments follows from the idiosyncrasies of individual suppletive morphemes.[12]

To summarize, there are many phenomena that create situations of apparent epenthesis. Mono-segmental morphemes and suppletion may both produce an apparently 'epenthetic' effect. However, these cases leave tell-tale signs: they happen in morphologically restricted environments, and may not occur in phonologically consistent environments. Valid cases of epenthesis show relative freedom in the morphological environments they appear in. For example, Axininca Campa's epenthetic [t] appears between any root and a following suffix, between any suffixes, and after subminimal roots. In contrast, Koḍava's [k] only appears between a root and certain suffixes. Valid cases of epenthesis also appear for phonological reasons such as ONSET, WEIGHT-TO-STRESS, and so on.

3.4.3 [N]

While there are no reported synchronic cases of stop neutralization to [k] or fricative neutralization to [x], there are many reported cases of neutralization to 'ŋ'. Languages with alternations (usually of /n/ to [ŋ]) include Huallaga Quechua, Seri,[13] Yamphu (Rutgers 1998), Selayarese (Broselow 2001), Makassarese (Aronoff et al. 1987), Misantla Totonac (San Marcos Atesquilapan dialect) (MacKay 1994:380), a number of Spanish dialects (Trigo 1988;

---

12 Similar to Buriat, Paradis (1992:43ff.) proposes that there is an epenthetic velar in Pulaar. The data revolve around stem-initial consonants and alternations like singular [ʔam] vs. plural [ᵑgam] 'to dance', and with certain 'Effect Markers': EM0-M: [ʔabb-ɛrɛ] vs. [gabb-ɛ] 'grain' (p.47). Paradis analyses these forms as being underlyingly vowel-initial. The plural marker is essentially a floating nasal feature, while the others are simply a floating consonant. I believe the analysis can be extended without having to appeal to an epenthetic velar if the plural is said to be /ᵑg/ and the EM is /g/. The plural coalesces with the stem-initial consonant with the proviso that the root's voice and non-glottal PoA specifications survive while the prefixes specification for [-cont] survives. So, /ᵑg+rɔkk/ becomes [ⁿdɔkk] because the root's PoA is coronal, so it survives. In contrast, /ᵑg-haal/ → [kaal] because the PoA of the root is lost because it is glottal, but the [–voice] remains. Vowel-initial forms follow straightforwardly: /ᵑg-am/ simply surfaces faithfully as [ᵑgam]. Chapter 6 discusses rankings needed for coalescence and for determining which feature values survive.

13 To be precise, /m/→[N] before pause in an unstressed syllable: /koːtpam/→ ['koːtpaN] 'sardine', cf. ['saːom] 'he will beg' (Marlett 1981:20). Faithfulness to the stressed syllable blocks neutralization in ['saːˌom] (Beckman 1998).

Morris 2000), and the Carib languages Arekuna (Edwards 1978:226), Tiriyó (Peasgood 1972:39), and Wayana (Jackson 1972:47). Many other languages restrict nasals in codas to just 'ŋ' but do not show alternations.

I will argue that the 'ŋ' in these cases is actually the glottal nasal [N] rather than velar [ŋ] (§2.2.1.1). A variety of evidence supports this proposal. Yamphu will be used as a representative example here because its phonological system will be discussed in detail in §4.2. Yamphu has three nasals: [m n], and a third, which Rutgers (1998) reports as [ŋ]. However, in terms of distribution, neutralization, and assimilation, 'ŋ' behaves like a glottal − i.e. [N].

Firstly, Yamphu 'ŋ's distribution parallels that of glottals in other languages. Glottals can be banned in onsets but permitted in codas (e.g. Standard Malay [ʔ] (Lapoliwa 1981), Chamicuro [h] (Parker 1994b), Pipil [h̃] (Campbell 1985)). Yamphu 'ŋ' has the same distribution. 'ŋ' is rare in word-initial onsets, and freely varies with [n]: e.g. [ŋa]~[na] 'fish', [ŋaːkma]~[naːkma] 'to request' (Rutgers 1998:33). There is a small amount of evidence that 'ŋ' is undesirable in medial onsets: Rutgers (1998:24) notes that intervocalic 'ŋ' is in free variation with [w̃] in a small number of words. A number of words with intervocalic 'ŋ' have allomorphs with [ŋʔ] (e.g. [hoŋaja]~[hoŋʔaja] 'hole'). However, medial 'ŋ' is tolerated in the majority of words (e.g. [kaːŋa] 'kind of cricket'). In contrast, 'ŋ' occurs in codas without hindrance. It is important to point out that in no way is Yamphu 'ŋ's behaviour typical of velars. Neither in Yamphu nor any other language can [k] appear in codas but not in onsets, and the same goes for [x] (see §2.3).

Yamphu [ŋ] also parallels [ʔ] in neutralization. /t/ neutralizes to [ʔ] in codas but /n/ neutralizes to 'ŋ' (see §4.2). This neutralization occurs word-finally; medial /n/ assimilates as discussed below. For example, /hæn/ 'you (sg.)' surfaces as [hæŋ] on its own, but its underlying coronal stop appears before vowels: [hæn-æʔ] 'you (sg.)+{ergative}', [hæn-iŋ] 'you+pl.', [hæn-iŋ-æʔ] '{you+pl.+ergative}'. 'you (sg.)' cannot be underlying /hæŋ/ because /ŋ/ does not neutralize to [n] word-medially (e.g. [ipːoŋ] 'ten', cf. [ipːoŋ-ikːo] 'eleven (ten+one)', *[ipːo.nikːo], [ipːoŋ-aːtʰ] 'eighteen'). Other morphemes that show this alternation include /-hon/ {logical consequence (LC)} (e.g. [asa-hoŋ] 'whoever'), /iman/ {interrogative}, and the elative suffix /-pan/ (e.g. [tuː-m-em-ba<u>ŋ</u>] 'be.3pl.fact.elative' − Rutgers 1998:278).

Yamphu is not alone: a number of languages neutralize stops to [ʔ] and nasals to 'ŋ'. It is common for languages to allow only [ʔ] and 'ŋ' in codas. For example, Makassarese only allows [ʔ] and 'ŋ' word-finally; notably, it does not allow word-final [k] (Aronoff et al. 1987; McCarthy & Prince 1994:§5). Languages with the same restriction are Nantong Chinese (Ao 1993), Kelantan

144   3 *Markedness reduction*

and Terengganu Malay (Teoh 1988), Selayarese, and Konjo (Broselow 2001). Similarly, Caribbean Spanish fricatives neutralize to [h] and nasals to 'ŋ' (Trigo 1988:72ff.). Other languages that allow only [h] and 'ŋ' in codas include Wayana (Jackson 1972) and Macushi (Abbott 1991 – only [h] and 'ŋ'). Finally, several Chinese secret languages neutralize codas in reduplicants to just [ʔ] and 'ŋ' (Yip 1982, 2000:27). In contrast, there is no language in which 'ŋ' as the result of neutralization parallels [k]: i.e. there is no language that has neutralization to [k] and [ŋ] in codas.

Assimilation in Yamphu also provides evidence that 'ŋ' is really [N]. /n/ assimilates in PoA to a following obstruent. For example, /pen/ 'sit' is realized as [mæm.<u>bem</u>.ba] 'without sitting', [<u>pen</u>.so.ben.ni] 'he doesn't even sit', and [<u>peŋ</u>.go.ben.ni] 'he really won't sit'. But before /ʔ/ and /h/, /n/ is realized as [ŋ]: [<u>peŋ</u>.ʔi] 'he's sitting', /hen-he:-nd-u-æn-de/ → [he<u>ŋhe</u>ːndwende] 'can you open it?' (Rutgers 1998:44–5). Stops assimilate before glottals too, but to glottal PoA, not dorsal: /mo-dok-ha/ → [modo<u>ʔha</u>] 'like those' (Rutgers 1998:48). Again, 'ŋ' behaves just like [N].

In summary, there is a variety of evidence that 'ŋ' produced by neutralization in Yamphu is glottal [N], not the velar [ŋ]. Of course, it remains to be seen if all cases of reported neutralization to [ŋ] are in fact neutralization to glottal [N], but at least in Yamphu this is a viable analysis.[14]

3.5   Conclusions

The aim of this chapter was to show that a prediction of the markedness reduction and PoM principles is borne out: when preservation is irrelevant for a particular phenomenon, markedness reduction clearly influences the outcome. This prediction was shown to be valid for consonant epenthesis and the output of neutralization. For both of these phenomena, preservation is irrelevant. Epenthetic consonants have no input correspondent, so are solely influenced by markedness and assimilation/dissimilation demands. Markedness determines

---

14 There is another case that is very similar to the [N] vs. [ŋ] situation – [w] vs. 'v'. In some languages, [v] is reported as epenthetic. However, in these cases there is (a) no [w] and (b) [v] appears in labial environments while [j] appears elsewhere. For example, Ebert (1996:9) reports that Koḍava resolves vowel hiatus by epenthesizing a [j] after front vowels (e.g. [eːi-i-j-uː] 'wherever') and a [v] after back vowels (e.g. [boṇ'ḍu-<u>v</u>-aː] 'is it necessary?'). In these cases, 'v' acts like a sonorant, and may in fact be the sonorant equivalent of the obstruent [v]. In other words, there may be two phonological segments, one an obstruent and the other a sonorant, that are phonetically realized similarly as [v]. Further investigation is needed on this issue (see de Lacy 2002a:§6.5.1.4).

3.5 Conclusions 145

the output of neutralization because all alternative outputs are equally unfaithful to the input.

This chapter also showed that there are several partially conflicting markedness hierarchies, and they interact with assimilatory and dissimilatory pressures. The result is that there is no single 'least-marked' consonant. There is instead a range of least-marked consonants, with the actual 'least-marked' one depending on how a language's constraints are ranked. As an example, [ʔ t h r ɹ j w] can be epenthetic onsets as each consonant is 'least marked' in terms of some interaction of the PoA and sonority hierarchies, and assimilation. Despite the range of alternatives, markedness hierarchies agree in significant respects, so a large number of consonants can never be epenthetic or the output of neutralization.

A final important point is that epenthesis and neutralization are consistent with each other: the features that are favoured in epenthetic consonants are also those that are the result of neutralization. For example, default epenthesis produces glottals and coronals, and PoA can be neutralized to glottal and coronal. Conversely, there is never epenthesis of [p] and [k], and neutralization never produces [p] or [k] as outputs. This correlation follows from the theory because hierarchies are not phenomenon-specific: there is a single set of markedness hierarchies that influences output form.

4 *Preservation of the Marked*

4.1 Introduction

This chapter argues that many phenomena fail to show markedness effects because of 'Preservation of the Marked' (PoM): marked elements can be specifically targeted for preservation. Consequently, highly marked elements can survive a process that less-marked elements undergo.

As an example, many languages eliminate PoA distinctions in syllable codas, but there is no implicational relationship about which PoAs can be eliminated. As seen in §3.3.1, only dorsals undergo neutralization in Standard Malay. In contrast, only coronals neutralize in the Nepalese language Yamphu, as shown in (1). From a traditional markedness point of view, Yamphu is surprising because highly marked PoAs – dorsal and labial – survive while the less marked PoA coronal does not. The data in (1) also shows an unrelated process of intervocalic stop voicing.

(1)   Coda PoA neutralization in Yamphu (in brief)
    (a) /t/→[ʔ] in codas
       /næmːit/ →   [næmːiʔ] 'daughter-in-law' (cf. [namːid-æʔ] {instrumental})
       /sitː-ma/ →   [siʔma] 'hit+{infinitive}' (cf. [sitː-a] 'hit+{past}')
    (b) /p/ → [p] in codas
       [kʰap]   'language'
       [kep-ma]   'stick+{infinitive}'
    (c) /k/ → [k] in codas
       [æʔlik]   'bendy'
       [kʰaːk-ma]   'scrape one's throat + infinitive'
    (d) /ʔ/ → [ʔ] in codas
       [asiʔ]   'previously' (cf. [asi.ʔ-em-ba] 'before')
       [jiːw-æʔ-mu]   'river-possessive-down' (cf. [kaniŋ-æʔæ] 'we-poss.')

PoM is responsible for the Yamphu situation. Dorsals and coronals are specifically preserved, and so are blocked from undergoing neutralization. However, the less-marked coronals are not subject to preservation, so they undergo the process. In ranking terms, the constraints that preserve the marked PoAs dorsal and labial (i.e. IDENT{dors,lab}) outrank the constraints that seek to eliminate them (i.e. *{dors}, *{dors,lab}, *{dors,lab,cor}, *{dors,lab,cor,gl}) in Yamphu. In contrast, the constraints that ban the less-marked coronal PoA (i.e. *{dors,lab,cor}) outranks all coronal-preserving constraints (i.e. IDENT{dors,lab,cor}). Tableau (2) summarizes this ranking with the word /soksæt/→[soksæ?] 'squeeze+pull'.

(2)   PoM in Yamphu neutralization

/soksæt/	IDENT{dors,lab}	*{dors,lab,cor}	IDENT{dors,lab,cor}
(a) so?sæ?	*!	**	**
(b) soksæt		****!	
☞ (c) soksæ?		***	*

The following sections focus on undergoers of neutralization (§4.2) and the undergoers of assimilation (§4.3). These phenomena have often been claimed to show markedness effects (Trubetzkoy 1939; Jun 1995; Mohanan 1993), but the following sections show that they do not – almost any set of segments can undergo neutralization and any set can undergo assimilation. Arguments for the faithfulness constraints that express PoM are provided in §4.4.

Another reason for focusing on neutralization is that it shows the limits of PoM's ability to obscure the effects of markedness reduction. Even with PoM, markedness effects can show through when there is nothing less marked for a feature value to become. For example, in place neutralization, it is impossible to eliminate both coronals and glottals. In OT terms, this situation results from Harmonic Ascent (Moreton 1999) – an input can only map to an output that is either equally faithful as or fares better on output constraints than the fully faithful candidate.

A further theme of this chapter is that markedness can have a 'covert' effect. While there are no overt markedness asymmetries in neutralization and assimilation undergoers, there are covert ones: some sets of segments are prevented from undergoing neutralization and assimilation for reasons of preservation, while other sets are exempted for markedness reduction reasons.

4.2 Neutralization and inventories

There are many languages in which the range of feature values in some environments are more restricted than in others. For example, the contrast between Yamphu /ʔ/ and /t/ is neutralized to [ʔ] in coda position, as shown in (1). This section focuses on such non-assimilative positional neutralization and shows that there is almost no restriction as to which PoAs may undergo neutralization. This fact is argued to follow from the faithfulness constraints that express the principle of Preservation of the Marked (PoM). Section 4.2.1 illustrates PoM using Yamphu's PoA neutralization.

While coda neutralization is the focus here, the same principles apply to neutralization in any position, and even to neutralization in all environments. It is common to call the output of all neutralizations in a particular environment the 'inventory' of that environment. For example, the Yamphu 'coda inventory' includes [k p ʔ] but not [t], while its 'onset inventory', or 'segmental inventory', contains [k p t ʔ]. In spite of this terminology, no distinction is made here between language inventories and the output of neutralization: inventories are simply the result of neutralization, so are formed by the interaction of markedness reduction and PoM. There is no appeal to any other influences (see §7.3 and §8.5 for further discussion; cf. Flemming 1995).

The empirical observations made here disagree with a number (perhaps the majority) of previous claims about neutralization undergoers. Segmental inventories are often assumed to be 'harmonically complete' (a term from Prince & Smolensky (1993) and Prince (1998)): if an inventory has a particular segment, then it also has all less-marked segments. The claim that all inventories are harmonically complete predicts that coda inventories like [k p ʔ] are impossible as they contain the highly marked [k] and [p], but not the less-marked [t]. Of course, Yamphu and other languages like it show that inventories do not have to be harmonically complete. Nevertheless, there are some universal generalizations about PoA: every language must have a glottal or coronal for each manner of articulation, factoring out assimilation, dissimilation, coalescence, and other interfering phenomena. The typology of neutralization is discussed in §4.2.2.

4.2.1 Preservation of the Marked in Yamphu

The segments in (3) appear contrastively in syllable onsets in the Nepalese language Yamphu (Rutgers 1998:ch.2). [b] is restricted to word-initial position and appears in only a few words (Rutgers 1998:18).

4.2 *Neutralization and inventories* 149

(3)   Yamphu onset consonants

	labial	coronal		velar	glottal
stops	p	t	t͡s	k	ʔ
	pʰ	tʰ	t͡sʰ	kʰ	
	(b)				
fricatives		s			h
nasals	m	n			N
liquids		r ɭ			
glides	w		j		

The stops are voiced intervocalically and post-nasally and are voiceless elsewhere. The intervocalic voicing requirement is seen in [tʰep.-ma] 'to hit the top' (cf. [tʰe.b-u-ŋ]) and [sak] 'hunger' (cf. [sæ.g-æ]). Syllables have the form (C₁)(C₂)V(:)(C). Simple onsets can contain any of the consonants in (3) (except that onset [N] is rare). In complex onsets, C₁ can be a stop, fricative, or nasal, and C₂ is the trill [r], flap [ɭ], or glide [w].

Of the stops, only [k p ʔ] appear in codas. The coronal [t] can only surface in medial codas when it is part of a geminate (i.e. [t:], [t:ʰ], [t͡s:], [t͡s:ʰ]). While the focus will be on [t] here, the ban on coronals runs throughout all manners of articulation: [n] is banned in codas except before a homorganic consonant, and final [s] and [r] are also prohibited. There is ample evidence that the glottal nasal [N] is truly glottal and not velar (see §3.4.3).

There is abundant evidence that /t/ neutralizes to [ʔ] in codas. This debuccalization takes place word-finally and before consonant-initial suffixes. Some verbs have a final geminate /t:/ underlyingly; the geminate still debuccalizes before a consonant, but emerges faithfully before a vowel (e.g. /kʰit:-ma/ → [kʰiʔma], cf. [jaŋ-gʰit:-uŋ]). All data comes from Rutgers 1998. In the glosses, 'nnp' means 'negative non-preterite'.

(4)   Yamphu coda PoA neutralization
        (a) /t/ → [ʔ] in codas
            /næm:it/→   [næm:iʔ]   'daughter-in-law'
                           cf. [nam:id-æʔ]   {instrumental}
            /hæ:t-ma/→   [hæ:ʔ-ma]   'bite+infin.'
                           cf. [hæ:d-u-ŋ]   'I nibbled at'
            /let-ma/→   [leʔ.ma]   'be brief+infin.'
                           cf. [kʰæʔ.-le.d-e] 'go briefly'
            /kʰæt-Nani/→   [kʰæʔ.Na.ni]   'nnp 1sg'
                           cf. [kʰad-ini]   'nnp 1 pl. incl.'

/kʰæt-ni/→	[kʰæʔ.ni]	'go+nnp 2sg'
/tʰet-mini/→	[tʰeʔ.mi.ni]	'lift+nnp 1non-sg.incl.subj,3pl.obj'
	cf. [tʰed.-a]	'nnp 1non-sg.incl.subj,3sg.obj'
/trit-ma/→	[triʔ.ma]	'be contrary+infin.'
	cf. [kap.-tni.d-u]	'he has (unexpectedly)'

(b) /tː/→[ʔ] in codas

/pʰæːtː-ma/→	[pʰæːʔ-ma]	'be recessive+infin.'
	cf. [laː-bʰæːt-e]	'take it away'
/metː-ma/→	[meʔ-ma]	'allow+infin.'
	cf. [rɯɯ-metː-a-mi]	'they made me walk'
/imːetː-nani/→	[imːeʔ-nani]	'cause to buy+nnp 1sg subj, 2sg obj'
	cf. [imːetː-a]	'preterite 1non-sg.incl subj, 3sg obj'

(c) /p/ → [p]

[kʰap]	'language'	[wapsa]	'chick'
[tsop]	'everybody, all'	[kep-ma]	'stick + infinitive'
[optaN]	'head scarf'	[reploŋ]	'peeling of the skin'
[kep-kʰad-i]	'Let's go sticking'		

(d) /k/ → [k]

[æʔlik]	'bendy'	[t͡suksum]	'six days ago'
[aktok]	'like that'	[imakna]	'what-do-you-call-it?'
[t͡sikt͡siʔ]	'nasty, repugnant'	[akjaʔwa]	'buttocks'
[kʰaːk-pa]	'scrape throat + perform act'	[kʰaːk-ma]	'scrape throat+infin.'

(d) /ʔ/→[ʔ]

[ʔok-ma]	'find+infin.'		
[asiʔ]	'previously'	cf. [asi.ʔ-em-ba]	'before'
[jiːw-æʔ-mu]	'river-possessive-down'	cf. [kaniN-æʔæ]	'we-poss.'[1]
[ædæʔ-wa]	'a little'	cf. variant [ædæʔ-a]	
[egeʔ-jæræN]	'on this side'	cf. variant [egeʔ-æræN]	
[loʔ-wæ]	'leech'	cf. variant [loʔ-æ]	

Forms like [næmːiʔ] 'daughter-in-law' cannot have an underlying final glottal stop (i.e. /næmːiʔ/) otherwise there would need to be a process whereby /ʔ/→[t] in onsets. The flaw in this approach is seen in the data in (4d): /ʔ/ surfaces faithfully in both onset and coda position. So if /asiʔ/ were really /asit/, it should appear as *[asi.d-em-ba], and not [asi.ʔ-em-ba].

Underlying /t(ː)/ does not always debuccalize in codas. Before obstruents it totally assimilates to form a geminate: e.g. /pit-kʰad-a/ → [pikːʰada] 'it started boiling' (Rutgers 1988:42), /læːt-pe-ma/ → [læːpːema] 'to do' (Rutgers 1988:43), /tʰet-tsini/ → [tʰetːsini] 'lift+nnp.2dualsubj.1excl.'.

Underlying /t(ː)/ can also delete. It does so for two distinct reasons. One is that glottal geminates are not allowed in Yamphu. So, /t(ː)/ deletes before /ʔ/:

---

[1] The possessive has a number of phonologically conditioned allomorphs. Its basic form is /æʔæ/, but the final vowel is deleted before consonants. For other alternations, see Rutgers 1998:65ff.

4.2 Neutralization and inventories

e.g. /tʰet-ʔenːa/→[tʰe.ʔenːa], *[tʰeʔ.ʔenːa] ('I lift' – Rutgers 1988:605). The other situation in which /t(ː)/ deletes is when its appearance as a [ʔ] would violate syllable structure conditions and create a complex onset or coda: e.g. /maʔat-ndzi/ → [maʔan.dzi] 'to not be+non-preterite-3dual', *[maʔaʔndzi] (cf. [maʔa.d-iŋ] 'preterite 1sg'), /maʔat-mːi/→[maʔamːi], *[maʔaʔmːi].

Once assimilation and deletion are factored out, the environments in which /t(ː)/ debuccalizes remain. In effect, these are in word-final codas (e.g. /næmːit/→[næmːiʔ]) and in codas before sonorants (e.g. /let-ma/ → [leʔma]).

4.2.1.1 Neutralization

Neutralization is a markedness-reducing process. Elimination of PoAs is forced by the already familiar PoA constraints. To force /t/ to become [ʔ], a coronal-banning constraint must outrank all constraints that preserve coronals. For Yamphu, *{dors,lab,cor} provides the necessary motivation; it must outrank IDENT{dors,lab,cor} and IDENT{dors,lab,cor,gl}. IDENT{dors,lab,cor}'s definition is repeated in (5).

(5)　　　IDENT{dors,lab,cor} 'If x is dorsal or labial or coronal, then x' has the same
　　　　　　　place of articulation as x.
　　　　　　　• x' is the correspondent of x.'

The tableau shows how /tʰet-na/ 'I lifted you' surfaces as [tʰeʔ-na] (cf. [tʰed-u] 'you lifted him').

(6)　　　Yamphu I: Motivating /t/ neutralization

/tʰet-na/	*{dors,lab,cor}	IDENT{dors,lab,cor}	IDENT{dors,lab,cor,gl}
(a) tʰet-na	* * *!		
☞ (b) tʰeʔ-na	* *	*	*

Candidate (a) violates *{dors,lab,cor} three times – once for [tʰ], once for [t], and once for [n]. In contrast, by turning /t/ into [ʔ], candidate (b) only incurs two violations. Neutralization of coronals in onsets is blocked by the onset-specific faithfulness constraint onset-IDENT{dors,lab,cor}, as shown in tableau (7).

(7)　　　Yamphu II: Blocking neutralization in onsets

/tʰet-na/	onset-IDENT{dors,lab,cor}	*{dors,lab,cor}
(a) ʔeʔ-Na	* *!	
☞ (b) tʰeʔ-na		* *

152   4 Preservation of the Marked

The opposite ranking would produce neutralization in all environments, resulting in just [k], [p], and [ʔ] and no [t] in onsets as well as codas; this system is found in Hawaiian and Yellowknife Chipewyan (§4.2.2.1).

Another important factor in a neutralization ranking is ensuring that there is something more harmonic for a segment to neutralize to. For /t/ to neutralize to [ʔ], all constraints that favour coronals over glottals must be outranked by *{dors,lab,cor}. These include the sonority-based Glottal Elimination constraints $*-\Delta_\sigma$/glottal and $*-\Delta_\mu$/glottal. The opposite ranking will prevent /t/ from neutralizing to [ʔ].

(8)   Yamphu III: Allowing neutralization to [ʔ]

/tʰet-na/	*{dors,lab,cor}	$*-\Delta_\sigma$/glottal
(a) tʰet-na/	* * *!	
☞ (b) tʰeʔ-na	* *	*

The importance of this ranking will be discussed further in §2.3.

Unlike /t/, /k/ and /p/ are preserved faithfully in codas: e.g. [aktok] 'like that', *[aːtoʔ], [kep-ma] 'stick + infinitive', *[keʔma], [kʰap] 'language' (see 4b,c). Preservation of /p/ and /k/ may seem somewhat perplexing for a theory of markedness: how can the less-marked /t/ be eliminated and the more-marked /k/ and /p/ survive? After all, the result is that the Yamphu coda inventory is not harmonically complete: [k p ʔ]. PoM provides a solution: the marked dorsal and labial PoAs are singled out for preservation. In constraint terms, IDENT{dors,lab} outranks all output constraints that ban dorsals and labials (i.e. all PoA constraints). The example used to illustrate below is [t͡suksum] 'six days ago'. If labials did undergo neutralization, the winner should be candidate (a) *[t͡suʔsuN].

(9)   Yamphu IV: Preservation of the Marked

/t͡suksum/	IDENT{dors,lab}	*{dors,lab}	*{dors}	*{dors,lab,cor}
(a) t͡suʔ.suN	**!			**
(b) t͡suʔ.sum	*!	*		***
☞ (c) t͡suk.sum		**	*	****

The rankings for /t/-neutralization and /k p/-preservation are compatible, as shown in (10).

(10)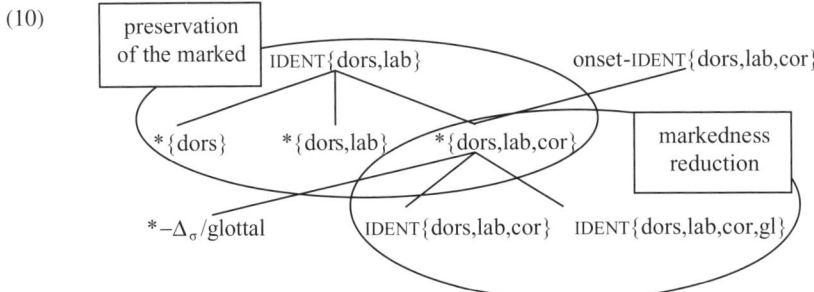

The compatibility of the rankings for /t/-debuccalization and /p k/-preservation is illustrated by the word /sok-sæt/ → [sok-sæʔ] 'squeeze+pull' in tableau (11).

(11) Yamphu v: Preservation of the Marked with unmarked neutralization

/sok-sæt/	IDENT{dors,lab}	*{dors,lab,cor}	IDENT{dors,lab,cor}
(a) soʔsæʔ	*!	* *	* *
(b) soʔsæt	*!	* * *	*
(c) soksæt		* * * *!	
☞ (d) soksæʔ		* * *	*

Candidates (a) and (b) go too far in neutralizing [k], thereby fatally violating IDENT{dors,lab}. Of the /k/-preserving candidates (c) and (d), (d) minimizes violations of *{dors,lab,cor} by neutralizing /t/ to [ʔ]. The result is a coda inventory with [k p] and [ʔ], but no [t].

4.2.1.1.1 The need for PoM-faithfulness

The need for PoM constraints in analysing Yamphu can be seen by examining a theory without them. For example, Prince (1998) entertains the hypothesis that only one PoA-faithfulness constraint exists:[2] the faithfulness constraint IDENT[Place] preserves all PoAs equally. Prince (1997c, 1998) shows that the IDENT[Place] theory cannot produce gapped inventories (also see Prince & Smolensky 1993:ch.9). I will expand on this point here.

Tableau (12) shows why such a theory fails. The winner should be (b) [soksæʔ], with /k/ preserved and /t/ debuccalized. However, this candidate is collectively harmonically bounded by candidate (c), with debuccalization of

---

2 Prince & Smolensky (1993:ch.9§2) arrive at the same conclusion, though in terms of the Parse-Fill theory, not correspondence.

both /k/ and /t/, and candidate (a) with no neutralization. In other words, no matter what the ranking of these constraints candidate (b) will always lose to either (a) or (c); the ☠ indicates a form that cannot win under any ranking. If IDENT[Place] outranks all other constraints, candidate (a) will win because it preserves underlying PoA better than (b); if one of the output constraints outranks IDENT [Place], candidate (c) will win because it reduces markedness better than (b).

(12)   Yamphu VI: The need for marked faithfulness

/soksæt/	IDENT[Place]	*{dors}	*{dors,lab}	*{dors,lab,cor}
☞ (a) soksæt		*	*	* * * *
☠ (b) soksæʔ	*	*	*	* * *
☞ (c) soʔsæʔ	* *			* *

This result does not depend on the markedness theory assumed. Even with a Fixed Ranking theory ‖*DORS »» *LAB »» *COR »» *GL‖, the result is the same. To ban /t/, IDENT[Place] must be outranked by *COR, but this then implies that /k/ will also neutralize because *DORS outranks *COR, so *DORS also outranks IDENT[Place].

The problem also arises with faithfulness theories that have several different faithfulness constraints where none specifically preserve marked PoAs. For example, a theory with 'unmarked' faithfulness constraints (IDENT{gl}, IDENT{cor,gl}, IDENT{lab,cor,gl}) comes up against the same problem. For /t/ to neutralize, *{dors,lab,cor} must outrank IDENT{cor,gl}, IDENT{lab,cor,gl}, and IDENT{dors,lab,cor,gl}; this ranking will also force neutralization of /k/ as well, though. Thus, IDENT{dors,lab} is essential in producing a [k p ʔ] inventory; analogously, IDENT{dors} is necessary to produce [k t (ʔ)] and [k ʔ] inventories (§4.2.2.1).

4.2.1.2 Assimilation and Deletion

In some environments, underlying /t(ː)/ assimilates or deletes instead of neutralizing. Underlying /t/ totally assimilates before stops: e.g. /pit-kʰat-a/ → [pikːʰada] 'it started boiling', *[piʔkʰada] (Rutgers 1998:42), /læːt-pe-ma/ → [læːpːema] 'to do' (Rutgers 1998:43). This pattern is common in cases of neutralization: assimilation pre-empts neutralization medially, so that it is only visible in word-final codas or in environments where assimilation is blocked (e.g. before sonorants). Assimilation beats neutralization in medial

4.2 Neutralization and inventories 155

codas because a constraint banning heterorganic stop clusters – called ASSIM here (see §4.3.2) – outranks the output constraint *{dors,lab,cor}. The constraint ASSIM bans [tp] in (a) and [ʔp] in (b). The only remaining candidate is (c), even though it has a labial in coda position.

(13)   Yamphu VII: Assimilation beats neutralization

/læːt-pe-ma/	ASSIM	*{dors,lab,cor}	IDENT{dors,lab,cor}
(a) læːtpema	*!	* * * *	
(b) læː?pema	*!	* * *	*
☞ (c) læːppema		* * * *	*

The candidate *[læːttema] is ruled out by a constraint requiring regressive assimilation – i.e. ONSET-IDENT{dors,lab,cor} (after Lombardi 1999; Beckman 1998; see §4.3.1 for discussion). ASSIM does not require stop+sonorant clusters to agree in PoA, so /læːt-ma/ will be realized as [læːʔma]. For obvious reasons, ASSIM cannot affect word-final consonants, so /t/ always debuccalizes word-finally.

The ranking in (10) predicts that [ʔ]+stop clusters will be avoided generally in Yamphu: since ASSIM bans [ʔ]+stop clusters and it outranks IDENT{dors,lab,cor,gl}, glottal stops cannot be retained before other stops. This prediction is correct: underlying glottals also geminate (e.g. /ham-beʔ-te/ → [hambetːe] 'where?').

A point of connection between the assimilation and neutralization rankings involves dorsals and labials. /k/ and /p/ do not assimilate before obstruents: e.g. [kep-kʰad-i] 'let's go sticking', *[kekːʰadi]; [aktok], *[atːok]. Like neutralization, assimilation of /k/ and /p/ would eliminate highly marked elements; like neutralization IDENT{dors,lab} therefore prevents assimilation, as shown in tableau (14).

(14)   Yamphu VIII

/aktok/	onset-IDENT{dors,lab,cor}	IDENT{dors,lab}	ASSIM
(a) ak.kok	*!		
(b) at.tok		*!	
☞ (c) ak.tok			*

ONSET-IDENT{dors,lab,cor} is violated by (a) [akːok] because the onset consonant fails to preserve the underlying PoA value, so preventing regressive total assimilation. The assimilation and neutralization rankings can be amalgamated as in (15).

(15)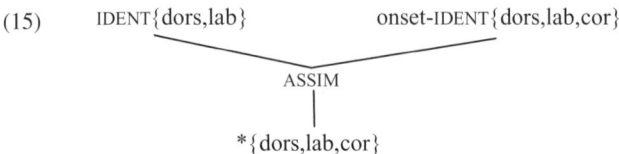

Underlying /t(ː)/ deletes when its realization as [ʔ] would produce an undesirable syllable: i.e. one that does not conform to the template $(C_1)(C_2)V(ː)(C)$, discussed in §4.2.1. /t(ː)/ is not the only consonant to delete in this situation: every consonant is subject to the same restriction: e.g. /tiras-ndzi/ 'to go and come back' → [tiran.dzi] {non-preterite 2dual}, cf. [tira.s-iŋ] {preterite 1sg}, /t͡siuk.t-na/ 'to escort down' → [t͡siuk.na] {preterite 1sg.su 2sg.obj}, [t͡siuk.t-uŋ] {preterite 1sg.su 3sg.obj}.

The constraint that regulates this aspect of Yamphu's syllable structure is *COMPLEX 'Incur a violation for every syllabic constituent that contains more than one segment' (Prince & Smolensky 1993). A more detailed analysis would allow for the permissible rising-sonority onset clusters, but developing this idea would go too far afield here. Tableau (16)'s candidate (a) fatally violates this constraint. As shown it outranks all constraints that demand preservation of root elements (e.g. MAX- Root – Beckman 1998).

(16) Yamphu IX

/t͡siukt-na/	*COMPLEX	MAX-Root
(a) t͡siukt.na/	*!	
☞ (b) t͡siuk.na		*

There are a couple of other revealing candidates. *[t͡siuʔ.na] shows that there is a preference for deleting peripheral consonants, implemented by a constraint such as IO-CONTIG, which demands preservation of adjacency relations (Kenstowicz 1994; McCarthy & Prince 1995). *[t͡siuk.ta] shows that there is a constraint that requires preservation of morpheme-initial material, much like Casali's (1997) morpheme-initial faithfulness constraints; this will be called ANCHOR-M-L here.

This ranking also helps account for the fact that /tː/ neutralizes to [ʔ] in codas. /metː-ma/ becomes [meʔma], with /tː/ losing both PoA and length. It does not become *[meːːa], indicating that ANCHOR-M-L must outrank constraints that preserve underlying consonant length (IDENT[length]).

(17)   Yamphu x

/meːː-ma/	*COMPLEX	ANCHOR-M-L	IDENT[length]
(a) metːma	*!		
(b) metːa		*!	
☞ (c) meʔma			*

Tableaux (16) and (17) have no constraints in common with the ranking in (10), so they cannot be amalgamated. The only point of contact is that MAX-Root must outrank *{dors} and *{dors,lab}, otherwise dorsals and labials would delete.

4.2.1.3   Beyond stops

Yamphu's desire to rid itself of coronals in codas extends beyond stops: the same neutralization affects nasals as well. Coda /n/ becomes glottal [N], while other PoAs remain faithful.[3] Evidence for glottal [N] is provided in §3.4.3.

(18)   Yamphu nasal neutralization (data from Rutgers 1998)
    (a) /n/→[N]
    /hæn/   'you (sg.)'
    [hæN] 'you (sg.)'
    cf. [hæ.n-æʔ] 'you (sg.)+{ergative}', [ha.n-iN] 'you + {pl.}'
    /-hon/   {logical consequence}
    [asa- hoN] 'whoever'
    cf. [hoŋ-gore] 'only because, since'
    /-pan/   {elative}
    [tuː-m-em- baN] 'be.3pl.fact.elative'(p.278)

    (b) /m/→[m]
    [ram]   'road' (p.34)
    [jamsima] 'to be shy' (p.592)
    [jemd͡zwak] 'cold' (p.594)
    [tumruk]   'knee' (p.34)
    [jumliNma] 'vessel for salt' (p.596)

    (c) /ŋ/ → [ŋ]
    [radaŋ-beʔ-mu] 'below-LOC-DWN' (p.81)
    [tsoŋd͡zaN]   'celebration of a bargain' (p.32)
    [wadoŋsæN] 'bangle' (p.589)
    [joŋniba]   'sister's husband' (p.33)

---

3 Rutgers (1998:33) notes that the only exception is the onomatopoeic [t͡sin.d͡zin.d͡zin.d͡zin] 'chatter chatter', which may have a final coronal nasal so the reduplicants retain identity with the base.

158   4 Preservation of the Marked

    (d) /N/ → [N]
        [ipo:N] 'ten' cf. [ipo:.N-ik:o] 'ten+one'
        /-an . . . N/ {2pl} [raps-<u>an</u>-i-<u>N</u>] 'you(pl) walked'
        cf. [ram-buʔ-it:- <u>an</u>-i-<u>N</u>-æ] 'walk-start-PF-2PL-12PL-2PL-FCT'
        (p.123)

Nasals are also affected by assimilation in the same way as stops. Dorsals and labials do not assimilate: e.g. [jem͡dzwak], *[jen͡dzwak]; [t͡soŋ͡dzaN], *[t͡sond͡zaN], but coronals do: e.g. /pen/ 'sit' (p.43): [<u>pen</u>-so-<u>ben</u>-ni] 'sit-too-sit-NNP', [<u>peŋ</u>-go-<u>ben</u>-ni] 'sit-TH-sit-NNP', [mæm-<u>bem</u>-ba] 'NEG-sit-NOM', [peN-ʔi] 'sit-NP'. A more complex example is /ʔænd/ 'downward motion (V)', as seen in [tiŋ-ʔænd-u-ŋ-go] 'drive.put down.3.exag.th' (p.597). Before another consonant, the /d/ deletes and the /n/ is forced to assimilate: e.g. [tsa:-ʔæŋ-gʰæ:-t:-u-ŋ-æ] 'eat-put down-prof-PF-3. EXAG-FCT', [we:-ʔæN-ʔa:-t-ts-u] 'throw-apply-PURP-PF-DU-3'. In short, [n] only appears in codas before another alveolar ([t͡s d d͡z n s]) due to assimilation.

The ranking established for stops above will also produce the neutralization and assimilation facts for nasals.

No other coronals debuccalize in Yamphu codas because all continuants are banned from coda position; the stops [k p ʔ ŋ m N] are the only coda consonants permitted. A limited amount of evidence indicates that continuants are deleted in coda position:

(19)   Yamphu /s/ deletion in codas
        (a) (i) /kʰo:s/ → [kʰo:] '3 non-singular', *[kʰo:s]
            (ii) /kʰo:s-d͡zeʔe/ → [kʰo:-d͡zeʔe] '3n.s. possessive',
                  *[kʰo:s.d͡zeʔe]
        cf. (iii) [kʰo:.s-æʔ] '3n.s. ergative' (p.90)
            (iv) [kʰo:.s-æʔæ] '3n.s. possessive'
        (b) (i) /t͡sa:s-ʔa/ → [t͡sa:.ʔa] 'eat + d͡zg-non-preterit'
        cf. (ii) [t͡sa:-ŋa] 'eat+1sg.non-preterit'
            (iii) [t͡sa:.s-iŋ] 'eat+1sg. preterit'
            (iv) [tsa:.s-a.d͡zi] 'eat+1du.incl.-preterite'

A deletion ranking can be straightforwardly incorporated into the present account. To produce deletion of continuants *[+continuant] must outrank MAX. To prevent deletion of onset continuants, both IDENT [continuant] and ONSET must outrank *[+continuant]. As discussed above, MAX outranks all the PoA-output constraints, so no other stops are eliminated. The example in tableau (20) is /sis/ 'the sensing of an emotion'.

(20)   Yamphu XI

/sis-ma/	IDENT[cont]	ONSET	*[+cont]	MAX
(a) siʔ.ma	*!		*	
(b) i.ma		*!		
(c) sis.ma			**!	
(d) sih.ma			**!	
☞ (e) si.ma			*	*

Having ONSET outrank MAX accounts for the fact that onsetless syllables are banned in Yamphu everywhere except word-initial position (e.g. [æk.sum] 'in five days', [asaː] 'who?', [iː] 'beer', [oː] 'far', [uŋ] 'flower'). I adopt McCarthy & Prince's (1993b:§4.2, 1995) proposal that word-initial onsetless syllables are permitted by having ANCHOR-L (Stem, PrWd) outrank ONSET.

4.2.1.4 Neutralization ranking

The essentials of the neutralization ranking for Yamphu have been given above. For the sake of technical completeness, this section discusses the ranking requirements to produce neutralization in OT. The following paragraphs step through the necessary and sufficient conditions of neutralizing /α/ to [β] (also see McCarthy 2001b:67ff.).

To neutralize /α/ to [β], some output constraint M that favours [β] over [α] must outrank all faithfulness constraints that ban the /α/→[β] mapping. Importantly, M must *favour* [β] over [α] – it cannot assign equal violations to both elements (cf. the constraint *{α,β}). In tableau (21) M is called *{α}.

(21)   Neutralization of /α/→[β], step 1

/α/	*{α}	IDENT{α}
α	*!	
☞ β		*

In Yamphu, the equivalent of *{α} is *{dors,lab,cor}; it outranks IDENT{dors,lab,cor} and IDENT{dors,lab,cor,gl} (the equivalent of IDENT{α} here).

The part that makes the neutralization ranking complex is ensuring that no higher-ranked constraints prevent /α/ from neutralizing or being realized as something other than [β]. For a start, no output constraint that favours [α] over [β] (e.g. *{β}) can outrank the neutralization-triggering constraint (*{α} here).

160   4 Preservation of the Marked

Otherwise, [β] would be eliminated. In Yamphu, such a *{β} constraint was *−Δ_σ/glottal.

(22)   Neutralization of /α/→[β], step 2

/α/	*{α}	*{β}	IDENT{α}
α	*!		
☞ β		*	*

Ensuring that /α/ neutralizes to [β] rather than some other segment [γ] requires a similar ranking. For every output constraint m that favours some other segment [γ] over [β], m must outrank all constraints that favour [β] over that [γ]. For example, the constraint *{β} bans [β] but not some other segment [γ], so a constraint that favours [β] over [γ] – i.e. *{γ} – must outrank *{β}. In Yamphu, this issue relates to why /t/ does not become [p] or [k]: *{dors,lab,cor} favours [ʔ] over [p] and [k]; in this situation, *{α} and *{γ} is the same constraint − *{dors,lab,cor}.

(23)   Neutralization of /α/→[β], step 3

/α/	*{α}	*{γ}	*{β}	IDENT{α}
α	*!			
γ		*!		*
☞ β			*	*

The final step is to ensure that faithfulness constraints do not prevent /α/ from neutralizing to [β]. For example, suppose [α] and [δ] shared some feature value [+ f] that [β] does not have. If IDENT[+f] outranked *{δ}, /α/ would map to [δ], not [β], because doing so would be more faithful. Thus, *{δ} must outrank IDENT[+f]. More generally for every segment γ, some output constraint that favours [β] over [γ] must outrank every faithfulness constraint that prefers the /α/→[γ] mapping over the /α/→[β] map. This issue does not arise in Yamphu because there is no feature that /t/ shares with [p] and [k] that [t] does not share with [ʔ].

(24)   Neutralization of /α/→[β], step 4

/α/	*{α}	*{δ}	IDENT[+f]	*{β}	IDENT{α}
α	*!				
δ		*!			*
☞ β				*	*

4.2 Neutralization and inventories

There is an alternative to the ranking ‖ *{δ} » IDENT[+f] ‖. Suppose [α] and [β] shared some feature value [+g] that [α] and [δ] do not share. Then IDENT[+g] would favour the mapping /α/→[β] over /α/→[δ]. So, if IDENT[+g] (i) outranked all output constraint that favoured [δ] over [β] (i.e. *{β}) *and* (ii) outranked all faithfulness constraints that favoured the mapping /α/→[δ] over /α/→[β] (i.e. IDENT[+f]), then the same result would follow.

(25) Neutralization of /α/→[β], step 5

/α/	*{α}	IDENT[+g]	IDENT[+f]	*{β}	IDENT{α}
α	*!				
δ		*!			*
☞ β			*	*	*

In short, it is no easy matter to ensure that /α/ neutralizes to [β]. Apart from the basic ranking of having an output constraint outrank a faithfulness constraint (26a), the influence of other output constraints (26b,ci) and faithfulness constraints (26cii) must also be blocked. The rankings laid out above are summarized in (26). M(x>y) is an output constraint that assigns more violations to *y* than *x*. F(x→y, *x→z) is a faithfulness constraint that assigns more violations to the unfaithful mapping /x/→[z] than to the unfaithful mapping /x/→[y].

(26) Neutralization of /α/ to [β] Ranking
    (a) some M(β>α) outranks all F(α)
        • M(β>α) is an output constraint that favours segment β over α
        • F(α) is a faithfulness constraint that bans the /α/→[β] mapping
    (b) There is no M(α>β) that outranks M(β>α)
    (c) For all segments γ (γ≠α,γ≠β),either
        (i) some M(β>γ) outranks all F(α→γ, *α→β) and all M(γ>β) or
        (ii) some F(α→β, *α→γ) outranks all M(β>γ) and all F(α→γ, *α→β)

4.2.2 Typological implications

Preservation of the Marked and markedness reduction together predict many different types of inventory. This section identifies these types and provides empirical evidence for them (§4.2.2.1). An important limit on neutralization is also discussed: it is impossible to eliminate the least-marked element (§4.2.2.2). Consequently, neutralization cannot eliminate both the coronal and glottal in an inventory. Apparent exceptions to the typological claims are argued to be due to the influence of related phonological phenomena in §4.2.2.3.

4.2.2.1 Inventories and neutralizations

Yamphu represents one of several predicted types of neutralization. Table (27) lists all predicted coda inventories produced by PoA neutralization.

(27)   Coda stop/nasal inventories produced by PoA neutralization

	dors	lab	cor	gl	
harmonically complete				✓	Kashaya (Buckley 1994), Kelantan Malay (Teoh 1988; Trigo 1988), Toba Batak (Hayes 1986)
			✓	✓	Chickasaw (Munro & Ulrich 1985)
		✓	✓	✓	Standard Malay (§2.3.1)
	✓	✓	✓	✓	Pendau (Quick 2000:§4.2.1)
			✓		Uradhi (Hale 1976; Crowley 1983)
		✓	✓		Formal Kiowa (Watkins 1984)
	✓	✓	✓		New Zealand English
gapped		✓		✓	Nganasan (Helimski 1998)
	✓			✓	Fuzhou (Yip 1982:646)
	✓	✓		✓	Yamphu (§4.2.1), Cockney English (Sivertsen 1960)
	✓		✓	✓	Nambiquara (Kroeker 1972)
	✓		✓		Mordva (Zaicz 1998)

Table (27) does not mention three possible neutralizations: those resulting in just [k], just [p], and [k p] only. These inventories can never be produced through PoA neutralization, and will be discussed in §4.2.2.2.

Table (27) distinguishes two types of neutralization: those that result in a harmonically complete inventory, and those that result in a gapped inventory. A harmonically complete inventory in terms of PoA is one that contains a contiguous range of the hierarchy starting with the least-marked element. At one extreme, [ʔ] is a harmonically complete voiceless stop inventory. Kashaya provides an example: all plain stops debuccalize in coda position (§5.2; Buckley 1994). At the other extreme, Pendau provides an example of a language with no PoA neutralization in codas: /k p t ʔ/ all surface unaltered.

These types are further subdivided into two sub-types: inventories with and without Glottal Elimination. Glottal Elimination can interact with PoA neutralization; the result is a harmonically complete coda neutralization to coronals, without a glottal. There are two crucial rankings in this situation. For glottals to neutralize, $*{-}\Delta_\sigma$/glottal or $*{-}\Delta_\mu$/glottal must outrank all constraints that preserve them (e.g. IDENT{dors,lab,cor,gl}). In addition, $*{-}\Delta_{\sigma/\mu}$/glottal must outrank *{dors,lab,cor}. Without the latter ranking, there is no less-marked element for glottals to become, so they will not change. This point is discussed in detail in §4.2.2.2.

Gapped inventories are those that are missing an element of intermediate markedness. Yamphu codas retain the least-marked glottals and the highly marked dorsals and labials, but eliminate the intermediately marked coronals. Several other languages have this same pattern, including Refugee Tibetan (Meredith 1990) and several English dialects. An even more gapped system was found in Classical Fuzhou, which only allowed [ʔ] and [k] in codas (Chan 1985).

As an example, Cockney English has neutralization of /t/ to [ʔ] in codas, as shown in (28) (Sivertsen 1960).

(28) Cockney Coda neutralization (Sivertsen 1960)
      /nɔt/ [nɔʔ] 'not'   cf. [nɔ.tɪʔ] 'not it'   (p.111)
      /kʌt/ [kʌʔ] 'cut'   cf. [kʌ.tɪʔ] 'cut it'   (p.110)
      /stæɪt/ [stæɪʔ] 'state' cf. [ðə.stæɪ.tjʊ.rĩ] 'the state you're in' (p.126)

In contrast, the highly marked /p/ and /k/ do not neutralize: [bɹɪk] 'brick', *[bɹɪʔ]; [ʌp] 'up', *[ʌʔ]. The output of Cockney neutralization is therefore a gapped coda inventory [k p ʔ]: it contains the least-marked element [ʔ] and the highly marked [k] and [p], but lacks an element with intermediate markedness: [t].

Smaller gapped inventories include [k ʔ] and [p ʔ]. The latter is found in Nganasan codas (Helimski 1998; Vaysman 2002). While Nganasan allows [p b t d c ɟ k g ʔ] in onsets, it only permits [p] and [ʔ] in codas, eliminating the others through PoA and voice neutralization as shown in (29). There is an independent process of metrically conditioned intervocalic lenition which accounts for the t~ð alternation, and voiceless stops become voiced after nasals (i.e. /nt/ → [nd]).

(29) Nganasan coda neutralization
      (a) Coronals debuccalize
      /mat/   → [maʔ] 'house', cf. [ma.ð-ə] {genitive}
      /bɨt/   → [bɨʔ] 'water', cf. [bɨ.ð-ɨ] {accusative}
      /koðaʔa-t/ → [ko.ða.ʔa-ʔ] 'kill {3pl}', cf. [ko.ða.ʔa-.ð-uŋ] {3pl+object}
      /kubu-t/   → [ku.bu-ʔ] 'skin+{predic.}', cf. [ku.bu-.t-uŋ] {3pl+indic.}'
      /kotu-t/   → [ko.ðuʔ] 'kill+imper.pres.2sg', cf. [ko.tu-.ð-ə]
      /ɲintɨ-t/   → [ɲin.dɨ-ʔ] 'aux. negative + 3pl.', cf. [ɲin.tɨ-.ð-ɨɲ]

      (b) Palatals debuccalize
      /ɹeⁿhiɟ-si/ → [ɹe.ᵐbiʔ.çi] 'dress+verbal adv.'
                   cf. [ɹe.ⁿhiʔ.ɟ-əʔ] 'connegative'

(c) Labials remain faithful
[ɲe.rəp.tə:]   'first'
[tap.kə.tə]   'from there'
[ko.ðu-p.su.ðə-m]   'kill {debitive, 1sg.}'
[ku.ə.ɟy.mu nip.ti.a] 'man or woman'
[ko.tu.-rup.tu.guɟ-]   base for 'continuously cause someone to kill'
[ho.tə.rub.tu-ɟa]   'make write'
[bɨ.ðib.ti.-si]   'give to drink'

Helimski (1998:488) and Vaysman (2002:§0.3) also assert that dorsals neutralize to [ʔ] in codas.

Nganasan is interesting because it interleaves preservation and reduction in a complex way. While the highly marked dorsals and relatively unmarked coronals are eliminated, the medial-marked labials are not. To eliminate dorsals, *{dors} must outrank all PoA faithfulness constraints, and to eliminate coronals, *{dors,lab,cor} must outrank IDENT{dors,lab,cor} and IDENT{dors,lab,cor,gl}. To preserve labials, on the other hand, IDENT{dors,lab} must outrank *{dors,lab} and *{dors,lab,cor}. These conditions do not conflict, but interact as shown in (30).

(30)   Nganasan's gapped [p ʔ] coda neutralization ranking

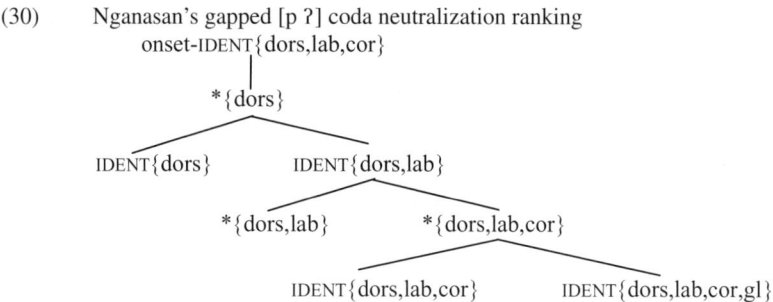

As with harmonically complete coda neutralizations, gapped neutralizations can also have Glottal Elimination. In Erza Mordvin, onsets allow [k p t], while codas permit only [k] and [t] ([pak.sʲat] 'fields' – Zaicz 1998).

4.2.2.1.1 Neutralization outside codas

Coda neutralizations have been the focus here because there are often clear alternations that show that neutralization comes about through elimination of PoA. In contrast, it is difficult to identify cases of PoA neutralization in onsets because underlyingly prevocalic stops rarely get forced into coda position and so do not alternate.

4.2 Neutralization and inventories

Even so, the theory makes predictions about possible onset inventories. Prince & Smolensky's (1993) principle of Richness of the Base means that there are no restrictions on inputs, so the fact that (for example) New Zealand English does not have an output [x] means that there must be a ranking in which input /x/ is eliminated in some way, through neutralization, deletion, or perhaps coalescence. Because neutralization is an option for eliminating input segments, the theory predicts that onset inventories could consist of almost all possible subsets of PoA. Table (31) shows that this prediction is borne out. It is important to emphasize that table (31) does not claim that all of the onset inventories came about through PoA neutralization; there are no alternations so it is impossible to know. Instead, table (31) shows that the empirical facts are not inconsistent with the present theory's predictions about the output of PoA neutralization in onsets.

(31)   Onset stop inventories

		k	p	t	ʔ	
complete					✓	Nancowry and Tübatulabal reduplicants (see below)
			✓	✓	✓	Harar Oromo (plain stops)[4] (Owens 1985)
			✓	✓	✓	Tahitian (Coppenrath & Prévost 1974)
		✓	✓	✓	✓	Tongan (Churchward 1953)
				✓		Buriat native words (Poppe 1960)
			✓	✓		Vanimo (Ross 1980)
		✓	✓	✓		Māori (Bauer 1993)
gapped			✓		✓	–
		✓			✓	–
		✓	✓		✓	Hawaiian (Elbert & Pukui 1979), Luangiua (Salmond 1974), Yellowknife Chipewyan (Li 1946), Colloquial Samoan (Clark 1976), older speakers' Biak (van den Heuvel 2004)
		✓		✓	✓	Ayutla Mixtec (Pankratz & Pike 1967), Egyptian Arabic (Broselow 1976; Gadalla 2000), Somali (Saeed 1999)
		✓		✓		Japanese (Yamato & Sino-Japanese strata) (Ito & Mester 1995)

---

4 Harar Oromo has three series of stops: plain voiceless, voiced, and voiceless glottalized (Owens 1985:10). Of the plain voiceless stops, there are only [t] and [ʔ]. [k] only appears as a geminate. The other stop series have more PoAs: [b d dʒ g], [p' t' tʃ' k'].

166   4 Preservation of the Marked

I was unable to find languages with the onset inventories [k ʔ] and [p ʔ]. However, coda inventories with just [k ʔ] and [p ʔ] exist (Fuzhou, Nganasan), and languages with corresponding fricative onset inventories also exist (e.g. [f h] – Māori – Bauer 1993). I therefore consider these to be accidental gaps.

The mono-segmental inventories [ʔ] and [t] require comment. Buriat allows [tʰ] in native words, and [pʰ] only appears in some interjections. In loanword onsets, [tʰ pʰ kʰ] all appear. In morphologically restricted environments some languages have just [ʔ], as in Nancowry and Tübatulabal reduplicant onsets (Alderete et al. 1999). For fricatives, there are languages which only allow [h] (e.g. Rapanui – du Feu 1996) and some which only allow [s] (e.g. Nambiquara – Kroeker 1972; Price 1976). I suspect the lack of a language in which the only voiceless stop is [ʔ] is due to functional pressures (e.g. the difficulty of perception of [ʔ]). It is therefore not an issue that is relevant to Competence.

4.2.2.1.2   Other manners of articulation
While stops have been the focus here, the same generalizations are valid for other manners of articulation such as fricatives, nasals, and approximants.

For example, Caribbean Spanish has a fricative neutralization that produces the gapped coda inventory [f h] (Trigo 1988:72ff.). /s/ debuccalizes to [h] in codas: e.g. /tos/ → [toh] 'cough' (cf. [tos-eh] 'coughs') (Trigo 1988:72ff.). However, /f/ only optionally debuccalizes: [difteria]~[dihteria] 'diphtheria'. The same fact holds for nasals. Trigo argues that /n/ debuccalizes to [N]: /tren/ → [treN] 'train' (cf. [tren-eh] 'trains'). Again, /m/ only optionally neutralizes: [album]~[albuN] 'album', [adam]~[adaN] 'Adam'. See §8.4.1.1 for details.

4.2.2.2   The Glottal/Coronal Universal and disharmonic inventories
While interaction of Preservation of the Marked and markedness reduction can produce a wide range of inventories through neutralization, not every type of inventory exists. In every language, for all manners of articulation, no PoA neutralization can produce an inventory that lacks *both* a coronal and glottal. This generalization is dubbed the 'Glottal/Coronal Universal' here. It is important to point out that the Glottal/Coronal Universal does not ensure that there will be a glottal or coronal in every manner of articulation in every language; it only states that PoA neutralization will never eliminate both glottals and coronals. Other phenomena that force changes in manner of articulation may interfere (e.g. lenition); the extent of this interference is discussed in §4.2.2.3.

The Glottal/Coronal Universal follows from the nature of markedness: elements can become less marked in neutralization but never more marked. So, if a segment is already as unmarked as it can be, it will not change. In constraint terms, for an input /α/ to map to a different output [β], there must be some output constraint that favours [β] over [α]. If there is no such constraint, there will be no motivation for change; in fact, faithfulness will favour preserving the input segment intact. This result is discussed in detail by Moreton (1999) under the title of 'Harmonic Ascent'. Focusing on the PoA-output constraints, glottal is the least-marked PoA. Because it is least marked, it can never be forced to neutralize by the PoA-output constraints, even if *{dors,lab,cor,gl} outranks IDENT{dors,lab,cor,gl}. This point is illustrated in tableau (32).

(32)

/aʔ/	*{dors,lab,cor,gl}	IDENT{dors,lab,cor,gl}	*{dors,lab,cor}
(a) at	*	*!	*
(b) ap	*	*!	*
(c) ak	*	*!	*
☞ (d) aʔ	*		

If the PoA output constraints never conflict with any other output constraint, glottals could never be eliminated in PoA neutralization. However, the sonority constraints (*−Δ$_{σ/μ}$/glottal) against glottals effectively promotes [coronal] to least-marked status, both in epenthesis and neutralization. So, could [labial] and [dorsal] be promoted in a similar way? In other words, could some process that eliminates coronals be combined with Glottal Elimination, with the result that [p] is the least-marked available segment and therefore epenthetic and the output of neutralization?

This question broaches a larger topic: the relation of markedness to segmental inventories. Traditionally, a language's 'inventory' is the set of phonemes, which are the contrastive segments in a language. With Richness of the Base in OT, there is no easy way to define the notion of 'phonemic', so I take 'inventory' to refer to the set of permissible *output* segments. Either way, the broader issue is whether inventories define limits in which markedness operates. Behind this view is the assumption that inventories are not determined by output constraints alone, but by additional mechanisms (see, e.g., Flemming's 1995 Dispersion Theory of vowel inventories). In contrast, the view in this book is that inventories are determined by the interaction of output and faithfulness constraints alone; there is no special mechanism for forming inventories. After all, the PoA constraints can prevent a segment from surfacing in all environments, just as they can motivate context-specific neutralization and act emergently in epenthesis − the difference is merely one of faithfulness rankings. In short, the same constraints are responsible both for the form of inventories and for positional neutralization.

168   4 Preservation of the Marked

The consequence of this view is that inventory structure can limit positional neutralization. As an example, suppose that [t] is eliminated from an inventory, as in Yamphu and Hawaiian. Could Glottal Elimination then emergently prevent neutralization to glottals? In this case, it would seem that /k/ could only neutralize to [p], since [p] is the least-marked non-glottal available.

The theory predicts that such neutralization is impossible. The reason follows from the ranking needed to eliminate coronals and Harmonic Ascent. As shown in §4.2.1, coronals are eliminated when *{dors,lab,cor} outranks IDENT{dors,lab,cor} and IDENT{dors,lab,cor,gl}. However, one further ranking is necessary: Glottal Elimination must be subordinated to PoA: in constraint terms $*-\Delta_{\sigma/\mu}/\{\text{glottal}\}$ must be ranked below *{dors,lab,cor}. Without this ranking, coronals cannot be neutralized to glottals, as illustrated in tableau (33).

(33)

/ta/	*{dors,lab,cor}	$*-\Delta_\sigma$/glottal	IDENT{dors,lab,cor}
(a) ta	*!		
☞ (b) ʔa		*	*

Tableau (33) shows that if $*-\Delta_\sigma/\{\text{glottal}\}$ outranked *{dors,lab,cor}, candidate (b) would be eliminated, thereby preventing coronals from being eliminated. This result follows from Harmonic Ascent (Moreton 1999): /t/ can only neutralize to a less-marked element. The only element less marked than [t] in PoA terms is [ʔ]. Therefore, if [ʔ] is eliminated, /t/ can only surface as [t].

The ranking ‖ *{dors,lab,cor} » $*-\Delta_\sigma$/glottal ‖ has another effect: it ensures that glottals are less marked than labials and dorsals. Since *{dors,lab,cor} favours glottals over dorsals and labials, this means that dorsals can only neutralize to glottals.

(34)

/ka/	*{dors}	*{dors,lab,cor}	$*-\Delta_\sigma$/glottal	IDENT{dors,lab,cor}
(a) ka	*!	*		
(b) pa		*!		*
(c) ta		*!		*
☞ (d) ʔa			*	*

Therefore, if coronals are eliminated in a language, epenthesis and PoA neutralization can only produce glottals. This again follows from the fact that no output constraint favours labials and/or dorsals over coronals. If there were such a freely rankable constraint – i.e. *{coronal} – it would not only be an easy matter to create a gapped inventory where /k/ neutralized to [p], it would be an easy matter to have all non-labial segments neutralize to labials, as shown in tableau (35).

(35)

/ʔakata/	*{dors}	*{cor}	*−Δ_σ/glottal	IDENT{dors, lab, cor,gl}	*{dors,lab}
(a) ʔakata	*!	*	*		*
☞ (b) papapa				* * *	* * *

In short, there can be no constraint that favours labials above coronals. The same goes for dorsals and their relation to labials and coronals – if there were a constraint *{lab,cor,gl}, all segments could neutralize to [k]. The lack of such a constraint in the present theory prevents this from happening.

The relation of markedness to inventories is discussed in more detail in §8.5.

4.2.2.3 Interaction with other processes and hierarchies

As explained in the previous section, the Glottal/Coronal Universal states that PoA neutralization can never eliminate both glottals and coronals from any particular manner of articulation in any inventory. So, whenever such inventories do occur, PoA neutralization is predicted not to be responsible. For example, vowel nasalization can target coronals alone, leaving a coda nasal inventory of just [m] and [ŋ]. Demands on sonority increase can also be prevented from applying to labials and dorsals, so that coronals are eliminated. This section identifies several such phenomena and shows how they can produce inventories that are 'disharmonic' in terms of PoA – i.e. lack both coronals and glottals.

4.2.2.3.1 Nasal coalescence

Nasalization can produce disharmonic coda inventories. For example, Chickasaw's coda inventory consists solely of [m] (Munro & Ulrich 1985; Trigo 1988:111). This is because underlying /Vn/ surfaces as a nasalized vowel: /cholhkan-a-n/ → [cholhkanã] 'spider-object', cf. [apa-ta-m] 'eat-question-past'.[5]

Such nasalization can be seen as arising from a general ban on codas (NOCODA). To motivate vowel-nasal coalescence, NOCODA must outrank UNIFORMITY – the anti-coalescence faithfulness constraint (for fuller analyses of coalescence, see chapter 6). The reason that only /n/ coalesces can be related to the loss of consonantal place features. If /m/ coalesces with a vowel, the /m/'s

---

5 Medial codas are under more stringent restrictions: both /m/ and /n/ end up as nasalization: [im-oka] 'his water', cf. [ĩːnita] 'his bear', [ĩʃoloʃ] 'his shoe'. *{dors,lab,cor}{dors,lab,cor} outranks IDENT{dors,lab} here, banning medial labials. See §4.3.2 for details.

labial PoA feature would be lost, fatally violating IDENT{dors,lab}. In contrast, /Vn/ coalescence would only require unfaithfulness to the coronal PoA.[6] Tableau (36) shows how this ranking works using hypothetical forms /tan kam/, which should surface as [tã kam].

(36)   Nasal coalescence

/ta$_1$n$_2$ka$_3$m$_4$/	IDENT {dors,lab}	NOCODA	IDENT {dors,lab,cor}	UNIFORMITY
(a) tã$_{1,2}$ kã$_{3,4}$	*!		**	**
(b) ta$_1$n$_2$ka$_3$m$_4$		**!		
☞ (c) tã$_{1,2}$ka$_3$m$_4$		*	*	**

Candidate (a) fatally violates IDENT{dors,lab} because the underlying /m/ coalesces with the preceding vowel, so losing its labial PoA feature. Candidate (b) gratuitously violates NOCODA by retaining both nasals. In contrast, candidate (c) coalescence of /an/ to [ã] does not violate IDENT{dors,lab} since the fusion only involves losing the relatively unmarked coronal feature. As shown in the tableau, IDENT{dors,lab,cor} must be ranked below NOCODA for /n/-coalescence to take place at all.

In short, although Chickasaw has a disharmonic nasal coda inventory, it does not come about through PoA neutralization. Even so, the effect of PoA-related constraints is still relevant: IDENT{dors,lab} prevents nasalization from affecting dorsals and labials.

Vowel-nasal coalescence is fairly common, and usually has the same result as in Chickasaw. However, some cases do not show overt alternations. For example, in Chaoyang coronals do not appear in codas, resulting in a nasal inventory of [ŋ m] (Yip 1994). Since nasal vowels are in complementary distribution with [Vm] and [Vŋ] sequences (i.e. *[Ṽm], *[Ṽŋ]), it is likely that nasal vowels derive from underlying /Vn/ sequences. Again, it is arguable that /n/ coalesces with a preceding vowel while other nasals do not (cf. Yip 1994:§3.1).

Two other processes can produce apparently disharmonic nasal inventories. One is where nasals are apparently neutralized to [ŋ]; such cases actually involve neutralization to the glottal nasal [N] – a harmonically complete inventory (see §4.3). The other is conversion of nasals to laterals. For example, Lawton

---

6 Hume (1992) and Clements & Hume (1995) have proposed that vowels and consonants share the same PoA features. This model of PoA features is compatible with the present proposal as they propose a difference between Consonantal and Vowel Place features. Coalescence of vowels and nasals can be seen as a loss of C-Place features, in their terminology.

(1993:21) reports that Kiriwina's [n] is in free variation with [l] in codas, resulting in a coda nasal inventory that consists of optionally [m] alone. Like lenition, this variation can be seen as a general process of nasal-to-liquid conversion, with /m/→[l] blocked by the PoA-faithfulness constraints since there is no labial liquid in the language.

4.2.2.3.2 Stop sonorization

There are also disharmonic stop inventories. For example, the only stop allowed in Dakota codas is [g]. However, such an inventory is not due to PoA neutralization, but to a process which seeks to increase the sonority of coda stops. In this language, word-final stops /p t/ and the affricate /t͡ʃ/ are optionally converted into the nasals [m n] in codas.[7] However, [k] never nasalizes in this position: it simply voices to [g] (Shaw 1980:367, 374). The data in (37) is from Shaw (1980:367–74).

(37)   Dakota stop sonorization
         (a) /p/→[m] in codas
             /RED-pot-a/ → [potpota] ~ [ponpota]   'worn out, spoiled'
             /RED-top-a/ → [toptopa] ~ [tomtopa]   'four'
             /nap-kawi/   → [napkawĩ] ~ [namkawĩ] 'beckon with the hand'
             /xap/   → [xam] (cf. [xap-a])   'to be stripped'

         (b) /t/→[n] in codas
             /RED-ʔot-a/ → [ʔodʔota] ~ [ʔonʔota]   'be many'
             /o-kʰat-jaɣu/ → [okʰad-jaɣu] ~ [okʰan-jaɣu] 'to be scorched in'
             /sdot ja/   → [sdod-ja] ~ [sdon-ja]   'to know'
             /ʃot/   → [ʃon]   'be smoky'

         (c) /t͡ʃ/→[n] in codas
             /aki-RED -het͡ʃa/ → [aki-hen-het͡ʃa] 'withered, nearly dead'
             /ʃet͡ʃ-ja/   → [ʃen-ja]   'dry'
             /ʃit͡ʃ-ja/   → [ʃin-ja]   'badly'
             /o-ʃit͡ʃ-xã-ka/   → [oʃin xãka]   'to act wickedly'
             /wa-nit͡ʃ/   → [wa-nin]   'be without, lack' (cf. [wa-nit͡ʃ-a])
             /ja-zit͡ʃ/   → [ja-zin]   'elastic, flimsy' (cf. [ja-zit͡ʃ-a])

         (d) /k/→[g] in codas
             /wãjak/   → [wãjag]   'to see' (cf. [wãjak-a])
             /ʃok/   → [ʃog]   'thick, solid' (cf. [ʃok-a])
             /t͡ʃek/   → [t͡ʃeg]   'to stagger' (cf. [t͡ʃek-a])
             /ka-kʰak/   → [ka-kʰag] 'to make dull noise' (cf. [ka-kʰak-a])
             [ojate-kĩ] ~ [ojate-g]   'the people' (stylistic variation)

---

7 If the voiceless stops are not converted into nasals, they undergo voicing assimilation to the following segment.

172   4 *Preservation of the Marked*

It is clear that the disharmonic coda voiced stop inventory is an incidental result of a non-PoA neutralization process. The reason that [k] does not nasalize is because the corresponding dorsal nasal [ŋ] is banned in the language.[8]

Stop nasalization can be motivated by a ban on low sonority coda consonants: i.e. *$\Delta_\mu \leq \{+$vd stop$\}$ (cf. Zec 1995), similar to Somali (§3.3.2.1). Assuming that codas are moraic in Dakota, *$\Delta_\mu \leq \{+$vd stop$\}$ will ban all stops in codas. This constraint outranks all faithfulness constraints that preserve the stop's nasality and voicing (i.e. IDENT[+nasal], IDENT[±voice]). The requirement that stops retain their value for [continuant] (i.e. IDENT[± continuant]) will ensure that stops turn into nasals rather than fricatives.

(38)   Dakota I

/ʃot/	*$\Delta_\mu \leq \{+$vd stop$\}$	IDENT [±continuant]	IDENT [±voice]	IDENT [±nasal]
(a) ʃot	*!			
(b) ʃod	*!		*	
(c) ʃos		*!		
☞ (d) ʃon			*	*

To prevent /k/ from nasalizing, a constraint against [ŋ] must outrank *$\Delta_\mu \leq \{+$vd stop$\}$. The present theory provides such a constraint: *{dors}/nasal, a manner-specific version of *{dors} (§2.3.3.3). *{dors}/nasal outranks *$\Delta_\mu \leq \{+$vd stop$\}$, so blocking /k/→*[ŋ]. IDENT{dors}, or any other PoA faithfulness constraint, outranks *$\Delta_\mu \leq \{+$vd stop$\}$ to prevent /k/ from both nasalizing and changing its PoA (e.g. /k/→*[n]).

(39)   Dakota II: Blocking velar nasal conversion

/ʃok/	*{dors}/nasal	IDENT{dors}	*$\Delta_\mu \leq \{+$vd stop$\}$
(a) ʃoŋ	*!		
(b) ʃon		*!	
☞ (c) ʃog			*

/k/ does not become [x] because IDENT[±continuant] outranks *$\Delta_\mu \leq \{+$vd stop$\}$.

The final issue is why /k/ does not remain faithful – i.e. [k], rather than surfacing as voiced. This can be ascribed to the effect of the emergent coda sonority constraint *$\Delta_\mu \leq \{-$vd stop$\}$, which bans voiceless stops in codas (as

---

[8] The only situation in which [ŋ] can appear in Dakota is before a dorsal stop. This comes about through assimilation of the coronal nasal.

in Somali – §3.3.2.1). As long as $*\Delta_\mu \leq \{+\text{vd stop}\}$ outranks IDENT[±voice], codas will voice.

(40)   Dakota III

/ʃok/	$*\Delta_\mu \leq \{+\text{vd stop}\}$	$*\Delta_\mu \leq \{-\text{vd stop}\}$	IDENT[±voice]
(a) ʃok	*	*!	
☞ (b) ʃog	*		*

In summary, Dakota's disharmonic coda stop inventory [g] is not due to PoA neutralization; it is the result of a ban on low-sonority elements that is partially blocked for dorsals. Even though this process is not PoA neutralization, the PoA constraints still exert a significant influence in banning dorsal nasals.

A similar pattern is found in Ecuador Quichua (Orr 1962). Of the stops [p b t d ts dz tʃ dʒ k g] only [k g] are found in codas ([tʃ] can appear in medial codas). However, this correlates with the fact that Ecuador Quichua only has the nasals [m n ɲ]. Again, dorsal stops are blocked from nasalizing to [ŋ], producing an apparently disharmonic inventory on the surface. Kashaya provides another example of stop sonorization (Buckley 1994:48).

In more general terms, Dakota shows how a general neutralization of manner of articulation can be blocked for marked PoAs, resulting in a disharmonic inventory. Lenition is in the same vein: there are a number of languages where only coronals undergo lenition, with the result that in many environments the only stops seen on the surface are [p] and [k] (Kirchner 1998:ch.4§1.2.1; Lavoie 2001). In many cases, the failure of /p/ and /k/ to undergo lenition can be ascribed to IDENT{dors,lab}, as there are often no counterparts with adequately high sonority that could preserve /p/ and /k/'s PoA (§3.3.5).

In summary, inventories that are disharmonic in terms of PoA do not come about through PoA neutralization. Therefore they offer no evidence for PoA markedness.

4.3   Undergoers of assimilation

Like neutralization, assimilation shows the influence of Preservation of the Marked. In some languages the need to preserve marked elements overrides the pressure to assimilate, with the result that only unmarked elements undergo assimilation.

A well-known example is Catalan place assimilation. Only coronals undergo assimilation; labials, dorsals, and palatals do not. More detailed data are provided in §4.3.1.

(41) Selective Major PoA Assimilation in Catalan

Root	/son/ 'they are'	/som/ 'we are'	/aɲ/ 'year'
amics 'friends'	son əmiks	som əmiks	aɲ əmik
pocs 'few (pl.)', *petit* 'short'	som pɔks	som pɔks	aɲ pətit
tontus 'stupid (pl.)'	son tontus	som tontus	aɲ tontu
xicots 'boys', *xop* 'wet'	son ʃikɔts	som ʃikɔts	aɲ ʃop
cosins 'cousins'	soŋ kuzins	som kuzins	
grans 'big (pl.)'	soŋ grans	som grans	aɲ gran

Analogous to Kiparsky's (1994) analysis, the failure of non-coronals to undergo assimilation will be attributed to the action of PoM-faithfulness constraints (also see Wheeler 2005a:§6). When faithfulness constraints to non-coronals outrank all place assimilation constraints, which in turn outrank all faithfulness constraints that preserve coronals, only coronals are able to undergo assimilation. Section 4.3.1 will discuss Catalan and other cases like it in detail, showing how the PoM-faithfulness constraints can produce cases of 'selective' assimilation.

Section 4.3.2 shows that Catalan is not the only type of selective assimilation system: for major place of articulation, any subset of PoAs can undergo assimilation. So, while only coronals undergo assimilation in Catalan, the mirror-image is found in Sri Lankan Portuguese creole, where only dorsals and labials undergo assimilation. A full typology is given in §3.3, but is summarized in table (42). A ✓ means that the PoA undergoes assimilation, while a ✗ means that it is preserved.

(42) Assimilation systems

	dors	lab	cor	Language
All assimilate	✓	✓	✓	Diola Fogny
No assimilation	✗	✗	✗	Southern Sierra Miwok
Unmarked	✗	✓	✓	Korean
undergoers	✗	✗	✓	Catalan, Yamphu
Marked	✓	✗	✗	Chukchi
undergoers	✓	✓	✗	SLP creole
mixed	✓	✗	✓	Harar Oromo
	✗	✓	✗	Seri (Stemberger 1992)

An analogous generalization is valid for voicing assimilation, and predicted to be valid for all types of assimilation (cf. Wetzels & Mascaró 2001).

While systems in which only unmarked elements assimilate are due to PoM-faithfulness, systems in which only *marked* elements assimilate are due to output constraints. Section 4.3.2 shows that the constraints that force assimilation work on the same principle as the output constraints that result in PoA neutralization – assimilation is a response to the reduction of markedness in clusters, rather than single segments. Section 4.3.3 shows why Catalan-style assimilation systems must employ PoM-faithfulness constraints.

4.3.1   Unmarked undergoers and Preservation of the Marked[9]

Assimilation can be blocked if doing so would result in losing a marked place of articulation. As mentioned above, a famous case is Catalan's PoA assimilation (Mascaró 1976, 1986; Wheeler 1979; Kiparsky 1985, 1994; Recasens 1991; Hualde 1992; Palmada 1994). The analysis presented in this section owes much to this previous work, especially Kiparsky's (1994) OT analysis. I also note that Wheeler (2005a) makes extensive use of the present theory to analyse not only PoA assimilation but a wide variety of assimilation and neutralization phenomena in the language. So while the analysis presented here is only a small piece of a much larger phonological system, Wheeler's work shows that it is consistent with other aspects of Catalan phonology.

Catalan has the surface consonants listed in (43) (adapted from Wheeler 2005a:Table 1; cf. Hualde 1992:367). Segments in parentheses are marginal or differ from dialect to dialect.

(43)   Catalan consonants

	labial	dental/alveolar	alveo-palatal	palatal	dorsal
stops	p b	t̪ d̪			k g
affricates		(t͡s) (d͡z)	t͡ʃ (d͡ʒ)		
fricatives	β f v	ð s z	ʃ ʒ	ʝ	ɣ
nasals	m	n		ɲ	ŋ
laterals		l	ʎ		
rhotics		ɾ r			
glides	w			j	

The voiced plosives are in complementary distribution with the voiced fricatives of the same PoA ([b]~[β], [d]~[ð], [g]~[ɣ]). For details, see

---

9 My thanks to Eva Juarros for her native speaker intuitions and for checking the transcriptions and glosses.

Wheeler (2005a:§10.1.2). Some Majorcan dialects have [c ɟ] in place of [k g].

Syllables have the form (C)(C)V(C)(C). Singleton onsets can consist of any consonant except [r], the affricates, [ŋ], and [w]. Codas can contain any segment except voiced obstruents; these neutralize to their voiceless counterparts.

Onset clusters consist of a stop or [f] plus a coronal liquid [r l], with the exception of [tl] and [dl]. Examples are [prumɛtrə] 'promise', [blaw] 'blue', [kla] 'clear', [frɛt] 'cold' (Hualde 1992:380).

Almost the same facts hold for coda clusters, though the order of segments is reversed. Word-finally, liquid+stop clusters are admissible, with the exception of [lt]. In addition, the following clusters with [s] are admissible: [sp st sk ns ls].

Of present interest is assimilation. Certain stops, nasals, and laterals in coda position assimilate to the PoA of a following onset consonant; the fricative [s] also alters in codas (see Hualde 1992). Two types of PoA assimilation are distinguished here. One is assimilation of major PoA – i.e. labial, coronal, and dorsal specifications. The other is assimilation of minor PoA – i.e. distinctions within the major PoA categories, such as bilabial vs. labio-dental for labials, and dental vs. alveolar vs. palatal in the coronal category. The focus of this section is major PoA assimilation; minor PoA will be discussed when it becomes relevant.

Only the alveolar nasal [n] exhibits major PoA assimilation in coda position; [m ɲ ŋ] remain unchanged. Table (44) provides data compiled from Mascaró (1976), Kiparsky (1985:85), Hualde (1992:395), and Palmada (1994:83, 109). Assimilation in minor PoA does occur, with bi-labial /m/ surfacing as labio-dental [ɱ] before [f].

(44)   Major PoA Assimilation in Catalan

Root	/son/ 'they are'	/som/ 'we are'	/aɲ/ 'year'
amics 'friends'	son əmiks	som əmiks	aɲ əmik
pocs 'few (pl.)', *petit* 'short'	som pɔks	som pɔks	aɲ pətit
veus 'voices'	som bɛus	som bɛus	
felisus 'happy (pl.)'	soɱ fəlisus	soɱ fəlisus	aɲ fəlis
tontus 'stupid (pl.)'	son tontus	som tontus	aɲ tontu
docils 'amenable (pl.)'	son dɔsils	som dosils	
cinc 'five'	son siŋ	som siŋ	
xicots 'boys', *xop* 'wet'	son ʃikɔts	som ʃikɔts	aɲ ʃop
rossos 'blonde (pl.)'	son rosəs	som rosəs	
lliures 'free (pl.)'	soɲ ʎiwrəs	som ʎiwrəs	aɲ ʎiwrəs
cosins 'cousins'	soŋ kuzins	som kuzins	
grans 'big (pl.)'	soŋ grans	som grans	aɲ gran

The forms [tiŋ presə] *tinc pressa* 'I'm in a hurry' and [tiŋ pa] *tinc pa* 'I have bread' show that the dorsal [ŋ] does not assimilate either (Palmada 1994:109; Mascaró 1976 resp.).

The same restrictions hold morpheme-internally. Homorganic nasal+C clusters and heterorganic labial+non-labial clusters are permitted morpheme-internally. There is no evidence for dorsal+non-dorsal clusters morpheme-internally. Given the general rarity of dorsal [ŋ] in the language, this may be an accidental gap. For further examples, see Wheeler (2005a:§6.1).

(45) Catalan morpheme-internal NC clusters
    (a) homorganic NC clusters
        [kən'do] *candor* 'candour'   [kəm'panə] *campana* 'bell'
        [kəm'bɔdʒə] *Cambotja* 'Cambodia' ['kambi] *canvi* 'change'
        [kuŋkəri'ðo] *conqueridor* 'conquering' [kəŋ'gur] *cangur* 'kangaroo'
    (b) heterorganic [m]+C (Hualde 1992:373)
        [kum'tat] *comtat* 'country'   [ə'sumtə] *assumpte* 'business'
        [dəm'na] *damnar* 'to damn'   ['imnə] *himne* 'hymn'
        ['premsə] *premsa* 'press'

4.3.1.1 Analysis

PoA assimilation comes about when a constraint against heterorganic clusters outranks all relevant PoA-faithfulness constraints. A theory of assimilation-motivating constraints will be presented in §4.3.2. For the moment the assimilation-causing constraints will be called ASSIM; their effect is to ban consonant clusters that differ in major PoA.

For assimilation of coronals to take place, ASSIM must outrank all faithfulness constraints that preserve coronals: i.e. IDENT{dors,lab,cor} and IDENT{dors,lab,cor,gl}. Tableau (46) shows the assimilation ranking at work. The constraint ASSIM is violated by all heterorganic clusters. So, candidate (a)'s [nk] cluster incurs a violation while (b)'s [ŋk] cluster does not. Candidate (a)'s violation is fatal.

(46) Catalan I: Basic anti-heterorganicity ranking

/son kuzins/	ASSIM	IDENT{dors,lab,cor}
(a) son kuzins	*!	
☞ (b) soŋ kuzins		*

4.3.1.1.1 Blocking labial and dorsal assimilation

ASSIM assigns a violation to all heterorganic clusters, not just those with [n] (there is no constraint that bans coronal+non-coronal clusters alone – §4.3.2).

Since ASSIM applies indiscriminately to different PoAs, a constraint must be invoked to block it from applying to labials, palatals, and dorsals. The relevant constraint is a PoM-faithfulness one, IDENT{dors,lab}. This constraint preserves input labial and dorsal specifications, so with it outranking ASSIM the marked categories are prevented from assimilating. This approach follows Kiparsky's (1994) analysis, and is employed in Wheeler (2005a). I adopt the proposal that (true) palatals in Catalan are a type of dorsal (i.e. corono-dorsals, or [−back] dorsals – Keating 1988; E. Pulleyblank 1989; unlike alveo-palatals which are [−anterior] coronals – Hall 1997). So, IDENT{dors,lab} will prevent /ɲ/ from assimilating to [t] in [aɲ tontu], *[an tontu].

(47)   Catalan II: Blocking assimilation of the marked

/som kuzins/	IDENT{dors,lab}	ASSIM	IDENT{dors,lab,cor}
(a) soŋ kuzins	*!		*
☞ (b) som kuzins		*	

Candidate (a) fatally violates IDENT{dors,lab} because /m/'s labial specification is lost in the output: /m/→[ŋ]. In short, IDENT{dors,lab} blocks assimilation, rendering the constraint ASSIM inactive in this competition.

The Catalan ranking therefore illustrates the blocking effect of PoM-faithfulness constraints in assimilation. The constraint IDENT{dors,lab} specifically preserves marked PoA values, so blocking the output constraint that promotes unfaithfulness – ASSIM. However, the output constraint outranks all faithfulness constraints that preserve unmarked feature values – IDENT{dors,lab,cor} – with the result that only unmarked values undergo assimilation.

In this particular system it is impossible to determine the ranking of the remaining PoA-faithfulness constraint, IDENT{dors}. Since IDENT{dors} incurs a subset of IDENT{dors,lab}'s violations, ranking it either above or below IDENT{dors,lab} will have no effect in relation to the output constraints discussed so far.

4.3.1.1.2 Avoiding other outcomes

ASSIM only eliminates candidates; it does not specify which of the surviving candidates will win. Thus, ASSIM bans candidates with a heterorganic cluster like [ŋp], but does not specify which of the alternatives – deletion [p], epenthesis [ŋip], assimilation [mp], or coalescence [m] – will apply.

The choice of winner falls to other constraints. Since deletion and epenthesis are ruled out in Catalan, the anti-deletion constraint MAX-IO and anti-epenthesis constraint DEP-IO must both outrank ASSIM. Tableau (48) illustrates this ranking.

(48) Catalan III: Blocking deletion and epenthesis

/som kuzins/	IDENT{dors,lab}	MAX-IO	DEP-IO	ASSIM
(a) soŋ kuzins	*!			
(b) so kuzins		*!		
(c) somi̯kuzins			*!	
☞ (d) som kuzins				*

The competition between (a), (c), and (d) shows the need for the ranking ‖ MAX-IO, DEP-IO » ASSIM ‖. If ASSIM outranked either MAX or DEP, the /mk/ cluster would be resolved by deletion or epenthesis. This point is discussed in detail in de Lacy 2002a:§7.3.1, where epenthesis is used to avoid heterorganic clusters in Ponapean. Deletion can be used to avoid heterorganic clusters, as in Attic Greek (de Lacy 2002a:§7.7.5).

Other outcomes are ruled out by other faithfulness constraints. For example, coalescence of /mk/ is blocked by the anti-coalescence constraint UNIFORMITY (McCarthy & Prince 1995). Neutralization and metathesis will not improve on ASSIM, so – by process of elimination – the only option available is assimilation.

4.3.1.1.3 Direction of assimilation

One further comment is needed in relation to the faithful mapping /som tontus/→[som tontus]. The coronal onset does not assimilate here: *[som pontus]. As Lombardi (1995, 1999) and Beckman (1998) have demonstrated, a faithfulness constraint that specifically preserves PoA values in onsets produces regressive assimilation. In the present instance, such a constraint blocks assimilation of onsets if it outranks ASSIM.

(49) Catalan IV

/som tontus/	IDENT{dors,lab}	onset-IDENT{dors,lab,cor}	ASSIM
(a) som pontus		*!	
☞ (b) som tontus			*

180   4 Preservation of the Marked

Diagram (50) summarizes the ranking established above.

(50)   Catalan assimilation ranking

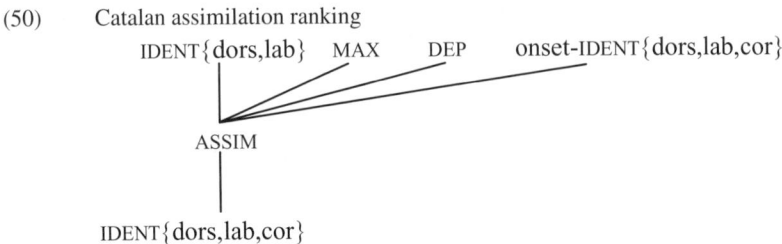

The diagram shows that the form of the PoM-faithfulness constraint IDENT{dors,lab} is crucial in blocking assimilation. If it preserved coronals as well, no assimilation would take place.

4.3.1.2 Stop gemination

The PoA-faithfulness constraint IDENT{dors,lab} has visible effects throughout Catalan's phonology, not just in major PoA assimilation. One effect is found in stop gemination. Coda coronal stops in Catalan geminate with a following onset consonant, but labials and dorsals geminate only if their input PoA specification would not be lost. The data in (51) is taken from Palmada (1994:82) and Hualde (1992:397).

(51)   Catalan stop gemination

	sɛt 'seven'	t͡sap 'none'	pok 'few'
pɔbːləs 'villages'	sɛpːɔbːləs	t͡sapːɔbːlə	pokpɔbːlə
kamp 'field'	sɛkːamp	t͡sapkamp	pokːamp
bɔʒus 'fools', bo 'good'	sɛbːɔʒus	t͡sabːo	pogbo
mal 'pain'	sɛmːals	t͡samːal	pogmal
labials 'labials'	sɛlːabials	t͡sablabial	poglabial
ʎiures 'free'	sɛʎːiures	t͡sabʎiura	pogʎiuras

Like assimilation, gemination is a way to avoid heterorganic clusters, and just like assimilation, gemination is blocked only when it would force unfaithfulness to input dorsal or labial specifications. So, /t͡sap mal/→[t͡samːal] is permissible because the input /p/'s labial feature is preserved in the output [m]. However, /pog mal/→*[pomːal] is prohibited because the input dorsal specification is lost. Similarly, /cap labial/→*[t͡salːabial] is banned because the input /p/ loses its labial specification in the output.

Voice assimilation is also apparent in the examples (e.g. /pok̲ labial/ → [poglabial]). For discussion of obstruent-sonorant voice assimilation, see Jun 1995 and Wheeler 2005a. Some dialects require assimilation in nasality as well (Hualde 1992:397).

Gemination in Catalan is motivated by constraints on syllable contact. As Vennemann (1988) has argued, many languages require a sonority fall from coda to onset segments. Such a condition would rule out the level sonority heterorganic stop-stop clusters and rising sonority [t.l], [t.m], and [t.ʎ] clusters. Geminates avoid syllable contact violations because they have a single root node, so there is no sonority cline at all. As expected under a syllable-contact approach, nasal and lateral codas do not geminate (for fricatives, see below): e.g. [son tontus], *[sot:ontus]; [sɔl tontus], *[sɔt:ontus].

The syllable contact constraint will be called SYLLCON here, after Davis (1998); for a recent theory of syllable contact set within Optimality Theory, see Gouskova 2001. As Gouskova argues, SYLLCON can be reduced to the interaction of several different constraints. In any case, ASSIM cannot be used instead of SYLLCON here as it only motivates PoA assimilation, predicting /sɛt labials/→ *[setlabials]. Conversely, SYLLCON cannot take over ASSIM's role: SYLLCON cannot motivate nasal assimilation: /son pɔks/→ *[sonpɔks] does not violate SYLLCON, and neither does [sompɔks].

Again, IDENT{dors,lab} outranks SYLLCON, preventing dorsals and labials from geminating.

(52)　Catalan v: Blocking gemination of marked PoAs

/t͡sap₁ k₂amp/	IDENT{dors,lab}	SYLLCON	IDENT{dors,lab,cor}
(a) t͡sak:₁,₂amp	*!		*
☞ (b) t͡sap₁k₂amp		*	

One assumption that underlies the analysis here is that consonants coalesce to form a geminate. This means that both /p/ and /k/ correspond to output [k:] in candidate (b) above. Because the labial /p/ corresponds to (b)'s dorsal [k:], IDENT{dors,lab} is violated. Further discussion of coalescence is provided in chapter 6. This approach is a parallelist implementation of traditional analyses in which gemination involved an opaque process of coda deletion followed by compensatory lengthening.

Finally, the ranking established above also accounts for liquid assimilation. For example, the non-palatal lateral [l] assimilates in palatality, but the palatal [ʎ] does not.

(53)　Lateral assimilation (Hualde1992:396)
　　　(a) /l/ assimilation　　　　　　(b) /ʎ/ non-assimilation
　　　　/sɔl/　　　　'sun'　　　　　　/eʎ/　　　　　'he'
　　　　[sɔl əmik]　　'friendly sun'　　[eʎ donə]　　'he gives'
　　　　[sɔl sɛk]　　'dry sun'　　　　[eʎ sap]　　　'he knows'
　　　　[sɔʎ ʒərma]　'brother sun'　　[eʎ ʒaw]　　　'he lies'
　　　　[sɔʎ ʎiwrə]　'free sun'

Since palatals are specified as [–back] dorsals, IDENT{dors,lab} blocks /ʎ/ assimilation, as shown in tableau (54).

(54)　Catalan VI

/eʎ donə/	IDENT{dors,lab}	ASSIM
(a) el donə	*!	
☞ (b) eʎ donə		*

As with nasal assimilation, /l/ can assimilate to palatals without hindrance, due to the dominance of ASSIM over IDENT{dors,lab,cor}.

As a concluding note, Rice & Avery (1991:116), citing J. Mascaró (p.c.), report that /l/ is realized as [l^w] before labials and [ɫ] before dorsals. Other sources report velarization but not labialization (Wheeler 1979:301), and others that /l/ does neither (Hualde 1992:396). Dialects that block velarization and/or labialization can be accounted for by having constraints that ban these marked segments outranking the constraint that motivates place assimilation – i.e. ‖ *ɫ, *l^w » *ASSIM‖.[10] The opposite ranking obtains in languages with velarization or labialization.

In short, Catalan presents a variety of phonological phenomena which are affected by PoM-faithfulness constraints. The common thread among these processes is that marked PoAs are preserved at the expense of having heterorganic clusters and syllable-contact violating sequences.

4.3.2　Marked undergoers and markedness reduction

The generalizations about undergoers of assimilation are just the same as those for neutralization: there are no markedness asymmetries for undergoers of either assimilation or neutralization. While only coronals undergo assimilation in Catalan, only dorsals and labials undergo assimilation in Sri Lankan Portuguese creole (§4.3.2.2). As shown above, PoM is responsible for situations in which marked elements are preserved from undergoing assimilation or neutralization.

---

10 The constraint on [ɫ] and [l^w] might be considered a manner-specific instantiation of *{dors,lab} – i.e. *{dors,lab}/liquid.

In this section, systems in which only unmarked elements avoid assimilation are shown to be due to markedness reduction.

Section 4.3.2.1 provides a theory of markedness reduction for assimilation, and §4.3.2.2 shows it in action.

4.3.2.1 Motivating assimilation

There are two leading ideas behind the form of the assimilation-inducing output constraints presented in this section. One is that all homorganic clusters are favoured over heterorganic ones. The other is that heterorganic clusters with highly marked segments are more marked than those with less-marked segments. For example, [kp] is universally more marked than [pt].

The entire set of anti-heterorganic cluster constraints – called the 'Marked-Cluster' constraints – is given in (55); their definition is provided in schematic terms in (56). In effect, the Marked-Cluster constraints combine the sets of PoA specifications allowed by the present theory.[11] The constraints in (55) do not refer to a particular manner of articulation, though manner-specific instantiations may be possible (see below for discussion). The constraints are freely rankable.

(55) The Marked-Cluster constraints (anti-heterorganic output constraints)
    (a) *{X}{dors}   (b) *{X}{dors,lab}
        *{dors}{dors}   *{dors}{dors,lab}
        *{dors,lab}{dors}   *{dors,lab}{dors,lab}
        *{dors,lab,cor}{dors}   *{dors,lab,cor}{dors,lab}
        *{dors,lab,cor,gl}{dors}   *{dors,lab,cor,gl}{dors,lab}

    (c) *{X}{dors,lab,cor}   (d) *{X}{dors,lab,cor, gl}
        *{dors}{dors,lab,cor}   *{dors}{dors,lab,cor,gl}
        *{dors,lab}{dors,lab,cor}   *{dors,lab}{dors,lab,cor,gl}
        *{dors,lab,cor}{dors,lab,cor}   *{dors,lab,cor}{dors,lab,cor,gl}
        *{dors,lab,cor,gl}{dors,lab,cor}   *{dors,lab,cor,gl}{dors,lab,cor,gl}

(56) Interpretation of the anti-heterorganic constraints
    *XY 'Assign a violation for every pair of adjacent segments such that
    (i) the first segment has a feature f_1 from set X and
    (ii) the second segment has a feature f_2 from set Y and
    (iii) $f_1 \neq f_2$.'

---

[11] The constraints are not formed through local conjunction (Smolensky 1993) since *{dors,lab,cor}&*{dors} does not specify linear order (e.g. [ɲt] violates *{dors,lab,cor} &*{dors}, but not *{dors,lab,cor}{dors}) nor necessarily adjacency (e.g. [ɲat] violates *{dors,lab,cor}&*{dors} – see Alderete 1997 for relevant discussion).

So, the constraint *{dors}{dors,lab,cor} assigns a violation to all clusters that consist of a dorsal followed by a labial or coronal: e.g. [ŋp], [ŋt]. The constraint does not assign a violation to homorganic sequences – [ŋk].

One way to conceive of the constraints is through the autosegmental idea that sequences of segments can share a single feature if they have the same value for that feature (Halle & Vergnaud 1980; Steriade 1982; Clements 1985; Hayes 1986; Sagey 1986; Schein & Steriade 1986). So, the constraint *{dors}{dors,lab,cor} does not assign a violation to [ŋk] because this sequence has a single dorsal feature, not a sequence of dorsal+dorsal. Of course, *{dors}{dors,lab,cor} will assign a violation to 'fake' homorganic clusters and geminates [k.k] – clusters in which the segments have separate PoA features (a distinction needed in Tigrinya – Schein & Steriade 1986; Keer 1999).

Similarly, *{dors,lab,cor,gl}{dors,lab,cor,gl} assigns a violation to every sequence with non-identical PoA specifications – i.e. all heterorganic clusters. In contrast, *{dors,lab}{dors,lab,cor,gl} only assigns violations to sequences where the first member is a non-coronal: e.g. [ŋp], [ŋt], [ŋʔ],[mp], [mt], [mʔ]. Similarly, *{dors,lab,cor}{dors,lab} is only violated by clusters where the second member is non-coronal: e.g. [pk], [tk], [kp], [tp].

Whether autosegmental formalism is adopted or not, the central points here are that (i) there are constraints that assign violations to heterorganic clusters and that (ii) the constraints favour heterorganic clusters with highly marked components over those with less-marked components.

It is useful to distinguish two general types of Marked-Cluster constraints. In one type, the leftmost set of elements is a subset of the rightmost one: e.g. *{dors}{dors,lab,cor}, *{dors,lab}{dors,lab,cor}. In the other type, the rightmost set of elements is a subset of the leftmost set: e.g. *{dors,lab,cor}{dors}, *{dors,lab,cor}{dors,lab}. The different types have distinct empirical effects. Constraints of the first type, like *{dors}{dors,lab,cor}, affect undergoers. For example, *{dors}{dors,lab,cor} will ban clusters consisting of a dorsal+non-dorsal [ŋp ŋt], but will not militate against any other heterorganic cluster [mk mt nk np]. Thus, if *{dors}{dors,lab,cor} is the only active constraint in a grammar, only dorsal+non-dorsal clusters would be eliminated (this happens in Chukchi, discussed in §4.3.3.2). In contrast, constraints like *{dors,lab,cor}{dors} affect the triggers of assimilation – this constraint is used in a language where only dorsals force assimilation. The 'leftmost' type of constraints – i.e. *{dors}{dors,lab,cor}, *{dors,lab}{dors,lab,cor}, etc. – are the focus of this section as they affect undergoers most transparently. The 'rightmost' type of constraint affects triggering elements; they are discussed in de Lacy 2002a:§7.5.

4.3 *Undergoers of assimilation* 185

The combined effect of the Marked-Cluster constraints is to (a) favour homorganic clusters over heterorganic ones and (b) favour heterorganic clusters with low-marked members over heterorganic clusters with highly marked ones. The result is that dorsal+C clusters, where C is any consonant that disagrees in PoA with the preceding segment, are local harmonic bounds for labial+C, coronal+C, and glottal+C clusters in terms of Marked-Cluster constraints with the form *{x}{dors,lab,cor}; the same is true of labial+C as a local harmonic bound for coronal+C and glottal+C, and coronal+C as a local harmonic bound for glottal+C. Thus, the constraints can be used to avoid any contiguous set of these clusters. For example, Sri Lankan Portuguese creole (§4.3.2.2) avoids dorsal+C and labial+C heterorganic clusters, but allows coronal+C clusters.

The earliest precursor to the present theory is Cairns & Feinstein's (1982) theory of onset cluster markedness (also see Morelli 1999). For the idea that assimilation produces a less-marked cluster, see Battistella 1990:132ff. For recent approaches to cluster constraints in Optimality Theory, see Baertsch 1998 and Gouskova 2001.

Importantly, the constraints do not provide unexpected problems for neutralization — there is no way to use the constraints to produce unattested medial neutralization patterns. For example, there is no Marked-Cluster constraint that bans coronals in codas without also banning more marked elements, so there is no way to use the constraints to force neutralization to labial or dorsal PoA.

As there are often different conditions on heterorganic clusters of different manners of articulation, it is quite possible that there are specific instantiations of the Marked-Cluster constraints for different manners of articulation.[12] Since the aim of this section is to determine the form of faithfulness constraints, little time will be devoted to developing this notion — the exact form of the output constraints will be made clear for each of the case studies as they arise. Similarly, the constraints in (55) do not refer to constituency, only linear order. So, the constraint *{dors,lab,cor,gl}{dors,lab,cor,gl} bans heterorganic clusters in any position, regardless of whether they consist of two onset segments, two coda segments, or a coda+onset sequence. While it is possible that further investigation will show the need for versions of these constraints that refer to constituency, the case studies discussed below provide no relevant evidence (also see Steriade 1995a for relevant work that does not refer to constituency).

---

12 I do not mean to imply that there should be a constraint for every possible combination of manner of articulation with PoA. Such an approach would fail to capture the implicational relations in manner of articulation for assimilation, as demonstrated by Padgett (1994) and Jun (1995). Clearly, the role of manner in place assimilation deserves careful formal development, a task beyond the scope of this chapter.

186   4 Preservation of the Marked

Again, while this issue is worthy of future attention, it is tangential to the main point here and – more importantly – has no bearing on the claims about faithfulness constraints made in this section.

In short, for the purposes of this chapter it is essential that there are output constraints that (i) favour homorganic over heterorganic clusters and (ii) distinguish different types of heterorganic cluster, based on PoA markedness. The Marked-Cluster constraints are employed because they fulfill these two functions. Supporting evidence is provided in the following sections.

Finally, constraints that mention glottals *{dors,lab,cor,gl}{dors,lab,cor,gl} are necessary; this point is discussed in §8.7.3 (cf. Gouskova 2003; Rice 1999a,b).

4.3.2.2 Analysis

Dorsals and labials undergo assimilation in Sri Lankan Portuguese (SLP) creole while coronals do not (Smith 1978; Hume & Tserdanelis 2002). SLP creole is therefore the exact opposite to Catalan in terms of assimilation undergoers. This section argues that the SLP creole system comes about through a ban on highly marked clusters, as do all 'marked-undergoer' systems. For SLP creole, this idea is implemented by the constraint *{dors,lab}{dors,lab,cor}, which only bans heterorganic clusters with a non-coronal as the leftmost element. In effect, coronals are already 'adequately unmarked' in SLP creole – they do not assimilate because doing so will not sufficiently improve their markedness.

SLP creole has the segments in (57).

(57)   Sri Lankan Portuguese creole consonants

	labial	coronal	palatal	dorsal
stops	p	t̪		k
	b	d̪		g
affricates		tʃ		
fricatives	f	s		
		z		
nasals	m	n	ɲ	ŋ
laterals		l		
rhotics		ɾ		
glides	w		j	

The short vowels are [i e æ ə ɔ o u], with long counterparts [iː eː æː aː ɔː oː uː]. Syllables have the structure (C)(C)V(ː)(C). Complex onsets consist of (1) an obstruent+[ɾ] (excepting [sɾ]), and – rarely – (2) an obstruent+[l] or (3) [s] followed by a stop. Word-medial codas must be sonorants.

Of the nasals, only [m] and [n] appear word-initially (e.g. [mael] 'honey', [noːs] 'we'), whereas [m n ŋ] all appear intervocalically and word-finally (e.g. [penera] 'sift', [uɲə] 'one', [kumijan] 'communion', [pːam] 'bread', [siːn] 'bell', [miːtiɲ] 'meeting' (Hume 2003:§3)). [ɲ] is rare in native words; it typically occurs in loanwords.

There are strong restrictions on heterorganic clusters. Heterorganic clusters where the first member is labial or dorsal are banned both within words and across word boundaries. The requirement can be seen in the alternations in (58); the annotation (xx#yy) refers to the page number and example number respectively in Smith (1978), whereas (H&T) refers to Hume & Tserdanelis (1999). The form for 'one' is underlyingly /uɲ/, as seen before vowel-initial forms like [əluɲɔɾas] 'sometimes' (101#748, 749).

(58)   SLP creole assimilation data
      (a) /m/+C assimilation

/maːm+su/	→[maːnsu]	'hand {gen.sg}'	(100#736)
/maːm+ki/	→[maːŋki]	'hand {verbal N}'	(H&T)
/maːm+pə/	→[maːmpə]	'hand {dat.sg}'	(H&T)
/vaːrzim+su/	→[vaːrzinsu]	'harvest {gen.sg}'	(H&T)
/vaːrzim+ki/	→[vaːrziŋki]	'harvest {verbal N}'	(H&T)
/vaːrzim+pə/	→[vaːrzimpə]	'harvest {dat.sg}'	(H&T)
/taːm nikərə/	→[taːnːikərə]	'also won't'	(89#641)
/ɾezaːm lej/	→[ɾezaːnlej]	'reasonably'	(100#740)
/boːm dʒentis/	→[boːndʒentis]	'good people'	(100#738)
/pərim təsuwaː/	→[pərintəsuwaː]	'I am sweating'	(100#739)
/pikiniːm kaːzə/	→[pikiniːŋkaːzə]	'small house'	(100#737)

      (b) /ɲ/+C assimilation

/miːtiɲ+su/	→[miːtinsu]	'meeting {gen.sg}'	(H&T)
/miːtiɲ+pə/	→[miːtimpəŋ]	'meeting {dat.sg}'	(H&T)
/miːtiɲ+ki/	→[miːtiŋki]	'meeting {verbal N}'	(H&T)
/uɲ pæːzu/	→[um pæːzu]	'one pound'	(102#758)
/uɲ faːkə/	→[um faːkə]	'one knife'	(102#757)
/uɲ maːm/	→[um maːm]	'one hand'	(103#760)
/uɲ diːjəpə/	→[un diːjəpə]	'for one day'	(102#758)
/əluɲ dʒeːntis/	→[əluɲ dʒeːntis]	'some people'	(102#756)

In contrast, the nasal [n] allows consonants with any PoA to follow it, as shown in (59).

188   4 Preservation of the Marked

(59)   /n/+C = no assimilation
       [kəkluːn-pə]   'turkey {dative sg}'   (100#741)
       [siːn-pə]   'bell {dative sg}'   (H&T)
       [siloːn-pə]   'Sri Lanka {dat.sg}'   (H&T)
       [siloːn-ki]   'Sri Lanka {verbal N}'   (H&T)
       [kəkluːn-ki]   'turkey {verbal N}'   (H&T)
       [siːn-ki]   'bell {verbal noun}'   (H&T)
       [siːn kidaːj]   'the ringing of bells'   (67#465)
       [konwən]   'convent'   (102#753)
       [grænpəpa]~[grænpə]   'grandfather'   (73#492)

The palatal nasal [ɲ] does not occur word-finally, so no assimilation data can be provided for it. In addition [ɲ] does not occur word-initially, and in intervocalic position it optionally becomes a nasalized glide [j̃] (Smith 1978:92). This means that [ɲ] has a very restricted distribution, only obligatorily occurring in medial codas before an alveo-palatal: [ɲt͡ʃ] and [ɲd͡ʒ]. It is therefore possible to treat [ɲ] as an allophone of /n/, assimilating to palatals (as in Catalan).

The same heterorganicity restrictions that relate to nasals hold for the coronal liquids [l ɾ] in codas.

(60)   Liquid clusters
       (a) [l]+C
          [kuːlpə]   'guilt'   [aːltu]   'tall, high'
          [əlkonsaː]   'consult'   [əlfaːdə]   'pillow'
       (b) [ɾ]+C
          [koːɾpu]   'body'   [gaːɾfu]   'fork'
          [koɾtaː]   'cut, slaughter' [pəɾsə]   'see, appear'
          [poːɾku]   'pig'

In short, only labials and dorsals undergo assimilation in SLP creole assimilation; coronals are exempt.

The leading idea behind the following analysis of SLP creole is that coronals do not assimilate because they are already 'adequately unmarked'. Coronal+C clusters are less marked than non-coronal+C clusters, so allowing them to survive in SLP creole. The leading idea is formalized in the present theory through the structure of the anti-heterorganic output constraints. For Marked-Cluster constraints of the type *{x}{dors,lab,cor}, coronal+C clusters incur a proper subset of the violations of other clusters. So, while [n{p,k}] violates only *{dors,lab,cor}{dors,lab,cor}, [m{t,k}] also violates *{dors,lab}{dors,lab,cor}, and [ŋ{p,t}] further violates *{dors}{dors,lab,cor}. Because of this local harmonic bounding relation, there is effectively a hierarchy of cluster types: ŋ{t,p} 〉 m{k,t} 〉 n{p,k}. SLP creole aims to avoid only the

4.3 *Undergoers of assimilation*   189

most-marked clusters, which include all clusters whose first element is more marked than coronal.

The Marked-Cluster constraint that is responsible for the SLP creole system is *{dors,lab}{dors,lab,cor}. This constraint bans non-coronal+C clusters but not coronal+C ones. *{dors,lab}{dors,lab,cor} must outrank all PoA-faithfulness constraints that preserve dorsal or labial PoA – i.e. all faithfulness constraints (only IDENT{dors,lab,cor} is given in the tableau below for the sake of brevity).

(61)   SLP creole I

/miti:ŋ-pə/	*{dors,lab}{dors,lab,cor}	IDENT{dors,lab,cor}
(a) miti:ŋpə	*!	
☞ (b) miti:mpə		*

The ranking in tableau (61) cannot force coronal+non-coronal clusters to assimilate. For example, from /si:n-pə/, the faithful output [si:npə] will not violate *{dors,lab}{dors,lab,cor} because it has a coronal as its first member. Thus, nothing favours the assimilated form *[si:mpə], and so the faithfulness constraint IDENT{dors,lab,cor} makes the crucial decision, favouring the unassimilated [si:npə].

(62)   SLP creole II

/si:n-pə/	*{dors,lab}{dors,lab,cor}	IDENT{dors,lab,cor}
(a) si:mpə		*!
☞ (b) si:npə		

To ensure that coronals do not undergo assimilation, some faithfulness constraint to coronals – i.e. IDENT{dors,lab,cor} – must outrank all constraints that ban coronal+non-coronal clusters – i.e. *{dors,lab,cor}{dors,lab,cor} (and also *{dors,lab,cor}{dors,lab}, *{dors,lab,cor}{dors}).

(63)   SLP creole III

/si:n-pə/	*{dors,lab}{dors,lab,cor}	IDENT{dors,lab,cor}	*{dors,lab,cor}{dors,lab,cor}
(a) si:mpə		*!	
☞ (b) si:npə			*

As in Catalan, onset-IDENT{dors,lab,cor} ensures that assimilation is regressive.

190   *4 Preservation of the Marked*

To summarize, systems in which unmarked elements are exempt (marked-undergoer systems) come about through the action of output constraints. Unmarked elements are exempt in such systems because they are already 'unmarked enough'. In general terms, the ranking needed for marked-only undergoer systems involves (i) an output constraint that targets marked elements alone outranking all faithfulness constraints that preserve those elements and (ii) faithfulness constraints that preserve unmarked elements outranking all output constraints that would eliminate those elements. For example, in SLP creole the constraint *{dors,lab}{dors,lab,cor} targets marked consonant clusters alone. This constraint outranked all PoA-faithfulness constraints. Since coronals do not undergo assimilation, IDENT{dors,lab,cor} has to outrank all output constraints that banned heterorganic coronal-initial clusters (e.g. *{dors,lab,cor}{dors,lab,cor}). This point is schematized in diagram (64), which summarizes the rankings identified above.

(64)   Sri Lankan Portuguese creole assimilation ranking

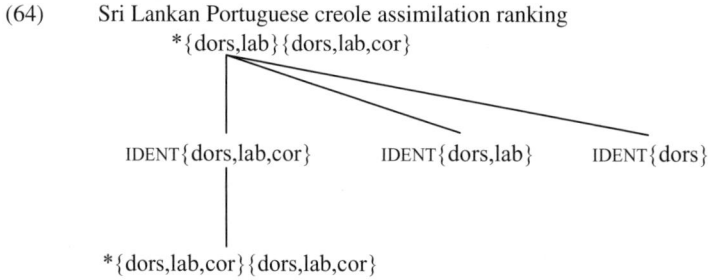

An alternative to the analysis just provided relies on faithfulness to block coronal assimilation: a constraint like IDENT{coronal} would outrank all anti-heterorganicity constraints (analogous to the Catalan analysis). So, from /siːn-pə/, the assimilated candidate *[siːmpə] would be eliminated due to the fact that it is unfaithful to the input coronal specification, fatally violating IDENT{coronal}. In contrast, /maːm-ki/→[maːŋki] does not violate IDENT{coronal}, allowing the anti-heterorganic constraints to do their job. While an analysis with the 'unmarked-faithfulness' constraint IDENT{coronal} does in principle work for SLP creole, §4.4 will show that it cannot replace the Marked-Cluster constraints. In contrast, the Marked-Cluster constraints are needed for independent reasons, so such 'unmarked-faithfulness' constraints are redundant.

On the empirical side, it has been claimed that marked-undergoer systems do not exist (Mohanan 1993:63,76; Jun 1995:33,70ff.), so some further support is provided here. The SLP creole-type system is common among Australian languages. For example, Alyawarra allows both homorganic and coronal codas, but no other types: e.g. [inpima] 'get', [aranka] 'beard', [antira] 'fat', [ampa] 'child', [aŋka] 'child' (Yallop 1977). Other examples include Bardi (Metcalfe 1975), Kuuku Ya'u (Thompson 1988), Lardil (Hale 1973), Ngawun Mayi (Breen 1981), Ngiyambaa (Donaldson 1980), Nhanda (Blevins 2001), and Nunggubuyu (Heath 1984). Sources for several of the languages show alternations. For example, Nunggubuyu eliminates dorsals in heterorganic clusters in a variety of ways, but always retains coronals.

(65)   Nunggubuyu: marked-undergoers only
    (a) /ŋ/ assimilation and /g/ deletion
        root   [gulmuŋ] 'belly'   [wulug] 'soft'
        +pergressive [ama-gulmum-baɟ]   [ama-wulu-baɟ]
        +locative   [gulmun-duɟ]   [wulu-duɟ]
        +relative   [ama-gulmuɲ-ɟinjuŋ] [ama-wulu-ɟinjuŋ]
    (b) /n/ and /d/ preservation
        [man-bajama] '(group) to keep going' [wadbar] 'grevillea'
        [a-muːn-baɟ] 'by foot'   [gudga] 'to prod'
        [dan-garu-gaji] 'to have a bellyache'

Outside Australia, the Uralic language Saami has the same restriction (Bye 2001:139) and the Dravidian language Tamil's initial syllable codas act in the same way: dorsal and labial nasals undergo assimilation, and coronals do not (e.g. [tun.bā] 'sorrow', cf. /maːm-taːn/ → [maːndā] 'tree (emphatic)' – Beckman 1998:§2.4.4; Asher 1985; Christdas 1988). The Hokan language Seri has a similar restriction: /m/ assimilates, but /n/ does not (Marlett 1981): /i-m-kaː/→[iŋkaː] 'who does not look for it' (cf. [i-m-aː] 'who is not grinding', [soːmen_kaʔa] 'he will winnow', Marlett 1981:16–17). Finally, Hamer (South Omotic) bans *{dors,lab}{dors,lab,cor} clusters as well, but resolves violations (for obstruent-obstruent clusters) through metathesis: /ep-sa/ → [es.pa] 'cause to cry', /wob-sa/ → [wospa] 'make bent', /ʊs-ka/ → [ʊksʌ] 'cause to spear' (Lydall 1976:404; Zoll 1998). For a discussion of how the Marked-Cluster constraints produce metathesis, see de Lacy 2002a:§7.5.1.3.

4.3.3 Typology

Catalan and Sri Lankan Portuguese creole represent only two of many possible 'selective' assimilation systems. While Catalan employs IDENT{dors,lab} to block assimilation, others use just IDENT{dors}, or IDENT{dors,lab,cor}. Similarly, while SLP creole uses *{dors,lab}{dors,lab,cor} to motivate assimilation, others use just *{dors}{dors,lab,cor}. Table (66) lists the full range of predicted systems. The columns 'dors', 'lab', and 'cor' indicate whether the relevant PoA undergoes assimilation: an ✗ indicates that the PoA does not assimilate, and the ✓ indicates that it does assimilate. For example, the Catalan entry indicates that coronals undergo assimilation while dorsals and labials do not.

(66)   Assimilation undergoers

dors	lab	cor	Case
✓	✓	✓	Diola Fogny nasals (Sapir 1965)
✗	✓	✓	Korean stops and nasals (Jun 1995; de Lacy 2002a) (Baffin Inuktitut oral stops – Dorais 1986)
✗	✗	✓	Yamphu stops (§4.2.1, Rutgers 1998) Catalan nasals (§4.3.1)
✗	✗	✗	Gujarati nasals (§4.3.3.1, Cardona 1965) Southern Sierra Miwok nasals (§4.3.3.1, Broadbent 1964)
✓	✗	✗	Chukchi nasals (§4.3.3.2)
✓	✓	✗	Sri Lankan Portuguese creole nasals (§4.3.2)
✓	✗	✓	Harar Oromo stops (§4.3.3.2, Owens 1985) Bole nasals (§4.3.3.2, Schuh 2005)
✗	✓	✗	Seri (Stemberger 1992; Marlett 1981)

Glottals are not mentioned in the table for two reaons. One is that many glottal nasals have been reported as velar [ŋ], so it is difficult at the present time to identify many clear cases of glottal nasal assimilation. In any case, it is difficult to find languages where glottals end up in the right position to undergo assimilation. Even so, glottals do undergo assimilation in Yamphu and Gujarati (see §4.3.3.1).

The two cases in which only dorsals fail to undergo assimilation are taken from Jun (1995). Baffin Inuktitut requires special mention. Dorais (1986) identifies the Inuktitut dialects of Baffin Island as allowing only dorsal+non-dorsal heterorganic clusters (e.g. [iɣlu] 'house', [uqsuq] 'blubber, oil'). PoA assimilation is synchronically active in these dialects, but only demonstrable for coronals. Bobaljik (1996:§4) comments that, while there are no labial+non-labial clusters, there are no synchronic alternations involving them because there seem to be no labial-final stems. Consequently, Baffin Inuktitut only tentatively fills this typological gap, based on the highly questionable assumption that (as they did diachronically) underlying labials assimilate in PoA, so accounting for the surface absence of labial+non-labial clusters. Korean is a more robust case – there are clear alternations in which both coronals and labials assimilate while dorsals do not. The one catch is that labials only assimilate before dorsals; this restriction is due to certain triggering effects imposed by the Marked-Cluster constraints (de Lacy 2002a:§7.5.2).

4.3.3.1 Unmarked undergoers

At one extreme of preservation IDENT{dors,lab,cor(,gl)} outranks the Marked-Cluster constraints. Such a language has no assimilation at all, as in Southern Sierra Miwok (Broadbent 1964):

(67) Southern Sierra Miwok lack of assimilation
      [sympy:] 'close eyes'   [ponpu:] 'to get dusk'   [kawenpa] 'shout at s.o.'
      [ʔymty:] 'to sing'   [tyntyn:y:] 'to think'   [contita?] 'crooked'
      [homcupa?] 'barber'   [palanca?] 'flatiron'
      [momko?] 'moccasins'   [tynkyn:a:] 'to maim'   [cinku?] 'seed basket'

At the other extreme is Diola Fogny (Sapir 1965:16): when *{dors,lab,cor} {dors,lab,cor} outranks all PoA faithfulness constraints all PoAs assimilate.

(68) Diola Fogny nasal assimilation
      (a) /n/: /pan+ɟi+maɲɟ/   →[paɲɟimaɲɟ]   'you (pl) will know'
      (b) /m/: /ni +RED+gam/   →[nigaŋgam]   'I judge'
      (c) /ɲ/: /ku+RED+bɔɲ/   →[kubɔmbɔɲ]   'they sent'
      (d) /ɲ/: /na+ RED+ti:ŋ/   →[nati:nti:ŋ]   'he cut (it) through'

The faithfulness constraints also predict a language in which only dorsals are preserved in heterorganic clusters, since dorsals are the most-marked elements.

To get a system in which only dorsals escape assimilation, IDENT{dorsal} must outrank all the Marked-Cluster constraints, and *{dors,lab,cor} {dors,lab,cor} must outrank all the other PoA faithfulness constraints.

Glottals often do not end up in the right environments to assimilate – they are often banned from coda position, or are subjected to a variety of other processes like deletion. Nevertheless, glottals both undergo and trigger assimilation in some languages. In the present theory, 'glottal' is the least-marked PoA, so glottals are expected to pattern with coronals in unmarked-undergoer systems. For example, in Yamphu only glottal and coronal stops undergo total assimilation to a following obstruent – like Catalan, labials and dorsals are exempt (Rutgers 1998). The data in (69) is from Rutgers (1998:43); for justification of underlying forms, see §2.1 and Rutgers 1998.

(69) Yamphu stop assimilation: coronals and glottals only
      (a) /ʔ+ C/ → [C:]
          /ham-beʔ-te/   → [hambet:e]   'where?'
          /hago-noʔ-so/   → [hagonos:o]   'even only now'
      (b) /t + C/ → [C:]
          /pi:t-kʰad-a/   → [pi:kːʰada]   'it started boiling'
          /læ:t-pe-ma/   → [læp:ema]   'to do'
          /kit-si-ma/   → [kis:ima]   'to feel fear'

(c) /p + C/ → [pC]
　[op<u>t</u>aŋ]　'head scarf'
　[ke<u>p</u>-<u>k</u>ʰad-i]　'Let's go sticking'
　[wa<u>ps</u>a]　'chick'

(d) /k + C/ → [kC]
　[kʰaː<u>k</u>-<u>p</u>a]　'scrape one's throat + perform act'
　[a<u>kt</u>ok]　'like that'
　[tsi<u>kts</u>iʔ]　'nasty, repugnant'
　[tsu<u>ks</u>um]　'six days ago'

There are clear alternations involving /ʔ/-assimilation. The possessive is underlyingly /æʔæ/: e.g. [k-æʔæ] 'I+{possessive}', but before consonants the final vowel deletes: e.g. [jiːw-<u>æʔ</u>-mu] 'river-poss.-down'. Final-vowel deletion often creates a [ʔ]+obstruent cluster. As expected, the [ʔ] is eliminated before stops through gemination: e.g. /hæŋguw- æʔæ-tw-e/ → ([æ]-*deletion* [hæŋguæʔtwe] →) [hæŋguætːwe] 'of the one of Hæŋguwa' (Rutgers 1998:65), *[hæŋguæʔtwe]; /maguw-æʔæ-tu/ → [maguwætːu] 'of Maguwa'. As in Catalan, dorsal and labial assimilation is blocked by IDENT{dors,lab} in Yamphu. The following tableaux illustrate the ranking.

(70)

/ham-beʔ-te/	IDENT {dors,lab}	*{dors,lab,cor,gl} {dors,lab,cor,gl}	IDENT {dors,lab,cor,gl}	IDENT {dors,lab,cor}
(a) hambeʔte		*!		
☞ (b) hambetːe			*	*

(71)

/aktok/	IDENT {dors,lab}	*{dors,lab,cor,gl} {dors,lab,cor,gl}	IDENT {dors,lab,cor,gl}
(a) atːok	*!		*
☞ (b) aktok		*	

Gujarati is similar to Yamphu but differs in that only the glottal nasal [N] assimilates: e.g. /səN-tap/→[səntap] 'affliction', cf. [dʒə<u>mt</u>o] 'dining', [mə<u>np</u>ətidʒ] 'soothing of mind', [kə<u>nb</u>i] 'peasant' (Cardona 1965:27). In this language, IDENT{dors,lab,cor} outranks the assimilation-causing constraint, preventing all but glottals from assimilating. For further discussion on assimilation and how the present theory compares to other approaches, see §8.4.

4.3.3.2 Marked and mixed undergoer systems

The Marked-Cluster constraints also predict languages in which only dorsals undergo assimilation, and languages in which all but glottals undergo assimilation. Finally, a mixture of markedness and reduction and marked faithfulness produces a language in which only 'medium markedness' elements — i.e. labials — assimilate.

The most-marked cluster consists of a dorsal+C. Such a sequence violates all of the relevant Marked-Cluster constraints: i.e. *{dors}{dors,lab,cor}, *{dors,lab}{dors,lab,cor}, and *{dors,lab,cor}{dors,lab,cor}. The constraint *{dors}{dors,lab,cor} sets dorsal+non-dorsal clusters apart from all other types, predicting a language that tolerates all heterorganic clusters except for this type: i.e. ✓[nt np nk], ✓[mp mt mk], *[ŋp ŋt], ✓[ŋk]. Chukchi provides a relevant system (Bogoras 1922; Krause 1980; Odden 1987). In this language, only /ŋ/ assimilates to the PoA of a following consonant; /m/ and /n/ remain unchanged.

Of the /ŋ/–assimilation examples below, (i)–(xii) have the morpheme /teŋ/ (e.g. [teŋ-əl?-ən] 'good'). A vowel harmony process forces the vowel to change. (xiii) is a reduplicated form, where the correspondent of the base's [ŋ] agrees with the following consonant's PoA. The root in (xiv) is underlying /t͡ʃeŋl/, as seen when it appears on its own: i.e. [t͡ʃeŋəl/. The examples marked O below are from Odden 1987:12, those from Bogoras 1922 are marked B, and those from Krause (1980) are marked K, the latter two with a following page number.

(72)   Chukchi /ŋ/ assimilation
       (a) /ŋ/ assimilates
           (i)   [tam-pera-k]   'to look good'   (O)
           (ii)   [tam-pera-e]   'he appeared well'   (B655)
           (iii) [tam-vairgin]   'good state of things' (B655)
           (iv)   [tam-wa-rəry-ən]   'good life'   (K21)
           (v)   [tam-waŋeirgin]   'good work'   (B655)
           (vi)   [tan-t͡ʃai]   'good tea'   (B655)
           (vii) [tan-t͡ʃott͡ʃot]   'good pillow'   (K21)
           (viii) [tan-l̩əmŋəl̩]   'good story'   (O)
           (ix)   [tan-leut]   'cleaver head'   (B655)
           (x)   [tan-ran]   'a good house'   (B655)
           (xi)   [tan-r?arqə]   'good breastband'   (O)
           (xii) [ten-jəlqet-ək]   'to sleep well'   (K21)
           (xiii) [p?om-p?oŋ]   'mushroom'   (K21)
           (xiv) [t͡ʃenl-ət]   'drawers'   (K21)
           (xv)   [telen-remkin]   'ancient people'   (B655)
           (xvi) [telen-jep]   'long time ago'   (B655)

(b) /m/ and /n/ do not assimilate

[valvimtilanaŋ]	'to Raven-Man'	(B667)
[gumnin]	'my left hand'	(B659)
[miml-ət]	'place near the water'	(K41)
[təmk-ən]	'hummock (abs.sg)	(K40)
[nə-mkə-kin]	'often'	(O)
[ramki t͡ʃin]	'people'	(B665)
[tumɣ-ə-tum]	'comrade'	(K40)
[mɲe-eŋeŋilin]	'sacrificing shaman'	(B660)
[umqə]	'polar bear'	(K40)
[n-i-np-u-qin]	'old one'	(B658)
[ɣa-n-pera-w-l̩en]	'decorated'	(O)
[mit-i-nmu-ut]	'we killed you(sg)'	(B659)
[ningdlinin]	'hand'	(B658)
[ŋinqej]	'boy (abs.sg)	(K40)

The restriction identified above holds of all NC clusters: whether morpheme-internal or across morpheme boundaries, [m] and [n] can appear before any consonant but [ŋ] can only appear before a velar (Bogoras 1922:652).

There is a variety of evidence that Chukchi 'ŋ' is a velar [ŋ] and not glottal [N]. Like velar /k/, /ŋ/ spirantizes to [ɣ] intervocalically: e.g. [kətəjɣat-ək], cf. [ɣa-ɣtəjɣat-len] 'the wind blew', [rat͡ʃwən-ək] cf. [mət-rat͡ʃwəɣ-mək] 'we competed'. In contrast, /ʔ/ does not spirantize, and /m/ and /n/ remain faithful before another nasal (e.g. [gumnin] 'my left hand', [mɲe-eŋeŋilin] 'sacrificing shaman', [mit-i-nmu-ut] 'we killed you (sg)' – Bogoras 1922). As /ŋ/ patterns like the velar /k/ in undergoing spirantization *and* the output of spirantization is a velar [ɣ], there is good reason to consider Chukchi 'ŋ' velar.

In the present theory, only dorsal+non-dorsal clusters violate the constraint *{dors}{dors,lab,cor}. So, with this Marked-Cluster constraint outranking all faithfulness constraints, only dorsal+non-dorsal clusters will be eliminated. To prevent assimilation of labials and coronals, at least IDENT{dors,lab,cor} must outrank all other cluster constraints (i.e. *{dors,lab}{dors,lab,cor}, *{dors,lab,cor}{dors,lab,cor}).

(73)   Chukchi I: Dorsals assimilate

/teŋ-perak/	*{dors} {dors,lab,cor}	IDENT {dors,lab,cor}	*{dors,lab} {dors,lab,cor}	*{dors,lab,cor} {dors,lab,cor}
(a) taŋperak	*!		*	*
☞ (b) tamperak		*		

(74)   Chukchi II: Labials and coronals do not assimilate

/təmk-ən/	*{dors} {dors,lab,cor}	IDENT {dors,lab,cor}	*{dors,lab} {dors,lab,cor}	*{dors,lab,cor} {dors,lab,cor}
(a) təŋkən		*!		
☞ (b) təmkən				*

For an analogous case, see Uradhi (Crowley 1983:321).

In summary, the typological predictions of the Marked-Cluster theory are borne out for marked-undergoer systems.

To complete the typology, the present theory predicts that a language could combine properties of Chukchi and Catalan. The Ethiopic language Harar Oromo does just this: it is like Catalan in that a marked PoA is exempt from assimilation (i.e. labials) but a less-marked PoA (coronal) is not; Harar Oromo is also like SLP creole in that a marked PoA (dorsal) undergoes assimilation while a less-marked one (labial) does not. The net result is that only labials are exempt from assimilation.

Harar Oromo has the consonants in (75) (Owens 1985; Lloret 1992).

(75)   Harar Oromo consonants

		labial	coronal	(alveo-) palatal	dorsal	glottal
stops	−vd		t	tʃ	(k)	ʔ
	ejective	p'	t'	tʃ'	k'	
	+vd	b	d	dʒ	g	
	implosive		ɗ			
fricatives		f	s	ʃ	x	h
			z			
nasals		m	n	ɲ		
liquids			l	r		
glides		w		j		

Syllables have the form (C)V(ː)(C). [k] has a limited distribution: it only appears as a geminate or as the second consonant of a consonant cluster: e.g. [mukːeːni] 'trees, forest', [ark] 'see'.

The examples relevant to present concerns involve stop assimilation. As shown in (76a), dorsal stops assimilate to form a geminate with a following consonant; [x] also optionally assimilates.[13] In contrast, labials do not (76b).

(76) Harar Oromo assimilation (data from Owens 1985)
  (a) Dorsal + C$_2$ → [C$_2$:]
/hok' + ne/	→ [hojnne]	'we scratched'	(p.24)
/meːk' + te/	→ [meːtt'e]	'you turned'	(p.22)
/d'iːk'+ na/	→ [d'iːjnna]	'we wash'	(p.23)
/fiːg + te/	→ [fiːjdde]	'you escaped'	(p.23)
/d'uːg + ne/	→ [d'uːjnne]	'we drank'	(p.23)
/beːx + ne/	→ [beːnne]	'we know' {optional}	(p.23)

  (b) Labial + [C$_2$] → No change
/tʃ'ap' + ti/	→ [tʃ͡'ap't'i]	'it (fem.) breaks'	(p.22)
/k'ab + ta/	→ [k'abda]	'you have'	(p.23)
/gub + tan/	→ [gubdan]	'you (pl) burn something'	(p.23)

There are no root+suffix alternations showing that coronals assimilate in PoA since all suffixes seem to only contain coronals. However, coronal nasals in prefixes assimilate to the PoA of a following stem consonant: /hin-waːdu/ → [hiwwaːdu] 'he doesn't bake', /hin-jaːdu/ → [hijjaːdu] 'he doesn't think', /hin-raftu/ → [hirraftu] 'you don't lie down'. Coronals also assimilate in manner and voice: e.g. /d'iːt'+na/ → [d'iːnna] 'we kick'; /did+ne/ → [dinne] 'we refused'; /haːd^ʔ +tiː/ → [haːttiː] 'mother {nominative}' (Owens 1985:24).[14]

The same assimilation pattern is also found in the Southern Oromo languages Boraana, Orma, and Waata for plain stop+coronal clusters (Lloret 1992:259ff.). The Western Oromo languages differ in that only coronals assimilate (i.e. the Catalan system).

Underlying geminate labials surface faithfully in the language: e.g. [lapp'eː] 'heart', [gubbaː] 'on top' (Owens 1985:14). So, the failure of labials to assimilate cannot be ascribed to a surface ban on labial geminates. Since coronals undergo assimilation, the Marked-Cluster constraint *{dors,lab,cor}{dors, lab,cor} must outrank IDENT{dors,lab,cor}. No other relevant Marked-Cluster

---

13 Assimilation is accompanied by diphthongization, described by Owens (1985:24) as 'a strong palatalization in the vowel preceding the velar consonant': e.g. /hok'-ne/ → [hojnːe] 'we scratched'. The diphthong formed has the same status as underlying /Vj/ clusters, shown by the fact that raising (/aj/→[eː] – e.g. /d'agaj-sis/ → [d'ageːsis] 'make someone hear') can optionally apply to them: e.g. /lag-niː/ → [leːnːiː]∼[lajnːiː] 'river+nom'. For further discussion, see Owens 1985:20, 23–4.

14 Consonant clusters with [ʔ] as the first member are eliminated by totally assimilating the /ʔ/ to the preceding vowel: /deːbiʔ+ti/ → [deːbiti], *[deːbitːi] 'she returns' (Owens 1985:20). Owens does not report any clusters with /tʃ/ as the first member.

4.3 *Undergoers of assimilation* 199

constraint (i.e. *{dors}{dors,lab,cor} and *{dors,lab}{dors,lab,cor}) can be used because these do not ban coronal+non-coronal clusters.

(77)   Harar Oromo I

/hin-waːdu/	*{dors,lab,cor}{dors,lab,cor}	IDENT{dors,lab,cor}
(a) hinwaːdu	*!	
☞ (b) hiwwaːdu		*

The Catalan-like aspect of Harar Oromo relates to labials. As in Catalan, labials are exempt from assimilation but the less-marked coronals are not. As shown for Catalan, the only way to account for this fact is to have a PoM-faithfulness constraint blocking assimilation of labials. In ranking terms, the constraint IDENT{dors,lab} must outrank *{dors,lab,cor}{dors,lab,cor}, as shown in tableau (78).

(78)   Harar Oromo II

/t͡ʃap'+ti/	IDENT {dors,lab}	*{dors,lab,cor} {dors,lab,cor}	IDENT {dors,lab,cor}
(a) t͡ʃatt'i	*!		*
☞ (b) t͡ʃap't'i		*	

However, there is an important difference between Harar Oromo and Catalan. Neither labials nor dorsals assimilate in Catalan, but dorsals assimilate in Harar Oromo. In this respect, Harar Oromo is like Chukchi – dorsals assimilate while the less-marked labials do not.

As in Chukchi, then, some constraint that bans dorsal+non-dorsal clusters must dominate all constraints that preserve dorsals – i.e. IDENT{dors,lab}, IDENT{dors}. This ranking is shown in tableau (79).

(79)   Harar Oromo III

/meːk' + te/	*{dors}{dors,lab,cor}	IDENT{dors,lab}
(a) meːk't'e	*!	
☞ (b) meːtt'e		*

No other output constraint will work. For example, *{dors,lab}{dors,lab,cor} must be ranked below IDENT{dors,lab}, otherwise labials would assimilate. Similarly, there is no faithfulness constraint that can force dorsals to assimilate. Diagram (80) shows the full ranking of the constraints.

(80)   Harar Oromo assimilation ranking

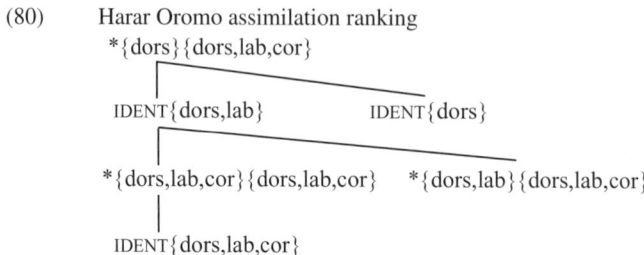

The diagram shows aspects of both the marked- and unmarked-undergoer rankings identified. Having the PoM-faithfulness constraint IDENT{dors,lab} outrank the anti-heterorganic cluster constraint *{dors,lab,cor}{dors,lab,cor} blocks marked elements from assimilating, as in Catalan. Marked elements alone are forced to assimilate through having the Marked-Cluster constraint *{dors}{dors,lab,cor} outrank the relevant faithfulness constraints (IDENT{dors,lab} and IDENT{dors}), just as in SLP creole and Chukchi.

In short, Harar Oromo shows that languages cannot be classed as having either 'marked undergoers' or 'unmarked undergoers'. As predicted by the free ranking of constraints, a language may have both aspects – in effect being a hybrid form of Catalan and Chukchi.

Harar Oromo is not alone. The Chadic language Bole has the same system as Harar Oromo's, but with nasal consonants.

(81)   Bole nasal assimilation, with labials exempt (Schuh 2005:§1.8.1)
      (a) /n/+C
        (i) /n/ 'I'   (ii) /gòj:an/ 'they bought a'
        cf. [ǹ iː wùi] 'I did pregnancy' [gòj:am bùːri] 'they bought a water pot'
        [ǹ zaluwòːji] 'I began' [gòj:an teːɓile] 'they bought a scoop'
        [m̀ pàtaːwò] 'I became thin' [gòj:aŋ gàŋga] 'they bought a drum'
        [ŋ̀ konuwòji] 'I took (it)' [gòj:aN ʔàdà] 'they bought a dog'
        [Ǹ ʔàlaːtùwo] 'I carried (it)'[15] [gòj:aɲ jàːwi] 'they bought a chicken'
      (b) /m/+C
        [kùrùm-nì] 'his fingernail' [kùrùm-tò] 'her fingernail'
        [gà dòm-no] 'in front of me' [gà dòm-ko] 'in front of you'
      (c) /ŋ/+C
        [gájáŋ] 'the pot'
        [gájám paːwò] 'the pot is closed'
        [gáján tàɓaːwò] 'the pot is red'
        [gájáɲ ʔjoruwò] 'the pot is erect'

---

15 This example is transcribed [ŋ̀ ʔàlātùwo] in the original. Following the discussion in §3.4.2, I assume that it is [N].

4.3 Undergoers of assimilation 201

As a final comment on the typology, marked-undergoer systems are not a peculiarity of PoA assimilation. Wetzels & Mascaró (2001) identify a number of such cases in voice assimilation. In these systems, only segments with the marked [+voice] feature assimilate; voiceless segments do not (Yorkshire English, Parisian French, and Ya:thê). Mekkan Arabic also has this type of system: voiced stops assimilate to voiceless stops, but not vice versa (Abu-Mansour 1996; Bakalla 1973).

The Marked-Cluster constraints can trigger more changes than assimilation. Due to OT's 'heterogeneity of target, homogeneity of process' property, they can trigger deletion, neutralization, and metathesis as well (de Lacy 2002a:§7.5, §7.6). Finally, they also make a number of predictions about direction of assimilation; these are discussed in detail elsewhere (de Lacy 2002a:§7.7.1.1) and will not be explored here, as it will be too great a digression.

4.3.4 Summary

The preceding discussion has shown how PoM-faithfulness constraints can block assimilation. The theory not only predicts that unmarked-undergoer systems exist, but that for every possible set of marked feature values there can be a system in which only those values are exempt from assimilation (or some other anti-heterorganic process). With the PoA hierarchy | dorsal 〉 labial 〉 coronal 〉 glottal |, then, there should be a system in which elements from the following sets are exempt from assimilation: {dorsal}, {dorsal, labial}, {dorsal, labial, coronal}. Almost all predicted cases are attested, as discussed in §3.3.

In all cases, the ranking has the same character: a faithfulness constraint that preserves marked feature values outranks the anti-heterorganic output constraints, which in turn outranks all faithfulness constraints that preserve the lesser marked feature values. Schematically, each system had the ranking || IDENT{*marked*} » M » IDENT{*marked,unmarked*} ||, where IDENT{*marked*} and IDENT{*marked,unmarked*}, in this instance, refer to marked and unmarked values of the Major PoA hierarchy.

Of course, the same point can be made for any feature, as there are PoM-faithfulness constraints for all features. So, the same effects should be seen for features like [voice], [nasal], and so on. For voicing, for example, the predictions are borne out. Bethin (1987) and Butska (1997) report that only the unmarked [−voice] segments assimilate in voicing to the following segment in Ukrainian (e.g. /borot + ba/ → [borodba] 'fight'). Voiced segments do not assimilate (e.g. [ridko] 'rarely').

Finally, only coda-onset assimilation has been discussed here. The existence of marked faithfulness constraints makes predictions for within-constituent assimilation as well. By having a ranking such as the one provided in §6.2 for Swedish, within-constituent assimilation can be to the unmarked value: e.g. /abt/ → [apt], /apd/ → [apt]. In contrast, by having IDENT [+voice] ranked appropriately, voice assimilation in coda constituents can be to the marked value: i.e. /abt/ → [abd], /apd/ → [abd]. The former of these cases is attested in a number of languages, as observed by Baković (1999b). Baković claims that the latter type is not attested, though the empirical grounds for this assertion are not made clear. Future research will no doubt determine whether within-constituent assimilation can be to either marked or unmarked values, and if – like Catalan – marked elements can be exempt from assimilation.

4.4   The form of faithfulness constraints

The preceding sections have made the empirical claim that any subset of PoA values can undergo PoA assimilation and neutralization. The theoretical claim is that there are two opposing pressures that produce this apparent lack of regard for markedness. Preservation of the Marked, expressed as the PoM-faithfulness constraints, can prevent marked elements from assimilating and neutralizing, while markedness reduction, in the form of the Marked-Cluster constraints and PoA output constraints, can exempt unmarked elements from assimilating/neutralizing.

An alternative is to say that there is no need for faithfulness constraints that refer to marked elements, and to rely entirely on output constraints to do the job. Section 4.4.1 shows this approach to be empirically inadequate.

The final issue is whether the present theory has enough faithfulness constraints. Section 4.4.2 discusses whether there is need for faithfulness constraints that refer exclusively to unmarked elements (e.g. IDENT{coronal}).

4.4.1   Output-only alternatives

An alternative account of Yamphu coronal debuccalization uses output constraints. If there is a freely rankable *{coronal} constraint, Yamphu's neutralization follows from the ranking ‖ *{coronal} » IDENT{PoA} » *{dors,lab} ‖. The apparent benefit of this approach is that it eliminates the need for several different PoA faithfulness constraints. However, the insurmountable problem is that it effectively denies that markedness exists.

Allowing *{coronal} to outrank *{dors,lab} not only affects possible undergoers of neutralization, it also affects output targets. With *{coronal}, it is an easy matter to produce neutralization to labial PoA:

(82)

/at/	*−Δ_σ/ glottal	*{coronal}	*{dors,lab}	*{dors}
(a) aʔ	*!			
(b) at		*!		
(c) ak			*	*!
☠ (d) ap			*	

The death's head ☠ marks an output candidate that is unattested in every grammar, given the input. Neutralization of /t/ to [p] is of course unattested: it goes against the generalization that all 'horizontally context-free' neutralizations – i.e. those that are not influenced by neighbouring segments (as in assimilation, dissimilation) – result in a less-marked segment (§3.3; Trubetzkoy 1939:81ff.). In short, there is no alternative to cases like Yamphu but a faithfulness solution, and constraints like IDENT{dors,lab}.

The same point can be made for assimilation. An output-based approach to unmarked-undergoer systems would employ an output constraint that only bans coronal+non-coronal clusters – i.e. *{cor}{dors,lab}. This constraint assigns violations to [nk np], but not to [mk mt ŋp ŋt]. As the following tableaux show, *{cor}{dors,lab} can be used to produce the Catalan system without appealing to marked faithfulness constraints. The only faithfulness constraint used here is one that preserves all PoAs, called IDENT[Place] (cf. Prince 1998).

(83) The output-only approach to unmarked-undergoer systems

/son kuzins/	*{cor}{dors,lab}	IDENT[Place]
(a) son kuzins	*!	
☞ (b) soŋ kuzins		*

(84)

/som kuzins/	*{cor}{dors,lab}	IDENT[Place]
(a) soŋ kuzins		*!
☞ (b) som kuzins		

In short, only coronals undergo assimilation in an output-based approach because only they are subject to active output constraints.

The problem with such an approach is that it again has undesirable effects on the output of neutralization. The constraint *{cor}{dors,lab} can produce an unattested system in which word-medial coronal codas neutralize to labials:

i.e. input /an-ka/ surfaces as ☂[amka]. This type of neutralization is easy to generate with *{cor}{dors,lab}, as shown in tableau (85).

The constraint *{cor}{dors,lab} rules out the candidate with a coronal+non-coronal sequence (a), leaving ☂[amka] and *[aŋka]. IDENT{dors,lab,cor} is irrelevant in selecting the winner – its role is simply to ensure that dorsals are not neutralized in every position (by outranking *{dors}).

The crucial constraint for choosing between [amka] and *[aŋka] is the context-free output constraint *{dors}, which is violated for every instance of a dorsal in the output. As shown, *{dors} favours [amka] over [aŋka], thus producing neutralization of /n/ to [m]. All constraints that favour [aŋka] over [amka] are ranked below *{dors} (e.g. Marked-Cluster constraints like *{dors,lab}{dors,lab,cor}).

(85)

/anka/	*{cor}{dors,lab}	IDENT{dors,lab,cor}	*{dors}
(a) anka	*!		*
(b) aŋka		*	**!
☞ (c) amka		*	*

The neutralization of /n/ to [m] would only apply in heterorganic clusters. Homorganic codas remain faithful: /anta/ will surface as [anta] since *{cor}{dors,lab} is not violated by homorganic sequences. Furthermore, there is no constraint that *favours* [amta] over [anta] – such a constraint would have to be *{coronal}.

Of course, it is important to affirm that the Marked-Cluster constraints cannot produce any unattested neutralizations. There is no Marked-Cluster constraint that favours a marked PoA over an unmarked one in coda position. For example, *{dors,lab}{dors,lab,cor} favours coronals over dorsals and labials in codas; there is no *{cor}{dors,lab,cor}. In more general terms, in terms of the Marked-Cluster constraints, a cluster with the form xy is a local harmonic bound for zy, where x is less marked than z.

In short, the output-only approach to Catalan necessarily invokes an output constraint that makes unattested typological predictions. The only remaining option is a faithfulness approach that reflects PoM.

Apart from typology, there is a reason internal to Catalan to employ PoM-faithfulness constraints rather than appeal to output constraints. An output constraint like *{cor}{dors,lab} localizes labial- and dorsal-exemption to just assimilation. However, dorsals and labials fail to undergo other processes like stop gemination (§4.3.1.2). Stop gemination is not motivated by PoA assimilation, but by sonority restrictions at syllable boundaries. If there are no faithfulness constraints that specifically preserve non-coronals, the non-coronal exemption would have to be built into the syllable contact constraint as an 'except when' clause: i.e. 'Incur a violation for a cluster *xy* where *x* has lower sonority than *y*, except when *x* is a dorsal or a labial'. Tampering with the constraint in this way is highly undesirable, as constraint interaction should deal with 'except when' clauses in constraints (McCarthy 2001b:§1.3.3, §3.1.4, §3.2).

4.4.2   Are PoM-faithfulness constraints enough?
Cases like Yamphu and Catalan show that faithfulness constraints that refer to marked elements alone are necessary. Chapter 6 will show that faithfulness constraints must be stringently formulated (i.e. IDENT{dors,lab,cor} and IDENT{dors,lab}), rather than having constraints that refer to individual feature values. However, is there any reason to reject faithfulness constraints that do not refer to the most marked value? For example, could the PoM-faithfulness PoA constraints co-exist with constraints like IDENT{coronal}, IDENT{labial}, IDENT{dors,cor}, and so on?

It is extremely difficult to show that constraints like IDENT{coronal} and IDENT{labial} are empirically undesirable. However, from a theoretical point of view their existence would render the Marked Reference Hypothesis invalid for faithfulness constraints (§2.3.1). Also, in terms of parsimony they are undesirable because they allow for fundamentally different analyses of the same phenomena. For example, /k/ neutralization in Malay has an output-based account whereby *{dors} outranks all PoA faithfulness constraints (§3.3.1). If freely rankable IDENT{lab} and IDENT{cor} exist, then there would be a faithfulness-based analysis of Malay whereby IDENT{lab} and IDENT{cor} outranked *{dors,lab,cor} so preserving /p/ and /t/ faithfully, while *{dors,lab,cor} could outrank all other faithfulness constraints, allowing /k/→[?]. In fact, for every case of markedness reduction there would be output- and faithfulness-based alternatives.

One other way of approaching this issue is to ask whether there is any benefit to having freely rankable IDENT{labial} and IDENT{coronal}. They may well be useful if they could take the place of a range of other constraints, but they cannot. While IDENT{labial} and IDENT{coronal} offer an alternative way to analyse Malay /k/→[?], they cannot be the sole way to analyse markedness reduction. To elaborate, suppose that there were no output constraints like *{dors} and *{dors,lab} — there is only a *{dors,lab,cor} constraint. While Malay /k/→[?] could be dealt with, a host of other cases could not: neutralization to coronal requires a constraint like *{dors,lab} (§3.3.2), and languages in which dorsals delete but other stops do not require a constraint *{dors} (e.g. Siuslawan – Frachtenberg 1922).

The same question can be asked for assimilation: if IDENT{lab} and IDENT{cor} existed, could a variety of assimilation-related constraints be eliminated? Initially, the answer seems more promising. A language like Sri Lankan Portuguese creole, where only coronals fail to undergo assimilation, could be analysed by having IDENT{coronal} outrank a single assimilation constraint AGREE[PoA], which in turn outranks IDENT{dors}, and IDENT{dors,lab}. The result would be that only coronals escape assimilation. This sort of analysis seems like it would allow the elimination of Marked-Cluster constraints like *{dors,lab}{dors,lab,cor} from CON. However, the Marked-Cluster constraints cannot be so eliminated. Constraints like *{dors,lab}{dors,lab,cor} can also cause word-medial neutralization and deletion. For example, in Kiowa only word-medial codas undergo neutralization, a fact attributable to the Marked-Cluster constraint *{dors,lab,cor}{dors,lab,cor,gl} (de Lacy 2002a:§7.6.1). The faithfulness constraints cannot produce such a system on their own.

4.5 Summary: overt and covert markedness

Segmental inventories, neutralization, and assimilation have long been among the most-cited markedness diagnostics. However, the empirical claim in this chapter is that any set of segments can undergo neutralization, almost any inventory is possible, and any set of elements can undergo assimilation.

The lack of asymmetries in these phenomena makes it tempting to think that markedness is irrelevant. In formal terms, denying markedness would amount to having freely ranked *{dorsal}, *{labial}, *{coronal}, and *{glottal}. Certainly, it is easy to produce gapped inventories with such constraints: a [k p ʔ] inventory would be generated by having *{coronal} outrank PoA faithfulness constraints, which in turn would outrank *{dorsal}, *{labial}, and *{glottal}. However, such a proposal faces insurmountable difficulties: it cannot account for phenomena that do show markedness effects. For example, it would allow unattested freedom in the output of neutralization, such as /t/→[p] (§4.4.1), and epenthetic consonants would have any PoA: e.g. ranking *{coronal}, *{labial}, and *{glottal} over *{dorsal} would produce an unattested epenthetic [k].

Without freely rankable ouput constraints, the only remaining way to deal with neutralizations like Yamphu's is to appeal to 'Preservation of the Marked' and its formalization as faithfulness constraints that specifically mention marked PoAs.

4.5 Summary: overt and covert markedness 207

In short, the lack of overt, visible markedness effects is not evidence against the concept of markedness. In fact, it would be surprising if there were any absolutely clear markedness universals (cf. Bybee 2001:191) as there are a variety of phenomena that can obscure markedness asymmetries. Undergoers of neutralization and assimilation are cases in point: any subset of segments can be blocked from undergoing assimilation and neutralization, so on the surface it seems as if markedness is irrelevant to them. However, markedness still plays a significant role. Dorsals undergo neutralization in Malay and dorsals and labials assimilate in SLP creole for markedness reduction reasons. In contrast, dorsals and labials are exempt from neutralization in Yamphu and assimilation in Catalan for faithfulness reasons. So, there is a markedness asymmetry for undergoers of neutralization and assimilation; but it is 'covert' — i.e. it is visible at the level of constraint interaction, not in terms of the typology of phonological outputs.

5 *Conflation in reduction*

5.1 Introduction

In informal terms, this chapter aims to show that it is not correct to assert that '*x* is more marked than *y*'; instead, it is only ever accurate to assert that '*y* is never more marked than *x*'. The latter formulation allows for a situation in which the markedness distinction between *x* and *y* is collapsed, or 'conflated'. This chapter focuses on such conflation in markedness reduction; chapter 6 discusses conflation in preservation.

The following sections will argue that markedness-referring output constraints with stringent form like those in (1a) are empirically more adequate than those with a universally fixed ranking, like those in (1b) after Prince & Smolensky (1993) and Lombardi (1995, 1998, 2002). The symbol '»»' marks a universally invariant ranking. Stringent constraints allow all attested types of conflation, while those with a universally fixed ranking do not.

(1) Stringent form (a) vs. fixed ranking (b)
 (a) *{dors,lab,cor,gl}, *{dors,lab,cor}, *{dors,lab}, *{dors}
 (b) *dorsal »» *labial »» *coronal »» *glottal

The effects of markedness conflation can be seen in hierarchies that have more than two members, like the PoA and sonority hierarchies. Conflation can be seen when neutralization is blocked. To preview the argument presented in §5.2, Kashaya coda stops usually debuccalize: e.g. /mihjoq/→[mihjoʔ] 'woodrat', /watac/→[wataʔ] 'frog', /qʰamʔot/→[qʰaboʔ] 'garter snake', /mahsit̪/→[mahsiʔ] 'embers' (Buckley 1994). However, PoA neutralization is blocked when it would result in the loss of underlying aspiration or glottalization. For example, /kilakʰ/ 'eagle' cannot become *[kilaʔ] because neutralization of /kʰ/ to [ʔ] necessarily loses the aspiration — *[ʔʰ] is not a possible segment.

So what is the actual surface form of 'eagle'? Here is where markedness conflation plays a crucial role. If conflation is not possible, the output *must* become the next least-marked available segment: i.e. /kʰ/ should neutralize to [tʰ]. This point is easy to illustrate with a fixed ranking theory, as in tableau (2). The constraint IDENT[ʰ] requires the preservation of aspiration, and so blocks neutralization to [ʔ].

(2)   Fixed ranking: no conflation

/kilakʰ/	IDENT[ʰ]	*dorsal	*labial	*coronal
(a) kilaʔ	*!			
(b) kilakʰ		*!		
(c) kilapʰ			*!	
☞ (d) kilatʰ				*

The winner has /kʰ/→[tʰ] because [tʰ] has the least-marked PoA that is also capable of preserving aspiration.

The problem is that the actual form of 'eagle' is [kilakʰ], with preservation of underlying PoA. From a conflation point of view, /kʰ/ does not neutralize because dorsals, labials, and coronals are conflated in Kashaya – they are all treated as equally marked. Therefore, while there is a markedness benefit in neutralizing to glottals, there is no gain in neutralizing to coronals. The stringent constraints can model this conflation straightforwardly, as shown in tableau (3).

(3)

/kilakʰ/	IDENT[ʰ]	*{dors,lab,cor}	IDENT{dors,lab,cor}	*{dors,lab}
(a) kilaʔ	*!	* *		
(b) kilapʰ		* * *	*!	* *
(c) kilatʰ		* * *	*!	*
☞ (d) kilakʰ		* * *		* *

Candidate (c) does not beat (d) because both incur the same violations of *{dors,lab,cor}. The next decisive constraint is a faithfulness one – IDENT{dors,lab,cor}, which favours preservation as in (d).

In short, conflation and stringent constraints allow for the possibility that underlying features will be preserved when neutralization is blocked. In contrast, a theory without conflation – like the Fixed Ranking approach – predicts that neutralization should always produce the least-marked value available.

210   5 *Conflation in reduction*

The stringent constraints also allow conflation to be prevented, unlike some representational theories of neutralization (discussed below). In fact, they also allow the same language to have conflation in one area and lack of conflation in another. Section 5.3 shows how the constraints produce two such systems – Dutch vowel reduction and Gujarati sonority-driven stress.

Section 5.4 examines alternative approaches to conflation that use representational devices and restrict hierarchies to two members. Both are shown to be empirically inadequate.

5.2   PoA conflation

As discussed above, markedness conflation can be seen when phonological phenomena are blocked from producing the least-marked output. Such blocking is found in Kashaya, a Pomoan language of northern Califonia described and analysed in detail by Buckley (1994); I owe the following data, description, and a number of the analytical insights to this work, though Buckley's analysis employs a representational approach to neutralization (cf. §5.4).

Kashaya has PoA neutralization in codas (e.g. /sulemat/ → [sulemaʔ] 'rope'). However, neutralization is blocked when doing so would lose underlying secondary articulation (e.g. [kilakʰ] 'eagle', *[kilaʔ]) or result in an illicit segment (e.g. *[kilaʔʰ]). The main issue discussed here is why there is no neutralization to coronal PoA in blocking situations: e.g. *[kilatʰ]. Such neutralization offers an apparently excellent compromise: secondary articulation is preserved and PoA markedness in codas is minimized. There is no independent reason why [tʰ] should be ruled out – it is certainly permitted on the surface in Kashaya codas (e.g. [kúlwetʰ] 'cattle'); in fact, there is even a process that forces plain stops to become aspirated (§5.2.3).

Kashaya has the surface segments in (4). Buckley transcribes the glottalized consonants as ṗ, ṭ, ċ, etc.; here I use pʔ, tʔ, cʔ instead to make the discussion more transparent.

(4)   Kashaya segments (Buckley 1994:13)

	labial	coronal		palatal	velar	uvular	glottal
stops	p pʰ pʔ	t tʰ tʔ	t tʰ tʔ	c cʰ cʔ	k kʰ kʔ	q qʰ qʔ	ʔ
fricatives		s sʔ		ʃ			h
nasals	m mʰ mʔ	n nʰ nʔ					
liquids		l lʰ lʔ					
glides	w wʰ wʔ			j jʰ jʔ			

Only [ʃ] and [h] do not have glottalized counterparts. Fricatives are inherently aspirated (Vaux 1998). The syllable has the shape CV(X), where X is a vowel or consonant. The superheavy syllables CVVC and CVCC are only allowed word-finally (Buckley 1994:233).

Plain stops debuccalize in word-final codas, as shown in (5). Neutralization in word-medial codas is discussed in §5.2.3.

(5) Word-final plain stop debuccalization. (Buckley 1994:99ff., 68ff.)
 (a) /t/ → [ʔ]
  /qahmat̪/ → [qahmaʔ] 'angry'   cf. [qamat̪-ʔ] 'he's angry' (p.68)
  /ʃeʔet̪/ → [ʃeʔeʔ] 'basket'   cf. [ʃeʔet̪-ʔemu] 'that's a basket' (p.72)
  /mahsit̪/ → [mahsiʔ] 'embers'   cf. [masit̪-ʔ] 'it's embers' (p.68)
 (b) /t̺/ → [ʔ]
  /qʰamʔot̺/ → [qʰaboʔ] 'garter snake' [qʰabot-ʔ] 'it's a garter snake' (p.68)
  /sulemat̺/ → [sulemaʔ] 'rope'   cf. [sulemat-ʔ] 'it's a rope' (p.68)
 (c) /c/ → [ʔ]
  /watac/ → [wataʔ] 'frog'   cf. [watac-ʔiqʰ] 'it must be a frog' (p.73)
  /maːcac/ → [maːcaʔ] 'they'   cf. [maːcac-ʔeːmu] 'that's them' (p.72)
 (d) /q/ → [ʔ]
  /mihjoq/ → [mihjoʔ] 'woodrat'   cf. [mihjoq-ʔ] 'it's a woodrat' (p.69)
  /micʰaq/ → [micʰaːʔ] 'sweat'   cf. [micʰaq-ʔ] 'it's sweat' (p.69)

Before going forward, some clarification of the PoA features of uvulars is necessary. McCarthy (1994) identifies uvulars like [q] as both [dorsal] and [pharyngeal]. Consequently, constraints such as IDENT{dors} and *{dors} apply equally to velars and uvulars. Uvulars [q ɢ ɴ ʀ ʁ χ] are also [pharyngeal], a class which also includes glottals [ʔ h ɦ] and pharyngeals [ħ ʕ]. Evidence for the markedness of uvulars will be discussed in §5.2.4, as well as support for the feature [pharyngeal].

Like the debuccalizations in §3.3.1, this phenomenon can be analysed using *{dors,lab,cor} and PoA-faithfulness constraints, as shown in tableau (6). Candidate (d) wins because it neutralizes wherever it can – i.e. in codas. The onset-faithfulness constraints prevents neutralization in onsets, as in candidate (a) and (b)'s /m/→[N]. Candidate (c) fails to neutralize at all, so fatally violating *{dors,lab,cor}.

(6) Kashaya I

/mihjoq/	ONSET-IDENT {dors,lab,cor}	*{dors,lab,cor}	IDENT{dors,lab,cor}
(a) Nih.ʔoʔ	* *!		* * *
(b) Nih.joʔ	*!	*	* *
(c) mih.joq		* * *!	
☞ (d) mih.joʔ		* *	*

5.2.1 Blocking and conflation

Debuccalization is blocked in several environments in Kashaya. One is when word-final stops bear either aspiration or glottalization in non-verbs (for verbs see §5.2.3). The aspiration/glottalization can either be part of the underlying segment or supplied by another morpheme.

(7) Aspirated and glottalized stops in non-verbs do not neutralize (Buckley 1994:100)
    (a) With underlying aspiration or glottalization
        [tʼopʼ]   'pop'   [hotʰ]   'warm'
        [tepʰ]   'unmarked game stick'   [hecʼ]   'nail, claw'
        [sʼot̪ʼ]   'lungs'   [kilakʰ]   'eagle'
        [kúlwetʰ]   'cattle'   [hosíqʼ]   'screech owl'
        [bá:ʃkʰotʼ]   'raspberry'   [ʃakitáqʰ]   'puffin'
    (b) With glottalization contributed by another morpheme
        /qahmat +ʼ/ → [qahmatʼ] 'angry+assertive' *[qahmaʔ]
        /siqʰot+ʼ/ → [siqʰotʼ] 'it's acorn grounds'
        /watac+ʼ/ → [watacʼ] 'it's a frog'
        /mihjoq+ʼ/ → [mihjoqʼ] 'it's a woodrat'

The ban on neutralization of glottalized and aspirated consonants also prevents neutralization in word-medial codas. Word medial codas always end up with either glottalization or aspiration, through a variety of phenomena (§5.2.3; Buckley 1994:87ff.).

In a similar vein to Buckley's analysis, neutralization is blocked in the forms in (7) because neutralization to [ʔ] (or even the other glottal – [h]) would result in loss of the underlying laryngeal features. The blocking is implemented by both a markedness and faithfulness constraint. The output constraint *GL^{GL} bans glottals with a 'secondary glottal PoA' (i.e. glottalization or aspiration); this rules out [ʔʼ hʼ ʔʰ hʰ].[1] The faithfulness constraint preserves the underlying aspiration and glottalization, called IDENT[+LAR] here after Lombardi (1991). Tableau (8) shows how these constraints block neutralization. Candidate (a)'s /t/ debuccalizes but retains aspiration, fatally violating *GL^{GL}. Candidate (b) avoids violating *GL^{GL} by eliminating the aspiration, fatally violating IDENT[+LAR]. The only remaining option is not to debuccalize so preserving the aspiration.

---

[1] *GL^{GL} could be seen as an OCP constraint that holds segment-internally between major and secondary PoA.

(8)   Kashaya II

/hotʰ/	*GL^GL	IDENT[+ LAR]	*{dors,lab,cor}	IDENT{dors,lab,cor}
(a) hoʔʰ	*!			*
(b) hoʔ		*!		*
☞ (c) hotʰ			*	

The success of the analysis relies on two factors. One is the form of the constraints: *{dors,lab,cor} is crucial in getting the right patterns here because it assigns the same violations to dorsals, labials, and coronals. This is seen with /kilakʰ/ in tableau (9). /kʰ/ cannot become a glottal because it would either create an impermissible segment (as in (a)), or lose aspiration (as in (b)). A viable option is to reduce the PoA to coronal, as in candidate (c); this results in both a permissible segment and preservation of aspiration. However, /kʰ/ does not become [tʰ] because doing so would not result in fewer violations of the active PoA-output constraint *{dors,lab,cor}. Both [kʰ] and [tʰ] violate *{dors,lab,cor} equally; this is conflation. The result is that markedness is not decisive, so the next constraint in the hierarchy determines the winner. As IDENT{dors,lab,cor} favours the faithful form, [kilakʰ] wins, not *[kilatʰ].

(9)   Kashaya III

/kilakʰ/	*GL^GL	IDENT[+ LAR]	*{dors,lab,cor}	IDENT{dors,lab,cor}
(a) kilaʔʰ	*!		**	*
(b) kilaʔ		*!	**	*
(c) kilatʰ			***	*!
☞ (d) kilakʰ			***	

In short, it is crucial that *{dors,lab,cor} assigns the same violations to dorsals and coronals here. If it favoured coronals over dorsals, *[kilatʰ] would win. This is the essential part of conflation: two markedness categories for a hierarchy H are conflated when they incur the same violations of all active H-referring output constraints.

Another important factor is that all output constraints that favour coronals over dorsals are outranked by a faithfulness constraint that preserves dorsals. If *{dors} outranked IDENT{dors,lab,cor}, the winner would be *[kilatʰ], as can be seen by inspecting tableau (10). Of course, the same goes for labials – *{dors,lab,cor} assigns the same violations to *[kilapʰ], and *{dors,lab} must

214   5 *Conflation in reduction*

be outranked by a labial-preserving faithfulness constraint. In tableau (10), *{dors} and *{dors,lab} favour both *[kilat^h] and *[kilap^h] over [kilak^h]; they therefore conflict with IDENT{dors,lab,cor}, and so must be outranked by it.

(10)   Kashaya IV

/kilak^h/	*{dors,lab,cor}	IDENT{dors,lab,cor}	*{dors}	*{dors,lab}
(a) kilap^h	* * *	*!	*	* *
(b) kilat^h	* * *	*!	*	*
☞ (c) kilak^h	* * *		* *	* *

The ranking illustrates a necessary property of the constraints: they must be freely rankable. It is crucial that *{dors,lab} and *{dors} are ranked below PoA-faithfulness constraints in Kashaya, in contrast to *{dors,lab,cor}. Diagram (11) helps illustrate this point.

(11)   ONSET-IDENT{dors,lab,cor}   *GL^{GL}   IDENT[lar]

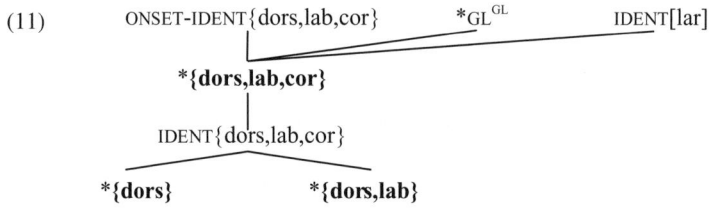

    *{dors,lab,cor}

        IDENT{dors,lab,cor}

*{dors}   ***{dors,lab}**

The interesting ranking is that *{dors,lab,cor} outranks both *{dors} and *{dors,lab}. This is an 'anti-Paninian' ranking, where a more general constraint outranks a more specific one (Prince 1997a,b,c,d, 1998, 1999). This ranking contrasts with 'Paninian' ones, as found in Standard Malay's || *{dors} » *{dors,lab}, *{dors,lab,cor} || (§3.3.1); contrasting Kashaya and Standard Malay, it is clear that there is no fixed ranking between *{dors} and *{dors,lab,cor} at least. As explained in chapter 2, if hierarchy-referring constraints must be freely rankable, they must necessarily be stringent, otherwise they would be unable to express hierarchical relations.

Anti-Paninian rankings are crucial in producing conflation. In contrast with the ranking in (11), a theory with fixed ranking has *{dors} outranking all other PoA constraints. This point is discussed at length in the following section.

To summarize, the stringent constraint *{dors,lab,cor} conflates the markedness distinction between dorsals, labials, and coronals — each PoA value incurs the same violations of active constraints. Consequently, neutralization of dorsals to coronals does *not* reduce PoA markedness. Because dorsals, labials, and coronals are conflated for markedness through *{dors,lab,cor}, both the faithful [kilakʰ] and neutralized *[kilatʰ] incur the same markedness violations. This indecision on the part of the output constraints means that faithfulness makes the crucial choice, favouring preservation of the underlying PoA – [kilakʰ].

5.2.2   Fixed ranking and conflation

The analysis presented above crucially relies on the stringent form of *{dors,lab,cor}. If there were instead a universally fixed ranking of output constraints of the form || *dors »» *lab »» *cor »» *glottal || (Prince & Smolensky 1993), there would be no way to deal with Kashaya and any system in which blocking resulted in a faithful form.

With a universally fixed ranking, opting for the next least-marked PoA when neutralization is blocked is always a better option than preservation. To get neutralization in the first place, *dors, *lab, and *cor must outrank their respective faithfulness constraints, as in tableau (12).

(12)   Kashaya V

/ʃeʔet̰/	*dors	*lab	*cor	IDENT{dors,lab,cor}
(a) ʃeʔet̰			* *!	
☞ (b) ʃeʔeʔ			*	*

The problem with this approach is that blocking loss of laryngeal features will not prevent reduction in PoA markedness. Tableau (13) illustrates; as above, the constraint *GL^Gl and IDENT[| LAR] prevent neutralization to glottal as this would result in loss of aspiration.

(13)   Kashaya VI

/kilakʰ/	*GL^GL	IDENT[+ LAR]	*dors	*lab	*cor	IDENT{dors,lab,cor}
(a) kilaʔʰ	*!		*		*	*
(b) kilaʔ		*!	*		*	*
(c) kilakʰ			* *!		*	
☞ (d) kilatʰ			*		* *	*

Tableau (13) shows that the incorrect output is produced: *[kilatʰ]. In fact, there is no way to rank the constraints so as to get faithfulness when neutralization is blocked. The problem can be traced to the constraint *{dors}. This constraint must outrank all dorsal-preserving faithfulness constraints otherwise neutralization would never take place (i.e. tableau (12)). However, *{dors} favours coronals over dorsals, so *[kilatʰ] will always be more desirable than [kilakʰ].

There is no way to introduce another output or faithfulness constraint to fix the problem. An output solution would require an output constraint that favoured dorsals over coronals to outrank *{dors}. In effect, such a constraint would have to have the form *{coronal}. However, no such constraint exists, as it reverses the markedness hierarchy and consequently has a variety of typologically devastating effects (§4.4.1).

A faithfulness solution would require a faithfulness constraint that favoured [kilak^h] over *[kilat^h] to outrank *{dors}. The only way this solution would work is if there is some feature value that [ʔ] and [k] share that [t] and [k] do not. In modern feature theories, no such feature is available (see, e.g., Hall 2006). The same problem arises for preventing /p^h/ from becoming [ʔ], and the same for /c^h/, /t^h/, and /ṭ^h/. In short, there is neither a faithfulness nor markedness way out of this problem for the fixed ranking approach.

To summarize, the Fixed Ranking approach predicts that, when neutralization is blocked, a segment will *always* neutralize to the next least marked value. In PoA terms, the universally fixed ranking encodes the idea that dorsals are *always* more marked than coronals. Consequently, coronals will always provide a better solution to dorsals when neutralization to glottals is blocked. In contrast, stringent constraints allow conflation; consequently when neutralization is blocked there are two choices: neutralize to the next least-marked PoA, or stay faithful (Kashaya).

To make one thing clear, the Fixed Ranking approach can produce some types of conflation: it can conflate a contiguous range of categories starting with the least-marked element in a hierarchy. For example, Standard Malay neutralizes /k/ to [ʔ], but /p/ and /t/ are preserved (§3.3.1). This is a type of conflation: labials, coronals, and glottals are conflated, so there is no markedness gain in /p/ surfacing as [ʔ]. As with Kashaya, this type of conflation is due to constraint inactivity: in Malay there is no active constraint that distinguishes between coronals, labials, and glottals – *{dors,lab} and *{dors,lab,cor} are rendered inactive for neutralization by ranking them below IDENT{dors,lab,cor}. In the Fixed Ranking theory, conflation of unmarked categories can be produced when faithfulness constraints outrank relevant output constraints: e.g. Malay: || *dors » IDENT[Place] » *labial » *coronal ||. However, the Fixed Ranking theory cannot produce any other type of conflation, i.e. it cannot conflate only marked categories, as demonstrated for Kashaya. It also cannot conflate an intermediate group of categories that does not include the least-marked element; in contrast, the stringent theory presented here can do so – see §5.3.2 (also de Lacy 2004).

For discussion of alternatives that attempt to retain universally fixed ranking and non-stringent constraints but allow conflation, see §5.4.

5.2.3 Verb-noun asymmetries and supporting evidence

The analysis presented above relies on the idea that the PoA output constraints *{dors,lab,cor}, *{dors,lab}, and *{dors} apply to glottalized and aspirated consonants as well as plain stops. However, it is reasonable to question this assumption. If the PoA output constraints only apply to plain stops, preservation of the PoA of glottalized and aspirated stops is a trivial matter, as there would be no pressure on them to neutralize in the first place. Happily for this analysis, there is clear evidence that the PoA output constraints *do* apply to glottalized and aspirated consonants. The evidence also gives additional insight into Kashaya's conflation.

Glottalized and aspirated stops are only prevented from undergoing neutralization in non-verbs. In verbs, glottalized stops undergo neutralization (there are no relevant forms that show neutralization of aspirated consonants). The forms in (14) involve a verb and the absolute suffix /ʔ/. These verbal forms contrast with nominal and adjectival forms plus the assertive suffix /ʔ/ (e.g. /siqʰot+ʔ/ → [siqʰotʔ], (7b)).

(14) Verb-final glottalized consonants undergo neutralization (Buckley 1994:102)
    (a) /limʔut+ʔ/ → [libuʔ] 'whistle+{absolutive}', *[libutʔ]
    (b) /pʰot+ʔ/ → [poʔ] 'knock off', *[potʔ]
    (c) /cacʔ+ʔ/ → [caʔ] 'see (pl)'
    (d) /nʔusʔeːkʔ+ʔ/ → [dusʔéʔ] 'pleat'
    (e) /simaːq-ʔ/ → [simaʔ] 'sleep'

The data shows that this neutralization is not just a quirk of the assertive suffix; even underlyingly glottalized consonants undergo neutralization, as in the roots /cacʔ/ and /nʔusʔeːkʔ/. In other words, glottalized consonants in verbs undergo PoA neutralization just like plain consonants.

So what motivates the neutralization of glottalized stops in verbs? One option is to invoke a verb-specific output constraint that specifically targets glottalized consonants. This would be a poor solution for several reasons. One is that differences between nouns and verbs have been argued by Smith (1997, 2002) to follow from faithfulness differences, not markedness; in fact, there has been a general trend in the OT literature to ascribe class-specific behaviour to faithfulness constraints alone, not output constraints (Benua 1997; Ito & Mester 1998). The second problem is that there is no typological justification for having separate PoA constraints for plain and glottalized segments: this would predict an unattested language in which glottalized stops debuccalize but plain ones do not.

A reasonable solution is that *{dors,lab,cor} is the motivation for /cʔ/ → [ʔ] in verbs just as it is for /c/ → [ʔ]. Accounting for the difference between verbal

218   5 *Conflation in reduction*

and nominal elements in Kashaya is straightforward in OT. As mentioned above, Smith (1997) shows that there are faithfulness constraints that apply specifically to nouns. Kashaya therefore shows the effect of Noun-IDENT[+LAR] — a constraint that preserves secondary articulation in nominals only.[2] The following tableaux show the blocking effect of this constraint.

(15)   Kashaya VII

/hec$^{?}$/$_{NOUN}$	Noun-IDENT[+LAR]	*{dors,lab,cor}	IDENT[+LAR]
(a) he?	*!		*
☞ (b) hec$^{?}$		*	

(16)   Kashaya VIII

/cac$^{?}$+$^{?}$/$_{VERB}$	Noun-IDENT[+LAR]	*{dors,lab,cor}	IDENT[+LAR]
(a) cac$^{?}$		* *!	
☞ (b) ca?		*	*

5.2.3.1   Medial codas

An analogous blocking effect is found with word-medial codas. Medial coda non-glottal stops must bear a secondary articulation in Kashaya — no coda contains a plain non-glottal stop on the surface (Buckley 1994:87). This demand is met in several ways, summarized in (17).

(17)   Consonants must have aspiration or glottalization before another consonant
    (a) Glottalization flop
        /s$^{?}$uwac-m$^{?}$a/ → [s$^{?}$uwac$^{?}$-ba] 'after drying' (p.81)
        /p^{h}a-nem-n$^{?}$o/ → [p^{h}anem$^{?}$do] 'they say he punched' (p.81)
    (b) Coalescence of stop+laryngeal
        /n$^{?}$a-hjut̲-ʔk^{h}e/ → [dahjut̲$^{?}$k^{h}e] 'will rub' (p.68)
        /p^{h}ak$^{?}$u:m-ʔk^{h}e/ → [p^{h}ak$^{?}$um$^{?}$k^{h}e] 'will kill' (p.69)
        /dasew hca/ → [dasew^{h}ca] 'wash room' (p.70)
    (c) Otherwise medial codas are aspirated
        /s$^{?}$uwac-me-ʔ/ → [s$^{?}$uwac^{h}meʔ] 'dry it! (formal)' (p.88)
            cf. [s$^{?}$uwacı́] 'dry it! (sg)'
        /n$^{?}$a-hjut̲-me-ʔ/ → [dahjút̲^{h}meʔ] 'break it! (formal)' (p.88)
            cf. [dahjut̲ı́] 'breat it! (sg)'

The only exception to the generalization is for stops that cannot bear aspiration or glottalization — i.e. [ʔ] (e.g. /qa-ne-ʔk^{h}e/ → [qaneʔk^{h}e] 'will bite', *[qaneʔ^{h}ke] Buckley 1994:68).

---

2 'Nominal' refers to [+Nominal] elements – i.e. nouns and adjectives (Chomsky 1981:48).

The constraint that demands pre-consonantal laryngeal features is called *C^plainC; this constraint is ad hoc, but discovering more well-motivated constraint(s) with the same effect is unnecessary here. *C^plainC must outrank faithfulness constraints that ban insertion of aspiration and glottalization – IDENT[±LAR]. *C^plainC also outranks *{dors,lab,cor}, so blocking PoA neutralization. Tableau (18) illustrates these points.

The faithful candidate (a) loses because it does not have a medial coda stop with aspiration or glottalization, so violating *C^plainC. Candidate (b) loses for the same reason – ʔ is not aspirated or glottalized. Candidate (c) has a coda with secondary articulation, but /c/ has undergone place neutralization to [t]. As established above, this PoA neutralization does not improve on markedness because *{dors,lab,cor} treats all PoAs as equally marked. The final decision is therefore passed to IDENT{dors,lab,cor}, which favours the most PoA-faithful candidate – i.e. (d).

(18)   Kashaya IX

/sʔuwac-meʔ/	*C^plainC	IDENT[±LAR]	*{dors,lab,cor}	IDENT{dors,lab,cor}
(a) sʔuwacmeʔ	*!		* * * *	
(b) sʔuwaʔmeʔ	*!		* * *	*
(c) sʔuwatʰmeʔ		*	* * * *	*!
☞ (d) sʔuwacʰmeʔ		*	* * * *	

Insertion of secondary articulation is clearly less desirable than obtaining it from a nearby segment (compare /sʔuwac-mʔa/ → [sʔuwacʔ-ba], cf. *[sʔuwacʰba]). This is no doubt due to the faithfulness constraints' ranking, but it would take this discussion too far afield to delve deeper here. *C^plainC may also explain why codas do not debuccalize in complex clusters: e.g. /nʔusʔeːkʔ-tʰ/ 'pleat-NEG' surfaces as [dusʔéːkʔtʰ] and not *[dusʔéʔtʰ]. Future work will no doubt help clarify the situation.

To summarize, Kashaya presents a situation where PoA neutralization to glottal is blocked when it would eliminate aspiration and glottalization. In such situations, consonants are not neutralized to coronal PoA. This fact can be explained if output constraints are stringently formulated – if dorsal, labial, and coronal PoA are treated as 'equally marked' for the purposes of neutralization, then only neutralization to glottal is satisfactory.

5.2.4 Preventing conflation: uvulars

The preceding discussion has established that Kashaya distinguishes two groups of PoA categories for neutralization: glottals vs. non-glottals. However, there is evidence that Kashaya makes three markedness distinctions: {uvulars} vs. {dorsals, labials, and coronals} vs. {glottals}.

Uvulars are avoided more vigorously than other PoAs in Kashaya. Although 'uvular' has not figured prominently in the PoA hierarchy so far, its treatment in Kashaya indicates that it is the most-marked PoA (perhaps along with the pharyngeals [ħʕ]). It was observed in (17) that medial coda [ṭ t c p k] avoid neutralization to [ʔ] through a variety of phonological processes that result in them bearing glottalization or aspiration. While these processes are enough to protect coronals, labials, and dorsals, they are not enough to affect uvulars, as shown in (19). The data and observations here are taken from Buckley 1994: §3.2.2.

(19) Uvulars in medial codas debuccalize
    (a) Glottalization flop environments
       (i) /sima:q-mʔa/ → [simaʔba] 'having fallen asleep' (p.97), *[simaqʔba], cf. /sʔuwac-mʔa/ → [sʔuwacʔ-ba] 'after drying', *[sʔuwaʔba]
      (ii) /kʰunu:q-nʔo/ → [kʰunuʔdo] 'they say it spoiled' (p.98), *[kʰunuqʔdo]
      (iii) /qaʃo:qʷ-nʔo/ → [qaʃoʔdo] 'they say he's getting well' (p.98)
    (b) Coda aspiration environments
      (i) /sima:q-meʔ/ → [simahmeʔ] 'go to sleep!' (p.97), *[simaqʰmeʔ], cf. /sʔuwac-meʔ/ → [sʔuwacʰmeʔ] 'dry it! (formal)', *[sʔuwahmeʔ]
      (ii) /micʰa:q-pʰi/ → [micʰahpʰi] 'if he sweats' (p.97), *[micʰaqʰpʰi]
      (iii) /hloqʷ-ʃe/ → [hlóhʃe] 'I wonder if it fell off' (p.98), *[hlóqʷʰʃe]

The data raise the question of why /q/ debuccalizes when it could have taken glottalization or aspiration and survived; after all, this is exactly what /p/, /t/, and /c/ do. For example, the /c/ in /sʔuwac/ receives glottalization from the initial consonant of /-mʔa/ to produce [sʔuwacʔ-ba] 'after drying', not *[sʔuwaʔba].

While plain /q/ debuccalizes, there are no examples of underlying glottalized /qʔ/ or aspirated /qʰ/ debuccalizing in medial codas. Buckley (p.98) reports some loanwords in which /qʰ/ is preserved: e.g. [taqʰma] 'dress' (from Alutiiq), [ʔéqʰʃe] 'fishhook' (from Alutiiq or Tanaina), [lu:cáqʰbe] 'pipe' (from Central/Southern Pomo), [ʃakitáqʰ] 'puffin'. When the aspiration or glottalization is the only realization of another morpheme, it also survives: /mihjoq+ʔ/ → [mihjoqʔ] 'it's a sweat'.

In short, the challenge is to explain why plain uvulars neutralize in medial codas while coronals, labials, and velars do not.

Uvulars are dorsals, but it is not possible to use *{dors} to motivate uvular neutralization because velars are not subject to the same avoidance as uvulars. Instead, an output constraint that specifically targets uvulars is necessary: i.e. *{uvular}. This constraint may derive from different hierarchies. One possibility is that the PoA hierarchy in its full form is | {uvular, (pharyngeal)} 〉 dorsal 〉 labial 〉 coronal 〉 glottal |. Consequently, output PoA constraints are *{uvu(lar)}, *{uvu,dors}, *{uvu,dors,lab}, *{uvu,dors,lab,cor}, and *{uvu,dors,lab,cor,gl}; there would of course be equivalent faithfulness constraints. On the other hand, this formulation gives uvulars the status of a major PoA feature, whereas they are a subclass of dorsals and gutturals. As a subclass, they could derive from a minor PoA hierarchy that refers to dorsals alone: i.e. | uvular 〉 velar |, producing *{uvular} and *{uvular,velar}. Either way, the result is the same: *{uvular} can motivate neutralization in Kashaya.

For ease of exposition, the analysis here will assume that there is a *{uvular} constraint separate from the major PoA constraints. *{uvular} outranks all constraints that attempt to impose aspiration and glottalization on a coda consonant – i.e. *C^{plain}C:

(20)   Kashaya x

/simaːq-m$^?$a/	*{uvular}	*C^{plain}C
(a) simaq$^?$ba	*!	
(b) simaqba	*!	
☞ (c) sima?ba		*

In contrast, *C^{plain}C outranks *{dors,lab,cor}, as shown in tableau (18); this ranking allows non-uvulars to be preserved in medial codas, as in /s$^?$uwac-m$^?$a/ → [s$^?$uwac$^?$-ba] 'after drying'. The alternative *[s$^?$uwa?ba] fatally violates *C^{plain}C.

The final issue is why /q/ becomes [?] and not [t$^?$]. The competitor *[simat$^?$ba] avoids violating both *{uvular} and *C^{plain}C. Certainly, the theory predicts that neutralization to [t$^?$] *could* happen in some language. However, there is an equally good reason why uvulars become glottals: faithfulness. McCarthy (1994) argues that the feature [pharyngeal] defines the class of gutturals, which include glottals [? h ɦ], pharyngeals [ħ ʕ], and uvular [q G N R ʁ χ] consonants. McCarthy provides a great deal of evidence for this feature; additional evidence is discussed in §8.6.3 for Misantla Totonoc. In Kashaya, IDENT[pharyngeal] forces uvulars to become glottals, shown in tableau (21).

222 5 *Conflation in reduction*

(21)   Kashaya XI

/sima:q-m$^{\text{?}}$a/	IDENT[pharyngeal]	*{uvular}	*C^{plain}C
(a) sima:t$^{\text{?}}$ba	*!		
(b) sima:qba		*!	
☞ (c) sima?ba			*

It is important to point out that the theory predicts that uvulars could have neutralized to coronal if IDENT[pharyngeal] was ranked below *C^{plain}C. In contrast, no PoA apart from uvulars shares a feature with glottals. So, if velars or labials were forced to neutralize medially in Kashaya, unlike uvulars they would have to become coronal because there is no faithfulness constraint that would force them to become glottal. In other words, using IDENT[pharyngeal] here does not represent a general way to avoid neutralization to the next least-marked segment – it is a method that can only be used for uvulars and other pharyngeals.

To complete the necessary rankings, uvulars with underlying aspiration and glottalization are preserved, despite *{uvular}. Consequently, IDENT[+LAR] must outrank *{uvular}. The ranking can be summarized in diagram (22).

The bold part of the ranking shows how both conflation and non-conflation can exist in the same grammar. *{uvu} is active, and consequently prevents conflation of uvulars with every other PoA. *{dors,lab,cor} is also active, and prevents conflation of glottals with other PoAs. However, there is no active constraint that distinguishes coronals from labials from velars – so all are treated in the same way for neutralization.

(22)

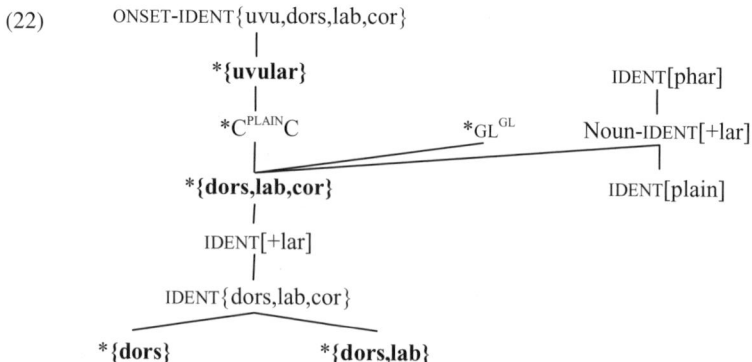

5.2 *PoA conflation*   223

There are some exceptions to medial coda /q/ debuccalization. It surfaces intact before the semelfactive *–c*, essive *–m*, and plural act allomorph *–m*: e.g. /ʔacʰulaq-c-w/ → [ʔacʰuláqʰciw] 'miss hitting (with one shot)' (p.99), *[ʔacʰuláhciw], /pʰa-cʔoːqʷ-m-w/ → [pʰacʔoqʰmaw] 'stab (pl.)' (p.99). Buckley (p.99) ascribes this effect to level-ordering; this places it too far beyond the scope of the present analysis to discuss here (see McCarthy 2006 for discussion of how to conceive of such phenomena within single-level OT).

There are other phenomena that relate to PoA and secondary articulation in Kashaya, including a ban on certain adjacent coronals. Detailed description and analyses can be found in Buckley 1994:§3.2.1, §3.2.2.

5.2.5   Summary
Kashaya PoA neutralization shows that conflation is necessary: velars, labials, and coronals are treated as 'equally marked' for the purposes of PoA neutralization. So, when neutralization to glottal is blocked, there is no gain in neutralizing to coronal.

Kashaya is not the only language to show conflation effects in PoA neutralization, nor is faithfulness the only reason that neutralization can be blocked. Hixkaryána has coda PoA neutralization to glottals: e.g. /w-esnɔk̲ u-sɯ/ →[wes.nɔh̲.sɯ] 'let me smell it', /t-ɔkɯ-kɔ/ → [tɔh̲.kɔ] 'gen.pref.-eat(nuts)-imp.', /koseɲitno/ → [kɔ.seː.ɲiʔ.nɔ] 'I dreamt' (Gildea 1995:88; Derbyshire 1979:180). However, neutralization to glottals is blocked before another glottal, no doubt by a ban on geminates. As in Kashaya, stops surface faithfully: /i kamsuku-hira/ surfaces as [ɨ-kam.suk.hu.ra] 'without blood', not *[ɨ-kam.suh.hu.ra] (Derbyshire 1985:12, 238). Fricatives exercise another option: metathesis (e.g. /ahos̲i- h̲ira/ → [a.hoh.s̲i̲.ra] 'not catching it', *[a.hoh.hira] – Derbyshire 1979:187). As in Kashaya, the question that these responses raise is 'Why don't the codas neutralize to the next best PoA available – coronal?' After all, doing so provides a much better alternative than the actually attested forms. For example, the PoA-faithful output *[a.hos̲.h̲ɨ.ra] avoids violating the ban on adjacent coronals without being unfaithful to the underlying segment order. Similarly, the output *[ɨ-kamsut̲.hura] avoids having adjacent glottals *and* avoids having a coda dorsal by simply opting for the next least-unmarked PoA – coronal. Again, the answer can be traced to conflation. Neutralization to coronal simply does not reduce markedness, as dorsals and coronals are treated the same for markedness. So the alternative solutions – metathesis and remaining faithful – can be employed instead.

5.3 Conflation prevention and vowel sonority

The stringent constraints predict that conflation is possible. However, they also predict that languages may choose not to conflate: if both *{dorsal,labial} and *{dorsal,labial,coronal} are active in a language, coronals will be avoided, but labials even more so. As §5.2 presented evidence for conflation, this section is devoted to showing that languages can prevent conflation and that the stringent constraints can account for such systems.

It is important to show that lack of conflation is possible because some theories predict that conflation cannot be prevented. In general terms, such theories effectively pick a threshold for each markedness hierarchy, sometimes on a language-particular basis; constraints ban every element above that threshold. For example, the PoA threshold for Kashaya would be set at 'coronal' and there would be just one PoA output constraint: *{non-glottal}. In this theory, there is no way to distinguish between more-marked elements within a single language — all non-glottals should be treated the same, and therefore always conflated.

In more concrete terms, there are a cluster of extant theories that require conflation. These theories have two properties in common. One is privativity or underspecification: the least-marked feature value is represented by not having that feature (see, e.g., Kiparsky 1982; Lombardi 1991; papers in Paradis & Prunet 1991b). For example, glottals (or coronals in some versions) have no PoA feature at all in such theories. The other property of these theories is the conception that neutralization is the result of feature elimination, not change. In such a theory, debuccalization is the deletion of PoA features; the resulting PoA-less segment is phonetically interpreted as glottal. Such a theory requires conflation because there are only two options: having features and not having features. If a feature is blocked from deletion, it does not have the option to become a less-marked feature because feature deletion is the only operation allowed. In other words, if neutralization of dorsal to glottal is blocked, dorsal cannot become coronal or labial because this operation requires changing dorsal to coronal or labial, not simply deletion of dorsal. In short, such a theory requires conflation: it predicts that if a feature is blocked from neutralizing, it will remain faithful.[3] (I hasten to add that conflation has never

---

[3] Not all theories that employ privativity, underspecification, and feature deletion require conflation. Rice's (1996) theory could allow for lack of conflation because the structure for dorsals properly contains coronal structure, so a dorsal could become coronal through feature deletion alone. For discussion of representational theories and markedness, see §8.4.

been addressed systematically in such representational theories, so the assertion expressed here is not aimed at any particular theory, and may be avoidable in some.)

Section 5.3.1 discusses conflation-prevention in Dutch vowel neutralization. The aim is to show that even in the same language two or more stringent constraints can be active. Section 5.3.2 presents evidence for the same point using sonority-driven stress in Gujarati. These languages are discussed here because both have a mixture of conflation and conflation-prevention, and so allow the stringent constraints' power to be fully exercised. Unlike Kashaya, both the examples relate to vowel sonority.

5.3.1 *Preventing conflation in neutralization*

This section argues that all of the hierarchy-referring constraints generated by the schemas in §2.3 are necessary. Languages do not simply pick a 'markedness threshold' — multiple markedness distinctions can be active in the same language.

To break the empirical monotony of PoA-related processes, this section focuses on vowel sonority neutralization; an example of conflation prevention for PoA neutralization is discussed in §8.4.1.1. Vowel sonority is often neutralized in unstressed syllables; such neutralization often goes under the name 'reduction' when the neutralization output is a central vowel and 'raising' when the target is a high vowel. In spite of the terminology, as Crosswhite (1999, 2000, 2004) has argued, both 'raising' and 'reduction' are simply different aspects of the same phenomenon — reduction of sonority.

A number of cases of vowel sonority neutralization are discussed in chapter 7 in the context of vowel markedness. To avoid unnecessary repetition, only the elements of the analysis that are essential to this section's aim are presented here.

5.3.1.1 The Dutch data

The empirical focus here is vowel reduction in the semi-formal register of standard Dutch. There is a large literature on Dutch vowel reduction (Martin 1968; Booij 1977, 1981; van der Hulst 1984; Zonneveld 1985; Kager 1989; Kager, Visch, and van Zonneveld 1987; Oostendorp 1995). One complexity of Dutch is that there are different reduction patterns in the unstressed syllable of a foot and unstressed unfooted syllables (Kager 1989:312; Booij 1981; Oostendorp 1995). The focus here will be the pattern in the unstressed syllable of a foot, summarized in (23); there is no room here for a complete analysis of the other cases in terms of the present theory (but see de Lacy 2002a:§4.3).

Supporting data is given in (24). The words listed are taken from Kager 1989 (hereafter K). Footing is my own, based on Kager's proposals; stress in Dutch is left-to-right trochaic and quantity-sensitive – tense vowels count as bimoraic (Kager 1989:313; Oostendorp 1995:§4.2). The transcriptions are from van Wely (1967), with vowel reduction marked following K's indications. Glosses are given where the English translation is not immediately apparent. Evidence for the underlying forms – e.g. that *karamel* is underlyingly /karamɛl/ and not /karəmɛl/ – comes from the formal register, in which reduction does not occur.

(23)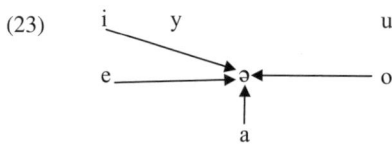

(24)
(a) /a/ reduction
    [(ˌkarə)(ˈmɛl)]   *karamel*   [(ˌsiɣə)(ˈrɛt)] *sigaret*
    [(ˌkɔlə)(ˌborə)(ˈtør)] *collaborateur*
(b) /e/ reduction
    [(ˌprosə)(ˈde)] *procédé* 'process'   [(ˌekə)(ˌnomə)(ˈtri)] *econometrie*
(c) /o/ reduction
    [(ˌʃokə)(ˈla)]   *chocola* 'chocolate'   [(ˌlimə)(ˈnadə)]   *limonade*
    [(ˌpɛlə)(ˈton)] *peloton* 'platoon'   [(ˌlokə)mo(ˈtif)]   *lokomotief*
    [(ˌeko)nə(ˈmi)] *economie*   [(ˌonə)(ˌmatə)(ˈpe)] *onomatopee*
    [to(ˈmat)] *tomaat* 'tomato'   [(ˌkatə)go(ˈri)] *categorie*
(d) /i/ reduction
    [(ˌrɛlə)(ˈkwi)] *relikwie* 'relic'   [(ˌdɪsə)(ˈplinə)] *discipline*
    [(ˌkɑrə)kə(ˈtyr)] *karikatuur*   [(ˌspɛsə)(ˌfisə)(ˈteit)] *specificiteit*
    [mi(ˈnut)] *minuut*   [(ˌində)vi(ˈdu)] *individu*
    [(ˌsɛrtə)fi(ˈkat)] *certificaat*
(e) No /y/ reduction
    [(ˌmany)fɑk(ˈtyr)] *manufaktuur* 'drapery'   [(ˈprimy)lə] *primula*
    [(ˈstimy)ləs] *stimulus*   [(ˌkomy)(ˈnɪst)] *communist*
(f) No /u/ reduction
    [(ˌʒalu)(ˈzi)] *jaloezie*   [(ˌkamu)(ˈflaʒə)] *camouflage*

5.3.1.2 Analysis

Chapter 7 argues that vowel reduction is due to a pressure to lower sonority in non-DTEs, building on Crosswhite (1999, 2000, 2004). In Dutch, the pressure

5.3 *Conflation prevention and vowel sonority* 227

is specifically on the unstressed part of a foot. As a reminder, the 'unstressed part of a foot' effectively refers to the non-DTEs of a foot in the present theory. Diagram (25) identifies the foot non-DTEs for the word [(ˌində)vi('du)].

(25)   Foot non-DTEs

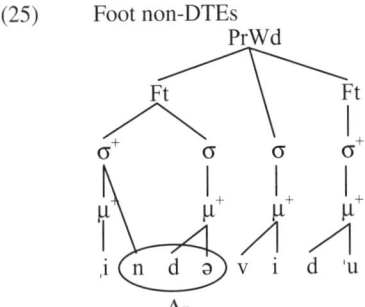

Even though [n d ə] are all foot non-DTEs, the non-DTE constraints will effectively regulate only the vowel's sonority as a constraint like *−Δ_{Ft}≥{i,u} will not affect the codas and onset consonants that are foot non-DTEs. In diagram (25), only ['u] is a PrWd DTE, but both ['u] and [ˌi] are foot DTEs. Every segment except for ['u] is a PrWd non-DTE. For definitions of 'non-DTE' and 'DTE' see §2.3.3.1.

The relevant constraints are given in (26). As a reminder, the general form *−Δ_{Ft}≥{x} bans all segments that are equally or more sonorous than x in the non-DTE of a foot. So, *−Δ_{Ft}≥{i,u} can be expanded to *−Δ_{Ft}/{a,ɛ•ɔ,e•o,i•u}. Constraints such as *−Δ_{Ft}≥{ɛ,ɔ}, *−Δ_{Ft}≥{ə}, and *−Δ_{Ft}≥{ɨ,ʉ} are not relevant because the sonority levels they refer to are not represented in Dutch's vowel inventory; for discussion of how inventories are restricted, see §7.3.

(26)   Non-DTE of Ft vowel sonority constraints
        *−Δ_{Ft}≥{a}   'Incur a violation for each low vowel in the non-DTE
                                  of a Ft.'
        *−Δ_{Ft}≥{e,o}   'Incur a violation for each low or peripheral mid vowel
                                  in the non-DTE of a Ft.'
        *−Δ_{Ft}≥{i,u}   'Incur a violation for each low or peripheral vowel in
                                  the non-DTE of a Ft.'

To get reduction of /i/ to [ə], *−Δ_{Ft}≥{i,u} must outrank all antagonistic faithfulness constraints, including those that preserve height (IDENT[+high]) and backness (IDENT[back]). In tableau (27), candidate (a) fatally violates *−Δ_{Ft}≥{i,u} because it contains a foot non-DTE that has the sonority of a high peripheral vowel or more − i.e. the [i] in *di*. Candidate (b) responds to this constraint

228   5 *Conflation in reduction*

by turning the /i/ into the less sonorous vowel [ə]. However, it goes too far by reducing the third underlying /i/ as well – this /i/ does not end up in the non-DTE of a foot, so is not subject to $*-\Delta_{Ft} \geq \{i,u\}$. Candidate (c) goes just far enough, reducing the footed /i/ to [ə], but leaving the other vowels alone.

(27)   Dutch I

/individu/	$*-\Delta_{Ft} \geq \{i,u\}$	IDENT[+high]
(a) (ˌindi)vi(ˈdu)	*!	
(b) (ˌində)və(ˈdu)		**!
☞ (c) (ˌində)vi(ˈdu)		*

To get reduction of /a/ to [ə] $*-\Delta_{Ft} \geq \{i,u\}$ must also outrank IDENT[low].

5.3.1.3 Preventing conflation

At this point, it may seem that $*-\Delta_{Ft} \geq \{i,u\}$ is the only active constraint of its type needed in Dutch. After all, it also bans [e] and [a] in foot non-DTEs, so what use are the constraints $*-\Delta_{Ft} \geq \{e,o\}$ and $*-\Delta_{Ft} \geq \{a\}$? In more general terms, why is there need for a theory that has a different stringent constraint for each level of the hierarchy? Why not just set a sonority threshold for Dutch at 'above schwa', and have a single constraint against footed unstressed vowels that are above this threshold?

The need can be seen when the blocking effect of roundness is considered. IDENT[+round] blocks most round vowels from neutralizing. For example, both /y/ and /u/ are prevented from turning into [ə]: e.g. [(ˌkomy)(ˈnɪst)], cf. *[(ˌkomə)(ˈnɪst)], [(ˌʒɑlu)(ˈzi)], cf. *[(ˌʒɑlə)(ˈzi)]. This blocking effect is easy to account for: IDENT[round] outranks $*-\Delta_{Ft} \geq \{i,u\}$ (after Crosswhite 1999).

As tableau (28) shows, although candidate (b)'s [y] is too sonorous for foot non-DTE position, it cannot reduce to [ə] because doing so would necessarily lose its underlying [+round] value.

(28)   Dutch II

/komynist/	IDENT[+round]	$*-\Delta_{Ft} \geq \{i,u\}$
(a) (ˌkomə)(ˈnist)	*!	
☞ (b) (ˌkomy)(ˈnist)		*

Other options are ruled out by other constraints. For example, reduction to central rounded [ɵ] or [ɞ] is ruled out by highly ranked constraints against central

5.3 *Conflation prevention and vowel sonority* 229

rounded vowels; in this, Dutch contrasts with Ojibwa, where both preservation of vowel roundness and reduction are paramount, with round back vowels becoming round central vowels (Crosswhite 2004:§2.5).

The ranking for roundness preservation shows why other foot non-DTE/sonority constraints are active in Dutch. In spite of IDENT[+round], /o/ reduces to the unrounded [ə]: e.g. [(ˌʃokə)(ˈla)], cf. *[(ˌʃoko)(ˈla)], [(ˌpɛlə)(ˈton)], cf. *[(ˌpɛlo)(ˈton)]. It is clear that a constraint against [o] in foot non-DTE position outranks IDENT[round]. *−Δ$_{Ft}$≥{e,o} fills this role.

In tableau (29), candidate (b) wins despite losing its underlying [+round] value for /o/. It is forced to do so because the other option — as in (a) — is to retain the /o/ and end up with a stressed mid vowel; however, stressed mid vowels are too sonorous, as expressed by *−Δ$_{Ft}$≥{e,o}.

(29) Dutch III

/ʃokola/	*−Δ$_{Ft}$≥{e,o}	IDENT[round]	*−Δ$_{Ft}$≥{i,u}
(a) (ˌʃoko)(ˈla)	*!		*
☞ (b) (ˌʃokə)(ˈla)		*	

There is one other important competitor: *[(ˌʃoku)(ˈla)]. This candidate preserves rounding and does not violate *−Δ$_{Ft}$≥{e,o}. However, the /o/ loses its underlying [−high] value. With IDENT[−high] outranking IDENT[round], /o/→[u] is ruled out. There is ample evidence that IDENT[−high] blocks vowel reduction in other languages; for examples, see Crosswhite (1999).

(30) Dutch IV

/ʃokola/	IDENT[−high]	*−Δ$_{Ft}$≥{e,o}	IDENT[round]
(a) (ˌʃoku)(ˈla)	*!		
(b) (ˌʃoko)(ˈla)		*!	
☞ (c) (ˌʃokə)(ˈla)			*

In short, Dutch shows the need for more than one constraint that refers to the same hierarchy in the same language: both *−Δ$_{Ft}$≥{i,u} and *−Δ$_{Ft}$≥{e,o} are active.

In general terms, evidence for the activity for more than one constraint comes from situations where marked elements are avoided in more environments than less-marked elements. In Dutch, the higher-marked mid vowels are always avoided in foot non-DTEs, whereas the less-marked high vowels are only avoided when doing so will preserve rounding.

The Dutch situation can also be expressed in conflation terms. There is clearly a general desire to avoid all non-schwa vowels in foot non-DTEs in Dutch. However, while high, mid, and low vowels are all avoided, they are not avoided to the same extent — i.e. they are not conflated. Low and mid vowels are avoided in all circumstances, while high vowels are avoided when roundness can be preserved. In short, the distinction between high and non-high vowels is not conflated in Dutch, despite both types undergoing the same type of neutralization.

5.3.1.4 Permitting conflation

What makes Dutch even more interesting for present purposes is that it *does* conflate the distinction between *mid* and *low* vowels in foot non-DTEs. Vowels do not reduce at all word-finally, even in the non-DTE of a foot: e.g. *cola* [('kola)], *cobra* [('kobra)], *koffie* [('kɔfi)], *trofee* 'trophy' [('trofe)], *hindoe* [('hɪndu)] (Kager 1989:303–4). The constraint responsible for blocking word-final reduction is called *ə]$_\omega$ here.[4]

So, /kola/ does not surface as *[('kolə)] as it would violate *ə]$_\omega$. But a viable option is for /kola/ to surface as *[('kole)] or *[('koli)]. *[('koli)] is already ruled out by IDENT[−high]. However, none of the constraints proposed so far prevent a neutralization to *[('kole)]. IDENT[back] is of no help as it is ranked below *−Δ_{Ft}≥{e,o}.

The solution is that /a/ does not become [e] because the two vowels are conflated for foot non-DTE purposes in Dutch. In other words, /a/→[e] would not improve on violations of active constraints. /a/ surfaces as [a] because IDENT[low] favours preservation of /a/ over preservation of [e], and it outranks *−Δ_{Ft}≥{a}, as shown in tableau (31).

Candidate (a) is ruled out because it undergoes vowel reduction and so violates *ə]$_\omega$. Candidate (b) reduces /a/ to the next least sonorous vowel available – [i], but in doing so fatally violates IDENT[−high]. Candidate (c) reduces /a/ to the next least marked vowel – [e], but produces no markedness gain as this candidate incurs the same active violations as [('kola)] – i.e. both violate *−Δ_{Ft}≥{e,o} equally. Candidate (c) would win if *−Δ_{Ft}≥{a} outranked IDENT[low], but with the current ranking mid and low vowels are conflated in foot non-heads for vowel reduction purposes. As there is no motivation for /a/ to reduce to [e], it is more harmonic to remain faithful, as in (d).

---

4 The ban on final ə may be due to domain-final lengthening, and a ban on long central vowels.

5.3 *Conflation prevention and vowel sonority* 231

(31)   Dutch v

/kola/	*ə]_ω	IDENT[−high]	*−Δ_Ft≥{e,o}	IDENT[low]	*−Δ_Ft≥{a}
(a) ('kolə)	*!			*	
(b) ('koli)		*!		*	
(c) ('kole)			*	*!	
☞ (d) ('kola)			*		*

In short, Dutch shows the need for stringently formulated constraints — they are needed to account for the conflation of low and mid peripheral vowels in vowel neutralization. However, it also shows the need for constraints at each level of the hierarchy — these produce non-conflation of mid peripheral and high vowels.

The effect is visible in the ranking diagram in (32). *−Δ_Ft≥{e,o} outranks all constraints, while *−Δ_Ft≥{a} is blocked by all the constraints above it. Consequently, there is conflation of mid and low peripheral vowels. However, *−Δ_Ft≥{i,u} can be blocked by IDENT[round], while *−Δ_Ft≥{e,o} cannot; the result is that mid and high peripheral vowels are treated differently — i.e. not conflated.

(32)   Dutch semi-formal vowel sonority reduction in foot non-DTEs: ranking

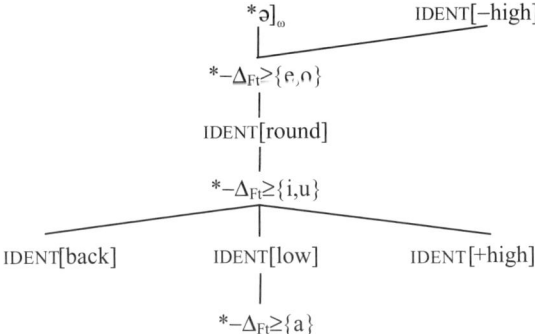

In short, Dutch vowel reduction illustrates the theory well because it has both conflation and crucial lack of conflation in the same system. As in Kashaya, the conflation part of the ranking ‖*−Δ_Ft≥{e,o} » *−Δ_Ft≥{a}‖ is anti-Paninian.

Dutch is not alone in showing conflation in vowel reduction. In a number of languages reduction is blocked and vowels remain faithful; Crosswhite (1999:ch.6) discusses relevant cases and an example is found in European Portuguese (Brakel 1985).

5.3.2 Conflation and its prevention in sonority-driven stress

Sonority-driven stress is another vowel-related phenomenon which shows the effects of both conflation and its prevention, even within the same language. In sonority-driven stress, stress (i.e. the DTE of the prosodic word – Δ_ω) can deviate from its default position if a higher-sonority vowel is elsewhere (Kenstowicz 1996; de Lacy 2006). Gujarati provides a particularly striking case that is very relevant for present purposes: some sonority categories are conflated for stress, while others are not, similar to the Dutch neutralization situation. However, while Dutch conflates mid and low vowels and distinguishes them from high vowels, Gujarati conflates high and mid vowels, and distinguishes them from both schwa and low vowels.

The primary aim in this section is to provide further empirical support for the concepts of conflation and conflation-prevention. The example discussed also allows for consideration of alternative approaches, taken up in §5.4.

5.3.2.1 Description

Gujarati is an Indo-Aryan language with significant numbers of speakers in India (especially in Gujarat province), several African countries, Fiji, and New Zealand.[5] The data presented here were elicited from one female and one male native speaker, both in their early twenties, from Ahmedabad City in Gujarat. The data and generalizations are very similar to the previous major description of Gujarati stress (Cardona 1965); differences are discussed when they arise.

Cardona (1965) and Mistry (1997) report that Gujarati has the vowels [i e ɛ a o ɔ u ə] (also see Nair 1979; Buch 1979; Taylor 1908). Syllables can be described by the template $(C_1)(C_2)V((C_3)C_4)$. Onsets are optional, as shown by [a.po] 'give' and [pi.e] 'he drinks'. Onset clusters consist of [s]+C (e.g. [skəndʰ] 'shoulder', [stuti] 'prayer', [sneh] 'affection', [srot] 'stream', and C+{v, l, r, j}. See Mistry 1997:665 for a concise overview. C_3 is a nasal homorganic with a following stop (e.g. [hiɲtʃ], [təŋg]). Geminate consonants are allowed: e.g. [chəpːən] '56', [gusːo] 'anger'.

A significant influence on stress in Gujarati is sonority. The placement of primary stress is described in (33); there is no secondary stress.

The domain of stress is the root plus its affixes, excluding clitics. Even very short words can be highly morphologically complex: e.g. [aw+'wa+n+ã] '(they) will come'; however, such morphological complexity does not affect stress placement when the morphemes have the shape CV, C, or V and appear

---

5 My thanks to Shimauli Dave and Varun Patel for providing native-speaker judgments on the data in this section, and to another consultant for valuable help with the data.

5.3 *Conflation prevention and vowel sonority* 233

inside the same prosodic word (ω) as the root. The description focuses on words of up to three syllables in length. Longer words are almost always compounds; root boundaries generally coincide with ω boundaries, so compounds have as many stress domains as roots. Other long forms contain enclitics or long prefixes, neither of which count in stress placement (Cardona 1965:34–5,143ff.). A number of orthographically quadrisyllabic words turned out to be phonetically trisyllabic (e.g. ['atʰmənū] 'western', spelt with a schwa between [tʰ] and [m]). A consultant did produce some monomorphemic quadrisyllabic words: e.g. [andʰidʰundʰi] 'choose', [kəṭokəṭi] 'emergency', and [rajinəmu] 'resignation'. Unfortunately, the status of these words is questionable: e.g. [kəṭokəṭi] may be partially internally reduplicated, perhaps explaining why my other consultant varied stress between [ˌkəṭoˈkəṭi] and [kəˈṭokəṭi]. As with morphologically complex quadrisyllabic words, I leave this issue for future research.

(33) Gujarati Stress
    (a) Stress a syllable with [a]
       (i) in the penult

[ˈsaḍa]	'peasants'	[ˈdʒaja]	'let's go'
[ˈsame]	'in front'	[ˈtʃalo]	'go (imperf.)'
[ˈtʃalis]	'40'	[ˈsabu]	'soap'
[ˈgadʒər]	'carrot'	[ˈagəl̪]	'in front'
[aˈwːanā]	'(they) will come'	[apˈwana]	'to give'
[ḍaˈmaḍol]	'tottering'	[aˈzadi]	'freedom'
[kʰɔ̃ˈkʰaɾo]	'coughing'	[ɔˈgaɭwũ]	'dissolve'
[beˈtalis]	'42'		
[muˈbarək]	'congratulation'	[kiˈnaɾo]	'shore, bank'
[uˈtaɾu]	'passenger'	[uˈtawəl̪]	'rush, hurry'
[dʒɔˈwana]	'deathbed'	[təhˈmahɾe]	'you (hon.)'
[pəˈtʃasmũ]	'50ᵗʰ'	[ləˈkʰawəṭ]	'writing'

       (ii) otherwise in the antepenult/initial syllable

[ˈlajbɾɛɾi]	'library'	[ˈtadʒetəɾ]	'recently'
[ˈpakistan]	'Pakistan'	[ˈmanito]	'favourite'
[ˈpatini]	'wife'	[ˈdʒʰakdʒʰəmal̪]	'sparkling'
[ˈbrahmənɳo]	'priestly caste'	[ˈakɾəmən̪]	'invasion'

       (iii) otherwise in the final syllable

[hɛˈran]	'distressed'	[boˈlatʃ]	'is spoken'
[ʃiˈkaɾ]	'a hunt'	[nukˈsan]	'damage'
[pəˈgaɾ]	'wages, salary'	[tʃəɾˈtʃa]	'discussion'
[hoʃiˈjaɾ]	'clever'	[sineˈma]	'movie theatre'
[ispiˈtal]	'hospital'	[pəhɛˈlā]	'in the past'
[pəɾikˈʃa]	'examination'	[dʒəɾəˈna]	a name

234   5 *Conflation in reduction*

(b) Otherwise stress a non-final syllable with one of [ɛ ɔ e o i u]
   (i) in the penult

[ˈbɛse]	'sit(s) down'	[ˈkʰeḍut]	'farmer'
[ˈsewək]	'servant'	[ˈnirbʰeḷ]	'absolute'
[ˈdʒuni]	'old'	[ˈdiwəs]	'day'
[eˈkoter]	'71'	[moˈḍetʰi]	'late'
[tʃuˈm:oter]	'74'	[kʰisˈkoli]	'squirrel'
[pənˈtʃoter]	'75'	[pəˈhɛlu]	'first'
[prɔˈfesər]	'professor'	[hõˈʃilũ]	'ardent, eager'
[mjuˈziəm]	'museum'	[nəˈmuno]	'sample'
[məˈḷiʃũ]	'we will meet'	[kəˈbutər]	'pigeon'

   (ii) otherwise in the initial syllable

[ˈowərkot]	'overcoat'	[ˈoḷəkʰwũ]	'know'
[ˈkojəldi]	'little cuckoo'	[ˈkudrəti]	'natural'
[ˈvismərəɲ]	'forgetfulness'		

(c) Otherwise stress a penult [ə][6]

[ˈkəre]	'does, do'	[ˈnəwo]	'new (masc.)'
[ˈdʒəmin]	'land'	[ˈʃəru]	'beginning'
[ˈpətəŋg]	'kite'	[pəˈrəbḍi]	'water-dispensing shed'
[rəˈməkḍũ]	'toy'	[pəˈrəntu]	'but'
[pəˈd:ʰəti]	'method'	[vəˈkʰətsər]	'on time'

The stress description can be informally described in terms of two interacting preference hierarchies, one relating to sonority, and one relating to position. Stress is always attracted to the highest sonority vowel − [a]. If a word contains an [a], it always ends up stressed: e.g. [ˈtadʒetər] 'recently', [sineˈma] 'cinema, movie theatre'. Similarly, stress tends to avoid schwa for higher sonority vowels: e.g. [ˈoḷəkʰwũ] 'to know', [ˈkojəldi] 'little cuckoo'. However, stress does not avoid [ə] entirely: when the final syllable does not contain [a] and the

---

6 Cardona (1965:34) disagrees with this description. He reports that stress only falls on a penult schwa in trisyllabic words if it is closed: e.g. [pəˈrəb.ḍi], [rəˈmək.ḍũ]. If the penult is open, stress falls on the antepenult: e.g. [ˈprə.tʃə.lit] 'current, popular' (the only example given − he notes that 'items of the type /prətʃəlit/ are rare'). I suspect that a process of schwa deletion is responsible for the disagreement between Cardona's account and my own. In my consultants' speech, medial [ə] was usually deleted as long as the result was an acceptable consonant cluster: e.g. /əgʰərũ/→[ˈəgʰrũ] 'difficult', /pərəspər/→[ˈpərspər] 'mutual', /sərəkʰi/→[ˈsərkʰi] 'equal', /ogənis/→[ˈogɲis] '19', /bukəḷo/ → [ˈbukḷo], /tʃʰɔkəra/→[ˈtʃʰɔkra] 'boys'; /prətʃəlit/ was pronounced [ˈprətʃlit]. It is generally the case, then, that /CəCəCV/ will surface as [ˈCəCCV]. However, [ə] deletion is blocked when it would create an illicit consonant cluster (e.g. [ˈakrəmən] 'invasion', *[ˈakrmən], [ˈvismərən] 'forgetfulness', *[ˈvismrən]). In such words with an initial syllable with [ə], stress falls on the penult as predicted by the present description: e.g. [pəd.ˈdʰə.ti] 'method', *[ˈpddʰti], *[ˈpəd.dʰə.ti]; [səm.ˈmə.ti] 'consent, *[ˈsəmmti], *[ˈsəm.mə.ti]; [nərˈpəti] 'king', *[ˈnərpti]. Cardona (1965:49–50) also reports this process (e.g. /mokəle/ → [mokle] 'send(s)'), and Mistry (1997:660ff.) provides a discussion along the same lines.

antepenultimate syllable has a [ə], stress remains on a penultimate schwa (e.g. ['ʃəɾʊ] 'beginning', [pə'ɾəntu] 'but').

Of present interest is the fact that stress does not prefer mid peripheral vowels over high peripheral vowels. For example, stress falls on the penult in [hõ'ʃilu] 'ardent,eager', and not on the more sonorous mid vowel: *['hõʃilu]. In other words, the mid and high peripheral vowels are conflated for stress purposes in Gujarati.

The other preference hierarchy relates to position. The penult is clearly the most unmarked stress position as the penult is stressed in words where all vowels are identical: e.g. [a'wːana] '(they) will come', [və'kʰətsəɾ] 'on time'. The next most favoured position is the antepenult (or pre-penultimate syllable — as noted above, word length prohibits a more general statement), as is evident from words with both an antepenultimate and final [a]: e.g. ['pakistan] 'Pakistan'.

The final syllable is clearly the least desirable position for stress. Stress only falls on an ultima [a] if there are no other [a]'s present: e.g. [sine'ma] 'cinema, movie theatre'. In fact, this is the only situation in which the ultima is stressed: e.g. ['kəɾe] 'does, do', [pə'ɾəbɖi] 'water-dispensing shed'.

In summary, Gujarati stress can be described informally as resulting from two interacting preference hierarchies: the sonority hierarchy of |a⟩,ɛ,ɔ e,o,i,u⟩ ə| and the position hierarchy of *penult* ⟩ *antepenult* ⟩ *ultima*. The following section expresses these hierarchies and their interaction in terms of the theory proposed here.

Stress does not prefer CVC syllables over CV ones. Stress does not fall on a final CVC in preference to a penult CV: e.g. ['dʒəmin], *[dʒə'min]. It does not fall on an antepenult CVC in preference to a penult CV: e.g. [səm.'mə.ti] 'consent', *['səm.mə.ti].

5.3.2.1.1 Evidence for stress

Both speakers realize stress as increased duration, and raised pitch (F_0) for the female speaker.

Phonological evidence that stress is located as described above comes from intonation and allophony. Stressed syllables are the locus for the pitch accents of intonation melodies. Allophonic alternations between tense [i u] and lax [ɪ ʊ] vowels and [ə] and [ʌ] are conditioned by stress (Cardona 1965:20–1).[7] The allophones [ɪ ʊ] appear in non-final unstressed open syllables (e.g. [nɪ.'ʃal]

---

7 Nair (1979) describes the high-vowel distinction as being one of duration while Cardona (1965) describes it in terms of a height distinction. In my consultant's data, the vowels differed in length and height, so I treat this as a tense-lax distinction here.

236   *5 Conflation in reduction*

'school', [gʊ.'dʒɾa.ti] 'Gujarati'). In contrast, [i u] appear in final syllables (e.g. [a'zadi] 'freedom', [ʊ'taɾu] 'passenger'), closed syllables (e.g. [suḍ.'tá.lis] '47', [sit.'to.ter] '77'), and – importantly – in stressed open syllables (e.g. ['dʰi.mo] 'slow', ['dʒu.ləm] 'tyranny'). Because high vowels are tense in open syllables only when stressed, they can be used to support the stress description above. For example, the form [nɪ.'ʃaḷ] 'school' shows that stress is not on the penult, otherwise it would be *['nɪ.ʃaḷ]; this allophony therefore supports the claim that stress avoids a penult high vowel for a final [a]. The form ['manɪto] makes a similar point: if the penult bore stress, it would be *[ma'nito]. Similarly, that stress falls on the penult in [hõ.'ʃi.lũ] 'ardent' is supported by the fact that it is not *[hõʃɪlu]. The form ['bukəḷo] is not *[bʊkəḷo], showing that stress falls on the initial syllable here.

The allophones [ə]~[ʌ] are also conditioned by stress. While [ə] appears in unstressed open syllables (e.g. [pə.'gaɾ] 'wages'), [ʌ] appears in closed syllables (e.g. [sʌɾ.'kaɾ] 'government') and in open stressed syllables (e.g. ['ʃʌ.ɾu] 'beginning'). Evidence for the stress described above can be seen in the [ə]~[ʌ] allophony in open syllables. The forms ['dʒʌ.min] 'land', ['ʃʌ.ɾu] 'beginning', and ['pʌ.tʌŋg] 'kite' show that stress is on the first syllable in these words, and that stress prefers a penultimate central vowel instead of a final high vowel (cf. *[ʃə.ɾu], *[dʒə.min]). The forms [pʌd.'dʰʌ.ti] 'method' and [ɾə.'mʌk.ḍũ] 'toy' show that stress falls on the penult, and not on the initial or final syllable (cf. *[pʌd.dʰə̱.ti], *[ɾʌ̱.mʌk.ḍũ]).

5.3.2.2   Sonority-driven stress I: attraction to [a]
The default position of stress in Gujarati is the penult, as shown by words where all syllables have vowels of the same sonority: e.g. [a'wːanã], [e'koteɾ], [və'kʰətsəɾ]. This follows if Gujarati has a trochaic (i.e. left-headed) foot aligned with the right edge of the ω: e.g. [e('koteɾ)]. A standard analysis of such a pattern is adopted here, using the constraints in (34) (cf. Prince & Smolensky 1993; McCarthy & Prince 1993a,b). The constraints' effect is illustrated in tableau (35).

(34)
ALIGNFTR   'The right edge of every foot must be aligned with the right edge
           of a prosodic word.' (McCarthy & Prince 1993a)
FTBIN   'Every foot is binary at the syllabic or moraic level.' (McCarthy
           & Prince 1986)
TROCHEE   'Every foot is left-headed' (i.e. ALIGN -L(σ,Ft) – McCarthy &
           Prince 1993a)

5.3 *Conflation prevention and vowel sonority*   237

(35)   Gujarati I: Right-aligned trochees

/ekoteɾ/	ALIGNFTR	FTBIN	TROCHEE
(a) ('eko)teɾ	*!		
(b) eko('teɾ)		*!	
(c) e(ko'teɾ)			*!
☞ (d) e('koteɾ)			

Stress does not appear on the penult when it contains a non-low vowel and some other syllable contains [a]. Two different types of penult-avoidance can be identified. 'Foot retraction' is when stress appears on an antepenult [a] to avoid a penult of lower sonority: e.g. [('lajbrɛ)ɾi] 'library', [('tadʒe)təɾ] 'recently', [('mani)to] 'favourite', [('akrə)mən] 'invasion'. For stress to avoid the penult in favour of stressing an [a], two conditions must be met: (i) some constraint must favour stressed [a] over all other stressed vowels, and (ii) that constraint must outrank ALIGNFTR. The latter ranking is crucial, since stress on antepenultimate [a] means that the foot is not aligned with the ω's right edge: e.g. [('tadʒe)təɾ]. The relevant constraint is *$\Delta_{Ft}\leq\{e,o\}$ 'Assign a violation to the head of a foot if it contains a vowel with less sonority than a low vowel.' Only ['a] avoids violating this constraint, as shown in tableau (36).

(36)   Gujarati II : Foot retraction

/tadʒetəɾ/	*$d_{Ft}\leq\{e,o\}$	ALIGNFTR
(a) ta('dʒetəɾ)	*!	
☞ (b) ('tadʒe)təɾ		*

While candidate (a) is most harmonic in terms of foot alignment, it fatally violates *$\Delta_{Ft}\leq\{e,o\}$ by containing a stressed mid vowel [e]. In contrast, its competitor (b) contains a stressed low vowel, so avoiding violations of *$\Delta_{Ft}\leq\{e,o\}$; its violation of ALIGNFTR is rendered irrelevant by the ranking.

The other possible response to *$\Delta_{Ft}\leq\{e,o\}$ is to change the feature content of the penult to [a] — i.e. *[ta('dʒa̱təɾ)] (for examples, see §7.3.2.1). To avoid this possibility in Gujarati, faithfulness constraints on vowel features (e.g. IDENT[low]) outrank the *Δ_{Ft}/x constraints.

The other type of penult-avoidance involves stress falling on the ultima to avoid a penult non-low vowel (e.g. [ʃi'kaɾ] 'a hunt', [sine'ma] 'cinema', [pəhɛ'lã] 'in the past'). These forms violate FTBIN since the foot is monosyllabic: [ʃi('kaɾ)], [sine('ma)].⁸ This response to the sonority condition is called 'foot degeneration' here, as the result is a degenerate (mono-moraic) foot. To account for foot degeneration, $*\Delta_{Ft}\leq\{e,o\}$ must outrank FTBIN, shown in (37).

(37)   Gujarati III : Foot degeneration due to avoidance of non-[a]

/sinema/	$*\Delta_{Ft}\leq\{e,o\}$	FTBIN
(a) si('nema)	*!	
(b) ('sine)ma	*!	
☞ (c) sine('ma)		*

The tableau shows that there is no way for the foot to be both binary and have a high-sonority head. The inevitable result is a violation of FTBIN.

The final point of this section is that foot retraction is preferred over degeneration. This is evident from forms like [('pakis)tan] 'Pakistan': if foot degeneration was preferred over retraction, the output should be *[pakis('tan)]. In ranking terms, the anti-degeneration constraint FTBIN must outrank ALIGNFTR, as shown in tableau (38).

(38)   Gujarati IV : Foot retraction beats degeneration

/pakistan/	$*\Delta_{Ft}\leq\{e,o\}$	FTBIN	ALIGNFTR
(a) pa('kistan)	*!		
(b) pakis('tan)		*!	
☞ (c) ('pakis)tan			*

To summarize, the ranking $\|*\Delta_{Ft}\leq\{e,o\} \gg \text{FTBIN} \gg \text{ALIGNFTR}\|$ accounts both for the fact that stress avoids syllables without [a] and for the preferences regarding stress position: the constraints determine that the most harmonic position is the penult, then the antepenult, then the ultima. In conflation terms, Gujarati prevents conflation of the sonority category 'low vowels' with all the other sonority categories. Such prevention is achieved by having

---

8 The foot could instead be iambic in this situation: i.e. [(ʃi'kaɾ)]. In this case, it would be TROCHEE that is violated and not FTBIN. In either case, the ranking arguments presented below would be the same. I have found no evidence that weighs in favour of either analysis, so I will assume that FTBIN is violated here.

an active constraint that favours low stressed vowels over all others – i.e. *$\Delta_{Ft}\leq\{e,o\}$.

5.3.2.3 Sonority-driven stress II: avoidance of ['ə]

Attraction of stress to [a] is not the only visible effect of sonority-stress interaction in Gujarati. Stress also avoids the lowest sonority vowel [ə]: e.g. ['pustəkne] 'to the book', ['vismərən̪] 'forgetfulness', ['kojəldi] 'little cuckoo'.

Schwa is not 'unstressable'. Stress falls on [ə] in two situations: (i) when there are no other non-[ə] vowels (e.g. ['pətəŋg] 'kite', [və'kʰətsər] 'on time'), and (ii) when the only other option is final stress on a non-low vowel (e.g. ['kəre] 'do', ['nə̃wo] 'new', ['ʃəru] 'beginning', [pə'rəbɖi] 'water-dispensing shed').[9] This latter situation contrasts with the influence of [a] on stress: Gujarati prefers a final stressed [a] over a penult of lower sonority, but it does not prefer a final higher-sonority stressed vowel over a penultimate stressed [ə]. To put this in different terms, the only way that Gujarati allows avoidance of penult [ə] is through foot retraction; foot degeneration in response to penult [ə] is not allowed. This restriction will prove significant in evaluating alternative theories of hierarchies below. For the moment, the focus will be on presenting an account that employs the DTE-sonority constraints.

For [ə] to force stress retraction the constraint *$\Delta_{Ft}\leq\{ə\}$ must outrank ALIGNFtR, following the same reasoning as for non-[a] vowels in the previous section. Tableau (39) illustrates this ranking with the word [('kojəl)di] 'little cuckoo'.

(39)   Gujarati v : Foot retraction to avoid stressed [ə]

/kojəldi/	*$\Delta_{Ft}\leq\{ə\}$	ALIGNFTR
(a) ko('jəldi)	*!	
☞ (b) ('kojəl)di		*

The next issue is foot degeneration. Gujarati does not avoid stressing a penult [ə] if doing so will result in stress on the ultima, or – in present terms – a degenerate foot. For example, *kəre* 'does, do' is stressed as [('kəre)], not *[kə('re)]. Similarly, 'but' is [pə('rəntu)], not *[pərən('tu)]. The lack of foot

---

9 Cardona (1965:33) reports free variation in stress with words of the shape [Cə.CV(C)] where V is not ə (e.g. ['dʒəmin]~[dʒə'min], ['vəɖe]~[və'ɖe], etc.). Neither of my consultants exhibited this variation – stress was invariably on the initial syllable, so I will not discuss an analysis here (see de Lacy 2002a:§3.4.1.4). Cardona also reports that words with the shape [CəC.CV] invariably have stress on the initial syllable, which is in agreement with the present description.

240   5 *Conflation in reduction*

degeneration is explained straightforwardly using the present constraints: the degeneration-banning constraint FTBIN must outrank *$\Delta_{Ft}\leq\{\partial\}$, as shown in tableau (40).

(40)   Gujarati VI: No foot degeneration to avoid stressed schwa

/kəre/	FTBIN	*$\Delta_{Ft}\leq\{\partial\}$
(a) kə('re)	*!	
☞ (b) ('kəre)		*

To recap, penult stressed [ə] can only be avoided through stress retraction in Gujarati, not degeneration. These facts are captured through the ranking ‖FTBIN » *$\Delta_{Ft}\leq\{\partial\}$ » ALIGNFTR‖. The position of *$\Delta_{Ft}\leq\{\partial\}$ contrasts with the sonority-stress constraint *$\Delta_{Ft}\leq\{e,o\}$; this latter constraint outranks both FTBIN and ALIGNFTR as it can motivate both foot retraction and degeneration. As an interim summary, the previous sections have provided evidence for the ranking in (41).

(41)   Interim Gujarati Ranking

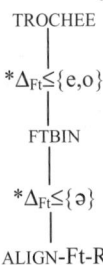

TROCHEE
|
*$\Delta_{Ft}\leq\{e,o\}$
|
FTBIN
|
*$\Delta_{Ft}\leq\{\partial\}$
|
ALIGN-Ft-R

Analogous to the Dutch ranking, the ranking of *$\Delta_{Ft}\leq\{\partial\}$ and *$\Delta_{Ft}\leq\{e,o\}$ illustrates a fundamental way in which the stringency theory and the Fixed Ranking theory differ. Section 5.3.2.4 completes the ranking by identifying the position of *$\Delta_{Ft}\leq\{i,u\}$.

5.3.2.4 Conflation

The final question to ask is why Gujarati ignores the sonority distinction between mid and high vowels for stress purposes. In purely constraint terms, this section deals with the issue of where the remaining foot-DTE constraint – *$\Delta_{Ft}\leq\{i,u\}$ – is ranked in the grammar of Gujarati.

Examples showing that stress does not retract from a high peripheral vowel when a mid vowel is available in another syllable are provided in (42).

5.3 *Conflation prevention and vowel sonority* 241

(42) (a) Antepenult mid vowels do not attract stress away from penult high vowels
  [hõ'ʃilũ]   'ardent, eager'   [o'tʃintũ]   'unexpected'
  [ɔ'ʃikũ]   'pillow'   [oḷ'kʰitũ]   'familiar'
  [lok'prijə] 'famous'   [og'ɳismũ]   'nineteenth'
  [ɔ'kuwi]   'get vomited'
  (b) Final mid vowels do not attract stress away from penult high vowels
  ['jurop]   'Europe'   [nə'muno]   'sample'
  ['pio]   'drink'   ['sitːer]   '70'
  ['dʒue]   'looks'   ['nirbʰeḷ]   'absolute'
  (c) High vowels do not attract stress away from penult mid vowels
  [su'telũ]   'lying down'   [kʰis'koli]   'squirrel'
  [tʃu'mːoter] '74'   ['kedi]   'prisoner'
  [si'tːoter] '77'   ['kʰeduṭ]   'farmer'
  [mus'keli]   'difficulty'   ['tʃɔwis]   '24'
  [əŋ'gredʒi] 'English'   ['mɔdũ]   'delay'

Allophony provides evidence for the stress marking above: e.g. [hõ'ʃilu] is not *[hõʃɪlũ].

As the data in (42a) is central to the theoretical point made here, some further discussion is necessary. Forms with the shape [C{ɛ,e}C{i,u}CV] proved to be difficult to find, so none are reported here. One near-example was [vɛ̃'tijũ] 'dwarfish', but my consultants almost always pronounced this as ['vɛ̃'tjũ]. This elimination of [i] is not sporadic: a number of forms with orthographic [ij] sequences were stressed on the antepenult: e.g. ''nɔrijo' 'mongoose', ''dʰotijũ' 'dhotis', ''koḷijo' 'morsel', ''motijo' 'cataract'. However, the orthographic 'ij' sequence was pronounced as just [j] in my consultants' speech; the same is reported by Gajendragadkar (1974) for Parsi-Gujarati. Therefore, these cases do not disobey the reported generalizations: they are ['nɔrjo], ['motjo], and so on. Significantly, the [i] could not delete when doing so would produce an inadmissable consonant cluster: e.g. [lok'prijə], *['lokprjə] and [o'tʃintũ],*['otʃntũ] – in these cases, the [i] bore the stress as predicted. It is also significant that stress appeared on the antepenult in [CVCijV] words even when it was not a mid vowel: e.g. ''tʃipijo' 'pair of tongs' (my consultants: ['tʃipjo]). This generalization was true for two consultants; the other reported that /ij/ was realized as [i] only in normal speech, while the [ij] is retained in careful speech.

A further set of apparent exceptions involves variation in clusters consisting of [i] and the coronal fricatives [s] and [ʃ]: orthographic 'si', 'shi', 'is', and 'ish' were occasionally realized as just [ʃ]. This variation is tied to speech rate, with deletion happening in rapid speech. An example is with the word for 'pillow', which was realized variously as ['ɔʃkũ], [ɔ'ʃikũ], and [ɔ'sikũ] by my consultants (similarly for [hõ'ʃilũ]~['hõʃlu]). Cardona (1965:34) reports it as [ɔ'ʃikũ], but one of my consultants did not stress the first syllable if the [i] was present: i.e. [ɔ'ʃikũ]~['ɔʃkũ]. Cardona also reports the form [məl̥iʃũ]~[məl̥ʃũ] (p.34) and variation between -[iʃũ]~[ʃũ] for the first person plural future ending, which one consultant reported as stylistic variants. The variants without [i]-deletion have been reported here as they are the most relevant ones for the stress description.

Finally, loanwords often retain the source language's stress in defiance of the stress rules: e.g. ['telifon] 'telephone', ['petikot] 'petticoat', ['redjijo] 'radio', ['ɔfisəɾ] 'officer' (also note the telltale retention of the source language's [f], which is not found in native words).

In short, all apparent exceptions can be put down to retention of source-language stress, or independent processes of deletion of [i] when adjacent to [j] or [ʃ]. As a final note, [u] does not delete like [i], agreeing with Cardona's (1965:34#3) description.

The situation illustrated in (42) is conflation of high and mid peripheral vowels. The Dutch analysis in §5.3.1 showed that mid and high peripheral vowels constitute separate sonority categories, yet they are treated the same in Gujarati stress.[10] As with Kashaya, it is a straightforward matter to account for category conflation using the stringent constraints. Two categories are conflated when they incur the same violations of active constraints. Mid and high vowels are indistinguishable for stress purposes in Gujarati, so every output constraint that assigns different violations to the two categories must be inactive — i.e. the constraint must not make a crucial decision in competitions involving stress. The constraint $*\Delta_{Ft}\leq\{i,u\}$ distinguishes between stressed high vowels and stressed mid vowels, so it must be inactive. Sonority-stress constraints are rendered inactive by ranking them below an appropriate metrical constraint, which happens to be ALIGNFTR in Gujarati, as illustrated in tableau (43).

(43)   Gujarati VII : Conflation

/otʃintũ/	ALIGNFTR	$*\Delta_{Ft}\leq\{i,u\}$
(a) ('otʃin)tũ	*!	
☞ (b) o('tʃintũ)		*

---

[10] Other cases of sonority-driven stress distinguish between high and mid peripheral vowels. For example, in Nganasan stress usually falls on the penult (e.g. [ku'humi] 'our (dual) skin'), but retracts to the antepenult if it contains a mid vowel while the penult contains a high vowel: e.g. ['ɟembiʔʃi] 'dressing', ['hoðyʔə] 'writing' (Eugene Helimski 1998, p.c.; Olga Vaysman p.c.; de Lacy 2004). Similarly, Kenstowicz (1996) reports that the usually penultimate stress in Chukchi retracts from high vowels to mid vowels: e.g. ['weni-wen] 'bell', cf. [nu'tenut] 'land'.

5.3 Conflation prevention and vowel sonority 243

Tableau (43) shows how *$\Delta_{Ft}\leq\{i,u\}$ is rendered inactive: ALIGNFTR effectively quashes all competition based on difference in stress placement because it favours a candidate with penultimate stress.

The same point can be made for the constraint *$\Delta_{Ft}\leq\{\varepsilon,\mathrm{\jmath}\}$. This distinguishes mid-low vowels from all others. If it were active in Gujarati, /ɔʃikū/ would surface as *[ˈɔʃikū] instead of the attested [ˈɔʃikū].

To summarize, Gujarati has the ranking in (44).

(44)   Final Gujarati Ranking

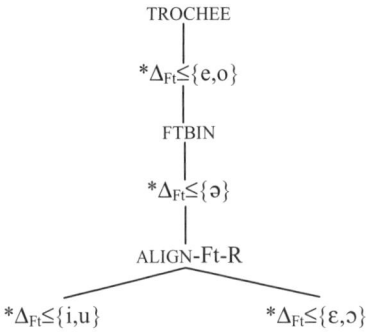

As argued for Kashaya, the stringency constraints' free ranking allows them to produce both conflation and lack of conflation in the same system. Gujarati conflates mid and high peripheral vowels for stress purposes by ensuring that *$\Delta_{Ft}\leq\{i,u\}$ is inactive. However, low vowels are kept distinct by having *$\Delta_{Ft}\leq\{e,o\}$ active.

Schwa is particularly interesting because it is conflated with other sonority levels in some environments but not others. When schwa is in the penult and the only non-schwa vowel is in the final syllable, the vowels are effectively conflated and so stress ends up on the penult. This conflation is due to the fact that TROCHEE renders *$\Delta_{Ft}\leq\{\partial\}$ inactive. However, when the choice is between the penult and antepenult, *$\Delta_{Ft}\leq\{\partial\}$ is active, so schwa is not conflated with high and mid vowels. Consequently, stress retracts to an antepenultimate non-[ə].

In short, Gujarati presents an extremely complex situation of conflation (stressed high and mid vowels), lack of conflation (stressed low vowels vs. the others), and environmentally sensitive conflation (involving schwa). The stringent constraints were shown to be able to deal with this mixture of conflation types.

244   5 *Conflation in reduction*

5.4   Alternatives

There are several imaginable alternatives to the proposals made in the preceding sections. One involves referring to representational distinctions rather than using constraint form. Another is to reduce multi-valued hierarchies to binary ones. These alternatives are discussed here and shown to be inadequate in dealing with conflation.

The conflation typology of sonority-driven stress, presented in table 45, will provide a useful background to the discussion (de Lacy 2004, 2006). The typology of sonority-driven stress is very revealing for conflation and conflation-prevention. Almost every possible contiguous conflation in stress-sonority interaction is attested. Categories are marked as conflated if they are grouped inside the same oval. For example, the mid and low vowels are conflated in Pichis Ashéninca, but the central and high vowels are not.

For ease of presentation the table uses 'ə' to stand for any central vowel due to the rarity of contrast between /ə/ and /ɨ/ (e.g. Pichis Ashéninca has [ɨ], not schwa). Similarly 'e o' stands for all mid vowels, including [e o ɛ ɔ] even though [e o] are demonstrably less sonorous than [ɛ ɔ].

(45)   Head-sonority conflation typology

Categories	Languages
(ə) (i/u) (e/o) (a)	Kobon (Davies 1981)
(ə) (i/u e/o) (a)	Gujarati (this section, de Lacy 2002a:ch.3)
(ə) (i/u e/o) (a)	Pichis Ashéninca (J.Payne 1990)
(ə) (i/u e/o a)	Yil (Martens & Tuominen 1977)
(ə i/u) (e/o) (a)	–
(ə i/u e/o) (a)	Nganasan (de Lacy 2004)
(ə i/u) (e/o a)	Kara (Schlie & Schlie 1993; de Lacy 1997)
(ə i/u e/o a)	*All vowels are treated the same*

Table (45) also shows that almost every imaginable conflation of vowel sonority categories is attested. I have not found a system that conflates ['ə] and ['i 'u] but distinguishes mid from low vowels. In such a language, stress would first seek out a low vowel and otherwise a mid vowel; if there were only high and central vowels, stress would fall on the default position. Given that there are languages in which stress favours low vowels over mid vowels (e.g. Gujarati) and languages in which high peripheral vowels and schwa are conflated (e.g. Nganasan), I assume that this gap is accidental.

There is one systematic gap: no language conflates non-contiguous categories. An example would be a language which conflates low and high vowels, but not mid vowels: stress would fall on the leftmost [a], [i], or [u], and skip over intervening mid vowels [e] and [o]. The stringent constraints predict that such a language cannot exist. It would require a constraint that favoured stressed high vowels over stressed mid vowels and there is no such constraint in the theory.[11]

5.4.1   Representational approaches

The conflation typology is useful in showing why representational approaches cannot deal with conflation. To explain, a number of authors have proposed that schwa has a 'degenerate' representation – i.e. it lacks subsegmental features, or a mora, or both (see, e.g., Hayes 1995:ch.7; Oostendorp 1995; Crosswhite 2004).

This representational idea could be integrated into a theory of schwa-avoidance. After Oostendorp 1995, if a constraint bans moras on featureless vowels, no higher prosodic structure – including prosodic heads – could be built over schwas. Consequently, schwas would be unstressable, except perhaps when no other vowel is available. This approach effectively makes two distinctions: between schwa on the one hand and peripheral vowels on the other. In fact, it conflates distinctions between peripheral vowels: as they all have one mora, they are all equal for stress purposes.

Unfortunately, such a representational approach faces insurmountable problems. One is that it cannot adequately account for languages which distinguish more than two categories for stress purposes. For example, the featureless/non-moraic schwa approach could be used to deal with schwa's stress avoidance in Gujarati. However, stress also seeks out [a] over [ɛ ɔ e o i u]. Following the representational approach through to its logical conclusion, it would be necessary to assume that Gujarati [ə] has no moras, [a] two, and the other vowels one (see, e.g., Hayes 1995:ch.7); preference for stressed syllables with greater moraic content would produce the observed stress system. In such an approach

---

11 Trommer & Grimm (2004) propose that Albanian is a counter-example. Stress usually falls on final syllables (e.g. [njeˈri] 'human', [pərpaˈrim] 'progress'). However, when the final vowel is [e], [o], or [ə], it falls on the penultimate syllable: e.g. [ˈanə], [ˈfaqe], [ˈpronə]. In contrast, stress does not avoid a final high vowel: e.g. [baˈri], *[ˈbari], [qerˈʃi], *[ˈqerʃi]. Although it seems at first glance that Albanian prefers to stress [i u] over [e o] (so reversing the sonority relation between high and mid vowels), it is clearly not sonority that forces avoidance of final stress in many words: e.g. [ˈhənə], [ˈən.dje], [ˈɠolle], [ˈneto]. In these words, stress does not end up on a more sonorous vowel; for [ˈən.dje], the result is a *less* sonorous stressed vowel. It is not possible to say that [ə] is treated as more sonorous than [e] in Albanian because the complementary type of attraction exists: [ˈehə]. In every other case of sonority-driven stress, deviation from the default stress position only occurs if there is a more sonorous vowel elsewhere.

conflation is a side-effect of mora assignment — it is the fact that high and mid vowels have the same moraic content that results in their conflation.

In effect, the moraic approach to sonority-driven stress outlined above converts moras into little more than a language-specific diacritic device that is almost synonymous with sonority. However, there is a difference between the sonority and moraic approaches. As moras represent duration, they make undesirable predictions for phonetic realization. In Gujarati, low vowels should be appreciably longer than high and mid vowels, and all should be longer than schwa. This is not so — there is no significant difference between [a]'s duration and the other vowels' in Gujarati. The same point can be made for other languages. For example, Nganasan distinguishes two groups of vowels for stress: [ɨ ə i y u] and [a e o]. The former group cannot have fewer moras than the latter because there is no significant durational difference between the two sets (de Lacy 2004:§2.6.3).

Representational theories also make strong predictions about other processes in the grammar. Proposing that low vowels have more moras than other vowels predicts that they can – and perhaps must – be treated differently for other mora-referring processes. This prediction is criticized at length by Gordon (1999).

Another popular representational theory relates specifically to the opposition between schwa and peripheral vowels, and relies on the idea that schwa lacks phonological features (e.g. Oostendorp 1995 and references cited therein). With additional theoretical devices, this fact makes schwas 'weak', and consequently unable to bear stress. This theory is one of a class that considers schwa to be fundamentally phonologically different from all other vowels. In contrast, the approach to stress proposed here denies that schwa is significantly different from other vowels in phonological terms – the only difference is that schwa is lower on the sonority hierarchy than (most) other vowels.

A problem with relating lack of features to stress avoidance arises in languages in which schwa is conflated with other vowels. In Nganasan, [ɨ], [ə], and [i y u] repel stress equally – they are conflated for stress purposes. If lack of features is the reason that schwa repels stress, then all of [ɨ ə i y u] must be featureless in Nganasan. However, if all vowels are featureless, then they are phonologically indistinguishable. At the very least, it is clear that featurelessness is not sufficient on its own to account for stress repulsion.

In the theory presented here, there is no appeal to lack of features or any other representational degeneracy. Schwa is not fundamentally different from other vowels in terms of its representation. It is simply low on the sonority hierarchy; its behaviour in phonological processes follows from its sonority level, not from its lack of features. Attempts to approach the conflation problem by appealing to representational differences among vowels leads to unsupported predictions regarding duration, mora-sensitive phonological processes, or difficulties in accounting for vowel contrasts.

For further critiques of representational theories of stress and conflation, see Gordon 1999, de Lacy 2002a:§3.3.4, and 2004:§2.6.3. For a general critique of representational theories of markedness, see §8.4.

5.4.2 Binary features

The typology of conflation discussed above allows examination of an alternative to the stringency approach. The alternative relies on decomposing every hierarchy into a series of two-member hierarchies, or binary features. If every hierarchy consisted of just two elements, conflation could be implemented through fixed ranking.

Of present relevance is the idea that the sonority hierarchy can be decomposed into several sub-hierarchies, each consisting of just two members. Such an approach has a precedent in Clements' (1990:292) account of consonant sonority; Clements proposed that the consonant sonority hierarchy | obstruent 〉 nasal 〉 liquid 〉 glide | could be decomposed into the four features, as shown in table (46). This approach contrasts with the assumption made here that there is a single unitary sonority hierarchy with several different values.

(46) Clements' (1990) consonant sonority decomposition

Obstruents	< Nasals	< Liquids	< Glides	
−	−	−	−	'syllabic'
−	−	−	+	vocoid
−	−	+	+	approximant
−	+	+	+	sonorant
0	1	2	3	rank (relative sonority)

Such a 'binary' approach could in principle be extended to vowel sonority. Table (47) illustrates a binary feature approach to vowel sonority. The features are named as 'F', 'G', 'H', 'I' here; discussion of whether they can be identified with commonly accepted features is given below.

(47) | ɨ 〉 ə 〉 i,u 〉 e,o 〉 a |

−	−	−	−	+	F
−	−	−	+	+	G
−	−	+	+	+	H
−	+	+	+	+	I

In constraint terms, the relation of the features above to heads could be implemented through four hierarchies, with the form (a) ‖ *Hd$_{Ft}$ /−I » *Hd$_{Ft}$ /+I ‖, (b) ‖ *Hd$_{Ft}$ /−H » *Hd$_{Ft}$ /+H ‖, (c) ‖ *Hd$_{Ft}$ /−G » *Hd$_{Ft}$ /+G ‖, and (d) ‖ *Hd$_{Ft}$ /−F » *Hd$_{Ft}$ /+F ‖. Conflation is a straightforward matter. For example, to conflate central and high peripheral vowels (as in Nganasan), *Hd$_{Ft}$ /−I would be inactive. Importantly, *Hd$_{Ft}$ /−I does not imply the inactivity of *Hd$_{Ft}$ /−H; if *Hd$_{Ft}$ /−H is active, then a distinction between high and mid peripheral vowels can be maintained. In this way, the binary feature approach seems to achieve the same ends as the stringent constraints; however, the theories make different predictions in other areas.

The problem with the binary feature theory is that it makes several false predictions in relation to natural classes. It relies on the existence of the features [I], [H], [G], and [F], and these features should therefore have effects on other processes. For example, the features can be expected to participate in dissimilation, assimilation, harmony, coalescence, and other relevant phonological processes. Certainly, some of the features fit with current feature theories. For example, [F] can be identified with [low], and is therefore a reasonable feature because it participates in assimilation and dissimilation (e.g. Kera – Suzuki 1998), and in vowel harmony (van der Hulst & van der Weijer 1995:519ff.).

However, feature [G] poses a problem. If [G] exists, it should participate in vowel harmony where every vowel must be either one of [ə i u] or one of [e o ɛ ɔ a]. Likewise, feature [H] predicts vowel harmony where every vowel is either central or peripheral. Such vowel harmonies are not reported in surveys such as Baković's (1999a). In short, the binary feature approach to vowel sonority inevitably relies on spurious features.

The same problem arises for the PoA hierarchy. For a binary approach to work for PoA, there would have to be a feature [F] where dorsals and labials were [+F] and coronals and glottals were [−F], and ‖*+F »» *−F‖. If there is such a feature, it should be able to assimilate, producing unattested assimilations like /atka/ → [apka] because [p] and [k] are both [+F], and the output [kk] can be blocked for other reasons (e.g. a ban on geminate consonants).

Of course, the result above raises the question of whether the multi-valued feature approach makes similar incorrect predictions. The [Sonority] feature seems to treat central and high peripheral vowels as a class, so does it also make incorrect predictions regarding assimilation and harmony?

There is a principled way for the multi-valued feature approach to avoid the problems just described. There are two different senses of 'natural class' for multi-valued features. One sense of 'natural class' relates to feature-value identity: α and β are part of the same class if they have identical feature values. From the feature-value identity sense of 'natural class', [i] and [u] form a natural class because both have the feature value *xxoooooooooo* for [Sonority] (see §2.3.3.1.1).

The other sense of 'natural class' is the 'string inclusion' sense: α and β are part of the same class if the *x*'s (or *o*'s) in α and β's feature-value strings form a substring of a certain specified *x* string. In this sense, [ə] and [i] are part of the same natural class because both segments have feature values that contain a substring of *xxx*.

Different types of constraints refer to these different types of natural class. The processes identified above – assimilation, dissimilation, and harmony – and their related constraints (e.g. AGREE or the constraints in chapter 4, the OCP) all require agreement of feature values. Since [ə] and [i u] do not form a natural class in terms of feature-value agreement, no harmony process will ever require that all vowels be either [ə] or [i u]. In contrast, constraints that ban certain features outright (e.g. $*\Delta_{Ft}/x$) refer to string-inclusion. Thus, such constraints refer to the 'feature-value inclusion' type of natural class.

5.5 Summary

This chapter has argued that distinctions between markedness categories can be collapsed or 'conflated'. In Kashaya, the distinctions between dorsals, labials, and coronals are conflated for neutralization purposes – because there is no distinction, there is no motivation for dorsals and labials to become the less-marked coronals when they are blocked from becoming glottals. The same effects were seen in vowel reduction in Dutch and sonority-driven stress in Gujarati and other languages.

It was also shown that languages must be able to prevent conflation – i.e. maintain distinctions between markedness categories. Conflation is not all-or-nothing: it is possible for some categories to be conflated while others are kept distinct in the same language. For example, Kashaya uvulars are not conflated with other PoA categories; similarly, while Gujarati mid and high peripheral vowels are conflated for stress purposes, low vowels are not.

In order to adequately produce conflation, it was argued that output constraints that refer to markedness hierarchies must be freely rankable and formulated stringently. The two properties necessarily go together: if constraints can be ranked freely, the only way to maintain hierarchical relations is for the constraints to directly encode those relations. For example, if the non-stringent

250 5 *Conflation in reduction*

constraints *{dorsal} and *{coronal} could be ranked in any way, there would be no way to establish that dorsals are more marked than coronals. In contrast, the stringent PoA constraints express the hierarchical relations by having no constraint that favours dorsals over coronals. Consequently, no matter how they are ranked, the stringent constraints will never reverse the markedness relations for PoA.

The stringent constraints were shown to produce conflation through 'inactivity'. If the constraint *{dors,lab} is dominated in a language so that it is not decisive in competitions involving a particular process, dorsals and labials will not be distinguished in that process. For example, *{dors,lab} is dominated by IDENT{dors,lab} in Kashaya, so the PoA neutralization process is not sensitive to the dorsal-labial distinction. The stringent theory can conflate any set of contiguous markedness categories in a hierarchy.

In contrast, a theory with a universally fixed ranking of constraints cannot allow all attested conflations. The fixed ranking ‖*{dorsal} »» *{coronal}‖ ensures that dorsals cannot be conflated with coronals in a language if *{coronal} is active. For example, *{coronal} would have to outrank PoA-faithfulness constraints in Kashaya to force /t/→[?] neutralization. If *{coronal} is active, *{dorsal} must be active as well, so dorsals and coronals cannot be conflated. The empirical effect is that, when neutralization to glottal is blocked, neutralizing to coronal would always be a better option than remaining faithful to dorsal PoA. Kashaya shows this prediction to be incorrect.

The constraints can also prevent conflation. Every member of the PoA hierarchy incurs a unique set of violations of the stringent PoA constraints, allowing each element to be distinguished. In Kashaya, for example, *{uvular} is active and so places stronger demands on uvulars than all other elements. It was demonstrated for Kashaya, Dutch, and Gujarati that a mixture of active and inactive constraints can both prevent and cause conflation in the same language. This contrasts with approaches which require conflation; for example, in the conceptually simplest representational theory of neutralization, PoA neutralization is simply deletion of PoA features. However, this approach predicts that conflation should always take place – there should be no reduction to the 'next least-marked' segment.

In informal terms, this chapter aimed to show that it is not correct to say 'x is more marked than y'. Such a statement implies that conflation can never happen: if feature x is blocked from surfacing with the least-marked value, it should then take the next least-marked value. Instead, it is correct to assert

5.5 Summary

that 'y is never more marked than x', so allowing for a situation in which the markedness distinction between x and y is conflated. So, for PoA coronals are never more marked than dorsals. In Kashaya, they happen to be treated as having the same degree of desirability.

The next step in arguing for the stringent form of constraints is to make the same argument for faithfulness constraints that refer to markedness hierarchies; this is the aim of the next chapter.

6 *Markedness conflation in preservation*

6.1 Introduction

Conflation is just as relevant for Preservation of the Marked and faithfulness constraints as it is for markedness reduction and output constraints. For example, preservation of labials does not always take precedence over preserving coronals; there are situations in which there is equal pressure to preserve labials and coronals – i.e. the distinction between labials and coronals is conflated for faithfulness purposes. This chapter identifies situations in which preservation conflation occurs. It also shows that faithfulness constraints with a stringent form can produce such conflation. Faithfulness constraints for PoA and obstruent voicing are given in (1) as both will be discussed in the following sections.

(1) Stringent faithfulness constraints
 (a) IDENT{dors}, IDENT{dors,lab}, IDENT{dors,lab,cor}, IDENT{dors,lab,cor,gl}
 (b) IDENT{+voice}, IDENT{±voice}

As mentioned in preceding chapters, a constraint like IDENT{dors,lab} is violated for every dorsal or labial that does not have a faithful correspondent. So, the mapping /kapata/ → [pataʔa] violates IDENT{dors,lab} twice, once for the unfaithful mapping /k/ → [p] and once for the unfaithful /p/ → [t]. It is not violated by /t/ → [ʔ] as IDENT{dors,lab} does not refer to coronals.

As with markedness-referring output constraints, a competing approach is that markedness relations are 'strict': preservation of marked elements should always take precedence over preservation of less-marked elements. As with the output constraints in chapter 5, this idea can be expressed through a fixed ranking of faithfulness constraints, as in (2). The symbol »» indicates a universal ranking.

(2) Fixed faithfulness ranking
 (a) IDENT{dorsal} »» IDENT{labial} »» IDENT{coronal} »» IDENT{glottal}
 (b) IDENT[+voice] »» IDENT[−voice]

Empirical evidence that the strict approach is incorrect comes from conflation of preservation distinctions in coalescence and assimilation.

Section 6.2 discusses conflation of voicing distinctions in Swedish. Section 6.3 presents evidence for faithfulness conflation from coalescence in the Indic language Pāli. 'Coalescence' refers to situations where two or more input segments fuse to form a single output segment, often combining features of both segments. For example, consonants coalesce in Pāli to avoid certain coda restrictions: e.g. /lab^h-tabːa/ → [lad̪ːʰabːa] 'take {gerund}' (§6.3, Fahs 1989). That coalescence has taken place rather than deletion is shown by the featural content of the output: [d̪ːʰ] retains the voicing and aspiration of the input /b^h/, and the PoA of the input /t/. In Optimality Theory, coalescence is a situation in which two or more input segments correspond to a single output segment (McCarthy 1995, 2000; Lamontagne & Rice 1995; Pater 1996, 1999; Gnanadesikan 1995). In other words, both /b^h/ and /t/ of /lab^h-tabːa/ correspond to [d̪ːʰ] in [lad̪ːʰabːa].

Coalescence creates conflict in faithfulness. In the Pāli /b^h-t/ → [d̪ːʰ] example, there is a conflict between preserving the labial feature of the /b^h/ and the coronal feature of the /t/. There are similar conflicts for voicing and aspiration. Such conflict in PoA shows preservation conflation. The marked labial value does not survive in spite of the fact that the PoA faithfulness constraints cumulatively favour preserving labials over coronals. Instead, the output is coronal because preservation of labials and coronals is favoured equally, and markedness reduction then favours the coronal over the labial. Tableau (3) summarizes the preservation conflation ranking.

(3)   Preservation conflation in Pāli

/lab$^h_1$-t$_2$ a /	IDENT{dors,lab,cor}	*{dors,lab}	IDENT{dors,lab}
(a) labːʰ$_{1,2}$a	*	*!	
☞ (b) lad̪ːʰ$_{1,2}$a	*		*

The constraint IDENT{dors,lab,cor} preserves dorsals, labials, and coronals equally. It is violated once by candidate (a) because input /t/ loses its coronal specification in the output [bːʰ] and once by candidate (b) because input /b^h/ loses its labial specification in [d̪ːʰ]. As both (a) and (b) are equally unfaithful, the lower-ranked *{dors,lab} constraints makes the crucial decision – *{dors,lab} favours (b) over (a).

Under a Fixed Ranking approach, it is impossible for the coronal specification to be preserved. As IDENT[labial] universally outranks IDENT[coronal] in this approach, preservation of coronal will always lose to preserving labial in

254 6 *Markedness conflation in preservation*

coalescence. In short, the Fixed Ranking approach to faithfulness predicts that in coalescence the marked value will always survive. This point is developed further in §6.3.

The Fixed Ranking approach will be compared in both of the case studies, along with a theory with freely rankable non-stringent faithfulness constraints.

Finally, §6.4 presents a different conception of faithfulness to deal with the 'majority rules' problem.

6.2   Preservation conflation in Swedish voicing

Swedish provides a case of preservation conflation, and so demonstrates the need for stringent faithfulness constraints. The empirical focus is the obstruent voicing hierarchy | +voice 〉 −voice |. Swedish has bi-directional voicing assimilation, and the unmarked [−voice] value always survives (Sigurd 1965; Hellberg 1974; Lombardi 1999). The following analysis argues that the unmarked value wins due to the action of output constraints against the marked value – i.e. *{+voice} in this case. A faithfulness constraint that preserves both values of [voice] – IDENT[±voice] – must outrank *{+voice} in order to prevent voice neutralization generally.

6.2.1   Bi-directional assimilation

In bi-directional assimilation, the feature content of the output is not determined by the rightmost or leftmost input segment. Instead, a single value dominates (Baković 1999b). In Swedish, the value is [−voice]: underlying clusters with an underlying voiceless segment surface as voiceless.

Table (4) lists the consonant contrasts found in Swedish (Sigurd 1965:19).

(4)   Swedish consonants

	labial	alveolar	alveo-palatal	velar	glottal
stops	p	t	tʃ	k	
	b	d	dʒ	g	
fricatives	f	s	ʃ		h
	v				
nasals	m	n		ŋ	
liquids		l r			

The Swedish syllable has an optional onset and optional coda; both constituents may contain between one and three consonants. There is no voicing neutralization in codas; both voiced and voiceless obstruents can appear in this position:

e.g. [tʊb] 'tube', [kap] 'cape'; [hed] 'heath', [bit] 'piece'; [tyɡ] 'cloth', [bak] 'back'; [ræv] 'fox', [kuf] 'odd'.

Swedish obstruent voicing assimilation has received a great deal of descriptive and theoretical attention (Sigurd 1965; Hellberg 1974; Anderson 1974; Cho 1999:134ff.; Lombardi 1999; Baković 1999a:58; Wilson 2000:132ff.). The output of Swedish voice assimilation is always a cluster of voiceless segments, as shown in (5); the data is from Hellberg 1974, Sigurd 1965, and Lombardi 1999. The left column gives the bare root, which faithfully preserves underlying voicing. The right column shows the root in an assimilation context.

(5)   Swedish obstruent voice assimilation
       (a) /ÇÇ̥/ → [ÇÇ̥]

Root	Gloss	Assimilated	Gloss
[tʊb]	*tub* 'tube'	[tup-s]	*tub-s* 'tube + genitive'
[røːd]	*röd* 'red'	[røt-t]	*röd-t* 'red (neuter)'
[ɡud]	*gud* 'good'	[ɡut-s]	*gud-s* 'good (genitive)'
[sprøːd]	*spröd* 'brittle'	[sprøt-t]	*spröd-t* 'brittle (neuter)'
[tiːd]	*tid* 'time'	[tit-s]	*tid-s* 'time+genitive'
[klædə]	*kläda* 'to dress'	[klɛt-səl]	*klädsel* 'dressing'
[fœdə]	*föda* 'feed'	[fœt-səl]	*fötsel* 'food'
[skuːɡ]	*skog* 'forest'	[skuk-s]	*skogs* 'forest (genitive)'
		[skʊks foːɡəl]	*skogsfågel* 'forest bird'
[hœːɡ]	*hög* 'high'	[hœkː tiːd]	*hög tid* 'festival'
		[hœkː fæːdiɡ]	*hög färdig* 'festival'
		[hœk-st]	*högst*
[viɡə]	*viga* 'to marry'	[vik-səl]	*vigsel* 'marriage'
[daːɡ]	*dag* 'day'	[dak-sljuːs]	*dagsljus* 'daylight'
[styɡ]	*stygg* 'naughty'	[styk-t]	*styggt* 'naughty (neuter)'
[byɡ]	*byggt* 'build'	[byk-t]	*byggt* 'build {supine}'
[hav]	*hav* 'sea'	[haf-s]	*hav-s* 'sea+adv. suffix'
[ræv]	*räv* 'fox'	[raf-s]	*räv-s* 'fox + genitive'
[stræv]	*sträv* 'rough'	[stræf-t]	*strävt* 'rough (neuter)'

(b) /ÇÇ̥/ → [ÇÇ̥]

[kœp]	*köp* 'purchase'	/kœp-d/ → [kœpt]	*köpt*{pt part.}
[brand]	*brand* 'fire'	[skukːs-prandː]	*skogsbrand* 'forest fire'
[daːɡ]	*dag* 'day'	[tisː-ta]	*Tisdag* 'Tuesday'
[də]	*-de*{preterite}	[syl-də]	*syl-de* 'covered'
		[læs-tə]	*läs-te* 'read'
		[stɛk-tə]	*stek-te* 'fried'

(c) /ÇÇ̥/ → [ÇÇ̥]

[hanːd-buːk]	*hand-bok* 'handbook'		
[syːd-vesːt]	*sydväst* 'south-west'		
[æɡə]	*äga* 'to own'	[æɡ-də]	*äg-de* 'owned'
[vævə]	*väve* 'to weave'	[væv-də]	*väv-de* 'weaved'
[byɡ]	*bygg* 'build'	[byɡ-d]	*bygg-d* 'build {pt part.}'

As shown by the pair /læs-də/ → [læstə] and /vig-səl/ → [viksəl], neither the rightmost nor the leftmost segment consistently determines the voicing of the output. The pair /tid-s/ → [tits] and /kœp-d/ → [kœpt] show that morphological affiliation does not matter: the voicing of the affix segment persists in [tits], while the root's value survives in [kœpt]. In short, if any of the input segments is [−voice], the output will be voiceless.

There is no controversy over the claim that [−voice] is the unmarked voicing feature for obstruents. Evidence comes from the many cases where [+voice] neutralizes to [−voice] in codas (Lombardi 1991; Wetzels & Mascaró 2001); voiceless segments only ever become voiced under the influence of sonority (§3.3.2.1). So, the issue that arises in Swedish voice assimilation is why the unmarked [−voice] value emerges while the marked [+voice] value is eliminated.

6.2.2 Conflation

The following analysis will show that the constraint IDENT[±voice] is needed to adequately account for Swedish bi-directional voicing assimilation. The crucial aspect of this constraint is that it 'conflates' unfaithfulness: it assigns the same violations to /+voice/ → [−voice] as to /−voice/ → [+voice] mappings.

Swedish voice assimilation has been analysed in Optimality Theory by Lombardi (1999), Baković (1999a:58ff., 1999b), and Wilson (2000:132ff.). The following analysis owes a great deal to Lombardi's proposals, and for the most part is a straightforward recasting of the analysis in Lombardi 1999 in terms of the constraints proposed here; the differences will be commented on where necessary. Baković (1999a,b) presents a significantly different approach to the issue presented here; it is discussed in §8.6. For an evaluation of Wilson's (2000) theory, see McCarthy 2003c.

The constraint generation schema in §2.3.1.2 provides two faithfulness constraints for voice. One exclusively preserves the marked value, IDENT[+voice], and the other preserves both values, IDENT[±voice]. Following §4.3.2.1, the output constraints that trigger voice assimilation are *{±voice}{±voice}, *{+voice}{±voice}, and *{±voice}{+voice}. In Swedish, the active constraint is *{±voice}{±voice}, for reasons that will become evident below. The other assimilation constraints will be discussed in §6.2.4.

In order for *{±voice}{±voice} to motivate assimilation of voiced segments, it must outrank all constraints that preserve voiced segments – i.e. IDENT[±voice] and IDENT[+voice]; the opposite ranking would prevent voiced segments from undergoing assimilation. This general ranking was established in chapter 4.

(6)   Swedish I: Assimilation

/fœd-səl/	*{±voice}{±voice}	IDENT{±voice}	IDENT[+voice]
(a) fœdsəl	*!		
☞ (b) fœtsəl		*	*

In Swedish, the marked input feature [+voice] is not preserved in assimilation. Therefore, all faithfulness constraints that preserve only marked values (i.e. IDENT[+voice]) must be outranked by some output constraint against that feature (*[+voice]). Tableau (7) illustrates this ranking. The crucial competition is between (b) and (c): (b) loses because it contains more voiced segments than (c).[1] Thus, *[+voice] must outrank IDENT[+voice]; the opposite ranking would favour Preservation of the Marked value, with the undesirable result that (b) would win.

(7)   Swedish IIa: Elimination of the marked

/fœd-səl/	*{±voice}{±voice}	*{+voice}	IDENT[+voice]
(a) fœdsəl	*!	*	
(b) fœdzəl		**!	
☞ (c) fœtsəl			*

Assimilation is bi-directional, so all constraints that promote directionality must be inactive. In particular, onset-faithfulness constraints must be ranked below *[+voice], as in tableau (8).

(8)   Swedish IIb: No active onset-faithfulness

/stɛk-də/	*{±voice}{±voice}	*{+voice}	onset-IDENT[+voice]	onset-IDENT[±voice]
(a) stɛk.də	*!	*		
(b) stɛg.də		**!		
☞ (c) stɛk.tə			*	*

---

1 *{+voice} assigns a separate violation for each voiced segment here. If one adopts an autosegmental approach – that the two voiced segments share a single [+voice] feature – the approach will still work: candidate (b) will still incur fewer violations of *{+voice}.

To complete the ranking, some faithfulness constraint that preserves [+voice] must outrank *{+voice} otherwise [+voice] would be eliminated in all contexts: e.g. /æg-də/ would emerge as *[æktə].

The only faithfulness constraint left is IDENT[±voice]; its effect is shown in the following tableau. A ranking analogous to ‖ IDENT[±voice] » *[+voice] ‖ is proposed by Lombardi (1999:285ff.).[2]

(9)   Swedish III: Avoidance of neutralization

/æg-də/	IDENT[±voice]	*{+voice}	IDENT[+voice]
(a) æktə	* *!		* *
☞ (b) ægdə		* *	

The constraint IDENT[±voice] prevents gratuitous elimination of [+voice], as in (a). The opposite ranking would produce a language with elimination of [+voice], as in German codas (§3.3.2.1).

Notably, no faithfulness constraint except for IDENT [±voice] can be brought to the aid of [ægdə] here. As Lombardi (1999) shows, all constraints that favour a directional bias must be ranked below *{+voice}. This was demonstrated in tableau (8) for onset-faithfulness constraints. Tableau (10) makes the same point for root-controlled faithfulness constraints.

(10)   Swedish IV: Irrelevance of root-faithfulness

/stræv-t/	*{±voice} {±voice}	*{+ voice}	root-IDENT [+voice]	root-IDENT [±voice]
(a) strævt	*!	*		
(b) strævd		* *!		
☞ (c) stræft			*	*

So, the resulting ranking for Swedish voice constraints is anti-Paninian (Prince 1997 a, b, c, d, 1998, 1999): a general faithfulness constraint outranks a specific one: i.e. ‖ IDENT[±voice] » *{+voice} » IDENT [+voice] ‖. The form of the constraint IDENT[±voice] is crucial in this analysis as it allows faithfulness conflation while maintaining contrast. This point will be fully developed in the next section.

---

2 The difference between the present approach and Lombardi's (1999) is that Lombardi has only one faithfulness constraint IDENT[Lar(yngeal)], which is equivalent in its effects to IDENT[±voice]. The theory has both IDENT[±voice] and IDENT[+voice]. For the need for IDENT[+voice], see §6.2.4.

6.2 Preservation conflation in Swedish voicing

6.2.3 Faithfulness conflation

The Swedish facts can be produced by the stringent constraints because the PoM-faithfulness constraints allow faithfulness conflation. The following tableau illustrates this point.

(11) Swedish v: Faithfulness conflation

/vig-səl/	*{±voice} {±voice}	IDENT [±voice]	*{+voice}	IDENT [+voice]
(a) vig-səl	*!		* *	
(b) vig-zəl		*	* * *!	
☞ (c) vik-səl		*	*	*
(d) fik-səl		**!		**

The reason that the output constraint *{+voice} emerges to make the crucial decision between (b) and (c) is because the mappings /vig-səl/ →[viksəl] and /vig-səl/ → *[vigzəl] are conflated in faithfulness terms: unfaithfulness to an input [−voice] specification incurs the same violations of active faithfulness constraints (i.e. IDENT[±voice]) as unfaithfulness to an input [+voice] specification. Because the active faithfulness constraint fails to distinguish the two different mappings, the lower-ranked output constraint can emerge to make the crucial decision. This is analogous to conflation in markedness reduction where two markedness categories are conflated if they incur the same violations of active output constraints (chapter 5).

To expand on this point, suppose that IDENT[+voice] outranked *{+voice}. This ranking would fail to produce the correct facts in Swedish: it would favour candidate (c) over candidate (b). A key point is that IDENT[±voice] *must* be active: if it were ranked below *[+voice], all voicing contrasts would be eliminated.

Therefore, there are two requirements on all active voice-faithfulness constraints in Swedish: (i) they must preserve the voicing contrast and (ii) they must allow faithfulness conflation. The only way to deal with both these conditions is to have a faithfulness constraint that preserves both values of [voice] at once, thereby assigning equal violations to candidates that differ in either value of [voice]. In short, the constraint IDENT[±voice] is indispensable.

6.2.4 Faithfulness fixed ranking

The conflation result just demonstrated contrasts with a Fixed Ranking theory of faithfulness. Suppose that there was a fixed ranking ‖ IDENT[+voice] »»

IDENT[−voice] ‖. These constraints offer no way to both preserve the voicing contrast and allow [−voice] to survive. Preservation of the voicing contrast requires the ranking ‖ IDENT[+voice] » *{+voice} ‖. However, emergence of [−voice] requires the ranking ‖ *[+voice] » IDENT[+voice] ‖. Thus, the Fixed Ranking approach results in a ranking paradox. The following tableaux demonstrate the problem. Tableau (12) shows that the ranking *[+voice] » IDENT[+voice] generates the correct assimilation, but incorrectly produces neutralization.

(12) Swedish VI: Correct assimilation, incorrect neutralization

/hœːg tiːd/	*{±voice}{±voice}	*[+voice]	IDENT[+voice]
(a) hœg: tiːd	*!	* *	
(b) hœk: tiːd		*!	*
☛ (c) hœk: tiːt			* *

In contrast, tableau (13) shows that the opposite ranking ‖ IDENT[+voice] » *[+voice] ‖ correctly prevents neutralization of [+voice], but incorrectly produces assimilation to [+voice].

(13) Swedish VII: Correct lack of neutralization, incorrect assimilation

/hœːg tiːd/	*{±voice}{±voice}	IDENT[+voice]	*[+voice]
(a) hœg: tiːd	*!		* *
(b) hœk: tiːd		*!	*
☛ (c) hœg: diːd			* * *

As a closing comment, the Swedish analysis shows that faithfulness constraints must be able to mention unmarked features (cf. Gouskova 2003). If only IDENT[+voice] existed, [+voice] is predicted to always win in assimilation and coalescence (Wetzels & Mascaró 2001:214ff.). For further discussion of this issue, see §8.7.3.

6.2.5 Summary

This section has identified a case of faithfulness conflation and shown that stringently formulated constraints are needed to deal with such cases. Swedish assimilation provides a situation where preservation of opposing feature values is in conflict: bi-directional assimilation forces a choice between preserving the marked or unmarked [voice] feature value. The survival of the unmarked [−voice] feature comes about because unfaithfulness to both underlying voice

6.2 Preservation conflation in Swedish voicing

values is treated equally; the output constraint *[+voice] then can be used to favour the least-marked value.

Swedish shows that the stringent constraint IDENT[±voice] is necessary. Other languages provide evidence for just IDENT[+voice]. For example, voiced segments are exempt from voicing assimilation in Standard Ukrainian (Bethin 1987; Butska 1997). There is no coda devoicing.

(14)   Ukrainian Voicing
       (a) C̬ → C̬ / C̬   (b) C̬ does not assimilate
       /borot + ba/ →   [borodba] 'fight'   [duʒka] 'handle'
       /pros' + ba/ →   [proz'ba] 'request'   [vezty] 'to drive'
       /jak + ze/ →   [jagze] 'how'   [xobta] 'trunk (gen.sg.)'
       /vok + zal/ →   [vogzal] 'station'   [ridko] 'rarely'
       /osʲ + de/ →   [ozʲde] 'here/there' [s'vbyd + ko] 'quick'
                                              [v'id + pov'idajte] 'answer (imp.)'

To block voiced segments from assimilating, IDENT[+voice] must outrank all the assimilation constraints, as shown in tableaux (15) and (16).

(15)   Ukrainian assimilation I

/xobta/	IDENT[+voice]	*{±voice}{±voice}	IDENT[±voice]
(a) xopta	*!		
☞ (b) xobta		*	*

(16)   Ukrainian assimilation II

/jak-ze/	IDENT[+voice]	*{±voice}{±voice}	IDENT[±voice]
(a) jakze		*!	
☞ (b) jagze			*

Cases similar to Swedish's are found in coalescence. For example, the Fort Chipewyan dialect of the Athapaskan language Chipewyan (Li 1946) has several coalescence patterns, one of which is the famous Athapaskan *d*-effect. As in Swedish, the unmarked [−voice] value survives in coalescence: e.g. /hɛ-uh-l-ze/ → [huɬze] 'start to hunt (2dual)', /ʔã-hɛ-θ-t-ʒa/ → [ʔãhθ͡tʃa] 'he went home' (Li 1946; de Lacy 2002a:§8.3.2). In contrast, [+voice] is preserved in Pāli's coalescence; e.g. /labʰ+ta/ → [ladːʰa], *[latːʰa]. Pāli is discussed in detail in the next section.

As a final note, the analysis presented above fails in one situation: when the majority of input segments are [+voice]. For example, the ranking predicts that /skuːɡ-s brand/ should surface as *[skuːɡz brand], whereas the attested form is [skukːs prand]. Section 6.4 argues that this problem is not due to the markedness mechanisms proposed here; instead, it appears because of fundamental aspects of faithfulness. The section presents a solution that revises the form of IDENT constraints.

6.3 Preservation conflation in Pāli coalescence

Pāli's coalescence shows how the theory can both prevent and produce conflation in the same system, even for the same feature. As a brief preview, when two heterogeneous consonants coalesce, coronal is preserved when in competition with labial, but if coronal vies with dorsal, dorsal survives. In other words, the most-marked PoA value (dorsal) survives in coalescence, but otherwise the least-marked available value (coronal) is preserved. Section 6.3.1 provides a description of the central facts. An analysis is given in §6.3.2.

6.3.1 Description

Pāli is an extinct language that was spoken on the Indian subcontinent; it is still spoken by Buddhist monks as a lingua franca, but not used as a first language. Table (17) lists the surface consonants found in Pāli. The majority of data cited below is from Fahs (1989); page numbers refer to this work.

(17)   Pāli Consonants (Fahs1989:§1.1)

		labial	Coronal	palatal	retroflex	dorsal	glottal
stops	voiceless	p	t̪	c	ṭ	k	
		pʰ	t̪ʰ	cʰ	ṭʰ	kʰ	
	voiced	b	d̪	ɟ	ḍ	g	
		bʰ	d̪ʰ	ɟʰ	ḍʰ	gʰ	
fricatives			s				h
nasals		m	n̪	ɲ	ṇ	ŋ	
liquids			l ɹ		ḷ		
glides		'v'		j			

Fahs (1989:§1.1) and Geiger (1943:60) call the glide 'v'. As this segment acts phonologically like a glide, it may have been closer to the semi-vowels [w] or [ʋ] than the voiced fricative [v]. In keeping with Fahs' description, I will refer to it as [v].

6.3 Preservation conflation in Pāli coalescence

Syllables require onsets, except word-initially (e.g. [agːʰati] 'he is worth'). The onset requirement is most commonly imposed through vowel deletion: e.g. /bruː-ati/ → [bruːti] 'speak-3sg', /ju-hu-ati/ → [juhati] 'sacrifice-3sg' (cf. [huta] 'sacrifice-{past.perf.pass.}' – p.562). Onset clusters can have two members if (i) the first member is [s] (e.g. [a.sma] 'we are', [sneheti] 'he was hung up') or (ii) the second member is a glide ([ɹa.tjo] 'the nights (nom.)', [pʰu.si.tvaː] 'touched').

Rimes can contain (i) a long vowel, (ii) a short vowel+consonant, or (iii) a nasalized vowel. Underlying long vowels shorten in closed syllables (e.g. /jaː-nta/ → [jan.ta] 'go-present participle', cf. [jaː-ti] 'go-3sg'). Word-final consonants are banned.

Two restrictions on coda consonants motivate consonant coalescence. Codas may contain the first half of a geminate (e.g. [tapːati] 'he is content', [tarejːum] 'they may cross over', [phuṭːʰa] 'be touched'); all consonants except for [h] and the glide [v] have geminate counterparts (Geiger 1943:94). Codas may also contain a nasal homorganic to a following stop: e.g. [vam.bʰe.ti] 'shames', [run.dʰa.ti] 'encloses', [anaṇ.ca] 'infinity', [kaṇ.kʰaː] 'doubt'. Many alternations show the nasal+stop restriction: e.g. /han-ʃːa-ti/ → [hapcʰati] 'kill-fut-3sg' (cf. [han-a-ti] 'kill-pres.-3sg'). Similarly, a nasal infix that marks a class of verbs in the present tense assimilates in PoA: e.g. /cʰid-N-a-ti/ → [cʰindati] 'split-class1e-pres-3sg', /lip-N-a-ti/ → [limpati] 'besmear-class1e-pres-3sg', /bʰuɟ-N-a-ti/ → [bʰuɲɟati] 'enjoy-class1e-pres-3sg' – p.131). Clusters of sonorants + [h] are treated as aspirated sonorants here (e.g. [a.mʰa.naː] 'with the stone', [sa.jʰa] 'that which is to be endured', [pa.ɲʰa] 'question', [pu.bːa.ṇʰa] 'forenoon' – Geiger 1943:92–103).

6.3.1.1 Coalescence Generalizations

Pāli's coda restrictions force many input consonant clusters to change. The usual method of cluster-avoidance is coalescence to form a geminate: e.g. /han$_1$+j$_2$a+ti/ → [haɲː$_{1,2}$ati] 'dig-pass.-3sg' (cf. [han-a-ti] 'dig-pres.-3sg' – p.390). Features of each of the input segments are often preserved in the output. For example, /nj/ → [ɲː] preserves the nasality of the /n/ and the palatal PoA of the /j/.

There are many potential faithfulness conflicts in Pāli coalescence. For example, in /labʰ-ʃ-ti/ → [ladːʰi] 'take-aorist-3sg', the feature values for [voice], [continuant], PoA, aspiration, and sonority all come into conflict. This chapter focuses on PoA, but the other subsegmental features will also be discussed in §6.3.2.5. Sonority will not be discussed in detail as it has been the subject of many previous analyses (Hankamer & Aissen 1974; Murray 1982;

Wetzels & Hermans 1985; Cho 1999; de Lacy 2002a:§8.5). Essentially, when consonants coalesce the output consonant has the same sonority as the least-sonorous input element. For example, an approximant+nasal results in a nasal (e.g. /kiɻ-na/ → [kiɳːa] 'scatter-part.', /ɻan-ja-ti/ → [ɻaɲːati] 'generate'), while a stop+fricative results in a stop (/kiliṣ -ta/ → [kilitːʰa] 'be dirty-infin.', /vatː-ʃ-ti/ → [vatːʰi] 'turn-aorist-3sg').

The following description and analysis of coalescence is only concerned with synchronic alternations. Unlike most previous analyses, the diachronic changes from Sanskrit to Pāli will not be discussed, though they follow roughly the same lines as the synchronic alternations. The generalizations proposed in this section are from an analysis of synchronic alternations reported in Fahs 1989.

As a starting point, morphological affiliation and the order of underlying segments has no influence on the survival of underlying features. The PoA of either the leftmost or rightmost consonant can survive, as can the PoA of either root or suffix: compare /sakː-ʃːa-ti/ → [sakːʰati] 'be able-fut-3sg' and /labʰ-ʃ-ti/ → [ladːʰi] 'take-aorist-3sg'. Instead, survival in coalescence relates to underlying feature values, as in (18).

(18)   The output PoA of Pāli coalescence
     (a) If the input cluster includes a dorsal, the output is dorsal.
     (b) If the input cluster consists of labials and coronals, the output is coronal.
     (c) If the input cluster consists of coronals alone, and it contains an alveolar, the output is alveolar; otherwise, it is alveo-palatal.

The data in the following sections provide evidence for the generalizations in (18).

6.3.1.1.1 Details about the data

The majority of coalescence is found between verb-final consonants and their suffixes. Verbs fall into two general classes. In one class the final consonant coalesces with suffix-initial consonants (e.g. /labʰ-tabːa/ → [ladːʰabːa] 'take-gerund'), while in the other the vowel [i] is epenthesized (e.g. /limp-tabːa/ → [limpitabːa] 'smear-gerund'). A clear example is /vas/ 'dress', which belonged to the epenthesizing class in one dialect, so that /vas-tum/ → [vasitum] {infinitive}, and to the coalescing class in another, so that /vas-tum/ → [vatːʰum] (Fahs 1989:363). However, even with many verbs of the epenthesizing class, the perfect passive participle –*ta* forces coalescence (e.g. /limp-ta/ → [litːa]); the aorist forms also often undergo deletion (e.g. /sibː-ʃ-ti/ → [sibːi], not *[sibːʰi] as expected in coalescence). There are many complexities and exceptions in the data that are beyond the scope of this discussion; nevertheless,

6.3 Preservation conflation in Pāli coalescence

the generalizations presented here have clear support in a large part of the vocabulary.

Evidence for the underlying form of roots is given by citing a verb form with a vowel-initial suffix. In most cases below this is the present indicative -[a] followed by the third person singular -[ti] (e.g. [lab^h-a-ti], [limp-a-ti]). There are of course many other vowel-initial suffixes in Pāli; this one was used for convenience.

The coalescing affixes used in the data below are listed in table (19). Evidence for the underlying forms comes from their shape after the vowel-final roots.

(19)
Affix UR	Gloss	Evidence	
/-ta/	passive perfect participle#1 (ppp1)	[jaː-ta]	'go-ppp[1]'
/-na/	passive perfect participle#2 (ppp2)	[liː-na]	'stick-ppp[2]'
/-tabːa/	gerund (ger)	[daː-tabːa]	'give-ger'
/-ti/	3rd person singular (3sg)	[jaː-ti]	'go-3sg'
/-mi/	1st person singular (1sg)	[jaː-mi]	'go-1sg'
/-tva/	absolutive (abs)	[daː-tva]	'give-abs'
/-ja/	present, class 1d (ps1d)	[gaː-ja-ti]	'sing-ps1d-3sg'
/-ɳaː/	present, class 1d (ps3e)	[kiː-ɳa-mi]	'buy-ps3e-1sg'
/-tum/	infinitive (inf)	[daː-tum]	'give-inf'
/-ja/	passive (pass)	[diː-ja-ti]	'give-pass-3sg'
/-a-/	present indicative (pres)	[lab^h-a-ti]	'take-pres-3sg'
/-ʃːa/	future (fut)	[jaː-sːa-ti]	'go-fut-3sg'
/-ʃ/	aorist (ao)	[jaː-s-im]	'go-ao-1sg'

Two suffixes that require special comment are the future /-ʃːa/ and aorist /-ʃ/, as [ʃ] is banned in Pāli outputs. There are many segments that are demonstrably in the underlying forms of Pāli words but never surface faithfully in the output (i.e. they undergo 'absolute neutralization'). For example, Pāli does not allow retroflex [ʂ] on the surface. However, it is clear that the verb for 'wish' [is] is underlyingly /iʂ/ because it coalesces with an alveolar stop to form a retroflex: /iʂ-ta/ → [iṭːʰa]. This contrasts with verbs with an underlying alveolar: /sis-ta/ → [sitːʰa] 'leave' (cf. [jaː-ta] 'go-ppp2', *[jaː-ṭa]).

There is also an underlying /s/-/ʃ/ distinction, neutralized on the surface to [s]. The aorist -s is underlyingly /ʃ/ and the future -ssa is underlyingly /ʃːa/, again shown by coalescence: /lab^h-ʃːa-ti/ → [lacːʰati] 'he will take', *[latːʰati]; /a-cʰid-ʃ-i/ → [acːʰecːʰi] 'split', *[acːʰetːʰi]. In both these cases, the output consonant is palatal despite the fact that – on the surface – the future and aorist otherwise show up as [s]: e.g. /jaː-ʃːa-ti/ → [jaːsːati] 'go-fut-3sg', /haɹ-ʃːa-ti/ → [hasːati] 'name-fut-3sg'.

Another absolutely neutralizing segment encountered in the data below is the retroflex /ɻ/, which surfaces as [ɹ]: e.g. /haɻ-ta/ →[haṭːa] 'name-ppp' (cf. [haɹ-a-ti]), cf. /kaɹ-tum/ →[katːum] 'make-inf.', *[kaṭːum].

The data below is limited by the fact that the most common suffix consonants that are attested as coalescing are the voiceless coronal obstruents [t c s ṣ ʃ], the nasal [n], and the glide [j]. After T. Hall (1997), I adopt the view that [c] and [ɟ] are coronals. There are also a few limited cases with suffixal [k] and [g].

When a sibilant coalesces, it is preserved as aspiration; e.g. /a-sakː-ʃ-ti/ →[asakːʰi] 'be able+aorist+3p.sg.' (cf. [sakː-o-ti] 'I am able'), /sis-ta/ →[sitːʰa] 'leave+participle'. This is due to the fact that sibilants bear the same laryngeal features as aspirated segments (Vaux 1998).

As a final comment, coalescence does not apply to every input consonant cluster in Pāli. Consonant clusters do not undergo coalescence and gemination when (a) there is no pressure to do so and (b) doing so would still result in an unacceptable output. For example, [s+C] onsets are permitted, so /s/+nasal clusters are realized faithfully: /as-mi/ →[a.smi] 'be+1p.sg.', *[asːi] (Fahs 1989:139). Codas permit nasals that are homorganic to a following stop, so underlying nasal+stop clusters surface faithfully: /kʰan+tum/ →[kʰan.tum] 'dig+infin.', *[kʰatːum] (Fahs 1989:191); /gam-tvaː/ →[gan.tvaː] 'go+absolutive' (Fahs 1989:183). Finally, the most common response for approximant+/j/ clusters is metathesis or conversion of the /j/ into vowel length: e.g. /bʰaɻ-ja-ti/ →[bʰiɟɟati]~[bʰiːɻati] 'carry+pass+3sg.' (Fahs 1989:201). This response will not be discussed here (see de Lacy 2002a:§8.5.2.4).

6.3.2 Analysis

The following analysis starts by identifying the basic ranking needed for coalescence in Pāli. The survival of PoA is then discussed; the analysis concludes by considering other feature conflicts.

The motivation for coalescence in Pāli is that codas are required to be either (a) nasal or (b) part of a geminate consonant. For present purposes, the effect of these conditions will be referred to as the constraint CODACOND, after Ito 1986. CODACOND is clearly the cover term for several constraints, including the anti-heterorganicity constraints from §4.3.2, but no further elaboration on this point is needed here.

Coalescence violates the faithfulness constraint UNIFORMITY (McCarthy & Prince 1995), defined in (20).

(20) UNIFORMITY   For each output segment x, x has only one input correspondent.

CODACOND, MAX, and DEP must outrank UNIFORMITY to produce coalescence. The subscript numbers in tableau (21) mark input–output correspondence relations. For example, in candidate (d) [lad:$^h_{1,2}$a] the subscript$_{1,2}$ after [d:^{h}] indicates that the output root node corresponds to *both* input /b^h/ and /t/.

(21) Pāli I: Basic coalescence ranking

/lab$^h_1$-t$_2$a/	CODACOND	MAX	DEP	UNIFORMITY
(a) lab$^h_1$t$_2$a	*!			
(b) lat$_2$a		*!		
(c) lab$^h_1$it$_2$a			*!	
☞ (d) lad:$^h_{1,2}$a				*

Having MAX and DEP outrank UNIFORMITY ensures that neither deletion nor epenthesis will be Pāli's response to CODACOND. In addition, all IDENT constraints that preserve features that are unavoidably eliminated in coalescence must be ranked below CODACOND, MAX, and DEP as well. These IDENT constraints preserve [voice], [sonority], and all PoAs except for dorsal (which always survives). For example, IDENT [±voice], IDENT{dors,lab}, and IDENT{dors,lab,cor} must be ranked at the same level as UNIFORMITY, otherwise the output [lad:^{h}a], which is unfaithful to /t/'s [−voice] and /b^h/'s labial specification, would be eliminated by the IDENT constraints just mentioned. Tableau (22) illustrates this point with IDENT [±voice]. If IDENT [±voice] were ranked above CODACOND, a cluster that differed underlyingly in [voice] would undergo deletion (b), epenthesis (c), or remain faithful (a).

(22) Pāli Ia

/lab$^h_1$-t$_2$a/	CODACOND	MAX	DEP	IDENT[±VOICE]
(a) lab$^h_1$t$_2$a	*!			
(b) lat$_2$a		*!		
(c) lab$^h_1$it$_2$a			*!	
☞ (d) lad:$^h_{1,2}$a				*

Vacuous coalescence

The evidence for coalescence is clear in many cases because the output consonant has features of both input consonants (e.g. /lab^h-tab:a/ →[lad:^{h}ab:a] 'take-gerund'). As mentioned above, stridents /s ṣ ʃ/ are realized as aspiration when they coalesce: e.g. /vas-tum/ → [vatːʰum] 'live-infin.' (cf. [vas-a-ti]) (see §6.3.2.4).

However, in some cases all the features of an input consonant are obscured: e.g. /rakːʰ-ʃ-ti/ → [rakːʰi] 'protect-aorist-3sg' (cf. [rakːʰ-a-ti]). Such cases of 'vacuous' coalescence are still coalescence, and not deletion: i.e. all the input segments /kːʰ/, /ʃ/, and /t/ still correspond to a single output segment [kːʰ]. In such cases, it just so happens a single input segment has all the feature values that survive. The form /a-sakː-ʃ-ti/ → [asakːʰi] 'be able-aorist-3sg' (cf. [sakː-o-ti]) is a useful contrast to [rakːʰi] – here the /ʃ/'s input presence is shown in the output by the aspiration and coalescence has clearly taken place.

The ranking provides the reason for thinking that vacuous coalescence is coalescence and not deletion. The ranking in (22) favours coalescence over deletion, so coalescence will be the default response to CODACOND violations. There is no constraint in the ranking that will favour deletion over coalescence just in the case where only one of the input segment's features survives. See Wheeler 2005b for more in depth discussion.

6.3.2.1 Preservation of the Marked: dorsals

The data in (23) show that dorsals survive in coalescence when competing with alveolars, alveo-palatals, and palatals. There is no data where dorsals compete with labials. The roots' underlying forms can be seen with vowel-initial suffixes in the present indicative, as shown in the 'Compare' column.

(23)   Pāli PoA coalescence I: /Dorsal + Coronal/ → [Dorsal]

UR	SR	Gloss	Compare	Fahs 1989 p.
/a-sakː-ʃ-ti/	[asakːʰi]	ao-*be able*-ao-3sg	sakː-o-ti	370
/a-sakː-ʃ-im/	[asakːʰim]	ao-*be able*-ao-1sg	sakː-o-ti	370
/sakː-ʃːa-ti/	[sakːʰati]	*be able*-fut-3sg	sakː-o-ti	370
/sakː-ɳaː-ti/	[sakːati]	*be able*-ps3e-3sg	sakː-o-ti	141
/sakː-ja-ti/	[sakːati]	*be able*-ps1d-3sg	sakː-o-ti	130
/sakː-ja/	[sakːa]	*be able*-gerund	sakː-o-ti	179
/rakːʰ-ʃ-ti/	[rakːʰi]	*protect*-ao-3sg	rakːʰ-a-ti	338
/lagː-na/	[lagːa]	*append*-ppp	lagː-a-ti	346

There are also some dorsal-initial suffixes that survive in coalescence, although they are quite rare: e.g. the desiderative: / RED-bʰuɲɟ-kʰati/ → [bubʰukːʰa-ti] '*enjoy*-desid-3sg' (cf. [bʰuɲɟ-a-ti]) (Fahs 1989:321).

There is also a small class of verbs that take a /k/ in the future and aorist, including /vis-k-ʃːa-ti/ → [vekːʰati] '*go*-k-fut-3sg', /vis-k-ʃ-ti/ → [vekːʰi] '*go*-k-ao-3sg' (cf. [vis-a-ti]), /vac-k-ʃːa-ti/ → [vakːʰati] '*speak*-k-fut-3sg' (cf. [vac-a-ti]), /bʰuɟ-k-ʃːa-ti/ → [bʰokːati] '*mean*-k-fut-3sg' (cf. [bʰuɟ-a-ti]).

Finally, there is a small group of verbs that take [-ga] as their passive perfect participle: /bʰaɟ-ga/ → [bʰagːa] 'break-ppp' (cf. [bʰaɟ-a-ti]), /muɟː-ga/ → [mugːa] 'sink-ppp', /lagː-ga/ → [lagːa] 'append-ppp').

The case studies in chapter 4 have shown how such 'Preservation of the Marked' can be implemented. Some faithfulness constraint that specifically preserves dorsals (e.g. IDENT{dors}) must outrank all output constraints that ban it (i.e. all PoA constraints). Tableau (24) illustrates this point with the form /a-sakː-ʃ-ti/. In this case, /kː/'s dorsal PoA vies with /ʃ/'s alveo-palatal and /t/'s alveolar PoA for realization.

(24)   Pāli II: Dorsal preservation

/a-sakː₁-ʃ₂-t₃i/	CODACOND	IDENT[dors]	*{dors}
(a) asakː₁ʃ₂ t₃i	*!		*
(b) asacːʰ₁,₂i		*!	
(c) asatːʰ₁,₂i		*!	
☞ (d) asakːʰ₁,₂i			*

In short, dorsal survival is a straightforward case of the marked PoA surviving through faithfulness, just as in Yamphu and Catalan (chapter 4).

6.3.2.2 Faithfulness conflation: labials

While dorsal+coronal coalescence results in the highly marked dorsal, coalescence of a labial with a coronal results in a coronal output, as shown in the data in (25). The roots' underlying form can be seen before vowel-initial suffixes, like the present indicative: e.g. [kʰip-a-ti], [gup-a-ti], [labʰ-a-ti], and so on.

(25)   Pāli PoA coalescence II: /Labial + Coronal/ → [Coronal]
       (a) /labial + alveolar/ → [alveolar]

UR	SR	Gloss	Fahs 1989 p.
/kʰip-ta/	[kʰitːa]	*throw*-ppp	170
/gup-ta/	[gutːa]	*guard*-ppp	170
/sup-tum/	[sotːum]	*sleep*-infin	192
/pa-ap-tabːa/	[patːabːa]	*attain*-gerund	175
/labʰ-ta/	[ladːʰa]	*take*-ppp	171
/labʰ-tabːa/	[ladːʰabːa]	*take*-gerund	175
/labʰ-tum/	[ladːʰum]	*take*-infin	191
/a-labʰ-tːʰa-mʰa/	[alatːʰamʰa]	ao- *take*-ao-1pl	348
/lubʰ-ta/	[ludːʰa]	*yearn*-ppp	171
/a-gam-tːʰa/	[agatːʰa]	*go*-ao-2pl	156

(b) /labial + (alveo-)palatal/ → [(alveo-)palatal]
/labʰ-ʃːa-ti/   [lacːʰati]   *take*-fut-3sg   172
/labʰ-ʃ-im/   [lacːʰim]   *take*-ao-1sg   172
/gam-cːa/   [gacːa]   *go*-abs   253

The labial /m/ becomes a homorganic nasal before a stop rather than coalescing: e.g. /kʰam-ta/ → [kʰanta] 'undergo-ppp' (cf. [kʰam-a-ti]), /gam-tabːa/ → [gantabːa] 'go-gerund' (cf. [a-gam-aː] 'ao-go-3sg').

So, in contrast with dorsal+coronal coalescence, the unmarked value emerges in coalescence of a labial and coronal: e.g. /labʰ-ta/ → [ladːʰa] 'take {participle}'. Analogous to Swedish, no faithfulness constraint favours preservation of coronals over labials. Therefore, output constraints must be responsible for favouring the output [ladːʰa] over *[labːʰa]. Specifically, the constraint *{dors,lab} favours the former over the latter. Therefore, *{dors,lab} must outrank all faithfulness constraints that preserve labials without preserving coronals – i.e. IDENT{dors,lab}. This ranking is shown in tableau (26).

(26)   Pāli IIIa: Survival of the unmarked I

/labʰ₁-t₂a/	*{dors,lab}	IDENT{dors,lab}
(a) labːʰ₁,₂a	*!	
☞ (b) ladːʰ₁,₂a		*

However, some constraint must prevent labials from neutralizing in all positions. More concretely, some faithfulness constraint must prevent /b/ from neutralizing to [d] in [badːʰa] 'tie {participle}' (i.e. *[dadːʰa]). Moreover, the faithfulness constraint cannot favour preservation of labials over coronals, otherwise the result in (26) would be undone. The only faithfulness constraint that can do this job is one that preserves labials and coronals equally – i.e. IDENT{dors,lab,cor}. This is illustrated with /labʰ-tabːa/ → [ladːʰabːa].

(27)   Pāli IIIb: Unmarked survival II

/labʰ₁-t₂abːa/	IDENT{dors,lab,cor}	*{dors,lab}	IDENT{dors,lab}
(a) ladːʰ₁,₂adːa	**!		**
(b) labːʰ₁,₂abːa	*	**!	
☞ (c) ladːʰ₁,₂abːa	*	*	*

Candidate (a) is eliminated by IDENT{dors,lab,cor} because it gratuitously removes labials even when coalescence is not at issue: the candidate incurs one violation of this constraint for [dːʰ]'s unfaithfulness to /bʰ/'s labial specification and one for [dː]'s unfaithfulness to [bː]'s labial specification.

It is crucial that candidates (b) and (c) are assigned the same violations of IDENT{dors,lab,cor}. Candidate (b) incurs one for the output [bːʰ]'s unfaithfulness to /t/'s PoA, and (c) for [dːʰ]'s unfaithfulness to /bʰ/'s PoA. So, IDENT{dors,lab,cor} conflates the two different types of unfaithfulness: both unfaithfulness to input labials and unfaithfulness to input coronals incur the same violations. Conflation renders IDENT{dors,lab,cor} irrelevant in the competition between (a) and (b). So, the lower-ranked *{dors,lab} makes the crucial decision, favouring the less-marked candidate (b). As a concluding comment, IDENT{dors,lab,cor} must be ranked below MAX, DEP, and CODACOND, otherwise coalescence would not take place.

The rankings of PoA constraints determined so far are summarized in (28).

(28)   Major place of articulation in Pāli coalescence: ranking

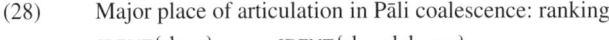
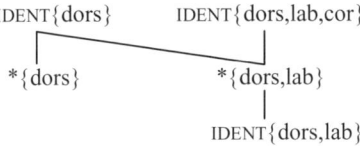

The ranking shows how both marked and unmarked features can survive in the same grammar. By ranking IDENT{dors} over all output constraints, survival of dorsal PoA is assured. By ranking *{dors,lab} over all constraints that preserve labials without preserving coronals, coronals survive when dorsals are not available.

To conclude the ranking discussion, one potential alternative account is to claim that the rightmost consonant's PoA value survives in labial+coronal coalescence. After all, all the data presented above involves the underlying order /labial+coronal/, never /coronal+labial/. Sequences of /coronal+labial/ never occur in Pāli because there are no labial-initial affixes that appear in the right environments. However, appeal to direction does not work in Pāli for several reasons. One is that direction plays no role for other features. Aspiration is preserved whether it is sourced from the leftmost (/sis-ta/ → [sitːʰa] 'leave+participle'—Fahs 1989:17), middle (/sak-ʃ-ti/ → [sakːʰi] 'be able+aorist+3p.sg.'—Fahs 1989:158), or rightmost consonant (/cʰid-ʃːa-ti/ → [cʰecːʰati] 'crack+future+3p.sg.' — Fahs 1989:148).

Another issue is formulation of an appropriate constraint. In a good deal of recent work, 'rightmost' and 'leftmost' are not appealed to as primitives; instead directionality effects are achieved by referring to constituents like onsets or

272 6 *Markedness conflation in preservation*

features like release (Beckman 1998). Evidence that it is not possible in Pāli to appeal to onsets or release comes from a small class of roots that coalesce to form a singleton, not a geminate. For example, /hat_1-t_2a/ coalesces to form /ha$t_{1,2}$a/ 'take' (Fahs 1989:170), not *[ha$t$:$_{1,2}$a]. Notably, /jam_1-t_2a/ 'hold back' becomes [ja$t_{1,2}$a], not *[ja$p_{1,2}$a] (also /d^{h}ov-ta/ 'clean' → [d^{h}ota], *[d^{h}opa]). Appealing to preservation of the onset's PoA does not resolve the tie between [ja$t_{1,2}$a], and *[ja$p_{1,2}$a] – both are equally unfaithful since [$t_{1,2}$] fails to preserve the PoA of the input /m/ while *[ja$p_{1,2}$a] fails to preserve the PoA of the input /t/. Thus, one would have to appeal to an output constraint to resolve the tie in favour of the coronal in any case.

Finally, in coalescence of /dorsal+coronal/, the leftmost PoA wins, not the rightmost. So, although direct evidence that /coronal+labial/ clusters would coalesce to form a [coronal] is lacking for incidental reasons, there seem to be no viable alternatives to the claim that labial+coronal coalescence aims to yield the least-marked PoA value.

6.3.2.3 Fixed ranking

A theory with a universally fixed ranking of faithfulness constraints like those in (29) cannot produce the Pāli coalescence pattern for PoA.

(29)   PoA faithfulness constraints with universally fixed ranking
       IDENT{dorsal} »» IDENT{labial} »» IDENT{coronal}

The problem with such constraints is that they will always favour Preservation of the Marked value in coalescence. This works for Pāli's dorsal coalescence: IDENT{dorsal} simply needs to outrank all anti-dorsal constraints, like *{dors,lab}. However, problems arise for labial+coronal coalescence, as in /lab^h-ta/ → [lad:^{h}a]. The fixed-ranking faithfulness constraints will incorrectly favour the candidate *[lab:^{h}a] because it preserves the more marked element when compared with [lad:^{h}a]. Therefore, the only way to get [lad:^{h}a] is to appeal to an output constraint that favours coronals over labials: i.e. *{dors,lab}. The resulting ranking is given in tableau (30), where the result is an alveolar from /lab^h-ta/ 'name-ppp', and in (31), where the result is an alveo-palatal from /lab^h-ʃ:a-ti/ 'name-fut-3sg'.

(30)   Pāli fixed ranking I

/lab$^h_1$-t_2a/	*{dors,lab}	IDENT[lab]	IDENT[cor]
(a) lab:$^h_{1,2}$a	*!		*
☞ (b) lad:$_{1,2}$a		*	

6.3 Preservation conflation in Pāli coalescence   273

(31)   Pāli fixed ranking II

/lab$^h_1$-ʃ:$_2$a-ti/	*{dors,lab}	IDENT[lab]	IDENT[cor]
(a) lab:$^h_{1,2}$ati	*!		*
☞ (b) lac:$^h_{1,2}$ati		*	

The problem is that the ranking eliminates labial PoA in all environments. This is shown in tableau (32) for /lab^h-tab:a/ 'name-gerund' and in (33) for /lab^h-ʃ:a-m/ 'name-fut-1sg'.

(32)   Pāli fixed ranking III

/lab$^h_1$-t$_2$ab:a/	*{dors,lab}	IDENT[lab]	IDENT[cor]
(a) lad:$^h_{1,2}$ab:a	*!	*	*
💣 (b) lad:$_{1,2}$ad:a		**	

(33)   Pāli fixed ranking IV

/lab$^h_1$-ʃ:$_2$a-m/	*{dors,lab}	IDENT[lab]	IDENT[cor]
(a) lac:$^h_{1,2}$am	*!	*	*
💣 (b) lac:$^h_{1,2}$an		**	

There is no way for the (a) candidates to win. For them to win, a faithfulness constraint that preserves labial PoA would have to outrank *{dors,lab}. However, the only faithfulness constraint that could do that is IDENT [lab], and its ranking is already fixed below *{dors,lab}.

6.3.2.3.1 Alternative faithfulness constraints

Some alternatives should be considered to maintain a Fixed Ranking approach. One option is to invoke an entirely different type of faithfulness constraint, one that will preserve the PoA of non-coalescing labials only. For example, a constraint that requires the PoA of input geminates to be preserved would block /b:/ → [d:] without preventing /b^h-t/ → [d:^{h}].

Another option is to propose a constraint that blocks PoA neutralization in onsets, where 'onset' for a geminate is taken to be the 'second half' of the geminate (assuming Selkirk's 1991 two-root theory of geminates). /abba/ → [ad.da] would violate such a constraint because the 'second' [d] in the output corresponds to an input labial; in contrast, /ab^h-ta/ → [ad.d^{h}a] does not violate it because the onset /d^h/ corresponds to an input coronal.

However, both proposals fail to account for forms like /labʰ-ʃːa-m/ → [lacːʰam] 'name-fut-1sg'. Neither type of faithfulness constraint can prevent coda /m/ from becoming [n] (i.e. *[lacːʰan]). In short, a faithfulness constraint would have to prevent /m/ from becoming a coronal in non-coalescing codas, but allow /m/ to become a coronal in coalescing ones (as in /ɟam-cːa/ → [ɟacːa]); this is clearly an insurmountable task because sensitivity to 'coalescence' would have to be encoded into the faithfulness constraint itself: i.e. 'be faithful if not coalescing'.

In short, a Fixed Ranking theory predicts that the marked value should always survive in coalescence. Pāli shows that this prediction is not correct.

6.3.2.3.2 All Fixed Ranking theories

In more general terms, any Fixed Ranking approach will block conflation of the most preserved element. For example, a theory with the opposite fixed ranking ‖ IDENT{cor} »» IDENT{lab} » IDENT{dors} ‖ faces the reverse problem: it predicts that the unmarked feature will always survive. This ranking again fails in Pāli as dorsals survive in dorsal+coronal coalescence. Because preservation of dorsals is less faithful than preservation of coronals in the fixed ranking above, and no output constraint favours dorsals over coronals, the competition between dorsals and coronals can only produce coronals.

It is not just Fixed Ranking theories with non-stringent constraints that fail to account for Pāli. Theories with *stringent* constraints in a fixed ranking do equally badly. For example, a theory with the fixed ranking ‖ IDENT{dors} »» IDENT{dors,lab} »» IDENT{dors,lab,cor} ‖ still cannot deal with the output of Pāli labial+coronal coalescence. Because coronals survive in this case, some output constraint that bans labials must outrank IDENT{dors,lab}, as established above. However, no higher-ranked faithfulness constraint preserves labials, resulting in labial neutralization in every position.

The opposite problem arises for a fixed ranking ‖ IDENT{dors,lab,cor} »» IDENT{dors,lab} »» IDENT{dors} ‖. Because dorsals survive in competition with coronals, some faithfulness constraint that preserves dorsals and not coronals – IDENT{dors}, IDENT{dors,lab} – must outrank *{dors} and *{dors,lab}. This results in a problem for labial+coronal coalescence because the labial-eliminating constraint – *{dors,lab} – is already ranked below all faithfulness constraints that preserve labials, so predicting that labials will win.

In short, universally fixed ranking makes fundamentally flawed predictions for coalescence.

6.3.2.4 Minor PoA

Preservation of minor PoA also results in the unmarked value being preserved. In coalescence involving alveolar and alveo-palatal consonants, the result is alveolar.

(34) (a) Pāli (alveo-)palatal+alveolar coalescence

UR	SR	Gloss	Fahs 1989 p.
/vac-tabːa/	[vatːabːa]	'speak-ppp'	175
/vac-tum/	[vatːum]	'speak-inf'	353
/vicː-ta/	[vitːa]	'extend-ppp'	367
/saɟ-tum/	[satːum]	'send-infin'	192
/iɟːʰ-ta/	[idːʰa]	'thrive-ppf'	234
/vaʃ-tabːa/	[vatːʰabːa]	'live-gerund'	363
/ɟi-gʰaʃ-tita/	[ɟigʰacːʰita]	'eat-ppp' (cf. gʰas-a-ti)	260

(b) Pāli alveolar+(alveo-)palatal coalescence

UR	SR	Gloss	Fahs 1989 p.
/haɹ-ʃːa-ti/	[hasːati]	'take-fut-3sg'	147
/tus-ja-ti/	[tusːati]	'be satisfied-ps1d-3sg'	129
/nas-ja-ti/	[nasːati]	'wreck-ps1d-3sg'	130
/das-ja/	[disːa]	'see-gerund'	179

As expected, two alveolars coalesce to form an alveolar (e.g. /as-ti/ → [atːʰi] 'be+3sg'), and two (alveo-)palatals coalesce to form an (alveo-)palatal (e.g. /ruc-ja-ti/ → [rucːati] 'like-ps1d-3sg').

The roots' underlying forms can be determined by examining their shape before vowel-initial suffixes: e.g. [iɟːʰ-a-ti], [bʰusɲ-a-ti]. A special case is the underlying form of 'live' – /vaʃ/. /ʃ/ is neutralized to [s] in all environments: e.g. [vas-a-ti]. However, 'live' must be /vaʃ/ rather than /vas/ because the final consonant coalesces to form a palatal with another palatal, not an alveolar: /vaʃ-ca-ti/ → [vacːati] (i.e. not */vas-ca-ti/ → [vasːati], cf. /vicː-ta/ → [vitːa], *[vicːa]).

The generalizations also apply to coalescence of three consonant clusters. For example, in /labʰ-ʃ-ti/ → [ladːʰi], the competition for survival is between a labial, alveo-palatal, and alveolar, and the alveolar survives (i.e. *[labːʰi], *[lacːʰi]). Labials lose out to alveo-palatals (e.g. /labʰ-ʃːa-ti/ → [lacːʰati]), but both lose out to alveolars (e.g. /labʰ-ta/ → [ladːʰa], /vaʃ-tum/ → [vatːʰum]), so the output is alveolar [ladːʰi].

The proposal that [c] and [ɟ] are alveo-palatal is adopted here (Clements 1976 1999; Halle & Stevens 1979; Hume 1992; T. Hall 1997). After Clements (1999), [c ɟ] are [−anterior, +distributed, −strident], compared with [tʃ dʒ], which are [−anterior, +distributed, +strident]. In short, the issue discussed in this section is the preservation of [anterior] values. So, coalescence of a [+anterior] segment with a [−anterior] one results in a [+anterior] one: e.g. /vac-tabːa/ → [vatːabːa], *[vacːabːa]; /saɟʰ-tum/ → [satːʰum].³

There is no doubt that of the two features, [+anterior] is the less marked. Every language that has a [−anterior] coronal also has a [+anterior] coronal, regardless of the manner of articulation. For example, there is no language with a [c] but no [t] or [t̪]. Therefore, survival of [−anterior] must be implemented by the same ranking as survival of coronal PoA: ‖ IDENT[±anterior] » *[−anterior] » IDENT[−anterior] ‖.

(35) Pāli IV: Unmarked survival of [anterior]

/saɟʰ₁-t₂um/	IDENT[±anterior]	*[−anterior]	IDENT[−anterior]
(a) sacːʰ₁,₂um	*	*!	
☞ (b) satːʰ₁,₂um	*		*

Tableau (35) shows how the candidate with [+anterior] [tːʰ] comes to be the output: it beats candidate (a) in markedness, by minimizing [−anterior] segments. The ranking of ‖ IDENT[±anterior] » *[−anterior] ‖ is essential for the same reasons as identified for ‖ IDENT{dors,lab,cor} » *{dors,lab} ‖ above – it prevents contrast in [anterior] from being neutralized in all environments. It also prevents the output of labial+alveo-palatal coalescence from being an alveolar, as shown in tableau (36).

(36) Pāli V

/labʰ₁-ʃː₂ati/	ident[±anterior]	*[−anterior]	ident[−anterior]
(a) latːʰ₁,₂ati	*!		*
☞ (b) lacːʰ₁,₂ati		*	

Other languages do the exact opposite in coalescence. In Chipewyan, [−anterior] survives in coalescence with a [+anterior] segment: i.e. /t+ʒ/ → [tʃ],*[ts] (e.g. /ʔã-hɛ-θ-t-ʒa/ → [ʔãhɛθtʃ͡a] 'he went home', (Li 1946:419). The same is true of coalescence in Catalan: /baʃ zɛru/ → [baʒɛru] *baix zero* 'low zero', *[bazɛru] (Hualde 1992:400). In these cases, the ranking ‖ IDENT[−anterior] » *[−anterior] ‖ holds.

---

3 The behaviour of true palatals in coalescence differs from alveo-palatals. For example, /kʰaːd-ja-ti/ → [kʰaɟːati] 'eat {pass-3p.sg}', /kʰan-ja-ti/ → [kʰaɲːati] 'dig {pass-3p.sg.}'. /j/ is palatal, as opposed to the alveo-palatals [c ɟ]. The output of /d-j/ is the alveo-palatal [ɟ] because this is the segment that is most featurally similar to a true palatal.

6.3 *Preservation conflation in Pāli coalescence* 277

There are some exceptions to the claim that coalescence of alveolars and alveo-palatals yield alveolars. One class of these cases involves combinations of a nasal plus a palatal: e.g. /han-cːa/ → [hacːa] 'kill {absolutive}', /kʰan-ja-ti/ → [kʰaɲːati] 'he was killed'. In some situations, the nasal assimilates to the following alveo-palatal rather than becoming a geminate: /han-ʃːa-ti/ → [haɲcʰati] 'kill {future-3p.sg.}'. The behaviour of /n/ may relate to the fact that nasals assimilate far more freely than other segments; this may be formally implemented by having nasal PoA features subject to less preservation than obstruents', accounting for the fact that the obstruent's PoA wins in coalescence. The other class of exceptions relates to combinations of /d/ and an alveo-palatal, which typically result in an alveo-palatal: e.g. /bʰid-ʃːa-ti/ → [bʰeɟːati] 'crack {future-3p.sg.}', /cud-ja-ti/ → [cuɟːati] 'push'. /d/ is generally the least robust of all consonants in Pāli, not only for PoA preservation, but for sonority preservation as well. I therefore leave it for further research (see de Lacy 2002a:§8.5).

6.3.2.5 Preservation of the Marked II: other features
This final section discusses the preservation of non-PoA features in Pāli coalescence apart from sonority.

If one of the input segments is an aspirated stop, /s/, /ʂ/, /ʃ/, or /h/, the output is also aspirated, as shown in (37).

(37)   Aspiration Preservation in Pāli (page numbers Fahs 1989)
       (a) stopʰ+C   /labʰ tum/   > [ladːʰum]   'take+infin.' (191)
                      /radʰ-ta/   → [radːʰa]   'result+participle' (170)
       (b) {s, ʃ, ʂ}+C /vaʃ-ta/   → [vutːʰa]   'live+participle' (170)
                      /sis-ta/   → [sitːʰa]   'leave+participle' (17)
                      /iʂː-ta/   → [itːʰa]   'wish+participle' (170)
       (c) C+ʃ   /sak-ʃ-ti/   → [sakːʰi]   'be able aorist+3p.sg.' (158)
                      /labʰ-ʃ-im/   → [lacːʰim]   'take+aorist+1p.sg.' (158)
                      /cʰid-ʃːa-ti/ → [cʰecːʰati] 'crack+future+3p.sg.' (148)
       (d) h+C   /duh-ta/   → [dudːʰa]   'milk+participle' (170)
                      /snih-ta/   → [sinidːʰa]   'love+participle' (170)
                      /dah-ja-ti/   → [dajʰati]   'burn+passive+3p.sg.' (201)

To deal with aspiration preservation, a faithfulness constraint that preserves [+spread glottis] outranks all output constraints that favour plain stops over aspirates. The proposal that voiceless fricatives are specified as [+spread glottis] is adopted here (Kingston 1990; Vaux 1998), so accounting for the fact that their coalescence yields an aspirated stop.

278 6 *Markedness conflation in preservation*

(38)   Pāli vi: Aspiration preservation

/vas₁-t₂um/	IDENT[+spread glottis]	*[+spread glottis]
(a) vatː₁,₂um	*!	
☞ (b) vatː^{h}₁,₂um		*

Input clusters of a retroflex consonant plus a stop always produce a retroflex consonant on the surface. Representative examples are given in (39).

(39)   Preservation of retroflexion
       /daṣ-tabːa/   → [daṭː^{h}abːa]   'see {gerund}'
                cf. /vaʃ-tabːa/ → [vatː^{h}abːa]   'live {gerund}'
       /daɻṣ-tvaː/   → [diṭː^{h}aː]   'see {absolute}'
       /kiɻ-na/   → [kiṇːa]   'scatter'
       /iṣ-ta/   → [iṭː^{h}a]   'wish'

Pāli does not allow retroflex fricatives or liquids on the surface, so /daṣ/ and /kiɻ/ are realized with non-retroflex consonants in other environments: e.g. /daṣ-ja-ti/ → [disːati] 'see-causative-3sg', /a-daṣ-ʃ-am/ → [adːasam] 'ao-see-ao-1sg'; /kiɻ-a-si/ → [kiɻasi] 'scatter-pres-2sg'. Retroflexion is a marked feature, so the 'marked coalescence' ranking must be used here: a retroflexion-preserving faithfulness constraint must outrank all output constraints against retroflex stops. The interesting difference in this ranking is that constraints against retroflex continuants (i.e. *ɻ, *ṣ) must outrank all retroflex-preserving faithfulness constraints, otherwise they would survive in the output. Tableau (40) shows the ranking for retroflex-preservation in coalescence; tableau (41) shows how retroflexion in continuants is otherwise neutralized. The relevant retroflexion feature is taken to be [+back] here (after Chomsky & Halle 1968; E. Pulleyblank 1989).

(40)   Pāli ranking vii: Preservation of retroflexion

/daṣ₁-t₂abːa/	*ṣ, *ɻ	IDENT[+back]	*ṭ,ḍ
(a) datː^{h}₁,₂abːa		*!	
☞ (b) daṭː^{h}₁,₂abːa			*

(41)   Pāli ranking viii: Elimination of fricative retroflexes

/daṣ-ja-ti/	*ṣ, *ɻ	IDENT[+back]	*ṭ,ḍ
(a) diṣːati	*!		
☞ (b) disːati		*	

6.4 Domain faithfulness and the majority rules problem

In summary, the other features that figure in Pāli coalescence can be accounted for in the same way as for PoA – through the use of PoM-faithfulness constraints and markedness-referring output constraints.

6.4 Domain faithfulness and the majority rules problem

The analyses of Swedish assimilation and Pāli coalescence presented above suffer from the 'majority rules' problem, identified by Lombardi (1996, 1999), and discussed in Baković 1999a,b, de Lacy 2002a:§7.7.3, McCarthy 2002, and Murray 2005. In a majority rules (MR) situation, the output takes on the feature value that is present in the majority of input segments. For example, in Swedish /skuːg-s brand/ 'forest fire', the underlined portion contains two [+voice] segments and one [−voice] one. If Swedish assimilation followed the MR principle, the output should be *[skuːgzbrand]; however, the attested form is [skuːksprand], with the [−voice] value surviving.

The problem that MR poses is that the stringency and marked faithfulness proposals predict that the majority *must* rule whenever (a) there is an odd number of segments, (b) the process is not directionally controlled (i.e. it is bidirectional assimilation or coalescence), and (c) the unmarked value wins when there are even numbers of segments. This situation arises in both Swedish and Pāli; the problem for Swedish can be seen in tableau (42). The ranking ‖ IDENT[±voice] » *{+voice} ‖ is necessary to allow less-marked segments to emerge when there are even numbers of input segments. However, this ranking inadvertently favours preservation of the *marked* value just when the input contains an odd number of consonants and the majority have the marked value underlyingly.

(42) The majority is forced to rule in bidirectional assimilation

/...gː-s b.../	*{±voice} {±voice}	IDENT [±voice]	*{+voice}	IDENT [+voice]
(a) ...gːsb...	* *!		* *	
(b) ...kːsp...		* *!		* *
☞ (c) ...gːzb...		*	* * *	

MR clearly presents a problem for the Swedish and Pāli analyses. However, it does not present a direct problem for the claims about markedness made here. In particular, it does not challenge the basic proposals that stringent constraints are necessary and that there is Preservation of the Marked. Instead,

280 *6 Markedness conflation in preservation*

I suggest that the MR problem indicates that there is a fundamental problem with current conceptions of faithfulness. Tableau (42) illustrates this point: the problem can be traced back to IDENT[±voice] − it simply preserves too much in (b).

The alternative proposed here is that faithfulness constraints preserve within domains (i.e. strings), not segments. Instead of preserving each segment's value for a feature, IDENT[F] demands that *all* segments' [F] values within a certain domain be realized faithfully. The relevant D(omain)-faithfulness constraint for [voice] is given in (43).

(43)   D-IDENT[voice]   'For every domain D,
                           incur a violation if some input segment *x* in D is [αF]
                           and its output correspondent *x'* is not [αF].'

The 'domain' for feature F is the string of contiguous segments that all have feature F. For [voice], I adopt the view that obstruent voicing is distinct from sonorant voicing (see, e.g., Gnanadesikan 1997 for theoretical proposals and references cited therein). So a string of segments is a [voice] domain if all the segments are obstruents. The result is that both /gː-s b/ → [kːsp] and /gː-s b/ → [gːzb] violate D-IDENT[voice] just once because neither preserves all [voice] features. Because they violate D-IDENT[voice] equally, *{+voice} emerges and favours the output with voiceless segments, as illustrated in tableau (44).

(44)   D-faithfulness solution

/...gː-s b.../	*{±voice} {±voice}	D-IDENT [±voice]	*{+voice}	IDENT [+voice]
(a) ...gːsb...	**!		**	
(b) ...kːsp...		*		**
☞ (c) ...gːzb...		*	***!	

Domain faithfulness is discussed in more detail in section 6.4.1. Section 6.4.2 shows how it applies to both the Swedish assimilation and Pāli coalescence cases. Alternatives are examined in section 6.4.3.

6.4.1 Domain faithfulness

Current concepts of featural faithfulness are segmentally oriented: IDENT[F] is violated once for each segment that fails to preserve its F value. I suggest that faithfulness operates not on the segmental level, but on longer strings.

6.4 Domain faithfulness and the majority rules problem 281

Specifically, faithfulness to feature F operates on a contiguous string of F-bearing elements. For example, the feature [voice], which I take to apply to obstruents only, has three domains within /sbaksbat/: /sb/, /ksb/, and /t/. To avoid violating D-IDENT[±voice], all segments must faithfully preserve their input voicing specifications. There is no distinction between partial and total unfaithfulness within a domain. For example, /ksb/ → [ksb] does not violate D-IDENT[±voice], but the outputs [ksp], [kzb], [gsb], [kzp], [gsp], [gzb], and [gzp] all incur one violation of D-IDENT [±voice]. For example, in the mapping /ksb/ → [kzb] there is some input segment (i.e. /s/) that is [−voice] while its output correspondent is [+voice]; therefore D-IDENT[±voice] is violated. Similarly, in /ksb/ → [gzp], there is some segment that is unfaithful in [voice], so there is one violation; it does not matter that there are two such segments.

The domain of faithfulness can be made more specific using positional faithfulness. For example, ROOT-D-IDENT[±voice] applies to only those domains inside a root. ONSET-D-IDENT[±voice] applies to only those domains inside onsets.

The discussion of Swedish and Pāli below will clarify the use of domain faithfulness.

6.4.2 Swedish and Pāli again

The problem encountered in Swedish bidirectional [voice] assimilation is that too many faithfulness distinctions are made by segmental IDENT constraints. There should be no faithfulness distinction between the mapping from /gsb/ to [gzb] and [ksp]. This collapse in faithfulness distinctions is what D-IDENT allows. However, it is first necessary to show that domain faithfulness still works with the other cases.

D-IDENT[±voice] preserves domains with a single obstruent in the same way that segmental IDENT does. A mapping such as /ag/ → [ak] violates D-IDENT[±voice] because the domain /g/ is unfaithful. D-IDENT [±voice] does not act much differently from segmental IDENT in bisegmental domains either. For example, from /stɛk-də/, both [stɛgdə] and [stɛktə] violate D-IDENT[±voice] once, just as they violate segmental IDENT[±voice]. The difference comes in complete faithfulness reversals: [stɛgtə] violates D-IDENT[±voice] once, but IDENT[±voice] twice. However, this difference can never be relevant as [stɛgtə] is harmonically bounded by other candidates: [stɛkdə] is more faithful and satisfies *{+voice} and OCP(voice) just as well, [stɛktə] is just as faithful but violates *{+voice} less. Tableau (45) illustrates.

(45)

/stɛk-də/	*{±voice} {±voice}	D-IDENT [±voice]	*{+voice}	D-IDENT [+voice]	onset-D-IDENT [±voice]
(a) stɛk.də	*!		*		
(b) stɛg.tə	*!	*	*	*	*
(c) stɛg.də		*	**!		
☞ (d) stɛk.tə		*		*	*

The visible difference only arises for domains larger than two segments. The case with two [+voice] and one [−voice] case has been discussed above and shown to work with D-IDENT [±voice]. In the same way, one [+voice] and two [−voice] segments surface as voiceless. In tableau (46), (b) and (c) are identical in faithfulness as both have a domain that is not completely faithful to voicing. Consequently, *{+voice} makes the crucial distinction, favouring the one with voiceless segments.

(46)

/hœg-st/	*{±voice} {±voice}	D-IDENT [±voice]	*{+voice}	D-IDENT [+voice]
(a) hœgst	*!		*	
(b) hœgzd		*	***!	
☞ (c) hœkst		*		*

Domain faithfulness also allows onset-controlled assimilation. The constraint onset-D-IDENT[±voice] is violated whenever a domain inside an onset is unfaithful. For example, /stɛk-də/ → [stɛk.tə] violates onset-D-IDENT [±voice] because the onset [t] in the domain [kt] is unfaithful. In contrast, [stɛg.də] does not violate the constraint.

MR also arises in Pāli coalescence, and it admits the same solution. When labials and coronals coalesce, the result is always a coronal. This is true for bi-consonantal clusters (e.g. /lubʰ-ta/ → [ludːʰa] 'yearn-ppp', *[lubːʰa]), and tri-consonantal ones: e.g. /sambʰ-ta/ → [sadːʰa] 'soothe-ppp', *[sabːʰa] (Fahs 1989:172); /limp-ta/ → [litːa] 'smear-infin.' (cf. [limp-a-ti]), /a-gam-tːʰa/ → [agatːʰa] 'go-ao-2pl'. A ranking with segmental-IDENT incorrectly predicts a MR situation, as shown in tableau (47).

6.4 Domain faithfulness and the majority rules problem

(47)   Segmental IDENT in Pāli

/sam₁bʰ₂-t₃a/	IDENT{dors,lab,cor}	*{dors,lab}	IDENT{dors,lab}
(a) sad:ʰ₁,₂,₃a	* *!		* *
☞ (b) sab:ʰ₁,₂,₃a	*	*	

As in Swedish, the problem here is that IDENT{dors,lab,cor} makes too many distinctions because it tries to preserve every segment's PoA features. In contrast, D-IDENT{dors,lab,cor} only distinguishes between complete and partial faithfulness. The domain for consonantal place features is a contiguous string of consonants (e.g. /s/ and /mbʰt/ in /sambʰ-ta/). Candidate (a) incurs one violation of D-IDENT{dors,lab,cor} because in the domain /mbʰt/ there is some input segment that is unfaithful in PoA; the fact that there is more than one is irrelevant. The same is true of candidate (b). Because (a) and (b) incur equal violations of D-IDENT{dors,lab,cor}, the markedness constraint emerges to favour the candidate with the least-marked PoA — i.e. [sad:ʰ₁,₂,₃a].

(48)   D-IDENT in Pāli

/sam₁bʰ₂-t₃a/	D-IDENT {dors,lab,cor}	*{dors,lab}	IDENT{dors,lab}
☞ (a) sad:ʰ₁,₂,₃a	*		* *
(b) sab:ʰ₁,₂,₃a	*	*!	

A similar analysis applies to anteriority in Pāli. When two [+anterior] segments coalesce with a [−anterior] one, the [−anterior] one still wins (e.g. /juɲɟ-ta/ → [juːta] 'join-ppp'; cf. [juɲɟ-a-ti] — Fahs 1989:336). This is due to D-IDENT[±anterior] assigning equal violations to [juːt:₁,₂,₃a] and *[juc:₁,₂,₃a], and *+anterior making the crucial decision.

In summary, domain faithfulness makes a distinction between complete and incomplete faithfulness; it does not distinguish different degrees of faithfulness within a domain. Such a lack of distinctiveness is clearly necessary in cases that would otherwise necessarily exhibit majority rule effects.

6.4.3 Summary, extensions, and alternatives

To summarize so far, I have just argued that the MR problem has nothing to do with markedness — it is instead due to the formulation of faithfulness constraints. Consequently, I will not expand significantly on domain faithfulness further here. However, I will address certain obvious questions.

One issue is whether MR effects *could* have implications for a theory of markedness (supposing the domain-faithfulness proposal turns out to be incorrect and segmental IDENT is the only possible conception of featural faithfulness). However, the difficulty in appealing to markedness constraints alone is clear in coalescence cases. /$m_1 b^h_2 t_3$/'s competing outputs [$d:^h_{1,2,3}$] and *[$b:^h_{1,2,3}$] differ solely in terms of PoA. However, *[$b:^h_{1,2,3}$] cannot be eliminated by a markedness constraint against labials because that constraint would have to be dominated by labial-preserving faithfulness constraints to prevent neutralization of labials everywhere. This preservation constraint would favour preservation of the majority value — i.e. labial.

Other solutions that have been proposed to the MR problem have a significant faithfulness element. For example, Murray's (2005) approach employs a DEP[±voice] constraint which is used to block neutralization (i.e. the insertion of a [−voice] feature), but allows assimilation. DEP[±voice] does not distinguish between degrees of input unfaithfulness, so it allows emergence of the least-marked value in assimilation. Murray's proposal is not adopted here because of general problems with MAX and DEP-feature constraints, discussed in §8.7.2. In addition, it cannot deal with systems in which only marked values assimilate, and so cannot account for Ukrainian's assimilation in which only [+voice] assimilates and the systems in which only marked PoA assimilates (§4.3).

Baković's (1999b) and McCarthy's (2002) solutions involve constraints that have both faithfulness and markedness components. They are discussed further in §8.6.

One major issue that remains to be addressed is whether domain-faithfulness constraints are the only kind of IDENT constraint. If so, then MR effects will be banned entirely. However, it is not yet clear that MR effects are impossible. Baković (1999b:§4) provides a detailed account of the conditions under which MR effects could be seen in assimilation; they are complex and rarely found. However, Baković goes on to argue that non-local assimilation – i.e. harmony – does provide ample relevant situations. Certainly, the issue requires more investigation before coming to any conclusions.

Another issue relates to the scope of domain faithfulness. Does domain faithfulness apply to every feature? Many questions remain, but the central point here is that the MR problem is not an issue for markedness and the central proposals of this book, but for faithfulness.

6.5 Summary

This chapter has argued that languages can conflate markedness categories in preservation, and that stringently formulated faithfulness constraints can capture this fact. The empirical effect is that the least-marked feature can survive in coalescence, bidirectional assimilation, and other processes where feature preservation comes into conflict. For example, coalescence in Pāli inevitably results in unfaithfulness to PoA: the output of /bʰ+t/ → [dːʰ] ignores /bʰ/'s labial specification, and output [bːʰ] ignores /t/'s coronal value.

In general terms, for a mapping /$x_1 y_2$/ → [$z_{1,2}$], where x and y have different values for some feature f, the theory predicts two possible outcomes. The examples focus on PoA. [*mf*] refers to a marked value of feature [f], and [*uf*] refers to a relatively less marked value.

(49) Outcomes of coalescence
    (a) The marked feature survives (e.g. /b+dʰ/ → [bʰ])
        || IDENT{*mf*} » *{*mf*} ||
    (b) The unmarked feature survives (e.g. /bʰ+d/ → [dʰ])
        || IDENT{*mf, uf*} » *{*mf*} » IDENT{*mf*} ||

Cases where the unmarked value survives in the output of coalescence show the need for stringent faithfulness constraints. If the unmarked value of a feature f appears in the output, some output constraint against the marked value **mf* must outrank all faithfulness constraints that preserve marked values. For the coalescence /bʰ+t/ → [dːʰ], where the unmarked coronal PoA survives, this means that *{dors,lab} must outrank IDENT{dors,lab}.

However, in order for *mf* to contrast with *uf*, some faithfulness constraint F must outrank **mf*. So, to prevent elimination of labials in every environment, IDENT{dors,lab,cor} must outrank *[labial]. Therefore, F must both preserve *mf* yet not favour *mf* over *uf*. The only way to satisfy these requirements is if F preserves both *mf* and *uf* equally, as shown in the tableau below. The faithfulness constraints are in a stringency relation, so allowing the unmarked value to emerge.

(50)

/ mf_1 uf_2 /	IDENT{*mf, uf*}	**mf*	IDENT{*mf*}
(a) $mf_{1,2}$	*	*!	
☞ (b) $uf_{1,2}$	*		*

Finally, the constraints predict systems in which a marked hierarchy value survives in coalescence with a less-marked value (e.g. /b+t/ → [d]), but a more-marked value is preserved in coalescence with a less-marked one (e.g. /k+d/ → [g]). Such mixed systems – like Pāli's for PoA – were shown to result from the fact that the rankings needed for marked and unmarked coalescence are compatible. The analysis showed that the stringent faithfulness constraints are easily able to deal with such a system while constraints in a fixed ranking cannot.

7 Markedness conflict: vowels

7.1 Introduction

One of the central points of this book is that there is no single 'unmarked segment'. Markedness hierarchies conflict, and so several segments have the potential to be treated as the least marked in a language for a particular process, depending on which hierarchy dominates. Vowel markedness is particularly revealing in this regard. Many vowels can have least-marked status, and so appear as the output of epenthesis and neutralization. The range of variation is due to a number of direct conflicts involving the sonority hierarchy in different environments.

The vowel sonority hierarchy is repeated from chapter 2 in (1), along with representative members of each class.

(1) Vowel sonority hierarchy

high central vowels	mid central vowels	high peripheral vowels	mid-high peripheral vowels	mid-low peripheral vowels	low vowels
ɨ ʉ ⟩	ə ⟩	i y ɯ u ⟩	e o ⟩	ɛ ɔ ⟩	æ a ɑ ɒ

Many markedness hierarchies that are relevant to consonants do not vary with prosodic context. For example, coronals are less marked than dorsals in every environment. In contrast, vowel sonority markedness is heavily dependent on prosodic context. For sonority, the least-marked vowel in a DTE (≈prosodic head) is [a], while the least-marked vowel in a non-DTE (≈prosodic non-head) is high central [ɨ ʉ] (§2.3.3.1).

An additional complexity is that prosodic contexts overlap. For example, the least-marked vowel in syllable DTEs (i.e. nuclei) is the highly sonorous [a]. However, the least-marked vowel in unstressed syllables (i.e. non-DTEs of the prosodic word – (Δ_ω), is the low sonority [ɨ ʉ]. So, unstressed syllable nuclei have two conflicting demands placed on them — as DTEs they should be highly sonorous, while as non-DTEs they should have low sonority. Languages differ as to which demand prevails and to what extent; consequently, any sonority level can be the 'least marked' in overlapping DTE and non-DTE environments.

The empirical effect of the conflicting demands on vowel sonority is that there are far fewer valid markedness diagnostics for vowels than for consonants. For example, unlike consonant epenthesis, vowels of any sonority level can be epenthetic — [ɨ ə i e ɛ a]. This variation is discussed in §7.2

Section 7.3 focuses on vowel neutralization, also called 'reduction' and 'raising'. As in epenthesis, there is a range of possible outputs of neutralization. In some languages unstressed vowels neutralize to the low sonority [ɨ] or [ə], but in others they neutralize to [a]. Even within the same language, some unstressed vowels can become less sonorous while others increase in sonority. This variation follows from conflicting demands imposed in overlapping prosodic contexts. Since vowel inventories are formed through neutralization, the result is that vowel inventories can contain any mixture of sonority levels.

One important implication of these constraints for inventories is that there is no need to appeal to devices such as 'Dispersion' (Liljencrants & Lindblom 1972; Flemming 1995). Vowel inventories such as [i u a] come about through a pressure to reduce sonority (e.g. $*\Delta \leq \{e,o\}$) being blocked by high-ranking faithfulness constraints (e.g. IDENT[±high]). The fact that 'dispersed' inventories are more frequent than other types is not an issue for Competence mechanisms to address.

Despite such variation and conflict in vowel sonority, there are vowel-related hierarchies that are not affected by prosodic context. For example, nasal vowels are more marked than oral vowels in all prosodic environments. There are also markedness relations between backness and roundness that do not vary in different prosodic contexts. These hierarchies have a significant effect on epenthesis and neutralization. This point is discussed at various points in §7.2.5.

Finally, there are phenomena which clearly show the effects of sonority markedness. When sonority influences the placement of feet or construction of syllables, it always shows the same markedness preferences. Section 7.4 discusses sonority-driven stress and shows why this phenomenon exhibits overt markedness effects.

7.2   Vowel epenthesis

Section 3.2 argued that consonant epenthesis is a valid markedness diagnostic. Faithfulness is irrelevant in epenthesis, so the only influence can be markedness reduction, once interferences like assimilation and dissimilation are factored out. The same is true for vowels — only markedness can influence vowel quality. However, there are many conflicting markedness pressures on vowel sonority. To recall the discussion from §2.3.3, sonority markedness relations in DTEs are the opposite for non-DTEs. As an example, two sets of vowel-sonority constraints are provided in (2). The sonority levels are symbolized by using common members: for example, '{ɨ,ʉ}' refers to the class 'high central vowels', 'ə' to 'mid central vowels', and so on. The 'ω' symbol stands for 'prosodic word'. A constraint like $*\Delta_\sigma \leq ə$ is violated by a syllable DTE (i.e. a nucleus segment) that has equal or less sonority than the 'mid central vowel' level. The notation '≤' is used here instead of listing all sonority levels as this would be too verbose (e.g. $*-\Delta_\omega \geq \{i,u\} = *-\Delta_\omega/\{a, ɛ\bullet ɔ, e \bullet o, i \bullet u\}$).

(2) (a) $*\Delta_\sigma \leq \{ɨ,ʉ\}$, $*\Delta_\sigma \leq ə$, $*\Delta_\sigma \leq \{i,u\}$, $*\Delta_\sigma \leq \{e,o\}$, $*\Delta_\sigma \leq \{ɛ,ɔ\}$, $*\Delta_\sigma \leq a$
(b) $*-\Delta_\omega \geq a$, $*-\Delta_\omega \geq \{ɛ,ɔ\}$, $*-\Delta_\omega \geq \{e,o\}$, $*-\Delta_\omega \geq \{i,u\}$, $*-\Delta_\omega \geq ə$, $*-\Delta_\omega \geq \{ɨ,ʉ\}$

The constraints express the generalization that low vowels are least marked for sonority in the DTE of syllables (Δ_σ), and high central vowels are least marked in the non-DTEs of the prosodic word; every nucleus except the primary stressed one is a non-DTE of the prosodic word ($-\Delta_\omega$).

So, what is the least-marked vowel for sonority in an unstressed syllable? The constraints in (b) favour high central vowels. However, every unstressed syllable nucleus is also a syllable nucleus so the constraints in (a) also apply, and favour the highest sonority vowel [a]. Consequently, there are two conflicting pressures in unstressed syllable nuclei.

As almost every position is both a DTE and non-DTE of some prosodic element, almost every position faces tension over whether to have high sonority, low sonority, or compromise with a mid-sonority level. The only exceptions are (a) onsets, which are not DTEs of any prosodic element, and (b) the nucleus that bears utterance-level stress (or perhaps focus), which is a DTE of every level.

With such markedness tension, vowel epenthesis is almost entirely uninformative about sonority markedness. However, for other markedness hierarchies, it is still useful. For example, hierarchies relating to vowel colour (i.e. roundness and backness) are not dependent on prosodic position, so epenthesis offers insight into their markedness.

Section 7.2.1 discusses the typology of epenthetic vowels. Sections 7.2.2–7.2.4 show how the relative freedom of epenthetic vowel sonority follows from the theory, and §7.2.5 discusses vowel markedness hierarchies other than sonority.

7.2.1 The spectrum of epenthesis

The list of vowel epentheses in table (3) shows that almost any non-round non-back vowel [ɨ ə i e ɛ a] can be epenthetic. The cases have 'default' epenthesis, where the epenthetic segment is not influenced by the feature content of adjacent elements. 'Copy epenthesis', where the epenthetic element duplicates part or all of a nearby vowel, is not relevant here (Kitto & de Lacy 1999). More generally, the cases below do not include those where epenthetic vowel content is influenced by processes such as vowel harmony, assimilation, and dissimilation.

Examples of each type of epenthetic vowel have been limited to a maximum of ten languages for practical (i.e. visual) reasons. To give a sense of the relative frequency of the types, of a total of 105 languages, 22 have epenthetic [i], 19 [ə], 13 [a], 10 [e or ɛ], 7 [ɯ], 5 [ɨ], and 26 had copy vowels (see Kitto & de Lacy 1999). I hasten to add that frequency is irrelevant to the theory here; the numbers are included for interest only. The mid-vowel epentheses of [ɛ] and [e] have been collapsed into one category as there is occasionally not enough description to determine which of these two the mid vowel is. However, some cases are clearly [ɛ] (e.g. Chipewyan) and others are [e].

(3)   Typology of epenthetic vowels

Vowel	Language	Family	Reference
ɨ	Amharic	Semitic	Hayward (1986)
	Karao	N. Phillipine	Brainard (1994)
	Washo	Hokan	Kenstowicz & Kisseberth (1971)
ə	Chukchi	Chukotko-Kamchatkan	Krause (1980)
	Hindi	Indo-Aryan	Steriade (1995b:138)
	Itelmen	Chukotko-Kamchatkan	Bobaljik (1997)
	Karo Batak	Sundic	Woolams (1996)
	Ladakhi	Tibetan	Koshal (1979)
	Malay	Sundic	Ahmad (1994)
	Mongolian	Altaic	Svantesson (1995)
	Palestinian Arabic	Semitic	Abu-Salim (1982:10)
	Sekani	Athapaskan	Hargus (1988)
	Wolof	Senegambian	Ka (1985)
i	Harari	Ethiopian	Rose (1997)
	Maltese	Semitic	Hume (1992)
	Manam	Oceanic	Lichtenberk (1983:32)
	Māori	Polynesian	de Lacy (2002a)
	Moañés Galician	Romance	Martinez-Gil (1997)

290 *Markedness conflict: vowels*

	Ojibwa	Algonquian	Piggott (1993)
	Pāli	Indo-European	Fahs (1989)
	Pipil	Aztecan	Campbell (1985)
e/ɛ	Basque	Indo-European	Hualde (1991)
	Biak	New Guinea	van den Heuvel (2004)
	Chipewyan	Athapaskan	Li (1946)
	Czech	Slavic	Ketner (2003)
	Galician	Romance	Colina (1997)
	Gengbe (Mina)	Niger-Congo	Abaglo & Archangeli (1989)
	Mohawk	Iroquoian	Hopkins (1987)
	Slave	Athapaskan	Rice (1989:133)
	Temiar	Mon-Khmer	(closed σs) McCarthy (1980)
	Tiberian Hebrew	Semitic	(word-final closed σs) Rappaport (1984)
a	Axininca Campa	Arawakan	Payne (1981), McCarthy & Prince (1993b)
	Coos	Penutian	Frachtenberg (1922)
	Dakota	Siouan	Shaw (1980:120)
	Klamath	Penutian	Kenstowicz & Kisseberth (1971)
	Lardil	Pama-Nyungan	Piggott (1993)
	Mabalay Atayal	Formosan	Lambert (1999:§3.2.1)
	Marathi	Indo-Aryan	Pandharipande (1997)
	Mesola Italian	Romance	Repetti (1996)
	Sudanese Arabic	Semitic	Haddad (1983)
	Tuscarora	Iroquoian	Mithun (1976:289)
	Wapishana	Arawakan	Tracy (1972)

The criteria for considering a process to be vowel epenthesis are the same as for consonant epenthesis (§3.4). In the cases cited above, vowel epenthesis takes place to satisfy a general phonological requirement such as minimal word restrictions, metrical conditions, and segmental phonotactic restrictions (Broselow 1982; Ito 1986). As discussed in §3.4, 'epentheses' that are arbitrarily limited to restricted morphological environments were not considered.

The following subsections identify the rankings of the DTE and non-DTE constraints that produce the attested vowel qualities.

7.2.2 High-sonority epenthesis in Coos

High-sonority vowels like [a] are the least-marked type in terms of the syllable DTE constraints alone. The influence of the DTE constraints on epenthetic quality can be seen in a variety of languages. The example discussed here is from Coos, a Penutian language described by Frachtenberg (1922: 309ff.).

Coos has the short vowels [i e a o u ə], and the long vowels [iː eː æː aː oː uː]. The syllable structure is (C)(C)V(X)(C), where X is a sonorant (nasal, liquid, glide, or vowel). Codas are restricted to certain [nasal+obstruent] and [liquid+stop] clusters (i.e. [mt ms mx nt nk nl lt lm ɬt ɬts]). Nuclei may contain a short vowel, long vowel, or diphthong. Examples of syllables can be seen in [dəms.tets] 'through a prairie', [ha.taː.jims] *no gloss*, and [tkem] *no gloss* (pp.307–8).

The restrictions on syllable structure motivate epenthesis in a variety of situations. As Frachtenberg explains, all inadmissible word-final and medial clusters are avoided through the insertion of a vowel (p.309). Relevant examples are given in (4).

(4)   [a]-epenthesis in Coos (data from Frachtenberg 1922)
      (a) Epenthesis in word-final clusters
           [m'iɬa̱x]   cf. [miɬx-'anəm]   'lunch make me' (p.315)
           [lhina̱p]   cf. [lhinp-'iːje]   'they two came through' (p.315)
           ['alqa̱s]   cf. [alqs-'aːja]   'they two are afraid of it' (p.315)
           [tsila̱ts]   cf. [ts'il-tsəxəm]   'he was astonished' (p.315)
           [kwaːxa̱l]   cf. [n-kw'aːxl-a]   'they two have bows' (p.315)
           /winq-s/   → [w'inqa̱s]   'mat, spider' (p.309)
           /helq/   [h'ela̱q]   'he arrived' (p.309)
      (b) Epenthesis in word-medial clusters (p.309)
           /winq-xəm/   → [win'aqaxəm]   'it is spread out'
           /helq-xəm/   → [hel'aqaxəm]   'it is the end'
           /ɬnq-a/   → [ɬn'aq-a]   'they two went down'

As an example, /alqs/ cannot surface faithfully with an acceptable coda *[alqs], so [a] is epenthesized to resolve the problem ['al.qa̱s]. In ranking terms, a constraint (or constraints) against inadmissible coda clusters must outrank DEP-IO. A detailed account of the constraints against inadmissible codas in Coos will not be given here as this would take the discussion too far from the point; the set of constraints responsible for Coos' coda restrictions will simply be called *CODA_CLUSTER here. To prevent deletion, MAX-IO must also outrank DEP-IO. The rankings are illustrated in tableau (5).

292 *Markedness conflict: vowels*

(5)   Coos I

/alqs/	*CODA_CLUSTER	MAX-IO	DEP-IO
(a) alqs	*!		
(b) als		*!	
☞ (c) al.qas			*

The issue of present interest is not what motivates epenthesis, but rather what determines the quality of the epenthetic vowel. As [a] is inserted, there must be some output constraint that favours it over all the other vowels [e o i u ə]. A contender for this role is the syllable-level DTE constraint $*\Delta_\sigma \leq \{e,o\}$. This constraint militates against all nucleus segments with less sonority than a low vowel. Thus, it will favour ['alqas] over all other candidates, including *['alqes], *['alqis], and *['alqəs].

The constraint $*\Delta_\sigma \leq \{e,o\}$ must outrank all output constraints that favour any of the non-low vowels over [a]. As it is the most sonorous vowel, [a] is the worst type of non-DTE. Consequently, $*\Delta_\sigma \leq \{e,o\}$ must outrank all relevant non-DTE constraints. These include constraints that refer to the positions 'foot non-DTE' and 'prosodic word non-DTE'. In tableau (6) candidate (a) fatally violates $*-\Delta_\sigma \leq \{e,o\}$ by having a low-sonority [ə] in the DTE of a syllable. Candidate (b) avoids this violation, but in doing so violates the lower ranked non-DTE constraints because its second [a] is in the non-DTE of a foot, which is also the non-DTE of the prosodic word.

(6)   Coos II

/alqs/	$*\Delta_\sigma \leq \{e,o\}$	$*-\Delta_\omega \geq \{i,u\}$	$*-\Delta_{Ft} \geq \{i,u\}$
(a) ('al.qəs)	*!		
☞ (b) ('al.qas)		*	*

$*\Delta_\sigma \leq \{e,o\}$ must outrank many other non-DTE constraints, including $*-\Delta_{Ft} \geq \{e,o\}$, which favours both [ə] and high vowels over [a], $*-\Delta_{Ft} \geq \{a\}$, and so on.

To generalize, [a] is epenthesized in the DTE of constituent α when some DTE constraint with the form $*\Delta_\alpha \leq \{e,o\}$ outranks all non-DTE constraints of the form $*-\Delta_\beta \geq x$, where β is a higher prosodic category than α and x is any sonority category. In Coos, for example, $*\Delta_\sigma \leq \{e,o\}$ outranks all $*-\Delta_{Ft} \geq \{x\}$ and $*-\Delta_\omega \geq \{x\}$ constraints, and so on up through the prosodic hierarchy.

What makes Coos interesting for markedness purposes is that the epenthetic vowel is not always [a]. After [s], it is [i]: e.g. ['dəm.sit] 'to the prairie he came'

7.2 *Vowel epenthesis* 293

(cf. [dəmst-'ets lh'inap]), [hætsitː] 'a story is being told' (cf. [hætsteniːjeqəm]). This is due to a constraint requiring agreement in place of articulation between [s] and a following vowel, which will be referred to as AGREE[coronal] here (Hume 1992; Clements & Hume 1995). Underlying vowels do not become [i] after [s] in Coos, so AGREE [coronal] has an emergent effect, just like $*\Delta_\sigma \leq \{e,o\}$. AGREE [coronal] must outrank $*\Delta_\sigma \leq \{e,o\}$ to block epenthesis of the low (non-front) vowel [a].

However, AGREE [coronal] only requires a front vowel to appear after [s]; it does not decide between [i] and [e]. Because the constraint $*\Delta_\sigma \leq \{e,o\}$ assigns the same violations to [i] and [e], lower-ranked constraints are free to determine which of the two vowels is most harmonic. Because [e] is more sonorous than [i], a non-DTE constraint like $*-\Delta_\omega \geq \{e,o\}$ will favour the latter over the former. The rankings are illustrated in tableau (7).

(7)   Coos III

/dəmst/	AGREE[coronal]	$*\Delta_\sigma \leq \{e,o\}$	$*-\Delta_\omega \geq \{e,o\}$
(a) 'demsat	*!		*
(b) 'demset		**	*!
☞ (c) 'demsit		**	

So, [e] is prevented from winning by having $*-\Delta_\omega \geq \{e,o\}$ outrank all DTE constraints that favour [e] over [i] – i.e. $*\Delta_\sigma \leq \{i,u\}$. Thus, even though the non-DTE constraints are dominated in Coos, they can have an emergent effect even in a system where DTE constraints generally dominate.

In slightly different terms, the ranking again illustrates the importance of conflation. It is crucial that the active DTE constraint favours low vowels but treats all others equally. Because $*\Delta_\sigma \leq \{e,o\}$ assigns the same violations to [e] and [i], the lower-ranked $*-\Delta_\omega \geq \{e,o\}$ can emerge to be decisive in this competition.

In short, Coos illustrates the ranking $*\Delta_\sigma \leq x \gg *-\Delta_\omega \geq y$; this favours relatively higher sonority epenthetic segments.

7.2.2.1 Alternative analyses

The analysis above uses sonority constraints to favour [a] over all other vowels. In comparison, Lombardi (2003) proposes that there are two constraints *NON-LOW and *LOW. If *NON-LOW outranks *LOW, the result will be an epenthetic [a]. There is nothing in Lombardi's analysis that is inherently incompatible with the theory presented here because the constraints proposed have the same favouring relationships: both Lombardi's constraints and those proposed here will allow [a] to win. However, while there is no conflict in terms of the typology predicted, constraints like *NON-LOW and *LOW are unnecessary – their role is subsumed by the DTE/sonority constraints. There is no question that constraints like *Δ_σ≤{e,o} are needed to deal with sonority-conditioned syllabification (Prince & Smolensky 1993), so *NON-LOW is at least innocuous, and probably redundant.

7.2.3 Low-sonority epenthesis

The preceding section has shown that the dominance of syllable-level DTE constraints over higher-level non-DTE ones results in a high-sonority epenthetic vowel. The opposite ranking produces a low-sonority epenthetic vowel. Complete dominance of the non-DTE over the DTE constraints will result in a grammar that epenthesizes the lowest-sonority vowel allowed in its inventory.

There are many cases where low-sonority vowels are epenthesized. The lowest-sonority vowel [ɨ] is epenthesized in several languages, the next-lowest sonority vowel [ə] is probably the most frequently epenthesized vowel, and the relatively low sonority vowel [i] is also epenthesized in many languages. Rather than providing a pedestrian analysis of a language that epenthesizes [ɨ] or [ə] in all environments, this section examines Maga Rukai, a language with low-sonority epenthesis that shows the effect of non-DTE constraints in a rather striking way.

Hsin (2000) reports that Maga Rukai has seven contrastive vowels: the peripheral vowels [i e a o u] and the central vowels [ɨ ə]. Every word in Maga Rukai must end in a vowel, so epenthesis is used to eliminate consonant-final words. This is a common process in Tsou languages (Tsuchida 1976).

At first glance, Maga Rukai vowel epenthesis may seem irrelevant to present concerns because the final vowel is generally a copy of the preceding vowel (8a). However, a key piece of data is that copying does not take place after [a] – [ɨ] is inserted instead (8b).

(8)   Maga Rukai epenthesis
    (a) [ikivi] 'tail' [kpiŋi] 'clothing'
        [θveke] 'betel nut' [rvele] 'arrow'
        [tesboko] 'egret (black)' [svoŋvoŋo] 'butterfly'
        [uŋulu] 'drink' [tkasludu] 'shrimp'
        [krɨmɨ] 'palate' [admɨmɨ] 'iron'
        [dkəsə] 'camphor laurel' [lcəŋə] 'vegetable'
    (b) [cacŋalɨ] 'start' [tkorpaŋɨ] 'frog'

Hsin (2000) provides evidence that the underlying forms listed above lack a final vowel underlyingly. The evidence is rather complex because a number of processes interact to change the underlying form substantially on the surface (including iambically conditioned vowel syncope, and coalescence). To summarize, Hsin (2000) shows that [dmele̠] derives from a form with underlying /a/ and /i/, which I take to be /damil/ here. Vowels in the weak member of a foot are prohibited, so *[(da'mil)] is banned. Instead of deleting, [a] coalesces with the following vowel, forming [('dmel)]. Finally, epenthesis takes place to avoid final codas, producing [('dmele̠)]. This proposal explains why the negative form is [(ˌdam)('liː)]: the negative morpheme consists of a mora, which forces the underlying [i] to metathesize. The result is that neither vowel is deleted, so showing the true quality of the input vowels. If the input was /damile/ – i.e. the copy vowel was underlying – the negative would be *[damleː]. The reader is referred to Hsin (2000:95ff.) for further details.

The most striking aspect of Maga Rukai epenthesis is the fact that the epenthetic vowel – for the most part – is a copy of the preceding one. Since copy epenthesis is not the focus of this section, the constraint that promotes copying is referred to as AGREEV here, requiring harmony between adjacent vowels. A theory of copy epenthesis (and references to other work on the subject) is provided in Kitto & de Lacy (1999), so the subject will not be discussed here.

AGREEV outranks output constraints that favour a particular vowel over all others, like the DTE constraint $*-\Delta_\omega \geq \{ə\}$, which favours [ɨ] over all other vowels. Tableau (9) illustrates this ranking. NOCODA, a constraint that bans coda consonants (Prince & Smolensky 1993), outranks DEP in Maga Rukai, so motivating epenthesis.

(9)   Maga Rukai ɪ

/rvel/	NOCODA	AGREEV	$*-\Delta_\omega \geq \{ə\}$
(a) 'rvel	*!		
(b) 'rvelɨ̠		*!	
☞ (c) 'rvele̠			*

NOCODA does not cause word-medial epenthesis (e.g. [tkasluɖu], *[tkasaluɖu]). There are two possible reasons for this: (a) CONTIGUITY (a constraint preserving input adjacency relations) blocks medial epenthesis (McCarthy & Prince 1995; Kenstowicz 1994), or (b) medial consonant clusters are all complex onsets (cf. Kager's 1997 account of Macushi).

However, $*-\Delta_\omega \geq \{ə\}$ is not inactive. Its effect emerges in epenthesis after [a], as in [tkorpaŋɨ] 'frog'. Epenthesis of [ɨ] in this situation raises two questions: (1) why is the epenthetic vowel not [a]? and (2) why is the epenthetic vowel [ɨ]? Non-DTE constraints provide an answer to both these questions.

Since [a] is the most marked non-DTE, [a]-copying can be blocked by a constraint such as $*-\Delta_\omega \geq \{a\}$. This situation is illustrated in tableau (10). The constraint $*-\Delta_\omega \geq \{a\}$ bans high-sonority non-DTEs, so eliminating the candidate with epenthetic [a]. This leaves the candidates without copy vowels – (b) and (c).

The tableau also goes some way to accounting for the emergence of [ɨ] in this situation. Since both (b) and (c) do not have copy vowels, they violate AGREEV equally. The equal violation allows the lower-ranked constraint $*-\Delta_\omega \geq \{ə\}$ to emerge, favouring the lowest sonority vowel available – i.e. [ɨ]. In other words, [ɨ] wins in this situation because it is the most desirable non-DTE.

(10)   Maga Rukai II

/tkorpaŋ/	$*-\Delta_\omega \geq \{a\}$	AGREEV	$*-\Delta_\omega \geq \{ə\}$
(a) tkor'paŋa	*!		*
(b) tkor'paŋə		*	**!
☞ (c) tkor'paŋɨ		*	*

To ensure that [ɨ] appears in this situation rather than some other vowel, further rankings are crucial. $*-\Delta_\omega \geq \{ə\}$ must outrank all DTE constraints that promote [ə] and more sonorous elements above [ɨ]: i.e. $*\Delta_\sigma \leq \{ɨ\}$ and $*\Delta_\mu \leq \{ɨ\}$.

To generalize, [ɨ] is epenthesized in the non-DTE of α when some non-DTE constraint of the form $*-\Delta_\alpha \geq \{ə\}$ outranks all DTE constraints of the form $*\Delta_\beta \leq x$, where Δ_β is lower on the prosodic hierarchy than α and also a $-\Delta_\alpha$. In Maga Rukai, $*-\Delta_\omega \geq \{ə\}$ outranks $*\Delta_\sigma \leq \{ɨ\}$, $*-\Delta_\mu \geq \{ɨ\}$, and so on. In other words, epenthesis is emergence of the unmarked – the unmarked vowel in terms of the non-DTE constraints emerges when copying is blocked.

An analogous ranking can be used to produce epenthetic [ə] and [i] for languages in which they are the least-sonorous vowels available.

7.2.4   A sonority compromise

The cases discussed so far have all relevant DTE constraints outranking all non-DTE ones or vice-versa. However, the DTE and non-DTE constraints can be interleaved. The result of mixing is that neither the most- nor the least-sonorous vowel is least marked in a particular prosodic position. Instead, the epenthetic

7.2 *Vowel epenthesis* 297

vowel emerges with medium sonority relative to the other vowels – [e], [ɛ], or [i].

[ɛ]-epenthesis is found in the Athapaskan language Chipewyan (Li 1946). Chipewyan has the vowels [i e ɛ a o u] (Li 1946:399). Syllables have the shape CVC, where coda consonants must be coronal or glottal fricatives or sonorants (i.e. [θ ð s z ʒ h n ɬ l r]) or [ɣ].

Words are minimally disyllabic in Chipewyan. As in its relative Slave (Rice 1989:133), [ɛ] is epenthesized before a monosyllabic stem. Due to a ban on onsetless syllables, [h]-epenthesis accompanies [ɛ]-epenthesis, as shown in (11).

(11)   Minimal word epenthesis in Chipewyan
        /tsaɣ/ → [hɛtsaɣ]   'he (sg.) was crying'
        cf. /ɣwa-tsaɣ/ → [ɣwatsaɣ]   'he will cry'
        /uh-tsaɣ/ → [huhtsaɣ]   'you (pl.) were crying'
        /ʃuh-t-tĩ/ → [ʃuhtĩ]   'you (dual) were eating'

[ɛ]-epenthesis appears in many other environments in Chipewyan, illustrated in (12). In all the cases, the epenthetic vowel is inserted to satisfy phonotactic requirements, such as the need to avoid onsetless syllables and complex constituents.

(12)   [ɛ]-epenthesis elsewhere in Chipewyan
        /n-tsʰaɣ/ → [nɛtsʰaɣ]   'you (sg) were crying'
        cf. /i-t-tsʰaɣ/ → [hitsʰaɣ]   'we (pl) were crying'
        /ʃ-n-tʰi/ → [ʃɛnɛtʰĩ]   'you (sg) were eating'
        /ʃ-n-ɣ-tĩ/ [ʃɛnɛɣɛ-tʰĩ]   'they (dual) ate'
        cf. [ʃ-uh-tʰĩ]   'you (dual) were eating'
        /n-θ-i-tʰɛs/ [nɛθitʰɛs]   'we lay down'
        /h-n-θ-tʰɛs/ → [hɛnɛðtʰɛs]   'they lay down'
        cf. [n-i-tʰɛs]   'you (sg) were lying down'
        /tu-n-tĩ/ [tunɛtĩ]   'he was drowning'
        cf. [tu-n-i-tĩ]   'you were drowning'

The issue of present interest is why the epenthetic vowel is [ɛ], as opposed to the more sonorous [a] or less sonorous [e] or [i]. The combined effect of the DTE and non-DTE constraints provides an answer.

The DTE constraint $*\Delta_\sigma \leq \{e,o\}$ bans all syllable nuclei with less sonority than low-mid vowels. If this constraint outranks all non-DTE constraints that favour high and high-mid vowels over low-mid vowels (e.g. $*-\Delta_\omega \geq \{ə,ɔ\}$), the epenthetic vowel will not be [e] or [i].

The non-DTE constraint $*-\Delta_\omega \geq \{a\}$ prevents [a] from being epenthetic. [ɛ] is only epenthesized in non-main stressed positions, so the epenthetic vowel will always be subject to this constraint. Stress always falls on the first syllable of the root.

To summarize, the DTE constraint $*\Delta_\sigma \leq \{e,o\}$ rules out high and high-mid vowels and the non-DTE constraint $*-\Delta_\omega \geq \{a\}$ rules out [a]. [ɛ] remains as the only viable epenthetic vowel, as illustrated in tableau (13). As in the preceding sections, epenthesis is motivated by a ban on consonant clusters outranking DEP-IO.

(13)   Chipewyan I

/n-tsʰay/	$*-\Delta_\omega \geq \{a\}$	$*\Delta_\sigma \leq \{e,o\}$	$*\Delta_\sigma \leq \{\varepsilon,\mathrm{ɔ}\}$	$*-\Delta_\omega \geq \{\varepsilon,\mathrm{ɔ}\}$
(a) na͡tsʰay	*!			*
(b) ni͡tsʰay		*!	*	
(c) ne͡tsʰay		*!	*	
☞ (d) nɛ͡tsʰay			*	*

As a final note, [ɛ] is selected over the round vowel [ɔ] because of another hierarchy: round vowels are more marked than unround ones. This point is developed in §7.2.5.

A final interesting fact about Chipewyan is that the epenthetic vowel is not [ɛ] in nasal environments. Chipewyan avoids coda nasal consonants through coalescence with a preceding vowel (Li 1946:401). Nasal mid vowels are also avoided. So, epenthesis before a nasal produces an epenthetic [ĩ]: e.g. /ɣ-n-tsay/ → [ɣĩtsay], *[ɣɛntsay], *[ɣɛ̃tsay] 'perf-2sg-cry (perf.)', *[ɣãtsay], cf. /n-tsay/ → [nɛtsay] '2sg.-cry (imperf.)' (Li 1946:413). Vowel+nasal coalescence can be motivated by NOCODA, as in §4.2.2.3. The focus here is on the fact that the epenthetic vowel is not [ã] in this situation; the fact that it surfaces as [ĩ] allows further rankings to be established, shown in tableau (14). The constraint *ɛ̃ bans nasal mid vowels.

(14)   Chipewyan II

/ɣ-n-tsay/	*ɛ̃	$*-\Delta_\omega \geq \{a\}$	$*\Delta_\sigma \leq \{e,o\}$
(a) ɣɛ̃'tsay	*!		
(b) ɣã'tsay		*!	
☞ (c) ɣĩ'tsay			*

7.2.4.1 Epenthetic mid vowels

The idea that mid vowels can be epenthetic has been challenged by Lombardi (2003), who suggests that cases of epenthetic [ɛ] always involve contextual factors that set them apart from cases of epenthetic [ə], [i], and [a]. However, it

7.2 Vowel epenthesis   299

is difficult to see what these factors are in Chipewyan. Epenthesis happens in a diverse array of morphological and phonological environments. It occurs both stem-initially and between prefixes. It can occur between any consonant, any vowel can be adjacent, and it is motivated by general phonological constraints such as *COMPLEX (e.g. /n-tsʰay/→ [nɛtsʰay], *[ntsʰay]), and avoidance of codas (e.g. /tu-n-tĩ/ → [tunɛtĩ], *[tun.tĩ]).

Chipewyan is not unique in having an epenthetic mid vowel. Epenthetic [ɛ] is also found in Slave (Rice 1989) and Czech (Ketner 2003, forthcoming). Mohawk's epenthetic [e] has been the subject of much discussion (Michelson 1988; Hagstrom 1997 and references cited therein). Temiar and Tiberian Hebrew have [e]-epenthesis in closed syllables (McCarthy 1980; Rappaport 1981, resp.). The epenthesis in Mohawk, Temiar, and Tiberian Hebrew is contextually restricted in that it occurs in limited environments, but these are phonologically well defined.

The ranking identified above is not just for epenthetic [ɛ] – it is needed whenever the epenthetic vowel is neither the least nor the most sonorous one in a language. For example, languages that have central vowels but epenthesize [i] will have to employ a ranking analogous to Chipewyan's: a DTE constraint bans central vowels and a non-DTE constraint will eliminate all non-high peripheral vowels.

7.2.5   Universals of epenthetic quality

While epenthetic vowels vary in sonority, they all have certain features in common. Putting aside interference from processes like vowel harmony and dissimilation, epenthetic vowels are always [−round] and may all be [−back] (also see Lombardi 2003). Table (15) summarizes: only vowels with dark black surrounds can be default epenthetic; it is possible that [ɯ] is epenthetic in some languages, hence the double-lines.

(15)

		[−BACK]			[+BACK]		
[+HIGH]	[+ATR]	i	y	ɨ	ɯ	u	[−LOW]
	[−ATR]	ɪ	ʏ			ʊ	
[−HIGH]	[+ATR]	e	ø		ɤ	o	
	[−ATR]	ɛ	œ	ə	ʌ	ɔ	
	[+ATR]	æ		ɐ			[+LOW]
	[−ATR]	a	ɶ		ɑ	ɒ	
		[−RD]	[+RD]	[−RD]	[−RD]	[+RD]	

The lack of round epenthetic vowels is expected here. Vowel roundness is a marked value, seen by the fact that round vowels may neutralize to unround ones, but not vice versa. Therefore, there is no markedness motivation for epenthetic vowels to be round: to be so would be gratuitously marked.

In constraint terms, epenthetic unround vowels are harmonic bounds for epenthetic round vowels in terms of context-free output constraints: i.e. *[+round]. Faithfulness constraints cannot be invoked to preserve round vowels since epenthetic vowels have no underlying features. The only way that an epenthetic vowel could be round is if roundness was an incidental property of some category on a prosodic hierarchy, like sonority. However, there is no evidence that the sonority hierarchy distinguishes round from unround vowels. For example, no stress system is sensitive to roundness (see §5.3.2, §7.4, de Lacy 2004, 2006). Since all prosodic hierarchies favour round and unround vowels of the same sonority equally, the emergent influence of *[+round] will always result in an epenthetic unround vowel.

A similar reason accounts for the fact that almost all epenthetic vowels are non-back. Backness in vowels is marked. So, again, an epenthetic vowel with a [+back] specification would be gratuitously marked. As with roundness, there is no prosodically based (i.e. sonority) motivation to have a back vowel – back and front vowels of the same height and peripherality have the same sonority value. So, sonority cannot favour back vowels over front vowels; the influence of the constraint *[+back] will always be decisive.

The major exception to the backness generalization is the low vowel [a], which is classed as [+back] in many languages, and can be epenthetic. This is an exception because in many inventories it has no front counterpart (i.e. [æ]), so *[+back] is necessarily violated; as shown above, epenthetic [a] comes about through imposition of sonority requirements.

So, vowel epenthesis exhibit markedness effects for hierarchies of vowel colour. The reason is that there are no conflicting hierarchies: there is no hierarchy in which round vowels are favoured over unround ones, or back vowels over front. This situation contrasts with sonority.

However, there have been a number of claims that epenthetic vowels can be round and/or back. The rest of this section discusses cases of putative [+round] and/or [+back] epenthetic vowels, and argues that there are no cases that are clear and convincing, and those that can be scrutinized closely do not hold up, in accord with Lombardi's (2003) conclusions.

7.2.5.1 [o] epenthesis

Quick (2000:30) argues that [o] is epenthesized between consonant-final roots and clitics in Pendau: [dʒundʒuŋ-oŋo] 'his/her house' (cf. [dʒundʒuŋ] 'house') vs. [babi-ɲo] 'his/her pig' (cf. [babi] 'pig'). However, there is an independent process of vowel harmony: affix vowels agree with root vowels in [round] and [low] (e.g. [me-ide] 'small', [me-meɲoŋ] 'cold', [ma-paris] 'difficult', [mo-doda] 'red', [mo-buluŋ] 'green'). Also, all enclitics happen to contain a round vowel: [ʔu] {1p.sg.gen.}, [mu] {2p.sg.gen}, [to] {1p.pl.incl.}, [ɲo] {3p.sg.gen.}, [mo] {completive aspect}, [po] {continuative aspect}. Therefore, the appearance of epenthetic [o] instead of [e] or [a] can be ascribed to the harmony process. In short, the epenthetic vowel's roundness is due to an incidental assimilation process, and is not an indication of the form of context-free output constraints.

Marlett (1981:55) reports that Seri has epenthetic [o]. However, this vowel seems to appear only before an [m]: e.g. /tm-kap/ → [tomkap] *no gloss*, /i-t-k-m-piː/ → [itkompiː] 'didn't he taste it?'. It also appears in very restricted morphological environments (i.e. between certain prefixes). Moreover, [i] is epenthesized in other environments: e.g. /ʔp-mi-panʃχ/ → [iʔpimpanʃχ] '1sg-proximal-run' (Marlett 1981:54). It is possible that epenthetic [o] is not epenthetic at all, but part of the input (see §3.4.2).

As in Seri, Hungarian epenthetic [o] only appears in restricted morphological environments, and [a] acts as the epenthetic vowel in other environments (Fowler 1986); it is therefore possible that [o] is a morpheme while [a] is the true default. In any case, only one of [o] and [a] can be epenthetic, because both cannot be least marked in the language and appear in phonologically indistinguishable environments.

7.2.5.2 [u] epenthesis

Li (1977, 1991) states that all pre-tonic vowels in Seediq are realized as [u], or perhaps [ʊ] or [ʉ] (also see Holmer 1996).[1] This could be analysed as neutralization of all vowels to a back round vowel, or deletion of all vowels followed by epenthesis of [u] (i.e. Li's analysis; see Holmer 1996:§7.1.1 for discussion). Either way, the reduction is a serious issue for markedness (Rice 2004a; Barnes 2002:§2.6.1). (The one exception is that the epenthetic vowel copies the stressed vowel's quality if a glottal [ʔ h] intervenes (e.g. [seʔediq] 'person', *[suʔediq]).)

However, based on recordings of Seediq provided to me by Arthur Holmer, the description of the pre-tonic vowel as [u]/[ʊ]/[ʉ] is incorrect. In some cases the duration of the pre-tonic vowel was so short as to be negligible; it is likely that there is free variation between vowel reduction and outright deletion. In the cases

---

[1] I am grateful to Arthur Holmer for discussing Seediq epenthesis with me and supplying recordings.

where there was a pre-tonic vowel, it was clearly [ə], as also observed by Arthur Holmer (p.c.). To elaborate, in the data provided by Holmer there were eight tokens of stressed (i.e. penultimate) [u], four of unstressed word-final [u], and eleven of the pre-tonic vowel. These tokens were analysed using SIL's Speech Analyzer 1.5, with sound files sampled at 22kHz, 16-bit, mono. Average values for the stressed [u]'s were F1:495, F2:943, F3:2648; averages for the unstressed [u]'s were F1:525, F2:1095, F3:2316. These values are comparable to [u] and [ʊ] in American English respectively. In contrast, the average formant values for [a] were F1: 707, F2: 1212, F3: 2733. The lower F2 in the [u]'s (compared with [a]'s F2) is consistent with the fact that vowel rounding causes lower F2. The pre-tonic vowels did not have the same formant values as either stressed or post-tonic unstressed [u]. In fact, their formant values varied a great deal, indicating that the sound is a 'targetless schwa' (Browman and Goldstein 1992). The range of values for F1 was between 190 and 500, and for F2 between 760 and 1700, and for F3 between 2500 and 3000. This contrasts significantly with the limited range exhibited by [u] in both unstressed and stressed positions. It is expected that further investigation may reveal a correlation between labial environments and rounding in the schwa; I suggest that Li's (1977) report that pre-tonic vowels are [u], [ʊ], or [ʉ] may be due to this labial influence. To conclude, I should note that Holmer (p.c.) mentions that pre-tonic vowels sound more like [u] in slow speech; there is clearly a need for further investigation here, but at least in normal speech the pre-tonic vowel is without doubt a schwa, and not like [u] or [ʊ].

Epenthetic [u] has also been reported in a number of Dravidian languages (e.g. Sinhala – Keer 1996:10). Other sources report that these languages actually have epenthetic [ɯ], [ʉ], [ə], or [ɨ] (e.g. Bright 1975:13; Koḍava – Ebert 1996). Similarly, Bright (1975:13) reports most Dravidian epenthetic vowels to be [ɨ], but also claims that the epenthetic vowel is [u] in dialects of Kannada and Telugu. One of the most-detailed phonological analyses of epenthesis in a Dravidian language is Mohanan's (1986) analysis of Malayalam. A ban on non-nasal coda consonants motivates epenthesis in this language. Mohanan shows that, contrary to previous claims, the epenthetic vowel is [ə], not [u]. [u] only ever appears due to particular allophonic restrictions. Further close analysis of Dravidian languages is clearly warranted.

Paradis (1992) reports that the epenthetic vowel is [u] in Fula (also see Causley 1999:73). However, the data is confined to the stratum 2 infinitive affix –dɛ (Paradis 1992:140ff.): e.g. [rokk-u̱-dɛ] 'to give', [moml-u̱-dɛ] 'to rub', cf. [ɟamir-dɛ] 'to order', [ɟeɟɟit-dɛ] 'to forget' (p.132). In contrast, a copy vowel appears before a stratum 1 affix: e.g. [fɔːft-ɛ̱rɛ] 'breath', [woːt-u̱ru] 'unique', [kɛs-iri] 'new', cf. [am-rɛ] 'turtle', [saw-ru] 'stick', [ⁿɟuːm-ri] 'honey' (p.130). It seems equally possible that the infinitive is /udɛ/ underlyingly, with the /u/ a latent segment (Zoll 1996); copy epenthesis could then be considered the default epenthesis strategy in the language.

Sapir (1965:17) reports that [u] or [ʊ] is used to separate consonants in Diola Fogny (the choice depends on ATR harmony): e.g. /amaŋut+ja/ → [amaŋutuja] 'if you don't want'. However, it is not clear that the [u] in these examples is epenthetic. Sapir also reports that deletion is used to eliminate underlying clusters: e.g. /lɛt+ku+jaw/ → [lɛkujaw], *[lɛtukujaw] 'they won't go'. There is no immediately apparent reason why deletion should apply in one instance but epenthesis in the other; the morphological and phonological environments seem indistinguishable. It may be the case that deletion is the default case; this idea is borne out by the fact that input consonant clusters separated by [u]/[ʊ] undergo deletion in rapid speech: /ujuk+ja/ → *slow*: [ujukuja], *fast*: [ujuja] 'if you see'. In short, '[u]-epenthesis' in Diola Fogny does not behave like epenthesis in other languages – it applies for no apparent reason to separate clusters that are otherwise resolved by deletion. Finally, [ɔ] is used to separate consonants in the formation of distributives: /RED+fuleŋ/ → [fuleŋɔfuleŋ], *[fuleŋufuleŋ]. Given the variation in deletion, epenthetic [u], and epenthetic [ɔ] with no apparent phonological conditioning, it is questionable whether any of the vowels are epenthetic. Without in-depth examination of each case – something beyond the scope of the present discussion – no further comment on these cases will be made here. At the very least, if there is [u]-epenthesis in Diola Fogny, it behaves like no attested case of [ə], [i], [e], or [a] epenthesis.

7.2.5.3 [œ]/[ø] epenthesis

The only claimed case of epenthetic [œ] and [ø] that I am aware of is in French. Adda-Decker et al. (1999) comment that the French epenthetic vowel is pronounced 'between open /œ/ and the closed /ø/' and that 'the pronunciation [œ] seems to be preferred' (cited in Hume & Bromberg 2005). However, Boula de Mareüil & Adda-Decker (2002) elaborate:

(16) But even if these phonemes [i.e. /œ/ and /ø/] are its closest neighbors, and even if the pronunciation /œ/ appears to be preferred nowadays, the realization of schwa does not merge exactly into the archiphoneme /Œ/, owing to the absence of lip rounding in the case of /ə/. The multiplicity of denominations, as well as the doubts concerning its color support the shifty nature of this *e*, which is defined more by its phonological behavior than by its timbre (Boula de Mareüil & Adda-Decker 2002).

In short, the epenthetic vowel does not have the same phonetic realization as the front round vowels /œ/ and /ø/. Côté & Morrison (2004) comment further, saying that 'experimental data fail to show any trace of lip rounding attributable to schwa'. They argue that any observed lip rounding is due to other phonetic factors.

Côté & Morrison's (2004) findings emphasize the importance of phonological evidence. A convincing way to show that the French epenthetic segment is [+round] would be to show that it influences other phonological processes like [round] harmony or dissimilation, but there seems to be no evidence of this sort available.

7.2.5.4 [Y] epenthesis

The front lax round [Y] has been claimed to be epenthetic in Icelandic (Kiparsky 1984; Karvonen & Sherman 1997). [Y] is inserted between a stem-final consonant and an [r]. The only suffixes that produce this environment are the nominative masculine singular [r] and third person singular [r]: e.g. [da<u>Y</u>r] 'day {nom.sg}', [tek<u>Y</u>r] 'take {3sg.pres.}'. Icelandic [Y] stands out from the cases in table (3) in terms of the restrictiveness of its environment: it is not epenthesized for minimal word reasons or to break up a banned consonant cluster, but only appears in the environment C+_r. This – along with its rare featural content – suggests that [Y] is not truly epenthetic. Instead, it may be a morpheme, either inserted in just this environment, or as part of the underlying representation of the nom.sg. and 3sg.pres. morphemes. The fact that it does not appear in the environment V+_r may be due to a ban on [VY] clusters. Of course, this issue deserves much more serious consideration. Nevertheless, it is at least possible that Icelandic does not present a case of a round epenthetic vowel.

7.2.5.5 Back unround epenthesis: [ɯ]

It is notable that all languages with epenthetic [ɯ] are Dravidian, except for Japanese. They include Kannada (Sridhar 1990), Koḍava (Ebert 1996), and Tamil (Vasanthakumari 1989). There seems to be disagreement – or language-internal variation – as to whether the epenthetic vowel is back [ɯ] or central [ɨ]. For example, the epenthetic vowel is reported to vary in realization as [ɯ] and [ɨ] in Koḍava (Ebert 1996:1). Similarly, Bright (1975:13) reports most Dravidian epenthetic vowels to be [ɨ]. Therefore, it may be that [ɯ] classes as a central vowel in these languages, thus being less sonorous than all other types. Again, this issue requires further investigation and careful phonetic measurement, and is unfortunately beyond the scope of this book.

Japanese 'epenthetic' [ɯ] appears in loanwords. Peperkamp & Dupoux (2003) and a number of others raise questions about whether [ɯ] is truly epenthetic. They point to studies showing that Japanese speakers perceive [ɯ] between consonants in foreign words even when there is no intervening vowel. This indicates that Japanese speakers perceive and store [ɯ] as part of the underlying form of words, rather than producing it from a synchronic process of epenthesis.

7.2.5.6 Epenthesis and DTEs

Epenthesis of low-sonority vowels depends on the influence of a non-DTE constraint. This raises the issue of positions that are DTEs of every category. If position p is not a non-DTE of any category, then anything epenthesized into p is subject only to DTE constraints. Since DTE constraints all favour high-sonority elements, they will favour [a] as the epenthetic vowel in p, and never anything less sonorous ([ɛ e i ə ɨ]).

A number of languages provide no evidence relating to this prediction, because in many languages epenthetic vowels avoid DTE positions (i.e. most importantly, the main stressed syllable) (Alderete 1995; Beckman 1998; Broselow 2001; e.g. Tuscarora – Mithun 1976:289). However, cases of epenthesis into Δ_ω position are attested. For example, [i] is epenthesized into main-stressed position in Classical Arabic: e.g. [katab'ti̱lu], *[katab'ta̱lu] (McCarthy 1979). Of course, [i] is a low-sonority vowel, yet the position it appears in is the DTE of the highest prosodic level (in some utterances). In short, the DTE-sonority constraints cannot deal with the Arabic system.

This fact is not problematic because sonority is not the only markedness force in the grammar. As emphasized above, there are several markedness hierarchies that affect vowels, such as those involving vowel colour – backness and roundness. Lombardi (2003) has argued that these hierarchies can also influence epenthetic vowel quality. For example, front vowels are favoured over back ones, so *[+back] will favour [i] over back [a]. Consequently, if *[+back] outranks the DTE-sonority constraints, [i] will be epenthesized even if it appears in the DTE of the utterance. Arabic epenthetic [i] is therefore due to hierarchy conflict: the backness hierarchy inadvertently causes low vowels to be avoided if they happen to be back, so blocking the DTE-sonority constraints.

7.2.6 Conclusion

To summarize the results of the preceding sections, the DTE and non-DTE constraints for sonority conflict in many environments. This conflict is the source of variation in the sonority level of epenthetic vowels. However, other markedness hierarchies (e.g. roundness, nasality, backness) do not relate to DTEs and non-DTEs. Consequently, there are no epenthetic nasal vowels, as nasal vowels are more marked than oral vowels; similarly, there are no epenthetic round or back vowels, as front unround vowels have the least-marked colour. So, although the conflicting hierarchies for sonority make vowel markedness less transparent, it is still possible to see evidence for other markedness hierarchies. The same conflict will be shown to account for the variation in vowel neutralization and inventories in the following section.

7.3 Vowel inventories and neutralization

Like epenthesis, vowel inventories and neutralization provide only limited insight into sonority markedness. As with consonants, preservation of the marked predicts that any mixture of sonority levels is possible in a vowel inventory. In addition, the conflicting demands on sonority predict that neutralization could produce outputs of any sonority level.

For example, if the constraints that promote high sonority in syllable nuclei dominate, a vowel inventory will contain a contiguous set of highly sonorous elements (e.g. the vowel inventory of [a e o aː eː oː] in Amuesha – Fast 1953). However, if the constraints that promote low sonority in non-heads dominate, high-sonority vowels will be neutralized to lower-sonority ones. This neutralization produces a gapped inventory with both high-sonority elements and low-sonority ones (e.g. Wosera's [ɨ ə a] – Laycock 1965; Upper Chehalis' [a e o ə] – Kinkade 1964). Section 7.3.1 discusses vowel inventories and their form in more detail.

Conflicting sonority demands in the same environments means that vowel neutralization can produce any sonority level, and neutralization can proceed in both directions along the sonority hierarchy even in the same prosodic context. For example, /e/ and /o/ reduce in sonority to [i] and [u] in Berguener Romansh unstressed syllables; in contrast, /ɛ/ and /ɔ/ increase in sonority to become [a] (Lutta 1923; Kamprath 1987; Crosswhite 2000). This sort of split system demonstrates the conflicting demands that can be placed on the same prosodic positions. Consequently, vowel neutralization gives no insight into sonority markedness. Nevertheless, it does give some insight into binary hierarchies like those for vowel nasality and colour. Unstressed vowel neutralization is discussed in §7.3.2.

7.3.1 Vowel sonority in inventories

The term 'vowel inventory' is usually used to refer to the vowels permitted in a language's stressed syllable nuclei, but potentially to all the vowels that appear in any environment. While vowel inventories are often thought to give insight into markedness, the present theory predicts that they will not exhibit overt markedness asymmetries, at least for sonority. The prediction follows from two factors. One is that — as with consonants — faithfulness constraints can preserve marked elements, preventing their elimination. The other was identified for epenthetic vowels: hierarchies conflict almost directly in regard to vowel sonority markedness. The result is that both harmonically contiguous and gapped inventories exist in terms of sonority levels.

Some short vowel inventories that are harmonically contiguous in terms of sonority are given in table (17). The missing system is one with just [a] and no other vowels. It is quite possible that there is a functional reason for this gap, and so it is likely to not be a theoretical concern.

(17)   Short vowel inventories: harmonically contiguous in sonority

ɨ	ə	i,u	e,o	a	Language
✓	✓	✓	✓	✓	Maga Rukai (Hsin 2000), Nganasan (Helimski 1998)
	✓	✓	✓	✓	Gujarati (Cardona 1965)
		✓	✓	✓	Māori (Bauer 1993)
			✓	✓	Amuesha (Fast 1953), Vach Khanty (Abondolo 1998b:360)
				✓	—

Gapped vowel inventories are those that contain both most- and least-sonorous vowels, but have eliminated segments with intermediate sonority. Table (18) identifies the different types.

(18)   Short vowel inventories: gapped in sonority

a	e,o	i,u	ə	ɨ	Language
✓				✓	—
✓			✓		—
✓		✓			—
✓	✓			✓	Classical Arabic (Mitchell 1956)
✓	✓		✓		Upper Chehalis (Kinkade 1964)
✓		✓	✓		Lushootseed (Bates et al. 1994)
✓		✓		✓	Wapishana (Tracy 1972)
✓			✓	✓	Wosera (Laycock 1965), Kabardian (Choi 1992a)
✓	✓	✓		✓	Gapapaiwa (McGuckin 2002)
✓	✓		✓	✓	—
✓		✓	✓	✓	—

The table has five missing gapped inventories. However, it is highly likely that the gaps are accidental. The inventories [a ə] and [a ɨ] are probably unattested because there are too few vowels – no language has just two short vowels in UPSID (see Schwartz et al. 1997). Languages with [e o] and no [i u] are rare (though certainly not unattested), so accounting for the lack of [a e o ɨ] and [a e o ə ɨ] (cf. Upper Chehalis with [a e o ə]). It is also rare (but not unattested) for languages to have both [ə] and [ɨ], so accounting for the lack of [a e o ə ɨ] and [a i u ə ɨ].

The important point about table (18) is that any sonority level can be gapped: some languages lack [ə] but have [ɨ] (e.g. Wapishana, Gapapaiwa), others lack [i u] but have [ə] or [ɨ] (e.g. Upper Chehalis, Wosera), and others lack [e o] but have a less-sonorous vowel (e.g. Classical Arabic, Lushootseed). In short, the evidence shows that there are no implicational relations for sonority gapping in vowel inventories.

As discussed in chapter 1, the fact that some types of inventory are more frequent than others is not relevant for a Competence theory. What is important is that all the types in the tables are attested in some language.

The following sections show how the lack of implicational relations follows from the theory. Section 7.3.1.1 discusses harmonically contiguous inventories, and §7.3.1.2 discusses gapping. Section 7.3.1.3 addresses the issue of disharmonic vowel inventories – those that have no low vowel.

The following discussion frequently refers to the vowel features [high], [low], and [ATR], so these features are given in relation to frequent vowels in table (19). Vowels that figure prominently in the following discussion are in bold.

(19)

		[−BACK]			[+BACK]		
[+HIGH]	[+ATR]	**i**	y	ɨ	ɯ	**u**	
	[−ATR]	ɪ	Y			ʊ	[−LOW]
[−HIGH]	[+ATR]	**e**	ø		ɤ	**o**	
	[−ATR]	ɛ	œ	ə	ʌ	ɔ	
	[+ATR]	æ		ɐ			
	[−ATR]	**a**	Œ		ɑ	ɒ	[+LOW]
		[−RD]	[+RD]	[−RD]	[−RD]	[+RD]	

7.3.1.1 Harmonically contiguous vowel inventories

In terms of the Δ_σ sonority constraints, low vowels are the least marked, followed by peripheral mid vowels, then peripheral high vowels, then central vowels. So, a harmonically contiguous syllable nucleus inventory contains a low

7.3 Vowel inventories and neutralization 309

vowel and representatives of a contiguous range of the sonority hierarchy. For example, Māori's [a e o i u] vowel system is harmonically contiguous (Bauer 1993), as is the [a e o i u ə ɨ] system found in Maga Rukai (Hsin 2000); both systems contain the most sonorous vowel and a vowel from a contiguous range of sonority levels. Similarly, Amuesha's vowel system [a e o] is harmonically contiguous (Fast 1953).

While they are not the focus of this discussion, consonants can of course also serve as syllable DTEs. Imdlawn Tashlhiyt Berber has the most complete harmonically contiguous DTE inventory: it allows segments of any sonority level to be syllable nuclei (Dell & Elmedlaoui 1985, 1988). My dialect of New Zealand English has a syllable DTE inventory that is almost harmonically contiguous: apart from vowels, nasals and liquids can be DTEs (e.g. [æpl̩] 'apple', [pɹəzn̩] 'prison'). However, New Zealand English (like many other English dialects) lacks [ɨ] and [ʉ], making it a gapped vowel system.

As discussed for the PoA hierarchy and for non-DTEs and sonority, harmonically contiguous inventories are produced when output constraints against highly marked categories outrank all faithfulness constraints that preserve them, while the opposite holds for less-marked categories. To produce the Māori [a e o i u] system, for example, an output constraint against the low-sonority central vowels $*\Delta_\sigma \leq ə$ must outrank all faithfulness constraints that preserve it, including faithfulness constraints that preserve height and peripherality (called IDENTV here for convenience). In contrast, some faithfulness constraint that preserves vowels with high sonority outranks all output constraints that militate against them.

Tableau (20) below shows how such a ranking produces a harmonically complete inventory. The input /pəkʉ/ contains two central vowels which must be made more sonorous to fit with the language's surface [a e o i u] inventory. Richness of the Base requires that such inputs be considered even in languages without alternations.

(20)   Producing a harmonic vowel inventory

/pəkʉ/	$*\Delta_\sigma \leq ə$	IDENTV	$*\Delta_\sigma \leq \{i,u\}$
(a) pəkʉ	**!		**
(b) pəku	*!	*	*
☞ (c) peku		**	*

The added complexity for vowels is that the syllable-DTE constraints must also outrank all those output constraints that promote low-sonority elements in

310 *Markedness conflict: vowels*

prosodic positions that overlap with syllable DTEs. For example, $*-\Delta_\omega \geq \{i,u\}$ bans all vowels except central ones in unstressed syllables. In Māori, unstressed syllables have the vowels [i u e o a], so $*-\Delta_\omega \geq \{i,u\}$ must be outranked by the syllable-DTE constraints.

(21)

/pikə/	$*\Delta_\sigma \leq \textrm{ə}$	$*-\Delta_\omega \geq \{i,u\}$	IDENTV
(a) 'pikə	*!		
☞ (b) 'piki		*	*

7.3.1.1.1 Unstressed vowel inventories

Chapter 3 focused on consonant neutralization in syllable codas. The vowel equivalent of the coda is the unstressed syllable; like the coda, the unstressed syllable is a common neutralizing environment. The same facts for consonants in codas are also true for vowel inventories in unstressed syllables – unstressed syllables allow both harmonically contiguous and gapped vowel inventories.

The $*-\Delta_\omega \geq x$ constraints promote reduction in sonority in unstressed syllables. To be more precise, the non-DTE of the prosodic word includes every vowel that does not have main stress. This includes vowels with secondary stress. Vowels with secondary stress often avoid reduction or do not undergo it as completely as unstressed vowels; this is ascribed to the effect of faithfulness constraints that target stressed syllables here, after Beckman 1998.

The harmonically contiguous unstressed vowel inventories are given in table (22). Discussion of how the $*-\Delta_\omega \geq x$ and $*\Delta_\sigma \leq x$ constraints interact is provided in §7.3.1.3. The high central vowel level is left out because few languages contrast [ɨ] and [ə].

(22) Harmonically contiguous unstressed syllable inventories

a, æ	ɛ,ɔ	e,o	i,u	ə	Language
				✓	New Zealand English
			✓	✓	Central Catalan (Wheeler 2005a: §2.3.4)
		✓	✓	✓	Sri Lankan Portuguese Creole (Smith 1978)
	✓	✓	✓	✓	Siuslawan (Frachtenberg 1922)
✓	✓	✓	✓	✓	Māori (Bauer 1993)

Central Catalan has a harmonically contiguous unstressed vowel inventory because this position can contain the low-sonority vowel [ə] and the next least sonorous vowels [i u]; it cannot contain [a ɛ ɔ e o]. The alternations that produce this harmonically contiguous inventory are shown below.

(23)   Central Catalan unstressed vowel neutralization

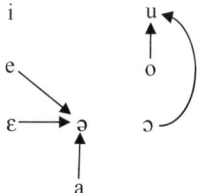

(24)   Central Catalan vowel reduction (Wheeler 2005a:§2.3.4)
        ['baɲə]   'bathe-3SG-PRS-IND'   [bə'ɲɛm]   'bathe-1PL-PRS-IND'
        ['pɛrðrə]   'lose-INF'   [pər'ðɛm]   'lose-1PL-PRS-IND'
        ['peðrə]   'stone'   [pəð'rerə] 'quarry'
        ['kɔzə]   'thing'   [ku'zɛtə]   'thing-DIM'
        ['tot]   'all- M.SG.'   [tu'tal]   'total'

As with syllable nucleus inventories, harmonically contiguous unstressed vowel inventories come about when a non-DTE output constraint outranks all relevant faithfulness constraints. For Catalan, the output constraint is $*-\Delta_\omega \geq \{e,o\}$; it bans all vowels in unstressed syllables which are equally or more sonorous than mid peripheral vowels. It outranks faithfulness constraints such as IDENT[±high], IDENT[±low], and IDENT[±ATR], as shown in tableau (25). Following Crosswhite's (1999:§3.4.0.0) proposals, the output of vowel reduction is restricted by IDENT[±round]. Consequently, both /o/ and /ɔ/ neutralize to [u], not to the less sonorous [ə].

(25)   Catalan I: reduction

/kɔzɛ-tə/	$*-\Delta_\omega \geq \{e,o\}$	IDENT[±round]	IDENT[±high]
(a) kɔ'zɛtə	*!		
(b) kə'zɛtə		*!	
☞ (c) ku'zɛtə			*

Tableau (26) shows that IDENT[high] is not entirely powerless. It forces neutralization of non-round vowels to [ə] instead of the equally acceptable [i], as shown by the form /pɛl-ut/→[pə'lut] 'hairy', *[pi'lut]. /ɛ/ must become either [i], [u], or [ə] because of $*-\Delta_\omega \geq \{e,o\}$, as shown by candidate (a). IDENT[round]

312 *Markedness conflict: vowels*

eliminates [u], and IDENT[high] prevents the non-high vowel /ɛ/ from becoming the high vowel [i].

(26)   Catalan II

/pɛl-ut/	*−Δ_ω≥{e,o}	IDENT[±round]	IDENT[±high]
(a) pɛ'lut	*!		
(b) pi'lut			*!
☞ (c) pə'lut			

It is crucial that *−Δ_ω≥{e,o} outrank all constraints that ban low sonority syllable nuclei. For example, *Δ_σ≤{ə} must be ranked below *−Δ_ω≥{e,o} otherwise neutralization to schwa would be blocked.

In short, Catalan's harmonically contiguous unstressed vowel inventory is the result of ranking a sonority-reduction constraint over all relevant faithfulness constraints. The same ranking is true of the other languages. For Siuslawan, it is *−Δ_ω≥{a}, SLP Creole employs *−Δ_ω≥{ɛ,ɔ}, Catalan has *−Δ_ω≥{e,o}, and NZ English uses *−Δ_ω≥{i,u}.

7.3.1.2 Gapped inventories

Gapped inventories contain low- and high-sonority vowels but lack vowels of intermediate sonority. Schematic examples are given in (27). 'Dispersed' vowel systems like [i u a] are very common (Schwartz et al. 1997:241); they contain the most sonorous vowel [a] and the relatively low-sonority high peripheral vowels, but lack the intermediate-sonority mid peripheral vowels. 'Vertical' vowel systems like Wosera's [ɨ ə a] (Laycock 1965) contain only the highest sonority vowel [a] and lowest sonority central vowels. The third type of system, called 'flattened' here, contains the relatively high-sonority low and mid peripheral vowels and very low-sonority central vowels, but lacks the intermediate-sonority high peripheral vowels (e.g. Upper Chehalis' [a e o ə] system – Kinkade 1964).

(27)   Gapped systems
         (i) 'vertical'   (ii) 'dispersed'   (iii) 'flattened'
              ɨ   i   u
              ə   e   ə   o
              a   a   a

Vertical, dispersed, and flattened systems are often thought to be fundamentally distinct (e.g. Liljencrants & Lindblom 1972; Lindblom 1990; Flemming 1995), with the difference arising from functional motivations: dispersed inventories reflect a functional pressure to maximize perceptual distinctness, while vertical systems reflect a pressure to minimize articulatory effort.

There is no appeal to functional pressures to account for the different inventory types here. Instead, the vowel inventory types simply exhibit different kinds of gapping. Vertical vowel systems are those in which the intermediate-sonority levels of high and mid peripheral vowels are gapped. In flattened systems the gap is the high peripheral vowels, and in dispersed systems the gap is in the mid peripheral vowels. The dispersed and flattened systems also eliminate some of the lowest-sonority elements.

The common [i u a] gapped inventory comes about when mid vowels are eliminated by ranking $*\Delta_\sigma \leq \{e,o\}$ above all faithfulness constraints that preserve lowness and ATR values. As shown in tableau (28), $*\Delta_\sigma \leq \{e,o\}$ can force the [−low, +ATR] vowel /e/ to become [+low, −ATR].

(28) Dispersed inventories I

/peka/	$*\Delta_\sigma \leq \{e,o\}$	IDENT[±low]	IDENT[±ATR]
(a) peka	*!		
☞ (b) paka		*	*

This ranking does not spell doom for high vowels. They can remain when specifically preserved by a faithfulness constraint (e.g. IDENT[±high]). The /e/ can neutralize to [a] as it only results in unfaithfulness to /e/'s underlying [low] value, assuming [e] is [−high, −low] and [a] is [−high, +low]. However, /i/ cannot neutralize to either [a] or [e], because it would require changing its underlying [+high] value to [−high].

(29) Dispersed inventories II

/peki/	IDENT[± high]	$*\Delta_\sigma \leq \{e,o\}$	IDENT[± low]
(a) pake	*!		*
(b) paka	*!		*
(c) peki		**!	
☞ (d) paki		*	

While the faithfulness constraints IDENT[±high], IDENT[±low], and IDENT[±ATR] have been used here, any faithfulness constraints that preserve values that act contrary to sonority reduction are equally useful. To complete the ranking for this inventory, segments that are less sonorous than [i u] are ruled out by having *Δ_σ ≤ə outrank all relevant faithfulness constraints.

Gapped vowel inventories in other environments result from analogous rankings in which faithfulness prevents marked vowels from deleting. For example, the demands on unstressed vowels are that sonority should be as low as possible. Harmonically complete unstressed vowel inventories are therefore those that include the least-sonorous available vowel (often [ə]) and vowels from contiguous sonority levels.

Table (30) gives a sample of gapped inventories in unstressed positions. No distinction is made between mid and high central vowels as they rarely contrast. A number of languages distinguish high-mid [e o] from low-mid [ɛ ɔ] for vowel reduction. For example, in Valencian Catalan /ɛ ɔ/ neutralize to [e o] in unstressed syllables, creating a gapped unstressed vowel inventory of [a e o i u] (cf. its stressed vowel inventory of [a ɛ ɔ e o i u]). The gap in the table is one with mid vowels and central vowels alone. There are languages that eliminate high vowels alone (e.g. Upper Carniolan Slovene) and ones that eliminate low vowels alone (e.g. Siuslawan), so it is possible that this gap is due to the limited sample of languages examined.

(30) Gapped unstressed syllable inventories

a	ɛ,ɔ/e,o	i,u	ə/ɨ,ʉ	Language
✓		✓		Berguener Romansh (foot non-DTEs) §7.3.2.2.
	✓	✓		—
✓		✓		Berguener Romansh unfooted syllables (§7.3.2.2.), Luiseño (immediately below)
✓		✓	✓	Belarusan (§7.3.2.2.)
✓	✓		✓	Upper Carniolan Slovene (Crosswhite 1999:50ff.)

Luiseño has a gapped unstressed vowel inventory (Munro & Benson 1973; Crosswhite 1999). While [i u e o a] are allowed in stressed syllables, unstressed syllables permit only [i u a]; /e o/ raise to [i u] respectively: e.g. ['tʃoka] 'to limp', cf. [tʃuˈka-tʃkaʃ] 'limping', ['hedi-n] 'will open' cf. [hi'di-ki] 'to uncover'. This is a situation in which IDENT[low] outranks the demand to reduce unstressed vowel sonority, implemented by *−Δ_ω ≥ {e,o}. Tableau (31) shows that this ranking requires /a/ to remain /a/ in unstressed position (a). However, the ranking forces non-low vowels to reduce in sonority, as in candidate (c)'s raising of /o/ to [u]. /o/ can become [u] here because both vowels are [−low].

7.3 Vowel inventories and neutralization

(31) Dispersed unstressed inventories

/tʃokatʃkaʃ/	IDENT[±low]	*−Δ_ω≥{e,o}	IDENT[±low]
(a) tʃu'katʃkəʃ	*!		
(b) tʃo'katʃkaʃ		* *!	
☞ (c) tʃu'katʃkaʃ		*	

In a similar way the gapped 'vertical' vowel system [a ə ɨ] is produced by having a faithfulness constraint that preserves a specific feature of the central vowels outrank all output constraints against them; the constraint used below is IDENT[central], which preserves the central place specification of the vowels. In contrast, the output constraint $*\Delta_\sigma \leq \{e,o\}$ outranks all faithfulness constraints that preserve peripheral vowels. As shown below, all non-[a] vowels are reduced while central vowels remain intact.

(32) Vertical inventories

/pakekɨ/	IDENT[central]	*Δ_σ≤{e,o}	IDENT[low]
(a) pakaka	*!		* *
(b) pakekɨ		* *!	
☞ (c) pakakɨ		*	*

So, just as with the PoA hierarchy and consonant sonority, gapped systems come about when a faithfulness constraint to the most-marked elements blocks an otherwise general neutralization process. Gaps in unstressed syllable vowel inventories are discussed and analysed further in §7.3.2.2.

The approach to vowel inventories described above incorporates them into a broader theory of sonority and markedness. This sonority theory is independently necessary to account for phenomena such as syllabification and sonority-driven stress (§7.4). Here, dispersed and vertical inventories have no special status; they are simply subtypes of gapped inventories, and are accounted for in an analogous way to gapped consonant inventories — by the interaction of output and faithfulness constraints.

7.3.1.3 Disharmonic vowel inventories

As discussed in §4.2.2.2, the least-marked element in a hierarchy cannot be neutralized to some other hierarchy element. For DTEs, the least-marked element is a low vowel as it is the most-sonorous type. Consequently, no ranking of the DTE constraints can cause an input low vowel to change its height as none of them favour any other sonority level over low vowels. So, input /a/ cannot help but surface faithfully since no change will decrease its markedness. Harmonic Ascent therefore rules out 'harmonically marked' vowel DTE inventories that lack a low vowel (i.e. one of [æ a œ ɐ ɑ ɒ]), such as [ə i u], [ə e o], and [i u e o].

It is important to underscore that this claim only holds for the position that is the DTE of *every* prosodic constituent — i.e. the vowel that bears utterance-level stress. As expected, there is no language that excludes low short vowels from such a position, and there may well be no language that excludes low short vowels even from the prosodic word DTE (i.e. main stressed) position. Every language in Maddieson's (1992) UPSID database has a low short vowel.

As discussed for vowel epenthesis in §7.2, most prosodic positions are both the DTE of some category and the non-DTE of another category. For example, in ['paki], [i] is the DTE of a syllable and the non-DTE of a foot, the non-DTE of a prosodic word, and so on. Consequently, there are pressures to both have both high and low sonority. The result of this antagonism is that apparently 'disharmonic' inventories are predicted to occur in positions that are simultaneously DTEs and non-DTEs. This point was made in §7.3.1.1 for unstressed syllables: an unstressed syllable inventory consisting of just [ə] is disharmonic in terms of DTEs, but harmonic from a non-DTE point of view.

A more interesting effect is that the antagonism of DTE and non-DTE sonority demands can force vowel neutralization to both lower and raise vowel sonority even in the same surface environment. This point is developed in the next section.

7.3.2 Direction of vowel sonority neutralization

Direction of neutralization is not a useful diagnostic for vowels. Since there are often conflicting sonority demands on the same prosodic position, the theory predicts that vowel neutralization can proceed in both directions along the sonority hierarchy. This prediction is borne out in a number of languages. Neutralization can force some vowels to become less sonorous and others to become more sonorous, even within the same language. This point is examined in §7.3.2.1 and §7.3.2.2.

Nevertheless, neutralization of other vowel features often does provide insight into markedness. For example, while there is neutralization of nasal to oral vowels, there is never any non-assimilative neutralization of oral to nasal vowels. This point is discussed in §7.3.2.3.

The following discussion relies heavily on Crosswhite's (1998, 1999, 2000) insights into vowel reduction. The idea that vowel reduction is produced by constraints that relate non-heads to sonority is proposed and discussed in detail in Crosswhite 1999. The points on which these proposals differ are that (a) the constraints employed here are stringently formulated and refer to DTEs, and (b) 'dispersed' vowel reductions are produced solely by sonority constraints here; Crosswhite proposes a separate mechanism to deal with them, discussed in §7.3.2.2.

7.3.2.1 Sonorization and desonorization

As explained above, DTEs demand high sonority and non-DTEs prefer low sonority. Many languages show the effects of one or both of these demands in synchronic alternations. For example, high vowels become mid in Chamorro stressed syllables, so becoming more sonorous (Chung 1983; Crosswhite 1998).

(33) Chamorro vowel lowering in main stressed syllables
(a)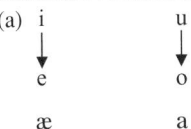

(b) *Data*
/laːpis/ ['laːpis] 'pencil' [la'pessu] 'my pencil'
/hugandu/ [hu'gandu] 'play' [ˌhugan'donɲa] 'his playing'
/lægu?/ [ma'læːgu?] 'wanting' [ˌmalæ'go?mu] 'your wanting'

The DTE-sonority constraints are responsible for forcing sonority to increase. In Chamorro, the relevant constraints target the main stressed syllable's DTE (Δ_ω), banning the low-sonority high vowels: $*\Delta_\omega \leq \{i,u\}$. Analogous to Crosswhite's (1999) analysis, this constraint outranks all faithfulness constraints that preserve [i u], so lowering will take place only under stress. Tableau (34) illustrates this ranking. The faithful candidate (a) violates $*\Delta_\omega \leq \{i,u\}$ because it has a high vowel in the main stressed syllable (i.e. the DTE of the prosodic word). Of the other two candidates, candidate (b) overreacts, lowering not only the stressed syllable's high vowel but also the unstressed vowel.

(34) Chamorro sonorization

/ma-lægu?-mu/	$*\Delta_\omega \leq \{i,u\}$	IDENT[±high]
(a) ˌma.læ.'gu?.mu	*!	
(b) ˌma.læ.'go?.mo		**!
☞ (c) ˌma.læ.'go?.mu		*

Lowering of /i/ and /u/ to [a] is blocked by the constraint IDENT[±low]. Lowering is optional on secondary stressed syllables: e.g. [tin'tagu?] 'messenger' cf. [ˌtenta'go?ta]~[ˌtinta'go?ta] 'our (incl.) messenger'. To produce lowering in

318 *Markedness conflict: vowels*

all stressed syllables, the constraint *$\Delta_{Ft} \leq \{i,u\}$ can be used, again outranking IDENT[±high]. To summarize, vowel 'sonorization' is due to DTE-sonority constraints.

The opposite of sonorization is desonorization; different subtypes are called vowel raising and reduction. Desonorization typically occurs in all unstressed syllables or in the unstressed syllable of a foot. For example, in Sri Lankan Portuguese Creole low /æ aː/ and mid-low /ɔ ɔː/ vowels shorten and raise in unstressed syllables (Smith 1978; Crosswhite 2000). Consequently, SLP Creole's stressed short-vowel inventory allows [i e æ ə ɔ o u], but its unstressed inventory is [i e ə o u]. The data shows an incidental process in which prosodic word-initial stressed syllables lengthen.

(35) Sri Lankan Portuguese creole unstressed vowel raising (Smith 1978)
(a)

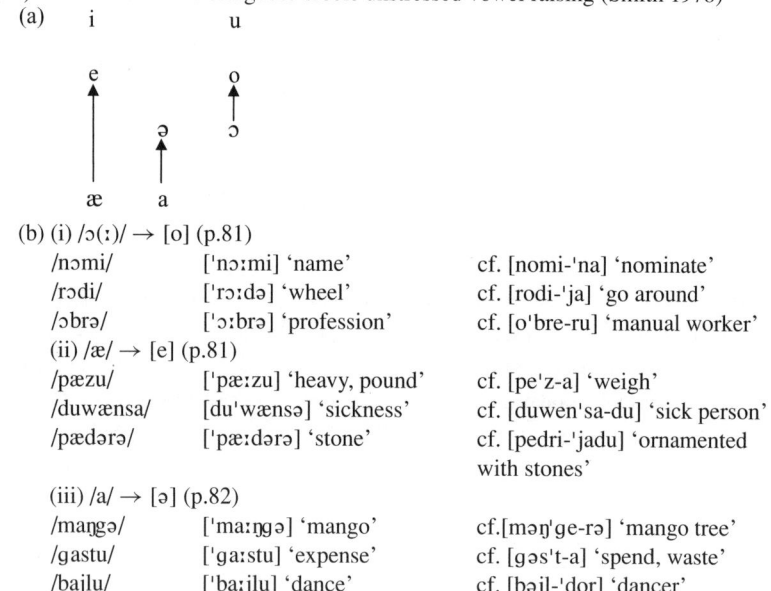

(b) (i) /ɔ(ː)/ → [o] (p.81)
/nɔmi/   ['nɔːmi] 'name'   cf. [nomi-'na] 'nominate'
/rɔdi/   ['rɔːdə] 'wheel'   cf. [rodi-'ja] 'go around'
/ɔbrə/   ['ɔːbrə] 'profession'   cf. [o'bre-ru] 'manual worker'
(ii) /æ/ → [e] (p.81)
/pæzu/   ['pæːzu] 'heavy, pound'   cf. [pe'z-a] 'weigh'
/duwænsa/   [du'wænsə] 'sickness'   cf. [duwen'sa-du] 'sick person'
/pædərə/   ['pæːdərə] 'stone'   cf. [pedri-'jadu] 'ornamented
                                                with stones'
(iii) /a/ → [ə] (p.82)
/maŋgə/   ['maːŋgə] 'mango'   cf.[məŋ'ge-rə] 'mango tree'
/gastu/   ['gaːstu] 'expense'   cf. [gəs't-a] 'spend, waste'
/bajlu/   ['baːjlu] 'dance'   cf. [bəjl-'dor] 'dancer'

In contrast, /i u e o/ do not desonorize in unstressed syllables (['nɔːmi], *['nɔːmə]; ['gaːstu], *['gaːstə]; [pe'z-a], *[pə'z-a]; [rodi-'ja], *[rədi-'ja]).[2]

The constraint *$-\Delta_\omega \geq \{\varepsilon,\mathrm{ɔ}\}$ is responsible for vowel reduction in SLP creole. It outranks IDENT[±low] and IDENT[±ATR], so allowing [+low, −ATR] vowels to become [−low, +ATR], as shown in tableau (36).

[2] /ɔ/ and /æ/ surface faithfully if the following vowel is mid-low (['nɔvi] 'nine' cf. [nɔ'væntu] 'ninety', *[no'væntu]; ['sæti] 'seven' cf. [sæ'tæntə] 'seventy', *[se'tæntə]). This is a situation where harmony blocks reduction.

7.3 *Vowel inventories and neutralization* 319

(36)   SLP creole unstressed vowel lowering

/pæzu-a/	*−Δ_ω≥{ɛ,ɔ}	IDENT[±low]	IDENT[±ATR]
(a) pæˈza	*!		
☞ (b) peˈza		*	*

The choice of vowel target is in part determined by faithfulness constraints. All underlying vowels retain their place specification: the front vowel /æ/ becomes front [e], the central vowel /a/ becomes central [ə], and the back vowel /ɔ/ becomes back [o]. They also retain their input specification for [high]: all the vowels become mid vowels, not high ones given that [a æ ɔ] are [+low, −high], and /e o/ are [−low,−high]. In constraint terms, IDENT[back] and IDENT[high] are crucial here. These constraints must outrank all output constraints that favour reducing low vowels even further — e.g. *−Δ_ω≥{e,o}, *−Δ_ω≥{i,u}, and *−Δ_ω≥{ə}.

The other interesting point for sonority is that underlying /ə/ becomes [e] in stressed syllables: /maŋgə-rə/ → [məŋˈge-rə] 'mango tree'. This form must involve /ə/ becoming the more sonorous [e] and not the reverse: i.e. not /maŋge/ → [ˈmaːŋgə]. If the underlying form was /maŋge/, it should surface as *[maːŋge] because [e] is permitted in unstressed syllables (e.g. [peˈza], *[pəˈza] 'weigh'). In constraint terms the increase in sonority is forced by *Δ_ω≤{ə}, which crucially outranks IDENT[±back]. The tableau shows that /ə/ becomes [e] rather than any other vowel because this is the most faithful mapping.

(37)   SLP creole stressed [ə] peripheralization

/maŋgə-rə/	*Δ_ω≤{ə}	IDENT[±high]	IDENT[±low]	IDENT[±back]
(a) məŋˈgərə	*!			
(b) məŋˈgirə		*!		*
(c) məŋˈgarə			*!	
☞ (d) məŋˈgerə				*

SLP creole's vowel raising is part of a broader typology of vowel desonorization. A very common type is vowel reduction to [ə], as found in most English dialects (e.g. NZ English: /ædvantejdʒ/ 'advantage' → [ədˈvantədʒ], cf. [ˌædvənˈtejdʒəs] 'advantageous'). A number of other languages desonorize to high vowels. For example, Siuslawan /a/ neutralizes to [i] in unstressed syllables: e.g. /mati-juː/ → [miˈtiːjuː] 'the art of making dams' (cf. [ˈmaːti] 'dam'), /tsǃaɬn-atc/ → [tsǃiɬˈnatc] 'with pitch' (cf. [ˈtsǃaɬn] 'pitch')

320 *Markedness conflict: vowels*

(Frachtenberg 1922). As shown above, SLP creole's target of neutralization is the mid vowels [e o] and [ə].

The non-DTE sonority constraints promote neutralization to the least-sonorous element available; the fact that they do not do so in every language is due to the confounding influence of faithfulness constraints, as illustrated above for SLP creole.

To summarize, the effect of both DTE and non-DTE sonority constraints is clearly evident in a variety of languages. DTE constraints promote higher sonority in heads, and non-DTE constraints promote lower sonority.

7.3.2.2 Conflicting demands

In the cases discussed so far, vowels in unstressed syllables have become less sonorous. The constraints on prosodic word non-DTEs favour lower sonority, so they are clearly responsible for this reduction. However, in some languages vowels become more sonorous in unstressed syllables. For example, Belarusan /e o/ become [a] in unstressed syllables (Krivitskii & Podluzhnyi 1994; Crosswhite 2004).

(38) Belarusan unstressed vowel sonorization

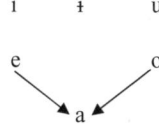

(39) Belarusan unstressed vowel neutralization
    (a) /o/ → [a] in unstressed syllables
      ['noɣi]   'legs'   cf. [na'ɣa]   'leg'
      ['kol]   'pole (nom.)'   cf. [ka'la]   'pole (gen.)'
      ['vʲosnɨ]   'spring (gen.)'   cf. [vʲas'na]   'spring (nom.)'
      ['mʲot]   'honey (n.)'   cf. [mʲa'dovɨ]   'honey (adj.)'
    (b) /e/ → [a] in unstressed syllables
      ['ʃept]   'whisper'   cf. [ʃap'tatsʲ]   'to whisper'
      ['reki]   'rivers'   cf. [ra'ka]   'river'
      ['spʲetsʲ]   'to ripen'   cf. [pas'pʲavatsʲ]   'to mature'
      ['klʲej]   'glue'   cf. [klʲa'jonka]   'oil-cloth'

The data also shows that the most-sonorous vowel /a/ remains [a] in unstressed position (e.g. [ra'ka] 'river'), and the lower sonority /i ɨ u/ also remain faithful (e.g. ['vʲosnɨ] 'spring (gen.)', ['noɣi] 'legs').

The curious aspect of Belarusan is that unstressed vowels are commonly thought to be under pressure to be less sonorous, yet [e] and [o] become more sonorous. Crosswhite (1999, 2004) proposes that [e o]'s strange behaviour is due to a pressure to have a dispersed inventory. In contrast, in the present theory such a neutralization is due to hierarchy conflict.

Non-DTE constraints force unstressed vowels to become less sonorous, so they are clearly not responsible for forcing /e o/ to change in Belarusan. The only constraints that force sonority to increase are DTE constraints. Therefore, constraints such as *$\Delta_\sigma \leq \{e,o\}$ must be responsible for the increase in unstressed syllables.

In fact, Belarusan has almost the same ranking as languages with an [i u a] inventory (§7.3.1.2): *$\Delta_\sigma \leq \{e,o\}$ forces mid vowels to become the more sonorous [a], and high vowels are unaffected because IDENT[±high] preserves them. The difference in Belarusan is that mid vowels in stressed syllables are preserved by σ́-IDENT[±low], after Beckman 1998.

Tableau (40) is an elaboration on the one identified in §7.3.1.2. Candidate (a) is one in which all mid vowels are eliminated; it fatally violates σ́-IDENT[±low] because the input's non-low /o/ surface as low [a] in the stressed syllable. Candidate (b) shows why high vowels do not neutralize: they are protected by IDENT[±high], which is fatally violated by the mapping /ɨ/→[a]. Finally, candidate (d) beats candidate (c) because (d) responds to *$\Delta_\sigma \leq \{e,o\}$ where it can – i.e. it bans mid vowels in unstressed syllables. The result of the ranking is that unstressed mid vowels become more sonorous.

(40) Belarusan

/mʲodovɨ/	σ́-IDENT[±low]	IDENT[±high]	*$\Delta_\sigma \leq \{e,o\}$	IDENT[± low]
(a) mʲaˈdavɨ	*!		*	
(b) mʲaˈdova		*!	*	*
(c) mʲoˈdovɨ			***!	
☞ (d) mʲaˈdovɨ			**	

To summarize, unstressed vowels can become more sonorous through the pressure for syllable DTEs to contain sonorous segments. In this way, Belarusan is just like any language in which sonority increases in DTEs, like SLP creole. The key difference is that unfaithfulness is blocked in stressed syllables.

7.3.2.2.1 Berguener Romansh unstressed 'dispersion'

A more complex example is found in Berguener Romansh, spoken in southeast Switzerland (also called Bergün Romansh; Lutta 1923; Kamprath 1987; Crosswhite 2000). It has seven vowels in stressed position: [a ɛ ɔ e o i u]. Pretonically, its unstressed vowel inventory is gapped: [a i u]. What is remarkable about the unstressed position is the directions of neutralization: while /e o/ raise to high vowels, /ɛ ɔ/ lower to [a]. Distinguishing between high, low, and ATR is important in this analysis, so the vowel's feature values are made explicit below.

(41) Berguener Romansh pre-tonic unstressed vowel reduction

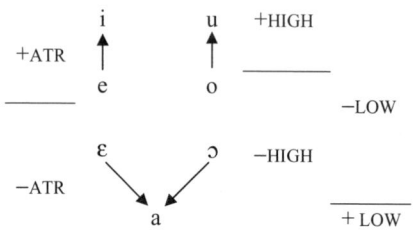

Table (42) provides supporting data. The forms are from Kamprath (1987) except that I follow Lutta (1923) in transcribing her pre-tonic 'ə' as [a]. It could be that Kamprath's 'ə' is an orthographic convenience: she notes that 'the only difference between [a] and [ə] is that the former is stressed and the latter unstressed' (p.54 n.1). In contrast, Lutta makes a clear distinction between [a] and [ə], noting that [a] is the result of pre-tonic reduction while [ə] appears post-tonically; this point is discussed further below. I found no data in Kamprath 1987 that show alternations involving /ɔ/, although /ɔ/ surfaces faithfully in stressed syllables (e.g. [ˈt͡ɕɔmbrə] 'room', [ˈgrɔnt] 'big').

(42) Berguener Romansh (data from Kamprath 1987)
    (a) [ˈi]~[ĭ]:   [ˈbigzə]   'snow(storm)'   [bizaˈset͡ɕə]   'sleet' (p.224)
    (b) [ˈu]~[ŭ]:   [ˈbuŋ]   'good'   [bun-ˈtɛt]   'goodness' (p.169)
    (c) [ˈe]~[ĭ]:   [ˈʒej]   'juice'   [ʒi-ˈuks]   'juicy' (p.175)
                     [ˈfeŋ]   'finish'   [fiˈn-i]   'finished'
    (d) [ˈo]~[ŭ]:   [saˈvok̥r̥]   'flavour'   [savuˈr-uks]   'flavourful' (p.174)
                     [ˈfos]   'false'   [fuzˈ-dɛt]   'falsehood'
    (e) [ˈɛ]~[a]:   [ˈmɛnd-ə]   'defect'   [manˈd-uks]   'defective' (p.175)
                     [ˈvɛnd-ər]   'to sell'   [vanˈd-eks]   'you (pl.) sell'
    (f) [ˈɔ]~[a]:   *no data*
    (g) [ˈa]~[a]:   [ˈsaŋ]   'healthy'   [sanˈ-dɛt]   'health' (p.175)
                     [ˈt͡ɕaɲt-ə]   'sings'   [t͡ɕanˈt-er]   'to sing' (p.181)

This system can be understood as having two aims. One is to reduce the sonority of prosodic word non-DTEs, resulting in /e o/ raising to [i u]. The other is to increase the sonority of syllable DTEs, so that /ɛ/ and /ɔ/ become [a].

Desonorization of /e o/ to [i u] is caused by $*-\Delta_\omega \geq \{e, o\}$ outranking all relevant faithfulness constraints (e.g. IDENT[high]).

(43) Berguener Romansh I: Desonorization of /e o/

/ʒe-uks/	*−Δ_ω≥{e,o}	IDENT[±high]
(a) ʒe.'uks	*!	
☞ (b) ʒi.'uks		*

However, *−Δ_ω≥{e,o} fails to force /ɛ ɔ a/ to become less sonorous. It is blocked from doing so by two constraints. One is the faithfulness constraint IDENT[±ATR] which prevents the [−ATR] vowels /ɛ ɔ a/ from becoming less sonorous [+ATR] vowels like [i u]. The other is the output constraint *Δ_σ≤ə; this prevents reduction to [ə] even though [ə] is a [−ATR] vowel. The rankings are shown in tableau (44)

(44) Berguener Romansh II: Blocking desonorization of low vowels

/san-dɛt/	*Δ_σ≤ə	IDENT[±ATR]	*−Δ_ω≥{e,o}	IDENT[±high]
(a) sən'dɛt	*!			*
(b) sin'dɛt		*!		*
☞ (c) san'dɛt			*	

The vowels /ɛ/ and /ɔ/ become more sonorous in unstressed syllables. As in Belarusan, this is due to the syllable-DTE constraint *Δ_σ≤{ɛ,ɔ}, as shown in tableau (45). To avoid violations of −Δ_ω≥{e,o} candidate (a) reduces unstressed /ɛ/ to [i], but in doing so fatally violates IDENT[±ATR]. Candidates (b) and (c) avoid violations of IDENT[±ATR] but equally violate the ban on high-sonority prosodic word non-DTEs. This equal violation is crucial as it allows the lower-ranked constraint *Δ_σ≤{ɛ,ɔ} to be decisive. As *Δ_σ≤{ɛ,ɔ} favours syllable nuclei with the lowest-sonority vowels, candidate (c) wins.

(45) Berguener Romansh III

/vɛnd-eks/	IDENT[±ATR]	*−Δ_ω≥{e,o}	*Δ_σ≤{ɛ,ɔ}
(a) vin'd-eks	*!		*
(b) vɛn'd-eks		*	* *!
☞ (c) van'd-eks		*	*

Stressed syllables are unaffected by the sonority conditions, so σ́-IDENT[±high] and σ́-IDENT[±ATR] dominate the (non-)DTE constraints. These constraints eliminate the competitors *[van'daks] and *[van'diks].

324 *Markedness conflict: vowels*

For remaining rankings, the sonority constraints force /ɔ/ to lose its [+round] feature, so $*\Delta_\sigma \leq \{\varepsilon,\mathfrak{o}\}$ must outrank IDENT[±round]. Constraints that contradict the DTE and non-DTE constraints used above are crucially inactive. For example, mid and high vowels exist in stressed and unstressed syllables, so $*\Delta_\sigma \leq \{e,o\}$ must appear below the faithfulness constraints in the ranking.

As an interim summary, the ranking shows that a 'dispersed' unstressed vowel inventory comes about through simultaneous pressures to have highly sonorous DTEs but low-sonority non-DTEs.

There is an additional complexity to Berguener Romansh's vowel reduction system. Lutta (1923:126) reports that there is a difference between pre- and post-tonic vowels. While pre-tonic vowels are [a i u], post-tonic ones are either [a] or [ə]: e.g. ['tɕeza] 'house', ['tɕaŋt-ə] 'sings'. To be more precise about the meaning of 'post-tonic', Berguener Romansh stress is assigned to the final syllable if it is closed, otherwise to the penult. In metrical theory, this pattern is due to a right-aligned quantity-sensitive trochaic foot. Consequently, post-tonic syllables are the non-head part of the head foot: e.g. [('tɕe.za)], [('tɕaŋt-ə)]. The inventory issues can therefore be recast as: (a) why can only [a] and [ə] appear in the non-head syllable of a foot, and (b) why can unfooted (i.e. pre-tonic) syllables not contain [ə]?

The solution is due to the constraint $*-\Delta_{Ft} \geq \{i,u\}$, which bans everything more sonorous than schwa in the non-head syllable of a foot. $*-\Delta_{Ft} \geq \{i,u\}$ outranks all faithfulness constraints that would prevent vowel reduction (e.g. IDENT[±ATR], IDENT[±high]), and all output constraints that ban schwa (e.g. $*\Delta_\sigma \leq \{\mathrm{ə}\}$). The effect of $*-\Delta_{Ft} \geq \{i,u\}$ is shown on post-tonic /e/ in tableau (46). The faithful candidate (a), candidate with sonorization (b), and candidate with desonorization to high vowels (c) are all ruled out by $*-\Delta_{Ft} \geq \{i,u\}$ as they all contain a footed non-head syllable with a vowel that is more sonorous than schwa. All the other constraints identified so far are rendered inactive in this ranking.

(46) Berguener Romansh IV

/tɕaŋt-e/	$*-\Delta_{Ft}\geq\{i,u\}$	$*\Delta_\sigma\leq\{\mathrm{ə}\}$	IDENT[± ATR]	$*-\Delta_\omega\geq\{e,o\}$	$*\Delta_\sigma\leq\{\varepsilon,\mathfrak{o}\}$
(a) ('tɕaŋt-e)	*!			*	*
(b) ('tɕaŋt-a)	*!		*	*	
(c) ('tɕaŋt-i)	*!				*
☞ (d) ('tɕaŋt-ə)		*	*		*

However, IDENT[+low] prevents $*-\Delta_{Ft}\geq\{i,u\}$ from forcing /a/ to reduce.

7.3 Vowel inventories and neutralization

(47) Berguener Romansh v

/t͡ɕeza/	IDENT[+ low]	*−Δ_Ft≥{i,u}
(a) ('t͡ɕezə)	*!	
(b) ('t͡ɕeza)		*

The tableaux above have shown how the theory provides an internally consist ranking of Berguener Romansh's three vowel inventories: (a) its pre-tonic (i.e. unfooted unstressed) vowel inventory of [a i u], (b) its post-tonic (i.e. foot non-DTE) inventory of [a ə], and (c) its stressed vowel inventory [a ɛ ɔ e o i u]. Not only does it get the inventory facts, it correctly models the direction of neutralization, with /e o/ becoming [i u] pre-tonically while /ɛ ɔ/ become [a]. The pre-tonic 'dispersed' inventory [i u a] is due to the interleaving of constraints on DTEs and non-DTEs, marked in (48). The post-tonic gapped [a ə] inventory is formed by placing a stronger requirement on foot non-DTEs, with the proviso that underlying low vowels remain low.

(48) Berguener Romansh vowel neutralization ranking

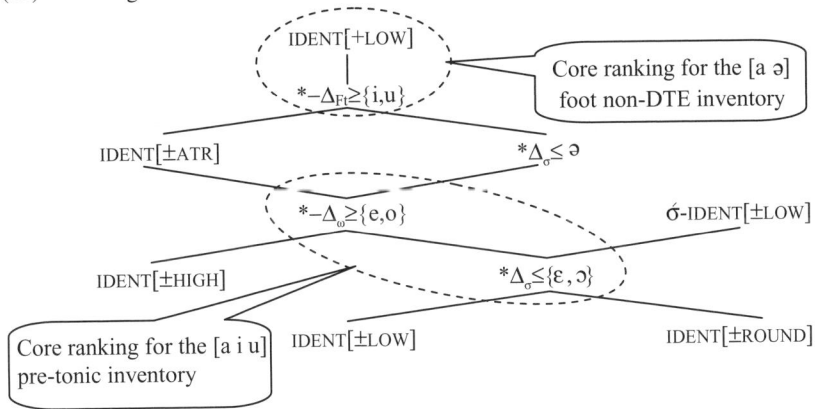

To summarize, sonority markedness is in conflict in many prosodic positions. Neutralization can therefore proceed in both directions, either increasing or decreasing sonority. So, direction of sonority neutralization in vowels is not a valid markedness diagnostic. However, there are exceptions: if a vowel is a DTE of every prosodic category, no output constraint will force it to reduce in sonority. Similarly, a segment that is not a DTE of any prosodic category will never be forced to increase sonority. For example, onset consonants are not the DTE of any category; as predicted, all non-assimilative neutralizing processes that target onset sonority reduce it (de Lacy 2000b; Smith 2002 and references cited therein).

7.3.2.2.2 Mid vowels are not special

Finally, Crosswhite (1999, 2004) proposes an alternative account of Berguener Romansh pre-tonic neutralization. The conceptual background is Dispersion theory, which expresses the idea that an inventory with corner vowels is desirable because it promotes maximal perceptual distinctness (Liljencrants & Lindblom 1972; Lindblom 1990; Flemming 1995). The core of the theory is the constraint in (49).

(49)   LIC-Noncorner/stress: Noncorner vowels are licensed only in stressed positions (Crosswhite 2004)

Mid vowels become low vowels when LIC-Noncorner/stress and IDENT[low] outrank IDENT[high].

The problem with LIC-Noncorner/stress is that it conflicts with the sonority hierarchy in an undesirable way. If it outranks all relevant sonority constraints, it effectively favours both low and high peripheral vowels over mid peripheral vowels. For processes other than vowel reduction, this effect has typologically fatal implications. For example, if LIC-Noncorner/stress outranks constraints on stress placement, the result is a language in which stress seeks out mid vowels even when a more-sonorous low vowel is in the 'default' stress position, as shown in tableau (50).

The skull and crossbones ☠ marks a winner that never occurs given the input and basic ranking — in no sonority-driven stress system does stress move away from the default stress position (i.e. the one favoured by stress location constraints like ALIGN-σ́-L) so as to fall on a lower sonority vowel. Supporting evidence for this claim is given in §5.4, Kenstowicz 1996, and de Lacy 2002a, 2004, 2006.

(50)

/pake/	IDENT[low]	LIC-Noncorner/stress	ALIGN-σ́-L
(a) pe'ke	*!		*
☠ (b) pa'ke			
(c) 'pake		*!	

In contrast, the present approach treats all cases of vowel reduction as deriving from the same source in that all are due to the action of the (non-)DTE/sonority constraints interacting with each other and faithfulness constraints. There is no need for mechanisms such as Dispersion or contrast enhancement.

7.3.2.3 Impossible neutralization directions

The theory does not allow every imaginable pattern of reduction. For example, it does not allow the pattern in (51), in which the mid-high vowels neutralize to [a] while the mid-low vowels neutralize to the high vowels.

(51)   Impossible unstressed vowel reduction

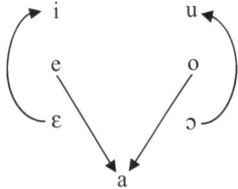

This system is predicted to not exist because it produces a ranking contradiction. The contradiction results from the fact that the constraint that motivates one neutralization blocks the output target of the other. To force /e/ to neutralize to [a], $*\Delta_\sigma \leq \{e,o\}$ must outrank every constraint that would prevent [a] as a possible target. These constraints include $*-\Delta_\omega \geq \{\varepsilon,\mathrm{o}\}$; this constraint favours [e] over [a], so it must be ranked below $*\Delta_\sigma \leq \{e,o\}$ otherwise the neutralization would be blocked.

(52)

/paka/	$*\Delta_\sigma \leq \{e,o\}$	$*-\Delta_\omega \geq \{\varepsilon,\mathrm{o}\}$
(a) peˈka	*!	
☞ (b) paˈka		*

In contrast, for /ɛ/ to become [i], $*-\Delta_\omega \geq \{\varepsilon,\mathrm{o}\}$ must outrank every constraint that favours [ɛ] over [i]; these include $*\Delta_\sigma \leq \{e,o\}$:

(53)

/pɛka/	$*-\Delta_\omega \geq \{\varepsilon,\mathrm{o}\}$	$*\Delta_\sigma \leq \{e,o\}$
(a) pɛˈka	*!	
☞ (b) piˈka		*

Hence, there is a ranking contradiction. In contrast, a neutralization in which /e/ becomes [i] and /ɛ/ becomes [a] involves no ranking contradiction because the constraint that motivates /e/-neutralization ($*-\Delta_\omega \geq \{e,o\}$) does not block the output of /ɛ/ neutralization, and likewise for the constraint that motivates /ɛ/-neutralization.

7.3.3 Conclusion

This section has focused on vowel neutralization and its worth as a diagnostic for sonority markedness. The difficulty with vowel neutralization is that often a single vowel is subject to conflicting demands. As a syllable DTE, a vowel is subject to constraints that aim to make it more sonorous while as a non-DTE of a foot and/or prosodic word it is subject to constraints that seek to make it less sonorous. The result is that some vowels may become more sonorous while others in the same prosodic position become less sonorous, even in the same language.

In contrast, markedness hierarchies that refer to subsegmental vowel features do not vary with prosodic position. For example, there are no conflicting markedness demands regarding vowel nasality: nasal vowels are more marked than oral vowels no matter what the prosodic context. So, as one would expect, no default epenthetic vowel is nasal (§7.2.5). Similarly, non-assimilative neutralization of vowel nasality always produces oral vowels. For example, Johore Malay bans nasal vowels everywhere except after a nasalized segment (e.g. [mākan] 'to eat', *[mākãn] – Walker 1998). Input nasal vowels are therefore neutralized to oral except in nasal assimilation environments. In contrast, there is no language which demands nasal vowels in a non-nasal environment and bans oral vowels. Similarly, there is no language which requires vowels to be nasal in a specific prosodic context (e.g. stressed syllables).

In summary, while the evidence for vowel sonority is difficult to see in epenthesis and neutralization, vowel alternations do provide evidence for other markedness hierarchies. Even so, the challenge raised by the preceding discussion is how to determine sonority relations if vowel epenthesis and neutralization are not valid diagnostics. This is the subject of the following section.

7.4 Prosodification

The preceding sections have shown that two pressures obscure the sonority hierarchy's markedness effects. One is Preservation of the Marked and the other is that different sets of sonority constraints conflict. Despite the fact that PoM is irrelevant for epenthesis, it gives no insight into sonority relations because of hierarchy conflict; the same is true of direction of neutralization. However, both preservation and hierarchy conflict are irrelevant for cases where sonority influences the position of prosodic elements, and these clearly show sonority-markedness relations.

In some languages, the location of syllable constituents and feet is heavily influenced by sonority. For example, the position of syllable DTEs – i.e.

syllable nuclei — is often influenced by the need to be as sonorous as possible. The famous case of Imdlawn Tashlhiyt Berber syllabification is an example: the most sonorous segment [a] is sought out as the ideal syllable peak. If there are no [a]'s available, the next most-sonorous available elements are designated as syllable heads, and so on down through the sonority hierarchy (Dell & Elmedlaoui 1985, 1988; Prince & Smolensky 1993:§2). A crucial point is that there is no language that reverses the preference relation: there is no language in which the least-sonorous segments are sought out as syllable nuclei.

As syllabification — especially in Imdlawn Tashlhiyt Berber — has been discussed in detail in much previous work, the empirical focus of this section will instead be on prosodic heads and foot structure – i.e. sonority-driven stress. The aim of this section is to show why PoM and hierarchy conflict do not obscure the sonority-markedness relations evident in sonority-driven stress.

As discussed in §5.3.2, sonority-driven stress describes a situation in which stress does not fall on the default position but seeks out another syllable with a higher sonority. Gujarati's default stress position is the penult (e.g. [ap'wana] 'to give', [e'kotɾ] '71', [və'kʰətsəɾ] 'on time'). However, stress will fall on the antepenult or ultima if they contain an adequately more-sonorous vowel than the penult: e.g. ['patini] 'wife', ['tadʒetəɾ] 'recently', ['lajbɾɛri] 'library', [ispi'tal] 'hospital', [pərik'ʃa] 'examination', ['vismərəɳ] 'forgetfulness'.

All cases of sonority-driven stress are like Gujarati's: stress only ever deviates from default position if it can fall on a more-sonorous vowel. The sole source of variation is conflation: Gujarati conflates mid and high peripheral vowels while Nganasan keeps these sonority categories distinct (de Lacy 2004). However, there is no language in which stress seeks out [i] or [u] when the default position contains the more sonorous [e] or [o]. A typology was given in §5.4. It showed that sonority-driven stress is sensitive to the effects of sonority markedness. Stress favours low vowels over all others (as in Gujarati), mid peripheral vowels over high peripheral vowels (e.g. Nganasan), and high peripheral vowels over central vowels (e.g. Gujarati, Pichis Ashéninca).

The issue is why sonority-driven stress is able to show sonority-markedness asymmetries. Why do PoM and hierarchy conflict not obscure sonority markedness, as they do for vowel epenthesis and neutralization?

One reason is that faithfulness, and therefore PoM, is irrelevant in sonority-driven stress. As an example, stress is attracted away from the default penult position to the final syllable in Gujarati [hɛ'ran] 'distressed'. There is no faithfulness cost in doing so: the competitor *['hɛran] is not less or more faithful than the winning candidate.

The only situation in which faithfulness is relevant in sonority-driven stress is when it inadvertently causes unfaithfulness. For example, Gujarati /i/ becomes [ɪ] in unstressed syllables, so /ʃikaɾ/ surfaces as [ʃɪˈkaɾ]. The constraint IDENT[±ATR] could block final stress, as [ˈʃikaɾ] preserves /i/'s [ATR] while [ʃɪˈkaɾ] does not. However, such rankings can only block stress from falling on a more-sonorous vowel; they cannot force it to seek out a lower-sonority vowel.

The other reason that sonority-driven stress shows sonority-markedness asymmetries is that the conflict in different sets of DTE and non-DTE constraints is eliminated. Although the same prosodic position may be subject to conflicting sonority pressures, the prosodic constituents overlap in such a way that there is never a harmonic gain to force a DTE onto a less-sonorous vowel than it would otherwise get in the default prosodic position.

For example, in Gujarati $*\Delta_\omega \leq \{\varepsilon,\mathfrak{o}\}$ outranks constraints that require penultimate stress, including FTBIN:

(54)

/ʃikaɾ/	$*\Delta_{Ft}\leq\{\varepsilon,\mathfrak{o}\}$	FTBIN
(a) (ˈʃikaɾ)	*!	
☞ (b) ʃi(ˈkaɾ)		*

As shown for vowel neutralization and epenthesis, non-DTE constraints conflict with DTE constraints. For example, DTEs of prosodic words can be non-DTEs of a higher constituent, like the phonological phrase (PPh). So, if ʃikaɾ appeared in the middle of a phonological phrase, the [a] would violate the constraint $*-\Delta_{PPh}\geq\{\varepsilon,\mathfrak{o}\}$. However, this constraint cannot force stress to avoid [a] in favour of the lower sonority vowel [i] as in *[ˈʃikaɾ] as both *[ˈʃikaɾ] and [ʃiˈkaɾ] violate $*-\Delta_{PPh}\geq\{\varepsilon,\mathfrak{o}\}$ equally: the [a] in both candidates is the non-DTE of the phonological phrase.

In more general terms, the point is that the non-DTE constraints agree with the DTE constraints: both favour having high-sonority vowels in DTEs and low-sonority vowels in non-DTEs. There is no constraint that favours having an [a] in a non-DTE of α when it could appear in the DTE of α. Therefore, no ranking of the DTE and non-DTE constraints will ever favour a configuration in which a DTE has a lower-sonority vowel than a non-DTE over one in which a DTE has a higher-sonority vowel than a non-DTE.

As a more-extended example, the following tableaux show a language in which main stress is always leftmost but secondary stress is sonority-driven. To force primary stress to be leftmost, ALIGN-Δ_ω-L outranks all sonority-stress constraints. In contrast, *Δ$_{Ft}$≤{e,o} outranks ALL-Ft-L, a constraint that requires the left edges of all feet to align with the left prosodic word edge. The consequence is that secondary stress seeks out low vowels.

(55)

/pitikitati/	ALIGN-Δ$_ω$-L	*Δ$_{Ft}$≤{e,o}	ALL-Ft-L
(a) (₁piti) ki('tati)	*!	*	* * *
(b) ('piti)(₁kita)ti		* *!	* *
☞ (c) ('piti)ki(₁tati)		*	* * *

The [₁a] in the winner is both the DTE of a foot and the non-DTE of the prosodic word. Accordingly, it is subject to the pressures of a non-DTE constraint – i.e. to have low sonority. However, the constraint *−Δ$_ω$≥{a} is violated by the [a] in the winner. So, if this constraint is placed above *Δ$_{Ft}$≤{e,o}, will stress avoid [a]? As tableau (56) shows, *−Δ$_ω$≥{a} does not force secondary stress to appear one syllable over from where it should, as determined by ALL-FT-L. There is no gain in overall harmony by doing so – every allocation of foot DTEs and prosodic word non-DTEs would result in the same violations of *−Δ$_ω$≥{a}.

(56)

/pitikatiti/	ALIGN-Δ$_ω$-L	*−Δ$_ω$≥{a}	*Δ$_{Ft}$≤{e,o}	ALL-Ft-L
☞ (a) ('piti)(₁kati)ti		*	*	* *
(b) ('piti)ka(₁titi)		*	* *!	* * *
(c) (₁piti)('kati)ti	*!		*	* *

So, sonority-driven stress differs from neutralization and epenthesis. In neutralization, if both non-DTE and DTE constraints apply to the same vowel, at least one of the constraints could be less violated by altering the vowel's sonority. Consequently, vowel neutralization can proceed in either direction – to make less or more sonorous vowels. In contrast, if both non-DTE and DTE constraints apply to the same vowel, it is not the case that both of the constraints would be less violated by altering the vowel's prosodic position. Altering the prosodic structure has no effect on the number of violations of the non-DTE constraint.

7.5 Summary

Vowel sonority clearly shows that there is no single 'unmarked segment' or even an 'unmarked vowel'. The sonority hierarchy differs depending on its environment: high sonority in DTEs is favoured over low sonority, while in non-DTEs low sonority is favoured. As many positions are both DTEs and non-DTEs, many vowels have the potential to be treated as the 'least marked' in a language, depending on which of the sonority-related constraints dominates. So, any of [ɨ ə i e ɛ a] can be epenthetic and the output of neutralization.

The conflict of sonority requirements was shown to produce many types of vowel inventory. If non-DTE constraints dominated, inventories contained very low-sonority elements, while if DTE constraints dominated, inventories contained only very high-sonority elements. If members of the two sets of constraints are interleaved in the ranking, they produce gapped inventories, such as the 'dispersed' [a i u] inventory, the 'vertical' [a ə ɨ] inventory, and the 'flattened' [a e o ə] inventory.

So, there are far fewer phenomena that overtly respect vowel-markedness relations. However, sonority-influenced prosodification is a reliable markedness diagnostic because the conflicting requirements imposed by DTEs and non-DTEs prove to be irrelevant. Sonority-driven stress shows that DTEs always prefer to be higher sonority segments.

In addition, vowel-markedness hierarchies apart from sonority do show markedness effects. For example, there is never any context-free neutralization of oral to nasal vowels, or unround to round vowels. So, while markedness asymmetries are difficult to detect in vowel-related phenomena, markedness is nevertheless essential in accounting for the effects of vowel sonority.

8 Predictions and alternatives

8.1 Introduction

The preceding chapters have identified several major predictions of the theory proposed here, including those in (1).

(1) (a) A phenomenon will not show markedness asymmetries if (i) faithfulness (i.e. preservation) is relevant or (ii) it is affected by extensively conflicting hierarchies.
 (b) Phenomena not described by (a) will show overt markedness asymmetries.
 (c) All phenomena will show markedness conflation and – if relevant – faithfulness conflation.

The aim of this chapter is to identify a number of other predictions of the theory. In doing so, alternative theories of various aspects of markedness are considered; the theory proposed here is shown to be more empirically adequate.

Section 8.2 outlines the major predictions of the theory, and shows how to prove the theory wrong.

The following sections question the theory's fundamental assumptions. Section 8.3 discusses perhaps the most fundamental markedness issue: does markedness exist? More precisely, is it necessary to have Competence mechanisms that produce markedness asymmetries, or do the observed asymmetries follow from external influences? The theory and discussion so far has assumed that there are markedness-related Competence mechanisms. There are two ways to object to this proposal. One is to deny that there are universal markedness asymmetries (Hume & Tserdanelis 2002; Hume 2003; Vaux 2001). The other is to maintain that there are markedness asymmetries, but that they are due to external mechanisms. For example, recent work by Blevins (2004) argues that markedness is an epiphenomenon of mechanisms of diachronic change (also Bybee 1988; Ohala 1995). Section 8.2 argues that (a) there are 'hard' markedness universals – evidence to the contrary is either not relevant to Competence or misanalysed, and (b) diachronic change cannot account for all markedness asymmetries.

Section 8.4 discusses the relation between markedness and representation. The proposals here do not demand any special representational devices to effect markedness relations, and they do not subscribe to the idea that there is a direct correlation between representational complexity and markedness. This section argues that theories that relate markedness and representation face serious problems that the stringent constraints and PoM avoid.

Section 8.5 discusses the role of phonological contrast in markedness. In the theory presented here markedness is not tied to contrastive oppositions: a feature's markedness on a particular hierarchy is independent of the other features that appear in a language's inventory. An alternative approach is that markedness asymmetries can only be stated with respect to a particular system of phonological oppositions. Work by the Prague School (esp. Trubetzkoy 1939) argued that markedness is intimately tied to contrastive oppositions; this has been continued in recent work by Battistella (1990) and Rice (1999a,b, 2004a,b, 2006). The section argues that the contrast approach faces significant difficulties in dealing with attested markedness asymmetries.

The topic of §8.6 is whether markedness is relative or absolute. An absolutist stance is taken here: a form is marked with respect to some feature regardless of what other derivational options it competes with. This approach is compared with theories which employ a relativist conception of markedness (Baković 1999b, 2000; McCarthy 2002).

Section 8.7 deals with alternative formalizations of markedness hierarchies. Howe & Pulleyblank's (2004) theory of markedness using MAX[F] and DEP[F] constraints is discussed and shown to make undesirable empirical predictions. Gouskova's (2003) proposal that constraints cannot refer to the least-marked element in a hierarchy is also examined and argued to be empirically inadequate.

8.1.1 Naming the theory

At this juncture I find myself compelled to give a name to the theory proposed in the preceding chapters simply because this chapter contrasts it with many other theories and many readers consider 'the present theory' a tedious and uninformative circumlocution. However, I am wary of giving a single name to the several distinct proposals made here because doing so may obscure their separateness. For example, 'Preservation of the Marked' does not depend on the proposal that hierarchies are expressed as feature values, nor does it depend on stringent constraint formulation, and vice versa. Similarly, proposals differ on the breadth of their theoretical applicability: principles such as Preservation of the Marked are abstract enough that they can be formally implemented in many different theories, but the constraint generation schemas of §2.3 are specific to Optimality Theory. Nevertheless, with these caveats in mind, I will refer to the bundle of proposals made in the preceding chapters as CoMP – an acronym containing <u>Co</u>mpetence, <u>Co</u>nflation, hierarchy <u>Co</u>nflict, <u>M</u>arkedness, and <u>P</u>reservation of the Marked.

8.2 Predictions

A number of predictions of the theory have been identified in the preceding chapters. This section highlights the major ones by showing how to prove the theory wrong.

If the epenthesis in (2) is discovered in natural language, CoMP would be mortally wounded, or at least severely maimed. This epenthesis case is a problem for the theory because it involves the insertion of a marked PoA value – labial. It is important to note that the epenthetic consonant's features are not influenced by the surrounding environment: the [p] appears in both non-labial (a) and labial (b) environments.

(2) A hypothetical theory-destroying epenthesis
    (a) /hata-it/ → [hata<u>p</u>it]
       cf. [hata], *[hatap]
       /hata-kop/ → [hatakop], *[hata<u>p</u>kop]
    (b) /ukpa?/ → [<u>p</u>ukpa?]
       cf. /mak-ukpa?/ → [makukpa?], *[mak<u>p</u>upa?]

The theory predicts that the only way a marked value can appear is through (i) Preservation of the Marked or (ii) 'markedness promotion' through partially conflicting hierarchies. Of course, there are two crucial assumptions here: one is that the PoA hierarchy is correct – labials are more marked than other PoAs – and the other is that there is no other hierarchy in which labials are favoured over all other PoAs. Given the discussion in previous chapters and below, these assumptions seem well supported (also see §8.2.3).

Preservation of the Marked

Faithfulness is not relevant for epenthesis because there is nothing for the epenthetic segment to be faithful to. The theory predicts that when faithfulness is irrelevant overt markedness effects will be evident. So, faithfulness provides no way to account for epenthesis of [p] in (2). Output constraints favour other PoA values over labial, so there is no configuration of constraints that would allow epenthesis of [p].

So, when faithfulness is irrelevant, the theory predicts that unmarked values should result. In contrast, when faithfulness is relevant, the theory predicts that both marked and unmarked values appear. For example, faithfulness is relevant in influencing the undergoers of neutralization, so unmarked elements (e.g coronals) can undergo PoA neutralization without more marked elements doing so.

There is a type of phenomenon that the theory *cannot* produce: a process which always results in marked values. Preservation of the marked means that marked values can only survive through faithfulness, while unmarked values emerge through the action of output constraints. So, if a process always results in the survival of marked values, it must therefore be the case that output constraints are always irrelevant. However, the theory has no way to ensure such irrelevance. The constraint-formation mechanism produces a set of output constraints for every hierarchy, and the stringent form of the faithfulness constraints allows output constraints to have an emergent effect. Such emergent effects were illustrated for coalescence and bi-directional assimilation in chapter 6. Incidentally, coalescence has been claimed to always preserve marked feature values (de Haas 1988); the case studies in chapter 6 showed otherwise.

Markedness promotion

Could [p] be epenthetic if its feature values were 'promoted' to least-marked status? As discussed in §3.2.4.3, there are two ways that this might happen. One is if the other segments in the class which have a less-marked PoA are incidentally more marked than the labial. This is the case for approximants: as the less-PoA-marked coronals are liquids, they can be eliminated, so promoting the labial [w] to least-marked status. However, it is not the case for stops: [p] does not have any incidentally less-marked feature than [t].

The other way is if there are conflicting hierarchies which favour labials over both coronals and glottals. As argued in chapter 3, there is a hierarchy which favours non-glottals over glottals, but there is no hierarchy which favours labials over coronals. Without such a hierarchy, there is simply no way to promote [labial] over [coronal] (§3.2.5, §4.2.2.2).

Active synchrony

Another important reason why case (2) is mortally wounding is because the [p]-epenthesis is clearly synchronic, as shown by the alternations. Crucially, its existence does not rely on diachronic evidence (cf. §8.3.2) or phonotactic generalizations.

Phonotactic generalizations have often been used as evidence for markedness. For example, the term 'passive neutralization' is used by Rice (1999a,b, 2004a,b, 2006) to describe certain situations that do not involve alternations but are reminiscent of other situations in which active alternations that show neutralization occur. For example, if a language lacks an [m] in codas, this would be evidence of a 'passive neutralization'. Extending the terminology, 'passive epenthesis' would describe a situation in which a segment systematically appears in a certain environment, so epenthesis is imputed. Such passive epentheses are common in phonological analyses, and often stem from a motivation to economize on lexical representations. For example, if a language bans vowel-initial words on the surface, often a consonant – usually [ʔ] – will be assumed to be epenthetic; in some theories, such an assumption allows simplification of lexical entries (though not in Optimality Theory – Prince & Smolensky 1993; Tesar & Smolensky 1998).

However, there is a fundamental problem with appealing to 'passive' processes to give insight into markedness: passive processes do not allow the mapping from inputs to outputs to be determined so 'passive epenthesis' may not be epenthesis at all, and the same goes for passive neutralization. For example, if a language lacks an [m] in codas, the /m/ may have been eliminated through deletion (/am/→[a]), epenthesis (/am/→[ami]), or coalescence (/am/→[ã]). McCarthy (2003b) has argued exactly this point for Tagalog, in which [ʔ] was though to be epenthetic for entirely non-alternating phonotactic reasons; in contrast, McCarthy's analysis relies on the fact that surface [ʔ] is always present underlyingly.

To give a concrete example, [n] does not appear in Lhasa Tibetan codas while [m] does (Denwood 1999). However, it is not necessarily the case that underlying /n/ is mapped to output [m] in this language. In fact, a lack of coda [n] often correlates with nasalized vowels, suggesting that underlying /Vn/ coalesces to form [Ṽ] (§4.2.2.3); there is therefore no increase in PoA markedness and no reversal of the PoA hierarchy. The cases cited in Rice (2004a) all have this character: cases of neutralization to labials or dorsals all involve 'passive neutralization' of PoA, and so are not evidence of PoA neutralization at all. For in-depth discussion, see §8.4.3.

Finally, another reason that (2) is fatal is that the evidence is not from loanword epenthesis or aphasia. As discussed in §1.3.1, there is evidence that much loanword adaptation is due to perceptual factors (Peperkamp & Dupoux 2003). Until the influence of phonology and phonology-external mechanisms on loanwords can be teased apart, the implications of loanword adaptation for

338 8 Predictions and alternatives

markedness remain obscure. The same may well be applicable to disordered phonology (for an overview, see Bernhardt & Stemberger 2006).

Independence from other processes
The epenthesis in (2) also poses a problem because it is not influenced by other processes. For example, it is not [p] through assimilation or dissimilation as it appears in both labial (e.g. [pukpaʔ]) and non-labial (e.g. [hatapit]) environments. Such processes can interfere with the basic effects of markedness, as discussed in §3.2. Epenthesis is also the correct analysis: there is a clear phonological motivation (i.e. ONSET), the process is not deletion (otherwise the root in (a) would be [pakap] in isolation, not [paka]), and the [p] is clearly not a morpheme, as it appears in diverse environments (i.e. both after and before roots).

Conflation
A final prediction of the theory that is not highlighted by (2) relates to conflation. The theory predicts that conflation is possible but not obligatory for both output and faithfulness aspects of every phenomenon. In other words, there should be no phenomenon for which conflation is obligatory, and none for which it is impossible.

In practical terms, conflation for output constraints will only ever be seen with hierarchies of three or more members (e.g. PoA, sonority, tone). In Kashaya, for example, the marked categories dorsal, labial, and coronal conflated while the less-marked glottal and the more marked uvular did not. The result was effects that could not be modelled using fixed ranking. So, the theory predicts that conflation will be evident – but not obligatory – for multi-valued hierarchies. For how to determine whether a hierarchy is binary or multi-valued, see §5.4.2.

For faithfulness, the theory predicts that conflation is possible for both binary and multi-valued hierarchies. In practical terms, the theory predicts that every value of every feature should emerge in coalescence and bi-directional assimilation, as illustrated in §6.3.

In short, when it comes to conflation it is not possible to find a language which will prove the theory wrong, as the theory predicts that conflation and lack of conflation should always be possible. Instead, if a systematic gap was found – either some hierarchy never conflated or always conflated – this would show that some fundamental mechanism of the theory is incorrect.

8.2.1 Invalid diagnostics
As the preceding discussion has suggested, the theory makes a number of predictions about phonological phenomena that do not show overt markedness

effects. Essentially, only synchronic alternations can be trusted to accurately show the effect of Competence mechanisms. Diachronic change, loanword adaptation, disordered phonology, and language acquisition may well provide some insight into markedness, but Performance effects also influence these to a currently undetermined (but certainly large) extent, and so obscure whatever insight they give into Competence.

Focusing on synchronic alternations, the two main influences on whether a phenomenon will show markedness effects is faithfulness to the marked and hierarchy conflict. Any phenomenon for which faithfulness is relevant will not show overt markedness asymmetries. If different markedness hierarchies conflict over which of two segments is the more marked, then the result will be no overt markedness asymmetries. In practical terms, table (3) lists phenomena that are predicted to not show markedness effects, and so cannot be used as markedness diagnostics. This table expands on the summary in §1.4.1.

Many of the diagnostics in (3) have traditionally been assumed to be valid; as shown in the preceding chapters, they are not.

As mentioned in chapter 1, there is a significant abbreviation in (3) and the diagnostic table in §8.2.2. The phrase 'there is some markedness hierarchy in which [β] is more marked than [α]' is more correctly 'there is some hierarchy in which some property of [β] is more marked than the corresponding property of [α].' Markedness hierarchies do not refer to segments, but to *features* and their values. Consequently, if /α/ and /β/ neutralize to [α], then [α] and [β] have different values for some feature F, and there is some markedness hierarchy in which [β]'s F value is more marked than [α]'s F value. For example, /k/ neutralizes to [ʔ] in Standard Malay codas; [k] and [ʔ]'s value for PoA is different, and as it so happens dorsals are more marked than glottals on the PoA hierarchy. In short, I have used the abbreviation 'there is a markedness hierarchy in which [β] is more marked than [α]' for reasons of space, instead of 'there is a markedness hierarchy in which there is some feature value of [β] is more marked than [α]'s value for the corresponding feature.'

(3) Invalid markedness diagnostics
    (a) Inventory structure
        If [α] is in some segmental inventory and [β] is not, then it is not necessarily the case that there is a markedness hierarchy in which [β] is more marked than [α].
        e.g. [k] is present in Hawaiian but not [t]; [k]'s presence is due to dorsal-faithfulness, and there is no hierarchy in which | t ⟩ k |.
        (§4.2; cf. Jakobson 1941; Trubetzkoy 1939; Greenberg 1966)

(b) Neutralization: undergoers
If /β/ undergoes neutralization but /α/ does not, then it is not necessarily the case that there is a markedness hierarchy in which [β] is more marked than [α].
e.g. /t/ neutralizes to [ʔ] in Yamphu while /k/ does not. Like Hawaiian, /k/'s survival is due to faithfulness (§4.2).
(§4.2; cf. Jakobson 1941; Trubetzkoy 1939; Cairns 1969)

(c) Assimilation: undergoers
If α undergoes assimilation and β does not, then it is not necessarily the case that β is more marked than α.
e.g. /m/ assimilates in Sri Lankan Portuguese creole but /n/ does not; however, there is no hierarchy in which | n ⟩ m | − this pattern is due to markedness reduction (§4.3.2).
(§4.3; cf. Kiparsky 1985; Mohanan 1993:63,76; Jun 1995:33,70ff.)

(d) Coalescence
If α and β coalesce to form β, then it is not necessarily the case that β is more marked than α.
e.g. labials and coronals coalesce in Pāli to form coronals. The output's form is due to conflation; there is no hierarchy in which | coronal ⟩ labial |.
(§6.3; cf. de Haas 1988; Causley 1999:ch.5)

(3a,b) are both neutralization. As shown in chapter 4, faithfulness can prevent marked elements from neutralizing. The result is a gapped inventory with highly marked elements and unmarked elements, but other elements missing. In other words, faithfulness to marked elements prevents phenomena from showing overt markedness effects.

Faithfulness again plays a role in (3c) − undergoers of assimilation. It has been claimed that if only one feature value assimilates, it will be the unmarked one (Jun 1995; Mohanan 1993). In present terms, this would have to mean that faithfulness to the marked is always paramount, preventing marked elements from assimilating. In this case, it is markedness reduction that is responsible for rendering assimilation undergoers uninformative for markedness. Cases where only marked elements undergo assimilation are motivated by markedness reduction, as argued in §3.3.

Coalescence is another diagnostic for which it has traditionally been thought that faithfulness is always paramount, with the result that the most-marked feature value will always survive (de Haas 1988). However, the stringent form of constraints permits faithfulness conflation to allow the unmarked value to emerge, so rendering coalescence an invalid diagnostic (§6.3).

One further set of invalid diagnostics are negative statements of the sort 'If α is treated as equally marked as β in some language, then there is no hierarchy in which | α 〉 β |.' For example, Gujarati treats mid and high peripheral vowels in the same way for stress purposes. However, it is not valid to assume that high and mid peripheral vowels are therefore indistinguishable for markedness – they may simply be conflated, as shown in §5.3.2.

So, faithfulness to the marked, hierarchy conflict, and conflation mean that a number of traditional markedness diagnostics are not valid.

One diagnostic which is occasionally discussed in the markedness literature is 'allophonic variability'. Greenberg (1966) (citing C. F. Hockett) states that unmarked features tend to show greater allophonic variation than marked ones. I interpret Greenberg's comment to be about free variation for an individual speaker. For example, Amuesha's /e/ may be variably realized as [e], [i], or [ɪ] in the same environment (Fast 1953). Unfortunately, it is often not made clear in the sources whether such variation is phonological or phonetic. Variation is clearly phonological if the allophones have phonological effects. For example, suppose there is a language in which /s/→[ʃ]/_[i] and there is variation between [e] and [i]. If the [e]~[i] variation is phonological, the form [sek] should have the variant form [ʃik], but it should never be realized as *[sik] or *[ʃek]. Otherwise, the variation could well be phonetic – i.e. due to underspecification in phonetic interpretive rules. Given the difference in the mechanisms used to deal with free variation in phonology (e.g. Anttila 2006) and phonetics (e.g. Choi 1992b), it is not clear how to generalize over both to identify a consistent correlate of markedness. Even if phonological and phonetic free variation could be teased apart, it is not clear whether there really is a correlation between markedness and allophonic free variation.

Contra Greenberg, Rice (2006:§4.6.2) proposes that free variation of allophones is possible when they are not contrastive. I will provide an example from my own fieldwork on Māori (Polynesian; spoken in New Zealand) in July 2000: a male consultant produced [k] and [x] in free variation inter-vocalically (e.g. [waka]~[waxa] 'canoe'); [k] and [x] are not contrastive. However, the 'lack of contrast' condition does not predict when free variation will occur. A female consultant did not have any [k]~[x] variation at all. In addition, [t] and [s] did not freely vary in either consultant's speech, despite the fact that the two sounds do not contrast.

The markedness status of freely varying allophones is also unclear: underlyingly marked values do not only vary freely with less-marked ones. For example, the male Māori consulant's realization of /h/ varied freely between [ʃ], [x], and [h] (especially intervocalically): here the free variant allophones of /h/ are certainly not less marked than [h] – of the three segments, only [h] is ever epenthetic.

In any case, I suggest that allophonic free variation should not be expected to show markedness effects (clearly). Phonological free variation is due to optionally applying phonological processes. Some of those processes will reduce markedness (e.g. neutralization), but others may inadvertently increase it (e.g. assimilation). For example, the Māori [k]~[x] free variation is clearly due to an optional process of lenition. As lenition is a type of assimilation, it can create marked elements and so gives no insight into markedness hierarchies. Therefore, the [k]~[x] free variation does not imply that [k] is less marked than [x] or [x] is less marked than [k]. In short, if free variation is due to optional phonological processes then it should not be expected to give any insight into markedness, as some processes reduce markedness while others inadvertently increase it (see Anttila 2006 for an overview of formal accounts of free allophonic variation as optional processes in OT).

8.2.2 Valid diagnostics

The theory predicts that markedness effects will be evident when faithfulness is irrelevant. Some relevant phenomena are identified in (4).

(4) Valid markedness diagnostics
 (a) Neutralization: outputs
  If /α/ and /β/ undergo structurally conditioned neutralization to map to output [α], then there is some markedness hierarchy in which [β] is more marked than [α].
  e.g. /k/ becomes [ʔ] in Standard Malay, so there must be a hierarchy in which dorsals are more marked than glottals (as this is one of the few features that is different for [k] and [ʔ]).
  (§3.3; Jakobson 1941; Trubetzkoy 1939; Cairns 1969)
 (b) Deletion
  If /β/ undergoes structurally conditioned deletion and /α/ does not, then there is some markedness hierarchy in which [β] is more marked than [α].
  (Rice 1999a,b; de Lacy 2002a:§6.4.2)
 (c) Consonant epenthesis
  If consonant [α] is epenthesized and [β] is not in some language, then there is some markedness hierarchy in which [β] is more marked than [α].
  e.g. [t] is epenthesized in Māori, not [p], so there is a hierarchy in which coronals are less marked than labials (as PoA is the only feature in which [t] and [p] differ).
  (§3.2; Archangeli 1984, 1988; McCarthy & Prince 1994; Lombardi 2003)

(d) Assimilation: triggers
If /γ/ assimilates to /β/ in terms of some feature F, but /γ/ does not assimilate to /α/'s F-value, then there is some markedness hierarchy in which [β] is more marked than [α].
e.g. segments must assimilate in PoA to a following dorsal in Korean, but not all segments assimilate to a following labial or coronal. From the claim that assimilation is markedness reduction in §4.3.2.1, it follows that there is a hierarchy in which dorsals are more marked than labials and coronals.
(Mohanan 1993:75,76; Jun 1995:78; de Lacy 2002a:§7.5)

(e) Prosodification: mutual influence
If some prosodic constituent P is attracted to or attracts [α] and ignores [β], there is some markedness hierarchy in which [β] in constituent P is more marked than [α] in constituent P.
e.g. the head of the prosodic word (i.e. the main-stressed syllable) is attracted to [a] in Gujarati, ignoring less-sonorous segments like [ɛ ɔ e o i u ə] in the default stress position. Therefore, there is some markedness hierarchy in which [a] in the head of the prosodic word is less marked than all of [ɛ ɔ e o i u ə] in the same prosodic position (§5.3.2).
(§5.3.2, §7.4; for tone and stress: Goldsmith 1987; de Lacy 1999, 2002b; sonority and stress: Kenstowicz 1996; de Lacy 2002a, 2006; sonority and syllable structure: Prince & Smolensky 1993 and references cited therein).

(f) Inventory structure (to a very limited extent)
If the presence of [α] in a segmental surface inventory implies the presence of [β] but not vice versa, then there is some markedness hierarchy in which [β] is more marked than [α].
e.g. if there is a dorsal and/or labial of a particular manner of articulation in a language, then there will also be a glottal and/or a coronal of the same manner of articulation (as long as no interfering manner-changing processes apply). Consequently, there must be one or more hierarchies in which dorsals and labials are more marked than coronals and glottals (§4.2.2.2).
(Jakobson 1941; Trubetzkoy 1939; Greenberg 1966; cf. chapter 6)

(g) Conflation contiguity
If every time α conflates with β, α also conflates with γ, then there is some hierarchy in which | α ⟩ γ ⟩ β | or | β ⟩ γ ⟩ α |.
e.g. in languages with sonority driven stress, if [a] and [i u] are treated in the same way, [e o] will also be treated the same way. Non-contiguous markedness categories cannot be conflated, so it follows that there is a hierarchy in which | a ⟩ e,o ⟩ i,u | or | i,u ⟩ e,o ⟩ a |.
(§5.4; Jakobson 1941; Trubetzkoy 1939; Greenberg 1966; cf. chapter 6)

The diagnostics above are predicted to show overt markedness asymmetries because they are not influenced by faithfulness. For example, (4a) is about the direction of neutralization. If /α/ neutralizes to [β] the only way for this to happen is if there is some output constraint which favours [β] over [α]. In the current theory, neutralizing-causing output constraints relate to markedness hierarchies, so it follows that there must be a hierarchy in which | α 〉 β |.

The prediction for deletion in (4b) relates to the form of faithfulness constraints in CoMP. All faithfulness constraints are 'segmentally based' – the constraint IDENT[F] refers to feature F as a property of a segment. So if F's segmental sponsor is deleted, IDENT[F] is vacuously satisfied. Therefore, faithfulness is irrelevant in deletion, and should clearly show the effects of markedness reduction (§8.7.2). This requires rejection of MAX[F] and DEP[F] constraints, which allow features to exist independent of their segmental sponsor. This point is discussed further in §8.7.2 (also see Struijke 2001).

Consonant epenthesis, assimilation, and prosodification have been discussed at length in previous chapters. (4f) relates to implicational relationships for segmental inventories. If [β] can only appear when [α] is present, there can be no output constraint that eliminates [α] and not [β], and there can be no faithfulness constraint that preserves [β] and not [α]. This situation is related to Harmonic Ascent, when an attempt to eliminate a segment fails because there is no less-marked segment for it to become. These cases are discussed in §4.2.2.2.

The conflation implication in (4f) derives from the fact that non-contiguous categories cannot be conflated. Such conflation would require a reversal of hierarchical relations.

8.2.2.1 Variation

The diagnostics in (4) can be used to determine the form of markedness hierarchies. However, there is no requirement that all markedness hierarchies agree. For example, if /α/ neutralizes to [β], there must be some hierarchy in which | α 〉 β |. However, the neutralization does not imply that there is *no* hierarchy in which | β 〉 α |.

Catalan rhotics provide an example (slightly simplified from Wheeler 2005a:§2.1.6.1) (for the same point for Portuguese see Brakel 1984).

(5)   Catalan rhotic distribution
      (a) [r] and [ɾ] contrast between vocoids
         ['fɛru] 'iron'   ['paɾə] 'father'
         [sər'ja]~[səriá] 'Sarrià' [səntuɾ'jo] 'centurion'

(b) Only [r] is allowed in other onsets
 ['ros] 'fair' [rə'fe] 're-make'
 [ən'rik] 'Enric' ['folru] 'lining'

(c) Only [ɾ] is allowed in complex onsets
 ['pɾɔw] 'enough' [rə.'fɾɛsk] 'refreshment'

(d) (i) In continental Catalan, only [r] is allowed in codas.
 ['for.mə] 'shape' [ə'mark] 'bitter'
 [ə'tur] 'unemployment'

   (ii) In other dialects, only [ɾ] is allowed in codas.
 ['foɾmə] 'shape' [ə'maɾk] 'bitter'
 [ə'tuɾ] 'unemployment'

There are no alternations to support the claim that /r/→[ɾ] in complex onsets and /ɾ/→[r] in non-intervocalic onsets; they could delete instead. However, for the sake of argument, let us suppose that they do neutralize. By the neutralization /r/→[ɾ] it must be the case that there is some hierarchy in which a property of [ɾ] is favoured over a property of [r] – i.e. | ɾ ⟩ r |. From /ɾ/→[r] there must be some hierarchy where | r ⟩ ɾ |. This result is perfectly acceptable because there is no meta-principle that requires all hierarchies to be consistent with each other. Cases where /α/→[β] and /β/→[α] simply indicate that there are two conflicting hierarchies (cf. Rice 2004b).

8.2.3 Labial unmarkedness and a theory of diagnostics

PoM and markedness reduction together allow markedness diagnostics to be identified. This section illustrates the importance of having a theory of markedness diagnostics such as the one proposed in the preceding chapters, and focuses on Hume's (2003) proposal that labial can be unmarked in a language (also see Hume & Tserdanelis 2002). Hume 2003 will be referred to as H hereafter. H is also important in that it disagrees with one of the fundamental claims about the PoA hierarchy: that labials are never less marked than coronals.

H presents an archetypal markedness argument for labial-unmarkedness. A number of diagnostics that are traditionally accepted as giving insight into markedness are applied to the question of whether labial can ever be the least-marked PoA in a language. The diagnostics H discusses are summarized in (6). The references in square brackets argue that the particular diagnostic gives insight into markedness.

(6) Hume's (2003) diagnostics for labial unmarkedness
 (a) Labials are <u>acoustically less salient</u> than other PoAs in English (Miller & Nicely 1955) and Japanese (Sekiyama & Tohkura 1991)
  [Battistella 1990; Jun 1995; Rice 2004a]

(b) Labials are almost as typologically frequent as coronals (Maddieson 1992)
[Greenberg 1966]
(c) The labial [m] is more frequent in Sri Lankan Portuguese creole words than [n] [Greenberg 1966]
(d) The labial [m] can appear in more environments in SLP creole than [n]
(e) Labial stops are *acquired* before other segments in language acquisition (Stemberger & Stoel-Gammon 1991)
[Jakobson 1941, 1949b]
(f) Labials are the sole undergoers of assimilation in Sri Lankan Portuguese creole
[Kiparsky 1982; Mohanan 1993; Jun 1995; Rice 2004a]
(g) Labials can be the sole segment in a language's coda
[Rice 1999a,b]

Noting that both coronals and velars have been claimed to be unmarked (§8.4.2), H comments that 'essentially any place of articulation can thus emerge as unmarked in some language', and concludes that 'markedness considerations do not provide compelling evidence for constructing predictive theories of grammar'.

The problem with H's claims is that no argument is given for why the diagnostics in (6) are valid. In contrast, the primary aim in this book has been to establish a theory which predicts where markedness effects should be overtly visible. Simply put, the formalism predicts that they will be visible in synchronic alternations which are not subject to preservation (i.e. faithfulness constraints) and directly antagonistic markedness requirements. Within this theory of where markedness effects should appear, the issue of labial markedness can be addressed.

As it turns out, CoMP predicts that the diagnostics in (6) are irrelevant for markedness. There are a group of diagnostics which are simply outside the purview of a Competence theory: (6a) refers to acoustic salience, which is outside the realm of a formalist conception of Competence and so of c-markedness, (6b,c,d) are statements about frequency which is again not relevant to c-markedness (§1.3.1), and diagnostic (6e) is about order of language acquisition, which can be affected by Performance concerns (§1.3.1). There are also diagnostics which are influenced by faithfulness: (6f) refers to undergoers of assimilation; as seen in §4.3, marked elements can be prevented from assimilating with the result that anything can undergo assimilation. (6d) has the same character in that 'survival in more environments' simply indicates more pervasive faithfulness to labial. Finally (6g) is a case of 'passive neutralization', where there are no synchronic alternations. It is true that a number of languages allow only [m] (and/or [ŋ]) in their codas, but this does not mean that underlying /n/ neutralizes to [m] (see §8.2) (phonotactics are rarely relevant in determining c-markedness).

There are two omissions in (6): neutralization and epenthesis. As discussed in chapter 3, these are valid diagnostics because they are not influenced by PoM. Labials fare badly using these diagnostics. There are no epenthetic labial consonants (apart from [w] – §3.2.4.3, §3.2.5). There are no active synchronic alternations in which /n/ neutralizes to [p], or /k/ becomes [p], and so on. Using these diagnostics, labials are not the least-marked PoA in any language.

Another diagnostic cited by H is deletion. SLP creole has word-final deletion of [m] while [n] or [ŋ] survive (after Smith 1978). The issues surrounding deletion as a markedness diagnostic are discussed in §8.7.2, as is this particular case. To anticipate the discussion, there is good evidence that the process is coalescence, not deletion (e.g. /əkə taːm/ → [əkə tã:], *[əkə taː]), and that the fact that only labials undergo this process follows from CoMP's constraints and the principle of PoM.

The other diagnostic relates to coda inventories. H suggests that only [m] may appear in Kiribatese codas: e.g. [am taːra] 'your towel' (Groves, Groves, & Jacobs 1985). When [n] and [ŋ] would appear in a coda followed by a heterorganic consonant, epenthesis takes place: e.g. /taian boki/ → [taiani̯ boki] 'some books', /ŋaŋ roo/ → [ŋaŋi̯ roo] 'about to be dark', cf. [e kan taraia] 'the people arriving', [naŋ kiro] 'about to faint'. However, there is an alternative analysis: Kiribatese aims to avoid heterorganic coda-onset clusters through epenthesis (like Ponapean – deLacy 2002a:§7.3.1). Clusters involving [m] do not undergo epenthesis because [m] is never in a coda – it inhabits a syllable nucleus. Evidence for this analysis is the fact that [m] is the only nasal that can appear in a syllable nucleus: e.g. [m̩.ka] 'rotten'. Consequently, the [m] in [a.m̩ taː.ra] does not require epenthesis of [i] because there is no coda-onset heterorganicity to resolve. The remaining issue is to explain why only [m] can be a nucleus consonant, but whether this is related to PoA markedness or not is an issue for future research.

To summarize, H's diagnostics for labial unmarkedness are not valid in CoMP. This case study underscores the importance of having a theory of where markedness effects should appear. It also emphasizes the point that Competence markedness is distinct from Performance markedness. Many of the diagnostics in (6) are about Peformance, and they favour labials at least as much as coronals, if not more so. Yet, despite the fact that labials are often the first sounds to be acquired, can be least salient, and most frequent, they are never less marked than coronals and glottals in terms of c-markedness.

This ends the summary of the theory's predictions. The aim of the rest of this chapter is to question its fundamental assumptions and examine alternatives.

8.3 Markedness exists

The theory assumes that markedness asymmetries are due to Competence mechanisms; markedness hierarchies are formal objects that are directly accessible by i-language components. It is also 'universalist' in the sense that markedness hierarchies and how to express them are the same in all grammars; languages differ solely in their constraint ranking.

Some major challenges to universalism have already been addressed at length in previous chapters. One of the major issues was that languages differ as to which consonant is the 'default'. This was shown to be due to conflict among different hierarchies. Other challenges to universalism are based on invalid diagnostics, such as using undergoers of assimilation to argue for markedness relations, or appealing to Performance-related phenomena such as typological frequency.

One other source of challenges to markedness not mentioned above is variation in the application of terms such as 'neutralization' and 'epenthesis'. There are at least three distinct uses of 'epenthesis': (a) to refer to a synchronic process supported by alternations, (b) to refer to certain diachronic changes or inter-dialectal variations, (c) to refer to certain phonotactic regularities unsupported by alternations. The (c) type of epenthesis refers to situations reported for Tagalog above, where every word begins with a consonant, so one (often [ʔ]) is assumed to be epenthetic. Of these uses, only (a) gives any insight into a Competence theory, as argued at length above.

An entirely different challenge to universalism is to deny that markedness asymmetries are produced by Competence mechanisms. After all, when faced with a generalization like 'dorsals are never synchronically epenthetic' there are two sources of explanation. One is to derive the generalization from a theory of i-language; the other is to derive it from factors external to i-language mechanisms.

It can be difficult to decide which mode of explanation to employ for some phenomena. One useful principle is that if a generalization is not an absolute universal, then it is not related to Competence. For example, the generalization 'if a language has a fricative, then it is likely to be [s]' need not be explained by a Competence theory. The catch is that some universals can be obscured by other processes. For example, the generalization 'every inventory contains a glottal and/or a coronal' is obscured by processes such as lenition and vowel-nasal coalescence (§4.2.2.3). For example, Chickasaw only allows [m]'s in codas, not [n]; the lack of coda [n] is due to vowel+nasal coalescence, so that /Vn/ → [Ṽ].

Even if a universal is absolute, it is not necessarily derived from Competence. For example, no language has only one consonant in its inventory, but this is quite possibly an accidental gap due to the functional need to distinguish lexical items. Similarly, if no language contrasts [w] and [ʋ], this might be related to difficulties of perceiving a difference, and therefore of learning the contrast. Of course, these are obvious and well-known issues: i.e. knowing which generalizations actually require i-language explanation.

Although it is difficult in some cases to know whether to consider a generalization an accidental gap, there are a good number of phenomena for which appealing to accident is undesirable. For example, a large number of languages have epenthesis processes, and in none of these is [k] epenthetic. If the choice of epenthetic element is unconstrained, it would be very likely that [k] – a very frequent sound in the world's languages – would be epenthetic in some language. So, the lack of epenthetic [k] requires either an explanation in terms of Competence mechanisms or one that uses external mechanisms, such as some principle that blocks a language with epenthetic [k] from ever being learned.

Blevins (2004) provides a recent example of an approach that seeks to eliminate markedness from Competence, called 'Evolutionary Phonology' (EP). EP is related to approaches that have sought to derive synchronic generalizations from diachronic principles (also see Bybee 1988, 2001:195ff.; Ohala 1974, 1983, 1990, 1992, 1995; Hale & Reiss 2000). EP's leading idea is that 'recurrent sound patterns have their origins in recurrent phonetically motivated sound change' (Blevins 2004:8). In other words, phonological asymmetries are the result of diachronic pressures rendering the development and survival of certain sound patterns highly unlikely, even impossible: 'Certain sound patterns are rare or unattested, because there is no common pathway of change which will result in their evolution' (Blevins 2004:9).

To give a brief example, following EP's methodology, if every language has a glottal or a coronal, EP would consider this as coming about because a language that lacks both a glottal and coronal for a particular manner of articulation is unstable — it cannot be easily transmitted intact. Perceptual or Performance factors would force learners towards adding a glottal or a coronal. In contrast, a Competence-based theory would account for the generalization by making it impossible for the learner to construct a grammar without either a glottal or a coronal: if the learner eliminated coronals, the form of the constraints and their ranking would automatically admit glottals, and vice versa.

8.3.1 Performance, not Competence

So, can EP and related theories be successful? I believe they can, but only in explaining Performance asymmetries, and not the sort of hard universals that Competence theories explain. To illustrate the distinction, selected items from Blevins' (2004:9–10) list of phonological markedness asymmetries are given in (7); because the focus of this book is on featural phenomena, the items relating to stress patterns are omitted.

(7)   Excerpt from Blevins (2004:9–10)
  i. SEGMENT INVENTORIES
    a. If a language has only three vowels, it will usually have /i, u, a/.
    b. All languages have voiced sonorants and voiceless obstruents in their segment inventories.
    c. In the series of voiced stops /b d g/, /g/ is most likely to be missing.
    d. No language contrasts voiceless laryngealized obstruents with their voiceless ejective counterparts.
    ...
  ii. PHONOTACTICS
    h. In nearly all languages, each consonant in a syllable-internal obstruent cluster must agree in laryngeal features.
    i. In many languages, each consonant in an obstruent cluster must agree in laryngeal features.
    j. In many languages, there is no possible laryngeal contrast for obstruents in pre-obstruent position.
    k. In languages where there is no possible laryngeal contrast for obstruents in pre-obstruent position, laryngeal contrasts are neutralized in this position in derived environments.

Table (7) is part of a response to three questions posed in EP; these questions are presented as central issues for phonological theory. They are: 'What are the frequent sound patterns exhibited by the world's languages? What are the recurrent sound patterns which phonological theory attempts to explain? . . . *why* [do] generalizations like those in [(7)] exist?' (Blevins 2004:9–10).

I disagree with both the assumption underlying the questions and their importance. There is no need for a Competence theory to explain frequency generalizations, which is what the majority of the statements above are (§1.3). To take example (i-c), it is not necessarily a Competence theory's job to account for the fact that [ɡ] is often absent while [b] and [d] are not. After all, it turns out that all imaginable (at least in terms of major PoA) voiced stop inventories exist, as in table (8).

(8) Voiced stop inventories

g	b	d	Languages
✓	✓	✓	Nhanda (Blevins 2001), Catalan (Wheeler 2005a)
✓	✓		Tigak (Beaumont 1979)
✓		✓	Wapishana (Tracy 1972), Ayutla Mixtec (Pankratz & Pike 1967)
	✓	✓	Sioux Valley (Santee) (Shaw 1980:17), Xavanté Macro-Je (Rodrigues 1999a)
✓			Makurap (Rodrigues 1999b:112ff.)
	✓		Koasati (Kimball 1991)
		✓	Diyari (Austin 1981), Nambiquara (Kroeker 1972)

A Competence theory must be able to produce grammars which generate all of the inventories in table (8). There is nothing more it needs to explain. The relative rarity of languages with a [ɡ] and missing some other stop (like Tigak, Wapishana, Ayutla Mixtec, and Makurap) does not have to come from Competence mechanisms. Performance factors such as difficulty of producing voicing on velars (e.g. Ferguson 1975; Ohala 1983) mean that learners would be more likely to eliminate it from their inventories or reinterpret it as voiceless [k]. But other factors like the [ɡ]-less speakers' success at survival, propagation, and colonization play an important role. Therefore, an explanation of why [ɡ] is rare relative to other voiced stops is not an explanation about markedness as a Competence concept – it is an account of Performance.

The same can be said for many of the generalizations in the list. In (i-a), many three-vowel languages do have [i a u], but certainly not all. For example, Alabama has [e o a] (Rand 1968) and Wosera has [a ə ɨ] (Laycock 1965). Again, a Competence theory must be able to provide a grammar for each (see §7.3), but does not have to explain why the [i a u] inventory is more frequent than the [e a o] system. This is the role of a theory of Performance. Examples (ii-h), (ii-i), and (iii-j) are also about probability, and are subject to the same criticism.

A few of the examples are absolute universals (i-b), (i-d), and (i-k). It is quite possible that there is an external explanation for these cases relating to functional pressures. However, these generalizations are not on the same order as universals such as 'No language has an epenthetic dorsal'; as argued below,

352 8 Predictions and alternatives

this generalization is impossible to explain in any theory that appeals to external mechanisms to constrain markedness.

In conclusion, a good many items on the list are simply not what a Competence theory of markedness seeks to explain. Consequently, a diachronically based account for them is not in competition with a Competence account, and therefore do not replace a Competence notion of markedness.

8.3.2 Diachrony–synchrony mismatches

One serious problem facing an attempt to reduce markedness to diachronic mechanisms is that some diachronic processes do not have synchronic counterparts. An example is the diachronic change of *t to [k]. This diachronic change is found in Hawaiian, Luangiua, Fort Chipewyan, and several Oceanic languages (Lynch et al. 2002:ch.4). It also occurred in codas in the change from Middle Chinese to Classical Fuzhou (Chen 1973). An even more extreme case of both coda *t and *p becoming [k], and the same for fricatives, is evidently in progress in the Maracaibo dialect of Venezuelan Spanish, where there is free variation between velars and glottals in codas where other dialects have non-velars: e.g. [oksekio]~[oʔsekio] (cf. [opsekio]), [exte]~[ehte] 'this' (cf. Castilian Spanish [este]) (Guitart 1981).

However, there is no synchronic neutralization process whereby /t/ surfaces as [k]; no language has alternations like [ak] and [ak.-mi] vs. [a.t-i]. If diachrony explains all synchronic asymmetries (or at least those relating to markedness), how can there be diachronic processes that have no synchronic counterpart? Even more perplexing for the diachronic account is the fact that synchronic /k/→[t] is attested (§3.3), but Lynch et al. (2002:54) note that 'across the languages of the world the sound change t to k is hugely more common than k to t'. In short, an extremely common sound change has no synchronic counterpart, while there is one for a rare sound change.

8.3.3 Many diachronic rights can create synchronic wrongs

The following argument follows Kiparsky (2004) closely. The basic point is that a number of natural diachronic changes can produce a grammar which is synchronically unattested, and reverses markedness relations. Following Kiparsky's argument, the lack of such grammars shows that there are Competence restrictions that constrain grammars, and so prevent diachronic changes from creating grammars that ignore markedness.

Kiparsky's argument refers to sonority-driven stress in Gujarati, as discussed in §5.4 and de Lacy 2002a. Stress is usually penultimate, but will fall on an [a] elsewhere if the penult is not [a] (e.g. ['tadʒetər], *[ta'dʒetər]). This fact was argued to result from Competence mechanisms, specifically constraints that refer to the sonority hierarchy | a 〉 e,o 〉 i,u 〉 ə |. A diachronically based account would posit that there is no such markedness hierarchy, and therefore no related constraints. Instead, in keeping with the spirit of Blevins (2004), Kiparsky suggests that in such an account the 'intrinsic acoustic prominence of sonorous vowels may be reinterpreted as stress in sound change'. In other words, the relative acoustic prominence of [a] makes it liable to be mis-learned as bearing stress.

However, a natural sound change could easily change the stress facts. For example, */a/ could become [ə] (as it did in a sound change from Sanskrit). If this happens in a daughter language of Gujarati, */ˈtadʒetər/ would become [ˈtədʒetər]. The problem with this form is that in synchronic terms a form like [ˈtədʒetər] has stress retracting to an antepenultimate schwa even though there is a more sonorous vowel – i.e. [e] – in penultimate position. As discussed in §5.4, no such stress system exists. In short, a natural sound change results in a language that reverses the markedness relation between [ə] and mid vowels on the sonority hierarchy. Diachronic mechanisms therefore cannot account for the markedness relations seen in sonority-driven stress. In contrast, the Competence theory presented here makes it impossible to construct a grammar in which schwa attracts stress away from a more sonorous vowel (§7.4), so providing an account of the observed facts.

Another example relates to the lack of [k] epenthesis. In the Eastern Polynesian language Māori, [t] is epenthesized in suffixation of the passive and gerund: e.g. /arihi-ia/ → [arihitia] 'chop-{passive}', cf. /hopuk-ia/ → [hopukia] 'catch-{passive}' (de Lacy 2003). These suffixes and the epenthesis process existed even before Proto-Polynesian: all Polynesian languages have some form of the suffix, and it seems that all have epenthesis (at the very least Māori and Hawaiian do, which is all that matters for present purposes – Elbert & Pukui 1979; 'Oiwi Parker Jones p.c.). In terms of its phonology, Māori is diachronically conservative; it preserves many aspects of Proto-Eastern Polynesian so it is likely that Proto-Eastern Polynesian had epenthesis of [t] too. As mentioned many times before, proto-Eastern Polynesian *t became Hawaiian [k]. Therefore, a diachronic theory would expect (or at least allow) epenthesis of [k] in Hawaiian: i.e. /lawe-ia/ → *[lawekia] 'bring-{passive}'. However, Hawaiian epenthesizes [ʔ], not [k]: i.e. [laweʔia]. Epenthesis of [ʔ] is surprising from a diachronic perspective, but not from a synchronic one. CoMP's Competence mechanisms do not allow [k] epenthesis, as shown in §3.2.5. Consequently, the only option for Hawaiian is to have an epenthetic [ʔ].

354   8 Predictions and alternatives

As with the quasi-Gujarati case, a diachronic change does not produce a language that it could – and probably should – do. In contrast, synchronic mechanisms provide an explanation: c-markedness mechanisms dictate that [?] epenthesis is possible while [k] epenthesis is not.

8.3.4   No craziness

A number of authors have argued that 'crazy rules' pose a significant problem for a Competence account of markedness. In rough terms, a crazy rule is a grammatical process that is 'arbitrary', or has no phonetic basis (Bach & Harms 1972). For example, McCarthy (1993) claims that [ɹ]-epenthesis in Boston English is 'demonstrably not the default consonant in English' and notes that this is 'a phonologically arbitrary stipulation, one that is outside the system of Optimality'. Put simply, if crazy rules exist, they show that there is no such thing as markedness: Competence mechanisms must be allowed to do (almost) anything so as to be able to accommodate crazy rules. Markedness must therefore be an epiphenomenon, and not hard-wired into Competence (also see McMahon 2000; Hyman 2001).

The problem with crazy rules is in their definition. Whether a rule is crazy or not depends on a priori assumptions about the phonetic basis of phonological constraints. If there is an assumption that all markedness hierarchies and constraints are phonetically grounded (in some sense), then a crazy rule can be defined as any rule/constraint that is not so grounded. However, if such a functionalist assumption is rejected, then the problem disappears. In a formalist approach there is no assumption that a constraint must be phonetically grounded, so there is no a priori way to define a 'crazy rule'. The closest definition is that a rule or constraint is 'crazy' if it cannot be generated by one's theory. To put it simply, 'crazy rules' only exist if one assumes that the phonology cannot be arbitrary.

Under some theories, some putative crazy rules turn out to be expected. For example, the theory presented here predicts that [ɹ] is a possible epenthetic segment. So, there is nothing crazy about [ɹ]-epenthesis. I should add that McCarthy's (1993) point is somewhat subtler – he points out that [ɹ] is not the default consonant in English. However, this is not quite accurate: while [?] is the default prosodic-word-initially, [ɹ] is the default inter-vocalically. It is perfectly possible to have more than one 'default' in a language, as chapter 3 has shown.

Another putative crazy rule is coda voicing: Somali stop voicing was discussed in §3.3.2.1, where underlying voiceless stops become voiced in codas: e.g. /ilik/ → [ilig] 'tooth' (cf. [ilk-ó] 'teeth') (Saeed 1999). If *{+voice} is the only constraint that has anything to say about voicing, this process would be highly problematic. However, CoMP predicts that coda stop voicing can occur due to pressure to make codas (especially moraic consonants (Δ_μ)) more sonorous: *$\Delta_\mu \leq \{-\text{vd stop}\}$. Certainly Somali coda stop voicing is crazy from the point of view of one constraint/process, but from another it makes perfect sense.

The issue of crazy rules and coda stop voicing underscores the Competence–Performance distinction and its relevance in thinking about markedness. Coda stop voicing is rare, but rarity is irrelevant to Competence. Competence mechanisms must generate all attested phenomena, no matter how rare they are. Even after generating everything that exists, though, there is a core of phenomena that never occur. No language ever has epenthetic dorsals or neutralizes PoA to dorsal, for example.

8.3.5 Summary

To summarize, there are good indications that not all markedness asymmetries can be ascribed to Performance phenomena, such as mechanisms employed in language learning and diachronic change. Diachronic tendencies differ from markedness asymmetries: while *t→k is a valid diachronic change, /t/→[k] is not a possible synchronic neutralization. Another is that natural diachronic changes could make a variety of languages that never exist, such as the diachronic *a→ə that never results in attraction to lower sonority vowels, and *t→k that never results in [k] epenthesis.

In short, Competence effects must be carefully separated from Performance tendencies. Diachronic approaches to markedness are potentially useful as ways to approach generalizations about Performance asymmetries, but they cannot replace Competence mechanisms: language is much more constrained than diachronic accounts predict.

8.4   Representational complexity is not markedness

In the theory proposed in this book markedness effects come about through constraint interaction, following Smolensky (1993). For example, the fact that epenthetic elements can be glottal but never dorsal is expressed by the fact that there is no constraint that favours dorsal over glottal PoA.

In contrast, a number of theories relate markedness directly to representational complexity; they are called 'representational markedness theories' here. In general terms, such theories claim that the least-marked value of a feature is not present in phonological representation. Glottals must therefore lack PoA features (Clements 1985; Sagey 1986; Hayes 1986; Steriade 1987b; McCarthy

1988; Avery & Rice 1989b; Clements & Hume 1995:§3.3.2; Rice & Avery 1995; Broselow 2001). (In fact, some have proposed that glottals lack a Place node, too.)

(9)   Placeless glottal theory

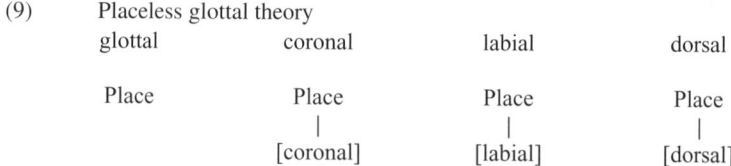

There is some disagreement over whether glottals or coronals lack place features (e.g. Lombardi 1995; cf. Paradis & Prunet 1991a:6ff.). Either way, the view is that the least-marked element is representationally less complex than more-marked elements.

Representational complexity is related to markedness by means of output constraints or rules which reduce structure. For example, neutralization to glottal can be achieved by deleting the Place node's dependents; the resulting featureless segment is phonetically interpreted as glottal. This process is illustrated in (10).

(10)

In representational theories, structure-deleting rules/constraints are the only ones possible, along with rules of reassociation. If structure-building or changing rules/constraints were permitted, representational complexity could increase thereby incorrectly producing processes that cause an increase in markedness.

There has been a great deal of work on representational complexity and markedness, often in terms of underspecification theory (see esp. Kiparsky 1982, 1985; Archangeli 1984, 1988) and feature privativity (e.g. Lombardi 1991). The limited space available here prevents detailed discussion of each different proposal. Instead, §8.4.1 aims to identify general properties of representational-markedness theories. Section 8.4.2 focuses on Rice's (1996) 'Default Variability' theory, which is one of the most elaborate representational approaches to markedness (also Rice & Causley 1998; Causley 1999; Rice 1999a,b, 2004a,b, 2006). Finally, §8.4.3 presents a case study which exemplifies many of the problems for representational theories identified in this chapter.

This section builds on a number of previous arguments that underspecification is not related to markedness and/or that underspecification is flawed (e.g. Kingston & Solnit 1989; Mohanan 1991; Akinlabi 1993; McCarthy 1994; McCarthy & Taub 1992; Steriade 1995b; cf. Ghini 2001:31ff.).

8.4.1 Predictions of representational theories of markedness

The most widely accepted version of representational markedness theories makes two assumptions. One is that for each (or at least many) features, the unmarked value is not represented in the phonological representation. The other is that lack of specification is universally fixed. So, glottals in every language have no Place features (or are perhaps entirely featureless).[1] These assumptions result in several strong predictions, outlined in (11).

(11)   Predictions of representational-markedness theories
       If the unmarked value of feature ([uF]) is not phonologically specified, then
       (a) [uF] will always be the **output** of F-related phenomena
       (b) [uF] will always **undergo** F-phenomena
       (c) [uF] will **never trigger** F-phenomena
       (d) [uF] will **never block** any phenomena

Each of these points will be discussed in turn, focusing on PoA. While glottals will be assumed to be placeless, a great deal of work assumes that coronals have no PoA (e.g. articles in Paradis & Prunet 1991b); nevertheless, the points made are valid no matter which PoA is taken to be placeless.[2]

8.4.1.1   Targets

A representational theory of markedness predicts that glottals will always be the target of PoA-related processes. This follows from the idea that markedness reduction is the simplification of representational complexity. Neutralization is expressed as deletion of PoA features. Deletion of PoA features results in an empty Place node, which is interpreted as glottal, as in (10). So, the least-marked PoA – glottal – is the target of PoA neutralization because its representation

---

[1] Some approaches allow representation to be determined on a language-specific basis (Morén 2003), or allow restricted structural variation (Rice 1996 – see §8.4.2). As this issue relates closely to the idea of universality of markedness and contrastiveness, see §8.2.1 and §8.5 for discussion.

[2] It has also been proposed that featureless segments may be susceptible to co-articulatory effects of neighbouring segments, or may not require a particular articulatory target (Choi 1992b). The discussion here focuses on phonological phenomena only.

is the least complex and the grammar seeks to eliminate representational complexity.

One problem with this approach is that it cannot make multiple distinctions in markedness as there are only two types of representational complexity: having a PoA node and not having one. 'Markedness promotion' therefore poses a problem. Cases of neutralization to glottal PoA must be explained under this theory by having placeless glottals. However, this poses a problem for cases of neutralization to coronal: if neutralization is deletion of place and coronals are not placeless, then neutralization to coronal should be impossible.

The same point can be made for epenthesis. Under the representational theory of markedness, epenthesis must be insertion of the structurally minimal element — i.e. it must be placeless. In languages with [?] insertion, glottals are clearly placeless. However, in languages with coronal epenthesis (e.g. Axininca Campa — §3.2.3), coronal must be placeless.

The conflict in this issue is evident in the controversy over which of coronal and glottal is placeless, and therefore unmarked (Paradis & Prunet 1991a; cf. Lombardi 2002). The difficulty is that the same phenomena provide evidence for both — coronals and glottals are both outputs of neutralization and of epenthesis.

From the point of view of the theory proposed in this book, the problem the representational theory faces is that it has only one hierarchy: i.e. | some structure 〉 no structure |. In contrast, CoMP allows many different factors (i.e. markedness hierarchies) to affect outputs. Glottals are least marked when the PoA hierarchy dominates in a language, but coronals can be least marked when the sonority hierarchy dominates. In short, the representational theory is simply not rich enough.

One way to maintain a representational-markedness theory and capture the variability of coronal and glottal unmarkedness is to abandon representational universality: glottals could have no PoA features in one language, but coronals could be placeless in another (e.g. Morén 2003). However, this approach faces difficulties in languages in which both glottals and coronals are the output targets of neutralization. 'Velarizing' dialects of Spanish discussed by Trigo (1988:78ff.) provide an example. The 'velar' nasal is interpreted here as glottal.

(12)   'Velarizing' Spanish dialects (Trigo 1988:78ff.)
       (a) Fricatives become glottal [h] in codas
           /tos/ → [toh] 'cough'   cf. [to.s-eh] 'coughs'
           /difteria/ → [dihteria]~[difteria] 'diphtheria'

8.4 *Representational complexity is not markedness* 359

(b) Nasals become glottal [N] in codas
/tren/ → [treN]   'train'   cf. [tre.n-eh] 'trains'
/desdeɲ/ → [desdeN] 'disdain' cf. [des.de.ɲ-ar] {verbalizer}
/adam/ → [adaN]   'Adam'   cf. [a.da.mis.mo] 'Adam-ism'
(c) Laterals become coronal in codas
/detaʎ/ → [detal]   'retail'   cf. [de.ta.ʎis.ta] 'retailer'
[eʎa] 'she'   cf. [el] 'he'
[donseʎa] 'lass'   cf. [donsel] 'lad'

Assimilation blocks neutralization, as in Yamphu (§4.2.1.2), so explaining the form of [des.deN], *[deh.deN]

To account for neutralization to glottals in (12a) and (b), a representational theory would need placeless glottals. However, if neutralization is deletion of Place features, (12c) implies that coronals are also placeless as laterals become coronal in codas.

It is possible to avoid this problem by abandoning the idea that there is a straightforward phonetic interpretation of placeless segments. A more elaborate theory could interpret placeless stops and fricatives as glottal but placeless liquids as coronal; after all, there are no glottal liquids. However, there is a second nasal neutralization that presents a problem even for this approach. The stem-final nasal's PoA neutralizes to *coronal* in the onset position of word-level suffixes: e.g. /desdeɲ-es/ → [des.de.nes], *[des.de.ɲes], *[des.de.Nes], /adam-es/ → [a.da.nes], *[a.da.mes], *[a.da.Nes]. These suffixes contrast with vowel-initial stem-level suffixes, where the underlying nasal's PoA is preserved (12a,b). So, the representational theory predicts that coronals must lack Place features because /m/ and /ɲ/ neutralize to coronal in this environment. However, glottals must also be placeless because /m/ and /ɲ/ neutralize glottal [N] in codas. Of course, both glottals and coronals cannot be placeless as they would then not be phonologically distinct.

In CoMP, such variation in neutralization can be achieved straightforwardly. Neutralization to glottals in codas comes about when *{dors,lab,cor} outranks *−Δ$_\sigma$/glottal, as shown in (13).

(13)   Velarizing Spanish I

/adam/	*{dors,lab,cor}	*−Δ$_\sigma$/glottal	IDENT{dors,lab,cor}
(a) adam	* *!		
(b) adan	* *!		
☞ (c) adaN	*	*	*

360   8 *Predictions and alternatives*

However, glottals are banned in onsets by the constraint *$-\Delta_\mu$/glottal. Consequently, nasals neutralize to the next least-marked PoA available – coronal. Tableau (14) shows how the coronal-favouring constraint *{dors,lab} eliminates the faithful candidate (a), and how *$-\Delta_\mu$/glottal blocks neutralization to glottal [N] in onsets.

(14)   Velarizing Spanish II

/adam-es/	*{dors,lab}	*$-\Delta_\mu$/glottal	*{dors,lab,cor}
(a) a.da.mes	*!		* * *
(b) a.da.Nes		*!	* *
☞ (c) a.da.nes			* * *

The ranking still allows /m/ to neutralize to [N] in codas as *$-\Delta_\mu$/glottal only bans glottals in onsets.[3]

/m/ does not neutralize in onsets within the stem: e.g. /adam-ismo/ → [a.da.mis.mo], *[a.da.nis.mo]. This can be achieved by using the positional faithfulness constraint Stem-onset-IDENT{dors,lab,cor}, which preserves PoA features in stem-internal onsets. This constraint is a composite of onset-IDENT{dors,lab,cor}, used in chapter 4 for Yamphu and Catalan, and the stem faithfulness constraints used for Axininca Campa in §3.2.3. It outranks *{dors,lab} here. The ranking is given in (15).

As a final point, the ranking ‖ *{dors,lab} » IDENT{dors,lab,cor} ‖ explains why the corono-dorsal /ʎ/ becomes coronal [l] in codas.

(15)   'Velarizing' Spanish ranking

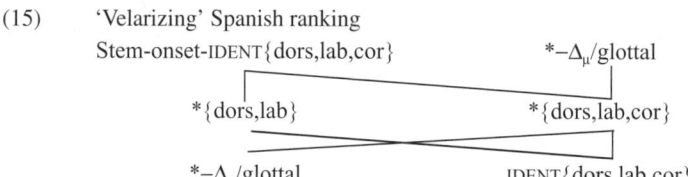

In short, if neutralization is deletion of features and the output of PoA neutralization is a placeless segment, the representational approach to markedness results in a contradiction in 'velarizing' Spanish: both [n] and [N] must be placeless. In contrast, there is no contradiction if PoA neutralization is influenced by two partially conflicting hierarchies.

---

3   In non-velarizing dialects of Spanish, the mapping /adam/ → [a.da.nes] could be analysed as involving faithfulness to /adam/'s paradigmatic base form, which would be [adan]. This analysis is not possible in velarizing dialects because the base of /adam/ is [adaN].

8.4 Representational complexity is not markedness 361

To summarize, the simplest representational theory of markedness makes incorrect predictions about targets of processes as it cannot deal with multiple markedness distinctions. A way for a representational theory of markedness to avoid this problem is to claim that there is a hierarchy of representational complexity. For example, Rice (1996) proposes that coronals are less complex than labials and dorsals, and glottals are less complex than coronals. Rice's theory is discussed in §8.4.2. It is shown to still face problems regarding undergoers, triggers, and blockers of phonological processes; these are discussed next.

8.4.1.2 Undergoers
A representational theory of markedness predicts that placeless elements will always undergo some PoA-related processes and never undergo others.

8.4.1.2.1 Placeless segments must undergo assimilation
If coronals have no place features, they cannot be prevented from undergoing assimilation if assimilation takes place at all; this point has been developed in detail by Kiparsky (1985:97), Avery & Rice (1989b), and Cho (1999). In contrast, if the assimilation process is prevented from deleting features, labials and dorsals will not assimilate. Thus, the Catalan assimilation system is produced in which only coronals assimilate. The idea is schematically represented in (16).

(16) (a) Assimilation applies to coronals

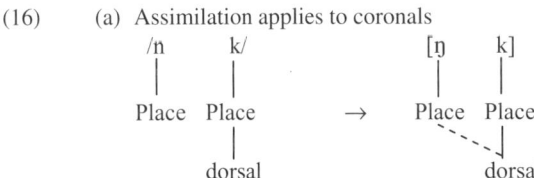

(b) Assimilation is blocked from applying to labials and dorsals

One strong prediction of this proposal is that the Catalan system is the only type of 'selective' assimilation that can exist. Assimilation applies freely to coronals because they have no place features, so it could never apply to labials or dorsals. So, there can be no system like Catalan except that only dorsals or labials undergo assimilation. The other implication is that there can never be selective assimilation systems in which more than one PoA undergoes assimilation. For example, there cannot be any system in which both coronals and labials undergo assimilation but dorsals do not as this would imply that coronals and glottals are both placeless, and therefore phonologically indistinct.

As discussed at length in §4.3.2, both these predictions are incorrect: any PoA may undergo assimilation. Sri Lankan Portuguese creole presents a problem for both points (Hume & Tserdanelis 2002). In SLP creole, dorsals and labials undergo assimilation while coronals do not. If such selective assimilation is related to lack of PoA features, labials and dorsals must both be placeless. Not only does this contradict the idea that coronals or glottals are placeless, it is impossible as labials and dorsals would be phonologically indistinct. Similarly, Chukchi's selective assimilation system means that dorsals must be placeless, given the reasoning above, and Harar Oromo's implies that labials must be placeless (§4.3.3).

SLP creole is certainly not alone in being the only selective assimilation system with more than one undergoer. In Yamphu, glottal and coronal stops assimilate to the PoA of a following obstruent while dorsals and labials do not (§4.2.1.2). Again, this creates the contradiction that both coronals and glottals lack place features.

8.4.1.2.2 Placeless segments cannot undergo dissimilation
While lack of place specification demands that placeless elements undergo assimilation, the placeless glottal proposal also predicts that glottals should be unable to undergo certain processes. For example, McCarthy (1994) observes that if glottals are placeless OCP restrictions on PoA should be unable to eliminate them. However, this is not so: McCarthy shows that gutturals and glottals act as a class in Arabic – no two elements from the set [χ ʁ ħ ʕ h ʔ] can appear in the same root (see also Hayward & Hayward 1989).

The same points can be made for many other processes. For example, Oostendorp (1995) relates lack of vowel features and stress avoidance. In this view, it is schwa's lack of features that repels stress. However, in Nganasan [ɨ], [ə], and [i y u] all repel stress to the same extent (§5.4, de Lacy 2004). The same point arises in Gujarati (§5.3): stress avoids schwa, but it also avoids high and mid-peripheral vowels when an [a] is available. These vowels cannot all be featureless, so it is clear that the idea that lack of features indicates failure to undergo stressing is not sufficient to account for the empirical facts about undergoers.

8.4 Representational complexity is not markedness 363

In summary, the representational complexity approach to markedness predicts that structurally non-complex elements (or at least structurally empty elements) must undergo assimilation and cannot undergo dissimilation. Both these predictions are incorrect. Any PoA may undergo assimilation, more than one PoA can assimilate while others do not, and any PoA may dissimilate. Therefore, there is no relation between representational complexity and the susceptibility of elements to undergo phonological processes.

8.4.1.3 Triggers

Representational markedness theories make predictions about which elements should be able to trigger processes. If a feature value does not exist, it should be unable to trigger a process like assimilation (McCarthy & Taub 1992). So, if glottals are placeless, they should not be able to trigger place assimilation (e.g. Rice & Causley 1998).

However, glottals can trigger place assimilation, and so can every other PoA. Yamphu provides a relevant example: stops assimilate to /ʔ/ and /h/. Before /h/, stops surface as [ʔ]: /mo-do<u>k</u>-ha/ → [modoʔha] 'like those', /læːt-he-ma/ → [læːʔhema] 'to be able to do' (Rutgers 1998:48). Before /ʔ/, stops are also banned; a /stop+ʔ/ cluster emerges as a single glottal stop [ʔ], presumably because geminate [ʔː] is banned: e.g. /læːt-ʔa-ma/ → [læːʔama] 'to go and do', /kʰik-ʔiʔi/ → [kʰiʔiʔi] 'it's bitter'. This process is assimilation to glottals and not neutralization: in coda position only /t/ neutralizes to [ʔ]; /k/ and /p/ do not (e.g. [ʔok.ma] 'find+infinitive', cf. /let-ma/→[leʔ.ma] 'be brief+infinitive').

Yamphu is not unique. Nganasan's nasals assimilate to the PoA of a following consonant. Before [h], the nasals /m n ɲ/ become [N]: [kotu-bam-bum] 'I kill {renarrative}', cf. [kotu-baN-humə] 'you (sg.) kill {renarrative}' (Helimski 1998:495, 506).

The same point has been made for [−voice]: Wetzels & Mascaró (2001) identify languages in which there is assimilation to [−voice] only, and there is no coda voicing neutralization (also see de Lacy 2002a:§7.4.4). Therefore, [voice] cannot be privative.

McCarthy (1994:207ff.) provides further arguments against the placeless glottal proposal, showing that glottals trigger vowel-consonant assimilation. Vowels can assimilate to the PoA feature of glottals (and pharyngeals and uvulars), resulting in lowering. For example, the feminine /-e/ in Syrian Arabic lowers to [a] after glottals, pharyngeals, and uvulars: e.g. [waːʒh-a] 'display', [mniːħ-a] 'good', [dagːaːʀ-a] 'tanning', cf. [daraʒ-e] 'step'. For other cases, see §8.4.3 and Rose (1996). So, representational markedness theories face a significant problem in processes where putatively featureless segments trigger assimilation.

It is not possible to avoid the triggering problem by claiming that languages differ as to which PoAs are unspecified, and that glottals happen to be specified for PoA in Yamphu, Nganasan, and Syrian Arabic. The problem is that some diagnostics may require glottals to be placeless in a language in which they trigger phenomena. For example, Yamphu glottals trigger assimilation, so must be specified for place; however, other PoAs neutralize to glottals, with the implication that glottals are placeless.

In any case, there is good reason to reject the premise that failure to trigger assimilation indicates lack of place features. While dorsals trigger assimilation in Korean, labials and coronals do not (Kim 1973; Kim-Renaud 1974, 1986; Iverson & Kim 1987; Jun 1995; Ahn 1998; Cho 1988, 1999; de Lacy 2002a:§7.5.2). If failure to trigger assimilation means lack of place features, then both labials and coronals must be placeless, and therefore phonologically indistinct.

One attempt to avoid the triggering problem is to allow assimilation to require agreement of adjacent consonants in having *no* place features. In other words, Yamphu glottal assimilation can be seen as a demand that adjacent obstruents agree in having an identical state of featurelessness. The problem is that it is not clear how to express this demand formally: if assimilation is spreading of features, there is clearly nothing to spread from a featureless segment. In any case, devising a way to demand agreement in featurelessness effectively gives featurelessness the same status as a specified feature, and so undercuts the premise of the theory and severely curtails its predictive power.

In short, representational markedness theories predict that unspecified elements are unable to trigger processes; however, the facts are against this prediction.

8.4.1.4 Blockers

If glottals lack place features, they should be unable to block place-related processes. For example, in the string /nʔp/ the /n/'s [coronal] feature is adjacent to the /p/'s [labial] feature. So, the /n/ should be able to assimilate to the /p/ to produce [mʔp].

A more extended example involves dissimilation. There are very robust generalizations about permissible consonants in the Polynesian language Māori (Krupa 1966). A root cannot contain more than one labial consonant, unless

8.4 Representational complexity is not markedness 365

they are identical. So, acceptable words are [pape] 'be wrong', [mame] 'a dog with short bristly hair', [fafe] 'scoop up', and [wawe] 'soon'. Unacceptable words are *[pafe], *[pame], *[pawe], *[fame], *[wafe], *[hapafe], and so on. The only exceptions are loanwords (e.g. [pamu] < English 'farm', [paːma] < English 'palm'); there are some native words that also have variants with the offending element (e.g. [pafera]~[pahera] 'open'). The restriction does not apply over morpheme boundaries (e.g. [ma+faki] 'torn off').

However, the restriction does not hold if the consonants are separated by another: e.g. [pakufa] 'formal handing over of a bride', [paremo] 'drowned', [pakewa] 'solitary', [mokopu] {ancient song-word} (Williams 1971). This blocking effect can be ascribed to the fact that the [labial] features are not adjacent on the consonant-place tier in these words.[4] So, if the glottal [h] is placeless, words like [pahemo] 'pass by, pass on' should be impossible; in [pahemo] the [p] and [m]'s [labial] features should be tier-adjacent, and therefore banned. There are many other words that pose the same problem: [pahemo] 'pass by, pass on', [pahawa] 'smeared', [pahewa] 'mistaken', [pahiwi] 'jerk', [pohewa] 'mistaken, confused', [mahewa] 'a univalve mollusc'.

The ban on nearby [labial] features also applies to consonant-vowel interactions (de Lacy 1998). All sequences of labial continuants are banned: *[{u,o}f, f{u,o}, {u,o}w, w{u,o}, uo]. The only exception is [ou], which is the only cluster to appear in the same syllable constituent. However, if glottals are placeless, sequences like [uho] and [ohu] should have tier-adjacent [labial] features, and so be banned. Again, they are not: e.g. [uho] 'heart, pith, sound', [kauho] 'legend', [uhono] 'splice', [ohu] 'volunteer workers', [kohuka] 'froth, foam', [kohuki] 'turn', [pohuka] 'small, stunted', [tohu] 'mark, sign', and [tohuŋa] 'skilled person'.

Certainly, glottals are transparent to some processes in some languages. However, a representational approach in which they are featureless or placeless predicts that they should *always* be transparent, and they are not. In addition, the transparency of a segment does not imply that it lacks features. Gafos & Lombardi (1999) and Walker (1998) show that there is a hierarchy of transparency in harmony and assimilation, with highly sonorous segments (i.e. glottals, glides, liquids) most likely to be transparent, and low sonority segments less so. Their results show that transparency is due to constraint interaction, not lack of representational structure.

---

4 The Māori labial consonant restriction is not restricted to prosodic domains such as the foot. Words such as *[('pafe)] and *[('hape)fe] are both impossible.

8.4.2 Default variability and elaborated representation[5]

The preceding discussion has identified a number of problems for representational theories of markedness, and particularly ones that identify either coronals or glottals as lacking place features. At this point, a question remains: could the problems identified above be avoided by a more elaborate representational theory?

To answer this question, this section examines Rice's (1996) 'Default Variability' (DV) theory of representation and markedness. DV proposes a close correlation of markedness and structure: less-marked PoAs are representational proper substructures of more-marked PoAs, as in (17).

(17) Default variability surface representations

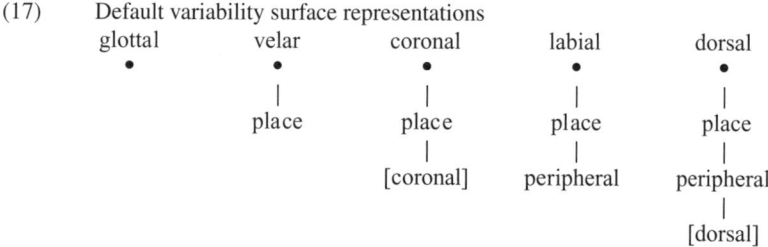

No explicit representation of glottals is given in Rice 1996; the glottal representation above is taken from Rice & Causley 1998, who propose that they have no place node. The other important point is that DV has velar as less marked than coronals, while other dorsals (e.g. uvulars) are more marked. This hierarchy will be discussed further below.

DV is the focus of this section because it develops the idea that representation is related to markedness further than any other theory. It also makes clear predictions, and has been developed in subsequent work (Rice & Causley 1998; Causley 1999). I should add that this section will not discuss a different proposal by Rice (1999a,b, 2004a,b, 2006) – that markedness is closely tied to contrastiveness; see §8.5 for discussion.

The general principle behind DV is clearly that for a markedness hierarchy | x 〉 y 〉 z |, z's structure will be a proper substructure of y's, and y's will be a proper substructure of x's. It therefore offers a potential way to avoid some of the problems noted in previous sections, where the unmarked PoA varies from language to language. It allows different types of neutralization depending on which structural elements are eliminated. For example, neutralization to glottal

---

5 My thanks to Keren Rice for discussing many of the issues raised in this section with me.

is deletion of the place node, while neutralization to velar is deletion of all dependents of the place node.

Nevertheless, DV faces a number of empirical problems. Problems involving triggering and neutralization of dorsals to labials will be discussed first. The remainder of the section will focus on the 'default variability' hypothesis, which is closely related to the 'velar-unmarkedness' theory.

8.4.2.1 Triggering

DV theory faces the same empirical problem that all representational theories face: triggering and blocking. DV predicts that a process cannot be triggered by a featureless segment. Consequently, glottals (at least) are predicted to 'behave differently from other consonant types in that they are neither triggers nor targets of assimilation/spreading processes' (Rice & Causley 1998). Both of these predictions are incorrect, as seen in §8.4.1.3, §8.4.1.4, and McCarthy 1994. Further discussion of triggering and representational theories will be given in §8.4.3.

8.4.2.2 Neutralization of dorsal to labial

DV predicts impossible neutralizations. As in other representational theories, neutralization is deletion of structure. Deletion of the place node results in neutralization to glottal PoA, and deletion of the place node's dependents results in neutralization to velar. Similarly, deletion of dependents of the peripheral node predicts that dorsals could become labials (e.g. /q/→[p]). However, as discussed in §3.3.4, PoA neutralization always produces glottals or coronals, never labials (excepting approximants).

Rice & Causley (1998) present a revised version of PoA representations in which labials have a place node which dominates the feature [labial]. While this representation avoids the problem just noted, it faces another problem: how to identify dorsals as more marked than labials. This distinction is necessary in languages that neutralize uvulars but not labials (e.g. Kashaya – §5.2.4), and to account for the fact that there are implicational relations in triggering of assimilation: dorsals always trigger PoA assimilation, while labials do not (Mohanan 1993; Jun 1995; de Lacy 2002a:§7.5).

8.4.2.3 Default Variability

A core idea in DV theory is that languages can choose which PoA can be the default. For DV theory, the choice is between coronals and velars (Rice 1996 does not discuss the role of glottals in any detail). The mechanism of 'default variability' is outlined in (18), adapted from Rice (1996:496).

368   8 *Predictions and alternatives*

(18)   Default variability
       If an underlying segment has a place node with no dependents, then
       (a) it can be given a [coronal] dependent, or
       (b) it can get a place dependent by assimilation (i.e. feature spreading), or
       (c) it can persist with no place dependents
           • A place node with no dependents is phonetically interpreted as velar.

So, there are effectively two defaults. The segment with least structure – i.e. a segment with an empty place node – is velar. However, an independent process can add a [coronal] feature to an empty place node, so the default segment can become coronal. The default (i.e. least-marked) PoA can therefore vary: it can be either velar or coronal. The [coronal] insertion rule can be restricted to particular environments. For example, onset consonants can be assigned a [coronal] node, while coda consonants are not; consequently, coronals will be defaults in onsets, but velars will be defaults in codas.

There are two separate issues to address in this proposal. One is whether variability in markedness can be derived from conditions on representation. The other is whether velars can ever be treated as less marked than coronals and/or glottals.

Causley's (1999) analysis of variation between epenthetic [ʔ] and [t] is useful in regard to the issue of whether variability relates to representation. [ʔ] has no place node in Causley's theory, so a general ban on structure (e.g. *STRUC) will produce a glottal. Other epenthetic PoAs come about through constraints that require structural complexity. For example, Causley (1999:64) proposes the constraint SEGPLACE 'Every root node dominates a place node'; if SEGPLACE outranks *STRUC, the epenthetic consonant will be the velar [k]. To get epenthetic [t], DV needs another constraint, like SEGCOR: 'Every place node dominates [coronal]'. In short, the Causley/DV approach to markedness variation is that there is direct conflict between requirements to minimize structure (*STRUC) and demands to have structure (SEGPLACE, SEGCOR).

In contrast, the theory proposed in this book produces variation through indirect hierarchy conflict. There are two independent markedness hierarchies – PoA and sonority. If PoA dominates, glottals will be the preferred PoA. Because glottals happen to be marked on the sonority hierarchy, coronals will be the preferred PoA if the sonority constraints dominate. The benefit of the 'indirect' conflict approach is that all the constraints are motivated by markedness hierarchies. The constraints that favour glottals come from the PoA hierarchy, whereas the constraints that favour coronals derive from the sonority hierarchy.

In contrast, while *STRUC in the DV/Causley theory is motivated by the pressure to minimize structure, it is not clear where the SEGPLACE and SEGCOR constraints derive from. They cannot come from a mechanism that seeks to

8.4 Representational complexity is not markedness 369

maximize structure, otherwise there should be a SEGPERIPHERAL and SEGDORSAL constraint as well, fatally predicting epenthetic labials and dorsals. So, while CoMP gets markedness variability through the conflict of different markedness hierarchies, the DV/Causley approach gets it through the conflicting requirement of structure-minimization and more limited structure-maximization, and it is not clear what broader principle the structure-maximization constraints derive from.

8.4.2.4 Velar unmarkedness

DV's proposal that velars can be unmarked is also found in previous and subsequent work (Williamson 1977:698; Kaye, Lowenstamm, and Vergnaud 1985, 1989:74; Trigo 1988; Harris 1990:264; Oostendorp 1999). Of these proposals, Trigo (1988) proposes that velars are the least-marked consonant in coda position only. DV's ability to allow the default to differ in onsets and codas in part captures Trigo's proposal. The aim here is to show that the velar-unmarkedness hypothesis is incorrect. This discussion builds on Paradis & Prunet's (1990, 1994) critique.

To make an important clarification, DV does not claim that all velars are unmarked: there are effectively two different representations of [k g ŋ x ɣ]: those without a place node and no dependents, and those with a [dorsal] node. DV's claim is that the unmarked PoA structure (i.e. a place node with no dependents) is phonetically realized as velar. It also proposes that segments without place dependents come about through neutralization, assimilation, and epenthesis; therefore, these processes should produce phonological structures that are realized as velar, such as [k] and [ŋ].

In terms of velar unmarkedness, the difference between CoMP and DV is therefore almost entirely about phonetic interpretation. DV proposes that the least-marked place structure is phonetically interpreted as velar while CoMP proposes that the least-marked PoA feature — [glottal] — is usually produced with glottal constriction (i.e. [ʔ], never [k]; [h], never [x]), but will be produced with velar~uvular occlusion as a side effect of nasal production. In a sense, then, the phonetically discernible difference between the theories is that DV predicts that obstruent velars [k g x ɣ] can be the realization of the least-marked PoA structure, while CoMP claims that they cannot; both agree somewhat in regard to nasals — i.e. that an 'ŋ'-like sound can pattern as having the least-marked PoA.

To give an example, Rice (1996) observes that Selayarese nasals all neutralize to what is described as 'ŋ' in prosodic word-final codas: e.g. [pekampekaŋ] 'hook' (Mithun & Basri 1986); in medial codas, nasals assimilate to the PoA of the following segment. However, there is an alternative account of Selayarese. In §2.2.1.1 and §3.4.2 it was argued that there is a glottal nasal [N]; [N]'s phonetic realization requires constriction at the back of the vocal tract, resulting in a velar or uvular. In CoMP, the Selayarese neutralization must produce the glottal [N], not the velar [ŋ].

So, both DV and CoMP have accounts of Selayarese nasal PoA neutralization (at least, the two theories are phonetically indistinguishable). However, they differ in their predictions for oral stops. CoMP predicts that oral stop PoA must neutralize to glottal, while DV predicts that it could become velar. As it turns out, all unassimilated coda stops are [ʔ] in Selayarese: e.g. [laʔbaʔ] 'wide', [taʔdoʔdoʔ] 'be sleepy'; [k] is not permitted in codas. The same facts are found in the closely related Buginese (Podesva 2000).

However, DV can account for Selayarese by using two different rules. One deletes all place dependents for nasals, producing a velar. The other deletes the place node itself entirely for stops, producing a glottal. Rice (1996) suggests that neutralization of stops to glottal may in fact be related to sonority. So, for CoMP, neutralization of PoA for Selayarese nasals and stops is part of the same process; for DV, nasals and stops undergo different processes.

Where the theories differ strikingly is in their typological predictions. DV predicts that there could be some language in which nasals neutralize to [ŋ], stops to [k], and/or fricatives to [x]. This neutralization would come about when only the rule that deletes place dependents is active. In contrast, the theory proposed here cannot produce such neutralization. It predicts that in all cases where nasals are described as neutralizing to 'ŋ' they actually neutralize to glottal [N]; in the same language stop PoA neutralization will produce [ʔ], and fricatives will become [h].[6]

To summarize, CoMP is more restrictive than DV. Both theories allow for cases where nasals become 'ŋ' (i.e. glottal [N] here, velar [ŋ] in DV). However, while DV predicts neutralization of stops to [k] and fricatives to [x], this is impossible in CoMP. This is a major problem for the velar-unmarkedness hypothesis as there is no language in which stops actively neutralize to [k]

---

6 Classical Fuzhou has been cited as allowing only [k] and 'ŋ' in codas. However, Chan (1985) reports that it also allowed coda [ʔ]. Classical Fuzhou *k has become Modern Fuzhou [ʔ] so that Modern Fuzhou codas allow only [ʔ] and [N]. There is no descendent of Classical Fuzhou that allows only [k] and [ŋ] in codas. Rice (1996) discusses South Vietnamese coda restrictions, a language which seems to come close to having neutralization of stops to [k]. In South Vietnamese, only [p m t n] are allowed as codas after the high front vowels [i e] and front [æ]. In contrast, only [p m k ŋ] are allowed after [ɛ] and back vowels. Finally, [p m t n k ŋ] are allowed after the central vowel [a]. This is not relevant to present concerns as codas are clearly influenced by assimilation here: front vowels ban back consonants [k ŋ] from following them, and back vowels ban following front consonants [t n]. The only clear view of coda restrictions is seen after the central (i.e. non-front and non-back) vowel [a]; both [t] and [k] can appear in this environment, showing that there is no general process of PoA neutralization to dorsals.

8.4 *Representational complexity is not markedness* 371

and fricatives to [x]. Every case which has been cited as having neutralization to velar involves nasals, and if stops or fricatives neutralize in the same language they always become glottal. For example, Rice (1996) cites Kagoshima Japanese as having neutralization of nasals to [ŋ]; however, its stops neutralize to [ʔ], not [k] (§2.2.1.1; Trigo 1988). Andalusian Spanish and Puerto Rican Spanish has neutralization of nasals to [ŋ], but its fricative /s/ neutralizes to the glottal [h], not velar [x] (Trigo 1988; Rice 1996:506–7). The lack of stop neutralization to [k] and fricative neutralization to [x] is a surprising gap for DV, but predicted by CoMP.

8.4.2.5 Distribution of 'ŋ'/[N]

A further problem for DV is in dealing with the restricted distribution of 'ŋ' in many languages. For example, Buriat [n] and 'ŋ' are in complementary distribution (Poppe 1960). [n] appears in onsets and in codas before coronals (e.g. [namar] 'autumn', [ende] 'here') and 'ŋ' appears in codas and before dorsals (e.g. [aŋχaŋ] 'beginning').

If the Buriat 'ŋ' is really velar, there are two major problems for DV to overcome. One is that other velars are not restricted in the same way: e.g. [k] can appear in onsets and codas (e.g. [koloːni] 'colony', [beʃək] 'letter, writing'). In fact, there is no language that bans non-nasal velars in onsets but allows them in codas (§3.2.3). In contrast, a number of languages ban glottals in onset position alone (e.g. Chamicuro, Macushi Carib, Standard Malay – Parker 1994b). So, if 'ŋ' is really glottal [N] its distribution is easy to explain as another case of restrictions on glottals. If 'ŋ' is actually velar, as in DV, then the lack of restrictions on all other velars is a significant puzzle.

Languages like Buriat include Dutch (Oostendorp 1999), Miogliola (Ghini 2001), and English (McCarthy 2001a). In English, for example, 'ŋ' cannot appear in onsets, and it can only appear as a moraic coda: i.e. [sɪ$^\mu$ŋ$^\mu$] 'sing', *[si$^{\mu\mu}$ŋ]. In Miogliola, 'ŋ' only appears in codas.

8.4.2.6 Restrictions on default variability

Focusing on a related aspect of DV theory, one of the core ideas is that the default can vary in different positions. For example, in Genovese the 'default' nasal in onsets is [n] while the coda default is 'ŋ' (Ghini 2001:172ff.).

(19) Genovese nasal PoA distribution
    (a) Only 'ŋ' is allowed in codas (p.173)
        ['puŋ.pa] 'pump'   [ɔ.'feŋ.de] 'to insult'
        ['aŋ.dʒow] 'angel'

372   8 Predictions and alternatives

    (b) All PoA constrasts appear in the post-tonic onset (p.172)
       ['ra.mu] 'branch'   ['ra.ɲu] 'spider'
       ['pe.na] 'pen'   ['pe.ŋa] 'penalty, pain'
    (c) In other onsets, 'ŋ' becomes coronal [n] (p.175)
       /raʒuŋu-'a/ → [ra.ʒu.'na] 'to reason' cf. [ra.'ʒu.ŋu] 'I reason'
       /seŋu-'a/ → [se.'na] 'to dine'   cf. [se.'ŋa] 'I dine'
       /aluŋtaŋu-aːse/ → [a.luŋ.ta.'naːse] cf. [m a.luŋ.'ta.ŋu] 'I go off'
       'to go off'
    (d) /n/ remains coronal in onsets (p.175)
       /iŋganu/ → [iŋ.'ga.nu] 'I cheat' cf. [iŋ.ga.'na] 'to cheat'

Rice (1996) cites Midi French as a similar case.

DV theory can account for this pattern by having (a) a rule that deletes all dependents of place in codas and (b) a rule that gives an empty place node a [coronal] dependent in non-post-tonic onsets. By rule (a), all codas become [ŋ]. By rule (b), underlying /ŋ/ becomes [n] in non-post-tonic onsets. As rule (b) does not apply to post-tonic /ŋ/, it can surface faithfully in this position, as in ['peŋa].

Such restrictions can also be modelled in CoMP on the assumption that the reported 'ŋ' is actually glottal [N]. As discussed in §3.2.3, glottals are often banned in onsets and codas for sonority reasons. The 'default variability' seen in Midi French therefore follows from a ban on high-sonority onsets (i.e. *−Δ$_μ$/glottal); this constraint forces underlying /N/ to become coronal [n]. In contrast, *{dors,lab,cor} forces coda PoA to neutralize to glottals. This ranking was discussed in §3.3.3 for similar alternations in Miogliola, so it will be summarized in tableau (20) using the hypothetical form /Nan/, which would surface as [naN]. Candidates (a) and (b) preserve the underlying glottal /N/ in an onset, so fatally violating *−Δ$_μ$/glottal. Candidate (c) fails to eliminate the coda coronal, so incurring more violations of *{dors,lab,cor} than (d).

(20)

/Nan/	*−Δ$_μ$/glottal	*{dors,lab,cor}	IDENT{dors,lab,cor,gl}
(a) Nan	*!	*	
(b) NaN	*!		*
(c) nan		**!	*
☞ (d) naN		*	**

To eliminate glottals in onsets while preserving other PoAs, *−Δ$_μ$/glottal must outrank onset-IDENT{dors,lab,cor,gl} which in turn outranks *{dors,lab,cor}.

8.4 Representational complexity is not markedness

The remaining issue is why [n] and [N] can both appear immediately post-tonically: e.g. ['peNa] 'penalty', ['pena] 'pen'. Ghini (2001:174) proposes that post-tonic consonants are ambisyllabic. If $*-\Delta_\mu$/glottal only applies to segments that are exclusively in onset position, then ambisyllabic [N] will remain faithful.

In short, variation in the default or unmarked feature value in CoMP comes about through hierarchy conflict. In Genovese, the PoA hierarchy favours glottals, but this comes into conflict with the sonority hierarchy in onsets, resulting in the variation seen. In contrast, the DV approach employs a structure-deleting rule in codas and a structure-building rule in onsets.

So the theories differ in how they account for variability, but they also differ in their empirical predictions. An important difference relates to which default appears where. DV predicts a language that is the opposite of Genovese: velars would be defaults in onsets while coronals would be defaults in codas. In this language, /na/ would surface as [ŋa] while /aŋ/ would surface as [an]. This situation can come about by (a) a rule that deletes dependents of place in onsets and (b) a rule that inserts [coronal] in codas. (Both these rules are independently necessary. Rule (a) is needed to explain why Colloquial Samoan allows [ŋ] in onsets but not [n], and rule (b) is independently needed to account for languages that have coda neutralization to coronal PoA (§3.3.2).)

However, none of the languages cited in this book have this pattern. In CoMP, the gap follows from the nature of the anti-glottal constraints. Onsets seek to eliminate high-sonority elements, so requiring a constraint like $*-\Delta_\mu$/glottal (de Lacy 2000b; Smith 2002). However, codas seek to maximize sonority, so there is no corresponding *CODA/glottal constraint, though there is a constraint that bans glottals in margins generally ($*-\Delta_\sigma$/glottal – see §3.3.3). With just $*-\Delta_\mu$/glottal and $*-\Delta_\sigma$/glottal, there is no ranking in CoMP that can force neutralization to glottal in onsets but to coronal in codas.

To demonstrate, neutralization to glottal in onsets requires *{dors,lab,cor} to outrank all faithfulness constraints that preserve coronals (e.g. IDENT{dors,lab,cor}) as well as all output constraints that favour coronals over glottals (e.g. $*-\Delta_\mu$/glottal, $*-\Delta_\sigma$/glottal). Tableau (21) illustrates.

(21)

/na/	*{dors,lab,cor}	IDENT{dors,lab,cor}	$*-\Delta_\mu$/glottal	$*-\Delta_\sigma$/glottal
(a) na	*			
☞ (b) Na		*	*	*

For /aN/ to become [an], a constraint that favours coronals over glottals in codas has to outrank all constraints that favour glottals. However, the only coronal-favouring constraints are $*-\Delta_\mu$/glottal and $*-\Delta_\sigma$/glottal, and both of these are rendered inactive by *{dors,lab,cor}, which eliminates glottals. In short, any attempt to have onset coronals become glottal and coda glottals to become coronal will result in a ranking contradiction, and so cannot exist.

To summarize, DV predicts too much default variability. DV predicts languages in which onsets require velars/glottals while codas require coronals; CoMP predicts that such a language cannot exist. In accord with CoMP, no such language has been identified.

8.4.2.7 Other diagnostics for velar unmarkedness

Rice (1996) cites other diagnostics for velar unmarkedness. One is epenthesis of velars; however, the cases of Murut and Uradhi cited by Rice (1996) are not viable epenthesis cases for reasons given in §3.4.1 and in Paradis & Prunet (1994).

Another diagnostic is the output of dissimilation. For example, coronals become velar before another coronal in Dakota reduplicants: e.g. /RED-sut-a/ → [suksuta] 'be strong', /RED-tetʃ-a/ → [tektetʃa] 'to be new' (Shaw 1980:31). Rice (1996) considers Dakota dissimilation to involve the loss of the first consonant's [coronal] feature, producing a placeless consonant which is then interpreted as velar. However, this argument only holds if it is assumed that dissimilation must involve deletion/delinking. In CoMP, there is no feature deletion, so the argument does not hold.

In any case, there needs to be a close examination of dissimilation cases to determine if there is any overt markedness influence. In the Dakota case, I suggest that the reason /t-t/ surfaces as [k-t] is because [k] is the next least-marked and most-faithful segment available. [ʔ] can be ruled out through Glottal Elimination (though /t-t/→ [ʔt] is of course a possible outcome, and attested in Kashaya – Buckley 1994:§3.2.1). The output /p-t/ can be ruled out by faithfulness: [p] does not retain the [−round] specification of /t/. So, the only possible outcome is /k-t/.

A way to distinguish the predictions of DV and CoMP may be found in labial dissimilation. The theory presented here predicts that /labial-labial/ could dissimilate to [coronal-labial] or [glottal-labial], as both options are less marked than [dorsal-labial]. In contrast, DV would predict that the dissimilation /labial-labial/→[dorsal-labial] is possible because velars can be less marked than coronals. The /labial-labial/→[coronal-labial] type is found in Berber, where the reflexive prefix /m/ becomes [n] before another labial (e.g. [n-fara]

8.4 Representational complexity is not markedness 375

'disentangle', cf. [m-xazar] 'scowl' – Alderete 1997). I do not know of a labial dissimilation that produces a velar+labial. It is clear that dissimilation needs re-exploration in the light of the markedness proposals made here.

Rice (1996) also discusses diachronic changes, including changes involving proto-[t] to daughter language [k] (e.g. Luangiua, Hawaiian, colloquial Samoan, Chipewyan, White Mountain Apache, and Kiowa Apache). As discussed in §1.3, diachronic change does not give clear insight into markedness.

Another argument for velar unmarkedness is found in Trigo 1988:90ff. Trigo (1988:90ff.) also cites evidence from transparency to vowel-feature spreading. In Chinook, only the velars [k k' g x], uvulars [q q' ɢ χ], and the glottal [ʔ] are transparent to rounding harmony: e.g. /u-k'asks/ → [uk'usks] 'girl' (cf. [i-k'asks] 'boy'), [u-qunakʃ] 'large boulder' (cf. [i-qanakʃ] 'stone'); cf. [ɑ-l-u-waːʔxit] 'it is caused to be pursued', *[ɑ-l-u-wuːʔxit], [u-lata-is] 'flounder', *[u-lutu-is]. Trigo proposes that the ability of dorsals to allow spreading indicates that they lack any place features. Paradis & Prunet (1994) provide an alternative account, based on the proposal that feature spreading is strictly local (also see Gafos 1996). Consequently, [+round] can only spread through consonants that can bear a [+round] feature. It just so happens that only velars and uvulars can bear such a secondary articulation: [p^w t^w] are not allowed in the language. Paradis & Prunet provide an interesting array of additional cross-linguistic support for their proposal. They adduce a minimally contrasting case from Inor: this language allows labialized labials and velars, and consequently allows rounding harmony to spread through both types, but not coronals. Given the Inor facts, if transparency truly indicated lack of PoA features, one would have to argue that both labials and velars are featureless in Inor – a fatal contradiction which would result in labials and velars no longer being phonologically distinct.

In short, DV is less restrictive than CoMP. DV predicts (a) that stop and fricative PoA could neutralize to velar, (b) a language where coronal onset consonants become velar (or glottal) but codas become coronal, (c) neutralization of dorsal to labial, (d) that a labial could become a velar in dissimilation (e.g. /ap-pa/ → [akpa]), and (e) that there could be epenthetic velars. CoMP does not allow any of these cases, and no apparently supporting cases survive scrutiny. The sole support for the velar-unmarkedness hypothesis comes from cases where nasals reportedly neutralize to the velar 'ŋ'; however, these can – and often must – be analysed as neutralization to the glottal [N].

8.4.3 Conflicting diagnostics

A problem that all representational theories face is that diagnostics for representational complexity may differ within the same language. For example, in Misantla Totonac (MacKay 1994) different diagnostics imply that different PoAs are the 'default', and there are phenomena that require all PoA features to be present.

MacKay describes two dialects: Yecuatla and San Marcos Atesquilapan. In both dialects [ʔ] is epenthesized to avoid onsetless syllables at the beginning of words and in morpheme-internal hiatus (1994:§2.7.1). Assuming a standard approach to representational complexity and markedness, glottals must lack PoA features because epenthesis involves insertion of minimal structure.

(22) Misantla Totonac glottal epenthesis
 (a) /ut ta-uka-laɬ/ → [ʔút taʔukaɬ] 's/he mounted'
 (b) /kin-iʃki/ → [kiʔiʃki] 's/he gives me X'
 (c) /ut a-iːn-ni-laɬ/ → [ʔút ʔaʔiːni-ɬ] 's/he obtained X for Y'

However, another diagnostic suggests that coronals lack PoA features. The discussion in §4.1.2 identified selective assimilation as a diagnostic of placelessness. MacKay (1994:§2.6) reports that /n/ assimilates but /m/ does not, similar to the Catalan situation: e.g. from the morpheme /min/: [mim-puːtʃaqeːn] 'your washbasin', [min-tsiʔ] 'your older sister', [miɲ-tʃik] 'your house', [miŋ-kin] 'your nose', /min-qaʃtal/ → [miɴ-qaʃtal] 'your lime (mineral)'.

In addition, while in both dialects glottals are epenthetic and only coronals assimilate, they differ in PoA neutralization. In San Marcos, word-final /m/ remains [m], but the coronal /n/ becomes the glottal [N]: /min-kam-an/ → [miŋkamaN] 'your children' (McKay 1994:409) (described by MacKay as [ŋ], but interpreted as the glottal [N] here). Therefore, neutralization in San Marcos seems to support the idea that glottals – both [ʔ] and [N] – are placeless.

However, in Yecuatla word-final /m/ neutralizes to [n]: e.g. /kiŋkam/ → [kiŋkan] 'my child' (cf. [kiŋkam] in careful speech) (McKay 1994:380). If neutralization is deletion of PoA features, then nasal PoA neutralization indicates that glottals are placeless in San Marcos, while coronals are placeless in Yecuatla.

To add to the complexity, liquids can optionally undergo PoA neutralization to glottal, resulting in [h]: e.g. /kulaːɬ/ → [kulaːh] '*huerta* (orchard)', /sululkiw/ → [suluhkeʔ] 'straight twig'. In other words, there are two parallel PoA neutralizations in the language, producing different results: nasal PoA neutralization results in coronals, while lateral PoA neutralization produces glottals; this is analogous to 'velarizing' Spanish dialects (§8.4.1.1).

To summarize so far, epenthesis suggests that glottals are placeless, while assimilation suggests that coronals are placeless. In San Marcos, nasal PoA

8.4 Representational complexity is not markedness 377

neutralization further suggests that glottals are placeless. In contrast, Yecuatla's nasal PoA neutralization indicates that coronals are placeless. To add to the confusion, Yecuatla's lateral PoA neutralization indicates that glottals are placeless.

The problems raised by Misantla Totonac show that one type of representational theory is incorrect: i.e. one in which there are only two distinctions in representational complexity. In such a theory, one segment lacks place features while all others have an equal degree of structural complexity. This theory fails with Misantla Totonac because both coronals and glottals would have to lack place features.

One way to keep a representational theory and deal with Misantla Totonac is to propose that there are more than two distinctions in representational complexity, as in Rice's (1996) DV theory (also Causley 1999; Morén 2003). With an elaborated theory of representational complexity, different processes can be seen as requiring different types of structural reduction. For example, epenthesis in Misantla Totonac could be seen as inserting a root node alone, with no place node – i.e. a glottal. Selective assimilation, on the other hand, can be seen as filling an empty place node – i.e. assimilation of coronals. Neutralization could come in two versions: deletion of place dependents, resulting in coronals, or deletion of place itself, resulting in a glottal. In effect, elaborating the structure allows for multiple output targets – both glottals and coronals.

However, even an elaborated representational theory cannot account for all of the phonological processes in Misantla Totonac. The problem is with triggering processes: if glottals have no features, they should be unable to trigger assimilation, and the same goes for coronals. However, there are phenomena in Misantla Totonac that are triggered by both.

Evidence that coronals have PoA features comes from consonant–vowel interaction. MacKay (1994: §3.4.1) describes an optional process whereby the low back vowel /a/ fronts to [ɛ] when adjacent to a coronal: e.g. [paɬma]~[pɛɬma] 'garbage', [ʃa:qeɬ]~[ʃɛ:qeɬ] 'buzzard', [mila:qaʃmatna]~[mila:qɛʃmatna] 'your hearing'. Following Hume 1992 and Clements & Hume 1995, this fronting is due to assimilation of the vowel's PoA to the consonant's [coronal] feature, making the vowels front. Of course, for such assimilation to take place, coronals must have a [coronal] feature.

Evidence that glottals also have features comes from the fact that they trigger assimilation just like coronals. [ʔ] spreads its glottalization onto a following vowel, resulting in creaky voiced vowels: e.g. /ik-tʃanlaɬ/ → [ʔḭktʃanlaɬ] 'I sowed X' (cf. /ni-ik-tʃanlaɬ/ → [nik-tʃanlaɬ] 'that I sow X') (MacKay 1994: §4.2.4).

378   8 Predictions and alternatives

Further evidence that glottals have PoA features is that high vowels adjacent to the uvulars [q] and [χ] and glottal [h] are banned: (e.g. [ʔi̱-ɬkɛ̱h-ni̱] 'her/his *epazote* (goosefoot)', *[ʔi̱-ɬki̱h-ni̱]; [sɔχɔnaː] 'pretty', *[suχunaː]; [qɛiɲ-ʃɛːh-na̱] 'roots', *[qiːɲ-ʃiːh-na̱] – MacKay 1994:§3.1.2). The place feature [pharyngeal] defines [q χ h] as a natural class (McCarthy 1989, 1994), therefore [q χ h] must have a PoA feature in their phonological representation. As McCarthy (1989:49) argues, [pharyngeal] is a sister to the other PoA features [labial], [coronal], and [dorsal] (see also §8.4.1.3). Consequently, glottals in Misantla Totonac are as featurally complex as every other PoA.

In short, it is not possible to maintain a representational approach to markedness in Misantla Totonac. One problem is that both coronal and glottal are identified as 'least representationally complex' by the diagnostics of epenthesis, assimilation, and neutralization. Another is that other processes require that both [coronal] and [glottal] (or [pharyngeal]) be phonologically present as they can trigger assimilation.

In CoMP, being the output of neutralization or epenthesis does not imply lack of PoA features. Markedness is determined by constraint violations, not by representational complexity. Consequently, the Misantla Totonac phenomena can be modelled using the constraints proposed in the preceding chapters. While lack of space precludes a detailed demonstration, the diagram in (23) identifies significant rankings.

(23)   Significant rankings for San Marcos Misantla Totonac

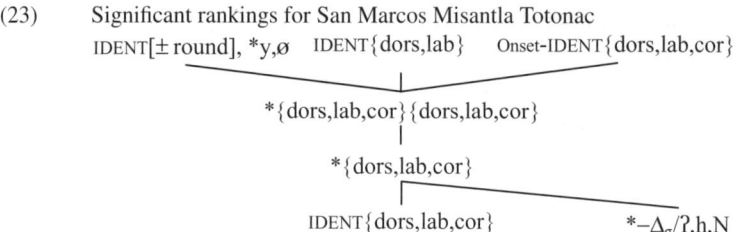

The ranking ‖ *{dors,lab,cor} » *−Δ_σ/ʔ ‖ ensures that a glottal will be epenthesized. In San Marcos, coda /m/ does not neutralize but /n/ becomes [N]; as in Yamphu, IDENT{dors,lab} outranks the neutralization-causing *{dors,lab,cor}, which in turn outranks IDENT{dors,lab,cor}. Liquids can neutralize using the same ranking, as the language has only coronal liquids. IDENT{dors,lab} also keeps /m/ from assimilating as it outranks *{dors,lab,cor}{dors,lab,cor}; in contrast, /n/ assimilates because its only protector – IDENT{dors,lab,cor} – is ranked below the assimilation-causing constraint.

Assimilation of /a/ to front vowels can be seen in the same way: *{dors,lab,cor}{dors,lab,cor} requires agreement in PoA, and onset-IDENT{dors,lab,cor} effectively requires that a vowel agree with an onset consonant's PoA. The change /ta/→[tɛ] is therefore assimilation of the vowel to [t]'s coronal PoA. The back vowels are protected from assimilating by IDENT[round] and *y,ø: if /tu/ became [ti] it would violate IDENT[round] and if it became [ty] it would violate *y. A similar approach is valid for glottal assimilation.

Yecuatla's ranking is very similar to San Marcos'. However, Yecuatla has neutralization of /m/ to [n], not [N]. This is achieved by ranking IDENT{dors,lab} below *{dors,lab,cor}. However, *−Δ_σ/N must outrank *{dors,lab,cor} to prevent /m/ from becoming [N]. *−Δ_σ/ʔ and *−Δ_σ/h remain low in the ranking. In other words, Yecuatla eliminates the labial's protection and imposes a high-ranking ban on glottal nasals.

8.4.4 Conclusions

The points about PoA and structure made above extend to other features. Similar claims about representational complexity have been made for vowels, with schwa often being considered featureless (Oostendorp 1995 and references cited therein). Schwa is often the unmarked vowel − a target of neutralization, epenthetic, and an undergoer of assimilation. However, exactly the same problems arise with a featureless schwa: schwa can trigger, undergo, and block processes, as discussed for sonority-driven stress (§5.4).

It is important to point out that the discussion above only argues against the idea that representational complexity is an explanation for markedness effects. It is not an argument against lack of structure or privative features. For example, the feature [nasal] may be privative, as [−nasal] never seems to trigger assimilation or harmony and is otherwise inert. However, the claim made here is that privativity of [nasal] does not relate directly to its markedness. In any case, representation plays such a limited role in CoMP that it is also possible that all feature values are fully specified, and even that all segments contain all features.

Of course, there have been many variations on the representational complexity theme, with many mechanisms not discussed here. For example, there is controversy over universality − while some maintain that glottals are placeless in every language, others allow coronals, and even other PoAs, to be placeless in other languages (Morén 2003). Kiparsky's (1982) theory of Contrastive Specification permits lack of specification only when the feature in question is not instrumental in establishing a phonemic contrast.

Despite the variation in representational complexity theories, none avoid all of the problems identified above, as observed in McCarthy 1994. Lack of specification, no matter for which feature, predicts that it will be a target, an undergoer, not a trigger, and not a blocker – and this prediction does not fit the facts. A theory of markedness therefore cannot rely on a concept of representational complexity and a mechanism that relates this to markedness reduction and preservation.

8.5 Non-contrastive markedness

CoMP denies that there is any relation between contrastiveness, inventory form, and markedness. Markedness hierarchies and relations are universal and exist independently of particular grammars and their segment inventories.

In contrast, theories like Rice's (1999a,b, 2004a,b, 2006) and Causley's (1999) argue that contrastiveness is crucial in understanding markedness: e.g. 'the contrasts within an inventory must be considered to draw conclusions about featural [markedness] relations within a class' (Rice 2006). In other words, markedness relations must be defined relative to a segmental inventory: 'a feature may pattern as marked if some contrast is present, but as not marked in the absence of that contrast' (Rice 2006). So, contrastive oppositions must first be established, and then markedness is defined in terms of these oppositions. In this conception of markedness there is no truly unmarked feature value on any hierarchy; a feature value is only unmarked relative to some other value in the system, and if there is no contrastive use of feature values in a language, neither value is least-marked. Theories that relate markedness to contrast will be called 'contrast-markedness' theories here.

Rice is not alone in claiming that contrastiveness is significant in phonology. It is also found in work by the Prague School (e.g. Trubetzkoy 1939; Jakobson 1941, 1978:79ff.; Battistella 1990:12ff.) and has influenced work on underspecification (e.g. Steriade 1987b; Clements 1988; Avery & Rice 1988, 1989b). It is also pursued in Rice and Avery 1993, 1995, Rice 2004a,b, 2006, Dresher 2003a, and MacKenzie & Dresher 2004. Contrastiveness is also important in various guises in lexical phonology (e.g. 'contrastive underspecification', the Alternation Condition – Kiparsky 1982, 1985), in work on inventory form in OT (Flemming 1995), and in related theories (Lubowicz 2002; Padgett 2003; Ito & Mester 2003).

However, a variety of phonological theories make no crucial reference to contrast (e.g. SPE). In classical OT (Prince & Smolensky 1993) it is difficult to define a level at which contrastiveness is expressed; the set of contrastive segments cannot be defined as only those that can appear in the input as Richness of the Base permits any segment in the input.

Of course, given the depth of current disagreement over the role of contrastiveness in phonology, the issue will not be resolved in the next few pages. Instead, the aim of this section is to identify the differences between a contrastive theory of markedness and a theory in which markedness relations are universal and make no reference to contrast, inventories, or phonemes. The conclusion will be that contrastive theories are necessarily more complex in that they require additional mechanisms to define inventories, while inventories are defined and phonological processes motivated using the same set of mechanisms in CoMP. I will also argue that a theory of markedness that does not refer to contrast is empirically more restrictive than one that does. Of course, this brief discussion cannot do justice to theories of contrast and markedness; the aim of the following discussion is limited to identifying the core predictions of contrast-markedness theories and comparing them with the present approach.

8.5.1 Predictions

In contrast-markedness theories such as Rice's (1999a,b, 2004a,b, 2006), feature values can only be called 'marked' or 'unmarked' when they contrast with some other value in an inventory. So, the question 'Is [labial] the most marked PoA?' is unanswerable without having a specific inventory in mind. If the inventory only contains labials, then [labial] is the least-marked PoA, relative to that inventory. If the inventory contains coronals as well as labials, only then do markedness relations become relevant: as labials are more marked than coronals on the PoA hierarchy, then [labial] would be more marked than [coronal] relative to that inventory.

The empirical consequences of this view are significant. If there is nothing to contrast with a feature value in a particular inventory, it will be the least-marked value. Consequently, a statement like 'Inventories must all contain the least-marked feature value' is vacuous as every feature value is unmarked if it does not contrast in this conception. Rice (2006) elaborates on this point in a discussion of the output of neutralization:

(24)   The existence of variation in the absence of contrast is reinforced in cross-linguistic surveys of neutralization. For instance, in languages that allow only a single nasal place of articulation in word-final position, some allow only coronals (e.g. Finnish – Yip 1991), some only velars (e.g. Japanese – Vance 1987), and some only labials (e.g. Central Eastern Tundra Nenets [Uralic] – Salminen 1998).

The term 'inventory' for the languages cited evidently refers to the set of nasal consonants allowed in word-final position. Within this inventory, there is no contrast in PoA in any of the languages. Therefore there is no way to constrain them by markedness means. The prediction is that neutralization of PoA should be able to produce any value – labial (as in Central Eastern Tundra Nenets), coronal (as in Finnish), velar (as – it is claimed – in Japanese), and presumably glottal (as in Kashaya). Rice underscores this point: 'It thus appears that the most frequently cited phonological diagnostic for markedness, neutralization, is not useful in singling out one or two features within a class as universally unmarked from a phonological perspective' (Rice 2006).

CoMP makes different predictions: it places strong restrictions on the possible output of neutralization so that neutralization to labial and dorsal PoA is impossible, no matter what the inventory of the language (§4.2.2.2). To explain this difference, it is necessary to delve deeper into the notion 'inventory'.

The inventory is the set of contrastive oppositions in a language. In a sense, the form of the inventory must be established before markedness oppositions can be determined. For example, if the inventory contains an [m] and [ŋ] but no [n], then the markedness relations would in effect be | ŋ ⟩ m | in terms of PoA.

The idea of an 'inventory' raises many questions, not just for contrast-markedness theories, but for all theories for which contrastiveness plays a major role. If the 'inventory' exists as a formal object, it is natural to ask how many inventories there are for a particular language, and whether they vary depending on environment. For example, is there one single inventory for every environment in the language, or are there separate onset and coda inventories, or even different inventories for every definable environment? There are significant differences between the two options. If onsets permit [t] and [d] but codas permit only [t], is [voice] in a contrastive opposition in coda position? If there is a single inventory for every environment, [voice] is contrastive in codas because [d] contrasts with [t] in onsets. However, if there are separate inventories for onsets and codas, [voice] is not contrastive in codas. The answer to this particular question may vary from theory to theory. In (24), it is at least clear that a separate inventory for coda consonants is assumed.

More importantly for present purposes, contrast-markedness theories require mechanisms to form the inventory that are different from those used to motivate phonological processes (see, e.g., Causley 1999:§6.5). Markedness cannot affect inventory form because markedness relations are only relevant within a particular inventory – in a sense the inventory's form must be established 'before' markedness relations become relevant. Markedness does play a role – it influences the form of processes like epenthesis, neutralization, and assimilation, and so on. So, the mechanisms that produce inventories are not the same that motivate phonological processes.

Finally, there are some significant issues for all work that refers to the 'inventory' or contrastive oppositions. This notion is identical to the 'phoneme' – i.e. the minimal contrastive unit of Trubetzkoy (1939). However, a great deal of work has identified many problems with the phoneme. In particular, no commonly agreed methodology for identifying phonemes emerged, with consequent problems for constructing a learnability theory (see Dresher 2003b for an overview). Theories of the phoneme also differed widely (compare Trubetzkoy 1939, Martinet 1964, Chomsky & Halle 1968). If the concept of 'inventory' (and therefore 'phoneme') is to be used in current phonology, some of the classic problems with phonemes therefore need to be addressed. CoMP, like most of post-Prague School phonology, avoids this problem by not having a concept of contrastiveness play any role in the grammar. OT goes to the extreme in this regard: Richness of the Base places no restrictions at all on inputs: they can contain any segment and structure in any language.

8.5.1.1 Inventory formation is neutralization

In contrast, markedness is independent of a particular language's inventory in CoMP: labials are always more marked than coronals on the PoA hierarchy no matter whether labials and coronals contrast in a particular environment. Consequently, the same mechanisms are used to determine inventory form and motivate phonological processes. An inventory is defined by having some *α constraint outrank all faithfulness constraints that preserve α – i.e. absolute neutralization. Neutralization is simply the situation when α-neutralization is blocked in some environment, by an environment-specific faithfulness constraint like ONSET-IDENT[α], or by an output constraint. There is therefore an intimate relation between inventory-formation and phonological processes.

This relation was discussed in §3.3.5 and §4.2.2.2. These sections showed that the shape of inventories has a significant effect on possible neutralizations. For example, the ranking needed to produce a stop inventory like [k p ʔ] means that PoA neutralization in codas can only ever result in glottals, never labials and dorsals. The reason is that the ranking needed to eliminate underlying /t/ is ‖ *{dors,lab,cor} » *Δ_σ/glottal ‖; as this ranking favours glottals over all other PoAs, it is therefore impossible to have neutralization to any other PoA.

This result does not depend on the inventory, either. In the hypothetical language discussed in §3.3.5, the surface coda inventory consists of just [m], yet it is impossible to force /ŋ/ to neutralize to [m]. The same goes for neutralization of /ɲ/ to [m], and the result can also be extended to epenthesis: it is impossible to have epenthetic labials or dorsals (approximants excepted).

In short, contrast-markedness theories and the present approach differ significantly in terms of their empirical predictions for neutralization outputs. A contrast-markedness theory like Rice's (1999a,b, 2004a,b, 2006) predicts that segments can neutralize to any PoA in inventories which only allow one PoA. In contrast, CoMP predicts that all cases of neutralization will produce glottals or coronals, never labials or dorsals.

8.5.1.2 Which theory is right?

In principle, it is a straightforward matter to disprove CoMP (assuming that the PoA hierarchy is correct): all that is needed is a valid case of synchronic neutralization to labial or dorsal PoA. Such a language would have alternations that show /ŋ/ or /n/ becoming [m] in codas, or /t/ surfacing as [p] or [k], and so on. As discussed above, apparent neutralization to 'ŋ' requires careful scrutiny to be sure the output is not [N]; whether the nasal is dorsal or glottal can be determined by examining its behaviour in other processes.

The other disprovable prediction is that in every case where there is a disharmonic inventory (e.g. just [m] in a coda and no [n] or [N]), CoMP predicts that the less-marked segments have been eliminated through some incidental process like lenition or coalescence. In no such case could they be eliminated by neutralization to a more-marked segment.

So has the quote in (24) shown CoMP to be wrong? Rice cites Central Eastern Tundra Nenets (CETN) (Salminen 1998) as having only labials in word-final position, with the implication that other PoAs (coronal, dorsal) are eliminated through neutralization. Certainly, for stops CETN allows [p pʲ t tʲ] in monosegmental onsets and only [b] and [ʔ] in codas; for nasals it allows [m mʲ n nʲ ŋ] in mono-segmental onsets but only [m] in codas (it allows [n] and [ŋ] before homorganic consonants). However, Salminen (1998:527) shows that coronals do not neutralize to labials, but rather to the glottal stop [ʔ]. The evidence is summarized in (25). There is an independent process of inter-vocalic stop voicing (i.e. /t/→[d]/V_V), Salminen's 'reduced vowel' is transcribed as [ʌ] here, and while Salminen distinguishes two types of glottal stop (orthographic 'q' and 'h', with the 'h' being 'nasalizable') both are transcribed as [ʔ] here.

(25)   The fate of PoA in Central Eastern Tundra Nenets (Salminen 1998:527)

	UR	citation	sNs2	PA	sG
(a)	/mʲat/ 'tent'	mʲa?	mʲa?-lə	mʲad-o	mʲad-əh
(b)	/mʌnʌs/ 'lump'	mʌnə?	mʌnʌ?-lə	mʌnəs-o	mʌnʌs-əh
(c)	/wen/ 'dog'	we?		wen-o	wen-əh
(d)	/wiːŋ/ 'tundra'	wiː?		wiːŋ-o	
(e)	Labials survive				
	[jam] 'sea'		[jamta] 'sea-sNs3'	[jam-kəna] 'sea-sLoc'	
	[ŋob] '1'				

So, there is no evidence that labial is the least-marked PoA in CETN codas: it is not the output target of neutralization. Instead, CETN has a gapped coda inventory of labials and glottals, like the related language Nganasan. For a ranking to account for such an inventory in CoMP, see §4.2.2.1.

Rice (2004b) also cites Lhasa Tibetan as having only labials in word-final position: the language allows word-final [m]: [pʰalam] 'diamond' (Denwood 1999) and does not permit word-final [ŋ] or [n]. However, Denwood argues that word-final /ŋ/ is not eliminated by neutralization to [m], but by coalescence with the preceding vowel: e.g. /lʰa-kʰaŋ/ → [lʰakʰãː] 'temple' (cf. [kʰaŋ-ba] 'house') (it is also possible that this process is neutralization to the glottal [ɦ̃], so accounting for the apparent compensatory lengthening of the vowel). There are no alternations that show the fate of /n/, so it is not possible to conclude that Lhasa Tibetan has neutralization of /n/ to [m]; in fact, the coalescence of /ŋ/ suggests otherwise. So, there is no evidence that labial is the least-marked PoA in Lhasa Tibetan codas: it is not the output target of neutralization.

Rice cites Vance (1987) as reporting that Japanese allows [ŋ] in coda position but not [m] or [n]. However, Yip (1991) states that the coda nasal is realized as 'unreleased, either velar, or uvular'. Vance (1987:34) comments that it is uvular [N] before a pause, and Nakano (1969:220) reports that it is articulated 'with the posterior part of the soft palate together with the uvula touching the back tongue'. It only appears word-finally because word-medially it assimilates to the following onset's PoA (Aoyama 1999). The articulatory variability seen in the Japanese coda nasal (i.e. velar~uvular) is a telltale sign of the glottal nasal [N] (also see Trigo 1988). To disprove CoMP, the final nasal would have to be shown to be velar rather than glottal; this could be done by observing its phonological behaviour in assimilation, lenition, and so on. Even if the word-final nasal in Japanese is velar, it would then have to be proven by active synchronic alternations that /m/ and /n/ neutralize to it.

In short, Central Eastern Tundra Nenets, Lhasa Tibetan, and Japanese are not counter-examples to CoMP as in neither language are they the outputs of neutralization. They highlight the point that synchronic alternations are the only sort of evidence that is relevant in markedness, and that facts may be misreported, such as [N] being called 'ŋ'.

It is in principle easier to disprove CoMP than the contrast-markedness approach because CoMP makes far more restrictive predictions about what can happen and how. For example, CoMP predicts that if a language allows only [m] in the coda, the /n/ must be eliminated by a non-neutralizing process like coalescence. Rice's contrast-markedness theory apparently allows any means of elimination, including neutralization.

8.5.1.3 Epenthesis

The same points for neutralization can be made for epenthesis. For Rice (2006), the contrast-markedness theory predicts a great freedom of epenthetic vowels: 'epenthetic vowels can be front, central, or back in place and high, mid, or low in height'. CoMP also predicts variation, but in a more restrictive way. All of [ɨ ə i e ɛ a] are predicted to be epenthetic – the variation in height is due to conflicting sonority demands. However, none can be round. For example, [y], [u], and [o] can never be epenthetic. Rice's contrast-markedness approach allows epenthetic [u]. Section 7.2.5 argued that cited cases of epenthetic [u] are at least doubtful, and that certain cases (e.g. Seediq's) are misreported [ə] epenthesis.

It is straightforward to disprove CoMP: a clear case of synchronic epenthesis of [u] – or [y], [o], [ø], or any phonologically round vowel – would do it. Again, CoMP is more restrictive in its predictions for epenthesis.

8.5.1.4 More on contrast-markedness

Rice's (2006) theory of contrast-markedness makes other predictions, relating to limitations as to which PoAs may selectively undergo assimilation. It seems that Rice's theory and the present one also diverge here, but perhaps with CoMP being less restrictive: it predicts any PoA can undergo assimilation while others are blocked from doing so. In comparison, Rice's theory predicts restrictions on which PoAs can assimilate depending on the inventory: 'In languages with a three-way consonantal place of articulation contrast in a particular position, labial, coronal, and velar, two places of articulation, coronal and velar, can pattern as unmarked . . .', and relates unmarkedness to the ability to selectively undergo assimilation. The predictions of Rice's theory are sufficiently complex and the data is sufficiently scarce that it may be difficult to prove conclusively that there are such restrictions at the present time. Even so, it is not immediately clear how systems like Sri Lankan Portuguese creole's fit in, where labials assimilate but coronals do not (§4.3.3). Further development of contrast-markedness theories may help identify other differences with CoMP.

8.5.1.5 Conclusion

CoMP claims that markedness relations do not depend on the contrastive oppositions (i.e. inventory) of a language. In addition, inventory formation is formed by the same mechanisms as positional neutralization. Contrast-markedness theories seem to have to appeal to separate mechanisms to form inventories and produce neutralization. CoMP may well have less theoretical machinery than contrast-markedness theories.

CoMP makes more restrictive predictions than contrast-markedness theories for neutralization and epenthesis. For non-approximants, labials and dorsals can never be the output of neutralization or epenthesis in CoMP, while they are allowed in contrast-markedness theories. No cases of labial or dorsal epenthesis or neutralization to labial and dorsal have yet survived scrutiny.

8.6 Markedness is absolute

In an 'absolutist' approach to markedness, constraints specify an absolute markedness threshold; if an output candidate exceeds the threshold, it violates the constraint. So, an absolutist constraint like *{dorsal} will be violated by any output candidate that contains a dorsal, regardless of what other candidates it competes with and its relation to the input. CoMP is absolutist.

In contrast, a relativist approach to markedness also has constraints that specify a markedness threshold relative to the original form; only if a form *increases* in markedness does it violate the constraint. A relative output constraint version of *{dorsal} – called ⇑*{dorsal} after McCarthy (2002) – would be violated if input /t/ became [k], but *not* if input /k/ remains [k]. In the /k/→[k] case, [k] is not an increase in PoA markedness relative to input /k/. Relativist approaches to markedness are developed in Baković 1999b, 2000, McCarthy 2002, and the commentaries on McCarthy's article in *Linguistic Analysis* 29:1–2. I use the term 'relative markedness' to cover both Baković and McCarthy's theories; McCarthy's approach is called 'Comparative Markedness'.

To be clear, both Baković's and McCarthy's theories accept absolute constraints like *{dorsal}. Languages that ban all [k]'s regardless of the underlying form show that absolute output constraints like *{dorsal} are necessary. The

388   8 Predictions and alternatives

issue is whether relative output constraints are needed in addition to absolute ones.

Evidence for relative markedness come from processes that are blocked just when the underlying form would be forced to become more marked. Assimilation provides a good case study, and is the focus of Baković's and McCarthy's work. Relative PoA output constraints like ⇑*{dorsal} would prevent /t/ and /p/ from assimilating in PoA to a dorsal because the /t/ would end up with a more-marked PoA. In contrast, /k/ is free to assimilate because it will either retain the same markedness or become less marked in PoA.

Baković's and McCarthy's theories have a broader range of application than assimilation; they deal with derived environment effects, opacity, and the 'majority rules' problem (Lombardi 1996, 1999). Even so, the focus here will be their predictions in assimilation because this relates directly to the issues of concern in this book (see esp. §4.3).

Section 8.6.1 shows how relative markedness works. Section 8.6.2 argues that relative output constraints are unnecessary and make incorrect typological predictions for assimilation; Preservation of the Marked and the Marked-Cluster theory of assimilation presented in §4.3 are argued to make empirically adequate predictions.

8.6.1   A relative markedness approach to SLP creole
McCarthy (2002) uses SLP creole's PoA assimilation to show how relative markedness works. As a reminder, in SLP creole assimilation, labials and dorsals assimilate (/maːm-su/ → [maːnsu], /uŋpæːzu/ → [umpæːzu]) while coronals do not (/siːn-pə/ → [siːnpə]). A relativist approach to SLP creole assimilation claims that coronals do not assimilate because doing so would create something *relatively* too marked. For example, if /siːn-pə/ were realized as [siːmpə], the unmarked coronal /n/ would end up with a more-marked PoA: labial [m]. In contrast, assimilation of /ŋp/ to [mp] results in a less-marked cluster. In short, the leading idea behind relativist approaches is that a process can be blocked if it creates something more marked out of something less marked.

McCarthy's (2002) theory of relative markedness, called 'Comparative Markedness' (CM) will be examined here; the results can be extended to Baković's theory. CM constraints are violated when two conditions are met: (i) the output form meets the constraint's structural description and (ii) the violation is 'new'. A violation is 'new' if there is no analogous violation in the fully faithful form.

For example, the CM constraint ⇑*{dors,lab} is only violated by candidates that have a dorsal or labial that is not present in the fully faithful form. From input /siːn-pə/ the fully faithful form is [siːnpə]; this candidate has one violation of the absolute *{dors,lab} constraint – i.e. in [p]. The candidate with assimilation *[siːmpə] violates *{dors,lab} twice, once for [m] and once for [p]. In comparison with the fully faithful form, *[siːmpə] therefore has a 'new' violation of *{dors,lab}, and so violates ⇑*{dors,lab} once.

In short, ⇑*{dors,lab} is (essentially) violated when an input coronal turns into something more marked. Hence, ⇑*{dors,lab} can be used to provide a straightforward account of SLP creole. The use of ⇑*{dors,lab} to account for SLP creole follows McCarthy's (2002) analysis (esp. see McCarthy 2002:9, n.9).

In tableau (26) candidate (a) is the fully faithful form. It incurs one violation of *{dors,lab} – i.e. by means of [p]. In contrast, *[siːmpə] incurs two violations of *{dors,lab} – one for [m] and one for [p]. Importantly, one of these violations (caused by [m]) is 'new' – i.e. it has no analogue in the fully faithful form. This causes a violation of ⇑*{dors,lab}, dooming *[siːmpə].

(26)   Comparative Markedness I

/siːn-pə/	⇑*{dors,lab}	ASSIM	*{dors,lab}
(a) siːmpə	*!		**
☞ (b) siːnpə		*	*

Comparative output constraints do not set a markedness threshold on unfaithful elements; instead, they are inherently relative, assigning a violation only if it increases markedness relative to the input form. So, /uŋ pæːzu/→[umpæːzu] does not incur any violations of ⇑*{dors,lab} because the fully faithful form *[uŋpæːzu] incurs two violations of *{dors,lab}, and [umpæːzu] also incurs two; in other words, [umpæːzu] is no less marked than *[uŋpæːzu] in terms of *{dors,lab}. This markedness allows ASSIM to rule out the unassimilated candidate, as shown in tableau (27).[7]

(27)   Comparative Markedness II

/uŋ pæːzu/	⇑*{dors,lab}	ASSIM	*{dors,lab}
(a) uŋpæːzu		*!	**
☞ (b) umpæːzu			**

---

[7] The stringent form of the output constraint ⇑*{dors,lab} is essential to the success of this analysis. If there were two non-stringent constraints ⇑*{dors} and ⇑*{lab}, the analysis would prevent assimilation of noncoronals to other noncoronals. For example, /ŋp/→ [mp] would violate ⇑*{lab} and /mk/→ [ŋk] would fatally violate ⇑*{dors}.

390   8 *Predictions and alternatives*

In short, Comparative Markedness can successfully produce a system in which only marked elements undergo assimilation.

However, while SLP creole is a useful as an illustration of relative markedness, it does not provide conclusive proof because CoMP – an absolute markedness theory – also has an account of SLP creole. In §4.3.3 it was shown that an absolute output constraint like *{dors,lab}{dors,lab,cor} can produce the same effects: only dorsals and labials must undergo assimilation. To put the difference in more general terms, for Comparative Markedness, coronals do not assimilate to non-coronals because the output would be too marked when compared with the input. In CoMP, coronals do not assimilate because they are already unmarked enough, so nothing motivates them to assimilate.

8.6.2   Predictions of relative markedness for assimilation

While both CM and the present approach can deal with SLP creole, the two approaches differ significantly in their predictions about other types of assimilation systems. Three different predictions are identified here.

One relates to a system that differs minimally from SLP creole's: one in which only the most-marked elements (i.e. dorsals) undergo assimilation. CoMP can produce this type of system while CM cannot (§8.6.2.1).

CM predicts a system in which a segment cannot assimilate to something more marked; the Marked-Cluster constraints do not (§8.6.2.2). Finally, asymmetries in triggering elements are discussed. The cluster-output constraints are argued to be necessary regardless of whether CM constraints exist or not (§8.6.2.3).

8.6.2.1   Dorsal undergoers

CM and CoMP differ in regard to predictions about a system in which only the most-marked PoA – dorsals – undergoes assimilation while coronals and labials do not. A dorsal-undergoer system is illustrated schematically in (28). For an example of such a system, see Chuckchi in §4.3.3.2.

(28)   Dorsal-undergoer system
    (a) Dorsals assimilate
        /aŋpa/→ [ampa]   /aŋta/→ [anta]
    (b) Labials do not assimilate
        /amka/ → [amka], *[aŋka]   /amta/ → [amta], *[anta]
    (c) Coronals do not assimilate
        /anka/ → [anka], *[aŋka]   /anpa/ → [anpa], *[ampa]

8.6 Markedness is absolute

In the absolutist approach advocated here, dorsals undergo assimilation because of the constraint *{dors}{dors,lab,cor} – i.e. a ban on dorsal+X clusters. Chukchi is possible because the absolutist constraint *{dors}{dors,lab,cor} expresses the idea that assimilation is reduction of marked structure.

As in SLP creole, a relative markedness approach would seek to produce dorsal-undergoer systems without appealing to *{dors}{dors,lab,cor}. However, it faces a significant difficulty. CM blocks PoAs from undergoing assimilation by banning an increase in markedness. This approach works for coronals because any assimilation (e.g. /np/→[mp], /nk/→[ŋk]) involves an increase in /n/'s markedness. However, it can only partially prevent assimilation of labials: while /mk/→[ŋk] does involve an increase in /m/'s PoA markedness, the assimilation /mt/→[nt] does not. Therefore, there is no comparative output constraint that can ban the assimilation /mt/→[nt]. CM therefore predicts that Chukchi's system is impossible.

In ranking terms, the fact that dorsals assimilate shows that the assimilation-inducing output constraint must outrank all faithfulness constraints against dorsals: i.e. ||ASSIM » IDENT{dors }, IDENT{dors,lab}, IDENT {dors,lab,cor }||. However, if ASSIM outranks all faithfulness constraints, what prevents coronals and labials from assimilating? CM provides a partial answer in the form of the comparative output constraints: ⇑*{dors,lab} will block assimilation of coronals to something more marked, as shown for SLP creole.

However, labials present a significant difficulty. While the mapping /amka/→*[aŋka] can be blocked by a CM constraint ⇑*{dors}, no constraint can block /amta/→*[anta]. There is no faithfulness constraint available that can favour [amta] over [anta] (because both are equally unfaithful – §3.3), nor can any comparative output constraint ban /mt/→[nt] since the output [n] has a less-marked PoA than the input /m/.

This conundrum is a general problem for relative markedness theories. Since relative markedness theories rely on the idea that change to a more-marked element is banned, there is no relative markedness-based way to prevent a change from a more- to a less-marked element.

The only way out is to appeal to an output constraint that specifically bans dorsal+non-dorsal clusters. This analysis captures the intuition behind the present approach: labials do not assimilate because they are already unmarked enough. Formally, there is no active output constraint that bans labial+C heterorganic clusters, so labials are never under pressure to assimilate in Chukchi. However, such a constraint is absolutist, so there is no need for relative markedness here. The implication is that the output constraint *{dors}{dors,lab,cor} is necessary regardless of whether CM constraints exist or not. If this is the case, it is a small step to assume that there is a constraint *{dors,lab}{dors,lab,cor} and that there is therefore no need for a CM analysis of SLP creole. In short, relative markedness theories are too restrictive, banning an attested type of assimilation.

8.6.2.2 Unattested systems
Relative markedness theories predict a system in which assimilation is blocked only when it would create a more-marked segment. This type of system is called a 'progressive blocking' system here, and is illustrated in (29).

(29)   Progressive blocking (PB) language
      (a) Dorsals assimilate to coronals and labials.
          /aŋ-pa/ →   [ampə]   /aŋ-ta/ →   [anta]
      (b) Labials assimilate to coronals, but not dorsals.
          /am-ka/ →   [amka]   /am-ta/ →   [anta]
      (c) Coronals do not assimilate at all.
          /an-ka/ →   [anka]   /an-pa/ →   [anpa]

In other words, assimilation only takes place if the output contains a less-marked sound: i.e. /m/→[n], but not /m/→[ŋ]. This system differs from SLP creole: in SLP creole, only coronals were prevented from assimilating; labials could assimilate to the more-marked dorsals, and dorsals to labials.

This type of system can be produced in the CM theory with the ranking ‖⇑*{dors}, ⇑*{dors,lab} » ASSIM‖. The input /am-ka/ cannot emerge as *[aŋka] because this form introduces a new violation of *{dors} (cf. fully faithful [amka]), thus fatally violating ⇑*{dors}. As with SLP creole, this ranking does not block the assimilation of labials and dorsals to coronals, or dorsals to non-dorsals. Tableau (30) illustrates this point.

(30)

/amkamta/	⇑*{dors}	ASSIM	*{dors}
(a) aŋkanta	*!	*	**
(b) amkamta		**!	*
☞ (c) amkanta		*	*

In contrast, CoMP cannot produce a progressive blocking system. The reason is that the theory can either prevent or allow labials from assimilating; it cannot make labial assimilation contingent on the sort of output it will produce.

In ranking terms, assimilation of /am-ta/ to [anta] requires an output constraint that bans [labial+coronal] clusters (i.e. *{dors,lab}{dors,lab,cor}) to outrank all faithfulness constraints that preserve labials (IDENT{dors,lab}, IDENT{dors,lab,cor}).

8.6 Markedness is absolute

However, with this ranking nothing prevents labials from assimilating to dorsals. To ban labial→dorsal assimilation, some faithfulness constraint that preserves labials (i.e. IDENT{dors,lab} or IDENT{dors,lab,cor}) must outrank all output constraints that ban labial+dorsal clusters – i.e. *{dors,lab}{x}, *{dors,lab,cor}{x}, where x is any set of elements. This ranking directly contradicts the one needed for labial→coronal assimilation, showing that the result is inconsistent.

No progressive blocking system has been reported so far. This fact does not weigh in favour of either theory at this point, though, since very few marked-undergoer systems have been identified (§4.3.3.2; Baković 1999b; Wetzels & Mascaró 2001). However, it is notable that the predictions of CM and CoMP are different, and thus will ultimately provide a way to tell which is empirically adequate.

8.6.2.3 Triggers

CM and CoMP make significantly different predictions regarding the elements that trigger assimilation. With only an assimilation constraint like ASSIM, CM predicts that there is no system that is the exact opposite of progressive blocking: where a segment will only assimilate to something *more* marked. Korean has such a system (Kim 1973; Kim-Renaud 1974, 1986; Iverson & Kim 1987; Jun 1995; Ahn 1998; Cho 1988, 1999).

(31)   Korean: a progressively more-marked system
    (a) Coronals assimilate to labials and dorsals.
        /an-paŋ/ → [ampaŋ] 'inner room'
        /han kaŋ/ → [haŋkaŋ] 'the Han river'
    (b) Labials assimilate to dorsals but not coronals.
        /kamki/ → [kaŋki] 'a cold/influenza'
        [sumta] 'hide+SE'
    (c) Dorsals do not assimilate.
        [paŋpota] '(more) than room'
        [paŋto] 'room as well'

CM constraints cannot produce the Korean system. In fact, it runs exactly counter to what is expected under CM: segments only assimilate if they become *more* marked, not *less*.

CoMP can account for Korean using absolute output constraints. Korean is in part like Catalan: coronals always undergo assimilation. The same analysis can be used here: IDENT{dors,lab} must outrank *{dors,lab,cor}{dors,lab,cor} as shown in tableau (32).

(32)

/sum-ta/	IDENT{dors,lab}	*{dors,lab,cor}{dors,lab,cor}
(a) sunta	*!	
☞ (b) sumta		*

However, labials assimilate before dorsals; this is due to the Marked-Cluster constraint *{dors,lab,cor}{dors}, which expresses the generalization that highly marked PoAs can compel assimilation.

(33)

/kam-ki/	*{dors,lab,cor}{dors}	IDENT{dors,lab}
(a) kamki	*!	
☞ (b) kaŋki		*

Given the necessity of *{dors,lab,cor}{dors}, a 'plausibility' argument for the current theory will be made here. If even the CM theory needs asymmetric assimilation constraints like *{dors,lab,cor}{dors} to deal with Korean, then there is no a priori objection to a constraint such as *{dors}{dors,lab,cor} for Chukchi (or *{dors,lab}{dors,lab,cor} for SLP creole). If this is the case, then there is no need for CM constraints to produce marked undergoer systems, like SLP creole's.

8.6.3 Conclusions

To conclude, relative markedness theories do not provide a full account of undergoer systems in assimilation. While they can potentially deal with certain types of marked undergoer system (i.e. one in which the least-marked element of a hierarchy fails to undergo assimilation – e.g. SLP creole), they cannot account for other attested types, including those where only the most-marked element of a multi-member hierarchy is an undergoer (e.g. Chukchi). Moreover, they predict the existence of an unattested system in which only elements assimilate to a less-marked PoA. Finally, the Comparative Markedness theory does not account for asymmetries in triggering effects, as found in Korean.

The discussion above has argued that all these cases require constraints that target specific marked elements in clusters, like *{dors,lab}{dors,lab,cor} and *{dors}{dors,lab,cor}. However, such constraints eliminate the need for relative markedness. CoMP accounts for all attested marked assimilation patterns, as well as triggering. It also correctly predicts that the unattested 'Progressive Marked' type of system cannot exist.

8.7 Markedness is expressed in both output and preservation constraints

This section examines the claim that markedness hierarchies are expressed as both output and faithfulness constraints, and that all elements in a hierarchy are expressed in constraints.

In recent work, Howe & Pulleyblank (2004) (HP) propose that markedness hierarchies can be expressed through faithfulness constraints. In many respects this proposal agrees with the theory of markedness preservation proposed here. However, there is one crucial difference: HP's theory uses constraints in which correspondence is feature-based, not segment-based. For HP, features can be in direct correspondence with each other; instead of (or at least in addition to) IDENT, there are MAX[Feature] and DEP[Feature] constraints:

(34)   IO-MAX[F]   'Every feature [F] in the input corresponds to a feature [F] in the output.'
       IO-DEP[F]   'Every feature [F] in the output corresponds to a feature [F] in the input.'

HP argue that markedness hierarchies can be expressed in terms of MAX[F] and DEP[F] constraints. For example, | dorsal 〉 labial 〉 coronal 〉 glottal | can be expressed as the constraints in (35). These constraints follow HP's proposals except that they assume stringent form rather than a universally fixed ranking.

(35)   (a) MAX{dors}, MAX{dors,lab}, MAX{dors,lab,cor}, MAX{dors,lab,cor,gl}
       (b) DEP{dors}, DEP{dors,lab}, DEP{dors,lab,cor}, DEP{dors,lab,cor,gl}

In effect, HP and CoMP agree that faithfulness constraints obey MRH. However, HP relate constraint form to the idea that the more perceivable property is preserved; while this differs from the present approach in its formal underpinnings, in most cases the two conceptions have the same effect.

CoMP disagrees with HP in assuming that all correspondence relations are mediated through segments, after McCarthy & Prince (1995). In this approach, featural faithfulness is only relevant if the feature's sponsoring segment is present in the output. For example, input /ka/ violates IDENT{dors} if it maps to the output [ʔa]; however, it does not violate IDENT{dors} in the mapping /ka/→[a] because the dorsal feature's segmental sponsor does not exist in the output. In contrast, MAX[dors] is violated in both cases.

One major difference between the theories is that DEP[F] constraints can determine the form of the output for HP. In CoMP, this is the job of output constraints. To illustrate, the form of epenthetic consonants in CoMP is determined solely by output constraints. *{dors,lab,cor} will force an epenthetic consonant to be glottal. In contrast, DEP{dors,lab,cor} can be used to force the output to be glottal:

(36)

/a/	DEP{dors,lab,cor}
(a) ka	*!
(b) pa	*!
(c) ta	*!
☞ (d) ʔa	

Candidate (a) violates DEP{dors,lab,cor} because the candidate has a [dorsal] feature in the output that is not present in the input. The same problem arises with (b) and (c). Inserting a [glottal] feature is the less onerous thing to do, from a faithfulness point of view, so [ʔa] wins.

The leading idea of HP's theory can be expressed in a strong and weak form. The strong form is that markedness hierarchies are only expressed as a set of MAX[F] and DEP[F] constraints; there are no output constraints. Instead, output constraints militate against general structure, like *STRUC (Zoll 1998). The weak form is that every hierarchy has faithfulness constraints of the MAX[F] and DEP[F] variety but may also have related output constraints. Howe & Pulleyblank (2004, p.c.) argue for a weak form of the theory, but examination of the strong form is also worthwhile as it highlights certain assumptions behind CoMP. Arguments against the strong form are given in §8.7.1, and the weak form is examined in §8.7.2.

8.7.1 The need for output constraints

Having faithfulness constraints alone is not enough. Output constraints are necessary in situations where faithfulness is irrelevant.

A straightforward example is found in sonority-driven stress. As discussed for Gujarati in §5.4, stress usually falls on the penult (e.g. [apˈwana] 'to give'), but can fall elsewhere if a more sonorous vowel is available (e.g. [ˈpatini] 'wife', [hɛˈran] 'distressed'). The problem faced by a theory in which markedness relations are only expressed by faithfulness constraints is that faithfulness is not at issue here: both [hɛˈran] and *[ˈhɛran] are equally faithful. As neither candidate violates any MAX[F] or DEP[F] constraint, the only way to account for the fact that [hɛˈran] wins is by using an output constraint $*\Delta_\omega \leq \{\varepsilon,\mathrm{ɔ}\}$; a full analysis is given in §5.4.

8.7 Markedness is expressed in both output and preservation constraints

Coalescence also provides a situation where faithfulness alone is not enough. If markedness hierarchies are expressed by faithfulness constraints alone, and – as HP suggest – there is only faithfulness to marked values, the most-marked values should always be preserved in coalescence. The Pāli coalescence /lab^h-tum/ → [lad:^{h}um] is a useful example. When /b^h/ and /t/ coalesce, MAX{dors,lab} demands that [labial] survive instead of the less-marked [coronal]. However, the output is the coronal [d:^{h}]; therefore, there must be some constraint C that outranks MAX{dors,lab}, and C must favour coronals over labials. In the strong version of HP's proposal, C cannot be a faithfulness constraint as faithfulness constraints respect PoM: i.e. there is no MAX{coronal}. Therefore, C must be an output constraint that favours coronals over labials – i.e. *{dors,lab}. The strong version of HP's theory does not allow such PoA-referring output constraints, but only general ones that militate against structure (*STRUC).

The final point relates to triggering and undergoing various phenomena. In Standard Malay, /k/ neutralizes to [?], but /p/ and /t/ do not. To prevent /p/ and /t/ neutralizing, MAX{dors,lab,cor} must outrank the constraint that forces neutralization – i.e. *STRUC or at least *PLACE. However, with such a ranking there is now no way to force /k/ to neutralize. To get rid of /k/, a constraint that targets dorsals (i.e. *{dors}) must outrank MAX{dors,lab,cor}. However, such a *{dors} constraint is not allowed in the strong version of the theory because it is an output constraint that refers to a feature hierarchy.

In short, there is no way to avoid having output constraints that refer to markedness hierarchies.

8.7.2 Segmental vs. featural correspondence

The weak form of HP's theory is that markedness hierarchies have both output constraints and MAX[F] and DEP[F] constraints. This proposal contrasts with CoMP, which uses IDENT[F] constraints.

The difference between IDENT[F] and MAX[F]/DEP[F] is significant (e.g. Lombardi 1995, 1999; McCarthy 1995, 2001b; Causley 1997; Pulleyblank 1998). For IDENT[F], the correspondence relation is 'segment-based' (McCarthy & Prince 1995). In informal terms, features do not have a life independent of their root nodes. In contrast, MAX[F] and DEP[F] allow features to persist even when the root node they were attached to has disappeared. Quasi-tableau (37) illustrates the difference. IDENT{dors} is not violated by candidate (c) because the constraint is only violated when corresponding segments differ in terms of [dorsal] specification; in (c), there is no segment that corresponds to /k/, so IDENT{dors} is vacuously satisfied. In contrast, MAX{dors} requires all underlying dorsal features to be present in the output.

(37)

/ka/	IDENT{dors}	MAX{dors}
(a) ka		
(b) ta	*	*
(c) a		*

There is a reason to have only IDENT constraints, as in CoMP (also see Keer 1999; Struijke 2001). IDENT constraints make a strong prediction about deletion: only marked things can be deleted. For PoA, this means that no language can delete [t] without also deleting some more-marked segment – i.e. [k] and [p].

The reason can be seen by trying to construct a ranking which deletes /t/ but not [k] and [p] in coda position. To eliminate /t/, *{dors,lab,cor} has to outrank MAX, the constraint that preserves segments. However, this ranking ensures that /k/ and /p/ will delete too. Ranking IDENT{dors,lab} above *{dors,lab,cor} has no effect, as tableau (38) shows. Candidate (b) can never beat (c) or (a) because IDENT{dors,lab} is vacuously satisfied in deletion.

(38)

/ak?ot/	IDENT{dors,lab}	*{dors,lab,cor}	MAX
(a) ak?ot		**!	
(b) ak?o		*!	*
☞ (c) a?o			**

In contrast, it is straightforward to produce a [k p] inventory through deletion using MAX[F], as in tableau (39). Candidate (b) loses to (c) because MAX{dors,lab} not only bans feature change, but also feature deletion.

(39)

/ak?ot/	MAX{dors,lab}	*{dors,lab,cor}	MAX{dors,lab,cor}
(a) a?o	*!		**
(b) ak?ot		**!	
☞ (c) ak?o		*	*

In summary, IDENT[F] predicts that deletion cannot produce disharmonic inventories: if an unmarked element is deleted in a particular environment, then all more-marked elements must also be deleted. In contrast, MAX [F] predicts that deletion can produce anything.

There are a number of cases where deletion targets only marked elements. For example, only apicals are permitted in Lardil codas; /p/, /k/, and laminal stops are deleted (Hale 1973:424–5; Prince & Smolensky 1993:98ff.). In Siuslawan (Frachtenberg 1922:456–7; Trigo 1988:108), coda /k/ is deleted but /p/ and /ʔ/ survive intact (there are no alternations that show /t/'s fate, but CoMP predicts it cannot delete – it may neutralize to [ʔ]).

To summarize, the facts suggest that MAX[F] is undesirable. However, much more work needs to be done on deletion phenomena. As yet very few typological generalizations about which segments delete while others survive are well supported. One great danger is that deletion and coalescence often have similar effects. For example, Hume (2003) identifies a process in Sri Lankan Portuguese creole as deletion, based on data from Smith (1978): 'a word-final labial consonant is optionally deleted in SLPC before a word beginning with a vowel or /j/, and less frequently before a pause; nasalization is realized on the preceding vowel'. However, this phenomenon is more readily analysable as coalescence, so accounting for the fact that the nasal consonant's nasality is realized on the vowel: e.g. /əkə taːm/ → [əkə tãː], not *[əkə taː].

Another danger is that some apparent PoA-motivated deletions are really conditioned by other factors. For example, Catalan word-final /n/ deletes while /m/ and /ɲ/ do not: e.g. [plɛ] 'full' (cf. [plɛn-a]), cf. [som] 'we are', [sɛɲ] 'sense' (Mascaró 1976; Hualde 1992:404). However, /n/ is deleted under complex conditions: it must be underlyingly (i) in absolute final position (cf. /plɛn-s/ →[plɛns], *[plɛs]), /kuntent/ →[kuntén] 'happy', *[kunté] (cf. [kuntént-ə]), (ii) preceded by a vowel: /karn/ >[karn], *[kar] 'meat', and (iii) in a stressed syllable (cf. [pətéʃin] 'they may suffer'). These factors suggest that /n/-deletion is not simply driven by PoA markedness considerations, but by some other condition, perhaps an elimination of a prosodic word appendix.

In short, deletion offers a way to decide between the MAX[F] and IDENT[F] approaches.

8.7.3 Reference to the least marked

The final alternative to be discussed here is Gouskova's (2003) proposal that constraints never refer to the least-marked element in a hierarchy. This proposal is called the NOZERO principle (p.4), and a constraint component that obeys NOZERO is called 'lenient'. Gouskova focuses on output constraints alone, but it is natural to extend the generalization to faithfulness constraints. In present terms, this means that there are no constraints of the form *{dors,lab,cor,gl} or IDENT{dors,lab,cor,gl}, or – for voice – *{±voice} or IDENT{±voice}.

In terms of undergoers of phenomena, it is difficult to show that there are constraints that mention the least-marked element. A constraint like *{dors,lab,cor,gl} can never force glottals to neutralize because there is nothing less marked for the glottal to become (without deleting entirely – see below). This is the situation of 'Harmonic Ascent' discussed in §8.4.2.

However, conflation shows that least-marked elements must be mentioned in faithfulness constraints. In §6.2.3 the constraint IDENT{±voice} was argued to be crucial in producing conflation in Swedish. The ranking ‖ IDENT{±voice} » *{+voice} » IDENT[+voice] ‖ prevents voiced segments from being neutralized generally, but allows *{+voice} to influence the outcome of assimilation. The general ranking schema for faithfulness conflation is ‖ IDENT{mF, uF} » *{mF} » IDENT{mF} ‖, so reference to the least-marked element is essential.

In terms of triggering processes, it is essential for output constraints to mention the least-marked element. For example, if glottal could not be mentioned by output constraints, the Marked-Cluster constraint *{dors,lab,cor}{dors,lab,cor,gl} could not exist (§4.3.2.1). Therefore, glottals would never be allowed to trigger assimilation, contrary to fact (§8.4.1.3).

In any case, it is not clear whether leniency has any (pervasive) empirical effects. Leniency seems to rely on the idea that there are perfectly unmarked segments and structures, at least in some environments. However, the preceding chapters have emphasized that markedness hierarchies conflict, with the net result that no segment is 'the least marked'. For example, a lenient implementation of the PoA hierarchy | dorsal 〉 labial 〉 coronal 〉 glottal | would lack the constraint *{dors,lab,cor,gl}, but this lack does not mean that glottals avoid violating *all* output constraints. The sonority hierarchy treats glottals as highly marked, so *MAR/glottal bans glottals. So, even without *{dors,lab,cor,gl}, every segment violates some output constraint, and Ø is the most harmonic output.

To expand on this point, Gouskova (2003:188) discusses a lenient version of the $-\Delta_{Ft}/x$ sonority constraints (called *MAR$_{Ft}/x$ in her work), where there is no *$-\Delta_{Ft}$/a since [a] is the least-marked sonority level in non-DTEs. She notes: 'GEN is able to provide at least some forms that do not violate any [lenient] *MAR$_{Ft}/x$ constraints, and a subset of them does not even violate any sonority constraints at all. [Lenient] *MAR$_{Ft}/x$ and *NUC/x put together cannot match the power of *STRUC(σ) or *V.' Gouskova's claim is valid, but only to a very limited extent once *all* possible sonority-DTE constraints are considered. The problem is that sonority provides a situation where there are many conflicts placed on the same prosodic positions (as discussed in chapter 7). For example, a vowel may be under pressure to be highly sonorous if it is the DTE of a foot, but under pressure to have low sonority if it is the DTE of any higher category. In fact, the only time that a vowel can escape violating any DTE/sonority constraint (even with lenient constraints) is when it is a low vowel in the DTE of the highest

8.7 Markedness is expressed in both output and preservation constraints 401

phrase — the utterance phrase. Even in this position, the vowel is subject to constraints that refer to featural hierarchies such as on roundness, backness, and ATR. Once these are factored in, it is possible that [æ] as the DTE of an utterance phrase will be the only vowel to escape violating both DTE/sonority and featural markedness constraints with a lenient CON. It is not clear what empirical advantage this gives over a theory without leniency — i.e. one that has constraints that assign a violation to the least-marked hierarchy element. In short, even lenient DTE/sonority constraints *almost* entirely match the power of a constraint like *V(owel), with the one situation in which they do not being negligible.

For non-DTEs, the same problem of hierarchy conflict occurs. Onsets are non-DTEs of every prosodic category, and not DTEs of any prosodic category. Therefore, if there is no constraint such as $*-\Delta_\mu /\geq\{-\text{voiced stops}\}$, [t] as an onset will not violate any (non-)DTE/sonority constraints at all. However, [t] will still violate *{dors,lab,cor}, therefore [t] will not avoid violating all markedness constraints, and Ø will still be the only form to completely satisfy all the negatively formulated markedness constraints. To be clear, Gouskova's claim is only that '[Lenient] *MAR_Ft/*x* and *NUC/*x* put together cannot match the power of *STRUC(σ) or *V', and here I am observing that the DTE/sonority constraints and PoA constraints together match the power of a ban on structure generally, or at least a ban on consonants.

In summary, the value of leniency is curtailed by hierarchy conflict. If | α 〉 β | in one hierarchy and | β 〉 α | in another, the lenient constraints *{α} and *{β} together still favour Ø over both [α] and [β], and in this respect have no different effect than having an additional constraint *{α,β}.

However, this discussion has so far not addressed the underlying issue: i.e. why (it seems) structure is never banned outright, and Ø is never favoured over having at least something. For example, with a constraint like *{dors,lab,cor,gl}, what would prevent a language without any consonants? The answer is probably that Competence mechanisms do allow such a language. However, a language without consonants would probably not transmit well in language acquisition given the tendency to hear consonant sounds where they are not (e.g. intervocalic glides, word-initial [ʔ]).

In any case, in some environments consonants are completely eliminated: many languages ban all consonants outside onsets (e.g. Māori — Bauer 1993), and could be accounted for by the ranking ‖ ONSET » *{dors,lab,cor,gl} » MAX ‖. In other words, there are constraints that do ban all structure in some environments (e.g. NOCODA), and they may simply be cover terms for the effect of constraints that ban all members of a hierarchy.

402 8 *Predictions and alternatives*

Finally, a constraint that refers to every element on a hierarchy can be used to motivate deletion, as Gouskova observes. For example, a constraint like $*-\Delta_{Ft} \geq \{\text{all vowels}\}$ can force syncope – the deletion of all vowels in the unstressed part of a foot. An example is found in Eastern Ojibwa (Piggott 1980): e.g. /mittikw/ → [mt'tik] 'tree', /akkan/→[k'kan] 'bone', /sanakat/ → [s'na₁kat]. Gouskova argues that syncope is not motivated by constraints that ban all vowels, but is always really metrically conditioned: a deletion such as /pata/ → [('pat)] can be seen as the desire to have a heavy stressed syllable (cf. [('pa.ta)]). The problem with this argument is that syncope occurs in Eastern Ojibwa even though there is no metrical advantage; the syncope does not increase the number of heavy syllables: e.g. *[(sa'na)(₁kat)] and [('sna)(₁kat)] both have one heavy syllable. It also does not eliminate unstressed syllables: /akkan/ could be realized as *[(₁ak)('kan)] where all syllables are stressed and footed. What motivates the vowel deletion is the desire to get rid of all unstressed footed vowels: i.e. /sanakat/ → [(s'na)(₁kat)], *[(sa̱.'na)(₁kat)].

In summary, both output and faithfulness constraints must be able to refer to the least-marked element in a hierarchy. Such reference is essential in accounting for the output of coalescence, triggering, and is not undesirable in accounting for syncope. To conclude, the proposals about markedness hierarchies remain: every hierarchy has a set of output and faithfulness constraints. The faithfulness constraints are of the IDENT variety, not MAX[F] and DEP[F], and all members – even the least-marked one – are mentioned.

8.8   Conclusions

This chapter has identified some of the more important predictions of the theory and the assumptions which underlie them. For example, the claim that faithfulness can prevent marked elements from undergoing markedness reduction predicts that a phenomenon will not show overt markedness asymmetries if faithfulness is relevant to it. Conversely, if faithfulness is irrelevant markedness asymmetries will be visible. A related prediction is that there can be no phenomenon in which only marked feature values survive. In addition, it is predicted that all phenomena will show markedness conflation, and faithfulness conflation if relevant.

Several core assumptions were also identified. The most obvious one is that there are markedness asymmetries in natural language and that Competence mechanisms produce markedness effects. Markedness asymmetries are not due to external mechanisms, such as diachronic change. These points were considered in §8.3, and alternatives were argued to be empirically inadequate.

8.8 Conclusions

CoMP relies on constraint form to implement markedness. In contrast, theories that relate representation to markedness were argued in §8.4 to face significant challenges. Similarly, §8.5 showed that CoMP's concept of markedness does not rely on the form of a language's inventory (i.e. its contrastive oppositions). Rice's (2006) contrastive theory of markedness was shown to be less restrictive than CoMP. Section 8.6 argued that there is no need for a notion of 'relative markedness', where a feature value is only marked if it is unfaithful to its underlying form. Finally, §8.7 argued that faithfulness constraints are segmentally mediated (i.e. IDENT[F], not MAX[F]/ DEP[F]), and constraints mention all elements in a hierarchy.

Space limitations prevented this chapter from discussing every approach to markedness, and also from examining individual approaches in detail. For example, there was no space to discuss Hume's (2004) functionalist theory in which markedness is based on 'perceptual salience, articulatory simplicity, functional load, social factors (e.g., prestige value), and the speaker/hearer's experience with the usage of linguistic elements, e.g. sounds, words'. Nevertheless, I believe the main points made in this chapter broadly relate to all current theories of markedness. For example, Hume (2004) claims that markedness is 'a probabilistic notion', while this chapter has argued that it is not – it is entirely categorical and predictive once PoM, hierarchy conflict, and influences such as assimilation are taken into account.

In short, CoMP differs from many current conceptions of markedness. The previous chapters have shown that its empirical predictions are borne out, and that the known counter-examples do not survive close scrutiny.

9 Conclusions

9.1 Markedness

This book has argued that 'markedness' describes the empirical effects of the formal principles that express markedness reduction, Preservation of the Marked, and conflation. These leading ideas are summarized in (1).

(1) (a) *Competence markedness vs. Performance markedness*
Markedness is part of grammatical Competence. Markedness in Competence is distinct from (apparently similar) Performance-related phenomena.
(b) *Markedness reduction*
There is grammatical pressure to eliminate marked elements.
(c) *Preservation of the Marked*
There is grammatical pressure to preserve marked elements.
(d) *Markedness conflation*
Distinctions between markedness categories can be collapsed (i.e. conflated), but never reversed.

In terms of the theory's formalism, markedness is expressed as a theory of phonological feature values and restrictions on constraints, set within Optimality Theory. The feature values encode markedness hierarchies, and the restrictions on possible constraints allow the feature value hierarchies to influence phonological phenomena. Of particular importance, there is no restriction on the constraints' ranking. However, all constraints – both output and faithfulness – refer to the same sets of elements: if a constraint refers to a member x of hierarchy H, it also refers to all members that are more marked than x in H. Schematically, for a hierarchy like (2a) there will be a set of freely rankable output constraints like (2b) and a corresponding set of faithfulness constraints like those in (2c).

(2) (a) $|x \rangle y \rangle z|$
(b) $*\{x\}$, $*\{x,y\}$, $*\{x,y,z\}$
(c) IDENT$\{x\}$, IDENT$\{x,y\}$, IDENT$\{x,y,z\}$

Certain markedness hierarchies must be combined with prosodic elements in forming constraints. The prosodic elements are an extended notion of Liberman & Prince's (1977) Designated Terminal Element. They allow reference to heads and non-heads at every prosodic level.

One of the biggest challenges facing any exploration of markedness is in teasing apart the different ways the word has been used. The previous chapters have argued that it is crucial to distinguish 'markedness' as referring to i-language (i.e. C(ompetence)-markedness) from its use in describing phenomena external to i-language (i.e. P(erformance)). Only once this distinction is made is it clear what 'markedness' refers to.

Synchronic phonological phenomena are relevant to c-markedness because they show the effects of i-language mechanisms directly. In contrast, external (Performance) mechanisms have a heavy influence on phenomena like language acquisition, loanword adaptation, diachronic change, and typological frequency. Once a full theory of Performance is established it may be possible to identify the Competence influences in these phenomena. But at this point in time, synchronic alternations are the only sure insight into c-markedness.

Alternations are key to understanding c-markedness. The previous chapters have emphasized that c-markedness effects are most clearly visible when the mapping from inputs to outputs is determinable. Static regularities are rarely helpful. For example, the coda neutralization of /k/→[ʔ] in Standard Malay shows that there is an output constraint that favours glottals over dorsals because there are alternations such as [baiʔ] 'good', cf. [kə-bai.k-an] (§3.3.1). In contrast, the fact that Tahitian lacks a surface [k] but has a surface [ʔ] is much less revealing (Coppenrath & Prévost 1974). There are no alternations that show /k/ neutralizing to [ʔ] in Tahitian; /k/ could delete, lenite to [ŋ], or coalesce. The Tahitian situation does not provide evidence for an output constraint that favours [ʔ] over [k], either: [ʔ] may survive for faithfulness reasons, not through markedness reduction. In short, alternations give great insight into c-markedness; phonotactics are far less revealing.

This book has focused entirely on markedness as it relates to i-language, but similar issues arise for Performance asymmetries. They include issues like why certain vowel inventories are more frequent than others (e.g. de Boer 2001), how historical change impacts on frequency (e.g. Blevins 2004), and how text frequency affects language acquisition (Stites et al. 2004). While this work has said nothing about Performance asymmetries, it has contributed to understanding p-markedness by identifying those phenomena that are relevant to c-markedness and those that are not.

Another major challenge in dealing with markedness is determining where markedness effects should be visible. The proposals predict that a phenomenon should show markedness asymmetries if (a) faithfulness is irrelevant and (b) there is no other directly conflicting markedness hierarchy. All other phenomena will not show any markedness influences overtly.

For example, preservation is irrelevant for default consonant epenthesis because the epenthetic consonant does not correspond to any input segment. Consequently, it will be entirely subject to the whims of the markedness hierarchies, and so produce a segment whose features are unmarked with respect to some hierarchy, or have a compromise value that partially satisfies several different hierarchies. In contrast, preservation is relevant for the undergoers of neutralization: if /k/ undergoes neutralization to become [ʔ], the input's PoA is not preserved. Because marked values can be preserved, some languages may retain /k/ intact while less-marked elements like /p/ and /t/ will neutralize. The result is that any PoA can undergo neutralization.

There is one important caveat about what it means to 'show markedness effects'. If a phenomenon shows markedness effects, it is solely under the influence of output constraints that relate to some hierarchy. However, hierarchies may conflict with the result that markedness effects may be obscured. An extreme example is found in vowel epenthesis. Syllable heads favour highly sonorous elements, while unstressed syllables favour low sonority elements. These two markedness preferences can compromise with each other, and so allow an epenthetic vowel to have any sonority – i.e. [a ɛ e i ə ɨ]. The general point here is that there is no such thing as the 'unmarked segment'. Markedness is not defined at the segmental level, but rather in terms of feature values. Different markedness hierarchies may inadvertently conflict, with the result that there is a range of potential 'least-marked' segments, depending on which hierarchy is dominant.

A practical implication is that it is not an easy task to determine markedness relations. A search for unqualified absolute universals will almost certainly reap few rewards. A statement like 'the output of phenomenon X is always segment y' is bound to be incorrect because there are many partially conflicting markedness hierarchies, and faithfulness obscures their effect in many situations. Assimilation and dissimilation may also make features become more marked in some environments while marked elements may be prevented from undergoing a variety of processes. In short, while it certainly is possible to detect markedness asymmetries, it is not a straightforward task.

Finally, the theory predicts that every markedness hierarchy will allow conflation, both in reduction and preservation. Conflation in reduction is only visible for markedness hierarchies that have more than two members, but it is potentially visible for all hierarchies in preservation.

The theory also makes a number of predictions about what is not relevant for markedness. It was argued that markedness is not related to representational complexity (§8.4), does not depend on language-specific contrastive oppositions (§8.5), and imposes absolute thresholds (§8.6).

9.2 Markedness in the future

Markedness has been an important concept right from the beginning of phonological theory. It played a central role for the Prague School (e.g. Trubetzkoy 1939), and it has always been an issue in generative grammar (though occasionally a marginal one). In Chomsky & Halle (1968:ch.9), markedness is formally expressed as a theory of feature values and restrictions on how rules can refer to those values. For Stampe (1972), markedness is expressed as restrictions on rule form. SPE's proposal was extended in the 1980s to concepts of representation and underspecification: the unmarked value of a feature is one that is not present in the representation. In broad terms, the present approach shares much with these theories: markedness is expressed through a theory of feature values and how constraints may refer to those values.

Given its long history, it may be somewhat surprising that at the time of writing markedness is an extremely contentious topic. The past few years have seen challenges to many traditional beliefs about markedness. These include proposals that many commonly accepted markedness diagnostics are invalid (e.g. Rice 1999a,b, 2004a,b, 2006; de Lacy 2002a). There have also been challenges to how markedness should be expressed formally, as in Prince & Smolensky's (1993) and Smolensky's (1993) rejection of representational accounts of markedness, and de Lacy's (2004) rejection of fixed ranking as a way to express markedness. Similarly, there is disagreement over whether there are any markedness diagnostics at all (Vaux 2001; Hume 2003), and whether markedness is even relevant for a Competence theory of language (Blevins 2004).

In some ways there seem to be more questions about markedness now than ever before: e.g. is markedness really relevant to Competence mechanisms? If so, how is markedness expressed formally? Is contrast central to understanding markedness? Is markedness related to representational complexity?

This book has presented answers to these questions. Markedness is relevant for Competence mechanisms; some phenomena that apparently present challenges to this view are really related to Performance. Other phenomena do not exhibit markedness asymmetries by 'Preservation of the Marked': markedness effects can only be overtly visible when faithfulness is irrelevant (chapter 4). Markedness is universal and independent of a language's contrastive oppositions (§8.5). There is also no need to refer to representational complexity; there are fundamental flaws in theories that attempt to do so (§8.4).

Nevertheless, I suspect that not everyone will agree with the conclusions presented here. Consequently, I think it is a safe prediction that the concept of markedness will continue to be controversial.

In any case, the theory proposed in this book provides a framework for further inquiry into markedness. There are many issues for future research within the framework presented here. The concepts of Preservation of the Marked and conflation are not just relevant for phonology, but also for syntax. Work by Aissen (1999) and Woolford (1999), among others, has shown how markedness hierarchies can be used to good effect in syntactic analysis. Woolford (in prep.) explores the effects of the theory's constraints in producing conflation in syntactic phenomena. The theory also has implications for understanding language acquisition, as explored in Pater & Barlow 2002:§3.4 and Farris & Gierut 2006.

Many phenomena have not been examined in the context of the theory, but require re-examination because of it. For example, the theory makes clear predictions about dissimilation and vowel harmony in terms of where they can apply, how they can impose conflation, and so on. In fact, even the PoA constraints require further examination. For example, this book did not discuss the markedness of palatals and minor PoA (though see Wheeler 2005a:ch.6 for proposals).

Even some major concepts require further exploration at a fundamental level. For example, it is not known whether categories in different markedness hierarchies can conflate with each other. There are also many questions about hierarchy combination. For example, can the PoA hierarchy combine with different manners of articulation to form both output and faithfulness constraints? Is there a general mechanism that allows different hierarchies to be combined? Smolensky's (1993) local conjunction seems too powerful a formal device, but it is likely that some combination mechanism is necessary (§4.3.2, Gouskova 2001). Related to this issue is why prosodic elements (i.e. (non-)DTEs) can combine with the sonority hierarchy and not segmental hierarchies; it is unclear whether this is necessarily a stipulation or derives from some deeper principle.

To conclude, the aim of this book was to present a theory of markedness. The key to understanding markedness is in determining what the term refers to. Once 'markedness' is taken to refer to synchronic Competence-related phenomena that are not influenced by preservation, it is possible to see its empirical effects and determine its expression in a formal theory of grammar.

References

Abaglo, P. and Diana Archangeli (1989). Language particular underspecification: Gengbe /e/ and Yoruba /i/. *Linguistic Inquiry* 20: 457–80.
Abbott, Miriam (1991). Macushi. In Desmond J. Derbyshire and Geoffrey K. Pullum (eds.) *Handbook of Amazonian languages*. Vol.3. Berlin, Mouton de Gruyter, pp.23–160.
Abondolo, Daniel (1998a). Hungarian. In Daniel Abondolo (ed.) *The Uralic languages*. London, Routledge, pp.428–56.
  (1998b). Khanty. In Daniel Abondolo (ed.) *The Uralic languages*. London, Routledge, pp.358–86.
Abu-Mansour, Mahasen (1996). Voice as a privative feature: assimilation in Arabic. In Mahasen Abu-Mansour (ed.) *Perspectives on Arabic linguistics VIII*. Amsterdam, John Benjamins, pp.201–31.
Abu-Salim, I. M. (1982). Syllable structure and syllabification in Palestinian Arabic. *Studies in the Linguistic Sciences* 12.1: 103–22.
Adda-Decker, Martine, Philippe Boula de Mareüil, and Lori Lamel (1999). Pronunciation variants in French: Schwa and liaison. In J. J. Ohala, Y. Hasegawa, M. Ohala, D. Granville, and A. C. Bailey (eds.) *Proceedings of ICPhS-99, The XIVth International Congress of the Phonetic Sciences*. San Francisco, pp. 2239–42.
Adler, Allison (2004). Faithfulness and perception in loanword adaptation: a case study from Hawaiian. Handout from the 12th Manchester Phonology Meeting. http://www.geocities.com/alycat715/papers.html (14 February 2006).
Ahmad, Zaharani (1994). Vowel epenthesis in Malay. In Cecilia Odé and Wim Stokhof (eds.) *Proceedings of the 7th international conference on Austronesian linguistics*. Leiden, Leiden University, pp.183–200.
Ahn, Sang-Cheol (1998). *An introduction to Korean phonology*. Korea, Hanshin.
Aissen, Judith (1999). Markedness and subject choice in Optimality Theory. *Natural Language and Linguistic Theory* 17.4: 673–711.
Akinlabi, Akinbiyi (1993). Underspecification and the phonology of Yoruba /r/. *Linguistic Inquiry* 24.1: 139–60.
Alderete, John (1995). Winnebago accent and Dorsey's law. In Jill Beckman, Laura Walsh Dickey, and Suzanne Urbanczyk (eds.) *Papers in Optimality Theory (UMOP 18)*. Amherst, MA, GLSA, pp.21–51.
  (1997). Dissimilation as local conjunction. In Kiyomi Kusumoto (ed.) *Proceedings of NELS 27*. Amherst, MA, GLSA, pp.17–32.

Alderete, John, Jill Beckman, Laura Benua, Amalia Gnanadesikan, John McCarthy, and Suzanne Urbanczyk (1999). Reduplication with fixed segmentism. *Linguistic Inquiry* 30: 327–64.
Anderson, Mike and Malcolm Ross (2002). Sudest. In John Lynch, Malcolm Ross and Terry Crowley (eds.) *The Oceanic languages*. Richmond, Curzon Press, pp.322–46.
Anderson, Stephen R. (1974). *The organization of phonology*. New York, Academic Press.
Andrews, Edna (1990). *Markedness theory: the union of asymmetry and semiosis in language*. Durham, NC, Duke University Press.
Anttila, Arto (2006). Variation and optionality. In Paul de Lacy (ed.) *The Cambridge handbook of phonology*. Cambridge, Cambridge University Press, ch.22.
Ao, Benjamin Xiaoping (1993). *Phonetics and phonology of Nantong Chinese*. Doctoral dissertation, Ohio State University.
Aoyama, Katsura (1999). Reanalyzing the Japanese coda nasal in Optimality Theory. In Shin Ja Hwang and Arle R. Lommel (eds.) *LACUS Forum XXV*. Fullerton, CA, Linguistic Association of Canada and the United States, pp.105–17.
Archangeli, Diana (1984). *Underspecification in Yawelmani phonology and morphology*. Doctoral dissertation, Massachusetts Institute of Technology.
　(1988). Aspects of underspecification theory. *Phonology* 5: 183–208.
Aronoff, Mark, Azhar Arsyad, Hasan Basri, and Ellen Broselow (1987). Tier configuration in Makassarese reduplication. In Anna Bosch, Eric Schiller and Barbara Need (eds.) *CLS 23: Parasession on autosegmental and metrical phonology*. Vol.2. Chicago, Chicago Linguistic Society, pp.1–15.
Asher, R.E. (1985). *Tamil*. London, Croom Helm.
Austin, Peter (1981). *A grammar of Diyari, South Australia*. Cambridge, Cambridge University Press.
Avery, Peter and Keren Rice (1988). Underspecification theory and the coronal node. In Peter Avery (ed.) *Toronto Working Papers in Linguistics 9*. Toronto, TWPL, pp.101–21.
　(1989a). Constraining underspecification. In Juli Carter and Rose-Marie Déchaine (eds.) *Proceedings of NELS 19*. Amherst, GLSA, pp.1–15.
　(1989b). Segmental structure and coronal underspecification. *Phonology* 6: 179–200.
Bach, Emmon and Robert T. Harms (1972). How do languages get crazy rules? In R. P. Stockwell and R. K. S. Macauley (eds.) *Linguistic change and generative theory*. Bloomington, Indiana University Press, pp. 1–21.
Baertsch, Karen (1998). Onset sonority distance constraints through local conjunction. In M. Catherine Gruber, Derrick Higgins, Kenneth S. Olson, and Tamra Wysocki (eds.) *CLS 34–2: the panels*. Chicago, Chicago Linguistic Society, pp.1–15.
Bakalla, Mohammed (1973). *The morphology and phonology of Meccan Arabic*. Doctoral dissertation, School of Oriental and African Studies.
Baković, Eric (1999a). *Harmony, dominance, and control*. Doctoral dissertation, Rutgers University.
　(1999b) Assimilation to the unmarked. In Jim Alexander, Na-Rae Han, and Michelle Minnick Fox (eds.) *University of Pennsylvania Working Papers in Linguistics* 6.1.

http://www.ling.upenn.edu/papers/v6.1-contents.html (14 February 2006) [also *Rutgers Optimality Archive* 340].
  (1999c). Deletion, insertion, and symmetrical identity. *Harvard Working Papers in Linguistics* 7 [also *Rutgers Optimality Archive* 300].
  (2000). Nasal place neutralization in Spanish. *Rutgers Optimality Archive* 386.
Barnes, Jonathan (2002). *Positional neutralization: a phonologization approach to typological patterns.* Doctoral dissertation, University of California, Berkeley.
Bates, Dawn, Thomas Hess, and Vi Hilbert (1994). *Lushootseed dictionary.* Seattle, University of Washington Press.
Battistella, Edwin L. (1990). *Markedness: the evaluative superstructure of language.* Albany, NY, State University of New York Press.
  (1996). *The logic of markedness.* New York, Oxford University Press.
Bauer, Winifred (1993). *Maori.* New York, London, Routledge.
Beaumont, Clive H. (1979). *The Tigak language of New Ireland.* Pacific Linguistics Series B, No. 58. Canberra, Department of Linguistics, Research School of Pacific Studies, The Australian National University.
Beckman, Jill N. (1998). *Positional faithfulness.* Doctoral dissertation, University of Massachusetts, Amherst.
Beckman, Mary E., Koneyama Yoneyama, and Jan Edwards (2003). Language-specific and language-universal aspects of lingual obstruent productions in Japanese-acquiring children. *Journal of the Phonetic Society of Japan* 7: 18–28.
Benua, Laura (1997). *Transderivational identity: phonological relations between words.* Doctoral dissertation, University of Massachusetts, Amherst.
Bermúdez-Otero, Ricardo and Kersti Börjars (2005). Markedness in phonology and in syntax: the problem of grounding. In Patrick Honeybone and Ricardo Bermúdez-Otero (eds.) *Linguistic knowledge: perspectives from phonology and from syntax.* Special Issue of *Lingua* 116.5.
Bernhardt, Barbara and Joseph Stemberger (2006). Phonological impairment in children and adults. In Paul de Lacy (ed.) *The Cambridge handbook of phonology.* Cambridge, Cambridge University Press, ch.25.
Bessell, Nicola J. (1998). Local and non-local consonant-vowel interaction in Interior Salish. *Phonology* 15: 1–40.
Bethin, Christina Y. (1987). Syllable-final laxing in Ukrainian. *Folia Slavica* 8.2/3: 185–97.
Bickerton, Derek (1984). The language bioprogram hypothesis. *The Behavioral and Brain Sciences* 7.2: 173–221.
Bittle, William (1963). Kiowa-Apache. In Harry Hoijer (ed.) *Studies in the Athapaskan languages.* Berkeley, University of California Press, pp.76–101.
Blevins, Juliette (1995). The syllable in phonological theory. In John Goldsmith (ed.) *The handbook of phonological theory.* Oxford, Blackwell, pp.206–44.
  (2001). *Nhanda: an aboriginal language of Western Australia.* Oceanic Linguistics Special Publication 30. Honolulu, University of Hawai'i Press.
  (2003). *Consonant epenthesis: natural and unnatural histories.* Berkeley, University of California.
  (2004). *Evolutionary phonology.* Cambridge, Cambridge University Press.

Bloomfield, Leonard (1924). Notes on the Fox language. *International Journal of American Linguistics* 3.2: 219–32.
Blust, Robert (1990). Three recurrent changes in Oceanic languages. In J. H. C. S. Davidson (ed.) *Pacific island languages: essays in honour of G. B. Milner*. London, University of London and School of Oriental and African Studies, pp.7–28.
Bobaljik, Jonathan (1996). Assimilation in the Inuit languages and the place of the uvular nasal. *International Journal of American Linguistics* 62.4: 323–50.
  (1997). Mostly predictable: cyclicity and the distribution of schwa in Itelmen. *Rutgers Optimality Archive* 208.
Boersma, Paul (1998). Spreading in functional phonology. *Proceedings of the International Congress of Phonetic Sciences* 22: 1–20.
Bogoras, Waldemar (1922). Chukchee. In Franz Boas (ed.) *Handbook of American Indian languages: Part 2*. Washington, Government Printing Office, pp.639–903.
Booij, Geert (1977). *Dutch morphology: a study of word formation in Generative Grammar*. Dordrecht, Foris.
  (1981). *Generatieve fonologie van het Nederlands*. Utrecht-Antwerpen, Het Spectrum.
  (1995). *The phonology of Dutch*. Oxford, Clarendon Press.
Boula de Mareüil, Philippe and Martine Adda-Decker (2002). Studying pronunciation variants in French by using alignment techniques. *Proceedings of the International Conference on Spoken Language Processing (ICSLP)*, Denver, pp.2273–6.
Brainard, Sherri (1994). *The phonology of Karao, the Phillipines*. Canberra, Australian National University.
Brakel, Arthur (1984). *Phonological markedness and distinctive features*. Bloomington, Indiana University Press.
  (1985). Reflections on the analysis of exceptions to the rule of Iberian Portuguese vowel reduction. *Hispanic Linguistics* 2.1: 63–85.
Breen, Gavan (1981). *The Mayu languages of the Queensland Gulf Country*. Canberra, Australian Institute of Aboriginal Studies.
Bright, William O. (1975). The Dravidian enunciative vowel. In H. F. Schiffman and C. M. Eastman (eds.) *Dravidian phonological systems*. Seattle, Institute for Comparative and Foreign Area Studies and University of Washington Press, pp.11–46.
Broadbent, Sylvia M. (1964). *The Southern Sierra Miwok language*. University of California Publications in Linguistics 38, Berkeley, University of California.
Broadbent, Sylvia M. and H. Pitkin (1964). A comparison of Miwok and Wintu. In William O. Bright (ed.) *Studies in Californian linguistics*. Los Angeles, University of California Press, pp.19–45.
Broselow, Ellen (1976). *The phonology of Egyptian Arabic*. Doctoral dissertation, University of Massachusetts, Amherst.
  (1982). On predicting the interaction of stress and epenthesis. *Glossa* 16:115–32.
  (2001). Uh-oh: glottal stops and syllable organization in Sulawesi. In Elizabeth Hume, Norval Smith, and Jeroen van de Weijer (eds.) *Surface syllable structure and segment sequencing*. Leiden, Holland Institute of Generative Linguistics, pp.77–90 [also *Rutgers Optimality Archive* 433].
Browman, Catherine P. and Louis Goldstein (1992). Articulatory phonology: an overview. *Phonetica* 49: 155–80.

Brown, Herbert A. (1986). *A comparative dictionary of Orokolo, Gulf of Papua*. Pacific Linguistics C-84. Canberra, Australian National University.
Buch, Hasit (1979). *An introduction to Gujarati language*. Gandhinagar, Director of languages, Gujarat State.
Buckley, Eugene (1994). *Theoretical aspects of Kashaya phonology and morphology*. Stanford, CA, CSLI Publications.
Butska, Luba (1997). *Voicing alternations in Ukrainian*. MA thesis, University of Toronto.
Bybee, Joan L. (1988). The diachronic dimension in explanation. In John A. Hawkins (ed.) *Explaining language universals*. Oxford, Basil Blackwell, pp.350–79.
  (2001). *Phonology and language use*. Cambridge Studies in Linguistics. Cambridge, Cambridge University Press.
Bye, Patrik (2001). *Virtual phonology: multiple opacity and rule sandwiching in North Saami*. Doctoral dissertation, University of Tromsø.
Cairns, Charles E. (1969). Markedness, neutralization and universal redundancy rules. *Language* 45: 863–85.
Cairns, Charles E. and Mark H. Feinstein (1982). Markedness and the theory of syllable structure. *Linguistic Inquiry* 13.2: 193–226.
Campbell, Lyle (1985). *The Pipil language of El Salvador*. Berlin, Mouton.
Cardona, George (1965). *Gujarati reference grammar*. Philadelphia, University of Philadelphia Press.
Casali, Roderic (1997). Vowel elision in hiatus contexts: which vowel goes? *Language* 73: 493–533.
Causley, Trisha (1997). Identity and featural correspondence: the Athapaskan case. In Kiyomi Kusumoto (ed.) *Proceedings of NELS 27*. Amherst, MA, GLSA, pp.93–105.
  (1999). *Complexity and markedness in Optimality Theory*. Doctoral dissertation, University of Toronto.
Chan, Marjorie K. M. (1985). *Fuzhou phonology: a nonlinear analysis of tone and stress*. Doctoral dissertation, University of Washington, Seattle.
Chen, Matthew (1973). Cross-dialectal comparison: a case study and some theoretical considerations. *Journal of Chinese Linguistics* 1.1: 38–63.
Cho, Young-mee (1988). Korean assimilation. In Hagit Borer (ed.) *Proceedings of WCCFL 7*. Stanford, CA, Stanford Linguistics Assocation, pp.41–52.
  (1991). The universality of the coronal articulator. In Carole Paradis and Jean-François Prunet (eds.) *The special status of coronals: internal and external evidence*. Phonetics and Phonology 2. San Diego, Academic Press, pp.159–79.
  (1999). *Parameters of consonantal assimilation*. Lincom studies in theoretical linguistics 15. Munich, Lincom Europa.
Choi, John Dongwook (1992a). An acoustic study of Kabardian vowels. *Journal of the International Phonetic Association* 21: 1–12.
  (1992b). *Phonetic underspecification and target-interpolation: an acoustic study of Marshallese vowel allophony*. Doctoral dissertation, UCLA.
Chomsky, Noam (1965). *Aspects of the theory of syntax*. Cambridge, MA, MIT Press.
  (1968). *Language and mind*. San Diego, Harcourt Brace Jovanovich.

(1981). *Lectures on government and binding*. Dordrecht, Foris.
(1986). *Knowledge of language: its nature, origin and use*. New York, Praeger.
Chomsky, Noam and Morris Halle (1968). *The sound pattern of English*. New York, Harper & Row.
Chomsky, Noam and Howard Lasnik (1977). Filters and control. *Linguistic Inquiry* 8: 425–504.
Christdas, Prathima (1988). *The phonology and morphology of Tamil*. Doctoral dissertation, Cornell University.
Chung, Sandra (1983). Transderivational relationships in Chamorro phonology. *Language* 59: 35–66.
Churchward, Henry M. (1953). *Tongan grammar*. London, Oxford University Press.
Churma, Donald G. and Yili Shi (1995). Glottal consonants and the 'sonority' hierarchy. In Marek Przezdziecki and Lindsay Whaley (eds.) *ESCOL '95*. Ithaca, NY, Cornell University, pp.25–37.
Clark, Ross (1976). *Aspects of Proto-Polynesian syntax*. Te Reo Monograph. Auckland, Linguistic Society of New Zealand.
Clements, George N. (1976). Palatalization: linking or assimilation? In S. S. Mufwene, C. A. Walker, and S. B. Steever (eds.) *Papers from CLS 12*. Chicago, Chicago Linguistic Society, pp.96–109.
(1985). The geometry of phonological features. *Phonology Yearbook* 2: 225–52.
(1988). Towards a substantive theory of feature specifications. In Juliette Blevins and Juli Carter (eds.) *Proceedings of NELS 18*. Amherst, MA, GLSA, pp.79–93.
(1990). The role of the sonority cycle in core syllabification. In John Kingston and Mary Beckman (eds.) *Papers in laboratory phonology 1: between the grammar and physics of speech*. New York, Cambridge University Press, pp.283–333.
(1991). Vowel height assimilation in Bantu languages. *Working papers of the Cornell phonetics laboratory* 5: 37–76.
(1992). The sonority cycle and syllable organization. In Wolfgang U. Dressler, Hans C. Luschützky, Oskar E. Pfeiffer, and John R. Rennison (eds.) *Phonologica 1988: proceedings of the 6th International Phonology Meeting*. Cambridge, Cambridge University Press, pp.63–76.
(1999). Affricates as noncountoured stops. In O. Fujimura, B. D. Joseph, and B. Palek (eds.) *Proceedings of LP '98*. Prague, Karolinum Press, pp.271–99.
Clements, George N. and Elizabeth Hume (1995). The internal organization of speech sounds. In John Goldsmith (ed.) *The handbook of phonological theory*. Oxford, Blackwell, pp.245–306.
Coetzee, Andries (2002). *Between-language frequency effects in phonological theory*. Ms., University of Massachusetts, Amherst.
Cohn, Abigail (1989). Stress in Indonesian and bracketing paradoxes. *Natural Language and Linguistic Theory* 7: 167–216.
Cohn, Abigail and John J. McCarthy (1994). Alignment and parallelism in Indonesian phonology. *Rutgers Optimality Archive* 25.
Colina, Sonia (1997). Epenthesis and deletion in Galician: an Optimality-theoretic approach. In Fernando Martinez-Gil and Alfonso Morales-Front (eds.) *Issues in the phonology and morphology of the major Iberian languages*. Washington, Georgetown University Press, pp.235–67.

Coppenrath, Hubert and Paul Prévost (1974). *Grammaire approfondie de la langue tahitienne (ancienne et moderne)*. Papeete, Librairie Pureroa.
Côté, Marie-Hélène and Geoffrey Morrison (2004). Experimental evidence and the nature of the schwa/zero alternation in French. Abstract from the 9th Conference on Laboratory Phonology. http://www.linguistics.uiuc.edu/labphon9/Abstract_PDF/cote.pdf (14 February 2006).
Creider, Chet A. (1986). Binary vs. *n*-ary features. *Lingua* 70.1: 1–14.
Crosswhite, Katherine M. (1998). Segmental vs. prosodic correspondence in Chamorro. *Phonology* 15.3: 281–316.
   (1999). *Vowel reduction in Optimality Theory*. Doctoral dissertation, University of California, Los Angeles.
   (2000). Sonority-driven reduction. In Pawel M. Nowak, Corey Yoquelet, and David Mortensen (eds.) *Proceedings of the Berkeley Linguistic Society 26S*. Berkeley, Berkeley Linguistics Society.
   (2004). Vowel reduction. In Bruce Hayes, Robert Kirchner, and Donca Steriade (eds.) *Phonetically-based phonology*. Cambridge, Cambridge University Press, ch.7.
Crowhurst, Megan (1994). Foot extrametricality and template mapping in Cupeño. *Natural Language and Linguistic Theory* 12.2: 177–201.
   (1996). An optimal alternative to conflation. *Phonology* 13: 409–24.
Crowhurst, Megan and Mark Hewitt (1997). Boolean operations and constraint interaction in Optimality Theory. *Rutgers Optimality Archive* 229.
Crowley, Terry (1983). Uradhi. In R. M. W. Dixon and Barry J. Blake (eds.) *Handbook of Australian languages*. Vol.3. Amsterdam, John Benjamins, pp.307–428.
Czaykowska-Higgins, Ewa (1988). *The interaction of phonology and morphology in Polish*. Doctoral dissertation, MIT.
   (1992). Placelessness, markedness, and Polish nasals. *Linguistic Inquiry* 23.1: 139–46.
Davies, John (1981). *Kobon*. Linguistica Descriptiva Series vol.3. Amsterdam, North-Holland.
Davis, Stuart (1998). Syllable contact in Optimality Theory. *Journal of Korean Linguistics* 23: 181–211.
de Boer, Bart (2001). *The origins of vowel systems*. Studies in the Evolution of Language. Oxford, Oxford University Press.
de Haas, Wim (1988). *A formal theory of vowel coalescence: a case study of Ancient Greek*. Publications in Language Sciences 30. Dordrecht, Foris.
de Lacy, Paul (1997). *Prosodic categorisation*. MA thesis, University of Auckland.
   (1998). A cooccurrence restriction in Maori. *Te Reo: Journal of the Linguistic Society of New Zealand* 40: 10–44.
   (1999). Tone and prominence. *Rutgers Optimality Archive* 333.
   (2000a). Heads, non-heads, and tone. Talk presented at the University of Tromso, Norway.
   (2000b). Markedness in prominent positions. In Ora Matushansky, Albert Costa, Javier Martin-Gonzalez, Lance Nathan, and Adam Szczegielniak (eds.) *HUMIT 2000: MITWPL 40*. Cambridge, MA, MIT Working Papers in Linguistics, pp.53–66.
   (2002a). *The formal expression of markedness*. PhD dissertation, University of Massachusetts, Amherst.

(2002b). Tone and stress in Optimality Theory. *Phonology* 19.1: 1–32.
(2003). Maximal words and the maori passive. In John McCarthy (ed.) *Optimality Theory in phonology: a reader*. Oxford, Blackwell, pp.495–512.
(2004). Markedness conflation in Optimality Theory. *Phonology* 21.2: 1–55.
(2006). The interaction of sonority, tone, and prosodic structure. In Paul de Lacy (ed.) *The Cambridge handbook of phonology*. Cambridge, Cambridge University Press, ch.12.
Dell, François and Mohamed Elmedlaoui (1985). Syllabic consonants and syllabification in Imdlawn Tashlhiyt Berber. *Journal of African Languages and Linguistics* 7: 105–30.
(1988). Syllabic consonants in Berber: some new evidence. *Journal of African Languages and Linguistics* 10: 1–17.
Demuth, Katherine (1995). Markedness and the development of prosodic structure. In Jill Beckman (ed.) *Proceedings of the North East Linguistic Society 25*. Amherst, MA, GLSA, pp.13–25.
Denwood, Philip (1999). *Tibetan*. Amsterdam, John Benjamins Publishing Company.
Derbyshire, Desmond C. (1979). *Hixkaryana*. Lingua Descriptive Studies 1. Amsterdam, North-Holland.
(1985). *Hixkaryana and linguistic typology*. Arlington, TX, SIL and the University of Texas at Arlington.
Dogil, Grzegorz (1992). Underspecification, natural classes, and the sonority hierarchy. In Jacek Fisiak and Stanislaw Puppel (eds.) *Phonological investigations*. Amsterdam, John Benjamins Publishing Company, pp.329–412.
Dogil, Grzegorz and Hans C. Luschützky (1990). Notes on sonority and segmental strength. *Rivista di Linguistica* 2.2: 2–54.
Donaldson, Tamsin (1980). *Ngiyambaa, the language of the Wangaaybuwa*. Cambridge, Cambridge University Press.
Dorais, Louis-Jacques (1986). Inuktitut surface phonology: a trans-dialectal survey. *International Journal of American Linguistics* 52.1: 20–53.
Dresher, B. Elan (2003a). Contrast and asymmetry in inventories. In Anna Maria di Sciullo (ed.) *Asymmetry in grammar, volume 2: Morphology, phonology, acquisition*. Amsterdam, John Benjamins, pp.237–59.
(2003b). Determining contrastiveness: a missing chapter in the history of phonology. In S. Burelle and S. Somesfalean (eds.) *Proceedings of the Canadian Linguistics Conference 2002*. Ottawa, Cahiers Linguistiques d'Ottawa, pp.82–93.
(2003c). On the acquisition of phonological contrasts. In Jacqueline van Kampen and Sergio Baauw (eds.) *Proceedings of GALA 2003*. Vo.1. Utrecht, LOT (Netherlands Graduate School of Linguistics), pp.27–46.
Dressler, Wolfgang U. (1989). Markedness and naturalness in phonology; the case of natural phonology. In Olga Tomic (ed.) *Markedness in synchrony and diachrony*. New York, Mouton de Gruyter, pp.111–20.
du Feu, Veronica (1996). *Rapanui*. London, Routledge.
Dupoux, Emmanuel, K. Kakehi, Y. Hirose, C. Pallier, and J. Mehler (1999). Epenthetic vowels in Japanese: a perceptual illusion? *Journal of Experimental Psychology: Human Perception and Performance* 25.6: 1568–78.
Durand, Jacques (1990). *Generative and non-linear phonology*. London, Longman.

Ebert, Karen (1996). *Kodava*. Languages of the World/Materials 104. Nürnburg, Lincom Europa.
Edwards, Walter F. (1978). A preliminary sketch of Arekuna (Carib) phonology. *International Journal of American Linguistics* 44.3: 223–7.
Efimov, V. A. (1986). *Iazyk Ormuri: v sinkhronnom i istoricheskom osveshchenii*. Moscow, Nauka.
Elbert, Samuel H. and Mary Kawena Pukui (1979). *Hawaiian grammar*. Honolulu, University of Hawaii Press.
Elfenbein, Josef (1997). Brahui phonology. In Alan S. Kaye (ed.) *Phonologies of Asia and Africa*. Winona Lake, IN, Eisenbrauns, pp.797–811.
Fahs, von Achim (1989). *Grammatik des Pali*. Leipzig, VEB Verlag Enzyklopädie Leipzig.
Fallon, Paul (2002). *The synchronic and diachronic phonology of ejectives*. Outstanding Dissertations in Linguistics. London, Routledge.
Farris, Ashley and Judith Gierut (2006). Gapped [s]-cluster inventories and faithfulness to the marked. In D. A. Dinnsen and J. A. Gierut (eds.) *Optimality Theory, phonological acquisition, and disorders*. Advances in Optimality Theory. London, Equinox, ch.12.
Fast, P. W. (1953). Amuesha (Arawak) phonemes. *International Journal of American Linguistics* 19: 191–4.
Ferguson, Charles A. (1975). Sound patterns in language acquisition. In Daniel P. Dato (ed.) *Developmental psycholinguistics: theory and applications*. Washington, DC, Georgetown University Press, pp.1–16.
Fikkert, Paula (1994). *On the acquisition of prosodic structure*. Doctoral dissertation, Holland Institute of Generative Linguistics (HIL), Leiden University.
Fitzgerald, Colleen M. (1997). *O'odham rhythms*. PhD dissertation, University of Arizona.
Flemming, Edward (1995). *Auditory representations in phonology*. PhD dissertation, UCLA.
Foley, William A. (1986). *The Papuan languages of New Guinea*. Cambridge, Cambridge University Press.
Fowler, George (1986). Morphological conditions on epenthetic vowels in Hungarian. In Anne M. Farley, Peter T. Farley, and Karl-Erik McCullough (eds.) *CLS 22/1*. Chicago, Chicago Linguistic Society, pp.1–13.
Frachtenberg, Leo J. (1922). Siuslawan. In Franz Boas (ed.) *Handbooks of American Indian languages: Part 2*. Washington, Government Printing Office, pp.431–630.
Frajzyngier, Zygmunt and Robert Koops (1989). Double epenthesis and N-Class in Chadic. In Zygmunt Frajzyngier (ed.) *Current progress in Chadic linguistics*. Philadelphia, John Benjamins, pp.233–50.
Fukazawa, Haruka (1999). *Theoretical implications of OCP effects on features in Optimality Theory*. Doctoral dissertation, University of Maryland, College Park.
Gadalla, Hassan A. H. (2000). *Comparative morphology of Standard Egyptian Arabic*. LINCOM Studies in Afro-Asiatic Languages 05. Munich, LINCOM Europa.
Gafos, Adamantios (1996). *The articulatory basis of locality in phonology*. Doctoral dissertation, Johns Hopkins University.

Gafos, Adamantios and Linda Lombardi (1999). Consonant transparency and vowel echo. In Pius N. Tamanji, Masako Hirotani, and Nancy Hall (eds.) *Proceedings of NELS 29, volume 2: papers from the poster sessions*. Amherst, MA, GLSA, pp.81–95.

Gajendragadkar, S. N. (1974). *Parsi-Gujarati: a descriptive analysis*. Bombay, University of Bombay.

Geiger, Wilhelm (1943). *Pali literature and language*. New Delhi, Munshiram Manoharlal Publishers.

Ghini, Mirco (2001). *Asymmetries in the phonology of Miogliola*. New York, Mouton de Gruyter.

Gick, Bryan (1999). A gesture-based account of intrusive consonants in English. *Phonology* 16.1: 29–54.

Gildea, Spike (1995). Comparative Cariban syllable reduction. *International Journal of American Linguistics* 62.1: 62–102.

Gnanadesikan, Amalia (1995). Markedness and faithfulness constraints in child phonology. *Rutgers Optimality Archive* 67.

(1997). *Phonology with ternary scales*. Doctoral dissertation, University of Massachusetts at Amherst.

Goldsmith, John (1976). *Autosegmental phonology*. Doctoral dissertation, MIT.

(1987). Tane and accent: getting the two together. *Berkeley Linguistic Society* 13: 88–104.

(1990). *Autosegmental and metrical phonology*. Oxford, Blackwell.

Gordon, M. (1999). *Stress and other weight-sensitive phenomena: phonetics, phonology, and typology*. Doctoral dissertation, UCLA.

Gouskova, Maria (2001). Falling sonority onsets, loanwords, and syllable contact. In Mary Andronis, Christopher Ball, Heidi Elston, and Sylvain Neuvel (eds.) *CLS 37: The main session*. Vol.1. Chicago, CLS, pp.175–86.

(2003). *Deriving economy: syncope in Optimality Theory*. Doctoral dissertation, University of Massachusetts, Amherst.

Green, T. (1993). The conspiracy of completeness. *Rutgers Optimality Archive* 8.

Greenberg, Joseph (1966). *Language universals, with special reference to feature hierarchies*. Janua linguarum. Series minor 59. The Hague, Mouton.

(1975). Research on language universals. *Annual Review of Anthropology* 4: 75–94.

Greenberg, Joseph (ed.) (1978). *Universals of human language: volume 1: method and theory*. Stanford, Stanford University Press.

Groves, T., G. W. Groves, and R. Jacobs (1985). *Kiribatese: an outline description*. Canberra, The Australian National University.

Guion, Susan G. (1996). *Velar palatalization: coarticulation, perception, and sound change*. Doctoral dissertation, University of Texas at Austin.

Guitart, J. M. (1981). Sobre la posteriorizacion de las consonantes posnucleares e el Español antillano: reexamen teorico-descriptivo. *Sexto Simposio de Dialectologia del Caribe Hispanico*, Universidad Catolica Madre y Maestra, Santiago de los Caballeros, Republica Dominaca.

Haas, Mary R. (1946). A grammatical sketch of Tunica. In Harry Hoijer, Leonard Bloomfield, and Mary R. Haas (eds.) *Linguistic structures of native America*. Viking Fund

publications in Anthropology 6. New York, Johnson Reprint Corporation, pp.337–66.
  (1968). Notes on a Chipewyan dialect. *International Journal of American Linguistics* 34: 165–75.
Haddad, Ghassan (1983). Epenthesis and sonority in Lebanese Arabic. *Studies in the Linguistic Sciences* 14: 57–88.
Hagstrom, Paul (1997). Contextual metrical invisibility. *Rutgers Optimality Archive* 219.
Hahn, Reinhard (1991). Modern Uyghur y~r insertion: nativization through analogical extension. *Acta Linguistica Hafniensia* 24: 77–96.
Hale, Kenneth (1973). Deep-surface canonical disparities in relation to analysis and change: an Australian example. In T. Sebeok (ed.) *Current trends in linguistics. Volume 9: diachronic, areal and typological linguistics*. The Hague, Mouton, pp.401–58.
  (1976). Phonological developments in a Northern Paman language: Uradhi. In Peter Sutton (ed.) *Languages of Cape York*. Canberra, Australian Institute of Aboriginal Studies, pp.41–9.
Hale, Kenneth and J. White Eagle (1980). A preliminary metrical account of Winnebago accent. *International Journal of American Linguistics* 46: 117–32.
Hale, Mark and Charles Reiss (2000). 'Substance abuse' and 'dysfunctionalism' : current trends in phonology. *Linguistic Inquiry* 31.1: 157–69.
Hall, T. Alan (1997). *The phonology of coronals*. Current Issues in Linguistic Theory. Amsterdam, John Benjamins.
  (2006). Segmental features. In Paul de Lacy (ed.) *The Cambridge handbook of phonology*. Cambridge, Cambridge University Press, ch.13.
Halle, Morris and Ken Stevens (1979). Some reflections on the theoretical bases of phonetics. In B. Lindblom and S. Ohman (eds.) *Frontiers in speech communication research*. London, Academic Press, pp.335–49.
Halle, Morris and Jean-Roger Vergnaud (1980). Three-dimensional phonology. *Journal of Linguistic Research* 1: 83–105.
Halpern, A. M. (1946). Yuma. In Harry Hoijer, Leonard Bloomfield, and Mary R. Haas (eds.) *Linguistic Structures of Native America*. New York, Johnson Reprint Corporation, pp.249–88.
Hankamer, Jorge and Judith Aissen (1974). The sonority hierarchy. In Anthony Bruck, Robert A. Fox, and Michael W. La Galy (eds.) *Papers from the parasession on natural phonology*. Chicago, Chicago Linguistic Society, pp.131–45.
Haraguchi, Shosuke (1984). Some tonal and segmental effects of vowel height in Japanese. In Mark Aronoff and R. T. Orhrle (eds.) *Language sound structure: studies in phonology presented to Morris Halle by his teacher and students*. Cambridge, MA, MIT Press, pp.145–56.
Hargus, Sharon (1988). *The lexical phonology of Sentani*. New York, Garland Publishing Inc.
Harris, John (1990). Segmental complexity and phonological government. *Phonology* 7: 255–300.
  (1997). Licensing inheritance: an integrated theory of neutralisation. *Phonology* 14: 315–70.

Haspelmath, Martin (1993). *A grammar of Lezgian*. Berlin, Mouton.
Hausenberg, Anu-Reet (1998). Komi. In Daniel Abondolo (ed.) *The Uralic languages*. London, Routledge, pp.305–26.
Hayes, Bruce (1986). Assimilation as spreading in Toba Batak. *Linguistic Inquiry* 17: 467–99.
  (1995). *Metrical stress theory: principles and case studies*. Chicago, The University of Chicago Press.
Hayes, Bruce, Robert Kirchner, and Donca Steriade (2004). *Phonetically based phonology*. Cambridge, Cambridge University Press.
Hayward, Dick (1986). The high central vowel in Amharic: new approaches to an old problem. In Joshua A. Fishman, Andree Tabouret-Keller, Michael Clyne, B. Krishnamurti, and Mohamed Abdulaziz (eds.) *The Fergusonian impact: in honor of Charles A. Ferguson on the occasion of his 65th birthday. Volume 1: from phonology to society*. Berlin, Mouton de Gruyter, pp.301–25.
Hayward, R. J. and K. Hayward (1989). 'Guttural': arguments for a new distinctive feature. *Transactions of the Philological Society* 87: 179–93.
Heath, Jeffrey (1984). *Functional grammar of Nunggubuyu*. Canberra, Australian Institute of Aboriginal Studies.
Heffner, R.-M. S. (1950). *General phonetics*. Madison, University of Wisconsin Press.
Helimski, Eugene (1998). Nganasan. In Daniel Abondolo (ed.) *The Uralic languages*. London, Routledge, pp.480–515.
Hellberg, Staffan (1974). *Graphonomic rules in phonology: studies in the expression component of Swedish*. Gothenburg, Acta Universitatis Gothoburgensis.
Hendon, Rufus S. (1966). *The phonology and morphology of Ulu Muar Malay (Kuala Pilah District, Negri Sembilan, Malaya)*. Yale University Publications in Anthropology 70. Peabody, MA, Yale University.
Hoff, B. J. (1968). *The Carib language*. The Hague, Martinus Nijhoff.
Holmer, Arthur (1996). *A parametric grammar of Seediq*. Lund, Lund University Press.
Hong, Soonhyun (1997). *Prosodic domains and ambisyllabicity in Optimality Theory*. Doctoral dissertation, University of Pennsylvania.
Hopkins, Alice W. (1987). Vowel dominance in Mohawk. *International Journal of American Linguistics* 53.4: 445–59.
Howe, Darin and Douglas Pulleyblank (2004). Harmonic scales as faithfulness. *Canadian Journal of Linguistics* 49: 1–49.
Hsin, Tien-Hsin (2000). *Aspects of Maga Rukai phonology*. Doctoral dissertation, University of Connecticut.
Hualde, Jose Ignacio (1991). *Basque phonology*. London, Routledge.
  (1992). *Catalan*. London, Routledge.
Hualde, José and Inaki Gaminde (1998). Vowel interaction in Basque: a nearly exhaustive catalogue. *Studies in the Linguistic Sciences* 28.1: 41–77.
Huang, Hui-chan J. (2004). Functional unity and context-sensitive changes: avoiding onset glides in Squliq Atayal. Handout from Manchester Phonology Meeting 12.
Hulst, Harry van der (1984). *Syllable structure and stress in Dutch*. Dordrecht, Foris Publications.
Hulst, Harry van der and Jeroen van der Weijer (1995). Vowel harmony. In John Goldsmith (ed.) *The handbook of phonological theory*. Oxford, Blackwell, pp.495–535.

Hume, Elizabeth (1992). *Front vowels, coronal consonants, and their interaction in nonlinear phonology.* Doctoral dissertation, Cornell University.
  (2003). Language specific markedness: the case of place of articulation. *Studies in Phonetics, Phonology and Morphology* 9.2: 295–310.
  (2004). Deconstructing markedness: a predictability-based approach. http://www.ling.ohio-state.edu/~ehume/papers/Hume_markedness_BLS30.pdf
Hume, Elizabeth and Ilana Bromberg (2005). Epenthesis and information context. Paper presented at MOT Workshop in Phonology, McGill University.
Hume, Elizabeth and Georgios Tserdanelis (1999). Nasal place assimilation in Sri Lanka Portuguese Creole: implications for markedness. Ms., University of Ohio.
  (2002). Labial unmarkedness in Sri Lankan Portuguese Creole. *Phonology* 19: 441–58.
Hyman, Larry (1982). The representation of length in Gokana. In Daniel P. Flickinger, Marlys Macken, and Nancy Wiegand (eds.) *Proceedings of the first West Coast Conference on formal linguistics.* Stanford, Stanford University, pp.198–206.
  (1985). *A theory of phonological weight.* Dordrecht, Foris.
  (2001). On the limits of phonetic determinism in phonology: *NÇ revisited. In Elizabeth Hume and Keith Johnson (eds.) *The role of speech pereception phenomena in phonology.* San Diego, Academic Press, pp.141–85.
Inkelas, Sharon and Young-mee Cho (1993). Inalterability as prespecification. *Language* 69: 529–74.
Ito, Junko (1986). *Syllable theory in prosodic phonology.* Doctoral dissertation, University of Massachusetts, Amherst.
Ito, Junko and Armin Mester (1992). Weak layering and word binarity. Report LRC-92-09, Linguistic Research Center, University of California, Santa Cruz.
  (1995). The core-periphery structure of the lexicon and constraints on reranking. In Jill Beckman, Suzanne Urbanczyk, and Laura Walsh Dickey (eds.) *Papers in Optimality Theory.* University of Massachusetts Occasional Papers 18. Amherst, GLSA, pp.181–210.
  (1998). The phonological lexicon. In Natsuko Tsujimuru (ed.) *A handbook of Japanese linguistics.* Oxford, Blackwell.
  (2003). Systemic markedness and faithfulness. *Rutgers Optimality Archive* 710.
Iverson, Gregory (1989). On the category supralaryngeal. *Phonology* 6: 285–303.
Iverson, Gregory and Kee-Ho Kim (1987). Underspecification and hierarchical feature representation in Korean consonantal phonology. In Anna Bosch, Barbara Need, and Eric Schiller (eds.) *Proceedings of CLS 23.* Chicago, Chicago Linguistic Society, pp.182–98.
Jackson, Walter S. (1972). Wayana grammar. In Joseph Grimes (ed.) *Languages of the Guianas.* Norman, SIL of the University of Oklahoma, pp.47–77.
Jakobson, Roman (1941). *Kindersprache, Aphasie, und allgemeine Lautgesetze.* Uppsala, Almqvist & Wiksell [tr. *Child Language, Aphasia and Phonological Universals.* The Hague, Mouton].
  (1949a). The phonemic and grammatical aspects of language in their interrelations. In Roman Jakobson (ed.) *Selected Writings II.* The Hague, Mouton, pp.103–14.
  (1949b). The sound laws of child language. In Roman Jakobson (ed.) *Studies on Child Language and Aphasia.* The Hague, Mouton.

(1978). *Six lectures on sound and meaning*. Cambridge, MA, MIT Press.
Jakobson, Roman, Gunnar Fant, and Morris Halle (1952). *Preliminaries to speech analysis*. Cambridge, MA, MIT Press.
Jakobson, Roman and Morris Halle (1956). *Fundamentals of language*. The Hague, Mouton.
Jun, Jongho (1995). *Perceptual and articulatory factors in place assimilation: an Optimality Theoretic approach*. Doctoral dissertation, University of California, Los Angeles.
Ka, Omar (1985). Syllable structure and suffixation in Wolof. *Studies in the Linguistic Sciences* 15.1: 61–90.
Kager, René (1989). *A metrical theory of stress and destressing in English and Dutch*. Dordrecht, Foris.
  (1997). Rhythmic vowel deletion in Optimality Theory. In Iggy Roca (ed.) *Derivations and constraints in phonology*. Oxford, Oxford University Press, pp.463–99.
  (1999). *Optimality Theory*. Cambridge, Cambridge University Press.
Kager, René, E. Visch and R. M. van Zonneveld (1987). Nederlandse woordklemtoon: hoofdklemtoon, bijklemtoon, reductie en voeten. *GLOT* 10: 197–226.
Kamprath, Christine (1987). *Suprasegmental structures in a Raeto-Romansh dialect: a case study of metrical and lexical phonology*. Doctoral dissertation, University of Texas at Austin.
Kang, Yoonjung (2003). Perceptual similarity in loanword adaptation: English postvocalic word-final stops in Korean. *Phonology* 20: 219–73.
Kangasmaa-Minn, Eeva (1998). Mari. In Daniel Abondolo (ed.) *The Uralic languages*. London, Routledge, pp.219–48.
Kari, James (1976). *Navajo verb prefix phonology*. New York, Garland Publishing.
Karvonen, Daniel and Adam Sherman (1997). Sympathy, opacity, and u-umlaut in Icelandic. *Phonology at Santa Cruz* 5: 37–48.
Kaye, Alan S., Jean Lowenstamm, and Jean-Roger Vergnaud (1989). Konstituentenstruktur und Rektion in der Phonologie. *Linguistische Berichte* 2: 31–75.
Kaye, Jonathan, Jean Lowenstamm, and Jean-Roger Vergnaud (1985). The internal structure of phonological elements: a theory of charm and government. *Phonology Yearbook* 2: 305–29.
Kean, M.-L. (1975). *The theory of markedness in Generative Grammar*. Doctoral dissertation, MIT.
Keating, Patricia (1988). Palatals and complex segments: X-ray evidence. *UCLA Working Papers in Phonetics* 69: 77–91.
Keer, Edward (1996). Floating moras and epenthesis in Sinhala. Ms., Rutgers University.
  (1999). *Geminates, the OCP and the nature of CON*. Doctoral dissertation, Rutgers University.
Kenstowicz, Michael (1994). Syllabification in Chukchee: a constraint-based analysis. *Rutgers Optimality Archive* 30.
  (1996). Quality-sensitive stress. *Rivista di Linguistica* 9:157–87 [also *Rutgers Optimality Archive* 33].
Kenstowicz, Michael and Charles Kisseberth (1971). Unmarked bleeding orders. *Studies in the Linguistic Sciences* 1.1: 8–28.

Ketner, Katherine (2003). *Homogeneity of process, heterogeneity of target in Czech epenthesis*. MA Thesis, University of Cambridge.
Key, Mary Ritchie (1969). *Comparative Tacana phonology, with Cavineña phonology and notes on Pano Tacanan relationship*. The Hague, Mouton.
Kim, C.-W. (1973). Gravity in Korean phonology. *Language Research* 9: 274–81.
Kimball, Geoffrey D. (1991). *Koasati grammar*. Lincoln, University of Nebraska Press.
Kim-Renaud, Young-Key (1974). *Korean consonantal phonology*. Doctoral dissertation, University of Hawaii, Honolulu.
  (1986). *Studies in Korean linguistics*. Seoul, Hanshin.
Kingston, John (1990). Articulatory binding. In John Kingston and Mary Beckman (eds.) *Papers in laboratory phonology I*. Cambridge, Cambridge University Press, pp.406–34.
Kingston, John and D. Solnit (1989). The inadequacy of underspecification. In Juli Carter and Rose-Marie Déchaine (eds.) *Proceedings of NELS 19*. Amherst, GLSA Publications, pp.264–78.
Kinkade, M. D. (1964). Phonology and morphology of Upper Chehalis: I. *International Journal of American Linguistics* 29.3: 181–95.
Kiparsky, Paul (1979). Metrical structure assignment is cyclic. *Linguistic Inquiry* 10: 421–41.
  (1982). Lexical phonology and morphology. In I. S. Yang (ed.) *Linguistics in the morning calm*. Vol.2. Seoul, Hanshin, pp.3–91.
  (1984). On the lexical phonology of Icelandic. In Claes-Christian Elert, Irène Johansson, and Eva Stangert (eds.) *Nordic prosody III*. Umeå, University of Umeå, pp.135–64.
  (1985). Some consequences of lexical phonology. *Phonology* 2: 85–138.
  (1988). Phonological change. In Frederick J. Newmeyer (ed.) *Linguistics: the Cambridge Survey. volume 1: theoretical foundations*. Cambridge, Cambridge University Press, pp.363–415.
  (1994). Remarks on markedness. Handout from TREND 2.
  (1995). The phonological basis of sound change. In John Goldsmith (ed.) *The handbook of phonological theory*. Cambridge, MA, Blackwells, pp.640–70.
  (2004). Universals constrain change; change results in typological generalizations. Ms., Stanford University.
Kirchner, Robert (1996). Synchronic chain shifts in Optimality Theory. *Linguistic Inquiry* 27: 341–51.
Kirchner, Robert Martin (1998). *An effort-based approach to consonant lenition*. Doctoral dissertation, University of California at Los Angeles.
Kitto, Catherine and Paul de Lacy (1999). Correspondence and epenthetic quality. In Carolyn Smallwood and Catherine Kitto (eds.) *Proceedings of AFLA VI: The sixth meeting of the Austronesian Formal Linguistics Association*. Toronto, University of Toronto, pp.181–200.
Koehn, Edward and Sally Koehn (1986). Apalai. In Desmond C. Derbyshire and Geoffrey K. Pullum (eds.) *Handbook of Amazonian languages*. Vol.1. New York, Mouton, pp.33–127.
Koshal, Sanyukta (1979). *Ladakhi grammar*. Delhi, Motilal Banarsidass.

Kossman, Maarten G. and Harry J. Stroomer (1997). Berber phonology. In Alan S. Kaye (ed.) *Phonologies of Asia and Africa (including the Caucasus)*. Vol.1. Winona Lake, IN, Eisenbrauns, pp.461–76.

Krause, Scott R. (1980). *Topics in Chukchee phonology and morphology*. Doctoral dissertation, University of Illinois, Champaign-Urbana.

Krivitskii, A. A. and A. I. Podluzhnyi (1994). *Uchebnik belorusskogo iazyka dlia samoobrazovaniia*. Minsk, Vysheishaia shkola.

Kroeker, Barbara J. (1972). Morphophonemics of Nambiquara. *Anthropological Linguistics* 14: 19–22.

Krupa, Viktor (1966). *Morpheme and word in Maori*. The Hague, Mouton.

Ladefoged, Peter (1975). *A course in phonetics*. New York, Harcourt, Brace, Jovanovich.

Laidig, Carol J. (1992). Segments, syllables, and stress in Larike. In Donald A. Burquest and Wyn D. Laidig (eds.) *Phonological studies in four languages of Maluku*. Dallas, Summer Institute of Linguistics and University of Texas, pp.67–126.

Lambert, Wendy (1999). *Epenthesis, metathesis, and vowel-glide alternation: prosodic reflexes in Mabalay Atayal*. Doctoral dissertation, National Tsing Hua University.

Lamontagne, Greg and Keren Rice (1995). A correspondence account of coalescence. In Jill Beckman, Suzanne Urbanczyk, and Laura Walsh Dickey (eds.) *University of Massachusetts occasional papers in linguistics 18*. Amherst, MA, GLSA, pp. 211–24.

Lapoliwa, Hans (1981). *A generative approach to the phonology of Bahasa Indonesia*. Pacific Linguistics Series D-34 (Materials in Languages of Indonesia, No.3). Canberra, Australia National University.

Lasnik, Howard (1990). Learnability, restrictiveness, and the Evaluation Metric. In Howard Lasnik (ed.) *Essays on restrictiveness and learnability*. Dordrecht, Kluwer, pp.146–62.

Lass, Roger (1976). *English phonology and phonological theory*. Cambridge, Cambridge University Press.

Lavoie, Lisa (2001). *Consonant strength: phonological patterns and phonetic manifestations*. Outstanding dissertations in linguistics. New York, Garland Publishing Inc.

Lawton, Ralph (1993). *Topics in the description of Kiriwina*. Pacific Linguistics D-84. Canberra, Australian National University.

Laycock, D. C. (1965). *The Ndu language family*. Pacific Linguistics Series C No.1. Canberra, Linguistic Circle of Canberra.

Leben, Will (1973). *Suprasegmental phonology*. Doctoral dissertation, MIT.

Lee, Duck-Young (1998). *Korean phonology: a principle-based approach*. LINCOM Studies in Asian Linguistics 12. Munich, LINCOM Europa.

Lefebvre, Claire (2000). What do Creole studies have to offer mainstream linguistics? *Journal of Pidgin and Creole languages* 15.1: 127–53.

Levin, Juliette (1985). *A metrical theory of syllabicity*. Doctoral dissertation, MIT.

Li, Fang-Kuei (1946). Chipewyan. In Harry Hoijer, Leonard Bloomfield, and Mary R. Haas (eds.) *Linguistic structures of Native America*. Viking Fund publications in Anthropology 6. New York, Johnson Reprint Corporation, pp.398–423.

Li, Paul Jen-kuei (1977). Morphophonemic alternations in Formosan languages. *Bulletin of the Institute of History and Philology, Academia Sinica* 48.3: 375–413.

(1985). A secret language in Taiwanese. *Journal of Chinese Linguistics* 13.1: 91–121.
(1991). Vowel deletion and vowel assimilation in Sediq. In Robert Blust (ed.) *Currents in Pacific linguistics: papers on Austronesian languages and ethnolinguistics in honour of George W. Grace*. Pacific Linguistics C-117. Canberra, University of Canberra Press, pp.163–69.
Liberman, Mark (1975). *The intonational system of English*. Doctoral dissertation, MIT.
Liberman, Mark and Alan Prince (1977). On stress and linguistic rhythm. *Linguistic Inquiry* 8: 249–336.
Lichtenberk, Frantisek (1983). *A grammar of Manam*. Honolulu, University of Hawaii Press.
Liljencrants, J. and B. Lindblom (1972). Numerical simulation of vowel quality systems: the role of perceptual contrast. *Language* 48: 839–62.
Lindau, Mona (1978). Vowel features. *Language* 54: 541–63.
Lindblom, B. (1990). Explaining phonetic variation: a sketch of the H & H theory. In W. J. Hardcastle and A. Marchal (eds.) *Speech production and speech modelling*. Dordrecht, Kluwer Academic Publishers, pp.403–39.
Lindkoog, John N. and Ruth M. Brend (1962). Cayapa phonemics. In Benjamin F. Elson (ed.) *Studies in Ecuadorian Indian languages*. Norman, Summer Institute of Linguistics of the University of Oklahoma, pp.31–44.
Lloret, Maria-Rosa (1992). The representation of glottals in Oromo. *Phonology* 12.2: 257–80.
Lombardi, Linda (1991). *Laryngeal features and laryngeal neutralization*. Doctoral dissertation, University of Massachusetts, Amherst.
  (1995). Why place and voice are different: constraint-specific alternations and Optimality Theory. *Rutgers Optimality Archive* 105.
  (1996). Restrictions on direction of voicing assimilation: an OT account. *University of Maryland Working Papers in Linguistics* 4:84–102 [also *Rutgers Optimality Archive* 247].
  (1998). Coronal epenthesis and unmarkedness. *University of Maryland Working Papers in Linguistics* 5: 156–75.
  (1999). Positional faithfulness and voicing assimilation in Optimality Theory. *Natural Language and Linguistic Theory* 17: 267–302.
  (2002). Coronal epenthesis and markedness. *Phonology* 19.2: 219–51.
  (2003). Markedness and the typology of epenthetic vowels. *Linguistics and Phonetics 2002 proceedings: Prosody and phonetics* [also *Rutgers Optimality Archive* 578].
Łubowicz, Ania (2002). *Contrast preservation in phonological mappings*. PhD dissertation, University of Massachusetts, Amherst.
Lupas, Liana (1972). *Phonologie du grec attique*. The Hague, Mouton.
Lutta, M. (1923). *Der Dialekt von Bergün und seine Stellung innerhalb der rätoromanischern Mundarten Graubündens*. Supplement to *Zeitschrift für Romanische Philologie* 71. Halle, Niemeyer.
Lydall, Jean (1976). Hamer. In Marvin Lionel Bender (ed.) *The non-semitic languages of Ethiopia*. East Lansing, MI, Michigan State University, pp.393–438.
Lynch, John (2000). *Anejoñ dictionary*. Pacific Linguistics. Canberra, Australian National University.

Lynch, John, Malcolm Ross, and Terry Crowley (eds.) (2002). *The Oceanic languages*. Richmond, Curzon Press.
MacKay, Carolyn J. (1994). A sketch of Misantla Totonac phonology. *International Journal of American Linguistics* 60.4: 369–419.
MacKenzie, Sara and B. Elan Dresher (2004). Contrast and phonological activity in the Nez Perce vowel system. In Pawel M. Nowak, Corey Yoquele, and David Mortensen (eds.) *Proceedings of BLS 29*. Berkeley, Berkeley Linguistics Society, pp.283–94.
Maddieson, Ian (1992). *UCLA phonological segment inventory database*. Los Angeles, UCLA.
Marlett, Stephen Alan (1981). *The structure of Seri*. Doctoral dissertation, University of San Diego.
Martens, M. and S. Tuominen (1977). A tentative phonemic statement of Yil in West Sepik Province. *Workpapers in Papua New Guinea Linguistics* 19: 29–48.
Martin, W. (1968). De verdoffing van gedekte en ongedekte *e* in niet-hoofdtonige postitie bij romaanse leenwoorden in het Nederlands. *De Nieuw Taalgids* 61: 162–81.
Martinet, André (1964). *Elements of general linguistics*. Chicago, University of Chicago Press.
Martinez-Gil, Fernando (1997). Word-final epenthesis in Galician. In Fernando Martinez-Gil and Alfonso Morales-Front (eds.) *Issues in the phonology and morphology of the major Iberian languages*. Washington, DC, Georgetown University Press, pp.269–340.
Mascaró, Joan (1976). *Catalan phonology and the phonological cycle*. Doctoral dissertation, MIT.
  (1986). Syllable-final processes in Catalan. In Carol Neidle and Rafael Núñez-Cedeño (eds.) *Studies in Romance languages*. Dordrecht, Foris, pp.163–80.
  (1996). External allomorphy as emergence of the unmarked. In Jacques Durand and Bernard Laks (eds.) *Current trends in phonology: models and methods*. Salford, European Studies Research Institute, pp.473–83.
McCarthy, John (1979). *Formal problems in Semitic phonology and morphology*. Doctoral dissertation, MIT.
  (1980). A note on the accentuation of Damascene Arabic. *Studies in the Linguistic Sciences* 10: 77–98.
  (1988). Feature geometry and dependency: a review. *Phonetica* 43: 84–108.
  (1989). Linear order in phonological representation. *Linguistic Inquiry* 20: 71–99.
  (1991). Synchronic rule inversion. In L. Sulton, C. Johnson, and R. Shields (eds.), *Proceedings of the Seventeenth Annual Meeting of the Berkeley Linguistics Society*. Berkeley, CA, Berkeley Linguistics Society, pp.192–207.
  (1993). A case of surface constraint violation. *Canadian Journal of Linguistics* 38: 127–53.
  (1994). The phonetics and phonology of Semitic pharyngeals. In Patricia Keating (ed.) *Phonological structure and phonetic form: papers in laboratory phonology III*. Cambridge, Cambridge University Press, pp.191–233.
  (1995). *Extensions of faithfulness: Rotuman revisited*. Amherst, University of Massachusetts.
  (1999). Sympathy and phonological opacity. *Phonology* 16: 331–99.

(2000). The prosody of phase in Rotuman. *Natural Language and Linguistic Theory* 18: 147–97.
(2001a). English engma. Talk Presented at the University of Massachusetts, Amherst.
(2001b). *Optimality Theory: a thematic guide*. Cambridge, Cambridge University Press.
(2002). Comparative markedness. *Rutgers Optimality Archive* 489.
(2003a). The length of stem-final vowels in colloquial Arabic. *Rutgers Optimality Archive* 616.
(2003b). OT constraints are categorical. *Phonology* 20.1: 75–138.
(2003c). On targeted constraints and cluster simplification. *Phonology* 19: 273–92.
(2006). Derivation. In Paul de Lacy (ed.) *The Cambridge handbook of phonology*. Cambridge, Cambridge University Press, ch.5.
McCarthy, John and Alan Prince (1986). *Prosodic morphology*. Rutgers Technical Report TR-32. New Brunswick, Rutgers University Center for Cognitive Science.
(1993a). Generalized alignment. In Geert Booij and Jaap van Marle (eds.) *Yearbook of morphology*. Dordrecht, Kluwer, pp.79–153.
(1993b). *Prosodic morphology volume 1: constraint interaction and satisfaction*. Rutgers Technical Report TR-3. New Brunswick, Rutgers University Center for Cognitive Science.
(1994). The emergence of the unmarked: Optimality in prosodic morphology. In Mercè Gonzàlez (ed.) *Proceedings of NELS 24*. Amherst, MA, GLSA, pp.333–79.
(1995). Faithfulness and reduplicative identity. In Jill Beckman, Suzanne Urbanczyk, and Laura Walsh Dickey (eds.) *University of Massachusetts occasional papers in linguistics UMOP 18*. Amherst, MA, GLSA, pp.249–384.
McCarthy, John and A. Taub (1992). Review of C. Paradis and J.-F. Prunet (eds.) *The special status of coronals: internal and external evidence. Phonology* 9: 363–70.
McCawley, James D. (1968). *The phonological component of a grammar of Japanese*. The Hague, Mouton.
McGuckin, Catherine (2002). Gapapaiwa. In John Lynch, Malcolm Ross, and Terry Crowley (eds.) *The Oceanic languages*. Richmond, Curzon Press.
McMahon, April (2000). *Chance, change and optimality*. Oxford, Oxford University Press.
Meredith, Scott (1990). *Issues in the phonology of prominence*. Doctoral dissertation, MIT.
Mester, Armin and Junko Ito (1989). Feature predictability and underspecification: palatal prosody in Japanese mimetics. *Language* 65.2: 258–93.
Metcalfe, C. D. (1975). *Bardi verb morphology (northwestern Australia)*. Pacific Linguistics Series B No.30. Canberra, Australia National University.
Michelson, Karin (1988). *A comparative study of Lake Iroquoian accent*. Dordrecht, Kluwer.
Miller, G. A. and P. E. Nicely (1955). Analysis of perceptual confusions among some English consonants. *Journal of the Acoustical Society of America* 27: 338–52.
Milliken, Stuart R. (1988). *Protosyllables: a theory of underlying syllable structure in nonlinear phonology*. Doctoral dissertation, Cornell University.
Mistry, P. J. (1997). Gujarati phonology. In Alan S. Kaye (ed.) *Phonologies of Asia and Africa*. Vol.2. Winona Lake, IN, Eisenbrauns, pp.653–73.

Mitchell, T. F. (1956). *An introduction to Egyptian Colloquial Arabic*. London, Oxford University Press.
Mithun, Marianne (1976). *A grammar of Tuscarora*. New York, Garland Publications.
Mithun, M. and H. Basri (1986). The phonology of Selayarese. *Oceanic Linguistics* 25: 210–54.
Miyakoda, Haruko (2005). The prosodic structure in Japanese acquisition. In Marina Tzakosta, Claartje Levelt, and Jeroen van de Weijer (eds.) *Developmental paths in phonological acquisition*. Leiden Papers in Linguistics 2.1. Leiden, the Leiden University Centre for Linguistics (LUCL). http://www.ulcl.leidenuniv.nl
Mohanan, K. P. (1986). Vowel epenthesis in Malayalam: schwa or U? *Indian Linguistics* 47: 97–101.
  (1991). On the bases of Radical Underspecification. *Natural Language and Linguistic Theory* 9: 285–326.
  (1993). Fields of attraction in phonology. In John Goldsmith (ed.) *The last phonological rule: reflections on constraints and derivations*. Chicago, University of Chicago Press, pp.61–116.
Montler, Timothy R. and Heather K. Hardy (1991). The phonology of negation in Alabama. *International Journal of American Linguistics* 57.1: 1–23.
Morelli, Frida (1999). *The phonotactics and phonology of obstruent clusters in Optimality Theory*. Doctoral dissertation, University of Maryland.
Morén, Bruce (1999). *Distinctiveness, coercion, and sonority: a unified theory of weight*. Doctoral dissertation, University of Maryland.
  (2003). The parallel structures model of feature geometry. *Working papers of the Cornell phonetics laboratory*. Cornell, NY, Cornell University, ch.5.
Moreton, Elliott (1999). Non-computable functions in Optimality Theory. Amherst, MA, *Rutgers Optimality Archive* 364.
Morphy, Frances (1983). Djapu, a Yolngu dialect. In R. M. W. Dixon and Barry J. Blake (eds.) *Handbook of Australian languages*. Vol.3. Amsterdam, John Benjamins, pp.1–187.
Morris, Richard E. (2000). Constraint interaction in Spanish /s/-aspiration: three peninsular varieties. In Héctor Campos, Elena Herberger, Alfonso Morales-Front, and Thomas J. Walsh (eds.) *Proceedings of the third Hispanic linguistics symposium*. Somerville, MA, Cascadilla Press.
Mosel, Ulrike and Even Hovdhaugen (1992). *Samoan reference grammar*. London, Oxford University Press.
Munro, Pamela and Peter John Benson (1973). Reduplication and rule ordering in Luiseño. *International Journal of American Linguistics* 39: 15–21.
Munro, Pamela and Charles Ulrich (1985). Nasals and nasalization in Western Muskogean. Ms., University of New Mexico and UCLA.
Murray, Robert W. (1982). Consonant cluster developments in Pali. *Folia Linguistica Historia* 111.2: 163–84.
Murray, Sarah (2005). Devoicing and voicing assimilation without AGREE. MS, Rutgers University.
Nair, Usha (1979). *Gujarati Phonetic Reader*. Mysore, Central Institute of Indian languages.

Nakano, Kazuo (1969). A phonetic basis for the syllabic nasal in Japanese. *Onsei no kenkyu [Studies of Phonetics]* 14: 215–28.
Newmeyer, Frederick (1998). *Language form and language function*. Cambridge, MA, MIT Press.
Newmeyer, Frederick J. (2003). Grammar is grammar and usage is usage. *Language* 79.4: 682–707.
Nicolaidis, Katerina, Jan Edwards, Mary Beckman, and Georgios Tserdanelis (2004). Acquisition of lingual obstruents in Greek. In Georgia Katsimali, Alexis Kalokarinos, Elena Anagnostopoulou, and Ioanna Kappa (eds.) *Proceedings of the 6th International Conference of Greek Linguistics, Rethymno, Crete, September 18–21, 2003.* http://www.philology.noc.gr/conferences/6thICGL/ebook/default.htm
Nivens, R. (1992). A lexical phonology of West Tarangan. In Donald A. Burquest and Carol J. Laidig (eds.) *Phonological studies in four languages of Maluku*. Dallas, SIL and University of Texas at Arlington Publications in Linguistics, pp.261–80.
Odden, David (1987). Dissimilation as deletion in Chukchi. In Ann Miller and Joyce Powers (eds.) *Proceedings of the Eastern States Conference on Linguistics*. Cornell, Cornell University (http://ling.cornell.edu/clcpubs/ESCOL.html), pp.235–46.
  (1995). African tone languages. In John Goldsmith (ed.) *The handbook of phonological theory*. Oxford, Blackwell, pp.444–75.
Ohala, John J. (1974). Phonetic explanation in phonology. In Anthony Bruck, Robert A. Fox, and Michael W. La Galy (eds.) *Papers from the parasession on natural phonology*. Chicago, Chicago Linguistic Society, pp.251–74.
  (1983). The origin of sound patterns in vocal tract constraints. In Peter F. MacNeilage (ed.) *The production of speech*. New York, Springer, pp.189–216.
  (1990). Alternatives to the sonority hierarchy for explaining segmental sequential constraints. In Michael Ziolkowski, Manual Noske, and Karen Deaton (eds.) *CLS 26: volume 2: the parasession on the syllable in phonetics and phonology*. Chicago, Chicago Linguistic Society, pp.319–38.
  (1992). There is no interface between phonetics and phonology: a personal view. *Journal of Phonetics* 18: 153–71.
  (1995). Phonetic explanations for sound patterns: implications for grammars of competence. In K. Elenius and P. Branderud (eds.) *Proceedings of the 13th International Congress of the Phonetic Sciences*. Vol.2. Stockholm, Department of Speech Communication and Music Aconstics, KTH and Department of Linguistics, Stockholm University, pp.52–9.
Ohala, John J. and James Lorentz (1977). The story of [w]: an exercise in the phonetic explanation for sound patterns. In Kenneth Whistler, jr., Robert van Valin, Chris Chiarello, Jeri J. Jaeger, Miriam Petruck, Henry Thompson, Ronya Javkin, and Anthony Woodbury (eds.) *Proceedings of the 3rd Annual Meeting of the Berkeley Linguistics Society*. Berkeley, Berkeley Linguistics Society, pp.577–99.
Onn, Farid (1980). *Aspects of Malay phonology and morphology: a generative approach*. Bangi, Universiti Kebangsaan Malaysia.
Oostendorp, Marc van (1995). *Vowel quality and phonological projection*. Doctoral dissertation, Katholieke Universiteit Brabant.
  (1999). The velar nasal as a nuclear nasal in Dutch. Ms., Meertens Institute, Royal Netherlands Academy of Arts and Sciences.

Orr, Carolyn (1962). Ecuador Quichua phonology. In Benjamin Elson (ed.) *Studies in Ecuadorian Indian languages*. Vol.1. Norman, Summer Institute of Linguistics of the University of Oklahoma, pp.60–77.
Owens, Jonathan (1985). *A grammar of Harar Oromo (Northeastern Ethiopia)*. Cushitic Language Studies 4. Hamburg, Buske.
Padgett, Jaye (1994). Stricture and nasal place assimilation. *Natural Language and Linguistic Theory* 12: 463–513.
 (2003). Contrast and post-velar fronting in Russian. *Natural Language and Linguistic Theory* 21: 39–87.
Pagliano, Claudine (2004). There is no post-verbal liaison in French: [t] in *fait-il* is epenthetic. Handout from the 12th Manchester Phonology Conference.
Palmada, Blanca (1994). *La fonologia del Català: el principis generals i la variació*. Universitat Autònoma de Barcelona. Barcelona, Servei de Publicacions de la Universitat Autònoma de Barcelona.
Pandharipande, Rajeshwari V. (1997). *Marathi*. London, Routledge.
Pankratz, Leo and Eunice V. Pike (1967). Phonology and morphotonemics of Ayutla Mixtec. *International Journal of American Linguistics* 33: 287–99.
Paradis, Carole (1992). *Lexical phonology and morphology: the nominal classes in Fula*. New York, Garland.
Paradis, Carole and Darlene LaCharité (2001). Guttural deletion in loanwords. *Phonology* 18.2: 225–300.
Paradis, Carole and Jean-François Prunet (1990). The coronal vs. velar placelessness controversy. *McGill Working Papers in Linguistics* 6.2: 192–228.
 (1991a). Introduction: asymmetry and visibility in consonant articulations. In Carole Paradis and J.-F. Prunet (eds.) *The special status of coronals: internal and external evidence*. Phonetics and Phonology 2. San Diego, Academic Press, pp.1–28.
Paradis, Carole and Jean-François Prunet (eds.) (1991b). *The special status of coronals: internal and external evidence*. Phonetics and Phonology 2. San Diego, Academic Press.
 (1994). A reanalysis of velar transparency cases. *The Linguistic Review* 11: 101–40.
Parker, Stephen (1987). *Kana acha'taka ijnachale kana chamekolo (vocabulario y textos chamicuro)*. Comunidades y Culturas Peruanas No. 21. Yarinacocha, Pucallpa, Peru, Ministerio de Educación and Instituto Lingüístico de Verano.
 (1989). The sonority grid in Chamicuro phonology. *Linguistic Analysis* 19: 3–58.
 (1994a). Coda epenthesis in Huariapano. *International Journal of American Linguistics* 60.2: 95–119.
 (1994b). Laryngeal codas in Chamicuro. *International Journal of American Linguistics* 60.3: 261–71.
 (1998). Disjoint metrical tiers and positional markedness in Huariapano. Ms., University of Massachusetts, Amherst.
 (2001a). On the phonemic status of [h] in Tiriyo. *International Journal of American Linguistics* 67: 105–18.
 (2001b). Non-optimal onsets in Chamicuro: an inventory maximised in coda position. *Phonology* 18.3: 361–86.
 (2002). *Quantifying the sonority hierarchy*. Doctoral dissertation, University of Massachusetts, Amherst.

Pater, Joe (1996). *NÇ. In Kiyomi Kusumoto (ed.) *Proceedings of NELS 26*. Amherst, MA, GLSA Publications, pp.227–39.

(1997). Minimal violation and phonological development. *Language Acquisition* 6: 201–53.

(1999). Austronesian nasal substitution and other NC effects. In René Kager, Harry van der Hulst, and Wim Zonneveld (eds.) *The prosody-morphology interface*. London, Cambridge University Press, pp.310–43.

Pater, Joe and Jessica Barlow (2002). Place-determined onset selection. Ms., University of Massachusetts, Amherst and San Diego State University.

Pater, Joe and Adam Werle (2003). Direction of assimilation in child consonant harmony. *Canadian Journal of Linguistics* 48.3/4: 385–408.

Payne, David L. (1981). *The phonology and morphology of Axininca Campa*. Summer Institute of Linguistics Publications in Linguistics 66. Dallas, SIL.

(1990). Accent in Aguaruna. In Doris L. Payne (ed.) *Amazonian linguistics: studies in lowland South American languages*. Austin, University of Texas Press, pp.161–84.

Payne, Doris L. and Thomas E. Payne (1986). Yagua. In Desmond C. Derbyshire and Geoffrey K. Pullum (eds.) *Handbook of Amazonian languages*. Vol.2. Berlin, Mouton de Gruyter, pp.249–474.

Payne, Judith (1990). Asheninca stress patterns. In Doris L. Payne (ed.) *Amazonian linguistics: studies in lowland South American languages*. Austin, University of Texas Press, pp.185–209.

Peasgood, Edward T. (1972). Carib phonology. In Joseph Grimes (ed.) *Languages of the Guianas*. Norman, Summer Institute of Linguistics of the University of Oklahoma, pp.35–41.

Peperkamp, Sharon (in press). A psycholinguistic theory of loanword adaptations. *Proceedings of BLS 30* http://www.ehess.fr/centres/lscp/persons/peperkamp/BLS30.pdf

Peperkamp, Sharon and Emmanuel Dupoux (2003). Reinterpreting loanword adaptations: the role of perception. In Maria Joseph Solé, Daniel Recasens, and Joaquim Romero (eds.) *The proceedings of the 15th International Conference of the Phonetic Sciences*. Ruddle Mall, Australia, Causal Productions, pp.367–70.

Piggott, Glyne L. (1980). *Aspects of Odawa morphophonemics*. New York, Garland Publishing Inc.

(1993). Satisfying the minimal word. *McGill Working Papers in Linguistics* 8.2: 194–233.

Pike, Eunice (1954). Phonetic rank and subordination in consonant patterning and historical change. *Miscellanea Phonetica* 2: 25–41.

Ping, Jiang-King (1996). *An Optimality account of tone-vowel interaction in Northern Min*. Doctoral dissertation, University of British Columbia.

(1999). Sonority constraints on tonal patterns. In Kimary Shahin, Susan J. Blake, and Eun-Sook Kim (eds.) *WCCFL 17*. Stanford, CSLI, pp.332–46.

Pinker, Steven and David Birdsong (1979). Speaker's sensitivity to rules of frozen word order. *Journal of Verbal Learning and Verbal Behaviour* 18: 497–508.

Podesva, Robert (2000). Constraints on geminates in Buginese and Selayarese. In Roger Billery and Brook Danielle Lillehaugen (eds.) *Proceedings of WCCFL 19*. Somerville, MA, Cascadilla Press, pp.101–14.

Poppe, Nicholas (1960). *Buriat Grammar*. Uralic and Altaic Series, Vol.2. Bloomington, Indiana University Publications.

Prentice, D. J. (1971). *The Murut languages of Sabah*. Pacific Linguistics C No.18. Canberra, Australian National University.

Price, P. David (1976). Southern Nambiquara phonology. *International Journal of American Linguistics* 42.4: 338–48.

Prince, Alan (1983). Relating to the grid. *Linguistic Inquiry* 14: 19–100.

(1997a). Paninian relations. Colloquium talk, University of Massachusetts, Amherst. http://ling.rutgers.edu/people/faculty/prince.html

(1997b). Stringency and anti-Paninian hierarchies. Handout from LSA Institute. http://ling.rutgers.edu/people/faculty/prince.html

(1997c). Topics in OT: Class 3: Harmonic completeness, AP order; chain shifts. Handout, LSA Institute. http://ling.rutgers.edu/people/faculty/prince.html

(1997d). Elsewhere and otherwise. *Rutgers Optimality Archive* 217. http://ling.rutgers.edu/people/faculty/prince.html

(1998). Two lectures on Optimality Theory. Phonology Forum 1998, Kobe University. http://ling.rutgers.edu/people/faculty/prince.html

(1999). Paninian relations. Handout, University of Marburg. http://ling.rutgers.edu/people/faculty/prince.html

Prince, Alan and Paul Smolensky (1993). *Optimality Theory: constraint interaction in generative grammar*. Rutgers Technical Reports TR-2. New Brunswick, NJ, Rutgers Center for Cognitive Science [also *Rutgers Optimality Archive* 537]. Published in 2004 by Blackwells.

Pulleyblank, Douglas (1998). Yoruba vowel patterns: deriving asymmetries by the tension between opposing constraints. *Rutgers Optimality Archive* 270.

Pulleyblank, E. G. (1989). The role of coronal in articulator based features. In C. Wiltshire, R. Graczyk, and B. Music (eds.) *Papers from CLS 25*. Chicago, Chicago Linguistic Society, pp.379–93.

Quick, Philip (2000). *A grammar of the Pendau language*. Doctoral dissertation, Australian National University.

Rand, E. (1968). The structural phonology of Alabaman, a Muskogean language. *International Journal of American Linguistics* 34: 94–103.

Rappaport, Malka (1981). The phonology of gutturals in Biblical Hebrew. In Joseph Aoun and Hagit Borer (eds.) *Theoretical issues in Semitic linguistics*. Cambridge, MA, MIT, pp.101–27.

(1984). *Issues in the phonology of Tiberian Hebrew*. Doctoral dissertation, MIT.

Raz, Shlomo (1983). *Tigré grammar and texts*. Afroasiatic Dialects, Vol. 4. Malibu, CA, Undena.

Recasens, Daniel (1991). *Fonética descriptiva del Català*. Barcelona, Intitut d'Estudias Catalans, Biblioteca Filològica XXI.

Repetti, Lori (1996). Syllabification and unsyllabified consonants in Emilian and Romagnol dialects. In Claudia Parodi, Carlos Quicoli, Mario Saltarelli, and María Luisa

Zubizarreta (eds.) *Aspects of Romance Linguistics*. Washington, DC, Georgetown University Press, pp.373–82.

Rice, Keren (1978). A note on Fort Resolution Chipewyan. *International Journal of American Linguistics* 44: 144–5.

(1988). Continuant voicing in Slave (Northern Athapaskan): The cyclic application of default rules. In Michael Hammond and Michael Noonan (eds.) *Theoretical morphology*. San Diego, Academic Press, pp.371–94.

(1989). *A grammar of Slave*. Berlin, Mouton de Gruyter.

(1992). On deriving sonority: a structural account of sonority relationships. *Phonology* 9: 61–99.

(1996). Default variability: the coronal-velar relationship. *Natural Language and Linguistic Theory* 14.3: 493–543.

(1999a). Featural markedness in phonology: variation. Part 1. *GLOT* 4.7: 3–6.

(1999b). Featural markedness in phonology: variation. Part 2. *GLOT* 4.8: 3–7.

(2004a). Neutralization and epenthesis: is there markedness in the absence of contrast? Handout from GLOW.

(2004b). Sonorant relationships: the case of liquids. Handout from a talk presented at the Canadian Linguistics Association.

(2006). Markedness. In Paul de Lacy (ed.) *The Cambridge Handbook of Phonology*. Cambridge, Cambridge University Press, ch.4.

(in prep.). *Markedness in phonology*. Cambridge, Cambridge University Press.

Rice, Keren and Peter Avery (1991). On the relationship between laterality and coronality. In Carole Paradis and Jean-François Prunet (eds.) *The special status of coronals: internal and external evidence. Volume 2: phonetics and phonology*. San Diego, Academic Press, pp.101–23.

(1993). Segmental complexity and the structure of inventories. In Carrie Dyck (ed.) *Toronto Working Papers in Linguistics 12*. Toronto, University of Toronto, pp.131–54.

(1995). Variability in a deterministic model of language acquisition: a theory of segmental elaboration. In J. Archibald (ed.) *Phonological acquisition and phonological theory*. Hillsdale, NJ, Lawrence Erlbaum, pp.23–42.

Rice, Keren and Trisha Causley (1998). Asymmetries in featural markedness: place of articulation. Handout from GLOW.

Rich, Furne (1963). Arabela phonemes and high-level phonology. *Studies in Peruvian Indian languages I*. Oklahoma, University of Oklahoma and SIL.

Roberts, T. and Y.-C. Li (1963). Problems in the phonology of the Southern Min dialect of Taiwan. *Journal of Tunghai University* 5: 95–108.

Rodrigues, Aryon D. (1999a). Macro-Jê. In R. M. W. Dixon and Alexandra Y. Aikhenvald (eds.) *The Amazonian languages*. Cambridge, Cambridge University Press, pp.165–201.

(1999b). Tupí. In R. M. W. Dixon and Alexandra Y. Aikhenvald (eds.) *The Amazonian languages*. Cambridge, Cambridge University Press, pp.107–22.

Rose, Sharon (1996). Variable laryngeals and vowel lowering. *Phonology* 13: 73–117.

(1997). *Theoretical issues in comparative Ethio-Semitic phonology and morphology*. Doctoral dissertation, McGill University.

Rosenthall, Samuel (1995). *Vowel/glide alternation in a theory of constraint interaction*. Doctoral dissertation, University of Massachusetts, Amherst.
Ross, Malcolm (1980). Some elements of Vanimo, a New Guinea Tone Language. *Papers in New Guinea Linguistic (Pacific Linguistics A, No.56)* 20: 77–109.
  (2002). Taiof. In John Lynch, Malcolm Ross, and Terry Crowley (eds.) *The Oceanic languages*. Richmond, Curzon Press, pp.426–39.
Rutgers, Roland (1998). *Yamphu: grammar, texts, and lexicon*. Leiden, Research School CNWS.
Saeed, John (1999). *Somali*. London Oriental and African language library. Amsterdam, John Benjamins Publishing Company.
Sagey, Elizabeth (1986). *The representation of features and relations in nonlinear phonology*. Doctoral dissertation, MIT.
Salminen, Tapani (1998). Nenets. In Daniel Abondolo (ed.) *The Uralic languages*. London, Routledge, pp.516–47.
Salmond, Anne (1974). *A generative syntax of Luangiua: a Polynesian language*. The Hague, Mouton.
Samek-Lodovici, Vieri (1992). *Universal constraints and morphological gemination: a cross-linguistic study*. Ms., Brandeis University.
  (1993). A unified analysis of crosslinguistic morphological gemination. In Peter Ackema and Maaike Schooslemmer (eds.) *Proceedings of CONSOLE 1*. Utrecht, Holland Academic Graphics, pp.265–83.
Samek-Lodovici, Vieri and Alan Prince (1999). Optima. *Rutgers Optimality Archive* 363.
Sapir, J. David (1965). *A grammar of Diola-Fogny*. Cambridge, Cambridge University Press.
Schein, Barry and Donca Steriade (1986). On geminates. *Linguistic Inquiry* 17: 691–744.
Schlie, Perry and Ginny Schlie (1993). A Kara phonology. In John M. Clifton (ed.) *Data papers on New Guinea linguistics: phonologies of Austronesian languages 2*. Papua New Guinea, SIL Academic Publications, pp.99–130.
Schuh, Russell G. (2005). Segmental phonology. In Russell G. Schuh (ed.) *Reference grammar of Bole*. http://www.humnet.ucla.edu/humnet/aflang/Bole-/bole_papers.html (14 February 2006).
Schwartz, Jean-Luc, Louis-Jean Boë, Nathalie Vallée, and Christian Abry (1997). Major trends in vowel system inventories. *Journal of Phonetics* 25: 233–53.
Schwartz, Linda J. (1979). Syntactic markedness and frequency of occurrence. In Thomas Perry (ed.) *Evidence and argumentation in linguistics*. Berlin, Walter de Gruyter, pp.315–33.
Sekiyama, K. and Y. Tohkura (1991). McGurk effect in non-English listeners: few visual effects for Japanese subjects hearing Japanese syllables of high auditory intelligibility. *Journal of the Acoustical Society of America* 90: 1797–805.
Selkirk, Elisabeth (1984). On the major class features and syllable theory. In Mark Aronoff and Richard T. Oehrle (eds.) *Language sound structure: studies in phonology presented to Morris Halle by his teachers and students*. Cambridge, MA, MIT Press, pp.107–36.

(1991). A two-root theory of length. In E. Dunlap and Jaye Padgett (eds.) *University of Massachusetts occasional papers in linguistics 14: papers in phonology.* Amherst, MA, GLSA, pp.123–72.

(1995). The prosodic structure of function words. In Jill Beckman, Laura Walsh Dickey, and Suzanne Urbanczyk (eds.) *Papers in Optimality Theory.* University of Massachusetts Occasional Papers 18. Amherst, MA, GLSA, pp.439–70.

Shaw, Patricia A. (1980). *Theoretical issues in Dakota phonology and morphology.* New York, Garland Publishing Inc.

Sigurd, Bengt (1965). *Phonotactic structures in Swedish.* Lund, Uniskol.

Silverman, Daniel (1992). Multiple scansions in loanword phonology: evidence from Cantonese. *Phonology* 9.2: 289–328.

Sivertsen, E. (1960). *Cockney phonology.* New York, Humanities Press.

Smith, Ian R. (1978). *Sri Lanka Portuguese Creole phonology.* Vanciyoor, Dravidian Linguistics Association.

Smith, Jennifer (1997). Noun faithfulness: on the privileged behavior of nouns in phonology. *Rutgers Optimality Archive* 242.

(2002). *Phonological augmentation in prominent positions.* Doctoral dissertation, University of Massachusetts, Amherst.

Smolensky, Paul (1993). Harmony, markedness, and phonological activity. *Rutgers Optimality Archive* 87.

Sommerstein, Alan (1977). *Modern phonology.* London, Arnold.

Spring, Cari (1990). *Implications of Axininca Campa for prosodic morphology and reduplication.* Doctoral dissertation, University of Arizona, Tucson.

Sridhar, S. N. (1990). *Kannada.* London, Routledge.

Stahlke, Herbert F. (1975). Some problems with binary features of tone. In Robert K. Herbert (ed.) *Proceedings of the Sixth Conference on African Linguistics.* Ohio, Ohio State University, pp.87–98.

Stampe, David (1972). *How I spent my summer vacation (a dissertation on Natural Generative Phonology).* Doctoral dissertation, University of Chicago.

Stemberger, Joseph (1992). Vocalic underspecification in English language production. *Language* 68: 492–524.

Stemberger, Joe and Carol Stoel-Gammon (1991). The underspecification of coronals: evidence from language acquisition and performance errors. In Carole Paradis and Jean-François Prunet (eds.) *Phonetics and phonology: Vol.2. The special status of coronals.* San Diego, Academic Press, pp.181–99.

Steriade, Donca (1982). *Greek prosodies and the nature of syllabification.* Doctoral dissertation, MIT.

(1987a). Locality conditions and feature geometry. In Joyce M. McDonough and Bernadette Plunkett (eds.) *Proceedings of NELS 17.* Amherst, MA, GLSA, pp.595–617.

(1987b). Redundant values. In Anna Bosch, Barbara Need, and Eric Schiller (eds.) *Proceedings of the Chicago Linguistic Society 23: parasession on autosegmental and metrical phonology.* Vol.2. Chicago, Chicago Linguistic Society, pp.339–62.

(1995a). *Positional neutralization.* Ms., UCLA.

(1995b). Underspecification and markedness. In John Goldsmith (ed.) *The handbook of phonological theory*. Oxford, Blackwell, pp.114–74.
Stites, Jessica, Katherine Demuth, and Cecilia Kirk (2004). Markedness versus frequency effects in coda acquisition. In Alejna Brugos, Linnea Micciulla, and Christine E. Smith (eds.) *Proceedings of the 28th Annual Boston University Conference on Language Development*. Somerville, MA, Cascadilla Press, pp.565–76.
Stonham, John (1999). *Aspects of Tsishaath Nootka phonetics and phonology*. LINCOM studies in Native American linguistics 32. Munich, LINCOM Europa.
Strange, W. and P. A. Broen (1980). Perception and production of approximant consonants by 3-year-olds: a first study. In G. H. Yeni-Komshian, J. F. Kavanaugh, and C. A. Ferguson (eds.), *Child phonology, Vol.2: Perception*. New York, Academic Press, pp. 117–54.
Stroomer, Harry J. (1987). *A comparative study of three Southern Oromo dialects in Kenya*. Hamburg, Helmut Buske Verlag.
Struijke, Caro (2001). *Existential faithfulness: a study of reduplicative TETU, feature movement, and dissimilation*. Doctoral dissertation, University of Maryland, College Park.
Suzuki, Keiichiro (1998). *A typological investigation of dissimilation*. Doctoral dissertation, University of Arizona.
Svantesson, Jan-Olof (1995). Cyclic syllabification in Mongolian. *NLLT* 13.4: 755–66.
Taylor, George P. (1908). *The student's Gujarati grammar with exercises and vocabulary* (2nd edition). Bombay, Thacker and Co.
Teoh, Boon Seong (1988). *Aspects of Malay phonology revisited: a non-linear approach*. Doctoral dissertation, University of Illinois at Urbana-Champaign.
Tesar, Bruce and Paul Smolensky (1998). Learnability in Optimality Theory. *Linguistic Inquiry* 29: 229–68.
Thompson, David A. (1988). *Lockhart River 'sand beach' language: an outline of Kuuku Ya'u and Umpila*. Darwin, Summer Institute of Linguistics, Australian Aborigines and Islanders Branch.
Tracy, Frances (1972). Wapishana phonology. In Joseph E. Grimes (ed.) *Languages of the Guianas*. Norman, OK, Summer Institute of Linguistics of the University of Oklahoma, pp.78–84.
Tranel, Bernard (1981). *Concreteness in generative phonology*. Berkeley, University of California Press.
Trigo Ferre, Rosario Lorenza (1988). *On the phonological derivation and behavior of nasal glides*. Doctoral dissertation, MIT.
Trommer, Jochen and Angela Grimm (2004). Albanian word stress. Handout from Manchester Phonology Meeting, 20–22 May 2004. http://www.ling.uni-osnabrueck.de/trommer/alb.pdf [31 January 2006].
Trubetzkoy, Nikolai S. (1931). Die phonologischen Systeme. *Travaux du Cercle Linguistique de Prague*. Vol.4. Prague, Jednota Ceskoslovenskych Matimatiku a Fysiku, pp.96–116.
(1939). *Grundzüge der Phonologie*. Göttingen, Vandenhoeck & Ruprecht [Translated by A. M. Baltaxe].
(1968). *Introduction to the principles of phonological description* (translated by L.A.Muny). The Hague, Martinus Nijhoff.

(1975). *N. S. Trubetzkoy's letters and notes*. The Hague, Mouton.
Truckenbrodt, Hubert (2006). The syntax-phonology interface. In Paul de Lacy (ed.) *The Cambridge handbook of phonology*. Cambridge, Cambridge University Press, ch.18.
Tsuchida, Shigeru (1976). *Reconstruction of Proto-Tsouic phonology*. Studies of languages and cultures of Asia and Africa, No.5. Tokyo, Institute for the Study of Languages and Cultures of Asia and Africa.
van den Heuvel, Wilco (2004). Floating moras triggering epenthesis at intonation boundaries in Biak. Handout from the 6th Austronesian Formal Linguistics Association.
van Wely, F. P. H. Prick (1967). *Cassell's English–Dutch, Dutch–English dictionary*. London, Macmillan Publishing Company.
Vance, Timothy (1987). *An introduction to Japanese phonology*. Albany, SUNY Press.
Vasanthakumari, T. (1989). *Generative phonology of Tamil*. Delhi, Mittal Publications.
Vaux, Bert (1998). The laryngeal specifications of fricatives. *Linguistic Inquiry* 29.3: 497–512.
  (2001). Consonant epenthesis and hypercorrection. Talk presented at the Linguistic Society of America.
  (2003). Consonant epenthesis and hypercorrection. Ms., Harvard University.
Vaysman, Olga (2002). Consonant gradation and Prosody in Nganasan. Ms., MIT.
Vennemann, Theo (1988). *Preference laws for syllable structure and the explanation of sound change*. Berlin, Mouton de Gruyter.
Walker, Rachel (1998). *Nasalization, neutral segments, and opacity effects*. Doctoral dissertation, University of California, Santa Cruz.
  (2000). *Nasalization, neutral segments and opacity effects*. New York, Garland.
Walsh Dickey, Laura (1997). *The phonology of liquids*. Doctoral dissertation, University of Massachusetts, Amherst.
Watkins, Laurel J. (1984). *A grammar of Kiowa*. Lincoln, University of Nebraska Press.
Waugh, Linda (1979). Markedness and phonological systems. In W. Wolck and Paul L. Garvin (eds.) *The fifth LACUS forum*. Columbia, SC, Hornbeam Press, pp.155–65.
Weber, David John (1989). *A grammar of Huallaga (Huánuco) Quechua*. University of California Publications in Linguistics 112. Berkeley, University of California Press.
Welch, Betty and Birdie Welch (1967). The phonemic system of Tucano. In Viola Waterhouse (ed.) *Phonemic systems of Colombian languages*. Norman, Summer Institute of Linguistics of the University of Oklahoma, pp.11–24.
Wells, John C. (1982). *Accents of English. volume 2: the British Isles*. Cambridge, Cambridge University Press.
Wetzels, W. Leo and Benjamin Hermans (1985). Aspirated geminates in Pali. In H. Bennis and F. Benkema (eds.) *Linguistics in the Netherlands*. Vol.1. Dordrecht, Foris, pp.213–23.
Wetzels, W. Leo and Joan Mascaró (2001). The typology of voicing and devoicing. *Language* 77.2: 207–44.
Wheeler, Max (1979). *Phonology of Catalan*. Oxford, Basil Blackwell.
  (2005a). *The phonology of Catalan*. The Phonology of the World's Languages Series. Oxford, Oxford University Press.

(2005b). Cluster reduction: deletion or coalescence? In Jesús Jiménez and Maria-Rosa Lloret (eds.) *Special Issue of Catalan Journal of Linguistics: Morphology in Phonology* 4 [also *Rutgers Optimality Archive* 718].
Wiese, Richard (2001). The phonology of /r/. In T. Alan Hall (ed.) *Distinctive feature theory*. New York, Mouton de Gruyter, pp.335–68.
Williams, Herbert (1971 [1844]). *A dictionary of the Maori language*. 7th edn. Wellington, A. R. Shearer, Government Printer.
Williamson, Kay (1977). Multivalued features for consonants. *Language* 53: 843–71.
Wilson, Colin (2000). *Targeted constraints: an approach to contextual neutralization in Optimality Theory*. Doctoral dissertation, Johns Hopkins University.
Wiltshire, Caroline (1998). Extending ALIGN constraints to new domains. *Linguistics* 36.3: 423–68.
Woolams, Geoff (1996). *A grammar of Karo Batak, Sumatra*. Pacific Linguistics C-130. Canberra, Australian National University.
Woolford, Ellen (1999). Animacy hierarchy effects on object agreement. In Paul F. A. Kotey (ed.) *New dimensions in African linguistics and languages*. Trenton, NJ and Asmara, Eritrea, Africa World Press, pp.203–16.
Yallop, Colin (1977). *Alyawarra: an Aboriginal language of Central Australia*. Research and Regional Studies 10. Canberra, Australian Institute of Aboriginal Studies.
Yar-Shater, Ehsan (1969). *A grammar of southern Tati dialects*. The Hague, Mouton.
Yip, Moira (1982). Reduplication and CV skeleta in Chinese secret languages. *Linguistic Inquiry* 13.4: 637–62.
  (1991). Coronals, consonant clusters, and the coda condition. In Carole Paradis and Jean-François Prunet (eds.) *The special status of coronals: internal and external evidence, II: phonetics and phonology*. San Diego, Academic Press, pp.61–78.
  (1992). Sonorant vs. obstruent codas in East Asian languages: a prosodic distinction. Ms., University of California, Irvine.
  (1994). Morpheme-level features: Chaoyang syllable structure and nasalization. *Rutgers Optimality Archive* 81.
  (1995). Lexicon optimization in languages without alternations. *Rutgers Optimality Archive* 135.
  (2000). Segmental unmarkedness versus input preservation in reduplication. In Linda Lombardi (ed.) *Segmental phonology in Optimality Theory*. Cambridge, Cambridge University Press, pp. 206–30.
  (2001). The complex interaction of tone and prominence. In Minjoo Kim and Uri Strauss (eds.) *Proceedings of NELS 31*. Amherst, MA, GLSA, pp.531–45.
  (2002). Necessary but not sufficient: perceptual influences in loanword phonology. Talk presented at The Architecture of Grammar conference, Central Institute of English and Foreign Languages, Hyderabad, India.
Yu, Alan (2004). Explaining final obstruent voicing in Lezgian: phonetics and history. *Language* 80.1: 73–97.
Zaicz, Gábor (1998). Mordva. In Daniel Abondolo (ed.) *The Uralic languages*. London, Routledge, pp.184–218.
Zec, Draga (1988). *Sonority constraints on prosodic structure*. Doctoral dissertation, Stanford University.

(1995). Sonority constraints on syllable structure. *Phonology* 12: 85–129.

(2000). Multiple sonority thresholds. In T. H. King and I. A. Sekerina (eds.) *The 8th annual workshop on formal approaches to Slavic linguistics*. Ann Arbor, Michigan Slavic Publications, pp.382–413.

Zoll, Cheryl (1996). *Parsing below the segment in a constraint-based framework*. Doctoral dissertation, University of California, Berkeley.

(1998). Positional asymmetries and licensing. *Rutgers Optimality Archive* 282.

Zonneveld, R. M. van (1985). Word rhythm and the Janus syllable. In Harry van der Hulst and Norval Smith (eds.) *The structure of phonological representations*. Vol.2. Dordrecht, Foris, pp.133–40.

Subject index

accidental gaps 349
acquisition, *see* learning
allomorphy, relation to epenthesis 135–8
alternations, as diagnostic 20, 133–5, 336, 405
anusvara, *see* nasal glide
assimilation
  as diagnostic 28, 30
  direction 179, 254–9
  motivation, *see* Marked-Cluster constraints
  undergoer typology 191–2, 201
  universals 6
  vs. markedness reduction 29

blocking
  in conflation 224–31
  of markedness reduction 154–7, 212

coalescence 263
  and disharmonic inventories 169
  as diagnostic 30
  ranking for 266–8
  universals 7
  vacuous 267–8
Comparative Markedness theory 387–94
Competence 1, 11, 346, 348–52
  and frequency 13
  small inventories 166
  vowel dispersion 287
conflation 2, 9–10, 24, 50
  faithfulness 259–60, 269–74
  with fixed ranking, *see* fixed ranking
  place of articulation 210–23
  and representation 245–7
  sonority 240–3
conflict of hierarchies, *see* hierarchy conflict

constraint
  and least marked, *see* Lenient CON
  restrictions on, *see* schema
contrast 380–7
coronal
  as least marked 36
  promotion 117
crazy rules 354–5
creoles 31

Default Variability theory 366–9
debuccalization, *see* neutralization to glottal
deletion 28, 398
diachronic change 16–17, 352–4
diagnostics
  apparent inconsistency 6–7
  invalid 29–31, 337, 342
  valid 27–9, 342–4
disorders 19
dissimilation 23, 29, 34, 75, 87
  and placelessness 362, 364, 374
Dispersion Theory 167, 287, 312–15, 321–6
DTE 63–9
  in codas 99
  in epenthesis 305
  in feet 227
  in syllables 86, 122
  overlapping environments 286, 288

epenthesis
  as diagnostic 28
  assimilative 80, 101–4
  coda 99–100
  consonant typology 79
  coronal 88
  default 80
  diagnostics of 135
  glottal 82

440

Subject index 441

labial 104
  mid vowels 298–9
  motivation 82
  palatal 104
  role of sonority 288
  vowel typology 288–90, 299–305
Evolutionary Phonology 349–52

faithfulness
  domain-specific 280–1
  featural vs. segmental 395–6, 397–9
  gradient 115
  in Kiparsky's work 55
  noun 217–18
  schema, *see* schema faithfulness constraints
features
  binary vs. multi-valued 57–9, 247–9
  in constraints 59–62
  natural classes 248
  xo, *see xo* Theory
fixed ranking 2, 22, 51, 68, 154, 208–10, 215–16, 247, 250–1
  faithfulness 252–4, 259–60, 272–4
free ranking 202–6
free variation 341
frequency
  and competence 12–16
  occurrence 15
  text 15, 31
  typological 12, 31
  within-inventory 15

gemination 113, 180–2, 266
glottal 37–42
  Elimination 96, 162
  in syllable margins, *see* Subset Generalization
  nasal, *see* glottal nasal stop
  not placeless 356, 361–5, 378
  phonetic implementation 37
  representation 42
  sonority of 94–6
  triggers assimilation 363–4
glottal nasal stop 37
  as trigger 40
  distribution 40, 371
  evidence for 39–42
  in assimilation 40, 194
  in epenthesis 40
  in neutralization 39, 142–4, 157

harmonic bound 50, 60
head, *see* DTE
hierarchy 2, 43, 247–9
  conflict 2, 30, 74, 122
  discovery 72–5
  evidence for 42
  non-existing 74
  place of articulation 35–42
  prosodic 64
  reversal for non-DTEs 45, 344
  sonority 68
  voice 34
historical change, *see* diachronic change

i-language, *see* Competence
innateness, *see* Competence
inventories 6
  as diagnostic 28, 30
  disharmonic 169, 315–16
  dispersed, *see* Dispersion Theory
  formation 148
  frequency 308
  gapped 163, 307, 312
  glottal/coronal universal, *see* universals glottal/coronal
  harmonically complete 148, 307, 308–12
  universals 6, 7
  vertical 312

labial
  promotion 128–32
  unmarkedness 345–8
learning
  effect on frequency 13
  order of 18, 31
Lenient CON 399–402
lenition 130–1, 171, 173, 342
loanwords 16–17, 31, 337

majority rules 279–84
manner of articulation 16, 70
marked, *see* markedness
Marked-Cluster constraints 183–5
Marked Reference Hypothesis 48
markedness
  affected by environment 44, 62–70
  as an epiphenomenon 5
  covert 206–7
  diagnostics, *see* diagnostics
  formal implementation, *see* schema

Subject index

markedness (*cont.*)
  in constraint form 22
  least marked 5
  probabilistic 403
  preservation, *see* preservation of the marked
  reduction, *see* reduction-markedness
  relative 5, 387–94
  representational theories of, *see* representation and markedness
  reversals 9, 25–6
  schema, *see* schema

nasal
  glide 37, 41
Natural Phonology 3
natural class 248
neutralization 110
  absolute 265, 383
  as diagnostic 28, 30
  direction 316
  fricative place 166
  in onset 164
  of glottal 124–7
  of vowels 306
  passive 133, 337, 342
  schema 159–61
  to coronal 117
  to glottal 112, 211
  to [w] 127–8
non-DTE, *see* DTE
NoZero Principle, *see* Lenient CON

output constraints, *see* schema

palatal 36, 104, 105
pharyngeal 36, 220, 221
phonotactics 20, 133, 405
pidgins 31
place of articulation 2, 35–42, 221
  in environment 36
  faithfulness constraints 3
  members 35
  minor 275–7
  output constraints 2
  and Subset Generalization, *see* Subset Generalization
Prague School 3, 380
preservation of the marked 1, 7–9, 11
  and gapped inventories, *see* inventories gapped
  in assimilation 175–80
  in neutralization 148–54
  markedness and environment, *see* DTE
  prosody Hierarchy-Structure Combination Restriction 69
  vs. segmental markedness 35

reduction
  markedness 23
  to mid vowels 326
  vowel 225–31, 318–19
reduplication 118
representation
  and markedness 245–7, 357
  complexity 35, 355
  in K. Rice's work, *see* Default Variability Theory

schema
  faithfulness constraints 52–4, 61
  prosodic output constraints 66
  segmental output constraints 47–51, 59
sonority
  against decomposition 248
  and conflation 232–43
  and DTEs 286, 288
  and stress, *see* sonority-driven stress
  conflict with voicing 122
  constraints 68
  glottal, *see* glottal, sonority of
  hierarchy 68
  in Clements' work 54, 247
  in codas 99–100
  influence on epenthesis, *see* epenthesis, role of sonority
  reversal 297–8, 306
  sonority-driven stress diagnostic 28, 329–30
  typology 244–5
sonority-driven stress 232–43
stringency 50
  contrast with non-stringent free-ranking 202–6
  in Prince's work 55
  suppletion relation to epenthesis 138–42
Subset Generalization 96–7

tone hierarchy 66

underspecification 3, 356
universals
    as accidental gaps 349
    glottal/coronal 166–9
    in Greenberg's work 3, 6, 12, 15, 341
    not epiphenomena 12
    obscured 207
    relation to Competence 349
unmarked, *see* markedness
uvular 35, 36, 220

velar never least marked 36, 41, 369–75
voice
    devoicing 122
    voicing as lenition 123, 354–5
vowel reduction, *see* reduction, vowel
    desonorization, *see* reduction, vowel
    sonorization 317–18, 320–1

xo Theory 56–9, 248

Language index

Aguaruna 41
Alabama 288
Alyawarra 191
Amharic 288
Amuesha 306, 307, 341
Anejom̃ 71, 80, 101
Apalai Carib 97
Arabic 40, 362
  Classical 305, 307
  Egyptian 165
  Mekkan 201
  Palestinian 288
  Sudanese 288
  Syrian 363
Arekuna 143
Ashéninca, Pichis 244
Atayal, Squliq 99
Austronesian 14
Axininca Campa 80, 88–94, 288

Bardi 191
Basque 111, 121, 134, 288
Belarusan 314
Berber 16, 374
  Imdlawn Tashlhiyt 329
Berguener Romansh, see Romansh, Berguener
Biak 165, 288
Boazi 71
Bole 192, 200
Brahui 80
Buriat 16, 40, 139–42, 165

Cantonese 14, 111
Carib 135
  Apalai, see Apalai Carib
  Arekuna, see Arekuna
  Macushi, see Machushi Carib
  Surinam, see Surinam Carib

Tiriyó, see Tiriyó
Wayana, see Wayana
Catalan 7, 8, 174–83, 192, 344, 351, 361, 399
  Central 310–12
Chadic 80
Chama 13
Chamicuro 40, 80, 97, 106–7, 143, 371
Chamorro 317–18
Chaoyang 133, 170
Chehalis, Upper 306, 307, 314
Chickasaw 133, 162, 349
Chinese, Cantonese, see Cantonese
  Chaoyang, see Chaoyang
  Mandarin, see Mandarin
  Nantong 143
  secret languages 144
Chinook 375
Chipewyan 80, 288, 297–8, 352
  Fort Chipewyan 261
  Yellowknife 6, 13, 165
Chukchi 192, 195–7, 288, 362, 390
Coos 288, 291–3
Cupeño 80
Czech 288, 299

Dakota 80, 100, 171–3, 288, 374
Diola Fogny 192, 193, 303
Diyari 351
Djapu 71, 97
Dravidian 302, 304
Dutch 80, 225–31, 371

Easter Island, see Rapanui
English 14, 72, 97, 101, 103, 163, 345, 371
  Boston 80, 354
  Bristol 108
  Cockney 118, 162, 163

444

Language index   445

New Zealand 20, 128, 162, 309, 310
North-Eastern US 108
Pig Latin 118
Yorkshire 201

Finnish 381
Fox 80
French 14, 80, 303
　Midi 372
　Parisian 201
Fula 302
Fuzhou 162, 166
　Classical 17, 163, 370

Galician 288
　Moañés 288
Gapapaiwa 307
Gengbe 288
Genovese 39, 371
German, Standard 122
Gokana 80, 92
Greek, Attic 8, 137
Gujarati 16, 96, 192, 232–43, 245, 307, 329, 352

Hamer 191
Harar Oromo, see Oromo, Harar
Harari 288
Hawaiian 6, 13, 16, 20, 71, 134, 165, 352
Hebrew, Tiberian 288, 299
Hindi 288
Hixkaryána 223
Huariapano 80
Hungarian 71, 301

Icelandic 304
Inor 375
Inuktitut, Baffin 192
Italian 138
　Mesola 288
　Miogliola Ligurian 40, 126, 371
Itelmen 288

Japanese 18, 80, 165, 304, 381, 385
　Kagoshima 39–40, 117

Kaingáng 80
Kalinga 80, 102
Kannada 302
Kara 244

Karao 288
Karo Batak 288
Kashaya 10, 162, 210–23, 374
Kewa 71
Kiribati 347
Kilivila see Kiriwina
Kiowa 162, 206
Kiowa Apache 13
Kiriwina 171
Klamath 288
Koasati 351
Kobon 244
Koḍava 135–7, 302
Komi 71
Konjo 144
Korean 9, 80, 111, 124–6, 192, 364, 393
Kuuku Ya'u 191

Ladakhi 288
Lamani 97
Lapp, see Saami
Lardil 191, 288, 398
Larike 80
Lezgian 124
Luangiua 13, 165, 352
Luiseño 314
Lushootseed 307

Mabalay Atayal 82–8, 93, 288
Macushi Carib 40, 97, 144, 371
Maga Rukai 294, 296, 307
Makassarese 39, 142, 143
Makurap 351
Malay Kelantan 43, 97, 143, 162
　Standard 8, 78, 80, 95, 97, 111, 112–17, 143, 162, 288, 371
　Terengganu 144
　Ulu Muar, see Ulu Muar Malay
Malayalam 302
Manam 288
Mandarin 14
Māori 15, 17, 80, 97, 165, 288, 307, 310, 341, 353, 364
Marathi 288
Mari
　Eastern 71
　Western 71
Maltese 288
Miogliola, see Italian, Miogliola Ligurian
Misantla Totonac, see Totonac

Miwok, Southern Sierra 192, 193
Mixtec, Ayutla 6, 80, 97, 99, 165, 351
Mohawk 80, 288, 299
Mongolian 288
Mordva 71, 162
Murut 71, 80, 137, 374

Nambiquara 162, 166, 351
Nancowry 165
Navaho 117
Nenets, Central Eastern Tundra 71, 381, 384–5
Nganasan 71, 162, 163–4, 166, 244, 246, 307, 329, 362, 363
Ngawun Mayi 191
Ngiyambaa 191
Nhanda 191, 351
Nunggubuyu 191

Ojibwa 288
　Eastern 402
　Odawa 80
Ormuri 71
Orokolo 13
Oromo Boraana 198
　Harar 71, 95, 165, 192, 197–200, 362
　Orma 198
　Southern 135
　Waata 198
　Western 198

Pāli 7, 262–79, 282, 288, 397
Pendau 162, 300
Pig Latin, see English, Pig Latin
Pipil 288
Polish 127
Ponapean 347
Portuguese
　Brazilian 128
　European 231, 344
Proto-Eastern Polynesian 13, 16, 353
Pulaar 142

Quechua, Huallaga 39, 142
Quichua, Ecuador 173

Rapanui 166
Romansh, Berguener 306, 314, 321–5

Saami 191
Samoan, colloquial 13, 71–2, 165
Santee, see Sioux Valley
Seediq 301, 386
Sekani 288
Selayarese 117, 142, 144, 369, 371
Seri 39, 137, 142, 191, 192, 301
Sinhala 302
Sioux Valley (Santee) 351
Siuslawan 206, 310, 399
Slave 288, 299
　Bearlake 80
　Hare 78, 80
　Mountain 71
Slovene, Upper Carniolan 314
Somali 122, 123–4, 165, 354
Spanish 14, 142, 144, 288
　Caribbean 117, 166
　Castilian 122
　Maracaibo Venezuelan 134, 352
　Velarizing dialects 358–60
Sri Lankan Portuguese creole 7, 8, 186–90, 192, 310, 318–20, 346, 347, 362, 388–90, 399
Sudest 71
Surinam Carib 134
Swedish 202, 254–62, 281

Tahitian 6, 165
Taiof 16
Taiwanese 111, 118
Tamil 80, 102, 191
Tarangan, West 117
Tati, Southern 80, 101–3
Telugu 302
Temiar 288, 299
Tibetan
　Lhasa 337, 385
　Refugee 134, 163
Tigak 351
Tigré 80
Tiriyó 143
Toba Batak 97, 162
Tongan 71, 165
Totonac 39, 73, 80, 376–9
　Misantla San Marcos Atesquilapan 142
　Yecuatla 117
Tsishaath Nootka 80
Tübatulabal 165, 166
Tucanoan 80

Tunica 80, 99, 100
Tuscarora 288, 305

Ukrainian 201, 261
Ulu Muar Malay 111
Uradhi 40, 80, 100, 162, 374
Uyghur 80, 104–5

Vach Kanty 307
Vanimo 71, 165
Vietnamese, South 370

Wangaaybuwan-Ngiyambaa, *see* Ngiyambaa
Wapishana 288, 307, 351
Washo 288
Wayana 143, 144
West Tarangan 117
Wintu 71
Wolof 288
Wosera 306, 307, 312

Xavanté Macro-Je 351

Yagua 80
Yamphu 7–8, 9, 39, 40, 111, 142, 143, 146–7, 148–54, 162, 192, 193–4
Yaùthê 201
Yil 244
Yuma 97